GROWING TO ONE WORLD

Growing to One World

The Life of J. King Gordon

EILEEN R. JANZEN

McGill-Queen's University Press
Montreal & Kingston · London · Ithaca

ISBN 978-0-7735-4261-7 (cloth)
ISBN 978-0-7735-8961-2 (ePDF)
ISBN 978-0-7735-8962-9 (ePUB)

Legal deposit fourth quarter 2013
Bibliothèque nationale du Québec

Printed in Canada on acid-free paper that is 100% ancient forest free (100% post-consumer recycled), processed chlorine free

This book has been published with the help of a grant from the Canadian Federation for the Humanities and Social Sciences, through the Awards to Scholarly Publications Program, using funds provided by the Social Sciences and Humanities Research Council of Canada.

McGill-Queen's University Press acknowledges the support of the Canada Council for the Arts for our publishing program. We also acknowledge the financial support of the Government of Canada through the Canada Book Fund for our publishing activities.

Library and Archives Canada Cataloguing in Publication

Janzen, Eileen R. (Eileen Rose), 1937–, author
Growing to one world: the life of J. King Gordon/Eileen R. Janzen.

Includes bibliographical references and index.
Issued in print and electronic formats.
ISBN 978-0-7735-4261-7 (bound). – ISBN 978-0-7735-8961-2 (ePDF). – ISBN 978-0-7735-8962-9 (ePUB)

1. Gordon, J. King. 2. Human rights workers – Canada – Biography. 3. Political activists – Canada – Biography. 4. Socialists – Canada – Biography. 5. Scholars – Canada – Biography. 6. Theologians – Canada – Biography. I. Title. II. Title: Life of J. King Gordon.

JC599.C3J35 2013 323.092 C2013-904221-0
C2013-904222-9

This book was typeset by Interscript in 10.5/13 Sabon.

For Holly
Daniel and Amy
Bobby and Lucy

Contents

Preface

I first met King Gordon in the summer of 1978 when he agreed to become a subject for my dissertation research into the philosophical roots of Canadian socialism as it came to expression in the Co-operative Commonwealth Federation (CCF). I was particularly interested in how the ideas of Fabian socialism were brought to Canada by returning Rhodes scholars (my study also included F.H. Underhill and F.R. Scott), and how these ideas were adapted to the Canadian political culture. In working through the full range of Gordon's papers, I became convinced that the wider story of his work deserved to come to the attention of his fellow Canadians; but when I urged him to write his autobiography, he responded that he was too busy (undoubtedly true) and that he rather hoped I would do the task for him. It was a task that after his death I felt honoured to undertake. In my view, King Gordon offers a compelling example of a young Canadian courageously struggling to find his place within the currents of twentieth-century thought, and his life exhibits a rare combination of intellectual reflection and political activism. In his mature years, he exemplified that quality for which Canadians have been known and admired throughout the world: a good citizen at home and a dedicated internationalist abroad.

King Gordon's life is a uniquely Canadian story, descended through both parents from Selkirk settlers, and spanning the twentieth century. His father, Charles W. Gordon, wrote bestselling novels under the name Ralph Connor. He was educated in Manitoba, at Oxford as a Rhodes Scholar, and as a student of Reinhold Niebuhr at Union Seminary and Columbia University in New York. At each stage in his formative years he was exposed to the ideals of public service, beginning with the progressive social gospel imbibed at his father's table, and developing through his exposure to Fabian socialism at Oxford and the radical social critique of Reinhold Niebuhr. After testing a vocation to the Presbyterian ministry in rural missions in British Columbia and Manitoba, he was ordained in the United Church of Canada, and taught Christian Ethics at United Theological College (affiliated with McGill) in Montreal. Gordon continued his radical activities as one of the writers of the Regina Manifesto, which was adopted by the newly formed CCF in 1933, and as a member of the League for Social Reconstruction (LSR). Finding himself dismissed from United Theological College in 1934, Gordon concluded that since he could not serve God in the church he would try politics, and he ran as a CCF candidate for Victoria and lost. With little hope for a job in Canada in the political climate of that time, he emigrated to the United States in 1938. This was a reluctant decision on his part, and it was regretted by others as well. J.S. Woodsworth, the CCF leader, wrote at the time, "Dear King, we were so sorry you had to leave us for a while. But I do hope that some of these days the way may open for your return. We need you in Canada."[1]

After editing his father's autobiography at Farrar and Rinehart, King Gordon became the non-fiction editor for the press, quickly becoming engaged in interventionist activities in an effort to bring the US into the war on the side of the Allies. By the time he joined *The Nation* as its managing editor in 1944, he was involved in a wide network of liberal causes in New York. With the founding of the United Nations in 1945, Gordon became the chief UN correspondent for the CBC, broadcasting daily news to the Canadian public. This first connection to the UN led to the mature form he would give to the vocation he had begun to answer years before as a student minister in the Fraser Valley of British Columbia – "to serve God through the service to man." In 1950 Gordon joined the Secretariat of the United Nations, Division of Human Rights, where he served on the Prisoner of War Commission, and in Korea, the Middle East, and the Congo. On his retirement, he at last realized his long-enduring hope of returning to Canada, where he became professor of international relations at the Universities of Alberta and Ottawa. He remained active through the 1970s and 80s, playing a formative role in many international and Canadian organizations. There was no slowing of his pace, and he died suddenly at the age of eighty-nine while driving down Wellington Street past the Parliament buildings.

It has taken me a long time to write this book. I began the actual writing in 1995, balancing a demanding job teaching history and political philosophy to juniors and seniors in a college preparatory school here in

Indianapolis, and also sharing the responsibilities of family life. I counted on working a month during the summer and a week during spring break. Each time I returned to the papers, I had a spasm of anxiety: would I still find Gordon filling the pages with his buoyant energy and purpose? As soon as I opened a carton of papers at the National Archives of Canada (Library and Archives Canada, or LAC) in Ottawa, there he would be with all his friends, serious and committed activists, but by no means long-faced or burdened by ideology. What struck me was their hope and confidence, their belief that by their arguments and actions they could bring about change. Each fall as I tucked away the files, I returned to my students refreshed, eager and privileged to share in the promise of their lives.

Why did the project continue to have this liveliness for me? Undoubtedly in the first place, it was my admiration for King himself, his steadfastness and constancy often in often difficult circumstances. Senator Eugene Forsey recalled, "I have never known anyone who genuinely cared so deeply for all kinds of people, not just groups but individuals – every person he encountered."[2] For all his achievements, Gordon was remarkably modest, cringing with embarrassment when Ivan Head, Pierre Trudeau's foreign policy adviser, introduced him to West German chancellor Willy Brandt as "a great Canadian."[3]

I also admired Gordon's perception of Canada and the Canadian people: he never suffered from the colonial deference that afflicted many in his generation. He saw his fellow Canadians as politically astute, capable not only of developing their own form of socialism, but also of carving out a sturdy independence in the shadow of two great nations, the United States and Britain. Most of all, he never lost his identity as rooted in the land of his birth, and he was one of those who could "go home again" – from Oxford, from the United States, from the world.

It has been important to me personally, as a Canadian, to tell King Gordon's story and show how love for one's country need not preclude respect for the patriotic loyalties that other national groups hold for their own histories.

One snowy December evening when I was having dinner with the Scotts in Montreal, Frank Scott reminisced happily about the "glory days" of the LSR and the CCF. He commented on King's leaving Canada and his long tenure abroad. He looked down, silent for a moment. Then he said softly, "King was the most Canadian of us all."[4]

Acknowledgments

I am indebted first of all to professors Timothy A. Tilton and Alan Ritter of Indiana University (Bloomington) who enthusiastically encouraged my early interest in writing about a Canadian topic for my PhD dissertation, and who guided me through the process with patience and skill. I am also indebted to the rich fund of scholarship on various aspects of Canadian life that I have been able to draw on in the attempt to provide the context for King Gordon's many-sided concerns and activities. My appreciation is only partly indicated in my footnotes and bibliography.

The archivists and staff of the National Archives of Canada, now Library and Archives Canada, have always been courteous and efficient in catering to my requests for (at times obscure) documents; and I must also thank Shelley Sweeney and Tyyne Petrowski of the University of Manitoba Archives, and Gordon Goldsborough of the Manitoba Historical Society, for their help in locating photographs of King Gordon and the Gordon family. Celine Kear of the University Women's Club of Winnipeg introduced me to the resources of the Ralph Connor House in Winnipeg, and Lorraine Cook and the Board of the Friends of Ralph Connor granted me permission to use these resources. Michael and Sandra Cox, members of the Gordon family in Winnipeg, also helped me in finding photographs. Joan Broughton of the United Nations Association of Canada and Cheryl Minnis worked tirelessly to get permission for me to use for a photograph of Gordon receiving the Pearson Peace Medal, and Joan Dold did the same for an article I had previously published on the nature of King Gordon's Christian socialism. Gillian Scobie copy edited the manuscript with patience and meticulous care and, with a deft touch, made suggestions that helped me identify the distinction between what was merely interesting and what was necessary to the narrative.

Cartographer Barry Levely drew the maps. I have used the two short quotations from Frank Scott's poems "Surfaces" and "A Grain of Rice" with the kind permission of William Toye, literary executor for the estate of F.R. Scott. It was a pleasure to be in touch with these willing helpers, several of whom had known King Gordon.

Between 1974 and 1976, Ernest J. Dick conducted a number of interviews with King Gordon that are deposited in the sound archives of LAC. These interviews are especially valuable not only for their information, but for the window they offer into Gordon's thinking as he reflects on the perceptive questions posed by Ernest Dick, and I am grateful to him for their use. Ronald St John Macdonald of Dalhousie University shared with me his personal reminiscences of his friendship with King Gordon, and their shared activities in the Group of 78. Before his untimely death in 2006, Professor Macdonald read and gave careful and detailed comments on early drafts of chapters 1 through 9 of the manuscript. His cheery greetings from Nova Scotia arrived frequently by phone and by letter, replete with anecdotes, always channelling Gordon's own energy into my project. I also thank Headmaster Bruce W. Galbraith for his unfailing and generous support of our Park Tudor School Model United Nations program, which I sponsored. The many years of participating with my students at MUN conferences deepened my knowledge of the UN and my appreciation of the work to which King Gordon dedicated his mature years.

I also thank Patricia and Eric Bays for their friendship and hospitality on my many research trips to Ottawa; and Richard L. Lancaster for summers on Deer Isle, Maine, watching the incoming tide while I read King's description of egrets flying down the Nile past the Gordons' Cairo apartment.

I cannot adequately express my gratitude to the Gordon family. From the beginning of my dissertation research, King Gordon offered me ready access to his papers, and over the years we had countless hours of conversation. It was a particular pleasure to come to know Ruth Gordon, and on one of my last visits with her in 1995, she lent me her own archive of letters that she and her husband had exchanged over the years of their separations. The contribution of these letters to this book is immeasurable. Charles W. Gordon has given me access to his father's papers in LAC, and to papers still held by the Gordon family that are identified in this work as J. King Gordon Papers (JKGP). Alison Gordon, with humour and interest, has helped with photographs and memories. I thank both of them for their gracious acceptance of my boldness in presuming to narrate a life – no, a pair of lives – with which they are uniquely familiar.

I owe far more than I can say to Mark Abley. It is rare to find a person who combines sharp analytical qualities with an ability to offer criticism without an edge. I have relied on (and trusted) his insight, discernment, patience, and steady encouragement – not to mention his sense of humour.

My indebtedness to, and gratitude for, my family – Holly, Daniel, Amy, and Gerry, and now also Bobby and Lucy – is inestimable.

Eileen R. Janzen
Indianapolis, Indiana
2013

GROWING TO ONE WORLD

Every single poem written regular is a symbol small or great of the way the will has to pitch into commitments deeper and deeper to a rounded conclusion and then be judged for whether any original intention it had has been strongly spent or weakly lost; be it in art, politics, school church, business, love, or marriage – in a piece of work or in a career. Strongly spent is synonymous with kept.

Robert Frost, "The Constant Symbol"

July 10. "A true man or a true friend, is a person whose outward acts correspond to – faithfully reflect – his inner feelings." This summer of 1923 I have dedicated to the task of self conquest – a task which in no way is ever complete but which unless begun leaves one's life colorless and to no purpose. To bring one's thought and actions into touch with the highest purpose for which one is in this world – if there is a purpose as I believe there is – to bring one's life under the guidance of God, if indeed there is a God, and I believe there is – is to gain complete mastery of oneself, and completely to realize oneself. Duty and the will – these two must be made to coincide.

J. King Gordon, Oxford, 1923

1

The Native Heath

Birkencraig. The name derives from the Scottish Highlands, but the birch and rock that call it forth are those of a northern lake and an island about 6 km from Kenora, Ontario. King Gordon's deep patriotism and sense of himself as a Canadian was first of all deeply rooted in an elemental love of the land itself, the family island, the Manitoba plains, the mountains of British Columbia. But his sense of being Canadian also derived from a colonial ancestry going back to the early part of the nineteenth century, and by the time he was born in 1900, the Gordons were well-rooted in the new country of Canada. His father, Charles W. Gordon, writing in his ebullient autobiography, recalled that while the creation of the Dominion of Canada in 1867 made barely a ripple on the surface of life in the Upper Canada backwoods of Glengarry, he greeted the news, as a seven-year-old, with a lusty "Hurrah for Canada!" It was perhaps more childish high spirits than patriotic devotion, but it proved prescient.[1]

The telling of a personal history begins with genealogy, an account of one's ancestors and the peculiar combination of genes, passions, accidents of nature and human decisions that flow together to produce, and presumably to some extent explain, the unique configuration of a person. King Gordon's story begins with the emergence of his paternal ancestors from the obscurity and misty glens of the Scottish Highlands, where his grandfather, (Donald) Daniel Gordon, was born near the Highland castle of Blair Atholl in 1822. After completing theological studies at the universities of Aberdeen and Edinburgh in 1849, Daniel was called as a missionary to the scattered Gaelic-speaking congregations in Lingwick in Quebec's Eastern Townships. Four years later, he moved his young family to the county of Glengarry in Ontario, where he served the Presbyterian Kirk for seventeen years.[2]

The earliest settlers to Glengarry County were made up of Loyalist dissenters from the American Revolution and settlers directly from Scotland, from the Highland counties of Perthshire, Inverness, Ross, Cromarty, and Argyleshire. Their Gaelic language and Presbyterian faith provided a strong continuing link between the new Glengarry community and Scotland, and it was to the Church of Scotland that the Canadian congregations appealed when in need of a new minister. As a result, a succession of ministers with prestigious degrees in theology were sent out from the Scottish universities of Edinburgh, Aberdeen, and Glasgow.

However, an internal dispute arose within the Church of Scotland, in 1843, with serious consequences for the Kirk in Glengarry. The issue turned on the right of local congregations to choose their own ministers over appointment through state patronage. As a result, one-third of the ministers formed the Free Church of Scotland. The new Free Church, made up of roughly 600 congregations, soon grew to be a significant missionary church, sending newly trained ministers to congregations abroad. As was often the case, the ripples of the metaphorical pebble dropped into the imperial pond of controversy washed ashore in the colonies. For the most part, the Presbyterians in Canada remained associated with the Church of Scotland, the Auld Kirk as it was called. Before long, however, the missionary zeal of the new Free Church ministers began to bear fruit, and by the time Daniel Gordon, an ardent Free Church advocate, arrived as minister in 1853, the congregation in Glengarry was overwhelmingly Free Church. Still, the church building itself, and about two hundred acres of land, remained the legal property of the Auld Kirk – or so it claimed – which by this time included fewer than a dozen members in its congregation.

Daniel, described by his son as a fiery Highlander and a passionate man capable of godly wrath, leapt into the fray. Arriving for church one Sabbath morning and finding the door locked with a new padlock, and his congregation waiting outside, he demanded that the beadle open the door. Having ascertained that the key handed him by the beadle was the one normally used to unlock the door, and that on this occasion it proved faulty, Daniel Gordon declared, "Stand clear!" With one swift blow of his foot, the new padlock snapped and the door flew open, allowing the people to pass in for the worship of God, Free Church style.[3]

This was not the end of the story, and righteous indignation bowed to the force of law. Charged with housebreaking and unlawful entry, Daniel mounted his black stallion and, followed by a cavalcade of Free Churchmen, answered a court summons in Cornwall, where he escaped a jail sentence but was ordered to forfeit the church property. Glorious in defeat, the congregation fell to, and by 1864 Daniel Gordon opened a sturdy new brick church at St Elmo that was still standing one hundred and thirty years later.[4]

This was the world that Charles W. Gordon, King's father, was born into on 13 September 1860: a community of high-spirited Highlanders, industrious, courageous, hacking a farming community out of the wilderness, and described by him as "a fighting people."[5] His father Daniel was a true man of his people who, in spite of his advanced university education, still held a strong belief in the spirit world often found in the remote hills of his homeland. He was not above terrifying his children at bedtime with tales of ghost armies marching through the closed iron gates of Blair Atholl, an event witnessed by his own brother Gilbert. Finally, his wife, the highly educated Mary Robertson, would plead that he tell his tales in daylight, and his children were moved to protest that there were no ghosts in Canada. His immediate awareness of the spiritual sphere also lent passion to his preaching, and C.W. Gordon recalled watching the faces of the congregation grow stark and pale under his father's condemnation of sin and his predictions of judgment. Yet tears flowed down Daniel's cheeks as he spoke of the love of God, and his son confessed to being moved to such depths by no other preacher.

Daniel Gordon's passion for religion was followed closely by his passion, if not corresponding skill, for playing the bagpipes. On many winter evenings he would appear in the manse living room and launch into one of the great Scottish *pibrochs*, as his family stared wordlessly, unable to identify it as a recognizable piece of music. This became one of King Gordon's favourite stories about his grandfather, an enduring part of his Scottish heritage, and decades later he was deeply moved by the sound of the pipes as he served with the United Nations in the Congo. However, he himself seems never to have yearned to play them.[6]

Despite the intensity and fierceness of his nature, Daniel was a kind father to his six sons and one daughter, and C.W. Gordon recalled only a single thrashing, which he considered (from the sage perspective of adulthood) to have been fully justified. He described himself and his brothers as a "band of young ruffians, wild as the deer in the forests which we roved and doubtless needing discipline enough."[7] For this discipline, a stern word alone generally sufficed.

Mary Robertson, wife of the redoubtable Daniel, came from an even earlier migration of Scots that had first settled in New England before moving on to Sherbrooke in the Eastern Townships. She came from a cultured family, and C.W. Gordon described her father as a man of fine culture and high spiritual quality. Mary followed her graduation from the Sherbrooke Young Ladies' Academy with studies at Mount Holyoke Female Seminary in Massachusetts and graduated with honours in English, mathematics, and philosophy.

Soon after Mary's return to Sherbrooke, the principal of the seminary died and the twenty-two-year-old Mary Robertson was invited to become principal in her place. She was eager to accept, but her father, wanting to keep her within the confines of the Highland community, pointedly advised, "I think the Lord will doubtless find you some good work to do in Canada, my lassie."[8] Presumably the Lord did, for within a year she had married the fiery young Daniel and gone with him to his church among the Gaelic-speaking "crude crofters" of the Highland community of Lingwick in the so-called Indian Lands, previously Mohawk lands. Within six months, using the Gaelic Bible and a Gaelic dictionary that she sent for, Mary could read the Gospels and recite the Lord's Prayer in the native tongue. For two years she worked among the struggling women of Lingwick, teaching them hygiene, cooking, childcare, and the Bible. Her next home in the manse of Glengarry proved even more remote from civilization, 40 km from the nearest railway. Her son describes her as fearless and compassionate, galloping along the forest trails with the latest baby perched before her on the saddle and another on the way. Daniel, often away on long missionary journeys, left Mary in charge of their little farm, and Charles Gordon recalled following her across a field on a frosty November morning, gathering up lambs wounded and torn by the wolves the night before, her face wet with tears as the two of them carried the lambs by sled to the barn. How lonely she may have been, no one ever knew, but martyr she was not, with her lively step and bright spirit, described by her son as "a gay and gallant saint."[9]

The ten years of childhood in Glengarry proved formative for Charles, and he immortalized them in the tales of Ralph Connor. "All that is set down in *Glengarry School Days* is true," he later wrote, and in some deep corner within himself he never left that tightly knit tribal and secure state of being. A review of his autobiography, *Postscript to Adventure*, edited by his son King and published posthumously in 1938, described C.W. Gordon as "100 per cent tribal, striding across continents with swing of kilt, triumphing in the tartan of his clan and blowing his own bagpipe like the rest."[10] Shortly before his own death in 1989, King Gordon wrote, "There [Glengarry] my father was born and lived for his first 10 years. And much later as we grew up in our home in Winnipeg, we somewhat got the impression that Glengarry was our native heath and that its Highland Scots were our kinfolk. And I've never quite lost that feeling."[11]

After teaching for a year in a country school, Charles and Gilbert set off for the University of Toronto in the fall of 1880. While there, the brothers were drawn to the prestigious St James Square Presbyterian Church, whose minister, the Reverend Dr John M. King, attracted crowds of students by his powerful intellectual teaching and preaching. Gilbert chose medicine as a career, and Charles decided for the ministry, studying classics and English. While both brothers were serious about their studies and took honours, they were not willing to sacrifice other aspects of university life to academic standing, a decision Charles looked back on with approval. Above all, he loved sports and competition. In the winter months the two spent hours in the gymnasium, where Charles won a reputation as a boxer by bloodying the nose of a big, brawny Highlander who weighed 180 pounds.

Graduating in 1883, Charles spent the summer in the wilderness north and west of Lake Nipissing, speculating for gold with his eldest brother Robertson, a mining engineer. It was an expedition to challenge the hardiest adventurer, let alone a weary, homesick student, but in the Herculean expenditure of energy it called forth, it united Charles's great love of the outdoors with his need for challenge and achievement, and it laid the basis for a style of ministry and life. In the exultation of success he wrote: "It is one of the supreme joys of life to be thoroughly fit. At the end of my fifth week I made that great discovery ... I say life is one gay song for the man fit for his day. And a man gets fit by observing the inexorable laws of life, work, food and rest in proper proportion and environment ... It is being as God meant you to be."[12]

This joy of life, love of the outdoors, and eagerness to be fit, "to wake and be willing to spring from your spruce bed ready for your morning dive," was a heritage C.W. Gordon passed on to his children, but especially to his son. One had only to observe King Gordon, at the age of eighty-five, dive from a rock on Birkencraig, the family island, into the shining morning waters of Lake of the Woods to feel its enduring spirit.

After studying theology at Knox College in Toronto, Charles, in one of those serendipitous moments that later characterized his son King's life (and which both interpreted as providential, though the son less explicitly so), was contacted by Dr James Robertson, the superintendent of missions in the Presbyterian Church in the West, to offer him a position as missionary to Banff, in the new Presbytery of Calgary, "the largest presbytery in the world." Charles found himself touched by the romance and promise of the sparsely settled West. In the 1880s, the region of Banff consisted largely of mining villages, lumber camps, and two or three railway stations, its magnificent beauty not yet developed as a centre of tourism. After four adventurous years on the mission field among the miners and lumberjacks of the West, he was called to serve as the first minister for the Presbyterian mission on the outskirts of Winnipeg, which would come to be known as St Stephen's, where he served until his death in 1938.

Once again the Reverend King, now the very distinguished principal of Manitoba College, entered the picture. It was he who decided that the West End Mission should be constituted into a church. However, as it was woefully lacking in funds, Gordon travelled to Toronto to meet the General Assembly's Committee on Missions. Undoubtedly, his most significant meeting was with his old friend T.A. Macdonald, editor of the church paper, *The Westminster Magazine*, who challenged him to write a tale for Eastern readers and assured him, "You'll get your money." Thus C.W. Gordon began his career as a writer, under the *nom de plume* of Ralph Connor, with the publication of his first novel, *Black Rock*.[13]

It is difficult to overestimate the popularity and influence of Ralph Connor's novels in the English-speaking world during the early years of the twentieth century. Nor can one understand King Gordon's easy identification of himself as a Canadian, his deep-rooted sense of being at home in the world, and his rejection of that colonial remnant referred to as the "garrison mentality" (so prevalent among Eastern intellectuals) without placing him within the context of his father's vigorous nationalism and vision of the western spirit as defining what it meant to be Canadian. Throughout his long international career, it was as though King Gordon carried within himself the fresh winds of the Canadian West and the independent confidence of the frontier – the West of Ralph Connor.

For thirty years in the early part of the century, Ralph Connor was the most widely read Canadian writer. It is estimated that the total hardcover sales of his twenty-six novels exceeded five million. His books were read by everyone – prairie farmers, prime ministers, presidents of the United States, common people of all descriptions – and he was received with respect in high places and adored in humble church halls. What accounted for such overwhelming popularity? With the publication in 1898 of *Black Rock, A Tale of the Selkirks,* he broke through the superficial refinements of Victorian Canada and appealed to a belief in individual initiative that he feared was being lost in the industrial and urban development of Eastern Canada. It was in the West that the individual still counted and where the new Canadian would be born. In his novels of the social gospel and imperial adventure, Charles W. Gordon tapped into an early version of the Canadian search for identity as the new nation struggled to establish itself, and he depicted a confident, aggressive nationalism. He described his heroes and heroines as "good, clean young Canadians, worthy in body, mind and spirit of the new nation that was coming into being in the minds of the Canadian people."[14]

Central to Ralph Connor's understanding of this new nationalism was the vision of a unified and autonomous Canada within the great parenting body, the British Empire.[15] The new Canadian nation would draw on the best of British traditions – the belief in fair play, the social constraints of law and order – while rejecting its class society and undemocratic social structures. But what of the tide of *non*-British immigrants pouring into Canada? What was their place in this land that was to draw so deeply on British tradition? Connor addressed this question in *The Foreigner* (1909), expressing the belief that it would be in the West that these "foreign" traditions and ethnicities would coalesce and be absorbed into the emerging Canadian identity.

Modern readers, their sensibilities shaped by the mosaic model of Canadian cultural identity, might interpret Ralph Connor's descriptions of eastern European immigrants, crowded into the tarpaper shacks of north Winnipeg, as patronizing and ethnocentric. King Gordon, however, writing the introduction to the reissue of *The Foreigner* (1972), offered a caveat in his father's defence by pointing out that in fact C.W. Gordon, as minister of St Stephen's Presbyterian Church, worked tirelessly to initiate the struggling immigrants into Canadian society and to prevent their exploitation.

In 1958, while stationed in Cairo with the United Nations Information Centre for the Middle East, King Gordon sent his son Charles copies of Ralph Connor's books. He confessed the difficulty of being objective about one's own father, but went on in some detail to describe him as having a great zest for life, a love of people, a competitive spirit, and outstanding courage. He concluded his letter: "One other thing. He was a great Canadian at a time when Canada was just feeling its way to an independent life of its own. That came out in his great work in Western Canada, in his fight for a decent city in Winnipeg, in his work in the First World War. And then he went on to be a great internationalist because having seen war at close range he hated it. And being a Christian he looked for and worked towards a society that would embody Christian principles."[16]

Some years later, Charles wrote an article on his grandfather in which he said, "One sees Ralph Connor through the eyes of his family – most clearly, in this way, because Ralph Connor is very much alive in the consciousness of his son and daughters, and grandchildren."[17] King Gordon was the beneficiary of the sturdy, optimistic, and finally inclusive nationalism of his father, as throughout his life he translated these qualities into a modern idiom.

King Gordon's ancestry through his mother also began in Scotland and came to fruition in Manitoba.[18] Helen Skinner King was born in Toronto in 1876 to Janet Skinner and the Reverend J.M. King. When Helen was eight, her father left St James Church and moved his young family to Winnipeg, where he had been appointed the first principal of Manitoba College.

When Charles Gordon accepted the call to the small mission church in Winnipeg, Dr King became his mentor and friend, and the King household his second home. As Helen grew from a cheerful, enthusiastic, and loyal member of the mission band into a comely young lady Charles Gordon's easy participation in the King household had become increasingly complicated for him. An incurable romantic and unsophisticated in matters of the heart, he responded with an act of renunciation. There would be no more Sunday dinners. When the girl's father inquired into the matter, Charles explained the dilemma of his heart. Dr King responded by pointing to the sixteen-year disparity in their ages and the absurdity of such a relationship. Charles meekly deferred, and proceeded to enlighten Helen on the situation. "I have never forgotten the quick flash of rapture in her eyes as … I told her that for her father's sake and my own sake I must keep away from her. The joy in her voice amazed me. Nothing mattered but the fact that it was because I loved her that I must keep away from her."[19] The principal deemed it appropriate that at this time his daughter, who had already gained a bachelor of arts from Manitoba College, should spend a year at his alma mater, the University of Edinburgh, clearly hoping that distance might cool their ardour. Undaunted, Helen set off for her year abroad in good spirits, assuring Charles that "Everything will come out all right."[20]

When Dr King became unexpectedly and seriously ill, Charles visited him daily, and at the end, heard the longed-for words: "I feel very happy that Helen will be in your care. She would be happy with no one else."[21] Dr King died in March 1899, and Charles and Helen were married in Toronto 28 September.

Helen's disposition reflected a gentle, unforced optimism, an easy confidence that later characterized her son John King. She went to Toronto to assemble her trousseau, and in only one letter, to her friend back in Winnipeg, did she allude to her grief at the loss of her father: "It will be lovely to be home again although in some ways it will be hard to go back and there will be a lonely feeling. But I am not going to think any more of it than I can help. There will be so much happiness to compensate all that."[22]

A large measure of that happiness arrived with the birth, on 6 December 1900, of John King, named after her father. It was a trying delivery for both parents, though in the telling it seems to have been the father, Charles, who bore the brunt. Banishing himself to the basement to tend the furnace (and, by his own admission, over-heating the house), he spent twenty-four hours in anxious agony praying for his wife's safe passage through travail. At last the doctor announced, "A fine boy!" "Well, daddy! What do you think of him?" asked his wife. Charles reported his relief in his autobiography, "'He looks all right, the little beggar,' I said as the nurse held up a red and wrinkled little old man for me to admire."[23] Thus was King Gordon launched into this world, the fruit of a sturdy ancestry, welcome, and surely, to the welcoming eyes of his parents, "trailing clouds of glory."[24]

2

A Dutiful Son

When he arrived in 1894 to take up his responsibilities as a missionary in its western outskirts, Charles Gordon described Winnipeg as "a hustling city fresh from its big boom of '81 to '83 with its soaring hopes and prices, its inflated ambitions and real estate, its vast and daring investments,"[1] which envisioned itself as a northern Chicago or Minneapolis, a gateway to the resources and markets of the vast prairie beyond.

In 1900, the year of King Gordon's birth, Winnipeg had a population of 42,000; by 1911 it had grown to 142,000. Suburbs began to spread out from the city. To the north, a community of Eastern European immigrants crowded into narrow streets and tarpaper shacks; south of the Assiniboine, Fort Rouge had become the residential district of the well-off.[2] Modest frame houses stretched to the west and Portage Avenue formed a kind of dividing line between the working-class and middle- to upper-class districts. It was in this central area that the Gordons lived, with St Stephen's Church at the corner of Spence and Portage, one block west of Balmoral.

Looking back from his old age, King remembered the Winnipeg of his childhood first of all in sounds that evoked images of the secure world that surrounded him. He described the Winnipeg of his childhood as the Venice of the prairie, a city without the noise of traffic in those long-ago days before the car. It was the sounds of horses' hooves on pavement that captivated his senses, the slow walk of the heavy trucks, the lighter, cluttered trot of his father's Strathcona, King Monbar, out for his daily exercise. In winter he listened for the sleigh bells, the slow bells on the big drays as they hauled away the mash from Shay's brewery, and the high, quick bells of Eaton's delivery. At night the train whistles cut across the clear, cold prairie when the temperature reached -34°C. He heard the clanking of the railway cars from the CPR station 2 km away as they were shunted across the yard; the sounds of the prairie in winter, the runners of the cutter on the surface of the snow as King Monbar raced homeward, with his passengers, King and his father, bundled up against the cold; the gentler sounds of the prairie in summer, of wind in the grass, and meadowlarks on the fence posts. In harmony with these pre-electronic sounds, it seemed to King that human communication also proceeded with a directness and intensity that compensated in part for its slower pace.[3]

King's early childhood was lived in the security of Scottish Presbyterianism, in a home dominated by the ebullient optimism of his father and the tender, adoring care of his mother, and his nurse, Agnes Pringle. "Ach, King," she would complain in response to childish pique, "You've a black dog on your back!"[4] He was of a sunny disposition, and the firm hand of Aggie and his mother, both parents' progressive ideas on child rearing, and the Gordon family's generous enjoyment of their children, seem, to a large extent, to have rendered moot the question of punishment. While both parents had a lively sense of humour, King described his father's love for fun as extravagant, enjoying practical jokes and appreciating the absurd. His father relished all kinds of games with his children and acted out charades with exaggerated mimicry, to the point of calling for a reprimand delivered in mock sternness by his wife.

In the winter, their father would flood the side yard to make a hockey rink, playing vigorously himself; in the summer it was tennis, baseball, and softball. He loved horses and racing, and Monbar was one of the fastest horses in Winnipeg. The winter ice on the river made a natural track and, until members of the congregation curtailed such activities of their minister as unseemly, cutter racing provided a keenness to winter sports.

During these pre-adolescent years, both parents travelled frequently, Helen to Toronto for church meetings or to visit friends and relatives, and C.W. Gordon, by now famous as Ralph Connor, on his many speaking engagements. The separations brought little disruption in attention and affectionate involvement with the children. In a letter typical of the many from father to son, C.W. Gordon wrote to seven-year-old King from Philadelphia in April, 1907:

> My dear King, Good boy – your letters are fine and do Daddy a lot of good. One day I came in pretty tired and a little lonely and what

> should I find waiting me but four fine letters – from four of the finest people in the world – a little boy with blue eyes and short hair and strong as a little bull and his name is ---------. And a little girl with lovely blue eyes and a Dutch cut and good and her name is ---------- and another little girl with lovely brown curls and blue eyes and her name is ----------- and now I want you before you read one more word to ask Mother to find that little boy and give him a hug and a kiss for me.[5]

His father concluded his letter by urging King to care for his mother and his sisters and not to think of himself alone: "Jesus thought of other people." Other letters of the period included admonishments to King to do the right thing, and become a strong brave man who would please God and do some good in the world. His mother reminded him to say his prayers night and morning and to read his Bible; and since he was at camp when she wrote, he was not to swim more than once a day and never to fool in boats or canoes.[6]

Life in the summer revolved around Birkencraig, the Gordons' island in Lake of the Woods. It was in 1907 when King was six that his father put his canoe into the lake from a dock near Kenora and, as King described it, launched his son into a new world. They landed on a sandy beach about 6 km into the lake and pitched their tent. That same year, C.W. Gordon bought a 36-acre island and built a lodge, and the summer saga of life at Birkencraig began.[7]

The lake, 96 km long and 80 km wide, abounds with thousands of islands, some merely single rocks jutting out of the lake's surface and covered with stunted pine, other larger ones heavy with the rich growth of evergreen, silver birch, and underbrush. King's Oxford classmate, Malcolm MacDonald, a frequent visitor in later years, caught the peculiar beauty of the lake in a reverie he wrote after an early autumn visit, describing the changes brought by the early frosts as celebrating a "pageantry of startling gorgeousness … in a blaze of color red green and yellow wherever a crumb of land protrudes above the blue surface of the water."[8] King preserved the original copy of this unpublished paean to the beauty of the island and lake among his own private papers.

Life on the island provided the children with opportunities to develop self-reliance and survival skills and they all became competent canoeists, swimmers, woodsmen, and campers. The society of Birkencraig observed the conventional division of labour of the time. The men did the heavy work of wood chopping and splitting, clearing, running the boat and the pump, and all the other manual and mechanical work. The women and girls shared the household chores of cooking, cleaning, laundry, and preparing lists of supplies for the men to buy in Kenora. While King's father held centre stage in the outdoor and social life of the island, his mother, in her gentle, efficient way and with endless acts of generosity and kindness, kept island life on an even keel and increasingly became its true centre.

In order to ensure a fresh supply of milk, from 1908 to 1918 C.W. Gordon arranged to have a cow brought down from Winnipeg each summer to provide twelve to fourteen quarts of milk daily for the camp. At the island, the responsibility for the cow's care fell on all members of the family, and at age fifteen King himself travelled down from Winnipeg with the cow, sharing the box car and, on arrival in Kenora, personally escorting it down to the dock and onto the barge. King wrote to his father in England, where he was stationed with the Canadian Expeditionary Force, "Just before dinner Stuart Holley brought the cow. We leave Winnipeg tonight at eleven, all the stuff has to be on board at 5. As I have a tin whistle and a mouth organ, and George [now the family coachman] has his gramophone, I don't think the trip down will be slow."[9] That particular cow – "Rainbows" – learned to swim and began to explore nearby islands, resulting more than once in a general cowhunt and a long swim home behind the rowboat for the cow, with King holding the lead. The cow era ended when a dairy was established in Kenora, and with it vanished the cowshed and park; but for many years thereafter, patches of grass and clover continued to thrive under the trees of Rainbows's fertilized pasture.

The bonfire was a Birkencraig institution going back to its earliest days, in the first instance as a means of burning the cleared trees and brush on the safety of the beach, a spot that became known as Bonfire Point. King described the ritual closely followed on each such occasion: Shortly after supper, people wended their way from the lodge – either by beach path or in canoes and rowboats – to the Point. At the signal, the birchbark was touched off, followed by a mounting roar as the pile caught fire and the sparks soared upward. As the flame settled into a steady blaze, the children emerged with their pointed sticks, and collected a marshmallow from Mrs Gordon for the roast. The singing followed, with C.W. Gordon strumming on his guitar, leading the singers in spirituals and songs from the Scottish Highlands. The sky darkened and the stars came out, the mists rising in the hollows bringing out the sweet smells of the cooling earth. And then it was time to find their way back to the lodge, singing quietly, smaller children in arms, some walking along the beach, others rowing in the shallow water along the shore. King and his cousin Charles (Chile) stayed to put out the fire and then tucked themselves into bed in their nearby tent, falling asleep to the cry of loons.[10]

A lifetime later, as King Gordon slept on a desert floor in the Sinai or under the sheltering tropical growth of the Congo, did he think back to those tranquil moments of childhood, listening to the night sounds of Birkencraig?

While later in his life as a theologian, minister, and political activist, Gordon's debt to his father's progressive Presbyterianism became abundantly evident, in his growing years religion was not a sombre thing but one that fell lightly on the shoulders of the children, having "a lot of joy and happiness in it." There was a day-to-day quality of faith in the Gordon household and, with the large family gathered around the table, meals became a kind of seminar, with C.W. reporting back on his church duties and his activities with the Winnipeg Ministerial Association in their efforts to right social wrongs. Although C.W. Gordon was a strongly emotional man with what King described as "an experience which represented real commitment which most of the rest of us didn't have," at the same time he had a practical, respectable approach to religion that expressed itself in a certain caution about "enthusiasts." Within the Gordon family, evangelism was seen as an intensification of beliefs already held, and one was not likely to be swept away by ecstatic religious experience.[11]

Formally, of course, the religious life of the Gordon family was anchored in St Stephen's where King's father was now senior minister. His mother too, had moved smoothly into her position as minister's wife; however, King wrote later that she was never impeded by the conventional confines of that role in the early twentieth century, and that she threw herself wholeheartedly into all church activities, exhibiting a joyful, willing spirit as she led the women of the congregation in lives of service. What she did was a free expression of what she was.[12] King joined the church at fifteen, an event normally spoken of as a conversion. He confessed that it was not the great emotional experience he had anticipated and that he felt "just about the same afterwards as before." However, he did note that it was a solemn occasion that gave one a certain status in the congregation.[13]

The informal richness of childhood stories, tales, and singing gave way to formal education when King was six with the hiring of a red-headed

Irish tutor named Miss Smith. This private arrangement lasted for two years. When King turned eight he entered the Model School affiliated with the Normal School, a public school later described by King as "kind of elitist," where one paid fees, and it included mainly children of the professional and well-to-do classes.

By 1912, when King entered Kelvin High School, the Gordon family numbered eight. King's birth in 1900 had been followed by five sisters: Mary, Greta, Lois, Ruth, and Marjorie. In 1914, C.W. Gordon moved his family to 54 Westgate, the newly completed twenty-three-room three-storey red brick mansion that he had built in the Jacobean Revival style. Its size, elegance, and location on Armstrong's Point overlooking the Assiniboine River, among the homes of Winnipeg's wealthiest residents, may have raised a few eyebrows among fellow clergy, but by this time C.W. Gordon was a wealthy man himself, a famous author, who continued to advocate and work relentlessly for the rights and welfare of the downtrodden. Moreover, the door at 54 Westgate was always open to visiting clergy (spare beds kept ready for such occasions), and to the stream of guests arriving from around the world, friends of the great author. The children were always included around the large dining room table on these occasions, where they listened to (and sometimes participated in) the conversation, exposed to a world well beyond Armstrong's Point. As for King, he had his own study, bedroom, and bath on the third floor. It was an enchanted childhood for the young Gordons, with large grounds for games and exploring and the riverbank for sledding in the winter. And in the summers, there was Birkencraig.[14]

Kelvin High School, one of the city's two new technical schools, offered both practical training in the trades – machine shop, electricity, and wood turning – and a traditional program focusing on the humanities and languages, including French, Latin, and Greek, each of which King studied. Although his parents regarded him as too young to attend university, he entered the University of Manitoba at the age of fifteen. By this time the First World War had begun. It was to have a radical effect on the Gordons' life.

Word of the outbreak of hostilities reached the Gordons at Birkencraig, and Gordon always remembered the hollowness in the pit of his stomach when he realized that his father would be going to war. To the thirteen-year-old boy, battle did not at all seem a glorious thing. There was no question that C.W. Gordon would volunteer to serve; however, at fifty-four, there was some doubt whether his services would be accepted. He described his own reaction in his memoirs:

> The daily papers brought to our island home by my son King, not yet fourteen years old, were read aloud at the tea table: a few friends and our six children, one boy and five girls, down to a baby sitting in a high chair.
> "Will you go to war?" asked my eldest girl, Mary, her big hazel eyes fixed upon my face. "Sure, he will go," said King with scornful impatience.[15]

The elder Gordon took the newspaper from his son and retreated to the woods, weighing his concern for his wife and small children against his duty as chaplain to his kilted regiment, the 79th Cameron Highlanders, for the first time facing the "terrible and ugly" reality of war, stripped of all romantic glory. He called King, and together they slipped away to Kenora. This was the private, reflective side of C.W. Gordon. Social historian Richard Allen describes another, more public, side in which military aggression was another aspect of the economic and industrial power that would crush civilization and Christianity, and which must be defeated. Allen quotes C.W. Gordon: "The failure of the State to eliminate war … is signal and ghastly."[16] Within a week, C.W.'s colonel had wired Ottawa announcing that, to a man, the 79th Cameron Highlanders had offered to serve overseas. Later that year, C.W. Gordon issued the clarion call to his fellow countrymen:

> O Canada, What answer make to calling voice and beating drum,
> To sword gleam and to pleading prayer of God
> For right? What answer makes my soul?
> "Mother, to thee! God, to Thy help! Quick! My sword."[17]

The 79th Cameron Highlanders remained in Winnipeg as a recruiting unit, but a battalion of 1,100 of its men, to be known as the 43rd Cameron Highlanders of Canada, sailed for Europe in the spring of 1915. Of this number, 350 were members of St Stephen's Church, including two elders who were officers and another parishioner who was a colonel. As official chaplain to the entire battalion (and shortly to become chief chaplain of the Canadian Forces in England, as well as senior chaplain for the Third Division in France), Major C.W. Gordon served with them on the Western Front from the Ypres Salient to Sanctuary Wood, the Somme, and back again to Arras. Although chaplains inevitably came under fire while working in the dressing stations and field hospitals with the wounded, their orders forbade their venturing directly into the firing line. Under a special arrangement with his friend and superior officer, Colonel R.M. Thomson, however, and in view of the large contingent of men from his church, these orders were relaxed in Gordon's case. The only time that he was prevented from accompanying his men into the firing line was at the Regina Trench on the Somme where, tragically and with bitter irony, Colonel Thomson himself was killed on October 8, 1916.[18] By this time, his battalion had dwindled from its original strength of 1,100 men to two officers and sixty-five men.[19]

Late in 1916, C.W. Gordon returned to Canada, a trip necessitated by Colonel Thomson's death and the confused nature of his estate, which also involved King Gordon's own financial affairs. Thomson was not only C.W. Gordon's close friend and advisor, but he was also his lawyer. Unfortunately for the Gordon family, the colonel had got into trouble with his own investments and had covered his debts with C.W. Gordon's money. The senior Gordon had great personal affection for his friend, and respect for his heroic death. Moreover, Thompson had been the husband of Gilbert Gordon's widow. When Gordon discovered that his own fortune had been lost, he decided that although he had a legal case, he would not pursue it, out of personal and familial loyalty.[20] He was left to support his large family with a ministerial salary and writing.

Early in 1917, C.W. Gordon was summoned to an interview with the prime minister, Sir Robert Borden, who had been approached by the British government with the proposal that a Canadian should be sent to the neutral United States to popularize the Allied view of the war. With some misgivings, Gordon accepted the assignment and began a demanding schedule of speaking engagements, using his immense popularity and recognition as "Ralph Connor" to present the cause. Once America had entered the war in April of 1917, he worked with the Liberty Loan Campaign, and only returned to his congregation in the fall of 1919.

While their father served the war effort both abroad and on the home front, the family in Winnipeg carried on. The strain on Mrs Gordon was particularly acute, with small children (the new baby, Alison, was born in January 1915 and still in infancy) and the responsibilities of maintaining morale among the congregation. Something of her grit and devotion to her domestic and community life comes through in a letter written to her husband in April 1918 while he was traveling with the Liberty Loan Campaign in the United States. Gordon's itinerary allowed him a brief stop in Minneapolis, and he had asked Helen to join him there for a few days. However, she replied, she was bound by obligation to remain with the family: the children were not well – King had exams – there was housecleaning to be done – and in the Red Cross drive she had fifty-two houses to canvas. She concluded, "I hope you won't think me stubborn but you know how much I want to see you and how lovely it would be to run away and have a good time and leave all the cares and worries behind. But I can't see it to be my duty."[21]

King's letters to his father on school activities, evenings of Shakespeare, and exams show the budding raconteur and the love of a good story that characterized King his entire life, a gift from father to son. His father responded proudly to these reports, writing in July of 1916 from "Flanders Somewhere:" "Just a note tonight to send you my congratulations on your splendid success. That is just fine my boy ... Well my boy you worked faithfully also well and you deserve all you got. And if you are spared I know you will always show the same spirit of fidelity to duty. After all that is the big thing, isn't it? The rewards are in the doing of the work itself and in the cultivation of the habits of fidelity, patience, self-control and endurance. Those are the real rewards. Honors and distinction are after all secondary matters. They are good in their way and very pleasant but they are *not* the things we work for."[22]

His father's call to duty – what *ought* to be done – sank deeply into King Gordon's psyche; it was, one might say, bred in the bone. Many years later, when at the request of the UN Secretary-General, Dag Hammarskjöld, he was asked to leave his UN assignment in Korea and move at short notice to Cairo, he would write to his wife Ruth: "I feel bound [by duty] to accept what the Secretary-General proposes ... I don't feel we can let our personal wishes block what he considers to be the urgent timing of the assumption of duties."[23]

King continued to provide his absent father with the homey details of their lives. One can only imagine how these descriptions of life and the everyday rhythms of life were received by his father, separated from his son by distance and the harsh realities of war. In these reports, one may see the beginnings of a budding raconteur who later in life will report to Canada on the human face of the UN and who will fill his letters to his wife and family with similar stories.

King hoped to join his father in the war and began working on his commission, which he received at seventeen through COTC (Canadian Officers' Training Corps) at the University of Manitoba. He enlisted in the summer of 1918, waiting to be called up on his eighteenth birthday in December. By this time, imbued with his father's view of the conflict as a righteous cause, answering the call to serve was a matter of unquestioned patriotism; he confessed to regarding the November armistice as something of a personal tragedy, depriving him of participation in the war. Even the tragedy of the Regina Trench, so soon to come, and the loss of his dear friend R.M. Thomson did not diminish C.W. Gordon's single-minded patriotism. King followed his father's lead, and there was little hint at this time of the evolution that would gradually replace his youthful enthusiasm for the use of military force; a case in point, he later felt, of how uncritically we absorb the social views of our parents and their communities. Although he never became a pacifist, he admired those who were, and over the course of time he developed a hatred of war and the devastating suffering it brought, convinced that it was the greatest barrier to achieving social justice throughout the world.

This, then, was the dutiful, conventional son who entered the arts faculty of the University of Manitoba in 1915 for four years of what he described as a fairly tranquil time of totally traditional education. He studied Latin, Greek, French, history, mathematics, and economics, concentrating his last two years in economics and Greek. His economics professor was A.B. Clarke from Edinburgh, a true disciple of Adam Smith and the school of classical economics. Clarke was highly doctrinaire, and the course was entirely abstract and theoretical, with no attempt to relate economic doctrine to the practice of everyday, twentieth-century capitalism.

King became editor of the monthly student newspaper, *The Manitoban,* which, during a time of social tumult and war, published articles notably lacking in public critique. "Where Will the New University be Built?" ran one bold headline. His activities also reflected his own obliviousness to the war that raged across Europe and was experienced with such excruciating pain by his own father. He wrote to his father regularly about his participation in university life: debating the form an Arts Literary Club should take; working on a college song book; donning his new COTC uniform. He reported that the COTC recruits found themselves astonished by the difference khaki made to morale.[24]

Although Gordon remembered discussing Walter Rauschenbusch's *Social Teachings of Jesus* at a YMCA meeting, he did not pause to reflect on the relationship of ethics to economic theories or, for that matter, the harsh contemporary realities of North Winnipeg. During the Christmas vacation of 1919, he attended a Student Volunteer Movement conference in Des Moines, Iowa, where he listened to leaders of the international missionary movement such as John R. Mott, Sherwood Eddy, and

Robert Spear talk not simply about evangelism but, as part and parcel of the gospel, the need to set up hospitals and schools and teach modern agricultural methods along with the message of hope. In a flurry of idealistic zeal, King decided to devote his life to the calling of a medical missionary. When his application for a Rhodes scholarship that year was rejected, he prepared for medical studies by taking a post-graduate year in science. Upon receiving a Rhodes the following year (he had not realized that he was still in the running), he dropped his medical plans with alacrity and without particular thought, as he would confess later.[25] Nevertheless, seeds had been sown that would in time bear the fruit of social action.

Meanwhile, life in Winnipeg was far from tranquil. In the wake of the First World War both Canada and the United States endured general labour unrest as they faced the growing disparity between the cost of living and wages, the reintegration of returning soldiers into the work force, and the response by radical labour elements to the Russian revolution. The war years had seen Canada's union ranks grow from 143,200 in 1915 to 378,000 by 1919, and there had been a number of strikes during the war.[26] Late in the war, orders-in-council were passed to suppress radical organizations and literature, and a ban on strikes was imposed in October of 1918. This last action on the part of the government seemed excessive. Labour was alarmed, and responded in a mood of "aggressive self-confidence."[27] The unrest climaxed with the Winnipeg General Strike during May and June 1919.

The immediate cause of the strike involved the grievances of two groups of workers, the building and metal trades, who were attempting to secure the principle of collective bargaining and, secondarily, to demand general wage increases commensurate with the soaring cost of living. Historian Desmond Morton writes that the strike leaders never understood that it was the power of their heated rhetoric rather than their relatively cautious deeds that struck fear into the hearts of the middle classes[28] – some of whom slept in churches for fear of being murdered in their beds.[29] In retrospect, it would seem that the strikers "had no pretensions of securing any kind of political or industrial control" and that the real issue was the right of the metal workers to bargain collectively through agents of their choice.[30]

The climax came early on the morning of Saturday 21 June as the strikers gathered in Market Square preparing to march in protest and Mayor Charles F. Gray read the Riot Act forbidding the parade. At this point, mounted police, some in red coats and some in khaki, broke the parade with an armed charge, pistols drawn, swinging hardwood clubs made from horses' neck-yokes sawn in two. Soldiers appeared with rifles and machine guns before the parade was finally broken in front of City Hall. "Bloody Saturday" had claimed one life and injured thirty others, sixteen of whom were police. On 25 June, the secretary of the Central Strike Committee sent a message to Premier T.C. Norris informing him that the strike would end the following day.

C.W. Gordon was absent from Winnipeg during the strike; however he was no stranger to labour disputes and had an impressive record of backing the workers. Shortly after the Winnipeg Strike, the provincial government created the Council of Industry for Manitoba, with C.W. Gordon serving as its first chairman. In his role as mediator and conciliator in a number of strikes, C.W. Gordon achieved a remarkable record of success. King attributed his father's success to his firm belief that there was always something to be said on both sides, and if the issues of dispute were opened up to the public and arguments made, the right course would emerge. In a 1974 interview, he pointed out that while in the General Strike his father's sympathies lay with the radical elements, his father's goal was non-ideological and pragmatic, and he rejected the notion of conflict and saw himself as a reconciler. King said that his father would never have identified – and, in fact, never did identify – himself as a socialist.[31]

As far as King himself was concerned, nothing in his own actions at the time of the Winnipeg Strike gave any hint of the radical to come. He recalled meeting J.S. Woodsworth and being in his home on Maryland Street while he was a student at university, but this man who became such an influence on his later life seems to have made little impression at the time. When the strike broke out, perhaps due in part to his father's absence from the home and from the family dinner table at which the elder Gordon liberally shared his views on current political and social events, King adopted the conventional wisdom on the strike. In such minds the strike had been started by a revolutionary group, the One Big Union movement which was pressing for a program of direct action, and its leaders had ties to Russia and were using foreign agitators to accomplish their purposes in Winnipeg. In a nicely prescient irony, the Reverend Canon Frederick G. Scott of Quebec City, father of Frank Scott, was also identified as an "outside agitator" as he worked alongside J.S. Woodsworth and the strike leaders. It would be many years before Frank Scott and King Gordon, working together for the rights of workers, enjoyed that label themselves.

In retrospect, Gordon expressed regret that his father had not been home to help him sort out the issues; but he saw his own actions and interpretation of the strike as part and parcel of the secure, well-intentioned but still uncritical young man that he was at the age of nineteen. Very shortly, the ballast of King's secure worldview would shift amid the cross-currents of political thought that he encountered at Oxford.

3

Intellectual Awakening at Oxford

In his memoir of Oxford in the 1920s, *An Appetite for Life*, Canadian Charles Ritchie artfully describes the affected indifference so characteristic of the times: "I dined in Hall and sat next to a red-haired man called Ducker with a prominent jaw. I made the mistake of remarking on the effect of the evening light coming through the colored windows on the paneling and portraits. He lowered his head in a disapproving silence. After dinner when we were walking across the quad he told me that it was not good form to make such comments. The beauties of Oxford are supposed to be taken for granted."[1]

The Oxford of Evelyn Waugh's clique, "the dandies" and the "aesthetes" of *Brideshead Revisited*, was, however, only a small part of the story, and many undergraduates were largely unaware of its existence even though they were doubtlessly touched by its languor. For Oxford had lost its brightest and best in the world war, an appalling 2,700 undergraduates out of a population of 3,000.[2] Immediately after the war, the university was crowded with veterans returning straight from the trenches, some suffering from the trauma of war and many grieving for a lost world. These young men were far from blasé. Leslie Hore-Belisha, later secretary of war under Neville Chamberlain, described his returning generation in the *Oxford Outlook* of May 1919, referring to the Thames by its local name: "We came back, but it was by the waters of Isis that we sat down and wept when we remembered Oxford. In truth we were ill at ease in the Zion of our longing. A new generation had sprung up in the land ... and we came as ghosts to trouble joy."[3] For others still young, the return to normal life was simply a vast relief after the horrors of war and they entered into it with an almost frantic "gusto and delight."[4]

It was into this Oxford that young Canadians and Americans poured in the early twenties, many of them Rhodes scholars. They were filled with fresh energy and enthusiasm, largely impervious to the weary decadence of the Old World, and often, like King Gordon, with no bitter memories of battle to overcome. For Lester Pearson, "Oxford University, and St John's in particular, turned out to be all that I had hoped and dreamed. Seldom are expectations so completely fulfilled as were those of my two years at Oxford."[5] Frank Scott's Oxford was "my great adventure,"[6] and Charles Ritchie found himself "shivering with excitement" and hardly knowing what he was saying as friends drove him up to Oxford from London.[7] For King himself, Oxford opened a new and unexpected world of ideas and experience, like breaking out of a comfortable cocoon, offering him "the exposure to a world whose existence I had hardly suspected."[8]

As King left for Oxford in October of 1921, anticipation for what lay ahead, and exhilaration at experiencing for the first time the wonders of New York, London, and Oxford, alternated with a prairie boy's homesickness. As the train pulled out of Winnipeg, he found himself with mingled feelings, the thrill of starting out on his big adventure dimmed by the sadness of leaving behind family and friends; his little sisters, Ashie and Marjorie – "poor kiddies" – rushing around trying to find a shaving kit for him.[9] C.W. Gordon met his son in Toronto, and they travelled down to New York together for King's departure on the *Aquitania*. They stayed at the Waldorf-Astoria, looking down from the tenth floor onto Fifth Avenue from which vantage point he viewed below him, "an eternal pursuit of the God money. Downtown New York ... is unhuman, unlovely, no thought for the artistic, everything sacrificed that the wheels of the great machine of commerce may revolve smoothly and with the least friction possible."[10] This hasty and somewhat superficial judgment may perhaps be attributed to youth, in view of King's happy attachment to this den of commerce and greed within less than a decade of his first visit.

The painful moment of parting arrived with only two gangplanks still down, and in the hurry of boarding King momentarily lost sight of his father. Desperate, and just as the boat prepared to pull out, he saw him standing at the last gangway with pain written all over his face: "Goodbye. God bless you, boy." As the band played "Ain't We Got Fun," with a slight tremor the ship backed out. King stood by the railing trying to grin. "Then feeling very lonesome, watched the New York skyline spread before us – the Statue of Liberty and beyond that the sea. Went below and wrote to Mother to send back with the pilot."[11] C.W. Gordon walked back to the Waldorf-Astoria and wrote to King:

> You will have to find your way boy as we all have. We who have been through think we know. But I suppose after all we don't. For that ancient life path though trodden by all the millions of wayfarers who have gone before us is always a new trail. The markings, the blazes changed, the very landscape shifted, but the main directions remain. East is east and west is west, and the stars are always in their places, and the sun is always there. So certain things will serve you as they served your father and mother. Honor and birth and faith and family, and God. Good night old boy. We will have some nights yet under the stars in our dear land.[12]

The rhetoric is that of another age, but these were the bedrock values that served King Gordon well for the rest of his life.

To King, London, the heart of the Empire, was everything that New York was not. As a guest of Sir Evan and Lady Spicer, friends of his parents, he walked the streets of London enchanted by gentlemen in top hats and dinner jackets, ladies richly dressed for theatre and restaurants, chauffeurs and porters in livery. In the buildings and monuments and "stately towers" he saw symbols of "world empire, world statesmanship and world justice." Apparently, he found the world of commerce more palatable on the Thames than on the Hudson, in this city of "tradition, dignity, humanity and life!!!"[13]

Oxford itself was not less enchanting as he arrived at Queen's, passing through the Palladian front designed by Sir Christopher Wren and settling into his rooms under the bell tower that looked out onto the back quadrangle built by Wren's student, Nicholas Hawksmoor. "Oxford! The land of dreams and very many imaginings has become a sudden reality!" he reported to his Manitoba friend, "dear ole Kay."[14] He assured her that his rooms would be first rate when he got them fixed up: a "bedder" with a fireplace, two cupboards, dresser, washstand, two chairs, and a table; and a "sitter" also with a fireplace, three chairs, two tables, and a bookcase. He put up pictures of friends and family on the mantelpiece, his father in the centre, with one of himself standing on the Treaty Island dock at the lake, looking into the Canadian sunset, far from Oxford. Together with other Rhodes scholars, he had dinner in Hall, "a very splendid old room," he continued to Kay, "richly carved, pictures on the wall life-size of famous graduates. (I understand if you endow the college to the extent of 2,000 pounds you have your picture added to the gallery.)" Eating as he did on this occasion with other North Americans, he was spared reprimand for commenting on the beauties of Oxford. After Hall he walked up the High Street as far as Magdalen Bridge where he found a Canadian canoe lying empty on the water. His mind flashed back to Birkencraig where only a month ago another Canadian canoe drifted down a glassy stream-like channel under bright moonlight, and from woods on the shore he heard the hooting of an owl.[15]

Inevitably, homesickness set in and, typically for students, it happened on a Sunday. The day, 23 October, began not too badly, with attendance at St Columba's Presbyterian Church and a rather sporting lunch with fellow-Manitoban Dick Bonnycastle: cold ham, salad and apple tart with a kick in it. After lunch he tried to read Hugh Walpole, but the damp and cold seeped into his rooms and his bones despite having pulled his chair right up to the fire. He was invited to tea, a "very boring affair," and then attended the University service in St Mary the Virgin where he heard an extremely broadminded sermon "for an Anglican." It was the kind of sermon his father would preach, and afterwards he returned to his cold rooms, not wanting to look up any of the fellows. By this time the chill had seeped into his spirit, not helped by the fact that so far he had not received any letters from home. (Like so many of his Canadian classmates, King suffered from the lack of adequate heat, although later that first term, he wrote to his father, "One does get used to the frigidity of everything tho', and gradually [one] comes to regard the state of being warm as something entirely conventional and unessential."[16]) But King was never down for long. Blessed with a buoyancy and practicality that would stand him in good stead many times later in his life in cold corners of the world, he took the situation in hand: "Made some excellent cocoa which with biscuits and jam went a long way towards cheering me up. It's darn lonesome on Sundays spent in College."[17]

By late October, King had met with his tutors and set up his academic program. The tutorial system at Oxford was a big change from the highly structured life at a Canadian university with its assigned readings, required attendance at lectures, and regular exams. At the beginning of the first term, the student met the tutor who was in charge of the subject he intended to study. King described this Moral Tutor, as he was called, as more or less a "traffic cop" cum guidance counsellor who helped set up courses and assign tutors, then was rarely seen again by the student unless he got into serious difficulty. Officially, according to the *Oxford University Handbook*, at the first interview the tutor would discover how advanced the pupil was and would acquaint him with the requirements for the examinations that he would eventually take at the conclusion of his course of studies.[18] He would also recommend lectures that he should attend. During term, each man (Oxford being an all-male institution at the time) would attend a tutorial at least once a week, meeting with the tutor either alone or in a small group, at which he would read an essay he had written on an assigned reading or topic, followed by questions, discussion, and critique.

Stephen Leacock's appraisal of this system has been most widely quoted: "The lectures, I understand, are given and may even be taken. But they are quite worthless and not supposed to have anything much to do with the development of the student's mind."[19] Perhaps Leacock's satire holds a grain of truth or even insight into the educational process, evoking images of stuffed chairs pulled up before a coal fire doing battle with the Oxford chill, the rumpled tweeds, the pipe, the unhurried and meditative critique, the intellectual intimacy. It was a process that cut across the more "bustling" ways of North Americans, and the handling of unstructured time proved more than a challenge for some of them. Charles Ritchie found himself reprimanded for falling into leisurely afternoons and evenings of gambling. "I went to McCallum today for my tutorial. After I had finished reading my essay he said, 'You are a Scottish Canadian, aren't you? Not a race, I think, to waste time and throw away opportunities in the way you are doing at present.' I was somewhat taken aback but said that I intended to work much harder in the future. He said, 'See to it,' in a rather grim voice."[20]

One young Canadian of Scottish descent needed no such warning, and King settled in eagerly to the Oxford routine of morning study, lectures, and writing essays, afternoons of sport followed by tea and conversation with friends and, after dinner in Hall, evenings of social events, clubs, or reading. He chose modern greats for his course of study – philosophy, politics, and economics, a "well balanced course of study in the social problems of the modern world"[21] – and he responded to the tutorial system with alacrity. His tutor in philosophy was Herbert F. Paton from Edinburgh, a Kantian and an expert in logic. King described him as "splendid and a very keen thinker," having been challenged severely by the tutor in his uncritical attempts to hold conflicting points of view on the grounds of being inclusive. "Very good Gordon, very good," Paton would say at the conclusion of an essay. "But last week you were arguing the opposite point. How do you account for this?" While Gordon tried to explain, finding himself only sinking deeper into the bog, Paton smoked and watched, finally commenting with a snort, "All very difficult, Gordon, isn't it? All very difficult."[22] He found the readings challenging as he plunged into Plato ("really quite deep at times"), Aristotle and eventually a great deal of Descartes, Berkeley, Hume, Kant ("he's great stuff and worth all the study you put on him"), Schopenhauer, and Bergson.[23]

He studied modern politics and history with Godfrey Elton (who sometimes sported a monocle), a partisan of the Labour Party who later became a Labour peer. While Elton was an excellent historian of political thought, it was in writing, language, and presentation of ideas that King felt he gained most. Elton was ruthlessly critical of what King admitted was his sloppy style, and horrified that he used "glimpse" as a verb. Years later (in Khartoum, appropriately enough), Gordon picked up a copy of Elton's biography of General Charles George Gordon and was delighted and somewhat vindicated to find Elton himself using "glimpsed."[24] But King also gained a fine background in political philosophy from the readings Elton assigned, moving from classical Greek and Roman thought down through the middle ages to Bodin and Grotius, and to the theories of the nation state and international law that became so essential later in his thinking as an internationalist. He read Reformation thought, exploring the delicate balance between authority and community, and examined the nature of the political contract as it appears in the thought of Hobbes (whose theory of sovereignty he considered "utter rot"), Locke, and Rousseau. From the Utilitarians and J.S. Mill, he moved into the notions of "positive liberty" of T.H. Green and L.T. Hobhouse (whom he heard lecture), culminating in R.H. Tawney's critique of the capitalist state. There is no evidence that he read Marx at Oxford, although, as will become clear, he eagerly absorbed the ideas of Fabian socialism. His vacation reading lists also included ethical philosophy, Moore and Bradley, as well as Dicey, Bryce, and Bertrand Russell.

Economics, that first term, did not work out as happily; but the new term brought him the greatest good fortune in a new economics tutor, F.L. Ogilvie, who would have a profound and formative influence on his intellectual development. He was already experiencing a shift in his thinking that was taking him beyond the conventional wisdom of his undergraduate economics. King's thinking in other areas was also expanding under the influence of Oxford. In spite of the internationalism of his father, as a student in Winnipeg King had remained largely ignorant of international affairs and, except for his brief dedication to the notion of service through medicine, appeared generally uninterested in the subject. Already, in his first term at Oxford, there is evidence of an awakening interest, albeit highly conventional, in the area that would in later life become his greatest passion. Perhaps it began as for the first time he viewed Canada from the imperial perspective, hearing himself and his fellow Canadians referred to as "colonials" – something he regarded as a bit of a joke, "a strange quirk of the Brits."[25]

However, with the Imperial Conference of 1926 coming up, King joined with a small group of Canadians called the "O Canada Club," who met regularly to discuss Canada's constitutional future and its position in the Empire or emerging Commonwealth. The group included George Ferguson and John Low at Christ Church, Graham Spry and Perry Hamilton at University College, John Farthing at New College and W.H. Brown and King Gordon at Queen's. Together they shared a nascent sense of being Canadian that had remained largely unnecessary until they left their native shores, at which point it became a matter of self-discovery. They were agreed in their rejection of a common government for a British-centred commonwealth and were adamant that the former dominions and colonies must be equal and independent. King wrote to his father: "Last night [15 May 1923] in many ways, was our most successful meeting."[26] The issue under discussion had been that of Canada's role in her own defence: would Canada remain dependent on England for her defence, or would she – God forbid – turn to the protection of the Monroe Doctrine and become dependent on the United States? The consensus seemed to be that Canada's best hope, critical to her own de velopment of nationalism, lay in shouldering her full share of the responsibility for her own defence in a commonwealth with the other dominions and dependencies. To modern ears, the enthusiasm of these youthful scholars may justifiably be thought to outstrip the niceties of argument, but along with other young Canadians of that first post-war generation, King and his friends were struggling with the issue of national identity that would dominate the national psyche for several generations.

Through the Colonial Club, a much larger group of over 200 members, King was meeting students from all parts of the Empire, listening to new perspectives and gaining information. In December of his first term, a student addressed the group on his recent experiences in Central Europe and the appalling conditions in the capital cities as well as those in the Balkans and Constantinople. King found himself interested in the "Irish Question." Regarding the "Reparation business," he had no doubt that Germany was playing a crooked game and doctoring the balance sheet. However, he considered the Disarmament conference a "wonderful achievement."[27] During Christmas vacation in London, he attended a meeting of the "World Alliance of the Churches for Promoting International Friendship," where he met several acquaintances of his father. However unsophisticated these responses to current affairs may have been at the beginning of his Oxford years (he would laugh with a certain rueful merriment as he recalled them years later), one could perhaps, with only slight hyperbole, think of him as a "budding" internationalist.

Social life at Oxford was an invaluable part of the educational process, and King spent a great deal of time being educated in this mode: the ritual of tea and conversation with friends in their rooms, most often that first term with Dick Bonnycastle and Gilbert Webb, an engineering student from South Africa; discussions over dinner in Hall; evenings at lectures or clubs, the theatre or concerts, or simply in more conversations in rooms, concluding with the inevitable cocoa (King was still a teetotaller) and biscuits with jam. Professor Paton held informal discussions every Tuesday night in his room, where they discussed general philosophical subjects of interest, including psycho-therapeutics and psychoanalysis, "which have more or less taken intellectual London by storm," drifting on to a consideration of spiritualism and telepathy. In addition to the O Canada group and the Colonial Club (of which Lester Pearson was also a member), King joined the Oxford Union, where he heard Stephen Leacock speak. King introduced himself, and Leacock recalled his student days with C.W. Gordon at Toronto. He also joined the Bach Choir, then under the direction of Sir Hugh Allen, and Queen's Eglesfield Musical Society, which gave an invitation concert in the Hall of the College each term.

Throughout his life, Gordon was a devoted and loyal friend, happiest when he was part of a team with a mission, and generous perhaps to a fault. At Oxford, he had many friends. During the first term, Dick Bonnycastle and Gilbert Webb were his closest companions. He also formed lifelong friendships with Gilbert Ryle, who later became a noted philosopher; Malcolm MacDonald, the son of Ramsay MacDonald;[28] and Graham Spry, who had inherited the editorship of *The Manitoban* from King, and who later became one of his closest cohorts in the League for Social Reconstruction and the CCF. In 1924, during King's last term, Ramsay MacDonald was elected prime minister and this happy circumstance gave Malcolm and his friends access to Chequers, the prime-ministerial country estate only 64 km from Oxford. King enjoyed piling into P.I. Bell's car along with Malcolm, Gilbert and sometimes including

King's sister Mary or other combinations of friends, for a day's outing in that elegant, pastoral setting.

George Ferguson and Arnold Heeney, both Rhodes scholars from Manitoba, also became good friends. Ferguson later became editor-in-chief of the *Montreal Star*, and Heeney became a distinguished Canadian diplomat. But although Gordon knew Mike Pearson (who was at St John's) largely through sports and the Colonial Club, it was not until their mature years that this acquaintance developed into friendship. Other contemporary Canadians included W. Hurst Brown and Jay MacFarlane from Saskatchewan, both of whom became distinguished medical doctors; John Farthing, the son of the Anglican Bishop of Montreal, with whom King spent a vacation in Florence; John Low of Calgary; Perry Hamilton; Terry MacDermot; Norman Robertson, later High Commissioner to the UK and Canadian Ambassador to Washington; and Roland Michener, a graduate of the young University of Alberta, Rhodes scholar, and future governor general of Canada. The preponderance of these Oxford friends (nearly all Rhodes scholars) who, along with Pearson, found careers at the highest levels of Canadian public service, leads one to wonder if Gordon might also have followed their career path. As it was, his radical politics precluded such an eventuality.

King also found himself the recipient of endless invitations to tea and dinner with the many contacts and friends of his parents. Then too, there were the relatives, connections with the Robertson family of C.W. Gordon's maternal ancestry, some of them extremely elderly. At times, this hospitality proved too much even for King's convivial spirit and, as he complained to his father, "I am rather overwhelmed at these unknown kinsmen thronging in upon me."[29] One family proved the exception, however: the Aberdeens in Scotland, who had deep connections with Canada and with the Gordons.

Lord Aberdeen, John Campbell Hamilton-Gordon, 1st Marquis of Aberdeen and Temair, had been appointed governor general of Canada in 1893, serving until 1898. Before his appointment, he and his wife Ishbel had already travelled widely in the Canadian West. C.W. Gordon first met Lord and Lady Aberdeen at Banff during his missionary service there, and they were drawn together by their love for the wild beauty of the landscape and their deep Presbyterian faith. In 1913 C.W. Gordon travelled to Scotland to attend the General Assembly of the Presbyterian Church, visiting the Aberdeen ancestral seat in Aberdeenshire. On King's first visit in 1921, his Lordship happily declared him "a chip off the old block!"[30] Both the Aberdeens became fond of King in a parental way, in many senses providing him with a second home, and he spent several vacations with them.

Although many undergraduates were still content with long walks through the countryside and along the Isis, organized sports increased greatly in status at Oxford during the 1920s, and the routine of games in the afternoons became well established. King ran track and played lacrosse, but his true love, indeed his passion, was rowing.

It is likely that King was approached his first evening in college by the captain and secretary of his college boat club, urging him to go down to the river to be "tubbed" – that is, to be taught the elements of rowing in a "tub pair," two in a boat plus a coach. By 21 October, he had been out on the river every day except one and had been promoted to a four-oared boat; shortly thereafter, to his great relief, he was given a place in an eight-oared clinker boat with sliding seats. He had anticipated sore hands, but nothing had prepared him for what he called the tender properties of his lower anatomy, encouraging him to choose the softest chair in the room or even to remain standing if possible. For those familiar with North American rowing, Oxford racing can be a trifle confusing. In the fifth week of second term, the "Torpids" are rowed, bumping races between the colleges in eight-oared clinker boats. As Gordon later described it:

> Put briefly, the Isis at Oxford is too narrow for several boats to race side by side. In consequence the eights of the twenty-odd colleges – and some have two – line up one behind the other in three divisions, with a boat length of open water between each boat. When the pistol goes, all boats start, the purpose being to catch the boat ahead and keep away from the one behind. Your success or failure determines your position next day. The race goes on for six days during Eights week [Torpids] each year.[31]

King rowed in the second eight in his first year and in the first eight in his last two years, competing against his friend Graham Spry, who was rowing for University College. He also, although apparently unknowingly, competed against Frank Scott, who was rowing for Magdalen. In his last two years, he rowed for Queen's in the great regatta at Henley. Could the little boy whose father taught him to paddle a birch bark canoe, Indian style, on Lake of the Woods have envisioned such future glory? Probably not. At no point in his life did Gordon spend much time contemplating what he might achieve in the way of future glory. He had a way of abandoning himself to the moment, living zestfully in the present, alertly involved with immediate issues. Even in his old age, when he made several abortive starts at writing his memoirs, he found himself constantly interrupted by current interests, still too busy living his life to write about it.

In December 1921, the end of first term found King at Paignton in South Devon as the guest of a fellow runner on the track team, having a reading holiday and a welcome respite from the Oxford chill – the "worst climate in the world." By contrast, "Italy couldn't beat [South Devon] for climate. Green palm trees in many of the gardens, lawns green and flowers in bloom, and the air wild and fresh like a September day at home."[32] Friends at Oxford could not believe that he would make such a long trip, nearly 300 km by train, for a stay of merely two weeks. After Christmas with Sir Evan and Lady Spicer, and he left for his first European vacation, skiing in the Bavarian Tyrol, an experience that marked the beginning of the focus and direction for his future life.

His destination, Garmisch, about an hour from Munich, provided delightful international company and skiing, sleighing, and skating. But rain abruptly ended life on skis in this enchanted winter wonderland. As the slopes turned to slush, one of the other Oxford men and King decided to visit Vienna, where they booked in at the Meissl um Schnadn Hotel near the Stefansplatz. For the first few days they were swept away by the aesthetic life: walks along magnificent streets, opera, gypsy music at a night spot, and marvelous old masters – Dürer, Breughel – at the Historisches Museum. Then, quite by accident, as they trudged through the snow down the Graben past steaming sausage kitchens, they came upon clusters of hungry men and women who contrasted sharply with the tastefully decorated shop windows and the overdressed tourists. Curious, they wandered through the great gateway of the Hofburg Palace, where they found Quakers handing out cocoa and other food to starving children as well as adults. Stunned, they lent a hand, and then, on the direction of the Quakers, they walked on to the university where they met a young Edinburgh graduate who was a representative of the European Student Relief Fund. King's breakfast that morning at the hotel, cocoa, a roll and an egg, had cost him 700 kronen; a similar breakfast was being served to the students for four kronen. Some 5,000 students out of the 23,000 in Vienna were being given such help daily.[33] As he stood in the library of the university, watching three or four hundred students studying, two and three to a book, he got an idea of what it meant to be a student in Vienna.

It was a shattering introduction to the realities of postwar Europe for a young Canadian who later described his life up to this time as a cocoon of security and plenty. He never forgot this first exposure to the human consequences of war, and it provided a dash of realism to his romantic boyhood notions of 1918. He returned to Oxford with relief, not quite as free with his complaints about the weather and his meagre fire. Shortly after his return, he read Keynes's *The Economic Consequences of the Peace*, and his reaction intensified by the immediacy of his few days in Vienna. Suggesting that he might return to Austria for the summer where he would possibly work with the relief organization, he wrote home and, in the thrall of Keynes, laid the responsibility for the humanitarian crisis he had witnessed on the peace terms imposed by the Allies, "whose aim was entirely destructive with apparently little thought as to the future economic welfare of our enemies who we must admit cannot be banished and must live on the same earth with us as neighbours."[34] In Geneva in February, he heard Dr Friedrich Nansen, Norway's famous explorer and its representative to the League of Nations, tell a gruesome tale of famine-stricken Russia, and he wrote to his parents: "If nothing is done I shall lose all faith in the Christian impulses that are supposed to dominate the actions of modern states."[35] King was already beginning to struggle with the question that dominated his later (post-Niebuhrian) thinking: that of the possibility of moral action on the part of nation states.

It was in response to such accounts of human suffering that, toward the beginning of April, King found himself once again en route for Central Europe, this time as the Canadian Student Christian Movement (SCM) delegate to the International Conference for European Student Relief in Turnov, Czechoslovakia. The purpose of the conference was to make students of thirty outside nations acquainted with conditions in the countries of Central Europe that were receiving student relief. It was a cosmopolitan assembly of students, where King met Visser t'Hooft, student representative from the Netherlands, who later became president of the World Council of Churches and a lifelong friend. King arrived after a four-hour delay at the German frontier, "those coldest and dreariest hours of any day, between two and six in the morning," only to be greeted by a student official with an unmistakably Canadian accent who asked him, "You are the delegate from Hungary?"[36] King happily disclaimed any Magyar lineage in his joy at discovering an old Toronto friend. The assembled students heard reports on the plight of European students caught in the dislocation and aftermath of war, that of 10,000 Russian refugees being perhaps the most heartrending. King attended an Easter midnight service in the Russian Cathedral and found himself deeply moved by the traditional Orthodox ceremony climaxed by the ritual declaration of faith, "He is risen," in the midst of conditions of such despair – a despair tangibly and tragically expressed in the suicide of three Russian students later that night.

For all his genuine concern for the stringent life that the European students were enduring, King began his trip home with a certain panache, boarding a former German war plane in Dresden for what was surely a novel mode of student travel in the early 1920s. With no navigation instruments, the pilot had to keep in sight of the ground through the rain and fog. King sat beside the pilot in an open cockpit as they whistled over the treetops. As the weather cleared, he found himself exhilarated beyond belief, returning to earth in Berlin with something less than an expert landing on the right wheel and wing tip.[37] But he went back to Oxford with a new understanding of the cost of war and its threat "to annihilate that class with whom most of all lies the hope of the recovery of Europe ... For the loss of this generation of educated youth might facilitate the advance of a wave of barbarism which would shake to its very foundations the form and structure of western civilization."[38] Certainly it is no surprise to find him many years later, with his conviction as to the importance of the role of an educated youth in developing nations, heading the Canadian University Service Overseas (CUSO).

This momentous second term at Oxford also brought King Gordon's first serious exposure to Fabian socialist thought. Reading his first essay to his new tutor, F.L. Ogilvie at Trinity, he expounded the orthodox free-enterprise doctrine he had been schooled in at the University of Manitoba, after which Ogilvie asked mildly, "Have you ever read Tawney's *Acquisitive Society*?"[39] King had never even heard of R.H. Tawney, but he bought a copy of *The Acquisitive Society* at Blackwell's on his way back to his college where he read it right through. As he described it, "I could almost feel the scales falling from my eyes."[40] Tawney's thinking penetrated deeply into King's as yet unformed political consciousness and proved to be a seminal intellectual influence in his socialist doctrines as they developed later and as he expressed them in his writings of the 1930s.

Fundamental to Tawney's thought is his distinction between social and personal property and his emphasis on property as related to social function rather than grounded in individual rights. The understanding of property as an absolute right, free from any obligation to service to society, is what Tawney calls the "acquisitive society" a society characterized by waste, inequality, and struggle between classes that understands property as an absolute right, free from any obligation of service to society. It not only produces a class of rentiers who live on the product of industry but contribute no meaningful labour to its increase, but also degrades those who labour, for it separates them from a sense of purpose in their work and makes them merely means to the end of producing wealth. Tawney's solution to the dilemma is to organize society once again on the basis of function, and to restore property as an institution with social usefulness. This means first of all that one must distinguish between property tied to function and property that is useless. Legitimate property in this sense is found in the tools of the craftsman, the holding of the peasant, the personal possessions that contribute to a life of health and efficiency. This type of property is to be encouraged. (In later years, it is precisely this kind of property, agricultural and personal, that the form of socialism embraced by King Gordon sought to safeguard and increase.)

By contrast, Tawney writes, all types of private property in return for which no function is performed must be abandoned. In many instances, the state itself may find it wise to own the capital used in certain industries. But even where capital remains in private hands, it should be paid the lowest interest for which it can be obtained, and those who own it should have no control over production. It is interesting to note that Tawney does not advocate nationalization as an end in itself, nor the abolition of all private property. For it is not private ownership per se that is corrupting to the principle of industry, but private ownership divorced from work, and Tawney does not include that class of "peasant farmers and small masters" – foreshadowing the prairie farmers and small businessmen of the later CCF – among those alienated from function and the legitimate holding of property.

This was new and radical thinking for King, and under the influence of Ogilvie he also began attending lectures at Barnett House by the leading Fabians of the period, J.A. Hobson, L.T. Hobhouse, Sidney and Beatrice Webb, G.D.H. Cole, and by Tawney himself. "My eyesight improved enormously," he reported.[41] At the same time, he was reading Bertrand Russell's *Road to Freedom* and L.T. Green's *Prolegomena*; he also read Hobson's *Incentives in the New Industrial Order*, which refuted the capitalistic arguments opposed to state ownership put forth in Hartley Withers's *The Case for Capitalism*.

It was at the end of his first year, on his first visit to the Aberdeens, that he fell in love with the austere countryside of Scotland. "I have really felt at home since coming to Scotland. I don't know, I guess there is a lingering sense of national pride about me. I felt a bit of this on the train when I realized we were in Scotland. After all, there's more in claiming common traditions with the descants of Bruce and Wallaces than speaking the tongue that Shakespeare spoke."[42] The visit also provided time for King to reflect on his first year at Oxford. "This year has meant a great deal to me," he wrote his father. "It has given me a start at thinking for myself although I am still very inclined to take other people's opinions. I am becoming increasingly conscious of what a tremendous lot I owe, in fact there is nothing that I do not, to you and Mother and the ideals and principles you have set up for me as the things worthwhile in life. I pray God that some day I may begin to justify all you have done for and given to me."[43]

As King reflected on what he had learned during his first year at Oxford, stimulated by Tawney's emphasis on the nature of social obligation, and his own growing sense of debt to what he had received from his parents, he was further drawn into that realm of thinking on his next vacation to Europe at Christmas in 1922, which also drew him more deeply into his new international interest. It was another skiing trip, this time to Chamonix, with his cousin Polly and her husband, Walter Riddell, of Geneva. Skiing in snow 2 m deep provided everything the rain in the Bavarian Tyrol had denied the previous year, and King gloried in the rustic lunches in a village halfway up the slope: half loaves of bread, cheese, eggs, and the inevitable cocoa. From the balcony of his room he looked out at the snow-covered mountain tops, luminescent in the moonlight, "a night so beautiful as to make me doubt my own existence" – the sparkling snow, the gleaming peaks, the black and white contrast of the spruce against the snow.[44] From Chamonix he returned with the Riddells to their home in Geneva for the first of several extended visits. Dr Walter A. Riddell, at that time the Canadian representative to the International Labour Organization (ILO), and later to become Canada's permanent representative to the League of Nations, was himself a Methodist minister and reflected Canadian Protestant churchmen's commitment to the League.[45]

King greatly admired Walter, who became both a model and mentor, and through whom King gained unique access to the workings of the League. During this first visit and a longer one at the end of the following summer, King sat in on meetings of the ILO, the Disarmament

Committee, and the General Assembly. He also used the library to prepare for a speaking tour in England in September 1923, at the request of the League of Nations Society, defending the League's actions (or lack thereof) during the Corfu crisis. Through Walter, he received introductions to Robert Cecil, Philip Noel Baker, Dr Friedrich Nansen, Hjalmar Branting of Sweden and, perhaps most significantly of all, a fellow Canadian and former Oxonian, Percy Corbett, who was working as a legal advisor for the ILO.[46] Gordon later identified these visits with the Riddells and the time spent in Geneva as marking the beginning of his growing conviction that only through an international organization that superseded the competition of nation states could there be any hope for economic stability and peace.

It was a small step from this experience with the League to the International Assembly at Oxford, which was organized as a student replica of the League of Nations, a forerunner of the Model United Nations program that has become widespread in schools and colleges throughout the world. The International Assembly was organized into two main branches, the Assembly of Delegates and the Secretariat. When possible, countries were to be represented by their own nationals, but when no undergraduates from a particular nation were available, others would substitute. King once headed the Polish delegation. Setting up meetings and debates absorbed a good deal of his time, especially as he became the secretary of delegations and eventually general secretary. More than once he lamented home on the woes of getting members to meet their responsibilities. In September 1923, while he was in Geneva, he wrote an article for *The Oxford Chronicle* proposing a federation of the individual Assemblies in England into a Universities League of Nations Federation.[47] He also wrote home that such a program would be invaluable in Canadian universities, stimulating knowledge and interest in world affairs. Many years later, as president of the United Nations Association of Canada, he was able to promote the Model UN program in Canadian schools and universities.

King had his own modest experience of student life in Europe in the summer of 1923, when he and Gilbert Ryle went to Hanover to learn German in order to meet the graduation requirement for a second language. With another friend, they moved into a German household presided over by a remarkable teacher by the name of Fraulein Abendhern, who had also taken into her household a number of destitute elderly women who helped out with the tutelage in informal ways.[48] The high spirits and confidence of the young students were undaunted by their lack of everyday German, particularly in Ryle's case, as he struggled through the more philosophical terms of Kant and Hegel. Having missed what one of the elderly guests had said to him one day at lunch, he searched desperately for the word meaning "understanding" and explained politely, "Ich habe keine unterhosen [underwear]!" Mercifully, his hosts exploded with laughter. Perhaps this was not their first encounter with English students. King and Ryle took long weekend walking tours in the Harz Mountains, and gradually their German improved. But the daily diet of boiled potatoes and cabbage caught up with King, and he found himself recuperating in a hospital on Lake Constanz after collapsing from weakness on one of his hikes. It was a glimpse into the daily deprivations of German life; and ten years later, with Hitler on the rise, King recalled how his hosts had been living with the dreadful inflation that had wiped out their entire savings and left them dependent on the meagre tuition of two Oxford students.

King's two Easter vacations to Florence in 1923 and 1924 show another side of the impact of Europe on young Canadians abroad. While the students expected to – and did – use their time to prepare for exams, read for their courses, and become proficient in languages, perhaps the greater part of their education was cultural, including exposure to the exquisite natural beauty that surrounded them at every turn. King wrote:

> You were expected to do some reading, and you usually did. But that didn't exclude the possibility of a few weeks in Paris with visits to the Louvre and the Jeu de Paume and l'Orangerie and Notre Dame ... And Rome is waiting with the Sistine and the ancient stones of the Forum. And Florence with the Uffizzi and the Pitti and Santa Croce and the Duomo and San Marco and Giotto, Botticelli, Massacio, Michelangelo, Leonardo – where do we stop? ... For a Canadian in the 1920's, it was all part of Oxford.[49]

He was enchanted by Genoa, with its tier upon tier of white houses that looked out on the forest of masts and funnels in the port. But it was Florence that won his heart, so much so that he and John Farthing spent their entire holiday of five weeks there. Within two hours of their arrival he and John had explored both sides of the Arno and had the good fortune to settle into two rooms of the Pensione Rigatti on the Lungarno just at the Ponte alla Grazie, where Dante met Beatrice, and into the warm hospitality of the Benedictus family. The Pensione Rigatti had been a former palazzo and the marquese and his family still lived on the lower floors. Their high-ceilinged rooms on the fourth floor had something of the splendour of their earlier occupants, pleasant to work in during the cool of early morning as they swatted their way through Locke, Berkeley, Hume, Trevelyan and the Webbs, with a detour through Ruskin on the glories that surrounded them.

Reminiscing in his later years, Gordon recalled the vast distance, geographically and culturally, between the new world of North America and the old world of Europe. When he first went abroad in 1921, he had not read the travel memoirs and the *bildungsroman* of nineteenth-century American writers, innocents abroad, so he experienced the cultural density and gentle beauty of Florence as an innocent himself, fresh and immediate upon his senses, unsullied by weary travelogues and without the benefit of film or television. He tried to bridge his two worlds as he stood on a balcony with the "very lovely, very remarkable" Constanza Fasola, whom he had met through John Farthing. Asked about Canada, he began describing to her the northern Canadian wilderness that the Group of Seven was then painting and the majestic Rockies in the West. She listened silently, then said, "I don't think I could stand it. I would be terrified. There has to be some touch of humanity that I can relate to." And they continued to look out on the beauty of the valley, their eyes picking out the white walls of the inhabited houses and the outline of the stone walls that surrounded the little farms and olive groves, the one secure in the old world, the other holding within himself the tension of old and new.[50]

King returned to Florence again at Easter in 1924. It was the last vacation before his final examinations, or Schools, and he and Gilbert Ryle persuaded Graham Spry to accompany them even though Spry's Schools were not due for another year. They returned to the Pensione Rigatti, where they settled into their routine of morning reading and lunch in the dining room that looked out toward the Ponte Vecchio. It was a "quiet room, good for conversation. The food was good and the fiasco of Chianti Ruffino on our table never required a miracle for its replenishment." (King had, by this time, been initiated into the pleasure of wine.) It was through the "lovely Constanza" Fasola that King, Gilbert, and Graham met Aldous Huxley on that 1924 vacation. Gordon recalled Huxley as a tall, thin man with thick glasses, very kindly and not as sharp and cruel as one might have anticipated from his books. As a result of these informal meetings, King pushed more deeply into reading Huxley and found that the author's breaching of conventional attitudes opened up a "whole new world" for him.[51]

This Easter vacation in Florence yielded far more than preparation for exams, and both King and Graham returned many times. There is a poignant sequel to the story for Spry, recounted by Gordon at the time of Spry's death in 1983. In 1944, the Canadian Armed Forces under the command of Brigadier-General Daniel Spry [Graham's brother] entered Florence following the withdrawal of the Germans. With them came war correspondent Graham Spry. As soon as he had a free moment, Graham found his way to the familiar piazza, following the road running out of it until he came to a wooden fence with the name FASOLA on the gate. He pulled the bell and in a few minutes he heard the sound of a lock being turned. Gordon continued the story:

> The gate opened and a young girl stood there. "Constanza!" said Graham, surprised. "Constanza is my mother," "I am Graham Spry." "Yes, I know. My mother is expecting you." "But how can that be? I didn't know myself until just recently that I would be with the Canadian army here." "My mother kept telling us that one of these days one of the Canadians who used to visit us will be back to see us. Come with me and we'll see her." I think it was that little incident that was responsible for Graham always saying, with a smile, when he talked of his war experience: "You know, I liberated Florence!"[52]

King's final year in Oxford was enlivened by the arrival, in the fall of 1923, of his sister Mary, a new graduate of the University of Manitoba and now enrolled in St Hugh's College, Oxford. Mary successfully invaded Oxford's male citadel by living on its sacred ground as a paying guest and virtual member of the family of Canon Cook and his wife, who lived in the southwest corner of Christ Church's Tom Quad. But if Mary was technically attached to St Hugh's and Christ Church, as far as her brother was concerned she was spiritually a part of Queen's, adding her intelligence, wit, and charm to the circle of King's friends, and forming relationships that extended far beyond their time at Oxford.

For the Christmas vacation at the end of 1923, King visited the Riddells in Geneva. On returning in January for his last months at Oxford, he found himself in a rare mood of despondency. On the 29th, he wrote to his father, confiding his mood of overwhelming futility: "Oxford is a curious combination of intellectualisms, social activity and sport. There seems little room for much else. And unless you somehow hang on to some belief in the goodness of God and a meaning in this life (though obscured for the most part) you turned pretty cheerfully to

Pessimism as the best way out."[53] And, where, he asked, were the answers? Philosophy led one to a stone wall beyond which he could not go; economic theory offered no moral justification of the economic or social structure of society, and was incapable of providing remedial change of distribution; and in spite of the splendid political efforts of the League, the international system was still dominated by militarism and treaties drawn up around particular national interests. He recalled the biblical words, "Vanity of vanities, all is vanity."

His mood of introspection had begun the previous summer of 1923 on a holiday to Scotland as a guest of Lord and Lady Aberdeen.[54] An expression of this interior reflection survives in King Gordon's papers, written on a single half-size sheet of paper. In retrospect, it may be taken as the statement of a personal credo from which he never wavered.

> July 10. "A true man or a true friend, is a person whose outward acts correspond to – faithfully reflect – his inner feelings." This summer of 1923 I have dedicated to the task of self conquest – a task which in no way is ever complete but which unless begun leaves one's life colorless and to no purpose. To bring one's thought and actions into touch with the highest purpose for which one is in this world – if there is a purpose as I believe there is – to bring one's life under the guidance of God, if indeed there is a God, and I believe there is – is to gain complete mastery of oneself, and completely to realize oneself. Duty and the will – these two must be made to coincide.[55]

Whatever his post-Oxford life might hold, it would encompass this marriage of what ought to be done – that "stern daughter of the voice of God" (Wordsworth) – with volition and consent. In January 1924 the question confronting King was how to translate principle, and vision, into action.

Meanwhile, there were still the glorious coming Easter weeks in Florence, the grueling training for Henley, where he would row for the second year for Queen's, and his final exams. He received his BA with second-class honours, the same standing as Mike Pearson and Graham Spry. His parents arrived and joined the circle of friends who celebrated with King and Mary on completing their academic courses, and after Eights Week, the Schools, and Henley, the four Gordons drove north on a pilgrimage to their ancestral homeland, travelling through the Highlands to Inverness and down the east coast to Aberdeenshire – Gordon country – where they spent ten days with the Aberdeens. On their arrival, knowing that King was uncertain about his future, the Aberdeens urged him to consider a position with the Labour Office in Geneva for which a Canadian was wanted; and on saying goodbye the last evening of their visit, Lady Aberdeen took his hand and said, "Best wishes. I hope we shall find you at Geneva after all." But by that time, King's vocational plans had clarified. He went up to his room and, on Lord Aberdeen's stationery, dated 31 July he wrote:

> This is I think one of the most important days of my life. For weeks I have been battling with myself, with my conscience and with a great darkness as to where lies my course in life.
>
> On Monday after a talk with Daddy, I came to the conclusion that my immediate plans are to be in the direction of the Presbyterian ministry … I think I have balanced alternatives, and although Geneva presents a most attractive opportunity which might lead to a valuable position later in Canadian life – academic or political – other claims of duty would seem to outweigh its possibilities. Then it dawned upon me that all my deepest interests have become centred in the League, in the possibility of averting war. I believe that the time of international statesmanship is not past but is just beginning. I believe that surely I shall find an opportunity of realizing my best self in that sphere of service. May I never allow the beacon which for many years has been smoldering and to-night has burst into flame to die out. May God help me. J. King Gordon.[56]

The Gordons left the next morning for Oxford, where King received his degree, after which they returned to Canada on the *Athenia*.

The danger of being an innocent abroad is that one becomes so enchanted by the foreign culture and alienated from one's own, that, like Henry James, one could never successfully go home again. Gordon always enjoyed quoting the adage, "A Rhodes Scholar is one with a great future behind him," catching in this clever aphorism the pathos of young colonials who returned from Oxford, pined for England, and never again found Canada to be home. But this was not true of King Gordon. Nourished by the pines and rocks of Birkencraig, the prairie grasses, and the winds that swept through them, he had within him an elemental love of the Canadian landscape. But he was nourished by Birkencraig in another way as well: the traditions of a family secure in their place in Canadian society while valuing their connections to and ancestral gifts from their Scottish heritage. Gordon always knew that there was a world beyond the Manitoba marshes, a world kept alive by constant visitors and which he would visit some day. Both his parents had studied abroad, and his father both travelled widely and enjoyed international recognition as an author. When King went to Oxford, still unformed in many ways, he was nevertheless securely grounded in the culture and geography of Canada – standing, one could say, upon the ancient and elemental pre-Cambrian rock celebrated by the man who would become his close friend, Frank Scott.

Oxford gave him, first of all, an education in the finest sense, the ability to view the world with an informed and critical eye. Through his vacations in Europe, King came face to face with the desperate human suffering of postwar Europe, and through his contact with the Riddells and the League, he began to envision how one might work to avert war and to achieve justice on an international scale. By the time he left Oxford, he had identified his own sense of a vocation to serve others, with the hope that his best self would be realized in international service. Finally, his exposure to the splendours of England and Europe, with their art and architecture and their great natural beauty, awoke in him an enduring love for travel that was never extinguished. Most of all, it would be the people he looked for, the boy with his donkey in Gaza, the refugee mother asking him to locate her son, the Korean orphans singing. But all this still lay in the future.

4

"A Preacher in the Bush": Testing a Vocation

King Gordon did not fall prey to the post-Oxford depression experienced by some of the returning young Canadian scholars. Frank Scott, for example, was offended by the ugliness of Montreal and the commercial aspect of Canadian life, and he described the countryside itself as "ill-kempt and dull, as though it had been all drawn out and got thin in the process."[1] By contrast, King returned to Canadian life filled with anticipation and immersed himself in activity that, at first glance, might seem to suggest an intellectual moratorium and an abrupt break with his Oxford life. However, one can argue that the five years he spent back in Canada before leaving for New York and graduate studies with Reinhold Niebuhr at Union Theological Seminary were a period of what Robert Frost has called "building soil." In his poem, "Build Soil – A Political Pastoral," Frost pleads for depth and reflection, in poetry, and in life itself, as in the agricultural practice where the first few crops get plowed back in to build the soil. In reflecting later on these years, Gordon did not feel that what he was then doing was necessarily less intellectual in nature than what he had been doing in Oxford, although certainly it was less academic, and "you miss the brilliant company, which is always made more brilliant by distance."[2] What these years did provide was a return to his Canadian roots and, at the same time, exposure to a new kind of experience which that neither his life in Winnipeg nor his time at Oxford had provided: that of ordinary working people for whom he developed deep bonds of affection and respect, which he never lost. In Frost's sense, it was this period of "plowing under" that produced the rich topsoil out of which grew a lifetime's motivation for social action.

When a position with the department of economics at the University of Manitoba that would allow him to combine teaching with his own theological studies was not forthcoming, King decided to postpone his plans to begin academic preparation for the ministry. Instead, he accepted the invitation of the home mission secretary of the Presbyterian Church to spend a year as a student missionary in the logging country of central British Columbia. In doing so, he was not only testing his vocation but also following the example of his father, who had been a missionary in Banff after completing his own theological training in the 1880s. Just before he left Winnipeg in early November of 1924, King received a letter from Gilbert Ryle, who had become a tutor in philosophy at Christ Church, a letter that nicely combined the Oxford ambience that King had left with an acknowledgment on the part of his English friend of that fresh energy brought to the old world by Canadians. Ryle wrote: "I feel a selfish hog, with a cushy job in Oxford near my people, while you and Mary are in Winnipeg missing – and I gather you do – England and the old familiar etc. ... I get all Oxford thrown at me while all my friends have to dig about in uncongenial professions in unbeautiful towns and miss it all."

And yet, Ryle admitted in his letter, in only a few years it might well be that the situation would be reversed, and those from the new world would look back on Oxford as a dream, "a jewel, but a backwater." He hoped that the gifts of the old world – age, buildings, culture, or manners – things that were positive and alive, without which the world would be poorer, would continue to be valued and missed. There was no room for smugness. He continued:

> You and Mary, Graham [Spry] and Arnold [Heeney], John Lowe, Fergie [George Ferguson], Webbie [Gilbert Webb] ... and your father and mother have not been mere birds of passage, interesting to the naturalist but nothing more. You all brought something to the life of Oxford (and certainly of me) which makes it richer. I was cynical and skeptical and shall I say <u>clever</u> before I knew you all: Now I hate cynicism and though I have not in the ordinary sense of the word <u>a</u> religion or <u>a</u> faith; yet I understand what the former is and I know that the latter is something which holds life together and makes it true and is not itself a mere collection of accepted dogmas and beliefs but is a real or the real thing in life that is not just surface. I know these things and I learned them from all of you.[3]

But thoughts of Oxford were far from his mind as King, dressed in his Oxford-cut brown suit, boarded the CN passenger train for the West, carrying with him winter clothes, his banjo mandolin, a Swiss backpack, and a heavy pair of downhill skis. Far from feeling deprived, he confessed to a feeling of excitement and anticipation of new experiences, landscapes, challenges, and direction. After a short visit with his cousin in Edmonton, he made his way to Jasper and his first view of the magnificent Rockies. They passed Mount Robson and travelled along the Thompson River, then the Fraser, which turns south at Prince George, and down to Giscome, British Columbia.[4]

Giscome was a modern sawmill town run by the Eagle Lake Lumber Company, which had timber rights both east and west along the CN line, and the headquarters of King's mission territory.[5] There were no roads apart from lumber trails, and King's parish consisted of small settlements and mills strung out a distance of 80 to nearly 100 km along the railway line, which followed the river. His parishioners included the men in the camps cutting wood, the employees of the saw mills with their wives and children, and a scattered population of settlers who had come out with the idea of farming – an unrealistic prospect, in view of the poor soil and lack of access to markets. Giscome itself, unlike the settlements and camps, was an established town with its large sawmill and company offices, a post office, a store, a school, and a doctor. It had no church building as yet, and the regular Sunday school and services were held in the school. Gordon's closest friend and advisor, Herbert Ashford, was the Presbyterian minister in charge of the stretch of track to the east. Ashford was a graduate of Dalhousie University in Halifax, with a degree in theology from Queen's University in Kingston. King was immediately attracted by Ashford's prowess in rugby and basketball, finding him "hard as nails – cares about as little for a 10-mile [16-km] walk as the average man for crossing the street."[6] Gordon and Ashford became great friends, and undoubtedly Ashford, with his muscular Christianity, indefatigable energy, and wholehearted love for the people, greatly influenced King, and his company and encouragement made the hardships of King's life more palatable.

King arrived in Giscome in late November. "I got here Wednesday evening at six. Not a soul to meet me of course, but I got a room at a big bunkhouse sort of place – new this year where the men of the mill stay. Really quite decent quarters. The food was excellent."[7] His first task was to find permanent lodging, and he found the people to be "all very solicitous as to my welfare but not very helpful." After trying about six places that people thought might have a room and discovering that these tiny bungalows offered inadequate space even for their present occupants,

King tried an old-timer living out in the woods. He had no room either, but he put King onto the trail of an empty shack about 2 km from town. And so it was that King found himself cleaning out an isolated two-room shack tucked into a clearing among tall cedars that he was free to chop for stove wood. He was delighted and immediately wrote home for a scone recipe, and two pairs of double heavy blankets.[8]

Keeping warm provided the greatest challenge to this new homemaker. The temperatures that winter dropped below -46°C, and when the fire was out, the temperature inside the shack matched the one outside. Gordon spent no time pining for the cozy chill of his Oxford digs. At night, when he returned from his duties, rather than lighting up the stove only to waken once again to the frigid air and frosty blankets, he simply set the fire ready for lighting. He then rolled a piece of newspaper and soaked it in coal oil, placing one end where he could reach it and the other in the tinderbox of the stove. Then, he climbed into bed with his clothes on. In the morning, he simply had to reach out, touch his end of the newspaper with a match and voila! he had a fire. Within half an hour, he recalled happily, the shack was toasty.[9]

He travelled by train when he could (the freight ran up one day and down the next), but he also caught rides with the section men who checked the tracks on their handcars, or with the local forester on his power jigger. On occasion, he used one of the speed cars himself. In snowy conditions, he often skied, both along the track and up and down logging trails; if there was no snow, he would walk along the track. Once, he followed the track of a dog team into the woods, where he spent the night with the loggers. Hikes of 16 to 24 km scarcely deserved mention, and he covered the length of his territory weekly. Some mornings it was the shunting of the train in the station that woke him; without time to kindle his ready-made fire, he would leap into his icy outer clothing, grab the hymnbooks and tear into town, catching the train by the caboose as it steamed up the track.

However his natural ingenuity and experience camping may have stood him in good stead for surviving his new circumstances, nothing in his life in Winnipeg or Oxford had prepared him for local modes of worship. The service in Giscome was fairly standard, with a Sunday school already established and the warm school available for a meeting place, but the situation in the hinterland was quite different. To begin with, there were no church buildings at all, and no set times for services. Gordon laid the foundations for worship first of all by visiting the camps and the isolated settlers, establishing contact, distributing magazines (sent out by the St Stephen's congregation in Winnipeg), and sometimes clothing as well. He carried his banjo on his back for evening entertainment in the bunkhouses after the loggers had finished their long day of work, and often after his brief service of hymns and prayers, he joined the local musicians in playing for a dance. "If you have any funny songs please send them along," he asked his father. "I've run out of mine and must have some more to keep up my reputation and the attendance at services! I've found that one must be broadminded here to get anywhere – and you can afford to be without sacrificing principles."[10]

The services, informal and ecumenical, were scheduled as they could be, usually on weekday evenings, and held in whatever building might be available, including cookhouses, pool halls, and private homes. Since he was not yet ordained, Gordon could not serve Communion or conduct weddings, but funerals fell within his jurisdiction, something he found particularly difficult as often the death was that of a child or involved a tragic accident.

In Giscome itself, King supplemented visiting and services with community service, organizing basketball teams for both boys and girls, a boys' club and a debating team, which got off to a roaring start largely due to a staunch henchman of King's who was also an erstwhile English public school boy. Perhaps the topic for that first debate also had something to do with its success: "Resolved: that political affiliation with the United States would be in the best interests of Canada." He does not record who won. In early August, they were fortunate to have two visiting American college students, who were doing summer work nearby (probably surveying), and they joined in the fun. After one debate, King reported to his mother, "We were beaten, but the debate was one of the best I have ever taken part in or heard for that matter. The schoolhouse was jammed to the doors and windows. Must have been about 80 out."[11] This evaluation, coming as it does from a former member of the Oxford Union, further reveals Gordon's understanding of intellectual, as distinguished from academic, activity and it also suggests an assumption that thought is not the exclusive province of any particular social group. Gordon took part in all kinds of community activities, including an evening of bobsledding with three of the loggers on three very small sleighs (tied together to make a bob) down a steep curving logging trail just outside of town. The three men took turns at being front man and King reported modestly that his experience in Switzerland enabled him to give the four ladies the two most thrilling rides of the evening.[12]

The mill itself was the throbbing heart of the town, operating three shifts and emitting a high, intermittent scream day and night. Gordon shared the lives of both the lumberjacks and the mill workers, becoming familiar with every step in the process, from felling the trees and floating the booms down the river, to the final stages of the planing mill and the stacks of green lumber piled in the open air to dry. Once he knew the men, he wandered freely through the mill at any time of the night or day, and he particularly enjoyed standing beside the man handling the saw (the chief sawyer) as big fir and spruce logs came up the jackladder onto the cradle where the logs were secured and squared, and the rough lumber emerged.[13] He loved the movement, the sound, the smell of fresh timber and the thrill of watching "little men at the levers of the great machines." It was quite different from anything he had known before, and he recognized the skill of the workers with an admiration bordering on awe. One young lumberjack taught King how to cross the Fraser River on a log boom without drowning himself, a most cherished (and useful) achievement. Once the ice had melted, crossing the river safely became an essential means of reaching parishioners on the other side of the river. The trick of survival, King learned, lay first of all in fastening two cleats into the instep of one's boots so as to be able to stand on logs to prevent their spinning, and then running across the log boom, picking one's direction from one big log to another while keeping up a swift movement when speeding across the smaller logs.[14]

This admiration encompassed not only the loggers and mill workers, but also the hardy resilience of the settlers in the region. He discovered how varied and pleasant these occupants of his new out-of-the-way parish were, and how similar in mood and humour to those he had met in other parts of the world. He was especially moved by the courage and endurance of the women as he trekked the miles to visit sick babies or to take their funerals. After he had spent one bright spring afternoon calling on eight isolated families, he wrote of these women: "It's a pretty lonely life out on the homestead and many of them don't get out much. Mrs Philips and her young family I don't think get out at all, except every two weeks to church, and she has to come across a lake and 2 km along the tracks. She is a most courageous little woman, fighting sickness and poverty, yet always brave and smiling. There are some heroes out in these lonely places who will never get any recognition, yet for sheer bravery deserve the highest awards."[15]

It was this same brave lady who probably saved King's life one clear moonlit night when he had started back for Giscome after taking a service in Aleza Lake, travelling the 24 km along the track by hand-speeder. About 2 km out of town, he spied a lantern on the track as he came upon a group of four small youngsters and their mother, who had started out from the church about fifteen minutes ahead of him. He stopped to say good night. They responded with some alarm, "There's a train coming, Mr Gordon!" And sure enough, with the rattling old hand-speeder turned off, he could hear it approaching. He viewed his safe delivery as a matter not so much of providence as of logic: had he not seen the lantern, he would not have stopped to say good night, receiving the warning of the mother and her children. Instead, he would have continued headlong into the coming locomotive.[16]

While King was spending Christmas in the wilderness of British Columbia, his Oxford buddy Malcolm MacDonald was enjoying the warmth and conviviality of the Gordon family in Winnipeg. He had joined the Gordons for a week at Birkencraig in late August, when he and King, along with C.W. Gordon and a local guide, went on a canoe trip, sleeping on balsam boughs at night under a canopy of stars. Later in his life, Malcolm MacDonald had a distinguished career in relation to Canada as Colonial Secretary for the Dominions, and as Britain's High Commissioner to Canada. It seems fair to suggest that his great love for Canada's natural beauty – and his affection for its people – was kindled by his early visits to Birkencraig. After his August visit to the lake, he wrote to King: "Before the end of the time at Lake of the Woods, I had become fonder of you all than of any other people outside my own family. That is a fact."[17]

Shortly after Christmas, King received another letter from Gilbert Ryle, full of news of Oxford and of mutual friends, and of Ryle's new position at Christ Church. It was –40°C when King picked up the letter in Mr. Brown's post office, and he read it back in his shack huddled beside his wood stove. "Are you at Fort George?" Gilbert asked, presumably referring to Prince George: "If so, you are, I gather about 4 or 500 miles [650 or 800 km] from Victoria: Otherwise I would suggest you dropping in to tea with a married sister of mine there! … I am trying to picture you in your location plastering the wall with pictures of Giotto's tower, the High and Murren. I am rather vague as to your work, but in any case it should be an interesting experience among a new type of man."[18]

To King, it was a communication from another life, intergalactic in its distance from the frigid stillness of the woods outside his shack. He felt their lives had diverged in a timeless way within the space of less than a year, these two who had shared the gentle light of Florence and the soft patina of age on the Oxford panelling about which one mustn't comment. As King thought of the trip on skis he would be making the next morning to Dunc Jennings's camp 8 km deeper into the woods in subzero weather, and then thought of Gilbert sitting in his big Minty chair working out the philosophy of the League and the First International, he would have been justified in concluding that their paths would not come together again. But in this, he would have been wrong, for their paths crossed repeatedly over the next fifty years. Each time they met, they seemed to rediscover the common ground between them, until their roles seemed almost to be reversed: Gordon grasping for the moral and political basis of the Socialist International as he translated his Fabianism to the Canadian idiom and, in a contemporary version of the League of Nations, pursued his quest for an international world order; and Ryle, talking to his fellow villagers (the closest he would come to Gordon's "new type of man") in the Red Lion in Islip about how to cope with England's worst drought in recorded history.[19]

In the present, however, King was preoccupied with the plans for a church building in Giscome. At first, the plan was to buy the old school, a building 18 × 7 m, and divide it into a boardroom, an auditorium, and the minister's living quarters. But King was not happy with this plan, feeling that a proper church would be more appropriate for a growing community like Giscome, particularly as the Catholics were building one. The problem was financial: there was no prospect of getting a loan since the company would not give up a deed to the property and no one would stand bond for $1,500.00 with no security. (The total cost for the new church would be $2,000.00.) But King was underestimating the willing enthusiasm of his parishioners. The congregation, Sunday school, and Ladies Aid put their minds to the task and by 9 August, when the church was dedicated, they lacked only $200.00 to clear the debt. C.W. Gordon arrived to help with the dedication, and after a rousing sermon on "The True Apology of the Christian Faith," which quite gripped the congregation, he swung into action with a sporting offer to raise half as much as the congregation subscribed in the offering. The congregation of 190, crammed to the very doors, responded to his generosity with a collection of $150.00, "a pretty stout effort," and the deed was done.[20]

After church union in 1925, the new church at Giscome was the first United Church of Canada to be dedicated in British Columbia. In 1967, Gordon revisited Giscome, finding the mill gone but the town looking much the same. He made his way to the little church and, finding it locked, peered in through the window. There, looking out, was his own picture, a young King Gordon in his Oxford suit made in 1924 by James the Tailor on High Street. On the other side of the vestibule was another picture, this one of Jesus Christ. King left, reassured that he was in the best company.[21]

Gordon later felt that his time in Giscome was of inestimable value and by no means an abandonment of the education of the previous three years. As he mastered the art of handling a two-bladed axe and learned each stage of the lumber industry, he had to restate various aspects of his world view. From this new perspective, Oxford elitism struck him as a kind of lingering colonialism, lacking in imagination and limited in understanding, and he was grateful that whatever had rubbed off on him of these attitudes was being knocked out of him by his everyday life with labouring people.[22] From the point of view of testing a vocation to the Presbyterian ministry, however, he did not find that this very specialized type of ministry provided an adequate base for commitment to the more conventional, urban ministry for which seminary would prepare him; and he confessed a preference for coaching basketball to writing sermons, an inclination he never entirely overcame. Nevertheless, at a deep level the year in Giscome had confirmed that vocation to service to which he had wholeheartedly dedicated himself on Lord Aberdeen's stationery the previous year, and on his arrival back in Winnipeg he enrolled in theological studies at United College. Because of his Oxford degree in philosophy, the college agreed that King be allowed to complete his work for the diploma in theology in two years, rather than the required three.

King was happy to be home again, relaxed and focused on his studies. He did not take much part in university life apart from sports. He took up track and ran the mile and the half-mile for Manitoba in the Western Collegiate Meets, winning a first and a second in what he considered a disgraceful (and undisclosed) time. It brought back memories of the 4-mile relay he had run in Oxford, winning the championship for Queen's.[23] He also took up rowing once again and in the spring of 1926 he joined the Winnipeg Rowing Club and rowed with them for parts of the next three summers. The club proved to be highly competitive in the rowing world, twice bringing home the coveted Lipton Cup of the North Western International Rowing Association, twice coming in second in the Canadian Henley, and competing in the Olympic Trials in 1928, where they were beaten in the final race by the Toronto Argonauts by half a length.[24]

It was during this first year of theology that King received another of Gilbert Ryle's timely missives, again reminding him of a life distant and sophisticated when viewed from the new world, and expressing Gilbert's concern that King was slipping into the conventional ways of his forefathers by choosing the church as a vocation. By this time, Ryle himself was well on his way to becoming a major twentieth-century philosopher, representative of the British ordinary-language philosophers who were influenced by Wittgenstein's insights into language. But in this letter, his concern focused on his friend's choice of vocation. He had received a weekend visit from Arnold Heeney during which they had discussed Gordon's move into theological training: "He has rather relieved my mind, if you will pardon me butting into your affairs, about your choice of life's work. I was immensely afraid that your choice was not really free and spontaneous, the product of circumstance rather than of real leaning. But he tells me that he is quite happy about it on that score and that he thinks that most of my objections are groundless. But I am, I suppose by nature, anti-clerical, so you won't expect me to be enthusiastic, will you?"[25]

One finds again the interesting juxtaposition of the two friends' perspectives, standing as they are on two different points of the compass: Oxford and the Canadian West. What constitutes the conventional, and what defines a frontier? The Bloomsbury crowd, comfortable and secure in their position in English life, deliberate and self-conscious, see themselves as iconoclastic, breaking with convention, on the frontier of intellectual life; while the Canadian, with a totally unselfconscious ease and relative freedom from convention and social class, explores both a geographical and social frontier, living his daily life with ordinary, labouring people. At this point in their lives, it is King who more fully embraces both worlds, while Gilbert can only speculate on what this other frontier might include.

Based on his reputation of success in Giscome, some time in the summer of 1926 King was asked by the secretary of the Manitoba Conference Home Mission to accept an appointment to serve the church in Pine Falls on the Winnipeg River, 120 km north of Winnipeg, where a new paper mill and town site were being built by the Abitibi Paper Company. This call required that King complete his already attenuated course in theology by reading and exams, preparing independently for the Certificate in Theology and his Ordination to the Ministry of the United Church, both of which he received in 1927. He was also asked to make a three-year commitment to the position. As he had begun to grow restless with the conventional comfortable life of Winnipeg, once again longing for the more rugged life of the bush, he responded with enthusiasm to the new challenge.

In late October 1926, King found himself on the platform of the railway terminal in Pine Falls, looking out across the river to the west onto acres of wet, freezing mud, with the concrete mill in the background and the low, sprawling bunkhouses of the construction camp in the foreground. Behind him to the east lay the beginnings of the new town with a store, a staff house, a hospital, and private houses in the process of being built. Taking a temporary room in the staff house, he began to explore the territory. Up the Winnipeg River at its mouth lay the Hudson's Bay post of Fort Alexander, a fort originally established by LaVerendrye, now on a First Nations reserve. Here King met the Hudson's Bay factor, a pleasant dignified Scot also named Gordon, who had a First Nations wife, and a son who was preparing to work in the mill. He also met the Reverend Kenneth Fryer, the Anglican priest, and his wife, who together ministered to the needs of the people on the reserve. With the advent of the camp and burgeoning new town, Fryer's ministry had extended to include the Anglican community in Pine Falls. Along the river between Fort Alexander and Pine Falls, the bush held many settlers whom Gordon came to know as he visited both as pastor and as a sort of medical scout, reporting illnesses to Dr Lansdowne at the hospital in town. Down the river toward the rapids (called Pine Falls) and further toward Silver Falls, a trail ran through a scattered community that was almost entirely French-Canadian. Here the Catholic priest, Father Caron, with whom Gordon worked closely and became fast friends, ministered to the population.

Pine Falls itself was neatly divided into two communities separated by the river: the town and the construction site. King was immediately struck by the feudal arrangements of the town, socially and geographically, with its five large houses on the riverfront where General Manager C.C. Irwin, the other top managers, and the doctor lived. The next two rows of lodgings back from the river housed middle-level management and the paper makers. The two remaining streets were for the manual workers. King described the houses as snug and comfortable, equipped with basements, furnaces, water, electric lighting, and electric cooking. The school, also modern, was bright and commodious. In contrast with this ordered life, the construction site packed between 800 and 900 men into overcrowded bunkhouses and, apart from a poolroom, provided no social facilities at all for these workers who laboured ten to twelve hours a day. However, one could not by any means claim that these workers, overcrowded as they were, lived in conditions of squalour, as their bunkhouses were clean and equipped with amenities, and their meals were plentiful and good. Moreover, two strong unions, the Papermakers and the Pulp, Paper and Woodworkers, provided a buffer against exploitation. About a kilometer beyond the construction site, a hamlet, or "shack town," constituted the last social grouping, a centre of bootlegging and prostitution.

Congruent with the social division between town and camp, it seemed appropriate, at least at the beginning, to hold two separate church services, interdenominational in nature and conducted jointly by Gordon and the Reverend Fryer. The schoolhouse provided ample space for the townspeople; but on the crowded campsite, even the dining room proved unavailable as the workers ate in shifts, and the clergy resorted to the poolroom as the only available space. In a letter to his mother, King described "a splendid old chap who runs [the poolroom] who hangs out the church sign every Sunday night and closes up the Pool Room for an hour and a half."[26] On his first Sunday, thanks to this arrangement, Gordon and Fryer conducted a joint service with music provided by a portable organ, a violin, and a dulcimer. King, with unacknowledged irony, preached on the scripture, "He looked for a city whose builder and maker was God."

Until January 1928, when the inevitable denominational break came, Gordon and Fryer alternated Sundays, one at the campsite and one in the town, an arrangement congenial to both clergy and population. Soon King had a weekly Bible study underway, Trail Rangers for the boys and Canadian Girls in Training for the girls of the congregation and, with encouragement and advice about fees from his mother, a Ladies' Aid for the women of the church.

King watched the building of the town in a literal sense, as street after street was completed and families began to move in. But it was in the building of the structures and institutions of community that he found his mission in Pine Falls. The church played an active role in all aspects of this process, and King himself drew no distinction between his work as a minister and his broader community activity. Most activities were organized by the Pine Falls Community Club, which had committees for each activity. King chaired two committees: snowshoeing and skiing, and rowing; but informally he participated in nearly every event going, organizing many of them. He branched out from the church choir into a Pine Falls Choral Society, which he conducted. This was a disciplined choir that performed regularly for the town and put on a program in the Winnipeg Music Centre. Through his affiliation with the Winnipeg Rowing Club, he was able to organize a rowing club for men. They purchased two used lapstrake fours from the Regina Boat Club, and with these and other discards from Winnipeg, they worked out on the river. Innate talent, enthusiasm, and King's assumption that rowing fell next to cleanliness and godliness in the great scheme of things, enabled them to participate in the Winnipeg Spring Regatta.

Beneath all efforts of community building lay the paternalistic and benevolent support of the Manitoba Paper Company. Later, during his studies at Union Theological Seminary in New York, Gordon wrote a paper for Professor Harry Ward on the industrial and social conditions of Pine Falls. In his essay, he assessed positively the company's fairness and orderly conduct of its affairs, his only reservation being that "the influence of the company is definitely to promote a sense of dependence and to discourage individual initiative in members of the community."[27]

Despite the mildness of this critique, the issue of paternalism haunted Gordon, posing as it did a threat to individual initiative and self-esteem. However, these were the boom years of the 1920s, and there was little suspicion of company benevolence. He viewed the church, along with the school and the unions, as essential in providing an independent base for action, preventing the growth of an overly dependent community. His own relationship with the company's managers was always amicable, and he rejected a conflict model in interpreting the economic and social life of the town. At this time, the issues of liberty and obligation remained largely implicit in Gordon's thinking and, as he coached basketball and directed plays, he tended to view the community as an external expression of his own internal coherence.

At King's invitation, J.S. Woodsworth, at that time Independent Labour Party MP for the riding of Winnipeg North, visited Pine Falls in January of 1928. He spoke to a men's meeting put on by the local papermakers union in the afternoon, and in the evening he preached in the United Church, spending the night at King's house. "He is a very good chap: a clear thinker and obviously sincere in what he says. He left an excellent impression here and, I think, took away a good one of the town."[28] This is Gordon's first specific reference to Woodsworth in his writings, although it is clear that before this time he had met him in Winnipeg and had attended meetings where Woodsworth had spoken. Gordon's sense that Woodsworth took away with him a positive impression of the town suggests a degree of tranquillity in labour relations there and supports King's own feeling that Pine Falls was a well-run community.

King's own life in Pine Falls also appears to have possessed a quality of tranquillity, and he described his three years there as pleasant and useful. He loved the outdoors, the informality of calling, even the odd bit of hunting. He wrote to his mother in mid-November, "Apart from a rather keen north wind blowing in off the lake it was very good walking weather ... I had gone out with a '22 and got a rabbit and a partridge just a little distance outside the townsite. (Don't tell Ashie I got the rabbit. They are a special pet of hers!)"[29]

The community of Pine Falls provided King's first opportunity to meet first hand the immigrant labourers who worked on the mill site, and he gained insight into the loneliness of their struggle away from family, coping with a strange culture in a strange tongue. It also made possible one of his greatest joys, working with the Catholic priest, Father Caron, and with the French-Canadian population employed by the company.

In January 1928, the happy inter-denominationalism in Pine Falls came to an end. Ever the team player, King regretted the separation of the two congregations, even though he recognized the institutional goals of both denominations and the necessity for church polity. In any case, by this time plans were well underway for the building of a new church. Financial support was forthcoming, including a gift from the Manitoba Paper Company and assistance from the Home Mission Board of the United Church. The only fly in the ointment was the plan for the new building. The board had approved a thoroughly utilitarian square edifice to which King emphatically objected on aesthetic grounds. Independently, he contacted his old friend and former rowing partner, Herbert H.G. Moody, newly graduated in architecture, at that time completing a year in Boston and eager to find work in Canada. Moody designed a tasteful and traditional half-timbered and plaster early-Tudor-period church, including in it a small chancel with a rood beam crossing it.

King was delighted and prepared to do battle with the board over the acceptance of the plan. In light of what the board considered his rather high-handed action and the radical change in the nature of the plan, discussion was extended and heated. ("I wish I had your grace and was rid of my temper," he wrote to his father after one stormy meeting when he reported feeling "trampled upon."[30]) Both adamant and persuasive, King finally convinced the Board to accept the new plan. However, the former Methodists on the board still drew the line at King's High Church frill – a cross on the exterior of the church and another on the rood beam inside. One moonless night during construction, the anti-ritual faction sawed down the exterior cross, and King, fearing the worst, quietly removed the interior one himself, ensconcing it in the safety of his study for his own private devotions.

All differences were put aside for the dedication of the new United Church on 14 October 1928, and King praised "the fine spirit of unanimity among our members" that had made the building of the church possible. He also pointed out how beautifully it harmonized with the natural environment and – somewhat to the surprise of many of his congregants – with the general style of architecture of the town. As in Giscome, C.W. Gordon preached at the dedication, and 106 members entered their names on the Charter Communion Roll. At the time of King's death in 1989, the beautiful little church still stood among the woods of Pine Falls.

The dedication of the church proved anticlimactic for King, and restlessness set in during his last year at Pine Falls. He had written to his father in September, just before the church dedication, "although I will have to keep right on the job here [after the dedication] I am hoping that we can get out for a couple of days together to Birkencraig before close up time. We had all too little time there this summer, in that loving and sacred spot."[31] He had also experienced a disappointment in love during his time in Pine Falls. The daughter of family friends from North Carolina, Betty, had captured his heart, but could not find a similar response in her own. He wrote to his mother in the fall of 1927, "What news of Daddy? And Mary? I haven't heard from either, although I got a letter from Betty. Heart broken, of course, that she can't come up north, but I am learning to stand up against the hard blows of circumstance."[32] The relationship continued off and on, with increasing frustration and intensity on King's part, until the spring of 1929 when the break was final. His father alluded delicately to King's disappointment: "I have been thinking of you a great deal these days. We must each of us carry our own burden, but we would like to give a lift to the load of those we love. There are mysterious channels of communication however and thru' the great Centre of all life we can reach those we love."[33]

Although he realized that his work at Pine Falls had come to an end and that it was time for him to leave, King found the actual breaking away from community and friends difficult. On 6 May he wrote home: "I told my Board tonight that I was going to leave. It seemed to stun them a little – and when I had spoken it left me a bit stunned too. Not burning a bridge so much as blowing it up with a single charge. Afterwards ... as I walked along the street and looked at the little houses with their lights burning a sudden revulsion of feeling against leaving came over me. I felt like a man without a home or country. For after all, Pine Falls has become home to me, and now the adventure beckons me to the high seas again. Well, I suppose there is no inherent right in man to a home. I certainly don't claim any."[34]

It was a rather wistful statement for someone who loved adventure as wholeheartedly as he did. Throughout his life, King committed himself with generous abandon to whatever circumstance he found himself in, so that his leaving was always to be characterized by regret.

In his departure from Pine Falls, King had little sense of divine guidance or of taking the next step in a grand scheme. Yet, his enrollment in the PhD program at Union Theological Seminary in New York in the fall of 1929 was as logical as it was unexpected. For hidden among the many rich aspects of his life during these three years in Pine Falls, and growing out of a certain restless maturing and readiness for another stage of growth, there was a distinct advance in King's thinking over his time at Oxford and Giscome. With his theological studies under his belt, he found writing sermons much more congenial than he had in Giscome and he turned less often to the famous sermons of Harry Emerson Fosdick for help. For example, he began referring directly to economic and social injustice, the sad state of affairs that resulted from greed, when men put their concern for money and profit over their concern for the welfare of their fellow human beings.[35] In another sermon he spoke of mysticism and that state of being withdrawn from the travail of daily life, in fellowship with God and the splendour of his presence; but he warned, we must return to the toil and dreariness of a world in bondage, for that is where we are needed to serve. "The Christian finds himself not in escape from the world, but in love for and in sharing with his neighbor."[36]

These sermons give little hint of the radical social ethics that characterized King's life and thought; but by grounding social action in the innate value of human beings in the eyes of God and in moral relationships, they reflect a maturing of his thought. At Oxford, he had responded with immediate compassion to the suffering he saw in Europe, attributing it to the result of the war, and going so far as to identify it as a direct consequence of an unjust peace at Versailles. By the end of his time at Oxford, he had developed a hatred of war; and in a sincere but unfocused way, he had dedicated himself to its prevention, possibly through international work in the League. In Giscome, he discovered and revelled in the life of the ordinary worker, finding the deep human affinity and respect that provided the foundation for his later social action. But in neither case did he reflect critically on his experience, examine his assumptions, or draw the inferences inherent in what he had learned. In these two sermons in Pine Falls there is, however nascent, an attempt to stand back, to begin with a certain conscious and deliberate effort that task of defining and refining his belief in the light of his experience.

In fact, at the deepest levels of emotion he had already ingested the experience that would provide the wellsprings for his socialism and internationalism, but he was still at that romantic stage of response captured in Wordsworth's definition of poetry as "the spontaneous overflow of powerful feelings." In this definition, the movement is directly from a deeply felt impression to an immediate, spontaneous response. Of course, for all their celebration of spontaneity, the romantic poets betray in the craft of their poems an application to reflection that is expressed in Wordsworth's other memorable definition of poetry as "emotion recollected in tranquility." These early sermons show the first stirrings of analysis and reflection expressed in the second definition, a move on Gordon's part to the level of analysis and reflection. This move to systematic thought would begin in earnest during his years at Union Theological Seminary in New York.

5

Union Theological Seminary: The Making of a Christian Social Radical

King Gordon described his move from Pine Falls to New York in 1929 as having been as "unexpected and accidental" as his previous moves from Winnipeg to Oxford, or from Oxford to Giscome. This motif, of what he called "the happy accidents of life," recurs repeatedly in his interpretation of his many vocational moves throughout his long life, though at times tinged with a deeper Presbyterian sense of providence. In fact, the move to New York marked three transitions for Gordon: from a small company town on the edge of the wilderness to a modern metropolis; from the quiet, somewhat traditional approach of a humanistic religion to his first exposure to a radical interpretation of a Christian social ethic; and from an apparently secure free enterprise economic system through a sudden collapse into a deep socio-economic depression.[1] In retrospect, he felt that in spite of the social radicalism he had encountered at Oxford, nothing had prepared him for the activist and directly relevant ethical thought he was about to encounter at Union.

Once again, the inspiration for the move had arrived by way of his father's contacts. C.W. Gordon, on a visit to New York to consult with his publisher, looked up his old friend Dr Archibald Sinclair, the former pastor of St Andrew's Presbyterian Church in Winnipeg and now the minister of First Presbyterian Church of Bloomfield, New Jersey. As the two friends visited, Sinclair spoke about the new directions in Manhattan's Union Theological Seminary resulting from a faculty of great scholars like James Moffatt, E.F. Scott and the dynamic radical, Reinhold Niebuhr. He suggested that Union might be a good place for King to do graduate work. C.W. Gordon passed this word on to his son, who duly applied and was accepted into the PhD program.

The largest interdenominational seminary in the country, by 1929 Union Theological Seminary had become a centre of graduate research, training students – many of whom had no intention of becoming parish ministers – in psychology and sociology as well as in the areas more traditionally associated with preaching the gospel. Like Gordon, many in the student body did their academic work concurrently with nearby Columbia University.[2] Under the leadership of President Henry Sloane Coffin, himself professor of practical theology, the Union faculty was made up of a dazzling collection of scholars, including James Moffatt, professor of church history; Ernest Scott, professor of biblical theology; William Adams Brown, professor of systematic theology; and, most relevant to King's interests, Harry F. Ward, professor of Christian ethics, and Reinhold Niebuhr, newly appointed as Dodge Professor of Applied Christianity. Reinhold Niebuhr's biographer, Richard Wightman Fox, describes Union Seminary in the early years of the twentieth-century as, "A flawless stone sanctuary rising out of scarred asphalt, an outpost of the sacred on the boisterous urban frontier ... [where] the rush and rhythm of the city streets did not unsettle Union's dim chiseled corridors."[3] As King quickly discovered on his arrival, however, this otherworldly calm proved illusory given the lively intellectual furor of the scholarly debate within those "dim chiseled corridors." Moreover, by the time he entered Union in September of 1929, the silence was about to be shattered further by the urgent cries of economic distress and human suffering brought about by the Wall Street crash.

King immediately found himself captivated by the life of the big city, and he seemed to have forgotten his earlier grudge against New York for its Philistine commercialism. As always, he loved walking, and covered many kilometers a day up and down Manhattan as he explored his new surroundings. His cousin Margaret Gordon ("Mar"), daughter of his father's brother Gilbert, was studying at Columbia, and they renewed their childhood friendship. Mar was by then a New Yorker with many contacts and friends – some in radical circles. They had tea together a couple of times a week, regaling one another with the choice bits of news, scandal, and "cosmic gossip" gleaned between their meetings.[4] Together, they attended a New Masses Ball and met some of the youthful left-wing leaders. At the more conventional level, King became an ardent opera fan, following the Ring cycle down to "the last Götterdammerung with unmixed joy."[5] He and Mar became aficionados of Broadway, and they attended the Philharmonic together. He was thrilled to hear the "wonderful baritone" Paul Robeson in recital, a program consisting almost entirely of the spirituals sung over the years at Birkencraig.

When Gordon arrived at Union, there was already a group of student social activists who met regularly in what was known as the Agenda Club, freely interpreted to mean, "something must be done about it." For some of the students, Niebuhr, as honorary president, was the hero. For others, the more radical Ward was placed first.[6] With his growing interest in the plight of the unfortunate, King quickly became involved with this informal group and, partly through the Club and partly through his associations with Mar, he received introductions to socially concerned New Yorkers: Jerome Davis, a friend of Niebuhr's from Yale Divinity School; Kirby Page and Sherwood Eddy from the Fellowship of Reconciliation and *World Tomorrow*; as well as Harry Laidler, head of the League for Industrial Democracy. He met Heywood Broun of the *New York World,* Roger Baldwin, later to become head of the American Civil Liberties Union, and trade unionists like David Dubinski of the International Ladies' Garment Workers' Union and Sidney Hillman of the Amalgamated Clothing Workers. He became close friends with John Bennett, who later became president of Union, and recalled a "remarkable" house party at the Bennett summer home on Heron Island, Maine. Grouped around the fireplace and locked in discussion, the guests' intensity rendered them oblivious to the Nor'easter rattling the windows around them.

But by far the most important relationships at Union, and the ones that influenced Gordon profoundly, were with his two major professors in Christian ethics, Niebuhr and Ward. He met Niebuhr on his first day. Having settled himself into his room overlooking Broadway, he strolled across the quadrangle to the Common Room where he saw a tall, lean man, bald, with a beak of a nose, intense eyes, and a rasping voice that dominated the room. He sat jack-knifed in a low upholstered chair, surrounded by about twenty students. King's first impression was that they were mesmerized by this dominating figure. Then one of the students broke in with a question that "triggered an almost electric response from the man in the chair – a great shout of laughter, a leap forward to the edge of the chair and a waving hand as the challenge was taken up."[7] This was the scene that Gordon would be part of countless times in the next two years; sometimes the group would be large, sometimes small, sometimes just Niebuhr and King, but always the conversation would be intense and vivid.

By a "fortunate chance,"[8] King was appointed graduate assistant to Niebuhr and Ward in the fall of 1930. In the heady and intense common-room discussions and lectures, and in the free-for-all social and discussion hour held in Niebuhr's Clairmont Street apartment on Thursday evenings, it seemed to him that "we were all participants in the writing of *Moral Man and Immoral Society.*"[9] Although he later developed his own theory of Christian socialism and by the mid-1930s had shed the role of Niebuhr's disciple (the two men remained friends and were frequently in touch until Niebuhr's death in 1971), Gordon was immediately captivated by Niebuhr's thought as it was reflected in *Moral Man and Immoral Society.*

Reinhold Niebuhr represented the first serious challenge to the idealism of liberal Protestant thinking as it entered the 1930s, as he blasted its deepest hope that human history would eventually realize a community founded on love. In *Moral Man and Immoral Society*, he argued that altruistic relationships were possible only in small groups like the family, and that a sharp distinction must be drawn between the moral and social behaviour of individuals and that of social groups. In the latter, relationships would always be determined by the proportion of power that each group possessed. Consequently, coercion became a necessary instrument for social cohesion, and pure ethical action among groups was impossible.

This was Niebuhr at his most intemperate, and it was a far cry from the gentle optimism King had imbibed at his father's table in Winnipeg or even, for that matter, the ameliorating assumptions of Fabian socialism he had been exposed to at Oxford. While Niebuhr was fond of claiming that he was a conservative in theology and a radical in politics, Gordon noted that those at Union who became Niebuhr's friends and disciples were, with a few notable exceptions, not particularly adept at theologizing. Unable to bring theological critique to bear on his thought, they therefore identified with the political radical and, as a result, found themselves unable to commit to either the utopianism of Marx or the cool rationality of liberalism.

Gordon's other mentor at Union, Harry F. Ward, was generally regarded by the student body as even more radical than Reinhold Niebuhr – perhaps because of his Marxist interpretations and his support of the Soviet Union. Gordon was particularly attracted to Ward's genuine respect for common working people, a quality he himself shared. He also admired Ward's seamless integration of theology and social action – an exemplification of

Karl Barth's adage that Christian theology is best done with the Bible in one hand and the daily newspaper in the other.[10] He described Ward as a small thin man with a sharp tongue and a country dialect, whose warm friendly manner belied his absolutely fearless and uncompromising fierceness in attacking injustice.[11]

The origins of Ward's theological journey lay in the English Methodism of his childhood, which stressed personal religious experience and human perfection.[12] Ward believed that the doctrine of human perfection was redirected from the individual to the social group, for human nature was essentially social, and the individual, as an individual, was inevitably part and parcel of society. Social change would not come about by converting individuals one by one; rather, by changing societal structures the individual would also be changed.[13]

This theme of "Christianizing the social order" was common parlance among advocates of the American social gospel, but Ward specifically emphasized Christianizing the economic base of society, because from it everything else emanated. Gordon was impressed by Ward's economic interpretation and signed up for his courses. He had already been sensitized, if not converted, to an economic interpretation of history through his reading of R.H. Tawney at Oxford and, as can be seen later in King's career, these ideas bore fruit, particularly in his early writings for the League for Social Reconstruction and the CCF. As far as the use of violence was concerned, while Niebuhr was conceding the principle in *Moral Man and Immoral Society*, Ward appeared to draw back, viewing revolution as too drastic a means of bringing about economic changes. In fact, with regard to both goals and means, Ward sturdily held to the concept of democracy, "that life must be organized in brotherhood for the purpose of realizing the eternal worth that belongs to every individual soul."[14] This idea too is central to Gordon's thinking of the 1930s.

King developed close social relationships with both Niebuhr and Ward, first in his capacity as teaching assistant and then simply as a friend, and their meetings were frequent and informal. In their professional relationship, he shortly discovered that he also shared with them a concern with the standards of student papers that it had become customary to accept. He confided to his father: "The custom seems to be to grade up from 80% instead of down to 50% as I should like to do."[15] This critical view of standards was something King also shared with his newly arrived classmate, Dietrich Bonhoeffer, the brilliant twenty-four-year-old German scholar who arrived in the fall of 1930 to spend a post-graduate year studying at Union. It is understandable that Bonhoeffer, with a doctorate in theology from the University of Berlin, and himself the product of a rigorous and sophisticated European education, should find the intellectual capacities of the young American students "laughably undeveloped." Richard Fox quotes Bonhoeffer: "The theological education of this group is virtually nil, and the self-assurance which lightly makes mock of any specifically theological question is unwarranted and naive."[16] Bonhoeffer went on to assert that the informality of social relations at Union and the reluctance to say anything against another member of the dormitory as long as he is a "good fellow" led to a "leveling in intellectual demands and accomplishments."[17]

On their part, the American students viewed Bonhoeffer as very German, not only in his thorough academic training, but in the formality of his manner and his drive for perfection. Quickly, however, the good will and charm of each side became apparent to the other: the students discovered that Bonhoeffer's formality was no barrier to friendship, and he came to appreciate the benefits of the open spirit and self-confidence of the Americans, marvelling at their willingness to discuss any subject with anyone, peer and professor alike.[18]

King, in his amiable way, was not put off by Bonhoeffer's judgment and European formalism, and he and Bonhoeffer developed a cordial relationship, keeping in occasional touch during the 1930s – Gordon's most radical period of political activity, and the time during which Bonhoeffer, banned by the Gestapo from teaching and preaching, worked closely with the opponents of Adolph Hitler. Bonhoeffer's closest friends at Union consisted of a small group comprising four young scholars: an African-American, Frank Fisher, who introduced him to Harlem life; Jean Lesserre, a Reformed French theologian; Erwin Sutz, also Reformed; and Paul Lehmann, an American who came from the Evangelical and Reformed Church. But more recent scholarship suggests that there were others, including King Gordon and Jim Dombrowski, who also interested and influenced him and about whom he repeatedly inquired in his correspondence with Lehmann. In his Introduction to the English Edition of *Dietrich Bonhoeffer Works: Barcelona, Berlin, New York 1928–1931*, editor Clifford Green writes:

> If we are clear about the importance of Fisher and Lasserre for Bonhoeffer's personal and theological development, what about this lesser-known group of faculty and students – White, Webber, Gordon, Klein, Dombrowski? These were probably some of the most radical Christians with whom Bonhoeffer ever associated – they were radicals not only in theory. Most of them were practicing socialists.

> They worked on urban and rural poverty, on racial justice and civil rights, on union organizing, on peacemaking, and at the United Nations. Interestingly, some of them had careers analogous to Bonhoeffer himself, being expelled from academic appointments, persecuted by law, imprisoned. What did these friends and associates mean to Bonhoeffer that he continued to inquire about them years after he had left New York?[19]

Gordon treasured his contacts with Bonhoeffer and spoke of him frequently in later life, pointing to his profound commitment and courage in opposing Hitler, which led to his martyr's death by hanging at Flossenbürg concentration camp on 9 April 1945, one month before the Allies liberated the camp. King learned of Bonhoeffer's death in early June when former prisoners sent news of his fate to Visser't Hooft at the World Council of Churches headquarters in Geneva.

As the economic depression deepened during the winter of 1929–30, and the desperation of the unemployed pressed itself into the students' consciousness, an informal student–faculty committee drew together around a project loosely termed the Union Waterfront Project. It began when an unemployed newspaperman, attempting to write the story of unemployment from the inside, came to the office of Erdman Harris, professor of Christian education at Union, reporting the ghastly situation into which New York City was drifting and asking for volunteers from Union.[20] The focus of the effort was the waterfront and Battery Park where seamen with honourable discharges from their ships found themselves huddled around makeshift fires with nothing to eat, nowhere to sleep, and nowhere to go. Many of them were only teenagers. What could be done? The response from the students astonished even themselves. Initially, King acted as student chairman of an ad hoc committee to address the problem until the Student Council appointed their own committee to head the project.[21] Starting out with the objective of raising $3,000 as an unemployment budget, a figure that staggered most of the students, they actually raised approximately $4,800.

The first goal of the committee was to address the needs of the teenagers, to pry them away from the despairing conditions of the waterfront and at least see that they got a bed for the night. The House Committee of the Seminary was approached: could the large guestroom in the dormitory be used? What about the gymnasium across the street? The use of the dormitory was turned down, but the gymnasium became available.

Under the daily supervision of the students, cots for twenty-five were set up and blankets, sheets, pillows, pillow-cases, towels, and soap were provided by a willing housekeeping staff. A treasurer meted out change each day to handle laundry, incidentals, and lunch money while the boys hunted for jobs. One of the seminary departments allowed the use of its secretary to create a job-finding office in touch with the free employment agencies. A student supervisor doled out clothing from the huge stock of suits, overcoats, pajamas, shirts, shoes, socks, underwear, and neckties that poured in. (One is tempted to wonder how frequently these young seamen had need of neckties.) Breakfast and dinner were served in the student refectory. Each boy had his own student supervisor, and students in groups roamed the waterfront each evening, recruiting.

Quite apart from the wholehearted and humane response by all concernd, it was a heaven-made situation for King, and it must have taken him back to the happy days of the boys' clubs in Giscome and Pine Falls. At the same time, it was a new and raw experience for him, perhaps most nearly paralleling his experiences with the student refugees in Vienna; except that this time the human tragedy was happening on his own doorstep. One miserably cold night, as he and the students walked around Battery Park in a relentless drizzle, they came across about thirty men warming themselves around a fire that burned in an old oil drum. A young boy was lying sick under some hay and they called an ambulance. Another boy with a Texas accent shivered close to the fire. Two older seamen explained that there was not much shipping these days. They walked along the waterfront and found men sleeping wrapped in newspapers. Back at the fire, a patrolman dispersed the group, who herded into the park enclosure. That night as he lay in his bed, heavy with guilt at what he had seen, King realized how little he had known about unemployment and human need. He awoke the next morning with his moral sensibilities heightened ineradicably.[22] It was, as King later reflected, an experience that brought him and the other students down from their theoretical heights and easy talk about the "crisis of capitalism."

In November of 1929, several members of the Agenda Club, including Gordon and his friend Jim Dombrowski, went to East Marion and Gastonia, North Carolina, where two strikes in the textile industry had resulted in violence and death. The strike in East Marion, where the United Textile Workers had been organizing, had been particularly brutal. King and his classmates were appalled at what they saw: Appalachian people brought in to work, living without sewers or running water, and working eleven to twelve hours a day with no minimum wage. The women got twelve to fourteen dollars for a week's work. In the town of Marion itself, some of the ministers were sympathetic, but in the mill town of East Marion, with the exception of one Baptist layman who had a house church, the ministers stood solidly with the company. Although at the national level there was considerable concern among religious groups such as the Federal Council of Churches, the Social Action Department of the Catholic Welfare Conference, and the Commission on Social Justice of the American Council of Rabbis, there was little that the students could do. They reported to the Agenda Club, and Jim Dombrowski gave a talk in New York at the annual conference of the Student League for Industrial Democracy entitled "The Human Cost of Textiles."[23]

Concurrent with his studies at Union, Gordon was serving as assistant minister to his father's friend Archie Sinclair at the First Presbyterian Church in Bloomfield, New Jersey. It was in his role as minister that he was able to bring together and integrate his several worlds of thought and experience during his two years in the United States. The Bloomfield church was prominent and wealthy, and Sinclair had lost none of his crusading zeal since his days as a young missionary in Yukon Territory and as a fellow worker with C.W. Gordon in the Winnipeg Ministerial Association. Sinclair had a doctorate from Heidelberg, where he had written his dissertation on Herbert Spencer, and, being a great admirer of Alfred North Whitehead and of Niebuhr, he was fascinated by new philosophical trends.

The Sinclairs welcomed King into their family life, and with them he explored the Orange Mountains on picnics and walks. Their circle of friends included intellectual and political luminaries who provided Gordon with introductions and stimulating conversation. It was through the Sinclairs that Gordon first met Norman Thomas, leader of the Socialist Party, who occasionally preached from Archie Sinclair's pulpit. It was the non-Marxist character of Norman Thomas's socialism that attracted men like Niebuhr, who entered the Socialist Party in 1929. At the time that King met him, Thomas was running for borough president of Manhattan, a race that ended in stunned defeat for the Socialists, as Manhattan was the centre of socialist strength. King, like his mentor Niebuhr and to some extent Sinclair, was also attracted by the moderate, non-violent socialism of Thomas and he liked Thomas personally, although he was somewhat put off by his "big, booming authoritative voice."[24]

Gordon's duties in the church included some preaching responsibility and the sole charge of the young peoples' activities, and he usually travelled twice weekly by bus to Bloomfield. The social prominence of First Presbyterian Church notwithstanding, Gordon was not reluctant to bring in outside speakers of unusual interest. During Dr Sinclair's prolonged absence due to illness in 1931, he filled in with preaching and Sunday afternoon musical services, and he reported to his mother, "In the evening at our young people's group we had a brilliant young communist who had been a year at Moscow University. The group – about sixty in all – were quite thrilled and asked some good questions afterwards."[25] In his sermons on the traditional and worthy virtues of the power of love and service to others, he also pointed out the striking inequalities of income, the contrast between rich and poor, luxury and misery, class intolerance, and racial hatred. He asked, "Am I my brother's keeper as we view the unemployed of other nations and their tariff walls, the nations' armaments pointing to another holocaust?"[26] Nor was he reticent to share his waterfront experience with the parish and, through his children's sermons, raising awareness of those children "who do not have all the nice things of the children of Bloomfield."[27]

During the summer of 1930, while King had been left in charge during the Sinclairs' vacation at their summer home in Canada, he discovered the more mundane aspects of keeping ten-year-old boys occupied when he took the boys of Vacation Bible School on an overnight hike. After giving them "a little preliminary coaching with camp craft so that the trip will be educational as well as a lark," he admitted, somewhat to his dismay, that "it is a bit difficult to know how to handle youngsters who have had no camp discipline."[28] Small wonder, for they walked along a 16 km stretch of paved road, had a cookout, made cocoa, had a swim, and hiked back home. This was tame stuff by Birkencraig standards, and King's letters were redolent with homesickness for "everything I long for: the pines and the birches, the clear water, a canoe, a tent and the smell of the woods and the sound of the lake, and of course, being with you all."

During that long summer in Bloomfield, he also tried out his fledgling wings on radical social issues, warning of the peril of doing nothing and, with a hazy notion of a benevolent deity, expecting that somehow God would work things out. He even took a shot at intellectuals – "material gathered at the feet of Niebuhr and Ward," he later noted wryly.[29] As he told his mother at the time, "This morning's sermon was not so hot: I was inveighing against intellectualism, and the only word of favorable comment I got afterwards was from the one really intellectual man in the congregation!" He recouped in the evening service by preaching a sermon inspired by rereading his father's stories on the Rich Young Ruler, concluding that "I will put my heavier philosophy into cold storage for the remainder of the summer months and confine myself to story telling."[30] When September came, he was glad to return to his studies.

But during these experiences of preaching and teaching in Bloomfield, perhaps in reaction to the teachings of Harry Ward, he struggled with the Presbyterianism of his father and its primary emphasis on the regeneration of the individual as the means of reforming society. In December 1930, in a letter to his father, he gave voice to one of those occasional introspective moods that punctuated his life, revealing an interior depth, a subterranean current of moral concern that underlay and indeed nourished all his public interests and commitments. He wrote to his father:

> You are right about the change of heart [as the basis for social change], and I know it and it makes one a bit desperate at times. My own focus is too rational and I feel the lack of that drive that a man of God should have. And I think somewhat wistfully that if I could 'get religion' in a rather simple and primitive way it might be to some good. But I shrink from fanaticism, from emotionalism, from pietism ... I can say this without fear of offending you because you run to none of these extremes, and combine an idealism in philosophy with a realistic grasp of human affairs, and a sense of being governed by the will of God with an intellectual grasp of the meaning of life. Perhaps I may yet reach God through a contact with the needs of man. At present I play spectator in an Aristotelian sense and hop off the fence for an occasional foray into the conflict ... And yet it certainly will not do to whip up an emotional appeal when I don't feel it. I suppose everyone has that problem of a divided self and only some terrific power can weld it together.[31]

This was a struggle that he returned to during the next decade as he worked out his own understanding of the moral basis of social reform.

It was always assumed that Gordon would return to ministry of some form in Canada after his time at Union, and as early as February of 1930 he wrote to his father, asking that if in his travels he should see anything opening up in the Canadian church, to let him know. Yet when it came, the invitation followed its own rather circuitous route. In January of

1931, Gordon received an invitation from the Montreal YMCA to speak at a forum being held on the topic of unemployment. About the same time, he got a letter from the minister of a prominent United Church there asking him to preach for him and informing him (off the record) that he was being considered for a chair in Christian Ethics and Religious Education at the United Theological College, the United Church theological college affiliated with McGill University. As it turned out, a group of UTC professors attended the forum and Gordon "preached for a call," in Presbyterian terms, a call that came a couple of weeks later in the form of a job offer. By this time he had completed his class work at Columbia and was well launched on his dissertation on "The Church and the Industrial Revolution," but the invitation to teach in the field of greatest relevance and commitment seemed to outweigh possible academic advancement. He abandoned any thoughts of a PhD and accepted the Montreal offer to join the faculty in September.

Response from Canada came quickly in the form of a letter from Salem Bland, "philosopher and mentor" of the social gospel in Canada.[32] Bland, an ordained Methodist minister and another ministerial associate of C.W. Gordon in Winnipeg, had become a "free-wheeling practitioner" of the new evangelism of the social gospel. Gordon described him as an "unrepentant Christian radical, though a gentle person."[33] Bland welcomed King: "Providence is opening up to you a position of great influence in a critical time ... I hope you may be able to play a part in the United Church of Canada akin to what Harry Ward has been playing with such boldness and wisdom in the United States. With very fond wishes and with high hopes. S.G. Bland."[34]

Very high hopes and high expectations, indeed. The response from King's Oxford companions Graham Spry and John Farthing lacked something of this high-minded expectation. Spry wrote from Ottawa: "I have just heard that you have been nominated for the chair of Christian ethics in Montreal and sincerely hope that you intend to accept. You will find a splendid group of congenial spirits in Montreal and very agreeable circumstances in which to work. And there is ample opportunity for your dangerous radicalism."[35]

John Farthing, also expressing delight and harkening back to their time together in Florence, hoped that together they could share a new Renaissance; but then his letter struck a more pessimistic note:

> Your coming to Montreal to teach Christian ethics is like your going among cannibals to teach them Christian charity. One of the leading

> lights in your college is one of the leading wealthy merchants of Montreal who had turned off employees of thirty years standing for a week's holiday without pay. It seems to me there is a smallness about that which is even worse than its hardness … Yes King, we need some Christian ethics badly. May I congratulate you further on your two excellent addresses as reported in the press. It was certainly good stuff and I'm surprised that after as fearless an utterance on Christian ethics you should still be considered for a post in a Christian theological college. Am I too cynical? You can't prove to me that I am.[36]

Gordon's reflection on this letter many years later was, "A powerful letter and not too unrealistic an appraisal of what I was getting into!"[37]

In the meantime, and before going off to the cannibals, King concluded his two years in the United States with a ten-day holiday in June, once again as guest of the Bennett family on their island off the coast of Maine. "There were about a dozen of us, practically all my best friends, almost all good sound radicals and … with a good sense of humor. We came back through Maine, and the New Hampshire mountains … glorious country. My old Ford stood up very well and we sailed along between 40 and 55 all the way."[38]

In one pithy sentence, Gordon summed up the profound impact his time in New York had had on his political views: "The experience of those two years changed my thinking into that of a Christian social radical."[39]

6

The Glory Days: Montreal, the LSR, and the CCF

After a month at Birkencraig, King packed up his Model A Ford in September and drove to Montreal, stopping on the way for a weekend in Glengarry County where he visited his father's birthplace and Grandfather Gordon's old Highland churches. It was a journey back to his roots, and was both emotional and restorative. He attended Sunday service in Apple Hill, and as he looked down from the pulpit it did not take much imagination to see the Highland congregation that his grandfather had looked down on Sunday after Sunday. "It did seem like walking on holy ground," he told his father. "Not that you would be likely to describe grandfather as a holy man. He was too highland for that, but sixty years seemed to have rolled back."[1] Although modern transportation and the clearing of forest now made the distances seem short, he could imagine the walk from church to church through woods and swamp on dark winter evenings.

Propelled onward by the energy of his past and eager to get to Montreal, Gordon continued on his way, covering the 135 km over dirt roads in just two and a half hours. He felt rather muddled and a little hard-pressed on his arrival, with the flurry of ceremony surrounding the opening of the term and the installation of new professors, while he hastily pulled together his first few lectures. Before leaving New York, he had expressed some misgivings about his new teaching assignment, writing to Principal James Smyth in early March: "As you are aware, the one feature of the proposal which has given me pause is that I shall be expected to teach some courses in the field of Religious Education, one in which my special interest and qualifications frankly do not lie."[2] Harry Ward took up Gordon's cause, also writing to the principal, and Professor W.A. Gifford responded by reassuring Ward that while he sympathized with his point of view, the difficulty lay in giving it immediate effect: the idea of a department of Christian ethics was new to Canada where the curriculum (largely prescribed by the board of education of the whole church) was still overloaded on the biblical side. No doubt the "powers that be" would ask why the college would need a professor for Christian ethics alone. Prospects for its success as a discipline would improve considerably by linking it with some admittedly needed work, in this case, religious education. Surely two half-courses a week should not be a burden for Mr Gordon, who would, at the same time, be compensated with as open and unprejudiced a public as he could find for his pioneering work in Christian ethics; and, within the college circle, he would find unanimous support.[3]

After one week of teaching, King was able to report to his mother, "It's going to be alright I think. They aren't such a bad crowd after all."[4] He especially liked the dean, D.L. Ritchie, who regaled him over dinner with stories in "quite the best Scottish tradition." In the same letter he described R.B.Y. Scott, newly installed as professor in Old Testament, as "a liberal not only in his scholarship but also in his social outlook." This generous but crisp comment scarcely portends the depth of mutual respect and commitment that R.B.Y. Scott and Gordon would develop in their long friendship. Even the church people that he had so far met seemed eager to respond to the crisis, particularly in immediate relief work with the unemployed.

Certainly there was an urgent need in Montreal, as there had been in New York, for Christians to become involved in humanitarian efforts to relieve the dreadful suffering brought about by the Depression. By 1933 Greater Montreal, the largest urban area in Canada, with a population of over a million, had more than a third of its population on relief. Across Canada, the burden of the Depression fell most cruelly on Prairie farmers and the urban unemployed. The crash of the stock market in 1929 had had relatively little immediate effect in Canada, since only a tiny percentage of Canadians had speculated to the degree that they were personally ruined. However, Canada's resource-dependent economy (eighty percent of her timber, mining, and farm produce was sold abroad) made it especially vulnerable to international instability. There was a stunning drop in Canadian exports, and commodity prices plummeted along with the volumes traded. A high protective tariff shored up manufacturing to some degree, but even so, industrial production fell by a third between 1929 and 1932.

Throughout his life, Gordon approached a political or social problem by starting with a human example and moving to ethical theory. In New York, it had been the faces and specific voices of the young seamen that had kept him tossing fitfully in his comfortable bed at night. So it was in Montreal, where the human face of misery rather than the statistical graphs and figures that disturbed him: the stories of a mother evicted from her home and on the street, surrounded by her furniture and her nine children; or the hundreds of young men, sleeping in the ball park under newspaper blankets.[5] It was a natural progression for him that very shortly after his arrival in Montreal, he was drawn into a remarkable organization that was in the process of being formed.

By one of those "fortunate chances" that seemed to mark his life, during that first week in Montreal in 1931 King received a phone call from Frank Scott asking if he would be interested in joining a small group modelled on the British Fabians, the newly conceived League for Social Reconstruction. Scott and Gordon had been contemporaries at Oxford, and although their paths crossed frequently – they had both sung in the Bach choir and rowed for their respective colleges – they had never met. In retrospect, the harmony that marked their fifty-four years of friendship seems already implicit in the unwitting counterpoint and rhythms of their singing and rowing. With Frank Scott's phone call that October morning, they began their long journey of over fifty years of friendship together.

On his return to Montreal from Oxford in 1923, Scott had become part of that small and intense community of young writers and artists who were preoccupied with issues of Canadian identity and its expression in art and literature. While Gordon was crossing log booms on the Fraser River and struggling with the finer points of theology, happily and securely oblivious to questions of what it meant to be Canadian, Scott was studying law and struggling with the heavy mantle of colonialism.

In 1928 Scott was appointed to the Faculty of Law at McGill, where he remained, first as professor and later as dean, throughout his professional academic life. In that same year, he married the Montreal artist Marian Dale, and together they gathered around them the lively young intellectuals of English Montreal, a group that included not only artists and writers, but newer friends who had been influenced by Fabian socialism and were looking for opportunities for political action. Typically, the group included Marian's friends from her student days at the Beaux-Arts; poets and writers like A.J.M. Smith and Leon Edel; the young lawyer Brooke Claxton, and Terry MacDermot, who was teaching history at McGill after completing his studies at Oxford. Graham Spry too was often a visitor in Montreal and with Alan Plaunt (a wealthy young businessman) was working to establish a Canadian equivalent of the BBC. Dr Norman Bethune, who taught art classes for underprivileged children with Marian and was already far to the left of the Scott group in politics, also joined the discussions.

King developed a close relationship with one of the group in particular, Pegi Nicol, a young artist and friend of Marian Scott. He was captivated by her vibrant spirit and lack of convention; she painted his portrait and began attending debates in the House of Commons to be prepared for meetings of the LSR. ("All artists are naturally socialists, so you don't need to make me one," she wrote to him in early 1932.) It is reported that, eight years later, she wept at his wedding.[6] By that time, both Pegi and her husband, Norman MacLeod, were living in New York, as were King and Ruth, and they continued their friendship until Pegi's death in 1949. Pegi seemed to offer King a window into the bohemian world that his upbringing and his serious sense of social purpose had not provided.

Gordon's activity in social causes was well known among his friends in Montreal, and Scott would have been familiar with his reputation in that small, interconnected world. The same evening of Scott's call, King bundled up for the short walk to 3653 Oxenden Avenue, a modest house with an ancient green Franklin parked in front. Marian Scott met him at the door and led him into a living room dominated by books and paintings where he met Frank (as tall and imposing as he) and the other members of the group: Eugene Forsey, who would in short order become his partner in the radical movement in the United Church; Jacques Bieler, an engineer and brother of André Bieler, a painter, whose father, a Swiss theologian, taught at UTC; Joe Mergler, a labour lawyer; and David Lewis, a first-year law student and president of the McGill Labour Club, soon to attend Oxford as a Rhodes scholar.[7]

Gordon recalled that introduction to Scott in an article written for *Saturday Night* in 1985, the year of Frank's death, and added Leon Edel's description of Frank: his sharply etched face, as if painted by Holbein; an attentive listener; and possessed of a sharp wit. What had first impressed King was his civility in manner and speech. Although Scott's searching mind exploded with new ideas, he spoke with quiet authority, becoming the centre of any conversation. Above all, Gordon was attracted by his way of "laying bare the pretensions of the self-important with shouts of laughter."[8]

Years later, Gordon still recalled the warmth of the Scotts' hospitality, and he tried to identify that single shared idea that had made them a group: "It wasn't literature. It wasn't art. It certainly wasn't socialism." And then it came to him: it was *ideas themselves* and a search for answers, not one answer, but many from "poets and painters and professors and lawyers and students and business people and even the politicians." And beneath the search they shared a common view, "a deep concern for man, a being capable of love and creative effort in an ordered world."[9]

With introductions over, Frank Scott introduced Gordon to their newly conceived project, one that he quickly embraced. The idea began with Gordon's old acquaintance from Winnipeg, J.S. Woodsworth, who had been active in the Winnipeg Ministerial Association with his father. In 1921 Woodsworth had been elected to Parliament as member for Winnipeg Centre on behalf of the Independent Labour Party of Manitoba. By 1931, he had become the leader of a small number of leftist MPs known as the Ginger Group, and a figure of enormous respect in Canada and a model for young intellectuals like Frank Scott. Woodsworth had also studied at Oxford a generation earlier and he expressed a hope to Frank H. Underhill, a young professor of history at the University of Toronto, that something along the lines of a Fabian Society could be created in Canada that could feed ideas into the political endeavours of the left, functioning as an intellectual resource much as the Fabians did for the British Labour Party.

Frank Underhill, as a Rhodes scholar at Oxford before the First World War, had actually been a member of the Fabian Society. When he returned to Canada in 1919 after military service in France, he taught history at the new University of Saskatchewan in that postwar period when the province "was being swept by the great prairie fire of the Progressive movement."[10] It was in Saskatchewan, he wrote, "so it seemed to me, I experienced for the first time what a democracy is really like when it is thoroughly alive."[11] It was here that he met Woodsworth for the first time, later describing him as "the first of those radicals whom Oxford has sent back to us, the forerunner of the Frank Scotts and Dave Lewises and Ted Joliffes"[12] – and, he might have added, the King Gordons. By 1931, when Gordon entered the picture, the time was ripe for Underhill and the others of the "Oxford connection" who had been influenced by

Fabian thought to press ahead with Woodsworth's idea of forming a Canadian counterpart to the Fabian Society.

It is an oft-told story, almost mythic in its retelling among the early members of the League for Social Reconstruction: in August of 1931, Dean Percy Corbett of the McGill Law School invited Frank Scott to attend the Annual Institute of Politics at Williams College in Williamstown, Massachusetts. Here Scott met Underhill and they liked each other immediately. On Sunday morning of the conference, Corbett, Scott, and Underhill hiked up Mount Greylock and, as they climbed, Underhill described what he had in mind: a group of intellectuals, with support from farmer and labour organizations, who could provide a leftist political party with the sort of viable ideas and coherent policy that would prevent it from splintering and being absorbed like the Progressives of the 1920s. Both men agreed that the first task of such a group would be to enunciate and clarify the principles that should guide politicians in social reconstruction.

On returning to Toronto and Montreal at the end of the conference, they gathered together a small group in each city and set about trying to draft a program or manifesto. The main problem seemed to be how radical the document ought to be, and at least five drafts went back and forth between September and January. Finally, it was the Montreal group that was in charge of the final draft, and historian Michiel Horn, in his history of the LSR,[13] argues that this accounted for the more moderate tone of the document: Scott and Forsey (both fluently bilingual) and their Montreal group had hopes of attracting membership from French as well as English Canada and feared scaring off this more conservative population. (It proved to be a futile hope in any case.)

The founding meeting of the LSR took place in Toronto on the weekend of 23 January 1932, a day on which, as Frank Scott famously described it, "the temperature fell to seventeen below [°F], which gave us a true-north-strong-and-free-feeling."[14] The Montreal group – Forsey, Gordon, Lewis, Scott, and J.K. Mergler – travelled down by train and met the Toronto group, which, under Underhill's leadership, consisted of Harry Cassidy, who taught social work at the University of Toronto; Eric Havelock, a classics professor; and Irene Biss and J.F. Parkinson, both of the department of political economy. A provisional national executive was appointed consisting of Gordon, Havelock, Parkinson, Scott, and Underhill, who became the first president. Isabel Thomas, head of the English department at York Memorial Collegiate in Toronto and the daughter of the Reverend Ernest Thomas, became secretary-treasurer.

In March, with more meetings like that first one at the Scotts and many letters back and forth between Montreal and Toronto, the group produced its manifesto.[15] The radical nature of the document is evident in its preamble, which states clearly that the goal of the LSR is to establish in Canada "a social order in which the basic principle regulating production, distribution and service will be the common good rather than private profit." This "social reconstruction" would be achieved through centralized planning – a constitutional amendment expanding the powers of the federal government to carry out guidelines set by a National Planning Commission – and a socialized economy that included public ownership of utilities and essential services and financial institutions. Social legislation would provide for the basic needs of the population through unemployment, illness, and old age, and cooperatives would be developed for production and marketing in the agricultural sector.

The details of what this national planning would involve were spelled out in the LSR book, *Social Planning for Canada,* finally published in 1935. Gordon was among the seven members of the research committee who signed their names to the preface and assumed responsibility for the book. Harry Cassidy was its editor-in-chief, Graham Spry his associate; Irene Biss, Eugene Forsey, and Joe Parkinson took charge of chapters dealing with the economy; Underhill assumed responsibility for politics, Scott for the constitution, and another Rhodes scholar who had recently joined the group, Escott Reid, oversaw the chapter on external affairs. The actual writing was often a joint effort and many individual authors worked on the book, some asking to remain anonymous.

It is interesting to note that the word *socialist* was not used in the early writings of the LSR, and when it entered common usage it was generally prefixed with "democratic" to distinguish the LSR from Marxism on the one hand and National Socialism on the other.[16] Gordon had already begun to refer to himself as a socialist in New York. Scholars of Canadian socialism have been quick and remarkably unanimous in characterizing the nature of the socialism found in the LSR (and in the CCF as well) as British, Protestant, and Fabian: eclectic, non-ideological, evolutionary, and democratic and – from the Marxist perspective – thoroughly revisionist.[17]

Michiel Horn identifies the opening chapter of *Social Planning for Canada,* "The End of a Century of Progress," as basically Gordon's work, although Harry Cassidy, Frank Underhill, Joe Parkinson, Leonard Marsh, and Frank Scott all offered criticism and suggestions. Gordon was at his evangelical best in the manifesto, achieving that clarion-call fervour that he so often lamented was lacking in his preaching, a bringing together of heart and head. We in Canada, he argued, are victims of a belief in progress prevalent in new countries but no longer borne out by the facts: we believe ourselves immune to the economic and social abuses of the old countries – slums, factories, bitter class war. But, he pointed out, there are two fallacies in this blind faith in progress: first, that scientific and technological progress can be equated with social and cultural progress; and second, that since technical advance provides improved material conditions of living, therefore the standard of material well-being of a society can be measured in terms of technical advance. However, an individual enjoys these material benefits of our modern age precisely to the extent that he is able to afford them. Gordon then analyzed the conditions of life under which the majority of Canadians live in the existing capitalist economy, with its mal-distribution of wealth and the bitter paradox that "the creation of plenty has brought forth calamitous scarcity."[18] With liberal use of tables and statistics, and examples from every sector of the Canadian economy, he demonstrated the effects of the concentration of power within capitalism and the consequent exploitation of the least protected groups within society. Drawing heavily on R.H. Tawney, he described capitalist culture in terms of "the acquisitive society," a society in which the values of religion itself are determined by economic factors. Fortunately, he concluded, this is not the whole story, for the prophetic voice of the church has from time to time been raised in judgment against the more flagrant forms of injustice, mitigating the worst evils of the system. As in his other writing of this time, Gordon appealed to the church to return to this prophetic calling.

By June of 1931 both groups had over one hundred members, and at the beginning of 1933 there were seventeen branches from Montreal westward to Victoria, most of them small, and most of them in Ontario. They drew their membership largely from the professional and academic classes, and from the middle and upper levels of white-collar workers. French Canadians, small businessmen, shopkeepers, and workers contributed almost no members. As talks began to develop among the leftist farm and labour groups for the formation of a new party, the question arose of whether the LSR would affiliate with such a party. It was generally accepted among the LSR leadership that direct affiliation with a party would handicap the LSR's goal of reaching the intelligentsia in particular, and Woodsworth agreed that the best course would be to work quietly behind the scenes and to pursue its program of education. This proved to be a wise decision, and with its strong belief in education and its liberal assumption that, if individuals could be shown the truth, they would be inclined to follow it, the LSR organized a vigorous program of public speaking, even organizing a series of radio broadcasts.

LSR members took conspicuous parts in political seminars and summer schools. Their program also included speakers of some note from the larger community and from abroad. Gordon was able to use his connections in New York to bring in Harry Laidler of the League for Industrial Democracy; Norman Thomas of the American Socialist Party; and, of course, his old friends Harry F. Ward and Reinhold Niebuhr, who spoke to packed meetings in the Church of the Messiah. The Fabian connections produced Sir Stafford Cripps, cabinet member in Ramsay MacDonald's National Government, and John Strachey, Scott's classmate at Magdalen and author of *The Coming Struggle for Power.*

Strachey proved somewhat of a disappointment. In the first place, many in his audience were expecting *Lytton* Strachey of literary fame – though it seems not to have occurred to them to wonder what the hidden lives of eminent Victorians might have had to do with socialism. In the second place, John Strachey was far too Marxist. Speaking to the Montreal Men's Canadian Club, he alluded to a known Canadian communist by beginning, "I understand you put my colleague, Tim Buck, in one of your penitentiaries."[19] Gordon found the moderate socialism of Prime Minister Walter Nash of New Zealand, who also spoke, far more to his liking.

His father's son in so many ways, King loved to speak in public, and he found himself hard-pressed to keep up with his schedule of speaking engagements as well as his class lectures at UTC where, he confessed, his students benefitted from rehashed Ward and Niebuhr. His diary of November 1932 through April 1933 found him speaking and preaching on thirty-eight occasions.[20] Fatherly concern from C.W. Gordon expressed itself in more than one letter. King sent his mother a copy of a two-week schedule after a speaking visit to Ottawa in October of 1932 (which included visits with Mike and Maryon Pearson and J.S. Woodsworth), assuring her, "I've decided not to speak any more than I'm already booked for before Christmas. (I have just twelve, I believe.)"[21] His talks presented the standard LSR fare, with his own particular prophetic emphasis: one favourite theme warned of the danger to religious liberty in a capitalist society that stressed the virtue of competition and individual achievement.[22] Another asked, "Dare the Church Be Christian?" and pointed out that the history of the Christian church had been marked by repeated accommodation between the ethics of Jesus and the ethics of the society within which the church existed. In the present context, the church found itself financially dependent on a capitalist system, justifying institutions that wasted human life and caused suffering. Dare the church stand in judgment and carry out the principles of Jesus? Gordon concluded this particular address by urging Christians to get out into society and throw their weight *as* Christians on the side of the oppressed.[23]

During this period, Gordon frequently spoke of the human side of misery in his sermons. A weathered manila folder among his papers labelled "Sermons, UTC, 1931–1932," offers an example. He had spent the previous day in a soup kitchen where the men were fed like robots, in silence, not spoken to, according to a system made efficient by stop watches and finding where delays and jams slowed things down. In this way, 4,000 men could be fed in two hours. "Silently plates of corned beef and potatoes are rattled down. It does not take long and they pass out into the street." There but for some accident of birth or fortune went King Gordon. He wondered, "Does he know enough, feel enough to hate me?"

> I who am well dressed, well fed, watch him eating like a wolf. Is this the thing the Lord made and gave to have dominion over sea and land; to trace the stars and search the heavens for power; to feel the passion for eternity? Is this the dream He dreamed who shaped the suns and pillared the blue firmament with light? And I thought of the thousands who eat in their homes, saying grace with their meals; who sleep in their soft beds and offer prayers in costly churches to the God of mercy. And I was one of them.

He closed this sermon by quoting, "If thy brother have ought against thee, leave thy gift before the altar and go thy way; first be reconciled to thy brother and then come and offer thy gift," concluding, "I wondered how I could be reconciled to my brother who has so much against me."[24]

Compassion, however, did not mean long-faced misery. There was a great sense of expectation and hope in the LSR, of confidence that it could bring about change. In later years, Gordon inveighed against dreary accounts of the 1930s. Far from being a group of Fabian intellectuals on the sidelines, he protested, among the LSR there was a "gut involvement" in the moral necessity of social change.[25] Gordon argued adamantly that there was nothing aloof or elitist about their commitment and, far from propounding the utopian and unworkable schemes that the contemporary press accused them of doing, they were going about the practical business of creating a new society. When the CCF was formed in 1932 as an active party across Canada, it opened the way for many LSR members (including Gordon himself) to serious political participation in a program they had helped formulate. Later, in 1944, the coming to power of the Saskatchewan CCF enabled – within the constraints of provincial jurisdiction – the implementation of many of the social goals of the LSR. These young intellectuals of the 1930s combined pragmatism with that utopian zeal of revolutionaries of all ages: "Bliss was it in that dawn to be alive, / But to be young was very heaven!"

But not all their time absorbed by social action, ethics, and politics. The large living room on Oxenden Avenue hosted talk and dancing to the gramophone and cheap and plentiful beer. King loved the Laurentian wilderness, as did Scott, and in summer they picnicked at Morin Heights or the Oka monastery, or went in by canoe to fish.[26] With proximity to the Laurentians, he once again took up skiing. He later recalled those days, wondering how he could attend the LSR executive meeting in the afternoon, a speech by Woodsworth in the evening, a party afterwards at Frank Scott's, and still catch the 8:05 ski train for St Sauveur the next morning.[27] Often, he would stay at Jacques Bieler's ski cottage, on one side of which his brother André had painted a huge fresco of St Christopher. As she watched the skiers leave on their way to the slopes early in the morning, Marian Scott used to say that she had a feeling they were being blessed as they passed.[28] On a sparkling day in 1932 when King and Frank Scott were skiing over the Maple Leaf Trail, pausing at the foot of Marquis Hill, Frank, glowing with cold and beaming with pleasure, turned to King: "If they ever ask you, say for *Who's Who*, what your recreations are, tell them, 'Skiing and changing the social order!'"[29]

But changing that social order would not be easy. The first response to the national economic crisis by the Conservative government of Prime Minister R.B. Bennett, elected in 1930, was to call a special session of Parliament to deal with unemployment.[30] Only two bills were passed during this session, the first providing $20 million for relief – described by the prime minister as "palliative"; and the second producing the sharpest increase of the protective tariff in more than fifty years. This action sought to increase jobs by guaranteeing Canadian manufacturers a monopoly of the domestic market, but it was a disastrous move for the farmers who depended on foreign markets. Bennett's next step was an appeal to the Commonwealth for preferential tariffs among its members but, in spite of an imperial economic conference on the topic in 1932, it proved a vain hope as all Commonwealth countries found themselves in the same plight.

One need not question the motivations or judge too quickly the early efforts of government leaders who were faced with the challenge of what was possible. One may readily grant that they acted in good faith out of a mindset of compassionate goodwill. Eugene Forsey described Bennett as a well-brought-up Methodist, but by the time Bennett produced a New Deal in 1935, he had gained a reputation as a "callous autocrat, the millionaire unmoved by the distress of the poor";[31] and he was ridiculed in *The Canadian Forum* as "Bennett of Tarsus,"[32] for his latter-day conversion.

What was surprising about Bennett's New Deal was not its lack of specificity – although he did mention unemployment insurance, minimum wages, and scaling down mortages, not new ideas in themselves – but that he stated: "I nail the flag of progress to the mast-head. I summon the power of the State to its support."[33] Blair Neatby writes that Canadians, on listening to Bennett's series of five radio broadcasts as he described his proposed reforms, "were almost dumbfounded to hear the Conservative prime minister, the man widely thought of as a reactionary spokesman for Big Business, using the rhetoric of social revolution."[34]

The reaction of the LSR members to Bennett's New Deal ranged from Frank Underhill's scathing comments to Forsey's defence of Bennett's motives and Frank Scott's position of cautious optimism. When MacKenzie King succeeded Bennett in 1935 as prime minister he submitted the new laws to the Judicial Committee of the Privy Council for review, and the Council ruled that the legislation was *ultra vires* as it fell under provincial rather than federal jusrtisdiction.[35] This, of course, cut to the heart of the basic tenet of central planning by the federal government as expressed in the LSR's statement of policy in *Social Planning for Canada* (1935).

King Gordon followed the general LSR view that Bennett's New Deal did not get to the root of the problem and would only strengthen and preserve the capitalist system. In any case, by the time of the election in 1935, leftist sentiment, with a coherent, rational policy of democratic socialism, had far outstripped Bennett. Gordon himself ran in the election as a candidate for the CCF and, as he was challenging a Liberal candidate, largely ignored Bennett in his campaign.

On his arrival in Montreal in 1931, Gordon had also discovered that a remarkable protest was well underway within the United Church, a protest in which he also quickly became active. In line with this movement, the 1932 Montreal and Ottawa Conference of the United Church appointed a Committee on Economic and Social Research, its membership consisting of Eugene Forsey, a lecturer in economics at McGill and former Rhodes scholar, as well as a dedicated and active United Church layman; J.A. Coote of the McGill Department of Engineering; and King Gordon. The committee was directed to examine issues that it considered should be of concern to the church, and given a small budget, with which it produced the *Information Bulletin*,[36] modelled on Harry Ward's bulletin put out by the Methodist Social Service Council. Between December 1932 and January 1934 the small committee produced seven issues. Almost immediately after the committee was formed, King received a letter from J.S. Woodsworth: "It seems to me that your Committee might well do its best work not attempting to cover the general field of research, but rather in centring on those conditions which exist right at your hand, and which, unless altered, will absolutely prevent any real democratic action. I am delighted to hear of the strong line you are following in Montreal."[37]

The *Information Bulletin*[38] dealt with such questions as unemployment, civil liberties, conditions in penitentiaries, and wages and dividends in the textile industry in Quebec – the latter a particularly sensitive issue as the chairman of Canadian Cottons, A.L. Dawson, was also a member of UTC's board of governors. It was Forsey's research that revealed the shocking wage levels of women and girls in Quebec's cotton mills and pointed out that shareholders were receiving satisfactory dividends, even in the Depression. The *Bulletin* also carried a column titled, "Thoughtful Canadians," which reported choice newspaper items: "Premier Taschereau refused the demands for an investigation [into conditions in the province's jails], stating that he knew that the prisons were administered properly, and what happens inside the walls did not concern the general public." In that same issue of December, 1932, the *Information Bulletin* also reported: "Premier Bennett speaking at Toronto said: 'The acquisition of property is what comes to a man of ability in this world if he has done his job properly. And it lies between him and his God what he does with it.'" The February 1933 issue juxtaposed newspaper articles describing a glittering social gala with one describing people searching garbage pails for food.

Before long, protests concerning the content of the *Information Bulletin* were raised. On 5 May 1933, Gordon received a letter from the secretary of the Montreal Presbytery of the United Church of Canada calling to his attention the decision of the Presbytery that the *Information*

Bulletin be headed by the statement: "This bulletin is for information. Its material has not been endorsed by the Presbytery."[39] Two letters followed from members of the Board of UTC, both written on 29 June 1933. The first letter, from J.A. Ewing, pointed out that he had been receiving copies of the *Bulletin* unsolicited, unwelcome, and whose content he found "most unseemly."[40] The second letter, from Alexander McA. Murphy, Esq., of Westmount protested the *Bulletin's* (also unseemly) attack on Prime Minister Bennett, "who is – incidentally – a member in good standing of the United Church of Canada."[41]

July 13 of that year found Gordon at Birkencraig responding to Murphy's letter. He assured Murphy that his concerns would receive serious consideration from the members of the committee, and he concluded his letter cordially: "I trust that you are enjoying a pleasant summer and trust that you are finding it possible to get some escape from the heat which I hear is afflicting Montreal."[42] Eventually, the Presbytery succeeded in balancing the three "Reds" on the committee with two more "right-thinking" people – F.W. Kerr, who was a minister at Westmount United Church in Montreal, and businessman J.M. Graham – but without noticeable improvement.[43]

The fact that the *Information Bulletin* survived as long as it did testifies to the strength of the radical mood in the larger church, which Gordon described as widespread, with active groups in every presbytery and conference "of committed and socially conscious men and women who knew one another, who met informally to study and discuss the maladies of a sick society, who drafted resolutions, worked out strategy, and established themselves as radical cells in the Christian community."[44] By 1933 there was increasing talk of bringing together these informal groups into an organized movement, and in 1934 the Fellowship for a Christian Social Order (FCSO) was formed, an organization in which Gordon played a vital role.

Gordon travelled to the Soviet Union in the summers of 1932 and 1934. It was while he was in Moscow in August of 1932 that he read in *The Moscow Times* that a new political party, the Co-operative Commonwealth Federation, had been formed in Calgary, drawing together the farm, labour, and socialist elements into a federation. The party was to have a national council made up of representatives from each of the organizations joining the federation; and a national president (J.S. Woodsworth was the unanimous choice) and secretary-treasurer, each to be elected by a national convention. The Calgary Convention agreed upon a provisional Eight Point Program, with the understanding that a definitive party program would be decided upon at a conference in Regina to be held the following year.

Although the LSR had no official representation at the convention in Calgary, Woodsworth's close ties with the group and their common cause made it logical that he should turn to them for help in drafting such a document. Scott recalled that Frank Underhill had drafted a first copy that he circulated among LSR members and that Graham Spry had then showed it to Woodsworth, who suggested that it be submitted to the CCF National Council. This recollection of Scott's was recorded in his travel diary in 1961.[45] An official invitation from the CCF National Council came to the LSR in January 1933, but the matter was neglected until June when Underhill retreated with his family to a rented cottage in the Muskokas, north of Toronto, and produced a first draft of the Regina Manifesto. The draft was based on the LSR Manifesto, and Michiel Horn's account describes other LSR members – Cassidy, Reid, and possibly Parkinson – going over it while they drank lukewarm beer on a muggy summer evening back at the Underhill home in Toronto. Underhill then retyped the document and sent copies to Gordon, Scott, and Woodsworth, retreating once again to the bliss of Lake Rosseau.[46]

As the summer of 1933 and the scheduled Regina Convention approached, King received a cautionary letter from his father that must have fallen strangely on his son's ears:

> I am disgusted with the CCF. They made fools of themselves in Parl[iament] – and again at Mackenzie where they chose Judge Stubbs as candidate – an utterly impossible, irresponsible, unbalanced man and thoroughly discredited by all sound citizens – honest enough, but an infernal conceited ass. It was a fool mistake. I hope you are not going to the Regina C.C.F. Convention. Let them slough off some of their fool leaders, hunker down into some clear thinking and take a little time to see beyond their noses. Busy yourself with the LSR. You have a good chance there – worthwhile – but the CCF? Not yet for any sake.[47]

King, however, was already on the path to Regina. In February of 1933, he had received an invitation from the Reverend Alistair Stewart, assistant minister at Westminster United Church in Winnipeg, inviting him to take part in a summer seminar at Lake of the Woods during the second week in July, to lecture on ethical issues in economics. Joe

Parkinson and Eugene Forsey had also been invited to participate in the seminar, at the end of which all three of them retired to the Gordons' island in Lake of the Woods about 2 ½ km away. Here they enjoyed the hospitality of the Gordon clan as they tucked themselves away in Ralph Connor's "Lookout," going over the draft Underhill had sent along with them in an effort to make it sound rather less academic. "We all considered ourselves more political animals than Underhill and we did a bit of editing to make it sound less academic and doctrinaire – replacing 'demands' with 'will provide,' for instance."[48] In the intervening month since his tirade, C.W. Gordon had apparently softened in his opinion of the CCF, and marginal notations in his handwriting indicate that he also went over the text and that his interest also seems to have been along the lines of softening Underhill's language.[49] The three "political animals" then pencilled in the margins the names of those who might argue for the various sections of the manifesto to the convention – Gordon's name appears beside "Freedom," Forsey beside "External Trade," and Scott beside "BNA Act." But apart from these largely cosmetic changes, the little committee of three seems to have proposed no substantial revision in Underhill's draft.[50]

Gordon, Forsey, and Parkinson then set off for Regina in the trusty Gordon Model A Ford. Forsey remembered that they drove through the States because there was no decent road through that part of Canada in those days; Gordon remembered several hundred kilometers of the trip as a treacherous drive over (presumably Canadian) dirt roads, in and out of the ditch as the rich soil of the Regina plain melted into rain-soaked gumbo. Scott met them in Regina, after travelling west by an undoubtedly American route as even his sturdy air-cooled Franklin would have been hard put to navigate the logging and mining trails north of the Great Lakes. The four professors had been invited to join the national council that began meeting on 16 July three days before the convention convened in the old City Hall. Michiel Horn describes the academics as "a great hit."[51] Persuasive and earnest, they impressed the council, which adopted without change the preamble and the clauses on planning, external trade, and socialized health services. The clauses on taxation and the emergency program were rejected entirely. Otherwise, except for agriculture, only minor revisions were made.

The Council's revised draft was read in its entirety to the convention by the secretary, Norman Priestly, "with no little homiletic intonation."[52] In the debate that followed, opinion was divided largely along the lines of the middle-class CCF clubs and their academic spokesmen, and the more politically sophisticated socialists who came from the urban labour groups of British Columbia and who backed a more doctrinaire socialist position. Two main controversies developed around the issues of agriculture and compensation for socialized industry. Underhill's plank on agriculture was, understandably, perfunctory – none of the LSR members knew much about land use. The Calgary program had called for "security of tenure for the farmer on his use-lease," that is, land used for productive purposes, and the Saskatchewan Farmer–Labour party (formed in 1932 under M.J. Coldwell) favoured this rather amorphous concept. Nor were the urban reformers from the East successful in getting clarification. Many years later, Forsey groused:

> The Saskatchewan Farmer-Labour Party had adopted an agricultural policy known as "use-lease." The Montreal newspapers had painted it in lurid colours as virtually nationalization of the land. We felt tolerably sure that it was not that, but we couldn't make out just what it was. Here, on the spot, was our opportunity to find out. So, very respectfully, we asked George Williams, the Leader of the Farmer–Labour Party, to tell us. He literally retreated into a corner, glowered at us, and growled: "Nobody is coming here from the EAST to take our socialism away from us!" Accustomed to being considered in Montreal as practically Stalin's right-hand men, we hastened to deprecate the soft impeachment ... Not one syllable of explanation of "use-lease" could we get out of him.[53]

A temporary compromise was reached by the convention on land tenure, and by 1936 it was acknowledged that the family farm was not an enterprise suitable for socialization and the idea of use-land, whatever it meant, was dropped from the CCF platform.

The other main controversy concerned compensation for socialized industry, an issue closer to the heart of the middle-class CCF clubs from Ontario than to their more doctrinaire comrades from British Columbia, who asked why owners should be compensated when society took back what rightfully belonged to it in the first place. Underhill's paragraph on compensation was deleted from the section on social ownership, and Gordon, Scott, Forsey, and one other unidentified delegate formed an ad hoc committee that, over lunch, drafted a compromise paragraph. Scott remembered that it was scribbled on a cigarette box, but it also appears in Gordon's writing on the back of his copy of Underhill's initial draft. In any case, it appeared in the final version of the manifesto as it was adopted in Regina, bearing, as Walter Young says, the mark of the Fabian intellectuals in the LSR.[54]

There remains the mysterious authorship of the closing, uncompromising paragraph of the Manifesto: "No CCF government shall rest content until it has eradicated capitalism and put into operation the full programme of socialized planning which will lead to the establishment in Canada of the Co-operative Commonwealth." M.J. Coldwell later complained that it was "a millstone around the party's neck";[55] and later Underhill said, "I don't think we had in our original draft that unfortunate ending to the Regina Manifesto – that the CCF would not rest until it had eradicated capitalism – about which it has always been unkindly reminded ever since. At least I hope we didn't have it."[56] Perhaps buoyed up by the enthusiasm of the moment and the response of the Convention, no one stepped up to claim responsibility, until many years later, on Easter Day 1979, Gordon confessed to Scott:

> You know, I think that you and I probably wrote that peroration. I recall ... a luncheon meeting when the three or four LSR members were working on the draft to take into account some of the proposed amendments. We ate lunch at a cheap little restaurant near the City Hall ... tile-top table, perhaps in a booth. I recall it was a serious lunch and one at which we were determined to protect not only the form and substance but the essential spirit of the manifesto. We probably decided that it should have a ringing challenge at the end.
>
> We were both influenced by our Christian ethical background and there's a bit of the defiance if not the poetry of Blake's "Jerusalem" in it. Quite in the spirit of: "I shall not cease from mental fight / Nor shall my sword sleep in my hand / Til we have built Jerusalem / In England's green and pleasant land." And Perry goes soaring off in a trumpet blast.[57]

Scott reported that when Norman Priestly finished reading the manifesto, with its final clarion call, the whole convention rose as one and cheered. At the time, he wrote cryptically in his notebook, "He who drafts, wins."[58]

It is generally agreed that the role of the LSR academics was of strategic importance to the CCF, both in giving voice to the theoretical basis of the party in the manifesto, and in helping guide it through the convention. Although new paragraphs were added, "the major draftsmen in most instances were the LSR delegates."[59] George V. Ferguson, King's friend and former Oxford classmate, by then a journalist with the *Winnipeg Free Press*, first applied the metaphor "brains trust" ("brains trust" being in vogue in Roosevelt circles at that time) to the intellectuals from the East;[60] and Spry himself, who had attended the convention as a reporter and delegate from the Ottawa CCF club, wrote to Harry Cassidy in Toronto, "The opinions of Scott, Parkinson, Forsey, and Gordon were almost always deferred to."[61] Ferguson identified the "brain-truster-in-chief' as Underhill" but also mentioned by name Cassidy, Forsey, Gordon, Parkinson, Scott, and Spry, whose ages averaged 31.75 years. Six of the "brains trust" had been Rhodes scholars.[62] In his history of the CCF, Walter Young writes: "The LSR was in every sense the CCF 'brains trust.' The minutes of the CCF national executive for this period indicate that although Underhill, Forsey, King Gordon, and Scott were not members of the executive, they were frequently in attendance and actively participated in the deliberation of that body."[63]

Elated and happy, the easterners sought their way home, but not before Gordon gave an interview to the Regina *Leader Post,* which quoted him as saying, "The road to be followed is the road to a society on a new basis planned in the interests of all, and that is the direction in which this great new movement is headed."[64] In early October Gordon received a letter from Norman Priestly on Co-operative Commonwealth Federation letterhead. In it he reported a resolution by the National Council, that thanks be extended to the four professors who attended the convention and Professor Underhill for their assistance in drawing up the Manifesto and Program, "a splendid piece of work that contributed so much to the convention and to our work in general."[65]

Frank Underhill once referred to the Regina Manifesto as "my utopia,"[66] and the same could almost be said for King Gordon. But there remained an incipient element of tension that would later become more pronounced on the issue of CCF foreign policy, which, in hindsight, Gordon considered the weakest part of the LSR and CCF manifestoes' analysis and program.[67] The article on foreign policy in the Regina Manifesto, largely the work of Underhill, was strongly isolationist in tone and in its attacks on the imperial tie to Britain. Having paid lip service to the principle of international cooperation, the article stated that genuine international cooperation was impossible with capitalist regimes, and that Canada must be particularly wary of the claims of empire: "We must resist all attempts to build up a new economic British Empire in place of the old political one, since such attempts readily lend themselves to the purposes of capitalist exploitation and may easily lead to further world wars. Canada must refuse to be entangled in any more wars fought to make the world safe for capitalism."[68]

Certainly Gordon decried war, capitalist or otherwise; but his feelings about internationalism were not as unambiguous as Underhill's. King had absorbed internationalism along with the social gospel, at his father's table, and he was fourteen when his father left for Europe. While the horror of war was acknowledged in the Gordon home, participation in the First World War was seen as patriotic. At the same time, during his time at Oxford, King had been profoundly influenced by his international experience, both in relief work in Austria and in his exposure to the League of Nations in Geneva. By 1933, in Montreal, he was again coming under internationalist influence through his friendship with Percy Corbett.

In the early autumn of 1932, there was a further stirring up of the Gordon family's commitment to internationalism when C.W. Gordon received an invitation to preach the sermon at the opening of the League of Nations Assembly in Geneva. This was an occasion for rejoicing in the family who were aware of the honour that was being bestowed upon their father. The church service at the opening of the League Assembly was a full-dress affair, and the preacher "stood in the lofty pulpit of the ancient Cathedral of Saint-Pierre, whence the great reformer, scholar, and statesman, John Calvin, was wont to thunder forth his messages to the people of Geneva."[69] The next day, C.W. Gordon attended the opening session of the Assembly. He was not blind to the shortcomings of the League (largely caused by the failure of the United States to join), and when British statesman Lord Robert Cecil, "with the utmost frankness," spoke to the Assembly, pointing out instances of failure and appealing for reform, C.W. Gordon beamingly affirmed: "I was never prouder of my British heritage than at that moment. The simplicity, the sincerity, the high moral tone, the intense and passionate conviction behind his appeal swept that company of hardboiled political agents off their feet."[70]

Gordon, of course, recognized the hyperbole and rhetorical flourishes of his father's style, but he also respected his father's intense concern for world peace and his loyalty to the League of Nations. His father's rhetoric was less a directive than an ambience, one that touched deep wells of loyalty and conviction in his son. Looking back in 1986, Gordon alluded to the unease he had felt at the time with the CCF/Underhill position and acknowledged that, "I somewhat reluctantly went along."[71] In 1987, speaking at the University of Ottawa on the topic, "The Imperatives of Social Democracy: Then and Now," he found it somewhat ironic that the article in the manifesto dealing with foreign policy, which had seemed inappropriate to him at the time, should carry a contemporary relevance. In the 1930s, the social democrats of the CCF/LSR were concerned with achieving social justice *within Canada*, seemingly indifferent to the application of these goals to the international community; by 1987, one had merely to consider the names of the world's prominent social democrats – Gunnar and Alva Myrdal, Olof Palme, Willy Brandt, Philip Noel Baker, for instance – to realize that they were the ones insisting that equal rights for *all humankind* must be sought.[72]

In fact, it would be not too many years before Gordon, in his own life, would take the goals of the LSR and the CCF for justice and security and work for their realization in the international sphere.

7

Montreal: Tough Sledding at United Theological College

Back on that October evening in 1931 when King had arrived at United Theological College renewed by the rest at Birkencraig and the visit to his ancestral home in Glengarry, he was filled with the prophetic zeal of his teachers Harry Ward and Reinhold Niebuhr. Like them, he held the conviction that the church primarily served the vested interests of society and that effective social change could only result, if at all, from the work of prophetic minorities. "Dare the Church Be Christian?"[1] he had asked. Perhaps it was inevitable that there would be trouble.

As he told the story, he got off to a bad start at the college, and it was his own fault. In a letter to King in April 1931, his father had warned him that caution would be appropriate: "One bit of advice I will venture. Remember Canada is not the USA in things Industrial and Economic. I know you will not begin with frontal attacks. Your first business will be a planning for position – get your forces in place before you deliver your blow. You conquer your enemy by winning him to your way of thinking. The big Industrialists need you badly."[2]

Perhaps his father's wisdom might have proved the better part of valour.

The principal of UTC, the Reverend James Smyth, was a Northern Ireland Presbyterian "with a somewhat conservative interpretation of Christian ethics"; and the Montreal establishment was well represented on the college board of governors by William Birks, head of the jewellery firm, A.O. Dawson of Canadian Cottons, and Alexander Mc. A. Murphy of Gurd's Ginger Ale. Shortly after Gordon's arrival, the Birkses kindly invited the new professor to dinner at their home on Côte des Neiges. It was a pleasant dinner and the guests were about to begin an evening of discussion when Gordon excused himself, explaining that Jennie Lee, the young Scottish Labour Party MP, was giving a lecture at Royal Victoria

College that he had to attend. Looking back years later, Gordon still felt chagrined by his lack of manners and confused priorities on this occasion.[3]

This social *faux pas* was followed by another, perhaps more serious, incident. Gordon was living in college his first term, and late one Sunday night he returned from a weekend's skiing in the Laurentians to discover that the janitor – a man in his seventies – was still on duty running the elevator. It was then eleven o'clock at night, and as they ascended he learned that this elderly gentleman had been working since eight that morning. On further inquiry, Gordon discovered that he worked a seventy-hour week with no relief and very little pay. Not one to let such matters lie unattended, he took the matter up with Principal Smyth first thing on Monday morning, suggesting that this college practice was somewhat at variance with what he was trying to teach in his Christian Ethics course. The principal was "flabbergasted" – not merely because he failed to see the incongruity in the college's position, but also at the audacity of a young professor interfering in the administration of the college.

That first year passed quickly with King's extracurricular immersion in radical causes and the founding of the League for Social Reconstruction. In the summer of 1932, travelling with Eugene Forsey, he took the first of two trips to the Soviet Union. This was an uncommon trip at the time, although Sherwood Eddy in New York had been escorting groups of ministers and laymen to Russia for some years, and there was immense curiosity about the "Russian experiment" among political liberals and radicals, including church people. Their first stop was England where King visited Gilbert Ryle at Oxford. The weather had not improved since his days there as student ("abominable, cold, grey, wet"), and he once again sat talking and reading in front of Ryle's smoky fire.[4] In London he heard a lecture by Harold Laski, the Fabian economist from the London School of Economics. Gordon recorded in his diary, "Laski, by the way, is a brilliant fellow. I felt on Sunday afternoon this is where I belong. This crowd talks my language."[5] He then spent a few days with Malcolm MacDonald at 10 Downing Street before sailing for Leningrad on a Soviet steamer.

From Leningrad he and Forsey travelled by train to Nizhny Novgorod, by boat down the Volga to Stalingrad, then the train once again to Kharkof and Kiev. After three weeks in the Soviet Union, they made their way back to England through Warsaw, Berlin, and Amsterdam. They were not conscious of being watched or directed away from certain places, but Forsey had no doubt that they were being kept well away from anything that might have created an unfavourable impression.[6] Their guide throughout their time in the Soviet Union was an electrician from one of the Baltic States who had worked in Boston where he had had his own business. Forsey wondered if it was this stigma of a capitalist past that accounted for his mild and diffident manner. The guide proved quite helpless, for instance, when other people took their seats in a train, and it remained for a young female railway official to rescue them by bundling the unfortunate Russians out of the disputed seats and off the train.[7]

Gordon described Leningrad as "a beautiful 18th and 19th century city which has fallen upon evil days and which has yet to assert its glory in the present."[8] Moscow, where they spoke with government officials, bureaucrats, and trade unionists, had a self-important attitude characteristic of cities like London and New York. But it was in Kharkof, the "Detroit of the Ukraine," that he saw the immense energy of the newly industrialized Soviet Union, with the enormous tractor factory covering hundreds of acres, and adjacent to it the new town with its apartments, theatres, schools, clubs, hospital, university, stadium – all built within the last two or three years, and all rather blatantly new. Nevertheless, the planning had been good and the structures well-built. Some of the newest buildings in Kharkof were, in his opinion, even beginning to show promise that modern Russia could produce architectural masterpieces that would seriously compete with the more recent buildings of Sweden, Holland, and pre-Hitler Germany. But Kharkof, in spite of its industrial and architectural promise, would be a dreadfully dull city to live in, "[a]s if one were to say, 'Detroit is my spiritual home.'" In these writings, one senses a certain tension between Gordon's aesthetic sense – and perhaps also his common sense – and his ideology.

Striking to the visitors' eyes as these new urban miracles might be, however, it was not in its industrial achievement that Gordon claimed he found the *soul* of the new Soviet Union, but rather in the collective farm a few kilometers from the city that he and Forsey visited. The farm – typical of hundreds, they were told – was imposing: a single row of whitewashed log houses each with its flowers and vegetable garden, its chickens, and a pig. Each member of the collective owned his own house and some of his stock. At the end of the row of houses stood the collective farm buildings – barns, silos, vegetable cellars, stables for horses, machine sheds and pens for cattle and pigs. The other collective buildings were the school, community hall, and dining room. "We went to the dining room and had a talk with the Party Secretary who was in charge of the operation. As is almost invariably the case of those in authority, he was young, clear-headed, keen about his job, ready to answer any questions."[9] The interview, he admitted, was something less than satisfactory as they struggled through translation to sort out the distribution of produce between state and *kolhoz* (farm), between *kolhoz* and individuals constituting the *kolhoz*, details of yearly income for each family and each worker, yield of crops, prices, and wages.

In spite of what was lost in translation, Gordon was convinced that the collective farm was beginning to justify itself and was coming to have an advantage over the private farmer in Soviet Russia, in that this new farmer was working *with* the state and not *against* it. In response to Gordon's question about the opposition of the kulaks (wealthy peasants) to collectivization, his fresh-faced Party secretary assured him that there was no longer any necessity for employing "political measures" to persuade the private farmers to come into the collective. It was true, he admitted, that in the beginning their opposition had been stronger than anticipated, and that they had slaughtered large numbers of livestock – cattle, sheep, and pigs. These actions, along with a bad harvest and inadequate transportation, had caused a severe food shortage in both rural districts and cities alike. Happily, he assured them, the situation had been turned around by good harvests and a "determined and brilliant line of action" on the part of the Communist Party. In spite of these cheery assurances, Gordon later confessed that he had come away with a degree of unease about the fate of the kulaks.[10]

There was, of course, no way that western travellers of that time could have known about Stalin's repression and slaughter of the kulaks – aptly and chillingly called "dekulakization" – in the process of collectivization. That information would not be available for many years to come. As Gordon said later, "We were young and hopeful, and without the later knowledge of Stalinism."[11] A greater familiarity with Russian history and the ability of its leaders to show the West what they wanted it to see (one is reminded of Catherine the Great, the enlightened despot, who took western diplomats on guided tours of model villages), and a more critical view of human nature, might have alerted them to the duplicity of their hosts. Reminiscing in 1975, Gordon told an interviewer that he and Forsey had not been completely "conned or brain-washed." At the time, they were not aware of the coercive nature of the regime in setting up the collectives; but what they did see – however controlled their opportunities to observe may have been – was enough to make them enthusiastic about the economic miracle and the concern for the masses that they did not see in their own Canadian society.[12]

But in their enthusiastic reaction to what they had seen in the Soviet Union, Gordon and Eugene Forsey were not untypical of their fellow Canadians in the LSR and CCF who came back from Russia in the 1930s with glowing accounts of the new Soviet society; although Gordon later confessed that Forsey, being "congenitally more conservative"[13] than he, was perhaps more critical. Graham Spry visited Moscow in the spring of 1936 (two years after Gordon's second visit) and wrote home that while it was too early to make bold predictions about the success of the Soviet Union, the stories about food shortages and clothes were "ridiculous" and the people were protected from the vicissitudes of illness, old age, and unemployment.[14] Ten days later he wrote to J.S. Woodsworth painting a slightly darker picture of scarcity of housing, which was bad in any case, and appalling inefficiency. Still, he assured Woodsworth, "... the soviet is doing the right things badly, we in England [where Graham now lived] are doing the wrong things well"[15]

Woodsworth himself had visited Russia in 1931 and, according to his biographer, returned with a "sober yet optimistic evaluation."[16] He was impressed with a sense "of a people on the march," and found the inefficiency balanced by boundless activity and tangible results in "dams and factories." He disliked the degree to which authority was centralized, but he admitted the evident economic success of central planning and was apparently unalarmed about its potential threat to civil liberty. In August 1935 Frank Scott travelled to Russia. He had followed the reports of the parade of English socialists through Russia – the Russells and the Webbs, for example – and his biographer Sandra Djwa reports that while his reaction to what he saw was not as enthusiastic as that of Forsey and Gordon, neither was it as tempered as that of Woodsworth. Djwa writes, "The poet in him loved the 'vision' of Russia while the intellectual balked at the reality of Russian totalitarianism."[17] On his return, Scott wrote in *The Canadian Forum*: "The USSR is a bible with a text for everyone. Conservatives ... find the expected backwardness and hardship, the communist enthusiast enters a thrilling world. Where lies the truth? Truth lies, I think, in the significance of things."[18]

Touching on the utopianism that seemed to lie at the heart of the Fabian mystification regarding the Soviet Union, George Bernard Shaw, enchanted like the Webbs, returned from Russia in 1931 declaring that the Stalin regime was nothing but applied Fabianism.[19] By contrast, Gordon's mentor, R.H. Tawney, refused to follow the Webbs into "the well-lighted abyss of Stalinism,"[20] fearing the bureaucratic power necessary for such a degree of centralization. For Tawney, there would be no Platonic republic, that frozen stillness of perfection with its totalitarian implications.

Gordon, while never losing his utopian vision, developed and refined his own theory of socialism, increasingly balancing idealism with pragmatism and a sense of the possible. In the crisis period of the Great Depression, Gordon (along with many others) was at his most activist and, perhaps, at his most radical in leftist causes. By the time he emigrated to the United States in 1938, his theory of Christian socialism was well on its way to coalescing around more moderate influences, in many ways coming to resemble that of Tawney, who first "opened his eyes." Looking back from the high hill of his old age, Gordon did not repudiate or condemn his response to what he saw – or thought he saw – in the USSR of the 1930s, choosing to honour his youthful idealism and saying simply, "We were not entirely fooled."[21]

It was natural that on their return to Montreal the two travellers would be invited to speak, and natural too that they would respond with enthusiasm. The Montreal *Gazette* for 3 October 1932 carried the headline, "Real Religion in Russia Discovered: No More Puritanical Group Than Communist, Says Prof. King Gordon."[22] "There is real religion in Russia today," Gordon was quoted as telling in his listeners in Emmanuel United Church the previous evening. While it proclaimed itself atheistic, it was "burning with zeal," that endowed individuals with significance and idealism. By contrast, the Canada he returned to, though labelled as Christian, had made a god of success and prosperity, judging them more important than the individual.

Two days later, the *Witness and Canadian Homestead* printed a summary of Gordon's talk under the less sensational headline, "Religion – In Russia and In Canada."[23] In this article, fairer because it was more complete, Gordon argued that this new religion had many of the marks of true religion: It allowed one to lose oneself in devotion to a great cause; it expressed a high regard for human life, especially for the life of little children, as exemplified in its public health clinics, its nursery schools, and its crèches; and it was marked by the dogmatism that characterizes all true religions – the Soviet professors had all the dogmatic sureness of the old Hebrew prophets. This new religion also included the missionary zeal and the apocalyptic hope of a true faith. But the question remained: Was this new religion of the Soviets adequate? King admitted that he found the new religion lacking in reverence and awe before the mystery of the universe and the unknowable, and that it placed too much confidence in self-reliance. Gordon concluded, in the spirit of the Old Testament prophets (Amos was a great favourite), by calling his audience back to the true religion, in this case, the Christian gospel.

The speaking engagements piled up until even King's missionary zeal flagged. He wrote to his mother at the end of October, after dinner with his cousin Molly on his first free evening in weeks, that they had barred Russia from their conversation, saying that he was beginning to feel like a curiosity: "That which has been to Russia and has come back half cracked." He added wryly, "I sometimes have a feeling that they are right."[24] A more ominous note then entered his letter. The senate of the college had met the previous evening and he had been told that some members of the board of governors were after his scalp. He warned his mother that she might be feeding an unemployed son in the future, "but I don't think they will consider it expedient to raise a fight at this stage in the game. There are too many other 'reds' in the church who would be inclined to resent the suppression of free criticism of the existing order. They will wait till they find some open back door through which to lead the attack."[25]

Given the composition of the board and the political climate in Canada at this time, could Gordon have been surprised at this warning concerning his tenure coming from the board of governors? In spite of the increasingly critical responses from right-wing elements about the *Bulletin* and his enthusiasm for Soviet reforms, he pressed on with his high-spirited and intense involvements with leftist causes. In March of 1933, he received an irritated letter from Sir Arthur Currie, principal and vice-chancellor of McGill. "You will recall a conversation I had with you recently," he wrote, "in which I objected to the constant association of your name with that of McGill University."[26] Gordon replied two days later:

> In regard to the matter which you raise I can only say that I regret as much as you do the fact that people persist in associating me with McGill University. This is not because they receive any encouragement from me. On the contrary I endeavor to make quite clear on any occasion of making a public speech (a) that I am speaking as a citizen and not in any official or representative capacity (b) that my association is with the United Theological College as a professor of Christian Ethics. I cannot protect myself (or McGill) on all occasions since some organizations and certain sections of the press remain obdurately stupid.

I shall persist in the attempt to make my status quite clear. I appreciate the kindly courtesy of your letter and regret exceedingly that I have been the cause of embarrassment to you in these difficult times.[27]

There was a story behind Currie's concern of which Gordon was unaware at the time. The RCMP had launched an inquiry into the presence of communists at McGill, and on 15 December 1932, RCMP commissioner J.H. MacBrien had suggested to Currie's assistant, Wilfred Bovey, that "chasing them out" would signal strong support to the forces of law and order in Canada.[28] Gordon, Scott, and Forsey, among others, were of concern. On 17 December Bovey wrote to Commissioner MacBrien on Currie's behalf, providing an evaluation of the risk posed by each professor. The statement on Gordon read:

> This young man is the son of Rev. C.W. Gordon whom you will remember as a Chaplain. He is not a professor of this University and has nothing whatever to do with us, although the Theological College upon the staff of which he hold[s] a place is affiliated to McGill. He is a 'Ramsay Macdonald socialist,' in other words, he disapproves the existing economic arrangements, but desires their change by parliamentary action, not by revolutionary action. At the time your letter arrived he had come in to see Sir Arthur in connection with the controversy [concerning his speeches on Russia] … Sir Arthur told him that whatever his views might be he was very foolish to link them up with statements concerning Russia, as this could not but give everyone the impression that he was sympathetic with Bolshevik methods and satisfied with their results. Professor King Gordon expressed his gratitude for the advice and stated that he would in future eliminate such comparisons from his remarks.[29]

After describing Scott and Forsey in similarly patronizing terms, Bovey concluded:

> What I am principally afraid of in connection with these 'parlour socialists' is that active and clever members of the communist party can use them to forward their own ends, and probably smile up their sleeves at the well meant efforts of the 'reformers.' On the other hand, Malcolm Macdonald explained to me that one object of the English socialists was to so control the 'liberal elements' that they

> would stick to parliamentary methods and oppose bolshevism. This, I feel sure, is what our Canadian socialists would like to do, although I cannot see that those in question have, or are likely to have, sufficient political importance to attain the end.

The commissioner seemed satisfied and he replied to Currie on 13 February 1933 that he believed Currie was doing all that was possible in controlling communism at McGill.[30]

Long after the fact, in March of 1980, Frank Scott sent a packet of photocopied letters to Gordon, including those quoted above, with a covering note written on the stationery of McGill University, Faculty of Law. "Here are some interesting letters! And I'm told there are plenty more all in the public domain except for McGill's copyright." He asked that Gordon not show them to Forsey, fearing that he would "make a fuss," preventing Scott from being able to examine the large number of boxes that still existed "unexplored!"[31]

During the same period of the RCMP's interest in the "young communists" of McGill, the attacks on the *Information Bulletin* continued as Gordon became more deeply embroiled in United Church politics.[32] As noted earlier,[33] in March of 1933 the issue concerning the *Bulletin* had blown up at a meeting of the Montreal presbytery,[34] and as a result, future editions of the *Bulletin* were required to carry a statement making clear that the *Bulletin* was for information only and not endorsed by the presbytery. Gordon and Forsey clearly understood this move as intended to "neutralize" the radical nature of their committee, and King knew that this tempest in the politics of the presbytery was part of a much larger fight that was breaking over his head about his tenure at United Theological College.

In light of the general financial crisis within the church and especially with regard to seminary education, the General Council of the United Church had issued a directive at its meeting in Hamilton in 1932 that the number of professors at UTC be reduced from five to four within two years. The financial crisis was genuine. The enrollment in the college had dropped in half by 1932, from 121 in 1931. Not only was income from tuition down, the mortgage interest was also in arrears: $1,959 at the end of 1931; and a year later, $4,100. The audited deficit for 1931 was $4,658; in 1933 it was $8,113. The total operating revenue was approximately $40,000, which indicates the relative size of the deficit.[35]

Gordon, mindful of the straitened circumstances of the college and of the directive from the general council, and aware that faculty salaries would be cut, wrote to the chairman of the board of governors on 22 February 1933, requesting that, since he had some additional income from speaking engagements and fewer family responsibilities than certain of his colleagues, his own reduction "should be proportionately larger in order to meet the demands of Christian mutuality and common fairness."[36] Clearly at this point he did not anticipate the elimination of his salary altogether. That, however, was what happened. On 29 March 1933, the board of governors announced its decision to abolish the Chair of Christian Ethics on financial grounds.[37]

The Gordons called from Winnipeg, offering their moral support. King responded to his mother, expressing appreciation for the call, and he quoted his father who, always distrustful of the sedentary posture, had warned him, "The danger of a chair is that you might stick to it." He added, "I'm afraid you must all think I am a lot 'redder' than I really am." He reported that the board was encountering an "extraordinary" amount of opposition and that, unless they were prepared to shift their stance and fight on grounds other than that of economy, he didn't see how they could see make their decision stick. He himself was "out of the scrapping" as the battle was being waged by a group of United Church ministers under the leadership of D.M. McVicar of the Ministerial Association, the "stalwarts" like Bob (R.B.Y.) Scott, (W.A.) Gifford, Frank Scott, and Dr Frank Pedley, and by the students themselves.[38]

In the days following the action of the board, the other professors of the college unanimously volunteered to make up Gordon's salary by taking a larger cut in their own salaries, and the students met and offered to pay higher fees. Since the reason given for his dismissal was economic, when a group led by Dr Frank Pedley of the Forum on Welfare came forward with a proposal to raise $1,500 for his salary, the board agreed to keep Gordon on for one year as a lecturer. The board's decision, announced to students' cheers at the spring convocation, was followed by the gathered assemblage rising to sing the hymn, no doubt relishing the irony of the opening line: "Dismiss me not thy service, Lord."[39]

Although the board stuck to its position that its motives had been purely economic, there was some skepticism in the press about their decision. The editorial page of *Saturday Night* noted on 8 April: "We should have supposed offhand that a Professor of Christian Ethics was about the last kind of professor that a theological college could afford to dispense with in these turbulent times. It is of course explained that the suppression of [the] chair has nothing to do with his social and economic views, but is entirely a matter of economy. Christian Ethics … has become a luxury that the authorities of the United Theological College can no longer afford themselves."[40]

The *Canadian Forum* was even more direct in suggesting that more than economics was at stake. In June, Ernest Deane threw down the gauntlet in the opening paragraph of his article, "Trying to Teach Christians Ethics": "The near dismissal of Professor King Gordon ... illustrated in a striking manner just what dangers face the churchman of today who has the courage to test the social order in which he lives by the principles of Christianity."[41]

Broadening the discussion to the wider issue of academic freedom, Deane pointed out that this was the first time since the Depression started that a Canadian college had attempted to remove a professor of radical views; he doubted that the pattern could be broken until the governors of colleges realized that they acted as trustees for a set of educational principles guaranteeing teachers the freedom to pursue the truth in whatever guise it might appear to them.

A statement by J.C. Ewing, K.C., a member of the United Church's General Council, gave some credence to the suspicion that among at least certain members of the church establishment there lurked an element of paranoia. Writing in *The Clubman,* in January 1934, he stated: "Colleges, both lay and theological, and the members of the clergy, are favoured breeding grounds of Communism. The Communists take advantage of the inexperienced, impractical, idealistic minds of college professors and clergymen. They, the clergy etc. visualize an ideal revolution where an ideal state of society will be established and all the evils that were ever dreamed of will disappear. All good citizens should unite to stamp out this Communist menace which is in our midst."[42]

The board's one-year extension was only a temporary reprieve, and on 20 March 1934, the board of governors of the college once more acted to abolish the chair, to take effect on 30 June.[43] Frank Pedley expressed surprise that the board had not approached his group for continued support of Gordon's salary, but board chairman A.O. Dawson explained that, since Dr Pedley had made no effort to contact the board, they had assumed the support would end. At this point, the General Council of the United Church became involved once again. By a "practically unanimous vote," the executive passed a motion at its meeting in early May requesting that implementation of the board's resolution be delayed until after the meeting of the general council scheduled to take place in September. Dr Pedley's committee would continue to pay Gordon's salary until the general council could review the board's decision at that time.[44]

It was a difficult time for King, particularly as he waited for the general council's decision in September. He was left in limbo not only as to his future at the college, but as to how he would earn his living if the council's review of the board's decision went against him. He wrote home late in May, telling his mother that he didn't want to leave the college unless he had to, but at this point he felt he had no alternative but to wait for the decision of the council. He then added: "However, I've got a good idea of what I'll do if I'm beaten. If I can't practice religion in the church, I'll try politics ... and sometimes I feel even now that I could be of more use there than in the church.[45]

When the General Council met in September, it requested that the board of the United Theological College appoint Mr Gordon as lecturer in Christian ethics for a period of two years. The board, however, apparently having reached the limit of its patience, refused their request, and Gordon was out of a job. And there the matter rested.

Nevertheless, the debate about his dismissal continued, and the question remained: Was the initial decision and the continuing stand of the board motivated by economic considerations alone, or did Gordon's radical politics figure significantly in his dismissal? Gordon's dismissal now became something of a cause célèbre in both Canada and the United States. King Gordon was well known at the congregational level of the United Church, on his own reputation as well as that of his father, and he had the backing of many of the progressive and radical ministers. In April 1934, the question was again raised in the *New Outlook*. The announcement of the board had, in the editor's view, "awakened decidedly uneasy feelings in the mind of many." And it expressed the skepticism of many in concluding that the board's explanation that they had acted in the interest of economy was a less than a complete and satisfactory statement.[46]

The Christian Century, on 11 April, also found the economic justification of dubious value and asked, "Are the two facts related or is there just coincidence – Gordon's persuasive Christian challenges of powerful persons and the timely opportunity to remove him from the storm center?"[47] In October, *The Christian Century* printed a letter from Gordon's fellow member in the newly formed Fellowship for a Christian Social Order, Gregory Vlastos. Protesting an earlier statement in the journal that the issue had now lost its larger significance and become a purely personal one, Vlastos asked, "What is this larger significance?" and argued that until the church settled the larger question of which areas of the social landscape Christian principles applied to, they were not in a position to judge the level of significance of Gordon's case.[48]

Gordon himself certainly felt at the time that the issue involved more than economics. In 1972 he wrote to Michiel Horn: "I doubt if you will be able to get 'proof' that the elimination of the chair of Christian Ethics was on account of the political views of its occupant." He added, however, that the board seemed curiously unwilling "to explore other methods of economizing to meet the crisis," such as salary cuts, or to accept the outside funding that was available to maintain him.[49] In an interview in 1975 he commented that "nobody thought of it as a purely economy measure," and evidently he did not either.[50]

With perhaps a surprising lack of bitterness and with that ungrudging generosity for which he was known, King quickly turned to his next assignment, which found him in energetic pursuit of his ethical vision as travelling secretary for the Fellowship for a Christian Social Order. For the next three years he travelled across Canada supported by the same group of friends who "gallantly and at much sacrifice to themselves"[51] raised his salary. It was a decision he never regretted.

Unrepentant, and uncowed by the criticism that had followed his earlier trip to the Soviet Union, Gordon undertook a second trip in 1934. This time he travelled under the auspices of the Canadian Pacific Railway – an irony not lost on him – as a tour guide, receiving his fare in return. It was a sixty-day tour with eight participants besides Gordon, and the total cost of the tour was $625. As this second trip was entirely a "guided tour" with no institutional obligations or interest – apart from those of the CPR to make a profit – Gordon was unencumbered by ideological constraints of any kind and free to let his imagination and aesthetic sensibilities have free rein, a freedom he joyfully exploited to the fullest.

The tour's longest stop was in Moscow, where they visited museums and attended the opera and ballet. However, the highlight of the visit was their attendance at the annual Physical Culture Day celebrations in Red Square, made possible by the magic password, "Intourist," and described by Gordon as "the most impressive event which I have witnessed in the USSR – or possibly anywhere else."

In reading an article he wrote for *New Outlook* on his return home, "Moscow, July 24,"[52] one can only use the word *enchantment* to describe his response to what he saw. From their place in the stands about 46 m from Lenin's tomb, they watched the athletes, in sports outfits of all colours, mill about in Red Square, ready to assemble for the marches. Red Square itself floated huge banners wishing long life to Comrade Stalin, the friend of Physical Culture. At the stroke of three, Stalin and three other figures in white emerged from behind Lenin's tomb and took their place on the reviewing stand. The crowds stood as the "Internationale" was played, proclaiming the release of the toilers of the world as the July sun blazed down from a burning blue sky. The red flag with hammer and sickle floated high above the Kremlin wall.

The parade followed, team after team of sports organizations from the factories, culture units of yachtsmen, oarsmen and tennis players and swimmers, all of the athletes brown and rugged. Gordon concluded his article: "This is the answer of the youth of Russia to those who say the Soviet Union is showing signs of cracking up. They have trials and dark days to face today and tomorrow. But crack up they never will while Russia trains itself, body and mind, to build and defend their new society and their new culture."

How strangely his words fall on modern ears.

Back in Montreal's chilly blasts the following winter, King recalled the other – less ideologically fraught – highlight of his trip, a visit to "those sunny Black Sea shores where the heat soaks through to one's very bones and the world basks in contented laziness."[53] It was another side of Soviet life that he saw in the Crimea, far from the organized propaganda of Red Square. However, their trip to these sunny shores had not been without drama. Travelling south on the dusty train from Kharkof to Yalta (which suggested to King the sound of Valhalla, "where the weary warriors would find rest"), they had become separated from their guides and, more important, from their tickets and their lunch. The obdurate conductor saw no reason why they should not be deposited at the first wayside stop, and it took all the German Gordon possessed and the help of a friendly medical professor from Kiev to persuade the functionary that they should be allowed on their way. A telegram from Intourist arrived and the crisis passed, but not the misery. The train was crowded and hot as they passed through hour after hour of dreary scenery: "The wheat fields of south central Russia have their limitations as a source of aesthetic inspiration," he complained. And there was still the issue of lunch. At the first stop they followed a tired line of workers and peasants to a sign marked РЕСТОРАН which they cleverly interpreted as "restaurant." The meal proved as dreary as the column of labourers that led to it: boiled milk, cabbage soup, black bread, and something sour between butter and cheese. Gordon and his tourists did their best to concentrate on its nutritive value. The afternoon passed in desultory conversation, and they then suffered what Gordon called "another memorable night in Calcutta," spent in their train compartment, tightly sealed to keep out thieves.[54]

But daybreak brought hope: Sevastopol and a cold bath and breakfast, a swim in the Black Sea, and lying on the shore drying themselves while the great naval guns of the harbour crashed the silence. Once again his vision of the Soviet future was restored, as was his sense of adventure as they travelled to Yalta, with Sasha and his ancient Fiat driving gently along a winding grey ribbon road through burnt hills, rocks, and occasional views of a single goat before a plaster hut. Suddenly, as King described it, the hidden character of Sasha revealed itself, and the Cossack emerged: "I have heard of those horsemen about whom it was said that you could not tell at what point the horse began and the rider left off. Such was Sasha and his Fiat." They careered up hairpin turns with no guardrails, Sasha impervious to the terror of his passengers until suddenly – was it a lifetime? – with an abrupt left turn and a sudden braking, they stared mesmerized down 610 m of sheer cliff. "Crawling away from the coast as the black squalls swept its surface, was the sea. Not bold, but singularly small we felt as we stood awestruck and silent upon that peak in Darien."[55]

They arrived safely, if a bit shaken, in Yalta, where the mountains came down to the sea, their steep slopes dotted with white villas and palaces, and vineyards with their purple grapes climbed up and down the terraces that bordered winding roads. They found open courtyard restaurants, orchestras playing, palaces, and gardens. Young people strolled along the seafront in moonlight, their sibilant voices like the quiet sound of the surf on the shale.[56] Still, it was not entirely a throwback to pre-revolutionary days, but rather an appropriation of that luxury and ease; for instance, they visited the czar's pre-war palace, Livadia, preserved in all its grandeur, now a convalescent home for peasants and workers. They were told that far back in the hills, sanitaria were being opened up for the treatment of tuberculosis, and rest homes for professors and scientists, as well as camps for university students and school children. A dash of realism invaded Gordon's thinking when, on a visit to a Young Pioneers camp, he asked about political education. The leader assured him, "There is no special political education. This is all political education."

Their boat left for Odessa the next day and, their trip seeming to follow a pattern, they discovered that their cabins had once again been usurped. It was hot and close below decks and Gordon strolled fore and aft among the peasants, workers, and students travelling third class, sprawled and tightly packed with their bundles: "Yalta left behind; Old Russia on the move."

Home again, as he sat in his Montreal digs that chilly winter afternoon, recalling his trip and reflecting on its meaning, his mind went back to that other winter day in Giscome as he sat in his shack reading Gilbert Ryle's letter from Oxford. As he had on that previous morning in the brilliant stillness of the forests, he contemplated the vast distances and disparate worlds of culture encompassed by the imagination, and he remembered Yalta:

Tonight I sat alone on the sea front at Yalta
A white moon hung over a gently breathing sea
A changing symphony of blue and silver
And sibilant Russian voices spoke softly
Reverencing the silence
A guitar played a bar or two of music
Wild hill music – before Karl Marx was heard of
And the Black Sea and the moon were older than Soviet Russia
And the music was older than Soviet Russia
And the love in the voices of the girl and the boy
Was older than Soviet Russia
And sea and music and moon and love had conquered
And I turned sadly from the silver path
To the north – where the North Star rested over Moscow
And still Laurentian valleys.[57]

The Reverend John Mark King, Principal of Manitoba College, circa 1895. (Courtesy of the Manitoba Historical Society)

Helen King before her marriage to C.W. Gordon in 1899. (Courtesy of the Friends of the Ralph Connor House – FRCH)

54 West Gate, the Gordon family home. (Courtesy of FRCH)

King Gordon at 2 ½ years (Courtesy of Alison Gordon)

King Gordon and his younger sisters, 1913. (Courtesy of FRCH)

Major C.W. Gordon in his regimental uniform, 43rd Cameron Highlanders, 1914. (Courtesy of FRCH)

"Rainbows," the Gordon cow, Birkencraig, 1915. (Courtesy of FRCH)

Queen's College, Oxford, first Eight rowing team, 1924.
Gordon left side, top row. (Courtesy of Alison Gordon)

Queen's College, first Eight rowing team, 1924. Gordon third from bow (back). (Courtesy of FRCH)

King Gordon (right) in front of the cookhouse at a railroad tie camp, Giscome, 1924, the foreman to the left, and the cook in the centre. (Courtesy of LAC and the Gordon family)

"Sive Dominus domum aedificat"

DEDICATORY SERVICE

PINE FALLS CHURCH
United Church of Canada

"Till at some sudden turn, one sees
Against the black and muttering trees
Thine altar, wonderfully white,
Among the forests of the night."
—Rupert Brooke.

OCTOBER FOURTEENTH
Nineteen Hundred and Twenty-eight

MINISTER
THE REV. J. KING GORDON, B.A. Oxon.

Dedicatory Service, Pine Falls United Church, 1928. (Courtesy of the Gordon family)

Portrait of Gordon by Pegi Nicol, circa 1932.
(Courtesy of the Gordon family)

Photograph of Gordon, CCF candidate, 1935.
(Courtesy of the Gordon family)

KING GORDON BROADCASTS

Hear King Gordon's Final Election Broadcasts over Station C F C T

Thursday, October 10	-	8.15— 8.30 p.m.
Friday, October 11	- -	7.15— 7.30 p.m.
Saturday, October 12	-	11.00—11.30 p.m.

C.C.F. Closing Campaign Meeting

CITY TEMPLE

Saturday, October 12th.

at 8.00 p.m.

SPEAKERS:

J. KING GORDON

ROBERT CONNELL, M.P.P.

JOSEPH ROUND

Published by Victoria Federal C.C.F. Campaign Committee.
Printed by the Victoria Printing & Publishing Co., Victoria, B.C.

Who Is KING GORDON

?

Victoria Campaign, 1935. (Courtesy of the Gordon family)

8

Itinerant Agitator and Political Candidate

In September 1934, after the board of governors of United Theological College had rejected the request of the United Church General Council, Gordon found himself without a job. Scarcely missing a step, he began his three-year career as – in his own words – "itinerant agitator," continuing to be supported by the generosity of Dr Frank Pedley and friends. His travels – first of all on behalf of the newly formed Fellowship for a Christian Social Order (FCSO), for the CCF and LSR, and eventually as lecturer-at-large for the United Church – led him to every corner of the country and exposed him to Canadians of all ranks and professions as they lived their daily lives. He listened and he talked (sometimes giving twenty lectures, speeches, and sermons within the space of one week) from the fishing and mining villages of the Maritimes to the drought-stricken Prairie provinces, and on to the middle-class bastion of Victoria, where he ran for political office. Few men in the 1930s could have had a greater or more immediate sense of the Canadian working people than he, and out of this intimate and extended sharing of their lives grew the genuine admiration and respect for ordinary people that he later applied to people of all nations.

By the end of the 1920s, the momentum of the prewar social gospel movement had foundered and fragmented, much like other social and political reform movements of the progressive period. The prosperity of the 1920s fostered a modification of earlier radicalism and encouraged the view that capitalism could be reformed and need not be replaced with socialism. This belief also permeated the churches, causing the radicals of the social gospel movement to feel that the church had betrayed its mission in its accommodation to the status quo and to the moneyed interests of society. Many of these disaffected radicals simply left the church, turning their energies toward politics or other causes such as pacifism. The more conservative elements of the movement retreated into a personal and private style of religious piety. Richard Allen argues that this defection at either extreme of the social gospel spectrum allowed its centre of gravity to shift to a more moderate progressive constituency that aimed to work with established institutions,[1] while maintaining its radical critique of the social order.

This adaptation proved temporary, however, and with the crash of 1929 a new and more realistic social gospel emerged, as reflected in Reinhold Niebuhr's increasingly stark critique of the liberal position in *Moral Man and Immoral Society*. Within the United Church of Canada this radicalism came to expression in the resolutions, reports, and debates of the Toronto and Montreal–Ottawa Conferences in 1933, conferences in which Gordon and Eugene Forsey vociferously participated. Even before 1933, however, the momentum that culminated in the founding of the Fellowship for a Christian Social Order was well underway.[2] Three years earlier, at the Toronto Conference in 1930, a small group of ministers had met together to explore the possibility of forming a group that would serve clergy and lay persons in the way that the Student Christian Movement (SCM) served academics. Once back in their churches they began holding weekly meetings, and by March 1931 their activity had led to the formation of a group that clearly intended itself to be a Christian socialist movement.

Shortly after Gordon's arrival in Montreal the following September, he and Forsey (with other radicals such as R.B.Y. Scott) began a parallel group called the Fellowship of Socialist Christians modelled on Niebuhr's organization of the same name. By the spring of 1934, a third group associating itself with the Montreal organization had been formed in Kingston. Gordon wrote to Niebuhr telling him of their new fellowship and its congruent point of view with Niebuhr's group in New York; but, he explained, there seemed to be some discomfort concerning the name: "Our situation in Canada is a bit different from yours in New York, since a number of our men are from smaller towns where the name 'Socialism' still throws a scare into the populace."[3]

It may have been this apprehension about the word *socialist* that led the Kingston group to name itself the Fellowship for a Christian Social Order in April 1934. In spite of the name change, it was clear that the newly formed FCSO shared the conviction of the Fellowship of Socialist Christians that it was necessary to go beyond the earlier liberalism of the social gospel and become politically active to bring about change. In fact, Niebuhr's influence on the FCSO must be acknowledged as considerable. Roger C. Hutchinson, in his study of the FCSO, refers to Niebuhr as helping to radicalize countless Canadians, and he quotes him as saying: "The young radicals of the United Church of Canada are as promising a group as could be found in any church of the world. In spite of the conservativism [sic] of a typical Toronto or Montreal church, which frequently manages to combine a decadent Calvinism with bourgeois complacency in a sorry compound, the left-wing movement in Canada has a considerable influence."[4]

Nevertheless, the Canadian group did not go as far as Niebuhr in drawing the dichotomy between the absolute Christian ethic and the requirements of social action, nor was there the sharp division among members of the FCSO between the transcendental God and evil man found in the theology of both Niebuhr and Karl Barth. A comparison of the FSC and FCSO statements of purpose finds in the Canadian text a moderation of the more cataclysmic aspects of Niebuhr's thought and a greater confidence in both the redemptive power of Christianity and the resources of the democratic process. As time went on, in spite of continuing cordial personal relationships and contacts, the ideological gulf with Niebuhr widened, and by 1937, in his review of the FCSO's publication of *Towards the Christian Revolution*, Niebuhr was accusing this "promising young group of radicals" of reverting to the culturally accommodated theology of an earlier era.[5] Nevertheless, the 1934 manifesto of the FCSO was stark in its condemnation of capitalism and in its belief in the necessity of collective action to restore the wealth of society to the whole community.

Since all its founding members were active in the United Church, it made sense that the organizational structure of the FCSO would follow the conference-and-presbytery pattern of the church, and a representative for each conference was appointed and urged to establish units in each presbytery. By 1937, the date when King resigned his post as travelling secretary, there were FCSO annual conference units meeting in eight provinces and in Newfoundland, with the greatest concentration of membership in Ontario. Most of the members were drawn from the clergy and laity of the United Church (though a group might occasionally include an Anglican, such as Andrew Brewin, who was also in the LSR and the CCF), and much of the membership overlapped with the LSR. The activities of the branches were primarily educational, providing study groups on Christianity and social change, recommending reading lists, publishing and distributing literature, and conducting summer schools and conferences. There was also active political participation in the support of CCF candidates.

Like the LSR, the FCSO's book, *Towards the Christian Revolution*,[6] was written and edited by men who belonged to both organizations, and it too reflected the close relationship between the LSR and the FCSO. In Gordon's chapter, "The Political Task," he focused on the rise of fascist totalitarianism, and pointed to socialism as the only certain alternative in preserving the remaining democracies. Interestingly, he acknowledged the difficulty of describing the political structure of the socialist state, the Soviet Union being "more Russian than socialist," and he turned to the Scandinavian democracies and New Zealand for examples of centralized social planning that still safeguarded and preserved decentralized control, largely through the use of cooperatives. He also looked to the church as playing a vital role in preventing the rise of totalitarianism, particularly in its educational function.

In the fall of 1934, when the newly formed organization asked the newly unemployed Gordon if he would take on the task of being their travelling secretary, he responded eagerly. With Montreal as his base, he himself set about the educational and organizational task he had urged on others. Many years later, he spoke gratefully of the scope of travel across Canada and his own exposure to diverse social groups. He had carte blanche to the various groups he met and talked with – labour unions, churches, and theological colleges of all denominations, SCM conferences, and CCF clubs. "The experience was exhilarating," he later wrote. "you felt you were part of a movement transforming Canadian society ... [It] was also humbling because you were so much better off than so many who were fighting a much tougher battle than you were."[7]

As he travelled on his lecture circuit, Gordon sent periodic reports back to R.B.Y. Scott in Montreal, president of the FCSO. In a series of such letters in June of 1937, he described a typical schedule during a tour of the Maritimes, which gives one a flavour of the times.[8] His first stop was Charlottetown, which he found "just a little incredible," and fully justified in classing Canadians as "foreigners." However, the incredibility rested not on their quaint uniqueness, but on the fact that there were spread throughout the Island twenty-three branch libraries, part of the Carnegie Library experiment. Added to this, 3,800 Islanders were enrolled in study clubs using materials from the Extension Department of St Francis Xavier University,[9] concentrating on social and economic problems. On his last day in Charlottetown, when he confessed to feeling rather ragged from the heavy schedule, King met with the local ministerial association and found himself revived by the discussion that followed his presentation and lasted for four hours.[10]

He then travelled to the mainland of New Brunswick where he found the city of St John "what you might expect": the local CCF group small and doctrinaire, committed to Trotskyism, and generally uninformed. But there was one bright note in Gordon's otherwise dour account of the visit to St John. Eugene Forsey had spoken to the Canadian Club the day before and "laid about him in great style on free speech and reactionary trends – using Quebec as a prize example but with references that might easily hit home in St J. He was in great form, and left them gasping."[11]

It was with relief that Gordon shook the reactionary dust of St John off his feet and arrived in Fredericton, completing his tour of all nine provincial capitals within five months. After a rocky start, applying his pacifist techniques against the "bull-headed obduracy of an imperialist-militarist who held out his jaw inviting right and left hooks," his heart was lifted to find the most promising group in Fredericton to be a little CCF club, led by the local Baptist minister.[12]

He concluded his visit to Fredericton with a Sunday afternoon drive to Marysville, a Canadian cotton town whose industrial squalour contrasted with the beautiful surrounding countryside. Gordon found himself dismayed, as he surveyed the unpainted clapboard houses with no plumbing, outhouses behind each house, and a central tap from which they all drew water. He was told that at the last election a company official stood at the polling booth and told the men that if Bennett were not elected the town would shut down.[13] King continued to Newcastle where he visited some of the Red Cross charity cases, "one of the most sickening trips I have ever had." Right in the shadow of a prosperous sawmill, he found hovels inhabited by children of fifteen and sixteen who looked like feeble ten-year-olds, suffering from lack of nourishment, decent clothing, and schooling, so different from the company towns of Giscome and Pine Falls.

A comment in Gordon's letter to Frank Scott from Moncton on 17 June introduced a theme that haunted both the FCSO and the early CCF: the attempts of communist sympathizers to penetrate their organizations, the sympathy with Marxism of its own left wing, and the danger that the two movements, democratic socialism and Marxist communism, would become identified together in the public mind. Walter D. Young, in his history of the CCF, points out that it was this flirtation with the Communist party by the left wing of the CCF that did the most harm to the new party by creating confusion in the public mind between CCF and communist policy. The press further exacerbated this confusion, Young writes, by repeatedly linking the two parties in their reporting, and the right-wing parties happily seized on this guilt by association in election campaigns. The CCF had an uphill task in public relations in attempting to present a clear distinction between themselves and the Marxists.[14]

Gordon illustrated this problem from his own experience, referring to an evening meeting in a Moncton schoolhouse during his Maritime trip, chaired by the mayor. King described him as a nice old chap who was frightened of a question period because there were half a dozen "communistic people" who might take advantage of it, with the result that people might say it was under communist auspices. Gordon assured him that under such extremely respectable chairmanship as His Worship's, the charge would hardly stick; and in any case that he, Gordon, thought he could handle any awkward questions in a way that would not lead to irreparable damage to the cause of religion in Moncton.[15]

In spite of King's light (and somewhat patronizing) tone, the FCSO, with its ties to the SCM, was also vulnerable to the charge of being "communistic." Looking back, Gordon identified part of the problem as rooted in contemporary student reaction to the actuality of depression and the dim prospects of employment. He wrote: "This dire social crisis pushed the SCM from its base in the social gospel and personal religion onto a much more radical course. Many students found their political radicalism – which carried some into Communist Party affiliations – nurtured within the SCM."[16]

The FCSO was not completely lacking in *savoir faire*, however, and Gordon later wrote that in this matter of various communist attempts to infiltrate organizations in an effort to promote their own political agendas, the LSR and the FCSO soon got over their initial innocence. As travelling secretary of the FCSO, he had been approached with a request that he endorse the Conference of the Canadian Youth Congress Against War and Fascism (CCYC). While in the past he had been in sympathy with a number of such conferences because he felt confident that they were designed to promote the cause of peace, in this case he felt compelled to refuse.[17] Still, while he doubted the sincerity and motives of the conference organizers, his curiosity was piqued, and he dropped in just to see how it was being run. His suspicions about its doubtful affiliation were immediately confirmed by the sight of Tim Buck, leader of the Canadian communists, sitting in the gallery, absorbed in reading a pamphlet. Even more curious, he stealthily made his way up to the gallery and surreptitiously peered over Buck's shoulder, discovering that Canada's leading radical was lost in thought with the latest papal encyclical, *Quadragesima Anno*.

In his travels through the Maritimes on behalf of the FCSO, Gordon was covering territory familiar to his father, who during the 1917 federal election had campaigned there on behalf of Sir Robert Borden's Union government. At that time the senior Gordon had spoken (as King would later do here) in churches and church halls, at the Canadian Club, at Rotary luncheons and in schoolhouses. But it was C.W. Gordon's contact with the extension program at St Francis Xavier University at Antigonish and his meeting with the young comptroller, Father James Tompkins, that proved to be most important to his son's future. Now, King's own first visit initiated what would become a reference point and metaphor in his search for what the Kingdom of God could mean in its temporal manifestation.

The Antigonish Movement, based at St Francis Xavier University, grew out of the needs of these sturdy fishermen, farmers, and miners of the seven eastern counties of Nova Scotia. Almost since Confederation, they had been faced with an ever-present economic problem and the feeling that any solution to the problem lay beyond individual or community control.[18] They waited in vain for some sort of redress from the federal government, and nursed their grievances against the central authorities in Ottawa. Under leadership provided by the professors from St Francis Xavier and the provincial Department of Agriculture, the people had begun taking matters into their own hands, setting up rural conferences dealing with issues of improving methods of soil culture and stock raising, cooperative marketing, and buying.[19]

Then in 1928, from their base at the Extension Department, a group of priests and educators including Father Tomkins, Father Moses Coady, the Reverend Hugh MacPherson, and A.B. MacDonald, launched out into a new venture of adult education. The program comprised three components: local meetings in schools, churches, and community centres; study clubs to undertake initiatives in solving local problems; and a six-week school for leaders, held at the university. By the time Gordon came in contact with the movement in 1935, there were between 900 and 1,000 active study clubs in Cape Breton and the counties of Pictou and Antigonish. Cooperatives and credit unions had developed to the extent that there was more than $100,000 on loan to members. Gordon observed hope and optimism among the people, who were developing a new sense of security and a growing confidence in their ability to control their own economic life, believing that their cooperatives represented the first feeble steps in breaking the hold of private capitalism upon their lives. While not aiming to achieve socialism (never its goal), Gordon felt that the movement nevertheless gave one a glimpse of the total pattern of integrated economic, social, and spiritual values possible in human community.

Eager to get out into the field and see the work in operation, Gordon responded to the suggestion of Professor A.B. MacDonald, assistant director of extension, that he spend a day in the mining area before his own schedule of lecturing claimed his time. They set off together on snow-banked roads for Reserve Mines, where Father Tomkins, now serving as parish priest, and the two guests made the rounds of the library, the credit union, and the cooperative store, Gordon visiting happily with everyone he met. The next day, he spoke to the Associated Study Club of Reserved Mines, a crowded parish hall of miners and their wives, along with two parish priests and two Protestant ministers.[20]

At the conclusion of the visit, Gordon drove with Father Tomkins to visit one of the big mines and, like his father before him, he was caught in a Maritime blizzard. The snow, driving almost horizontally, had piled drifts across the road but their driver charged through, with clouds of snow flying in all directions. Finally, the wheels spun and came to a stop. They were stuck fast and their intrepid driver had to concede defeat. But what of Father Tomkins, whose vocabulary did not contain the word "defeat"? At his insistence, the others took turns with the shovel, clearing the snow around the wheels, to no avail. Then through the blinding snow a man approached on foot, the field secretary, suspecting their plight, who had been waiting for them at the mine. At this point, Father Tomkins – who, in deference to his age had been sitting in the closed car during this battle with the elements – upon hearing the secretary's voice, emerged and stood with his back against the raging storm. King, with the sure touch of the storyteller reminiscent of his father, concluded his account:

> "Alex," shouted Dr Tomkins over the storm. "Do you think we are on the right track?"
> "Yes, of course. But what do you mean?"
> "I mean the whole movement – study clubs, credit unions, cooperatives. Is it really going to work out? Is it going to enable these people to solve their big problems?"

"Yes, I think so."
"But are you sure?"
"Yes, I'm sure."[21]

Poetic license perhaps, but with this astonishing conversation ringing in his ears and with seemingly no sense of the irony of their situation – an aged priest and a local functionary discussing social theory in the midst of a howling blizzard – Gordon continued his journey with his faith in the human endeavour renewed.

While Gordon spent most of his time on the road during his three years as "itinerant agitator," his home base was Montreal, where he shared an apartment with his sister Lois, who taught at Miss Edgar's and Miss Cramp's School for Girls. When in Montreal he kept in close touch with friends and with current events, of which the Spanish Civil War proved to be one of the most troubling. There were a number of small, ad hoc left-wing organizations as well as the LSR that supported the new democratic government of Spain. In the summer of 1936, Graham Spry, in an amazing feat of imagination, had created (apparently out of whole cloth) the Spanish Hospital and Medical Aid Committee.[22] Not a penny had been collected when he printed a headline story in the *New Commonwealth* announcing the plan (as he said, it was only the announcement of a plan, not the announcement of an achievement); and he was both relieved and alarmed when Dr Norman Bethune[23] – a member of the Communist party who had offered his services to the Republican government – responded, only to discover that as yet there was neither organization nor money to send him or supplies to Spain. Spry and his friends quickly created the Committee to Aid Spanish Democracy, giving substance to Spry's phantom organization, and eventually Bethune sailed from Quebec City with a large store of medical supplies. Spry pleaded ignorance of Bethune's communist affiliation. After all, Bethune belonged to a family in which there were three Anglican bishops and, "He never mentioned to me that he was a communist."[24]

In Montreal, Frank Scott headed the Committee for Medical Aid to Spain, one of the various left-wing groups that, in October of 1936, sponsored a visit to Canada by a delegation from Republican Spain. When the group arrived in Montreal on 23 October, it faced virulent opposition from both church and city authorities; public opinion in Quebec strongly supported Generalissimo Franco and regarded the republicans not only as communists, but as atheists as well. Initially, the meeting with the delegates was scheduled to take place in the Mount Royal Arena on the evening of their arrival; Gordon described the events that followed in an article appropriately titled, "Fascist Weekend in Montreal."[25] Fearing civil disorder and riots provoked by local fascist groups, the acting mayor of Montreal banned the Mount Royal meeting, and Scott's committee learned that Victoria Hall, the alternate site, was also suddenly unavailable to them, leaving Scott with no choice but to cancel the large public meeting. However, he was able hurriedly to secure a small salon in the Mount Royal Hotel for a meeting of a semi-private nature. As the mayhem continued in the streets, the hotel management, fearing invasion, aborted the event by turning out the lights and ordering Scott's group to leave.

Sunday the 25th was the occasion of the Catholic celebration of the Feast of Christ the King, and 100,000 French Canadians assembled in the Craig Street armories and the adjoining Champ de Mars, where numerous speakers denounced communism and called for the faithful to join in a crusade for its extermination. Meanwhile, in Quebec City, Premier Maurice Duplessis addressed a crowd of 20,000, asserting that the "grand theories" of liberty, equality, and fraternity were of no account; it was the virtues of faith, hope, and charity that mattered.[26] The events of the weekend, only too representative of the climate in Quebec, had brought into focus for Gordon and other members of the LSR the fragility of civil liberties in Quebec. Michiel Horn describes Eugene Forsey's reaction as "not untypical," as Forsey described the weekend to David Lewis, calling it "part of a growing body of evidence that fascism was a threat at home as well as abroad."[27] It was incidents such as these that led several LSR members in 1937 to participate in the founding of a Civil Liberties Union.

Gordon remained sympathetic to the cause of the Spanish loyalists and maintained his ties with the Republican delegates from Spain and with Dr Bethune. On a more bizarre note, during the visit of the Spanish delegates to Montreal, Gordon was rather incongruously offered the position of consul for Republican Spain. Despite the LSR's independent stand in favour of the Spanish loyalists and fairly heavy pressure from his friends, he refused.

In May of 1934, faced with uncertainly about his position at United Theological College and frustrated in his efforts to find fulfilling work in the church, King had written to his mother that, since he couldn't practice religion in the church he would try practising it in politics. His opportunity to do this came with the general election of 1935, in one of those "happy accidents" that seemed to form the leitmotif of his life – in this case, an invitation to stand as CCF candidate for the riding of Victoria.[28]

During the last week in April Gordon was scheduled to address an SCM camp on Gambier Island, just off the BC coast near Vancouver, followed by a series of lectures in Vancouver churches. On his arrival in Vancouver, much to his surprise, a committee representing the Victoria organization of the CCF met him at the train. To his even greater surprise, they invited him to accept the CCF nomination for Victoria in the forthcoming federal election. His first response was bewilderment, a confusion of feeling honoured and disbelief: Victoria! For the CCF? He had always thought of Victoria in stereotypical terms as British, conservative, a haven for the affluent retired where the height of ambition was to sit in the drawing room of the Empress Hotel and enjoy crumpets and tea. But the delegation argued that Victoria was like any other Canadian city, with a sizable working class and a politically conscious electorate, ripe for the CCF picking. Gordon said he would consider their offer.

With his busy schedule, there was little time to consider a future career one way or the other. Others, however, had been taking action on his behalf. Since the UTC board of governors had refused to take Gordon back onto its teaching staff the previous autumn, the executive of the General Council, meeting in Toronto on 24 and 25 April, 1935, resolved that "for a period of one year only, the Rev. J. King Gordon be appointed Lecturer in Christian Ethics to be available for service in the Theological Colleges and elsewhere, his duties to commence July 1, 1935."[29] The salary for this professor-at-large position was to be $1,500, with an additional $500 for travel and incidental expenses, the cost to be shared by the church and friends. Gordon now found himself caught in a dilemma, noting that neither the CCF nor the United Church would likely be willing to divide his labours.

Because of his travels, Gordon first heard of the General Council's resolution from George Ferguson of the *Winnipeg Free Press*. A telegram dated 26 April and addressed to him in care of the SCM at the University of British Columbia read: "MARY AND I SEND CONGRATULATIONS ON SUBSTANTIAL MEASURE OF SUPPORT GIVEN AND STRONGLY URGE YOU ACCEPT EXECUTIVES PROPOSAL."[30] For some reason the church did not get around to notifying Gordon directly of their offer for more than two weeks after they had notified the press. Their letter, dated 10 May, only reached him on 17 May at his father's house in Winnipeg.

By that time he had already been deluged with advice from friends and supporters. The response of Professor John Line was typical in its tone of encouragement and he wrote to Gordon that the church's proposal "exceeded our hope; and from things I have gathered I am certain the disposition in official quarters is to give every facility for a real educational programme and the expectation is that in your hands this will develop a very significant post and work."[31]

Not all reaction was positive, however, and Frank Scott telegraphed simply, "DONT LIKE CHURCH OFFER STOP FRANK." A second telegram followed: "HOPE YOUR REJECTION OF VICTORIA CONSTITUENCY NOT FINAL STOP JOB FOR YEAR ONLY WILL LEAVE YOU STRANDED AFTER SPOILING YOUR POLITICAL CHANCES STOP WHY NOT BREAK NOW AND TRY BIGGER WORK STOP REFUSING THIS JOB NO BETRAYAL OF YOUR SUPPORTERS STOP POLITICS ONLY ROAD TO HEAVEN NOW."[32]

The telegraph wires hummed with news from Victoria, with the district council of the CCF urging him to accept the nomination and asking him for an immediate response so that they could set a date for the constituency nominating convention.[33] Gordon replied from Winnipeg that he was giving the matter serious attention, whereupon three more telegrams arrived. The first, another from John Line, assured him that the offer of $1,500 was likely to be made permanent.[34] Gregory Vlastos's cable strongly urged him to accept the nomination, unless he was bound by his promise to the church.[35] Finally, Frank Scott weighed in once again, arguing that the moral victory in the church had already been won and that another "wandering lectureship" was pointless. He added, "Leadership in radical politics [is] yours for the taking."[36] At this point, the United Church friends offered reassurance that whatever decision he made, the honour of the church would be vindicated in doing the right thing by King in continuing financial support. This generous attitude on the part of his friends not only reflected their respect for Gordon but (with prescient insight) their conviction that he should be retained for Canada.[37] A letter from W.A. Gifford, Gordon's former colleague on the UTC faculty, wrote that, "I see no reason outside yourself, against your acceptance of a promising opening into parliament."[38]

Gifford's letter represented fairly accurately Gordon's own approach to the complicated issue. "In fact, I was not faced with an important crossroads where a right or wrong choice would decide the future course of my life. As Gifford suggested there was no sharp line between the practice of politics and the practice of religion."[39] Gordon's itinerary in Saskatchewan during the first two weeks of May exemplified his sense of the complementary and integrated roles of politics and religion: on his arrival on 2 May, he met with SCM camp leaders to discuss their camp program, and later the same day, spoke to the CCYM (the youth movement of the CCF). He preached at both Westminster (United) and Knox (Presbyterian) churches; and at the end of that first week he was handed over to George Williams, the leader of the Saskatchewan CCF. For the next seven days he spoke throughout the province on behalf of the party, warmly welcomed by all the local leadership. At the end of that week, George Williams expressed the hope that Gordon would take the morning service at Carmichael United Church.

Reflecting later on his experience in Saskatchewan, King saw little difference between the first week's program under the auspices of the Christian SCM and the second week's under the political CCF. While they differed in emphasis and method, both groups were concerned with bringing about a more humane and just society, their membership often overlapping. Gordon, of course, did not mean to conflate the two groups, recognizing the secular nature of politics, and the necessarily independent stance of the religious community. But in his own mind, he felt free to serve the liberal ideals of the church and the social radicalism of the political party, without a sense of inner conflict.[40]

A letter from J.S. Woodsworth undoubtedly exerted considerable influence on him. Woodsworth told King that he was "very anxious indeed that you should be in the next Parliament," his only reservation being that he choose a riding that promised a good chance for election. If Victoria did not offer that likelihood, there were others to choose from. Concerning the offer from the United Church, it seemed to Woodsworth "more or less of a compassionate allowance and a way of evading a decision of the real issue at stake." He concluded: "All I should like to impress is that since you have become quite a figure in the public life of this dominion that it would be a very great contribution indeed if, by your own action, you could convince the public that political action was worthwhile, and that a socialist programme was the only thing that would save the situation."[41]

The official telegram, when it arrived, announced that Gordon had been nominated by an overwhelming majority.[42] Four names besides his had been brought before the nominating convention, but all four voluntarily withdrew once Gordon's telegrams offering his serious consideration of the nomination were read.

And so the die was cast. Gordon telegraphed his acceptance to Victoria and received in reply: "MANY THANKS FOR GOOD NEWS EVERYONE HERE MOST ENTHUSIASTIC."[43] The seat in Victoria was not in his pocket, however, and his future employment in Parliament was by no means assured. It was too early in the process to burn all his bridges, and on 21 May Gordon sent a hand-delivered letter to the secretary of the executive council of the United Church in Toronto, T. Albert Moore, requesting a postponement in the commencement date of the lectureship. He received a prompt reply turning him down, but with a proviso: the sub-committee had passed a resolution that if he were to apply for the appointment at a later date, they would give his request careful consideration.[44] Gordon then suggested that he could accept the church's offer on 1 July on the understanding that the church would then allow him to take up a political nomination, but the executive of the General Council – perhaps not viewing the roles of the church and politics to be quite as integrated as Gordon perceived them – found itself unable to comply with this request as well.[45]

And so, considering his options with the church closed, Gordon accepted the Victoria nomination. But apparently the church did not share his opinion that in regard to its previous offer there was no more to be said. In a letter dated 8 July, the tenacious sub-committee passed yet another resolution stating that it needed further time to consider the whole question and had therefore decided to defer action for another three weeks. In the meantime, no salary was to be paid until the question of Gordon's employment by the Church was definitely settled.[46] The curtain went down on "Church or State: To Stand or Run," as Gordon had framed his dilemma, with a final letter from the secretary of the General Council dated 1 August 1935. Once again the sub-committee had acted, and this time its resolution read, "The appointment of Rev. J. King Gordon should become effective as from October 1st, 1935." Surely the church must be credited with going the extra mile in trying to accommodate Gordon's wishes. They again added a caveat: "The opinion was strongly expressed that The United Church should not be held responsible in any way for any statements made by you during the present political campaign."[47]

Along the left margin of the final paragraph, a heavy pencilled bracket tied these last four lines together. C.W. Gordon, in his distinctive handwriting, commented: "What a life saver!" As loyal father, C.W. Gordon voted CCF in support of his son in the October election; but, as a former church moderator, he perhaps understood church politics in a way his son did not.

Gordon and his friends in the CCF, with their LSR supporters, entered the election campaign of 1935 convinced that the political future of

Canada belonged to the CCF. As far as Gordon and others of the left were concerned, neither of the programs offered by the Liberal or Conservative Parties touched the root of the problem, as demonstrated by their own policy outlined in *Social Planning for Canada*, which appeared that same year. Along with Gordon, several members of the LSR also ran in the election: Graham Spry in Toronto-Broadview; E.B. (Ted) Jolliffe, newly returned from Oxford, in Toronto-St Paul's; Everett O. Hall in London, Ontario; and George Mooney in Verdun, Quebec. Altogether, the CCF contested fewer than half of the country's 245 constituencies, and only three of these were east of the Ottawa River, all in the Montreal area. In spite of the odds against them, Gordon entered the campaign filled with hopeful energy and later described it as "one of the most rewarding experiences of these exciting days."[48]

On his arrival in Victoria at the beginning of July, he was welcomed cordially by a committee led by H.A. Bowden, secretary of the Victoria CCF district council whom Gordon described as "the man who was to be my loyal guide, comforter and friend during the exigencies of a fraught election campaign."[49] They quickly dismissed the suggestion that he might be regarded as an eastern carpetbagger. He found to his relief that the core of the party comprised a good cross-section of the community, not only those loyal leftists who had served their apprenticeship in the British Labour party and the ILP, but also, for example, a Congregational minister, one of Victoria's leading doctors, and the chief librarian of the public library. King was assured that the Anglican bishop of Victoria was sympathetic, and Jimmie Phillips, head porter at the Empress Hotel, provided assurances that the third-floor staff was solidly CCF. He wrote to his mother on 7 July: "Well, I've arrived and in my very first day here I seem to have met dozens of people – practically all of them our own CCF people. They are a good crowd, simple hard working English people, most of them for whom the CCF is a religion."[50]

A brochure from the campaign asks, "Who is King Gordon?" Underneath this caption a photograph reveals King, black hair parted neatly on the side, brisk military moustache, steady blue eyes gazing sincerely into the camera. Inside, bold headings identify him as: Son of Ralph Connor; Rhodes Scholar; All-Round Athlete; Pioneer Minister in B.C.; Professor of Christian Ethics; Practical Christian; Superb Training for Politics; King Gordon, The Man! On 22 September, he shared the platform with Grace MacInnis, daughter of J.S. Woodsworth, who appealed directly to the women: "'Let me cook the meals of our nation / And I care not who makes her laws.' That was the motto in grandmother's cookbook. Yet today, growing numbers of women are caring who makes the laws of the country."[51] He formed a close friendship with MacInnis, later a CCF MLA in the BC legislature, the first female MP elected to the House of Commons, and secretary of the CCF caucus at Ottawa; and with her husband Angus, the first federal MP from the BC socialist labour movement, elected in 1930. King often stayed at their home in Vancouver, and Grace spent a week in Victoria, campaigning for King. At every meeting, it seemed to him, King met some friend from his days in Giscome or Winnipeg, or someone who had known his father or grandfather King, people who had attended St James in Toronto, Manitoba College, or who had come from Glengarry. He used the radio extensively, and in view of his later career, his observations on the new medium are interesting. He wrote to his mother: "Victoria has been getting more and more strenuous. Meetings every night with a radio broadcast every Monday. These blessed radio talks which have to be typed and timed to the minute take the most preparation and take a surprising amount out of me. It is a funny feeling to be alone in a room confronted with a mic. with the invisible audience listening for every cough – or more probably twisting the dial for a new program of jazz music."[52]

By late September, he felt the competition was between himself and the Conservative candidate, D.B. Plunkett – which, in fact, proved to be the case. A note of wistfulness crept into this same letter, which he posted to his mother in Kenora. "Your letters from the lake are like cool lake breezes. It is as good as having a few hours at the island to get them. Not quite – but the next best thing."

The last week before the election found the campaign "waxing hot and heavy," as King explained to his father en route to Vancouver. He remained optimistic. For the most part the campaign had been "pretty clean, with the papers treating us fairly."[53]

As it turned out, Gordon did not win, but he made a good showing, coming second with 6,482 votes to the conservative D.B. Plunkett's 7,504. Mackenzie King and his Liberals swept into office with 173 seats. Seven CCF candidates were elected, including T.C. Douglas and M.J. Coldwell in Saskatchewan and, of course, J.S. Woodsworth in North Winnipeg. In the previous year, Woodsworth had published a practical analysis of the electoral machinery in Canada, pointing out its unrepresentative character and arguing for the need for some type of proportional representation. His argument was borne out by the disproportionate results of the single-member constituency system in the 1935 election, which worked greatly to the detriment of the CCF: the Social Credit party took all the Alberta seats and two others (seventeen in all) with approximately half the votes the CCF needed to elect its total of seven seats, even though it got over 400,000 votes.[54]

It had been a wholehearted fight, and Gordon was understandably exhausted and suffering a letdown as he returned to his speaking schedule with the FCSO and prepared to take up his lectureship with the United Church. In early November he wrote to his mother in a despondent mood aboard the CPR ferry on his way back to the mainland from a short trip to Victoria, feeling rather "down in the mouth," admitting that in returning to the lecture circuit he was finding the church, with its excessive demands, "a harder show than a political party." He also told his mother that there were times when "one wants to call some of his life his own."[55]

This rare admission of fatigue and discouragement allows a glimpse into the depth of King's exhaustion and disappointment. However, as he looked back from the railing of the ferry on his way to Vancouver, watching his friends on the dock and the harbour lights receding in the distance, he wondered if perchance he might come back after all. "They all want me to run again and probably I shall. But it is all so far away as I live my life."

In fact, it was not all that far away. In the following May, the victorious Mr Plunkett died and Gordon was asked to contest the by-election of 1936. This time the Conservative candidate was none other than the former premier of British Columbia, the Honourable Simon Fraser Tolmie. The CCF organization was intact and went to work with a will, though perhaps the name of Tolmie slightly tempered their confidence in victory. There was also another factor that Gordon felt might have played some small part in the election results. J.S. Woodsworth and M.J. Coldwell had been invited to take part in the final rally in the Victoria armoury. Gordon recounted a story, told to him by Coldwell, of a conversation between Coldwell and Woodsworth as they crossed by ferry from Vancouver. In this conversation, Coldwell reported, he had said to Woodsworth: "You know, J. S., Gordon has a good chance to win. Now, there is one issue that has not been raised in this campaign and I don't think it needs to be raised. We all know how you feel about British Columbia's discrimination against Asians and we are all with you. But probably you don't need to raise the matter at this final meeting."[56]

According to Coldwell, Woodsworth had not intended to speak on the question, but when he was reminded, there was no way that he could, in good conscience, avoid a moral issue of such magnitude. At a dramatic point in his speech before the crowd in the armory, he stretched out his arm and waving his finger, as it were, in the face of the British Columbia authorities, he said, "And there is another thing; the treatment of our Japanese and Chinese and Indian fellow citizens." At that moment, according to Coldwell, Gordon turned to him and whispered, "Doesn't he look like the prophet Amos?"[57] However apocryphal the story may have been, Gordon lost by a mere ninety votes and bore Woodsworth no ill will. The result was 5,977 for Tolmie and 5,887 for Gordon.

In November 1937, Gordon once again contested Victoria in a by-election, after Tolmie, like his predecessor, died in office. But by this time the Liberal surge across the country was in full swell and the Victoria group was shaken by ideological dissension. Gordon ran a bad third, 3,000 votes behind his Liberal opponent.

The previous summer, Gordon had been elected vice-president of the party at the CCF's national convention, and on 11 August 1937, he received a letter from Frank Scott congratulating him on his "penultimate office." At that date, neither of them could know how soon Gordon would remove himself from the Canadian political scene. Shortly before the November 1937 by-election, on 31 October, C.W. Gordon died suddenly and unexpectedly, a devastating event for the entire Gordon family.

The summer of 1937 had been a particularly happy one for the Gordons, with the whole family except for Marjorie (who was in London) gathered at Birkencraig. C.W. Gordon spent the days ensconced in the Lookout, working on his memoirs. When the call for dinner came, he would stop at the nursery window and visit with Mary's fifteen-month-old son Peter, arriving late and unrepentant to take his place at the head of the table.[58] Evenings found the family by the fire, caught up in intense discussions of world affairs, the day's news of Spain and China, Hitler and Mussolini, with C.W. Gordon loyally defending the League of Nations, boasting of its achievements and accounting for its failures. Gordon left for the East in late August, finding the parting particularly difficult. "I can see him quite clearly standing on the dock in his old gray sweater beside my mother and young Peter, who always liked to see the boats come and go. He stood there with his hand raised in good-bye until the boat rounded the point of an island and he was out of sight."[59]

When the first news of C.W. Gordon's illness came in early October, no one was especially alarmed, and it was only after surgery when he did not show his usual powers of recuperation that the family became anxious. By this time the draft of his memoirs was completed but needing revision, and John Farrar, the New York publisher, not wishing to disturb him, asked King to take it in hand. Called back to Winnipeg, King read the manuscript on the train, a deeply moving experience as he travelled through the barren country north of Lake Superior: "For in that day I had lived through his life with him, not in morbid retrospect but vividly as he lived it, recapturing with him its excitement, its light and its shadow ... I could not get out of my mind the thought – here is a life that is complete. The postscript has been written."[60]

So insistent was King's premonition that his father's life had been lived that he asked the dispatcher at Armstrong to telephone Winnipeg for news. Good news, it turned out, for C.W. Gordon had spent a quiet day and looked forward to seeing King on his arrival the next day. But this was not to be. King continued his account, describing the final moments of his father's life, which found the two with miles remaining between them:

> I awakened just as dawn was breaking over lakes and granite hills, so reminiscent of the Lake of the Woods country. It was gray and the first snow flurries were filling up the pockets in the rocks.
>
> He died peacefully that morning just as the first light was showing. In the days and weeks that followed when it was so difficult to reconcile oneself to the end of a life that was so much of the very essence of life, the impressions of that train journey kept recurring – flashes of his debonair charm, his cool courage, his quiet faith in God and man.[61]

The entire family except Marjorie, who by now was on her way home from London via the Far East, gathered for the funeral. Letters and tributes poured in and had to be acknowledged. King had to leave for the Victoria election but there were matters of the estate to be cared for in consultation with his father's lawyer, R.F. McWilliams, and the question of editing the manuscript, a task considerably larger than King had imagined from his first reading of it on the train out to Winnipeg. He was asked by the publisher to do an introduction, and at the end of January he left for New York, where he stayed with Dr Archie Sinclair, in Montclair, New Jersey. He spent his days at Farrar and Rinehart, discussing design with Ruth Anderson, the art editor, and generally assisting in getting the book ready for publication in the spring of 1938.

After a month's work in the office, John Farrar asked him if he would consider taking on a permanent position as non-fiction editor, and he agreed. It seems not to have been a wrenching decision for Gordon to leave Canada at this time: he was disheartened after the November election; he had no prospect of an academic job; he had reached the conclusion, as he had explained to his mother, that he wanted some life of his own; and he was tired of being what he considered a financial burden to his friends. Above all else, he considered the move temporary as he continued to hope for some opening in the CCF. He returned to Canada to wrap up his work with the FCSO, and to Winnipeg to help settle his father's estate.

This took some time, and for months after he had formally immigrated to the United States in March of 1938 he corresponded with the Winnipeg lawyers on the financial settlement of his father's estate, the abandonment of the large house at 54 Westgate, and the renting of a smaller house for his mother and sisters remaining at home. (The former house was eventually purchased by the University Women's Club of Winnipeg and now stands as the Ralph Connor House.) He received two short letters from J.S. Woodsworth during this time, hand-written on House of Commons stationery. One was in response to receiving King's gift copy of his father's autobiography, *Postscript to Adventure,* which included C.W. Gordon's own introduction. "It all brings back memories," Woodsworth wrote. "Your grandfather, Dr King, was for two years one of my teachers [at United College]. As a teacher, I think the one who made the greatest impression on me. You have a goodly heritage!"[62] Gordon particularly cherished the message of the other letter. "Dear King, We were so sorry you had to leave us for a while. But I do hope that some of these days the way may open for your return. We need you in Canada."[63]

Frank Scott wrote wistfully:

> Dear King,
>
> So you have taken the plunge. I feel that a certain chapter in Canadian history has ended. Wherever one turns, the A.O. Dawsons and the J.A. Ewings seem to be on top, more secure than ever and twice as righteous.
>
> However, I am sure you have done the best thing. Even if you had not the new personal responsibilities to assume, I feel that perhaps it was time for you to make a break with a certain type of life. If you are ever going to start again, you [must] start fresh. And things are surely going to start again, whether we do or not. The trouble is that they most likely won't start until we begin to gather up the fragments at the bottom of the precipice.

It might be a good plan if we closed a lot more chapters. I feel the LSR might take a two-year rest with advantage … We ought all to write our personal histories and interpretations now. (Graham, by the way, is planning a book.) Other members of the LSR persist in keeping the group alive, however, and we are actually holding our next convention in Toronto on April 9th. Hadn't you better join us?

Let us know when you are coming through again, and if you want a bed we have one.

Sincerely, Frank.[64]

9

J. King Gordon's Christian Socialism

By the time Gordon emigrated to the United States in March of 1938, the foundational tenets and metaphors of his Christian socialism had shaped themselves into a theory that did not alter fundamentally in the following years.[1] He modified certain positions, as did others of the CCF, for example in the welfare statism and mixed economy doctrines of the Winnipeg Manifesto of 1956. And he applied his principles of economic and social justice to an increasingly international community as he moved into the secretariat of the United Nations and pursued his deep interest in international relations. But these adaptations and modifications expressed no abrupt or discordant departures from earlier principles. His writings and career in the late 1920s and early 1930s offer an arresting instance of a young Canadian theologian finding his place among the major currents of Christian social thought.

In the 1930s, a time of turmoil and soul-searching among the intellectual and church communities, contemporary philosophies such as the social gospel, Fabian socialism, and even Marxism afforded possible interpretations of events and provided motivations for action for Gordon and his peers. While he was foremost an activist among his colleagues of the League for Social Reconstruction, the CCF, and the Fellowship for a Christian Social Order, Gordon also struggled to forge his own coherent theory of Christian social action from the received tradition. In Gordon's case, this inheritance consisted mainly of the moderate segment of the social gospel; his father's Presbyterianism; and the radical pessimism of Reinhold Niebuhr. In dialogue with these three sources of influence, King Gordon formulated his theory around the central metaphor of the Kingdom of God, a metaphor that bears examination as an interpretive key to his own motivation and action.

King always claimed that his Christian socialism began at his father's table in Winnipeg where, as a boy, he listened to passionate discussions of current social issues, absorbing the intensity of the argument long before he could comprehend its content.[2] On both sides his ancestors had represented a tradition of community service stretching back to the early 1840s in Upper Canada and the Eastern Townships. At Oxford in 1921, the social concerns that he had absorbed at home were interpreted and reinforced by his exposure to the Fabians. When he returned to Canada in 1924 to take up student missionary work in the West, however, his theories, socialist or otherwise, were still largely inchoate, and it was not until 1929 when he began his studies at Union Seminary, under the tutelage of Reinhold Niebuhr and Harry Ward, that he began to formulate his own philosophy of Christian socialism in any systematic way. The one invaluable component that he did take with him to New York, however, was a deep comradeship and ease with working people and a sympathetic understanding of their problems, garnered from his experiences with his parishioners in the forests of British Columbia and the company town of Pine Falls, Manitoba.

Gordon's first teacher was his father. The lessons he learned from C.W. Gordon largely reflected the theological assumptions of the social gospel sweeping the Protestant churches of Western Europe and North America before the First World War. The term "social gospel" can be used to refer broadly to any efforts to apply Christian charity to society in a reformist way. However, the Christian social gospel of the late nineteenth-century was a distinct phenomenon, a departure from the intensely individualist assumptions of both Christian and secular thought earlier in the century.[3] In the earlier view, the source of social problems lay largely within individuals; consequently, solutions were also individual – acts of charity, and reformed wills and hearts. The more modern concept of the social gospel, in contrast, understood persons as social creatures and largely products of society; therefore the gospel had to be applied to social systems and structures. The movement generally was optimistic about social reconstruction, denying the doctrine of the fall with its consequent corruption of the will. Human institutions as well as human beings were malleable, as readily shaped by good as by evil. The social gospel therefore emphasized the reform of society, for the morally regenerated institution would then mold the new moral person.[4]

King wrote of his father that he "never spoke of the 'social gospel'; the Christian gospel for him was a social gospel."[5] But Richard Allen has described him as representative of the progressive social gospel: the centrality of the community, the goal of human development, a view of God as immanent in his creation, and a church that placed "conduct and utility" ahead of "creedal orthodoxy."[6] C.W. Gordon's Calvinism provided a further foundation for the reassertion of the social mandate of the Christian gospel as it was preached by John Calvin himself, and John Knox and Jonathan Edwards, all of whom conceived and promoted a society in which social and economic relationships were governed in accordance with Christian principles.[7] The goal of these earlier theories was more to prevent social disintegration than to construct an institutional context that would encourage moral regeneration. However, the evangelical influences of the Free Kirk movement in Canada had, by C.W. Gordon's day, considerably transformed the rigidity of the earlier Calvinism, and within this altered consciousness, the senior Gordon and other Canadian Presbyterians eased their way into the wider context of the social gospel.

But C.W. Gordon still retained elements of the evangelism of his father's Free Kirk in his understanding of the nature of social reform. King recalled conversations he had with his father after the formation of the LSR and the CCF, in which the senior Gordon expressed distrust in the confidence of their members as to the efficacy of bringing about fundamental changes through alterations in the social and economic environment, and he expressed concern that socialist control was in danger of mirroring capitalist control. Institutional change, the reform itself, was necessary and moral, but simply changing the system was not enough and King's father was distrustful of fundamental changes in the environment without a corresponding change in the human heart. In spite of his great optimism about what could be accomplished by a church dedicated to the wellbeing of all humankind, he did not fall into the romantic tradition of the social gospel that saw human progress to new ethical heights as inevitable. For C.W. Gordon, the individual always remained the actor, and for this reason he argued that neither radical adjustments of the environment aimed at reshaping the individual, nor blind optimism in inexorable progress, took adequate account of human freedom and power of choice.[8] These themes recur in the thought of his son.

It was out of this theological background – and the intervening influence of Fabian thought at Oxford – that King approached his studies with Reinhold Niebuhr and Harry Ward at Union in 1929; and it was Niebuhr, with his vibrant energy and passionate focus on the church's role in bringing about social justice, who first forced King to think analytically and to look critically at his own unexamined and gentle optimism. Niebuhr challenged the optimism of American theological thinking, stirred out of his liberal idealism and pacifism by the social realities of a rapidly expanding industrial community during his ministry in Detroit. He saw the Christian "law of love" in danger of becoming merely sentimental if unrelated to justice, and his *Moral Man and Immoral Society* was a heroic rejection of the social gospel's faith in the politics of love and reason and its confidence that the Kingdom of God could be realized within history. In Niebuhr's thinking, power relationships rather than ethical considerations became the central feature in social reform, and progress toward a more just society would come out of struggle, conflict, and organization; moreover, the changed society emerging out of this necessary conflict would always contain some of the unethical characteristics of the conflict and its motivations. The political achievement must always be fragmentary, an uneasy balance of power, limited and incomplete. Yet the Christian must strive to ensure that those who possessed power were endowed with the largest measure of ethical self-control, so that the Christian spirit might mitigate the harsher features of the struggle, all the while despairing of its goals being completely achieved.

Niebuhr came to see radical ambiguity at the heart of every human enterprise. Since every achievement of human virtue and rationality bears an element of evil and unreason, it is folly to attempt to establish the Kingdom of Heaven within history or to achieve perfection through human effort. This is the human tragedy. Consequently, Niebuhr advocated a philosophy of social action without the utopian illusions of either liberal culture or Marxism, both of which reflected the same confidence in one's unlimited capacity for self-improvement. For Niebuhr, only by the breaking into history of a wholly transcendent God could the Kingdom be fully realized.[9]

At first, caught up in the heady excitement of being Niebuhr's teaching assistant and in the social action projects of the Union Seminary student body, Gordon drank deeply from the Niebuhrian well. Gradually, however, during his time back in Canada in the 1930s, strong elements of his father's Presbyterianism and his own confidence in the optimism of social gospel thinking re-emerged, and eventually he departed radically from Niebuhr's positions. As he taught at United Theological College and then travelled widely throughout Canada, participating in the growing radical movement in the United Church, the LSR, the CCF, and the FCSO, he took what he had learned from Niebuhr, refining, redefining, integrating, until he came to his own understanding of the role of Christian action in history. His theories on the Christian in politics and his justification for Christian political action appeared in publications of the LSR, the FCSO, and journals of the period such as the *Canadian Forum* and the *Christian Century*.[10] He also developed his ideas in unpublished sermons and lectures, given before his students and congregations as well as trade union groups, CCF Clubs, cooperatives, and study groups of all kinds.

The question Gordon faced, of the relationship between the Christian and society, has persisted in the Christian community since its inception. Ought the Christian to participate in the political realm at all, or does the command to renounce the world and its evil ways involve a withdrawal from secular affairs, and a retreat into mysticism? How does the Christian act to bring about change in the world? Can the Christian, through political action, bring the values of religion to bear upon the structures of society? Can one expect to see these values realized in this world, or does this wait upon the arrival of a post-temporal state of being?

The metaphor of the Kingdom of God, prevalent in theological thinking of the period, became the central organizing principle in Gordon's ethical and political thought. He defined the Kingdom as "that state of harmonious dwelling together in which each individual by exercising his will in accordance with the principle of its true value attains to the highest degree of self realization."[11] It is an inner reality, a realm of values, embodying the spiritual and creative aspects of human experience. It is set in contrast to the kingdom of this world, the material, the mechanical, the realm of human predatory instincts and will to acquisition. But Gordon allowed neither a radical dichotomy between these two realms nor a flight into mysticism that would deny the material world. Believing that one must seek to transform the secular world of everyday experience so that it reflected the values of the Kingdom, he affirmed the mutually necessary nature of both. He told his congregation:

> The material realm is God's world ... Here are men born, nurtured at their mothers' breasts, build their homes, extract from the earth products necessary to sustain their lives. Here are men to develop their arts, perfect their skills, and discover more concerning the wonders of their world so that their lives may be richer. Here are they to found their community. In their ever-widening community, in their relationships with one another, a concern for the material becomes

> less and less. But if any groups of them are cut off from their material basis of life, they perish, just as truly as they perish as spiritual beings if they are cut off from the fellowship of the community. [We] are long past the point where we can … insist that to maintain the spiritual is to emphasize its importance to the exclusion or suppression of the material.[12]

The first step in bringing about this transformation, he argued, is to repent of one's part in that society that represents the refusal of the Kingdom. To do this, one must accept responsibility for the social calamity that the refusal to acknowledge the spiritual dimension has produced and assert the reality of the spirit. Such repentance would also mean renouncing an atomistic and mechanistic interpretation of the universe, and embracing an organic, functional whole.

The way of the Kingdom is compassion – not pity – involving shared suffering with others. One source of this suffering in society lies with the war that rages within the individual between nature and spirit, between primitive acquisitive selfish impulses and a spiritual urge to seek the realization of the good. This war is not absolute, as the ascetic tradition would have one believe, nor can a solution be achieved through the suppression of one side by another. The spiritual and the natural must thus be integrated so that the natural life expresses the life of the spirit. Moreover, human personality is given fullest expression only in organic relation to the community. But where society denies that organic relationship, it also denies the full expression of the spiritual life, and causes suffering among its members.

No calm observer of twentieth-century civilization, Gordon noted, could possibly describe the relationship of individual to community as organic. The flaming creed of the nineteenth century proclaimed the rights of the individual over and against society. The new economic science asserted that the good of all was promoted when each served his own end. The result is a fragmented society whose individuals survive by competition, which in turn produces a vast disparity in the distribution of material goods, and thus dictates that economic concerns be the chief preoccupation of human lives. The misery of the poor renders their spiritual development impossible: "If you offer the good life to the man who starves, you might just as well offer him a stone. Curtailed education, ill-health from undernourishment, over work, enforced idleness, the never absent sense of insecurity – these are the practical denials to entering the Kingdom of Heaven for the majority of our working population."[13]

However, he argued, it was not enough to condemn the present society: the situation called for action. At this point, King found the optimistic hymn of progress of the social gospel insufficiently radical to deal with the evil embedded in social institutions; but neither could he find a solution in Marxism, which he rejected for its materialism, its statement of class conflict purely in terms of the clash of rival powers, and its utopian claim that a higher state of society would leap into being when the capitalist order was destroyed. "There is always the danger that into the form of the new society will be poured the old materialism which is the essential evil of our present order."[14]

How then can the old society be uprooted and a new society be established consistent with the principles of the Kingdom? An essential requirement is an organized and committed group of people, free from vengeance and hatred, and prepared to present their vision of the good society in a language that ordinary people can understand. Using all available educational, social, and economic means, they must evolve plans for change that will then be implemented by peaceful political means. Finally, they must constantly challenge and search, realizing that because the Kingdom can never be completely realized on earth, it must always preserve its revolutionary character. To refuse to act is to watch the emergence of an order lacking ethical purpose.[15]

One finds here elements of Niebuhr's influence: the radical nature of evil within the human heart and in human society, and the need for individual political action to bring about a more tolerable state of social life; the Niebuhrian rejection of easy optimism about inevitable improvement in the human condition, and even about how much one can expect to be accomplished. But in his assertion that Christian groups can act both ethically and effectively within society, King rejected Niebuhr's absolute dichotomy between the Christian ethic and the requirements of political action. In doing so, he also rejected coercion rather than persuasion as the necessary means of gaining agreement or, at least, compliance.[16]

Gordon's most cogent critique of Niebuhr, and an apposite clarification of his own statement of Christian social action, is found in his review of *Reflections on the End of an Era,* a collection of Niebuhr's essays published in 1934.[17] On 23 February 1934, he wrote to Niebuhr: "Your book has given me a terrible time, physically, spiritually, intellectually and ethically. You probably gathered as much from my review of it ... In many ways, I think it is the biggest thing you have done, even if it has not the same continuity as 'Moral Man.' You may think me a bit unfair in my basic criticism; if so, shoot away. My friends who are reading the book, or having it read to them, are responding either enthusiastically – or violently. That is a fairly sure test of a book's significance."[18]

Niebuhr's essays reflected his deepening pessimism, portraying humanity as a desperate but futile contender in a world dominated by demonic forces within oneself as well as within one's warring world. King commented that Niebuhr's fatalism as he contemplated the end of the era was closer to Spengler than to Marx. He argued that Niebuhr, in his revolt from the easy and shallow evolutionary optimism of liberal Christianity, had swung over to an extreme transcendentalism that despaired of valid ethical or religious achievement in human affairs. This religious absolutism, with its accompanying despair, raised the two major points of Gordon's disagreement with Niebuhr: First, he objected to Niebuhr's distrust of human nature. He wrote:

> Now it is only an extreme form of self-renunciatory and ascetic religion which judges all men's impulses as evil *per se*. There is surely an ethical distinction between the self-interest so admirably illustrated in the "economic man" of the nineteenth century political economist and the "natural" will-to-live as representing an urge to full self-expression, even after we have made full allowance for the optimistic sentimentality of errant disciples of J. J. Rousseau. The first is easily transmuted into a will-to-power which takes the form of the exploitation of others; the second may express itself in the highest search for cultural and spiritual development and frequently represents the ethical basis of revolution where individuals realize they are denied what is necessary to their highest development.[19]

For King, individual and environment interact, neither being rigidly determinant. The natural human impulse may produce evil in society; but it may also produce an environment in which the drive to spiritual fulfillment will be encouraged. Society may operate to degrade and to deprive, hampering efforts to act upon only the best motives; but it may also provide support for the highest human strivings. On this matter Gordon's thought has a flexibility and openness not found in Niebuhr's, and a far more radical rationale for individual Christian political action. Here King drew on the optimism of his social gospel background, but no longer uncritically so, for the realization of the good is no more certain than the inevitability of evil. And so Christians cast themselves with all available strength and resources into a battle that is a real war and no mock skirmish.

At this point Gordon parted company with Niebuhr on a second issue: the latter's despair of gaining ascertainable social-ethical advance in the field of politics. Niebuhr wrote, "The pessimistic assumption of classical religion that no political order can fully incarnate the highest ideal is the natural consequence of the transcendent perspective of high religion."[20] His antipathy to liberal Protestantism constantly inclined him to make this pessimism his own. The logical demand of such a position, King argued, was ascetic withdrawal from an evil world, taking consolation in the "assurances of grace" (the title of the last essay in Niebuhr's book). King could not follow Niebuhr in such pessimism. For, he claimed, there is another element in religious absolutism identified by Niebuhr himself in his earlier writings: to the prophet in action, the absolute is not only the conviction of sin, but also the *assurance* of the ultimate triumph of God's purposes in history. He wrote: "The Christian realist rejoices when the secular realist is filled with despair and when the pure mystic retires to gain solitary consolation. His insights into the absolute keep him humble, but they also give him assurance of victory. And by this assertion of an impossible victory, he makes that victory real. It should be Reinhold Niebuhr, and not his humble critic [King Gordon] who says, 'Except the faith of a Christian exceed the faith of a Marxist, he shall in no wise enter the Kingdom of Heaven.'"[21]

Niebuhr's pessimism had tempered King's own natural optimism and banished any vestiges of the social gospel's faith in inevitable progress, but Niebuhr's despair, and his commitment to a transcendent Deity who breaks into history cataclysmically, did not overcome King's own theological heritage from his Presbyterian forebears and from his father, whose conviction rested with a God immanent in His creation who works through His church to accomplish His will in history. King summed it up simply later in his life: "[S]hort of perfection, a good deal can be accomplished [through political action]. I have always believed this, and I still do."[22]

Gordon's view of the Kingdom as at once historical and trans-historical raises the question of how this metaphor functions in his theory and to what degree he expected its literal realization on earth. Niebuhr candidly and courageously suggested that there need not – and probably would not – be a solution to social problems. He proclaimed the folly and futility of every attempt to establish the Kingdom of Heaven within history, for history is not its own redeemer. Its destiny remains ambiguous to the end; and this is the human tragedy. The concept of the Kingdom for Niebuhr, therefore, functioned eschatologically: the transcendent God brings about the Kingdom in His own good time. Meanwhile, political action must be directed toward altering the power structures of society. Manipulation of power, not love, is the only way to bring about social change; but human power will never bring in the Kingdom.

Gordon did not leave the world to this tragic fate. In a review of Niebuhr's *Beyond Tragedy,* he wrote:

> The importance of the religious conception of human tragedy is that it goes "Beyond Tragedy." That is the essential difference between the Christian view of man's fate and the Greek view. The Greeks concluded that man's *hubris* quite properly called for the jealousy and vengeance of the gods. The cycle kept repeating itself ... But in the tradition of our religion the break in the cycle is found. Beyond tragedy there is mercy and there is redemption. The purpose of God and even the judgment of God are directed not merely to human punishment but to human salvation. Beyond the tragedies of the kingdoms of this world there is the Kingdom of God. And since the Kingdom of God is in history as well as beyond history, man is never quite abandoned to his tragic fate.[23]

And since the Kingdom of God is in history as well as beyond history – this immanence of God gives impetus to political action without Niebuhr's split between ethics and power. For the Kingdom comes neither apocalyptically nor inevitably; it comes through the obedient actions of the children of God. Such a vital role endows political action with *final,* not merely interim, significance, as in such action the Christian fulfills the otherwise unrealizable purpose of God in the world. Thus, the concept of the Kingdom provides both impetus and justification for political action within history where a great deal – but not perfection – may be achieved.

However, the Kingdom image in Gordon's theory is not collapsed into immanence. It also serves a utopian function. Northrop Frye argued that a utopia is not a concrete program for building an ideal state, but operates to educate its readers for social existence. Plato, in his *Republic*, for instance, was not expecting to set up his ideal state anywhere; nor, for all his political involvement as Lord Chancellor under Henry VIII, did Sir Thomas More expect the arrival of his utopia. Rather, Plato and More were concerned about the analogy between the ideal state and the structure of the wise mind.[24] Even at his most enthusiastic, Gordon did not suppose that the Kingdom of God would be ushered in with the arrival of the CCF in Ottawa. To take so literally his comments about the historical nature of the Kingdom is to mistake the utopian function of his metaphor. The Kingdom – that realm of value in which one fully realizes one's potential as a human being – functions as a vision within history, and an education for what might be possible. That goal the Christian must never abandon, even while knowing it will not be fully realized. It is historical and it is visionary. It speaks of now and it speaks of the end time.

Gordon's image of the Kingdom acted powerfully on his own understanding of socialism. It reminded him, first, that socialism and a just society are intermediate goals, and that beyond these goals one must pursue an ultimate vision of society that includes spiritual capacities and concerns.[25] For him, socialism, as an economic and political arrangement of human affairs, most adequately expressed the spiritual principles of Jesus. But socialism deals with externals, with the right ordering of material life, and while the significance of the political and the economic must never be underestimated, one must look beyond the material and encompass the spiritual dimension as well. The ultimate goal for the Christian is always the Kingdom.

Gordon stipulated that Christianity has a profound role to play in the movement for a reconstructed society. The church must not become a political body nor identify itself with one political movement, lest it lose its moral prerogative of judging the institutions of society. But it must identify itself with the cause of the oppressed and offer support to the political group that acts in the interests of the downtrodden. It must bring to the struggle all the resources of a high ethical religion. It must mitigate the role of violence and the spirit of vengeance. He concluded, "[I]ts goal stated in terms of social justice and individual self-realization will, in the main, include the goal of Socialism, but will go beyond."[26] Interestingly, Gordon found the template encompassing both the material and the spiritual in the Antigonish Movement at St Francis Xavier University in Nova Scotia when he visited there while travelling with the FCSO. He did not claim, however, that Antigonish represented a truly socialist society, only that it indicated one way in which the spiritual and material aspects of life could be successfully combined.[27]

Second, he pointed out, the Kingdom metaphor sets norms that a socialist system would have to meet in order to realize humanity's fullest potential. If, for example, the human spirit is to be free to pursue the higher values of the Kingdom, the state must not be allowed to exercise totalitarian power. King vehemently rejected totalitarianism in any form, although in the 1930s, before Stalin's purges became known, he directed his attack largely against fascism. In "The Political Task," written in 1936, he opened his article: "The political task of our generation is that of preventing the rise of the totalitarian state in the remaining democratic countries of the world ... [and] the furthering of a state organized to provide economic security and maintain individual liberty. The two tasks are essentially one. For the only sure bulwark against fascism is to be found in the successful organization of the socialized state."[28]

But while he rejected the domination of the individual by the state, King contended that in the reconstruction of society a legitimate use of state power is both possible and necessary. With the close relationship of the political and the economic in modern industrialized society an accomplished fact, the economic needs of the people have come to be one of the chief concerns of the state. But the phrase, "the economic life of the people" might mean one of two things: the provision of the economic necessities of life; or, the organization and operation of the industrial system to provide for the needs or the profits of its owners. It is in the former sense that King, like his Fabian mentors, found the use of state power justified.

Gordon was also on his guard against paternalistic forms of state power that limit personal development and sap initiative and creativity. The egalitarian norm inherent in his Kingdom metaphor operated powerfully in Gordon's socialist vision. During his own experience with ordinary working people, he encouraged the participation of the people at every level of policy making.[29] While he was always careful to point out that institutions such as strong trade unions and cooperatives must not be considered a substitute for socialism,[30] their presence mitigated and balanced state power.[31] In the socialist government of Saskatchewan, elected in 1944, Gordon later felt that he had found a model of socialism free from both totalitarian tendencies and debilitating paternalism.[32]

One persistent question for the young socialists of the CCF was whether Canada could develop a distinctly Canadian socialism, or whether it would always carry colonial vestiges of, for example, the British Labour party or the Fabians. J.S. Woodsworth himself, at the First National Convention of the CCF in Regina in 1933, had said, "I am convinced that we may develop in Canada a distinctive type of socialism. I refuse to follow slavishly the British model or the American model or the Russian model."[33] This preoccupation was part of the larger question of national identity that haunted Canadian artists, writers, and poets following the First World War, and Frank Scott, who straddled the worlds of both the arts and politics, wrote about the issue of Canadian colonialism with particular poignancy: "It is more a cast of thought, a mental climate. The colonial is an incomplete person … He must look to others for his guidance, and far away for his criterion of value. He copies the parental style instead of incorporating what is best in something of his own. He undervalues his own contribution and over-estimates what others can do for him. Old greatness is more to him than new truth.[34]

It was unlikely that Canada would develop a form of socialism radically different from that of Western Europe and Great Britain, for despite a certain difference in social conditions, English Canada's own social and intellectual heritage at that time was largely British and Western European, and, of course, nearly all of the founders of the LSR and many of the CCF were of British ancestry, educated partially in England or in the Canadian schools of English-speaking Canada, where to be Canadian was to be British; or were even recent immigrants from the British Isles. In a hypothetical "Field Guide to Socialist Birds," Canadian socialism would be distinguishable by its local markings: it would qualify as a regional variant, but not as a new or separate species. These distinguishing features might be identified as the emphasis on tenure in land for the farmer; the adaptation of socialism to a federal state; state ownership and control of the development of natural resources; a reliance upon the rural classes for support; and an alliance of farmers with professional and labouring classes. But certainly Canadian socialism operated out of the same assumptions as did the British democratic socialists, and it shared the same goals regarding the nature of the class struggle and the role of the state in bringing about economic reform.

Unlike Frank Scott and other friends, such as Frank Underhill, for whom the specifically Canadian character of their socialism constituted a pressing issue, Gordon seems to have been singularly free of colonial angst. This may in part be accounted for simply by temperament and background; he was above all a pragmatist, sensitive to issues and at times caught in keen intellectual struggles, but never paralyzed by them.

Moreover, he had inherited an easy sense of national identity that doubtless flowed first of all from his family's roots in Canadian history and culture, and from his own secure boyhood, welcome in all levels of Canadian life as the son of Ralph Connor; it also grew out of his own extensive experience with Canadian people of all ranks and professions and from his profound respect for their struggle. As he watched them establish their own cooperatives and credit unions, trade unions, and other institutions in an attempt to improve their lives, he recognized a hardy and even canny political prowess among Canadians. Here was no colonial, dependent mentality, but a people capable of developing their own political forms to solve their own political problems. For King, the power and energy of the CCF flowed upward from the working people of Canada, not downward from its intellectuals, or across the sea from the Fabians. Despite the fact that he spent much of his adult life abroad, he had a keenly developed perception of a Canadian political consciousness as indigenous within the people themselves, and a political culture sharply defined as Canadian. To return to the metaphor of the Kingdom of God, always central to his thinking, it conferred a great transcendent dignity along with a sense of historical urgency on these individuals who struggled against the oppression of capitalism.

The vitality of the image of the Kingdom continued to dominate Gordon's thinking as he moved into his later career. While he no longer spoke specifically of its theological implications, he applied it powerfully on a humanistic level. King recognized that, because the boundaries of the Kingdom encompass all humankind, one must work at breaking down the barriers of inequality and injustice between humans on an international level.

Gordon never lost his admiration for the Antigonish Movement, or his conviction that it embodied a core principle necessary to healthy socialism: the integration of the material *and* spiritual elements of humankind. When he left Canada in 1938, King moved into less specifically political forms of endeavour, but he remained a Christian socialist to the end of his life, supporting a form of socialism informed by metaphor, "that state of harmonious dwelling together in which each individual by exercising his will in accordance with the principle of its true value attains to the highest degree of self realization; a realm of being combining the creative and spiritual aspects of human experience with the fair distribution of those material goods necessary to sustain and nourish physical life."[35]

10

New York and Wartime Publishing

King had become weary of his itinerant life during his three years of traversing Canada; as he repeatedly mentioned to his mother, he was ready to have a home. And so, on his arrival in New York to edit his father's autobiography and take up a position as non-fiction editor with Farrar and Rinehart, he settled happily into his Manhattan sublet. On 24 September 1938, he wrote to his mother that apart from the walk upstairs, his new apartment had no disadvantages. He looked out upon dozens of trees and the back gardens stretching to Park Avenue. Best of all, the young woman from whom he was subletting had left her gramophone-radio and her records. It was a sunny afternoon, and with the quiet of the apartment broken only by Bach, he wrote contentedly: "I think it is going to mean that I become a home-staying young man for a change. It is like a new start in life. I went downtown and made two most important purchases – a laundry bag at Woolworth's and the first volume of A Well Tempered Clavicord! Now there is little else I need for my comfort."[1]

Little else, indeed! At the time of his move to New York King was thirty-eight years old, an age at which one could reasonably expect he might also need a wife. It was not that he lacked admirers: with his Celtic good looks (tall and athletic, coal black hair and clear blue eyes), his self-confident bearing and his charming disposition, he was surely one of the more eligible and sought-after bachelors in his circle of friends, and in fact he had had several affairs of the heart. Despite his *bonhomie*, however, Gordon was always private and rather reticent about his feelings and deep emotions. A journal fragment written in the fall of 1937 in his Montreal apartment, "Reflections on Oxford," gives a rare glimpse into the reflective and introspective side of his personality as he explored the terrain of his inner life:

> I don't know why tonight so many cars and trucks go hurtling by leaving a roar behind them when last night, were there any? But each car as it fades away leaves an emptiness in this room. And in the fireplace are a few blackened sticks and a heap of white ashes. My own weariness, after 120 miles [200 km] of driving and a speech, just adds to the dismal furnishings. Matter and spirit. For last night there was fire and warmth and the spirit-fire which burns and does not consume but gives life. And the whole house was so crowded with loveliness that there was no room for emptiness and weariness and ashes. And here is a great mystery of the spirit and body of man.[2]

He had been reading Dorothy Sayers' *Gaudy Night*, which awakened "an old nostalgia, lifting a curtain you felt was decently dropped forever. For what has Oxford, with its discordant bells, its silent spires and towers, its drowsy rivers, its mouldering stones – what has Oxford to do with the world of 1937?" Looking back, he wondered how what had meant so much to him – for he was not one of those who feigned boredom at Oxford – could have been dropped so completely. For it was Oxford that began his intellectual awakening; and moreover, while Oxford had "probably disturbed me more than it fed me, it did so without disillusionment," as those who had then awakened him were friends[3] and no amount of realism could destroy the reality of genuine relationships.

Still, for all the gentleness of this awakening, he found himself regretting that it had taken him so long to achieve satisfactory emotional-intellectual integration. On that lonely night in Montreal he explored the reasons for this delay, concluding that despite having been "flooded from the very beginning of my existence with affection, I was, nevertheless brought up in a distrust of emotion." Was this, he wondered, because of the Calvinist tradition with its emphasis on moral discipline, chastity, temperance and intellectual appraisal? In any case, when he left his loving home, he was "repressed, sentimental and with the woolliest concepts of intellectual training and integrity." While Oxford took care of his intellectual growth, his emotional side – which he now regarded as far more important – remained undeveloped.

By upbringing and good fortune, he was wise in his selection of friends at Oxford who, despite their youth, proved authentic and emotionally mature. At the same time, however, he had few if any mature relationships with women, something he put down to "early repressions and just damned ignorance." Even from the distance of 1937, he wrote: "I grow angry at that abominable tradition which made boys grow into men thinking of love, except in its sentimentalized forms, as something a little shameful, of sex-relationships as identifiable with 'lust,' and of women as the inevitable object of that lust. Angry, because in an amazingly rich life love did not come to me except in a sentimentalized or romantic form, always slightly dishonest, always crashing against ruinous inhibitions."[4]

In short, he felt, "Oxford floated a dream world to be dissipated by my increasing knowledge of the world as it is; Oxford, a deceiver of the past, promising light for the journey, leading by primrose paths to sunlit but empty meadows."[5] His long reverie brought King to the conclusion that one could not be a mature adult while clinging to a divided life, and that one never rids oneself of the past by disowning it. It is only by integrating one's past into one's present that one achieves maturity. "It takes not just courage but also prudence to see that one object of living is to make your life a whole."[6]

It is hardly surprising that in the year following these insights into his own emotional life, King should find the person who would share his life for the next fifty years.

Ruth Anderson was the art production editor at Farrar and Rinehart, and King first met her when they worked together on the design and production of his father's autobiography, *Postscript to Adventure*. He was immediately captivated by her warmth, intelligence, quick wit, and sense of humour, and by the way she would spot human foibles with a gentle irony that lacked all trace of malice. They shared a common outlook on social issues – generous and inclusive – and King admired Ruth's prodigious reading and passion for books. Ruth was born in Brooklyn in 1910, making her ten years his junior, and grew up in Mountain Lakes, New Jersey. In her early twenties, having earned a high-school diploma from Emma Willard Girls' School in Troy, New York, she returned to New York City and, after a year as a receptionist in the New York Public Library, joined the editorial staff at Farrar and Rinehart. By the time King arrived, she was art editor of the ambitious Rivers of America series, which until that time had included no Canadian rivers. King encouraged the choice of Henry Beston to write about the St Lawrence River, and Bruce Hutchison the Fraser. He also suggested that the Canadian painter A.Y. Jackson, one of the Group of Seven, do the art. At the end of the project, Jackson gave Ruth the original endpaper, as well as a painting that she treasured until the end of her life. With her encouraging manner and ubiquitous blue pencil, Ruth became a favourite editor among Farrar and Rinehart authors, and inscriptions on the fly-leaves of many of her books touch one with their sincerity and humour. Another editor, who had been moved in as her office mate "so that she could keep an eye on him," inscribed the gift of one of his books to her, "with all my heart to Ruth Anderson, who wrote more of this book than I did. Ogden Nash."[7]

There was a ripple in this story of true love, however; perhaps not an obstacle, but an issue that had to be faced. After a brief marriage in her early twenties, Ruth had been divorced. At this time, the United Church stand on remarriage was ambiguous, but that was not the problem. The predicament lay in the genuine horror of divorce common in respectable families of the time, particularly in more socially conservative Canada. The Gordon family was not immune to this attitude. However, their feelings did not arise out of a desire to avoid scandal, but were grounded in a deep religious understanding of marriage. On breaking the news of their intentions to his mother, King received a heart-rending reply:

> My dearest King,
>
> I feel I must write you right away, for I know you must have felt my silence and my inability to say anything to you. I think the terrible shock of what had happened was too much for me so that the joy that should have been in my heart, that you were to be happy, just could not show itself. I feel as if the very foundations had been taken from under me. Never did I want Daddy so much, for he is the only one that could help me. Divorce has always been such a dreadful thing to me and that it is happening, among those we know, seems so alarming. But I never knew it would come so close to me. It is like some sort of bad dream, that I just can't get out of my mind. You said it had been a great strain and worry to you and Ruth, so you won't be surprised that it upset me so much. I know this would not have happened if you could not have done it with a clear conscience, and my prayer is that you will be very happy together and be a great blessing to others. I am positive that the breakdown in so many homes is because there is not a religious life to hold them together. That was certainly what kept our home together and I so long to see it in the homes of our children. So the one thing that I coveted for you was that you should get a wife who would have the same ideals

that you have. Nothing else matters. I feel sure that Ruth is such a girl from what you say, and hope that as I get to know her better, she will be all I could desire for you. She certainly is getting a husband who will be good to her. You have been a perfect son and you will be a perfect husband. It would have been hard for me to pick any one that I would have considered good enough for you. If I have said anything to hurt you, forgive me, my dearest boy. I only want you to be happy in the best sense of the word. I can't write Ruth yet, but will in a day or two.

... On reading this letter over, I don't know whether I should send it or not, but my heart is so full, and I can't talk to anybody, so I don't think you will mind. My love to Ruth, and tell her I will write her very soon. With very much love, my own darling boy.[8]

He replied:

Mother dearest,

Your letter has just come and my heart is very sore. I know that you must feel hurt though I did not know at the time that it would seem such a shattering blow. Mother darling, it cuts me very deep that I should bring you this unhappiness and all the more so because I wanted so much to have you made happy by my marriage. And we will, mother. Ruth is so awfully anxious that you should be happy in us. I know that you will come to love her.

I don't know what I can say to make you feel better now. I feel partly lost myself sometimes because anybody who takes a course that is against that approved by society finds life lonely – and I'm quite sure that many of my friends will think amiss of us. I can only say that Ruth and I both realize it and are going to be married because marriage must be made something that is deep and rich and beautiful or else it becomes a travesty.

King continued, explaining to his mother that his relationships with women had not been happy and that had certain of these attempts to find love been realized, disaster would have ensued. Now, for the first time he was completely sure. His relationship with Ruth had brought back to him a certain sense of security in the world that he feared he had been losing: "Because somehow a discovery of love that was real and strong carried you to the very heart of what was real in the spiritual world." With the courage of a son seeking the integration and authenticity that he spoke of in his Oxford reflections,[9] he pressed on:

> Mother dear. It has always been difficult for our family to talk about the deep things and we have kept our feelings always hidden from one another. I have often thought that that has not been good. For one thing, I think all the children have so admired you that they have tried to keep their intense griefs, disappointments, fears, to themselves lest they hurt you. More than that, lest they create a wrong impression. That has not been fair on our part. And as far as we are concerned, I hope that it can change. Our love for one another has always been deep and I hope that my marriage to Ruth is going to lead us into a deeper understanding.
>
> My mother darling. Just have faith in us that we are doing the right thing. I understand so well how you feel. But you must not be unhappy. We are going to make a good life and those things that Daddy and you lived for and are so much a part of you, we are going to try and realize in our lives together.[10]

His mother's reply, with its reassurance that all would be well, arrived quickly:

> I feel I must write you tonight. Thank you so much for your lovely letter which was a great comfort to me, and I now feel that I should not have written you as I did, but the burden on my mind and heart was too great to bear alone and I just had to let you know how I felt. It was not that I did not think Ruth would make you happy or that she was not all that I could wish for you … I know we will learn to love each other dearly as we get to know each other. In time some of the shock may pass. I could not have decided for you if I would, and you have made your own decision thinking it to be right. All I ask is that God will bless you both and that He will be at the centre of your life and home.[11]

King's predictions that Ruth and his mother would come to love each other, and that he and Ruth would make a good life, realizing the values of his parents in substance if not always in form, were amply fulfilled. Helen Gordon became a mother to Ruth, to a considerable degree healing Ruth's deep sense of loss on her own mother's premature death when

Ruth was scarcely twenty. Helen Gordon's acceptance of Ruth signalled to the family that Ruth was now one of them, and following her example, the sisters took Ruth to their hearts. Grandchildren soon added to the family's sense of fulfillment, with Charles William (his grandfather's namesake) born in November 1940, followed by Alison Ruth in January 1943. Years of devotion on Ruth's part, and the sharing of daily events that make up the fibre of family life, yielded the mutual loyalty that Helen longed for in that first anguished letter.

Ruth and King were married on 6 November 1939, in the Collegiate Church of St Nicholas on Fifth Avenue in New York, with their old family friend, Dr Archie Sinclair, taking the service. King's mother and two of his sisters, Lois and Ruthie, came down for the service. King's cousin Charles Gordon ("Chile" – son of his father's elder brother Gilbert) was best man and Chile's sister Margaret Gordon Forsyth (Mar) and her husband Jim put on a reception. King recalled that when the time came for a toast to the bride, Chile made a charming speech in praise of Ruth. King found himself so touched by Chile's speech and by his cousin's presence at the wedding that he responded at length in praise of Chile, launching on that long journey that they had traveled together since their boyhood days of camping on Birkencraig. Finally, Mar jogged his elbow and whispered, "King, you are responding to the toast to your bride!"[12]

On Ruth's side, her brother Alan and her sister Marie and their families attended, as well as her father, Isaac Anderson (a book editor at the *New York Times*). A newspaper photograph shows the couple leaving the church, King tall and distinguished in his overcoat and silk scarf, fedora in his hand, and scarcely holding back a smile as he looks directly into the camera. Ruth makes no such attempt at restraint: elegant in a short coat and corsage, with a matching cloche tilted stylishly, her face is suffused with a dimpled smile. After a honeymoon in the Laurentians, they returned to New York where their good fortune held and they rented a flat in the MacDougal-Sullivan Gardens in the Village, just south of Bleecker Street. There they had their own small garden as well as access to the common garden running from Bleecker to Houston Streets. On their honeymoon, Ruth wrote to Helen: "I am so awfully happy that you were with us this weekend and most particularly on Monday [the wedding]. It was wonderful of you to make the long trip, and it made our wedding so much more than it could possibly have been without you."[13] By December, Helen was writing to "My dearest Ruth," and telling King, "Everywhere I go so many people ask me about you and Ruth and everyone loves the picture and several have said Ruth just looked as if she belonged to the Gordon type of girl, but they all knew you would pick a lovely girl." Packing up her homemade mincemeat for their Christmas, she asks what they need in the way of household goods.[14]

Gordon's move to New York initiated a period of transition marked by integration and growth, at the end of which his earlier sense of vocation finally came into focus. With the benefit of the perspective that distance makes possible, he was able to reflect on three fundamental and formative aspects of his past – his Oxford years; his Canadian roots, both familial and public; and his earlier American experience at Union Seminary – in such a way as to become free to move in new directions while at the same time continuing to draw on these foundations as a resource for future endeavours.

To begin with, he revisited Oxford at quite a different level of engagement. His deep Oxford friendships continued, but now he moved into new relationships in the British Labour Party, connections that proved significant in his future.

In leaving Canada, Gordon left the security of being known (and loved) as the son of C.W. Gordon, welcome and at home in all levels of Canadian life. In some ways, his leaving was a cruel blow to his assumption that he would find his vocation in Canada, if not in the church, then in politics. He carried with him grief and uncertainty, stepping out into a world that had not – in the sense of Oxford and Canada – been prepared for his coming. The bonds of family and friendship remained, of course, and his ties with the CCF kept the possibility of returning uppermost in his mind.

In spite of the uncertainty of his future in the United States, he plunged ahead with characteristic optimism, re-establishing contact with Reinhold Niebuhr and Harry Ward, but no longer as an uncritical graduate student. In the process, he became active in a myriad of leftist activities and discovered that in some significant ways he had outgrown his Fabian mentors, who now seemed to him uninformed, even parochial, in their view of the world.

Finally, happily anchored in his marriage to Ruth with his new family of two adored children, King found himself freed from his father's reputation and from paternal expectation. His experiences with the CCF had grounded him in the realities of politics. In these early years in New York,

Gordon gained greater freedom (in spite of less security) to move toward that vocation glimpsed fleetingly in his reverie at the Aberdeen estate in the Scottish Highlands: to serve God through service to man.

In spite of Gordon's physical remove to New York, Canadian affairs were never far from his thoughts – or his responsibilities. In the summer of 1942 during a vacation at the island, and quite out of the blue, he was notified that he had been named as Labour representative to the Royal Commission on Steel. The Commission had been established to investigate an industrial dispute in the Canadian steel industry: whether to freeze wages, pitting the government and unions against one another. Against strong pressure from the government-appointed counsel, Gordon took the stand that steel should be categorized as a national industry and, like other industries essential to the war effort, should be exempt from the general wage freeze.[15]

Failing to reach a compromise, Gordon wrote a minority report[16] and asked Frank Scott for his opinion before filing it. Scott responded: "I have been through your opinion for the Steel Commission and think it is excellent. It seems to combine a judicial quality with the right degree of humanity and common sense. The main lines of the argument I would not alter at all."[17]

At least one other notable Canadian concurred with Gordon's opinion: Prime Minister Mackenzie King. Gordon wrote to his mother, "I don't know what to think of that – as a compliment! However, I am glad that they came to some kind of a settlement and along the lines I suggested."[18]

In the meantime, Gordon had settled into his position as non-fiction editor at Farrar and Rinehart. It was an unlikely sequel to his six years as a Christian socialist activist, as his only training as an editor had been in connection with editing his father's autobiography. What drew him to the job initially was probably the family connection with George Doran, his father's editor for many years and the previous owner of the publishing house. By this time, Doran's son-in-law, Stanley Rinehart, his younger brothers, and John Farrar, owned the business. Gordon had immense respect for Stanley Rinehart, with his steady leadership and his business acumen, but in the first instance his tie was with the slight, redheaded, energetic John Farrar.

Gordon had three areas of responsibility as an editor: he prepared accepted manuscripts for publication before passing them on to Ruth Anderson (Gordon) for design; he recommended books for publication;

and he developed ideas for new books, contacting and recruiting potential authors. He threw himself into the task with his customary enthusiasm, and he had the pleasure of producing a bestseller on his first editing assignment.

As might be expected, hard work and high spirits characterized the working day, and after hours King described pennies pitched against the wall, and beer, in the bar of the Duane Hotel across Madison Avenue. The books in which Gordon most deeply invested himself concerned political freedom and social justice, and in some cases dealt with the threat to civilization itself posed by the terrible conflagration then sweeping the world. The titles of the books published at this time – Erich Fromm's *Escape from Freedom*, for instance, or Erika Mann's *Zero Hour* – indicate that Farrar and Rinehart was in the war long before Pearl Harbor, and John Farrar was in the forefront of American liberal and anti-fascist opinion, determined to do all he could to ensure that the United States would become an active partner in the war against Hitler.

In New York, Farrar was responsible for inaugurating a project among publishers called *Books in Wartime*, which brought together authors and publishers in support of the war. (Gordon was placed in charge of Farrar and Rinehart's pamphlet series on war issues). Farrar was also actively involved in many interventionist groups such as the Committee to Defend America by Aiding the Allies, the Fight for Freedom, and the Council for Democracy, to name but a few. He was one of those instrumental in organizing the War Writers Committees that mobilized some of the leading US writers in active pro-Allied propaganda aimed at the isolationist America First movement. Gordon was, of course, pulled into this activity through his professional relationship and friendship with John Farrar. But it was not only friendship and professional interest that accounts for Gordon's commitment to the interventionist cause: it was his understanding of his own role, what he could do now that he was a resident in the United States with no immediate likelihood of returning to Canada, to offer support to his homeland in the war against Hitler.

Canada, involved in the war from the start, had a special interest in these pro-war groups and, particularly in the two years before Pearl Harbor, Gordon worked tirelessly in disseminating information interpreting Canada's position. It was a tense period between the two North American neighbours, their strained relations presenting what Lester Pearson called "a very difficult problem indeed." Pearson, newly returned to Canada from London, referred particularly to the US tendency to consider Canada as either a part of the British Empire to be dealt with through a British spokesman from the United Kingdom, or a North American colony.[19] Gordon's files from this period indicate that he kept in frequent contact with Pearson, along with Escott Reid and Norman Robertson, also of External Affairs. Brooke Claxton, president of the Montreal branch of the Canadian Club, was particularly helpful in assembling a list of prestigious speakers from Canada and abroad who were available to speak to American audiences on international issues;[20] and Edgar Tarr of Winnipeg, a close friend of the Gordon family, was an active member in The Canadian Institute of International Affairs (CIIA), and the Institute of Pacific Relations, the latter offering him many opportunities to visit with King and Ruth. Gordon himself kept up his involvement in the CIIA, becoming a popular speaker at the Couchiching conferences, particularly after he joined the staff of *The Nation* in 1944. He was also asked by the CIIA on several occasions to be the Canadian representative at the Canadian-American conferences sponsored by the Foreign Policy Association.

As part of this drive to promote understanding between the two nations and to nudge the United States to join Canada's war effort, Gordon piloted through the press a book of articles, *Canada Fights*, edited by J.W. Dafoe of the *Winnipeg Free Press*. His attempt to distribute the book, however, ran into some bureaucratic snags. Gordon had been asked to speak to the Canadian-American League at the Trenton Kiwanis Club and had been told that they were getting together details for speakers and could give him a ready-made list of books if he wanted one. This seemed to King a perfect opportunity to add *Canada Fights* to the Kiwanis list. He contacted the trade commissioner at the Canadian Trade Office in New York, suggesting that his recommendation of the book would be of great help in spreading the word. The answer was a firm and "high-toned" no. The book did not have the imprimatur of the Dominion government and therefore the commissioner could not recommend it.

King exploded in frustration in a letter to Brooke Claxton – by this time a newly elected Liberal MP and parliamentary secretary to the prime minister. "Dear Brooke," he wrote, "Is the Canadian Department of Trade and Commerce the Holy Catholic Church or what?" He was particularly irked that the commissioner had read the book, knew Dafoe, and was quite aware of Farrar and Rinehart's efforts in promoting the interventionist cause.[21] Claxton replied post haste, assuring King that the matter was being taken care of.[22] As he always relished challenging what he considered bureaucratic ineptitude, Gordon concluded wryly that he was himself making a small contribution to the war effort.

This frenetic interventionist activity on Gordon's part contrasted sharply with the isolationist foreign policy platform of the LSR and the CCF. Frank Scott, for example, wrote in the spring of 1942, "I can understand your feeling about the war. I don't share it."[23] In light of this apparent defection on Gordon's part, it is interesting to look more closely at his views on the issue of war in relation to those of the Canadian socialists – whose own views were of necessity being challenged and undergoing modification with the approach of war. King had never been entirely at ease with the isolationist foreign policy statements of the LSR and the CCF – even though, as he said, he went along with them in a show of solidarity.[24]

Implicit in the LSR's arguments against international involvements and participation in European wars was the haunting awareness that, fighting as part of the Empire in the First World War, with no separate declaration of war, Canada had lost 60,000 men. By inference, LSR's isolationism appears first of all to have been a function of their strong anti-imperialism. The Statute of Westminster in 1931, which had given no clear constitutional guarantee concerning Canada's right of independent action should Great Britain go to war, left the implication that Canada was still subordinate to Great Britain in this area. (This issue was not settled until Canada's independence was confirmed by Parliament's vote of a separate declaration of war on 10 September 1939, one week after Britain.) Although Escott Reid had argued in 1933 that "the true internationalist must be a socialist, just as the true socialist must be an internationalist,"[25] by the time *Social Planning for Canada* was published in 1935, the chapter on foreign policy (written largely by Frank Underhill but reflecting the view of most LSR members) expressed the fear that Canadian membership in the British Commonwealth of Nations offered an even greater likelihood than membership in the League of Nations of dragging Canada into a foreign war. As Underhill wrote, "Canadian nationalism is an achievement of no significance if Canadian policy is in the end always to be determined by the *faits accomplis* of the British Foreign Office."[26]

Another element in the LSR's anti-war stand was the desire to prevent the high cost to Canadian unity inherent in a fight with Quebec over conscription. In that strange psychological quirk which demands that the cause for which sacrifices have been made must be deemed to have been worthy, the slaughter of the First World War had actually resulted in an increased imperial loyalty in many *English* Canadians who did not want to feel that their loss had been in vain, and who remained ready to answer the call of defending the Empire once again. Brooke Claxton (who, while attracted to the LSR/CCF, had never joined) feared, for example, that the Quebec provincial election in the fall of 1939 was "nothing less than a challenge to Quebecers to decide where to place their wartime allegiance – in Ottawa or Quebec City," and warned that the election could be "the first shot in a Canadian civil war, or the breakup of Confederation."[27]

Moreover, the LSR members felt that not only would the blow of war be devastating to national unity, but the cost in resources and economic disruption would divert energy, interest, and collective wealth from what was always their first goal: the establishment of socialism in Canada. Their caution extended even to Canada's participation in the League of Nations. Although they had initially supported the organization as "our only hope for maintaining peace long enough for socialist governments to be established in the majority of the countries of the world," they increasingly saw it as a league of capitalist powers, "a society of retired burghers defending the principle of property" and unlikely to remove the causes of war.[28] LSR opinion could not, of course, be divorced from the CCF, for which the war issue produced a major upheaval, and the Regina Manifesto of 1933 had left no doubt as to the new party's stand on war. Article 10 (written by Frank Underhill) stated that Canada must refuse to be entangled in any more wars fought to make the world safe for capitalism; and J.S. Woodsworth himself was, of course, a firm pacifist.

The official CCF policy as of the 1936 party convention, was that Canada would remain neutral in any war, no matter who the belligerents were. As a member of the national council preparing a foreign policy statement for the 1937 convention, Gordon made only one change in the 1936 statement: He inserted the word "imperialist" before the word "war." It now read: "Canada would remain neutral in any *imperialist* war no matter who were the belligerents."[29] This proved, for Gordon's future stand, to be a significant alteration.

In spite of the ambivalence inherent in party policy over the definition of what kind of war might be fought, it was clear that the national party felt it was not committed to support the imperial tie in any way. At the provincial level, however, and particularly in Saskatchewan, there was significant opinion to the contrary. This uncertainty in party policy led to an inner-party crisis when Britain went to war on 3 September 1939, by which time Gordon – kept abreast of the news by Frank Scott – had left Canada for New York. A compromise within the party was reached by the CCF National Council between the two opposing points of view – those supporting Woodsworth's pacifist stand and the interventionists, led by Saskatchewan's George Williams – the isolationist position passing by fifteen to seven. On 10 September, when Parliament voted by an overwhelming majority for Canada's entry into war, there were only three dissenting votes: two from Quebec MPs, and that of J.S. Woodsworth.

King's feeling on the declaration of war was initially one of loneliness, an emotion common to expatriates when crisis erupts in their homeland, but he felt comforted by his belief that Americans were not lacking in their support. "We have spent a very quiet Labour Day weekend," he wrote to his mother. "After the shock of Friday's news it was difficult to do much but try to preserve some kind of rational calm in a world that had suddenly fallen to pieces."[30]

Gordon's move to New York in 1938 was mourned by the LSR and the CCF, who, in Michiel Horn's words, had lost an indefatigable worker, but it in no way signalled a loss of interest or lessening of loyalty on his part to the party or to the cause of socialism. During his years in New York he became deeply involved in liberal-leftist causes in the United States, even as he remained open to the possibility, even likelihood, that he would return to Canada if an opportunity to be of help in the CCF presented itself. During his years in Montreal he had stayed in close contact with his former teachers and friends, Reinhold Niebuhr and Harry Laidler, often serving as a liaison between the Fellowship of Christian Socialists and the League for Industrial Democracy, and their Canadian counterparts. Both Niebuhr and Laidler welcomed Gordon's return to the United States and provided him a ready entry into socialist politics, a realm of activity that often overlapped with his interventionist efforts.

Because of Niebuhr's increasingly all-out interventionism, he had by the late 1930s run afoul of many of his isolationist and pacifist friends in the Socialist Party and the Fellowship of Socialist Christians. In fact, after a party request to give an account of his nonconformity, Niebuhr resigned from the Socialist Party in May of 1940 and shifted his energies to the formation of a new group, the Union for Democratic Action (UDA).[31] In March 1941, Gordon received a letter from the "Provisional Committee of the Union for Democratic Action" with an appended personal note from Niebuhr asking him to be a sponsor.[32] It was time for realism, Niebuhr argued, and for embracing the goal of "salvaging the liberal heritage of the west by backing Britain against Hitler."[33] Among those who joined Niebuhr in his major recruiting effort for the new UDA were Freda Kirchwey and Robert Bendiner of *The Nation*, which under Kirchwey's editorship had become a gathering place for radical and liberal interventionists. Within a week of Niebuhr's invitation, King joined this group of enthusiastic recruiters, replying, "Dear Reinie, I should be glad to do whatever I can in it and for it."[34]

At the end of the war, in the climate of increasing suspicion concerning Russia's goals in Europe and the growing skepticism among American liberals toward the conciliatory policy of the Popular Front, the UDA was dissolved and replaced by the Americans for Democratic Action (ADA). Like the UDA before it, the ADA wanted no communist affiliation, but the new group went even further in wanting no ties at all, even residual ones, to socialist doctrines, despite its increasing commitment to the liberal programs of the New Deal, and the UDA rapidly became involved in the day to day politics of the Democratic Party.[35] Both the UDA and later the ADA became major bases for Gordon's own political activity and for providing contacts in his attempts to encourage linkages between Canadian and American social democrats.

During these years in New York, King maintained a steady stream of correspondence with the CCF in Canada, and he and Ruth offered hospitality to the equally steady stream of speakers who came down from Canada to participate in seminars and roundtable discussions on Canadian-American relations; and to address sympathetic leftist groups such as unions, the League for Industrial Democracy (King was on their board of directors), the UDA, and the Socialist Party. The most frequent visitors included David Lewis, national secretary of the CCF; M.J. Coldwell, since 1940 the national chairman and also parliamentary leader of the party; Frank Underhill; and, of course, Frank Scott, who replaced Coldwell as national chairman in 1942. In 1940–41, Scott spent a sabbatical year at Harvard on a Guggenheim Fellowship, and this gave him a more immediate access to the American groups – and to King and Ruth.

Gordon followed the provincial and national elections closely, offering encouragement to CCF candidates and receiving several invitations to become a candidate himself. His possible return to Canada and the role he might play was a common topic of conversation with CCF visitors and a common theme in his correspondence. Scott, for instance, constantly made references to the possibility of such a return: "I was sorry to miss you [on King's visit to Montreal in regard to the Royal Commission on Steel in 1942] and hope you may be coming back this way. I really wanted to talk about the whole situation in Canada and where you might possibly fit in again."[36]

But they were realistic. In the context of Gordon's invitation to become managing editor of *The Nation* in February 1944, he wrote to Scott, "I am constantly thinking of Canada and the possibility of getting back. I talked to M.J. about it when he was down. I know there is important work to be done and a hell of a big battle ahead. But I cannot honestly see what immediately and specifically there is to bring me and Ruth and the children back now."[37] Scott agreed four days later: "I have hoped all along that you would come back to Canada, because I know that sooner or later you could fit in to the movement at a point where you would not feel that you had lost ground by being away so long. But the cold fact is that the moment is not yet in sight."[38]

Despite setbacks like Victoria, Gordon continued to have high hopes for the CCF, encouraged by the remarkable success in the Ontario provincial election of 1943, when E.B. (Ted) Joliffe led the CCF to within inches of forming the government of Canada's largest and wealthiest province. Writing in a US student publication, *The Assembly,* described on its masthead as "the magazine that stands for militant liberalism in the problems of both war and peace," his optimism took flight. The article, entitled "CCF: Awakening in the North," proclaimed: "Canada, entering her fifth year of war, is experiencing a political renaissance. The clean, new broom of an aggressive people's movement is sweeping reactionary ideas and political deadwood into the discard. The Co-operative Commonwealth Federation – popularly known as the CCF – has, in all likelihood, the political and social destiny of Canada in its hands."[39]

The victory of the CCF in the Saskatchewan provincial election in June 1944 and its continuing strength in the province in these early years was viewed by the national party as somewhat of an anomaly.[40] Gordon acknowledged this anomaly in 1946 when he wrote two articles for *The Nation* on the success of the party in Saskatchewan, in the first of which he asked, "Why should Saskatchewan, the most agrarian of Canada's nine provinces, be the first to elect a socialist government?"[41] This was not an unseemly question for socialists to ask, given the fundamental Marxist tenet that the revolution would come from the proletariat, and it may have implicitly reflected Marx's prejudice against the agrarian classes and what has been loosely translated as the "idiocy of rural life."

Seymour Lipset, in his analysis of the agrarian socialism of the CCF, notes that, "the agrarian-based CCF could not obtain much in the way of inspiration from Marxist socialist doctrine, since that doctrine has been ambiguous with respect to agrarian policy," and that "agrarian people were believed to be too conservative and too capitalistic to be susceptible to socialist ideals."[42]

Gordon addressed the question directly, finding part of the answer in the strong cooperative movement that preceded the political organization of the CCF in Saskatchewan, and further, in the determination of Prairie farmers to handle their own marketing and financial operations, freeing themselves from dependence on the big service organizations of eastern Canada. "It's not a very long step," he wrote, "from cooperatives to a government that applies the same principles in other spheres of activity. ... The CCF is building a new society in Saskatchewan not according to any doctrinaire socialist blueprint but in accordance with certain basic social principles applied to the communal problems of daily living." He found in the rural people of the Prairies that same stubborn independence and interdependence that characterized the fishermen and miners of Antigonish. In contrast to the American Progressive movement that appeared to be fragmented into competing factions, he argued that the strength of the CCF lay in its unity, its success in eliminating sectionalism, and its ability to work out a coherent and practical socialist program.

Gordon's optimism concerning the future of socialism also embraced the British Labour Party, and he maintained many contacts in England. On the Labour victory in July 1945, he wrote to Ruth, who was vacationing with her sister-in-law and their children up at Buzzards Bay, Massachusetts: "The news of the Labour sweep in England has just come through. It's simply terrific. What a responsibility those boys have now."[43] "Those boys" included Jennie Lee, Labour MP from Lanark, first elected to the House of Commons in 1929 at the age of twenty-four. King and Ruth had become close friends with Jennie Lee through her connection with Farrar and Rinehart. As one with access to the inner-Labour circle (particularly its left wing) through her husband Aneurin (Nye) Bevan and close friends like Sir Stafford Cripps, Jennie Lee was a pipeline of inside information and party gossip as she wrote long, entertaining letters to King. Gordon's contact with Cripps (who was the British ambassador to the USSR when they met) led to his introduction to Isaiah Berlin while Berlin was attached to the British embassy in Washington during the Second World War. And so the network went on, with introductions that led to friendships, which then continued through the years.

Some of King's British contacts proved a personal disappointment. His Fabian hero, R.H. Tawney, like Berlin, was also sent out from England to aid in the war propaganda effort. Tawney, however, did not like the US enough to try to understand it on its own terms, looking down on American culture and finding both its intellectual life and its working class inferior to the European. His biographer points out that Tawney "did not regard Americans as wholly foreigners, but as European manqués. So he did not realize that British ethnocentrism kept him from entering the different reality that is America."[44] Harold Laski's visit in December 1945 also disappointed Gordon, and revealed the extent to which his views had broadened and matured since his youthful enthusiasms at Oxford. He wrote to Frank Scott: "[Laski's] visit was very stimulating and certainly stirred up a hornet's nest among liberals as well as among reactionaries, as you would expect ... His speech at the dinner was ... over-simplified and too doctrinaire; and, I think, unnecessarily identifying class interests with individuals of that class ... In other words, while it was refreshing to hear good orthodox Socialist analysis again, his speech probably had the effect of alienating a good many liberal businessmen who would go a long way in accepting the necessity of a planned society, national and international, but who would refuse to accept Laski's sharply defined Marxist categories."[45]

Both this optimistic broadening and to some degree the disillusionment as well, were part and parcel of the clarification and modification of King's youthful and uncritical embrace of socialism as he reached the fine critical judgment that marked his mature years. In no way, however, did that earlier commitment of service to God through the service to his fellow human beings diminish.

The issue of academic freedom in Canada, which continued to trouble Gordon, was once again brought to the fore in January 1941, when Frank Underhill's recurring problems with the University of Toronto resulted in the board of governors' abrupt request for his resignation from the department of history on the grounds that his connections with the university were causing it adverse publicity and harm. The issue at stake was the right of (often radical) professors to hold and publicly articulate views contrary to (often more conservative) administrators, boards of trustees, and the politicians who controlled the purse strings of public institutions. After the outbreak of war in 1939, Underhill continued to make outspoken isolationist and anti-imperialist statements, remarks that were found particularly offensive at a time of delicate relations between Canada and the US who had not yet entered the war. The episode brought back painful memories for King of his own dismissal from United Theological College in Montreal. In due time, Underhill's cause carried the day. Michiel Horn argues that probably the most important factor in his defence was the political pressure applied by Underhill's friends in the government, who were able to persuade members of the board of governors to consider the effects that Underhill's dismissal could have for Canadian-American relations in this period of diplomatic strain concerning the war.[46]

Frank Underhill emerged shaken from his ordeal; and the episode was a reminder to Gordon of the continuing fragility of academic freedom in Canada, to some degree vindicating his conviction that the basis for his dismissal from UTC in 1933–34 was political and not, as the UTC board had claimed, financial. He confided to Scott that his longing to return to Canada to share in the "good fight" was not diminished by the Underhill crisis but, if anything, intensified. However, the opportune moment for such a return had not come, and King was instead about to enter the vortex of American liberal causes as managing editor of *The Nation*. Moreover, by this time he had become part of a wide network of leftist–liberal interests in the United States and of the liberal community in New York. His energy, commitment, and hard work appeared limitless, and his generosity and genuine liking for people meant that he was welcome in organizational planning and activities. Many of the relationships that grew out of pursuing a common goal resulted in lifelong friendships that accrued over the years in layered density. During their eventual retirement in Ottawa, the Gordons received a steady stream of visitors from around the world, as well as a daily heft of letters. And in 1944, Gordon was about to embark on an odyssey at *The Nation*, mitigating his disappointment in not returning to Canada. He could continue his "good fight" – on another soil to be sure, but in a place that he felt had become his "home away from home."

11

Editor and UN Correspondent

At the time Gordon joined its staff, *The Nation* was one of the oldest and most prestigious political magazines in the United States, giving voice to the assumptions of classical liberalism: the basic goodness of human nature, and the effectiveness of reason and education in eradicating ignorance and social evils. The magazine rose to its twentieth-century apotheosis under the editorship of Oswald Garrison Villard, grandson of the famous abolitionist, William Lloyd Garrison, who transformed it from a non-political stance, in which it owed no allegiance to any political party or interest, to a crusading liberal journal. At the end of the First World War, Villard hired a young idealistic staff that included Freda Kirchwey, hired for the less-than-lofty task of clipping articles for the International Section.[1]

Kirchwey quickly rose within the magazine hierarchy from a clipper to an editor and then managing editor, and by 1937 she had purchased *The Nation*, becoming its owner, editor, and publisher. During her years at *The Nation* (she retired in 1955) she championed a wide array of liberal causes such as the Spanish civil war, pacifism, and collective security, refugees, and Zionism, McCarthyism and censorship, and finally, the peaceful use of atomic power. These were all causes close to King's heart and, as he told his mother, reflected those of the CCF.[2] Before Pearl Harbor, Kirchwey became an early interventionist, supporting American involvement in the European war against fascism; however, in spite of the Nazi–Soviet Pact of 1939, she remained steadfast in her loyalty to the Soviet Union. Her inflexible stand on this issue – particularly in the post-war period – led to a professional distancing between Kirchwey and others unsympathetic to Stalin, including Reinhold Niebuhr and

Gordon. This difference did not, however, diminish King's admiration for her, and they remained devoted friends until her death in 1976.

Gordon was approached with a formal offer to become managing editor of *The Nation* in February 1944, an offer he found more difficult to accept than one would expect. There was, of course, his habitual loyalty that tempted him to remain with Farrar and Rinehart. Also, Reinhold Niebuhr, who was on the board of *The Nation*, cautioned him about the shaky finances of the magazine and expressed concern regarding the leftist leanings of Kirchwey's associate editor, Alvaraez Del Vayo, who had been foreign minister in Republican Spain and who was still a strong believer in the Popular Front. On the other hand, accepting the offer would be challenging and exciting work, keeping King in the front of the political battle line. Moreover, any cautionary considerations would be balanced by the possibility of access to the newly formed United Nations. This hope was soon realized when Gordon became *The Nation*'s accredited correspondent at the UN.

When he accepted the position, Frank Scott wrote lamenting that it would delay Gordon's return to Canada, but he concluded: "I think your choice is probably right. The difference is merely between working for a cause you like in the USA immediately and working for the same cause in Canada at some rather uncertain future date ... Anyway, if you get chased out by the reaction there as you were from here you will have a safe place to escape to. I think it is splendid the way you have risen to the top of the liberal group in New York, and I congratulate you for it."[3]

The die was cast, and happily so. *The Nation* heralded his hiring, saying, "We are fortunate to have Mr. Gordon on our Board. In his former position [at Farrar and Rinehart] he handled most of the books dealing with politics, labour, social problems, the war, and foreign policy, and his whole experience has been in the field of public affairs."[4]

Freda Kirchwey felt strongly that the policy of *The Nation* must be one of advocacy, influencing the public by articulating a particular point of view. *The Nation*'s policy was set week by week on a collegial basis as the editorial staff (including Gordon) met and discussed emergent issues, possible writers, and editorial positions. Gordon was responsible for contacting authors and editing articles, reading unsolicited manuscripts, and writing editorials and occasionally signed pieces, particularly on Canada.[5] He was also expected to generate ideas for new articles and on this score he had considerable responsibility and latitude.

In joining *The Nation*, Gordon widened his circle of friendships and connections even further, first of all within the staff of the magazine itself. Although his predecessor, Robert Bendiner, had left to join the army, Keith Hutchison, an economist from the London School of Economics, oversaw the economics editorial policy; I.F. (Izzy) Stone was the Washington correspondent and came in one day a week (invariably late) with his copy. Gordon described Alvarez Del Vayo, who was in charge of foreign affairs, as a "romantic, left-wing Spaniard still living in the days of the Popular Front and uncritical as far as ideology was concerned. He absolutely would not take any kind of stand against the Soviet Union."[6] Kirchwey frequently called on experts in various fields for specific articles and as speakers for conferences that *The Nation* sponsored. Reinhold Niebuhr, for example, addressed the audience concerning American foreign policy at the public forum on "America's Opportunity to Create and Maintain Lasting Peace"; Archibald MacLeish helped plan a special issue on "American Liberal Democracy," which included articles from Carl Sandburg, Eleanor Roosevelt, Thomas Mann, and Carl Van Doren. The forum on atomic power included scientists, politicians, columnists, and ethicists, and reached abroad for its keynote speaker, Harold Laski. It was a heady, intense intellectual world of common interest and serious intention, a natural milieu in which the many strands of Gordon's own interests and commitments coalesced.

The Nation was sharply focused on the movements and forces that were shaping the world as it emerged from the war. Strongly pro-Roosevelt, it saw a new, fully collaborative role for the United States in world affairs and closely followed the thinking and deliberations dealing with post-war international organization. It drew heavily on the anti-fascist refugee community in its discussions and articles on the likely shape of post-war Europe. Gordon himself participated on a radio panel on the topic, "What Should Be Done With Germany?"[7] He argued *The Nation*'s position that after adequate measures had been taken to prevent a resurgence of German military aggression, it should be readmitted to the community of nations as soon as possible. Harold Laski, Kingsley Martin, and Barbara Ward, as well as Keith Hutchison, examined and interpreted postwar trends in Britain. *The Nation*'s interests encompassed post-colonialism as well, following the progress of independence for India and maintaining close contact with the Institute of Pacific Relations, another group with which King was already identified.

But it was the role of the Soviet Union that ran like a Wagnerian leitmotif through *The Nation*'s discussion of international affairs – a theme that caused considerable *sturm und drang* among both the editorial staff and the magazine's supporters. From her earliest years on staff,

Kirchwey brought a pro-Soviet perspective to her articles, as early as 1921 demanding "Recognize Russia!" – an exhortation she repeated yearly until Roosevelt's recognition of the Soviet Union in 1933. That date coincided with the beginning of *The Nation*'s advocacy of a new role for the United States in Europe, one of opposing Nazi hostility to the Jews and of supporting fleeing refugees. When the Communist International (Comintern) abandoned its propaganda for international communism in the mid-1930s and called for unity with all groups opposed to fascism, Kirchwey was "relieved and encouraged by Moscow's 'olive branch,'" and redefined the basic conflict as between fascism and democracy, "a struggle in which the forces of revolution must support and win the support of all the friends of democracy, while the forces of capitalism will gradually, and often unwillingly, form an alliance with the cohorts of fascism."[8]

Interestingly, this argument is similar to the position King had taken in his 1936 chapter for the FCSO publication, *Towards the Christian Revolution*, in which he identified the fundamental totalitarian threat to democracy as residing in European fascism rather than in Soviet communism.[9] The Spanish civil war had offered a clear opportunity to destroy fascism, with the Nazis and the Italians aiding Franco while only the Soviet Union supported the Spanish Loyalists. When Alvarez Del Vayo, with his unswerving commitment to the leftist cause in Spain, was added to the staff as a contributing editor in 1941, he reinforced Kirchwey's pro-Soviet convictions. Even during the purges of the 1930s and the Nazi–Soviet Pact in 1939, Kirchwey romanticized the Soviet Union, a position that her biographer argues affected her judgment. "In spite of trials," Kirchwey continued to argue, "I believe Russia is dependable; that it wants peace, and will join in any joint effort to check Hitler and Mussolini, and will also fight if necessary. Russia is still the strongest reason for hope."[10]

With the Yalta agreement, the end of the War, and the rise of the Cold War, Kirchwey's strident position on the Soviet Union increasingly alienated her from her liberal constituency, many of whom wrote for *The Nation*, including contributing editors Louis Fischer and Reinhold Niebuhr, who both resigned. There was also a growing tension within *The Nation* itself: a frequently sympathetic portrayal of the Soviet Union in the editorial section of the journal was just as frequently counterbalanced by an anti-Soviet book review in the literary section, and to Kirchwey's credit it must be said that she endured this duality for a considerable length of time.[11] Frequently finding himself caught in the middle of this controversy, as far as office politics were concerned, Gordon refused to take sides,[12] although he wrote both editorials and articles critical of the Soviet Union,[13] and he privately expressed support for Niebuhr when he resigned from the journal.[14]

While he remained close to Reinhold Niebuhr, however, Gordon could not follow him as he moved, with growing pessimism, into his "Cold Warrior" phase. In the context of the larger foreign policy debate that ensued following 1945, he was once again coming under the influence of his friend Percy Corbett, whose optimistic internationalism represented a point of view that not only suited him temperamentally, but had seen him through the isolationist days of the CCF and was now being corroborated by his daily contact with the United Nations.

The death of Franklin Roosevelt on 12 April 1945 shocked the nation and held particular pathos in that victory in Europe, assured by the time of his death, eluded him in its realization. For the American left, it was an especially bitter blow, and Gordon, along with many others, predicted a hard road ahead for the New Deal liberals, a prediction soon realized as the Roosevelt coalition disintegrated and the country swung to the right in the Congressional elections of 1946. Victory in Europe followed close upon Roosevelt's death (King's first reaction: "a tremendous relief to know that the killing and the bombing has stopped"), and shortly thereafter, the surrender of Japan in August. King was up at Buzzards Bay with Ruth and her family when the news reached him; a week later he wrote home to Winnipeg, contrasting the days they been enjoying – filled with clear bright air and the peaceful, deep blue sea as the children played on the beach, in and out of the water – with the stunning news of Hiroshima that rendered unreal those quiet days of the past week.[15]

For Gordon, the introduction of nuclear weaponry marked a turning point in his understanding of the use of military force. While he never recanted his support of military action in certain circumstances, he came to see the possible use of nuclear weapons as the greatest threat to economic sustainability and social justice throughout the world and, indeed, to human survival itself. *The Nation* responded with a swift and surefooted grasp of the implications of atomic weapons for world politics. Kirchwey wrote in her first editorial after Hiroshima that "a World Government" was needed to control atomic weapons and that "it is one world or none."[16] She immediately set about organizing a *Nation*-sponsored conference on the implications of Hiroshima and Nagasaki and the necessity of providing for international control of this deadly new force.

In preparation for the conference, Gordon wrote a signed article in the 24 November issue of *The Nation*, "The Bomb is a World Affair," supporting Harold E. Stassen's argument that the bomb be put under the international control of the United Nations. Gordon objected, however, to President Truman's statement made earlier that month that such an "international" plan be based only on consultations with Great Britain and Canada, excluding the Soviet Union; and he strongly supported those, like Bernard Baruch and Robert Oppenheimer, who argued that the Soviet Union must be included in the creation of any form of effective international control and that all nations concerned must express a willingness to submit to inspection by the United Nations. It was this hypothetical willingness on the part of the international community to recognize the authority of the UN that in Gordon's view went above and beyond the control of the bomb and laid the basis for a more comprehensive level of international cooperation.[17]

King revelled in the intellectual life and the open forum on ideas provided by *The Nation*, and in the wealth of connections and friends that grew out of his editorial work. The growing strain within the *Nation* community concerning the Soviet Union's role in international politics must not be allowed to obscure the fact that Gordon's time at the journal was a period of immense enjoyment and professional satisfaction. Nevertheless, by early 1947, he was experiencing a growing restlessness. He wrote to Frank Scott: "I've just about come to the conclusion that I'm going to get out of the job I'm in. It's partly because of the wear and tear in a managing editor's life that cuts down heavily on any creative effort ... that is, the [editorial policy] is a joint affair with the editorial staff"[18] This collegial approach had been one of the factors that first attracted Gordon to his position as managing editor, but with the "increasing tug and strain" among the staff caused by Kirchwey and Del Vayo's stand on the Soviet issue, he found it more and more constraining. In addition, *The Nation* was facing financial problems. He elaborated in his letter to Scott: "The Nation like most other American magazines has been taking something of a licking with costs mounting and subscriptions and advertising flattening off and even sagging a little. We are going to have to make heavy economies. I'm sure the magazine will keep going but it is going to be an increasing load for those who remain."

In any event, it was *The Nation*'s financial exigencies, rather than editorial stress, that proved determinative. Kirchwey reluctantly concluded in July that, in her efforts to economize, she would need to combine her position with his, "with the greatest reluctance," and entirely in the way he would choose. "I would not expect or even allow you to leave until you had adequate time to find another post that you like and that seems suitable financially.[19] They agreed on the date of Gordon's departure as 15 September, and that he would be kept on the payroll and continue to be *The Nation* correspondent at the UN through December. In the meantime, King's pace did not slacken as he soldiered on at *The Nation* throughout the hot summer of 1947, finding himself particularly busy with other staff on vacation.

Kirchwey concluded her regretful letter outlining their understanding on a sympathetic note: "I am immensely worried about the whole future of the paper for its troubles do not end with January 1 and even if we succeed in meeting the current deficit; but to have to forfeit your help and create difficulties for you and Ruth are among the unhappiest parts of the whole business."[20] Gordon continued to meet socially with his friends at *The Nation* and their paths crossed frequently as they pursued their mutual interests.

Quite independently of developments at *The Nation,* Ruth and King had decided to leave the pleasant MacDougal–Sullivan sanctuary in Greenwich Village for the country. Through Ruth's sister-in-law, Sally Anderson, they heard of a large farmhouse on a 200-acre "estate" (as Gordon wryly called it) of wild land on the New York Post Road near Garrison, on the east side of the Hudson River across from the United States Military Academy at West Point. Ruth described the new house, which they were renting, to Gordon's sister Mary: "It's ten rooms, four baths, and large attic, plus four hundred [sic] acres! It's furnished, but large enough to absorb our furniture. It's an old farmhouse, with a wing added on. The original house has a dining room, library, study, and kitchen, with three bedrooms, and a bath above. There is also a bath on the first floor. The wing has an enormous living room with bay window, and two bedrooms and bath above. There's quite a lot of cleared space which is lawn, lots of climbing trees, and a good space for a vegetable garden."[21]

The move changed the pattern of Gordon's life as he began the 105-km commute down to the United Nations at Lake Success and Flushing Meadow to do his weekly report for *The Nation*; he had also begun writing both signed and unsigned reports for the *Atlantic,* and with the opening of the Second General Assembly in September of 1947, his freelance assignments for the Canadian Broadcasting Corporation (CBC) had picked up. His days were also filled with the large amount of yard work that needed to be done as he attempted to tame the estate, and he had his first encounter with farm machinery – rather belatedly, one might observe, for a prairie boy. He explained in a letter to his mother that he had started out with a scythe, but was mercifully rescued after an hour when a neighbour arrived with a hay mower and offered to help. Thereupon, he and the neighbor took turns driving the tractor and operating the mower, "pulling the appropriate levers at approximately the right times."[22] It was an exhilarating transition to country life.

As the season moved on through autumn, mowing changed to clearing bush and chopping logs, exploring trails, and painting watercolours in the hills around the property, and, finally, shovelling snow. Although there was plenty to keep him busy, there was also time to brood, and King quite probably harkened back to the depression he had suffered in his last term at Oxford when, as now, he had faced an uncertain future, perhaps reflecting that during the years since certain options seemed to have closed for him. As he pondered his vocation of service once again, it now had the added dimension of supporting a family.

As always, there was his lingering hope of getting back to Canada. In his letter to Scott in April of 1947, when he first talked about his impending break with *The Nation* and discussed the possibility of something opening up in Canada, he mentioned the appeal Western Canada had for him, particularly Saskatchewan. The new CCF government under Tommy Douglas had attracted young socialist intellectuals from all over Canada into its bureaucracy, and quite possibly King would have found himself at home there. But the invitation to return to Canada came not from Saskatchewan, but from his own hometown of Winnipeg, to be the editor of a new daily newspaper.

The idea for a new liberal paper, *The Citizen*, rose out of a long drawn-out printer's strike that had resulted in the merger of the two major Winnipeg daily papers: *The Free Press*, owned and run by the Sifton family, whose editorial policy was consistently anti-CCF; and the Winnipeg *Tribune*, which followed a more independent, if conservative, line. Gordon received a letter from H.S. Ferns, president of the Winnipeg Citizen Publishing Co., Ltd., outlining the proposal for the new daily paper. So far, the project still lacked assets of about $100,000 and a guarantee of newsprint and wire services; but it was assured of strong community support, with 10,000 fully paid up members (at five dollars per share). These prospects struck Gordon as high on morale, but weak on practicalities. He thanked the board for the honour and asked for a couple of weeks to think about the offer. Then he did his homework, contacting editor friends in the US and CCF politicians in Canada.

While the editors urged caution, the politicians – with a notable exception – urged him to accept. Stanley Knowles, CCF MP for Winnipeg North Centre, wrote to David Lewis, national secretary of the CCF, that he hoped King would accept the offer and felt he would be reasonably safe in doing so, adding "that it would be a boost for us to have [King] back here is beyond question."[23] Knowles then moved to the caveat: the old problem of Labour-Progressive Party (communist) influence. At the moment there were only two LPP members on the board, and the other ten members could be swung either way: on the one hand, a leftist position bordering on "fellow-travelling," and on the other, one sympathetic to the CCF. It would be Gordon's job to persuade the board to the latter.

It was the old threat to the CCF by those further to the left that Gordon himself had struggled with in his days as a candidate in Victoria and in the end, the factor that determined his decision. Sage advice arrived from the Gordon family's friend Edgar Tarr: stay out of leftist infighting in Winnipeg.[24] King heeded this friendly warning and turned down the offer. The prospects of returning to Canada remained meagre.

What Gordon really wanted was a job that did not exist: to continue the kind of reporting on the United Nations that he had been doing on a freelance basis for the CBC, but as its regular, fulltime correspondent. Sometime in the early fall of 1947, he proposed such a plan, writing to Ernest Bushnell, CBC director of programs, suggesting that in view of the CBC's great interest in UN coverage they needed someone at Lake Success (the UN's headquarters at that time) all the time, not just a team from Montreal and Toronto when the General Assembly was in session. He also pointed out that such a move would save them money. Bushnell responded eagerly to Gordon's proposal and shortly thereafter the deal was sealed over breakfast at the Biltmore. His immediate boss would be Ira Dilworth, head of the International Service in Montreal, but it was understood that he would also supply the National Service when needed.

As it turned out, Gordon did three types of broadcasts. He began with "News Roundup," a daily four minute report broadcast across Canada and described as "a specialized type of news program. It contains on-the-spot reports of important events, background material explaining important news of the day, and human interest stories."[25] It was precisely four minutes and fifteen seconds long and excluded editorializing. Two other types of reports, both longer (eight to ten minutes), offered scope for Gordon's own views and opinions, Midweek Review or Weekly Roundup, as well as the daily/weekly International Commentary, which was broadcast mainly in England but also sent into Europe. Gordon found that the CBC allowed their reporters much more latitude than other networks, such as the BBC, which required that reporters hew the government line. He was cautioned only that "we should like to speak as a Canadian organization reflecting Canadian viewpoint – a viewpoint which supports the United Nations to the fullest extent."[26] King himself put out ten to twelve reports a week and reported in passing in a letter to Ernie Bushnell that during a single session of the General Assembly (the fourth) his staff had put out over 400 transmissions in twelve weeks.[27]

One of Gordon's first duties was to assemble a group of "stringers," or freelance commentators, both for the Canadian broadcasts and for the International Service. The international reporters were invariably press representatives from newspapers or wire services in their own country or region. With his alert eye for colourful characters and his great love of a story, King's favourite was the Dane, Peter Freuchen, "world famous Arctic explorer and writer, one leg lost in the frozen north. He would come stumping in dressed in a navy-blue seaman's sweater, eyes shining, always pleasant and alert." He recounted:

> One day he came in, downcast, and announced: "I've been fired." I said: "who fired you?" He answered: "Mr. Griffiths." I said: "Why?" He said: "I guess it was because of something I said." I growled: "They can't do that," and got on the phone to Montreal. When Griffiths got on the line I said: "What's this about Freuchen?" He said: "Some important Catholics in Quebec complained about something he said on Jerusalem." I said: "Look: you can't do that. In the first place, Peter Freuchen is the most listened to commentator in his country on our whole roster, as a CBC commentator he is free to make his own judgments, and, most importantly, if there is any firing to be done on our staff in New York it is going to be done down here." and I hung up. Next day Peter came in with a smile on his face. "I've been rehired."[28]

Gordon relished his new position and recalled happily, "The job suited me to the ground. I was my own boss."[29] Everything in his past seemed to have prepared him for the cut and thrust of the international debate, the camaraderie of his colleagues in the press corps, the contact with diplomats and especially the work of the UN committees and agencies that were hammering out policy. His optimism was high – unrealistically so at times – and his dejection at the lack of progress in the rebuilding of the postwar world, though keen, never collapsed into cynicism or despair. The hundreds of scripts that survive are models of communication and education, reflecting King's rapport with ordinary, intelligent listeners. In a directive on "Tips to Talkers" sent out by the CBC Talks and Public Affairs Department, radio reporters were told: "Radio audiences are all usually very small – two or three people who are sitting at ease in the living room, or eating in the dining room, or kitchen, or playing Chinese Checkers in the parlor. This means that while you are speaking before the 'mike,' your entire approach should be informal and rather intimate."[30]

These were King's people, and his most avid fans included his mother and sister Ruthie in their cozy living room in Winnipeg. He needed no instructions on how to talk to them.

He often began his talk by setting the context, drawing his listeners in with a homey metaphor that made them feel included. He was at the kitchen table with them, drinking tea, gracefully leading them into the harsh world of international affairs. For example, he opened his report on a meeting of the Human Rights Commission in February 1947: "It's Lincoln's Birthday. School's out and all day long the UN has been deluged with young people. Girl Scouts in green uniforms swarmed into the Security Council and listened a little puzzled to a deadlocked debate on disarmament. College students took a busman's holiday and listened to a lecture on UNESCO. Abe Lincoln himself would have a wonderful time in this place."[31]

He used the analogy of the connect-the-dots game that his children played to describe the emerging picture of Palestine as part of the East–West power picture.[32] In another report on Human Rights, he reminded his listeners: "We are apt to forget that behind the label of the nation is the man and woman in the home, the child going to school, the morning newspaper coming to the door, the worker going with his lunch pail to the factory, or the farmer overhauling his tractor in preparation for the spring plowing, the radio carrying the evening program, the meeting in the church auditorium or the town hall – all the activities of people in a community, activities so natural that we take them for granted, unless somebody denies us the right to perform them."[33]

He enchanted the isolated Saskatchewan farm wife, following his static-studded CBC report as she prepared the evening meal, with his description of Paris, broadcast during the Third General Assembly in

September 1948. One wonders what she saw in her imagination as he described the terraces of the Palais de Chaillot that gave an uncluttered view of Paris glistening in the clear light of autumn.[34] And finally, he invited listeners into the often-lonely life of the UN bureaucrat, far from home on Christmas Eve as he listened to piped-in carols over the intercom in the UN cafeteria at Lake Success.[35]

All was not atmosphere and context, however. Gordon constantly and subtly educated, gradually building a solid picture of the structure of the UN, its councils, committees, and agencies, and the interplay of power not only among the member nations but among the institutional parts of the organization itself. He pointed out the realities of power; the necessity of concentrating the responsibility of keeping the peace in the Security Council, for example; the interests of national security and the claims of sovereignty of the various nations; and the implicit prohibition against violating the interests of the great powers, in particular, the United States and the Soviet Union. But he was quick to point out that while the drama of these power interests played out on the big political stages of the UN, they were balanced by the humanitarian interests of other UN bodies. Day by day, King drew attention to the workings of the committees of the General Assembly and the other councils, particularly the Economic and Social Council (ECOSOC) and the Trusteeship Council. He also praised the day-to-day work of the Secretariat, charged with implementing the policy decisions of the General Assembly.

How does one measure the effectiveness of Gordon's steady efforts to inform and educate his audience through the airwaves, as he patiently painted this picture of the UN, its nature and its purpose? He received many letters expressing gratitude, and his superiors in the CBC repeatedly praised the quality of his reporting. Any evaluation of the effectiveness of such efforts must also take into account the importance of radio as a medium of communication at this time, and the necessity of educating the population about the newly formed UN if it were to have a realistic chance of reaching its goal of achieving peace in a world of competing and often contradictory national interests. But also for Gordon himself, this early period of broadcasting was of considerable significance. In the first place, in these broadcasts he honed the skills that gave voice to his own natural gifts – his love for words, for ideas, for people. And they also gave him entrée to the UN at the moment of its founding so that its ideals claimed his loyalty and his imagination; and its institutions, politics, and policies became so familiar to him that he was able to move among them with ease when he joined the UN staff in 1950.

King delighted in his personal contacts with the UN press corps and with the delegates themselves that being the CBC correspondent made possible, and he passed many of these vignettes on to his listeners. He loved to tell the story of introducing his mother to Andrei Gromyko, the Soviet Union's permanent representative to the UN. Mr Gromyko, with diplomatic charm, and Helen Gordon, with her natural charm, visited together like two old friends. From then on, whenever their paths crossed, Gromyko would inquire about Mrs Gordon's health and send her his best wishes.[36] Quite to the contrary, King agreed privately with Lester Pearson's description of another Russian respresentative, Andrey Vyshinsky, that "old master of the colorful smile,"[37] who was the "most gifted, energetic, articulate, and unscrupulous of the communist polemicists at the UN."[38] He described Madame Pandit of India, as "a very beautiful and talented woman";[39] and he praised Eleanor Roosevelt's candour and graciousness in a letter to his mother, after he had interviewed her in her New York apartment for an editorial on human rights.[40] One is struck by the informality and ease with which the reporters seemed to mingle with the statesmen at that time.

Running through all Gordon's CBC scripts is his concern with Canada's role at the United Nations and his admiration for Lester Pearson, since 1948 the head of the Canadian delegation to the UN. King described it as "not surprising to find a strong Canadian delegation here at Flushing Meadow and Lake Success," and wrote to his mother in October 1947, that he had been seeing a lot of his friends since the Assembly began. Mike Pearson had been down to the house and played some baseball with Charley. Jerry Riddell, Escott Reid, and General Andrew McNaughton (representing Canada on the Atomic Commission) had arrived, as well as George Ignatieff, who was assisting him. Many years later, Gordon recounted an incident that revealed the respect in which the Russian delegation held Ignatieff, this youngest son of the last education minister of Czar Nicholas II. "The Russians never forget his Russian ancestry," he wrote, "or his mastery of the language." He recounted the occasion: "[I]n the late forties when I was covering the Security Council for *The Nation* being witness to an incident when Gromyko corrected a translator for the mistranslation of a word. When the translator held his ground Gromyko said: 'I appeal to a distinguished member of the Canadian delegation: Mr. Ignatieff, what did I say?' Ignatieff, who had been following the translation closely, replied at once that Gromyko was right."[41]

Gordon's loyal support and admiration for Pearson was consistent and genuine – and lifelong. In his retirement, he kept a picture on his desk of Pearson in waders, mid-stream, holding aloft a fish, his face beaming with a fisherman's pride. It was signed, "To King. With best wishes. Mike."

In early June of 1948, Gordon learned that he would be sent to Paris in September to cover the Third General Assembly for the CBC. By 20 June plans had been made for Ruth and the children (Charley, eight, and Alison, six) to accompany him.[42] September found them embarking in Montreal and sailing down the St Lawrence on the *Empress of France* with most of the Canadian delegation – but not the Gordons' luggage – also on board. The mishap concerning the luggage was documented by their fellow passenger, I. Norman Smith of the *Ottawa Journal*. Smith reported that Gordon, who he claimed had a predilection for losing his way ("He gets lost looking for restaurants so often that fellow correspondents have considered getting a label of some kind to pin around his neck"), had sent the luggage on ahead by another ship, and that he then successfully "convinced his wife that it wasn't his fault – but then she's got a very special sense of humor and human kindness. The rest of us were only surprised that it turned up at Liverpool."[43] One wonders if this story and King's reputation of being "directionally challenged" might not prove apocryphal, considering that he spent most of his life globe-trotting and there are few other tales extant of lost entities, human or otherwise. In any case, the Canadians had a merry time on their sea voyage, filling their spare time with shuffleboard and charades. (General Andrew McNaughton acted out "The General Dies at Dawn.") Their merriment was cut short on the last day out from Southampton by the sad news of the assassination in Jerusalem of Count Folke Bernadotte, a Swedish diplomat who had been appointed UN mediator in Palestine the previous May.[44]

King left Ruth and the children in Cornwall with friends until he could find suitable accommodation for them in Paris. The Canadian contingent continued on to Paris where they settled in at Le Grand Hotel. King wrote to his mother that he felt right at home, surrounded by so many familiar faces from Lake Success and old friends from Oxford days, but it was being with the Canadians that he particularly enjoyed. He even had a good word to say for the Liberal prime minister Mackenzie King (that nemesis of the CCF, particularly Frank Scott). Perhaps Gordon's heart had been softened by the prime minister's "recalling warmly" a letter he had once received from King's mother.[45]

Gordon loved every minute of his time in this "friendly, beautiful place," and as always, people were his meat and drink: "King thrives on it all – and is always making plans for something *more* to do,"[46] Ruth wrote to her mother-in-law. With his remarkably good health and buoyant energy (he seemed to have suffered from only an infrequent cold and, although he occasionally complained of feeling pressed with work, he rarely if ever slowed his pace), he found a hotel for Ruth and the children on the Left Bank, the Hotel de Nice on the Rue des Beaux Arts, just across the Seine from the Louvre. But alas, when Ruth flew in to Paris with the children on their ninth wedding anniversary, she was dismayed to find no sign of King, for he was off on a flight with the Berlin Airlift. With her usual equanimity, she and the children settled in and were well taken care of by friends and by the arrangements King had made for them.

Meanwhile, Gordon had flown into Berlin from the American base in Rhein-Main, "right into a world which it is difficult to believe exists," in a big four-motor American aircraft carrying about ten tons of flour.[47] He flew in the cockpit with the crew through the big billowy clouds at about 1,524 m, looking down on the green fields below, and as they travelled he visited with the co-pilot, a young homesick boy whose father owned a walnut farm in Oakland, California. They flew in along a 32-km-wide corridor, and King described to his mother his first glimpses of the city as they approached the Tempelhof airport: "You see whole areas from the air which have been swept bare of buildings, whole streets with not a house standing that has a roof on it. The enormity of the desolation in this great city is just impossible to describe." This was the city both he and his mother had visited and loved in their student days, now wasteland and rubble. It was a bleak picture, one that Gordon reported also by shortwave to his listeners back in Canada. He concluded his letter to his mother as he sat in the American mess centre in Berlin, listening to the steady roar of the relief planes overhead as they flew in at regular intervals. "Berliners used to hear that and crowd down into their cellars: now it spells life and not death."[48]

Once back in Paris, along with a busy schedule for King at the Assembly, the family settled into a domestic pattern in their little hotel, and into an active social life as they were included in the many parties of both the Canadian delegation and the press corps. There were also trips to the ballet, opera, and art galleries. Ruth wrote to Mrs Gordon, "We are able to put the children to bed here before we go out – and a very nice French lady at the desk listens for them since King doesn't get home till 8 as a rule."[49] King added, "When we come in [the concierge] invariably reports: 'Les enfants étaient très sages. Ils dormirent bien.'" They came to love the Left Bank with its small shops and friendly people, and they poked around in galleries and bookstores, buying little gifts. "It's a wonderful place – if only it weren't for the fog,"[50] King wrote home. Although King's moments with Ruth and the children were snatched from his busy schedule, it was a happy interlude for the family. Charley celebrated his eighth birthday with a family party consisting of fruit juice and an unusual "rum" birthday cake bought at the corner of rue St André des Arts that was, Gordon recalled in 1986 in a letter to his sister Ruthie, all they could find in the Paris of that day. Singing and gifts were followed by an all-Beethoven concert and dinner out. The Gordon children seem to have been remarkably well-behaved on occasions of such formality. Many years later, Charles Gordon, with his mother's ironic wit and humour, gave quite a different account of these three-hour adult conversations in restaurants, claiming extreme boredom and a lasting aversion to European culture.[51]

Ruth spent most of her days exploring Paris with the children, with lunches at sidewalk cafes, frequent stops for hot chocolate, and trips to the zoo. On the day after Charley's birthday (his new watch proudly perched on his wrist), she took them to the circus: "Paris circuses are such fun because they are so tiny and have only one ring, which makes it much nicer – you are so close to everything."[52] One Sunday they took a trip out into the country to visit American friends who lived in a small village where everyone was a farmer or grew fruit. King and Charley hiked through an orchard and up an escarpment where they had a view of wheat fields that stretched for miles. For the moment, King felt that he was back on the Canadian Prairies, an image rendered more real by the sight of a Massey Harris disc harrow beside a farmhouse. It was an hour of companionship between father and son, stolen from a busy schedule.[53]

Meanwhile, UN personnel were working at fever pitch so that the delegates could be home for Christmas, and the General Assembly passed the International Declaration of Human Rights on 10 December, thus bringing to an end the Paris idyll. On 11 December, King and the family left Paris for Geneva, their first stop on a CBC assignment reporting on postwar conditions in Europe. He filed reports from Geneva, Rome (with a nostalgic side trip to Florence), London, and Edinburgh, and in each capital that he visited, found encouragement that Europe was rising once again from the devastation of war. But it was Geneva that filled him with more hope for world peace than any other place he had visited since he had begun reporting on the work of the UN.

During his student days at Oxford, King had seen the League of Nations in Geneva in its first bloom after the First World War, a bloom that quickly faded. Now, twenty-five years later, having spent twelve weeks in Paris watching in frustration the wrangling and disputes and desperate compromises in the new search for world peace, it was with some misgiving that he went out to the Palais des Nations in Geneva, expecting a hollow shell of a building. The Palais looked much the same, however, and once inside he found the headquarters of five specialized UN agencies, "working agencies, not just talking agencies," doing solid, businesslike work. He visited three of them: the Economic Commission for Europe (ECE), leading the way after the emergency work of the Marshall Plan; the International Labor Office (ILO), where he spent an hour with David Morse, the new director, and recalled his first visit to the ILO when he was a guest of the Walter Riddells; and the World Health Organization (WHO), headed by Brock Chisholm of Canada.[54]

On a stop in Milan on their way to Rome, Gordon found himself particularly interested in efforts being made to restore Italy's cultural treasures. The Leonardo da Vinci fresco, *The Last Supper*, miraculously spared in the Allied bombing, now had its protective chapel rebuilt, and he and Ruth looked at it in all its faded grandeur. With the children, they visited the Brera Palace, which had housed some of the greatest treasures of northern Italian art, and found it being repaired, a chute carrying rubble down from the upper stories to waiting trucks in the main courtyard. They asked the workmen where they might find the pictures and were led to one small room, guarded by a double lock. There, before their eyes, were twelve paintings, works by Giovanni Bellini, Raphael, Gozzoli, Luigi Luini, and Piero della Francesca. In a storeroom they found other pictures stacked up, "higgledy piggledy," waiting for the spring opening of the museum.[55]

They travelled on to Rome where King reported a week later that the Italian recovery flourished, thanks to the aid of the Marshall Plan and the "enormous, vital energy" of the Italian people themselves, although he admitted that the war-torn South lagged sadly behind, and that within 50 km of Rome, he found himself in the heart of a primitive agrarian society.[56] The Gordon family spent Christmas with friends in Rome and, because of a missed train connection, New Year's Eve in Pisa, where they were compensated by a moonlit view of the leaning tower.[57] And then, it was on to England and beyond it, the highlands and glens of Scotland.

The trip to England held an unexpected pleasure: an invitation from Britain's chancellor of the Exchequer, Sir Stafford Cripps, to accompany him to the opening of a new factory in the north of England, an area which, since the 1930s, had been one of the most depressed regions of the country. And then, the grand finale of the trip: Edinburgh. "I am back in Scotland after twenty-five years," he told his audience on his International Commentary, broadcast from Edinburgh on 19 January:

> I say *back* because it is an astonishing thing the way ancestry asserts itself in the case of a Scotsman. It is all very well to believe that nationalism is one of the expensive anachronisms that are the blight of international relations today. I felt that in my twelve weeks in Paris at the UN Assembly: I felt it at every border I crossed in Europe. But I must confess that in returning to Edinburgh, when I walk up Princes Street and cross over to the High Street and St Giles, and walk up the Royal Mile to the Castle, I find myself caught up in the mesh of history. And my Scottish nationality seems very important.[58]

One wonders how this deeply committed humanist and supporter of "nations without walls" is going to reconcile his thorough-going internationalism with his own strong sense of patriotism, and his love of his ancestral past. As though acknowledging the issue, he goes on to say, "Now, this nationalism may not be as baneful as it might appear to a thorough going internationalist." Gordon's Scottish conservatism and faithfulness to his own history did not require him to violate the patriotic loyalties and love that other national groups held for their own histories. King's thought always encompassed respect for diversity and tolerance of difference. Although later in his life his criticism of the political outgrowths of national loyalties became more sharply focused, and he spoke more directly of the danger of their perversion in the nationalism of the modern state, he never apologized for that organic, invisible web of shared experience and association that binds human beings to their community and to their past.

And so they sailed for home on the *Britannica*, encouraged and hopeful after their odyssey through Europe, luggage safely in hand. Gordon continued to work happily with the CBC throughout 1949, writing a long report for the corporation on his own impressions of recovery in

Europe, and giving his assessment of broadcasting possibilities (contacts, technical details, even travel notes on where to stay) in the various countries. He also covered the Fourth General Assembly that fall, and continued writing on a freelance basis for both *The Nation*, and *The Atlantic Monthly*. It came as something of a surprise then, to both him and the CBC, when he was invited to accept a position within the UN bureaucracy itself, in its division of human rights. The invitation came through the personal contact of John Peters Humphrey, the first director of the Human Rights Division and author of the Secretariat draft of the Universal Declaration of Human Rights.[59] Gordon had known Humphrey during the 1930s in Montreal, when they were both charter members of the LSR branch in that city. At that time, Humphrey was practising law in Montreal, where he had been a student of Percy Corbett at McGill and where, in 1937, he became a colleague of both Corbett and Frank Scott on McGill's law faculty. In 1946, Humphrey was appointed to the United Nations as director of the Human Rights Division, and he and Gordon once again came in contact.

Gordon's departure from the CBC was entirely amicable, though certainly regretted on the CBC side and to some degree on his own. As he explained in his letter of resignation on 26 December 1949, his first interest had always been international affairs; and having been a commentator and interpreter for so long, he now felt a desire to accept a more direct share in making the UN work.[60] Ira Dilworth, general supervisor of the International Service, replied immediately that he would not embarrass King by asking him to reconsider, but had he thought there was the slightest chance of reversing the decision, "I should make every possible effort to retain you." He continued,

> As I have indicated to you on other occasions, your work as CBC Representative at Lake Success has given us the liveliest satisfaction. You have done an excellent job for us and we appreciate that very deeply indeed. I personally want to tell you that I have always felt keenly indebted to you, not only for the skill and ability with which you carried on your work, but for your spirit and attitude. Your willingness to undertake every possible assignment and your ability to work with people of differing points of view and temperaments have made our association an extremely pleasant and fruitful one.[61]

And so the decade of the 1940s ended. It had been a period of considerable professional accomplishment for King, but as he and Ruth looked back from their tenth wedding anniversary, it was clear that it had also been a decade of the greatest domestic happiness and enjoyment of their family life together. As is often the case when couples come to parenthood in their more mature years, they marvelled at their good fortune and doted on their children. In spite of King's frequent absences and heavy schedule, and surely in large part because of Ruth's maternal devotion and steady hand, the children had a close and affectionate relationship with both their parents in these early years. Charley's birth in November 1940 had resulted in that mixture of joy and apprehension typical of the arrival of a first child, and he required minute attention on a twenty-four-hour basis. "Fortunately," King had written to his mother, "we have a very good baby nurse – Miss O'Meara who weighs 200 lbs and has been a baby's nurse for about half a century."[62] Ruth came from the hospital to a clean house, a roaring fire in the living room and an abundance of fresh flowers from "the proud father – and all of us watching with joy the first bottle at home." Alison Ruth was born in January 1943, and in short order had complete control of her father's heart. By her second birthday, King was writing to his mother, "There is really nothing that Alison doesn't say or understand now and you can watch her pick up a phrase from Charles as quick as a flash."[63] King later described their seven years at the MacDougal-Sullivan Gardens in the Village as very happy years in ideal family surroundings. The children played in the garden and climbed rocks in Central Park, and Charley attended the Little Red Schoolhouse – or "Little Red," as it was called.

King had stayed behind to work in New York when Ruth took the children up to Cape Cod for July and August with her sister-in-law, Sally Anderson, and Sally's two boys ages five and three, joined by Alan Anderson and King whenever possible. After visiting them at the end of July, King wrote his mother, "Alison was almost unrecognizable she is so plump and bronze: her appetite is enormous. The children are getting along very well together and the rather difficult meal problem is settled by a chart with blue stars for good conduct ... Alison is the only one so far who has missed a star: she socked Andy one breakfast and temporarily broke up the orderly proceedings." By October of that same year, he commented simply, "Alison is a perfect tornado."[64]

But even an adoring father can be blind to a daughter's potential. In view of Alison Gordon's professional career as a novelist who has written murder mysteries set in a baseball genre, and as a journalist who covered the Toronto Blue Jays for the *Toronto Star* (1979 to 1983), there is a nice irony about King's assessment of her interests. In this less than prescient observation in 1947 when she was four-and-a-half years old, he wrote to his mother: "Charley is keeping up his baseball and is getting better and better at it. He and I have batting practice and catching practice and he can always give me a full description of the big league games with all the names of the players and the plays. Alison tries hard to keep up but her major interest is not really baseball."[65]

Charley too came in for his share of praise. In a letter to Charley's grandmother when he was four, his father described him as "a wonderful little boy." When Ruth took the children to Birkencraig for the summer of 1944, Charley basked in the adoring attention of his grandmother and aunts, and Ruth's letters to King are filled with details of daily schedules. Ruth wrote to her mother-in-law: "I just went up to the flagpole [the highest point on the island] with Ruthie. It is so beautiful. I must take Charles up tomorrow. Such a wonderful feeling of the largeness of it all with the sky and clouds all beautifully tinted."[66]

Ruth followed through on her intention and a trip up to the flagpole became an evening ritual for Charley. It is small wonder that Charles and Alison grew up loving the island as had their parents and grandparents before them, and Birkencraig has remained the family centre for all the Gordons and their expanding family of in-laws, grandchildren, and great-grandchildren.

Gordon himself visited Birkencraig whenever his schedule allowed, and his ties with his mother and family were spontaneous, profound, and entirely taken for granted, as hundreds of letters exchanged regularly over the years attest. There were also family visits whenever possible: to Gretta and Mary, both married, in Toronto; to Lois in Montreal and then in Toronto; to Alison and Ruthie in Winnipeg, and Marjorie in Ottawa. King remembered his father's birthday each year. Typical was his letter to his mother in September 1945: "This is Daddy's birthday and I wanted to write you before the day is over. He would be hopeful at the new chance the world had – perhaps the last chance – to build peace. He would now be at it, urging our leaders to build more wisely than the last time."[67]

A great sadness visited the family at Mary's death to cancer in January of 1948. King had always been particularly close to his sister, and they had shared not only their childhood as only son and first daughter, but their days at Oxford, travels on the continent, and vacations in Florence. In 1933, Mary had married Humphrey Carver, an Oxford graduate. He had come to Canada in 1930, where he became a noted landscape architect. Knowing that the end was imminent, King wrote to his mother, who was in Toronto at Mary's bedside:

> Dearest Mother,
>
> If you were anybody else, I don't know how I could write to you tonight. Humphrey's phone call has taken the heart out of me. But I know that though your heart will be very heavy, your faith and courage will be strong. And Mary has some of the same qualities from you. You will be a great blessing to them all in these months ahead. And you will all be constantly in our hearts.

After reminiscing about their childhood together and that special closeness that came with being the first two siblings, sharing similar temperaments and interests as they grew older, King continued:

> What a dauntless spirit she had, often distressed by the ailments of the flesh, but stubbornly refusing to be downed. And that wonderful, vital spirit is what she will always be.
>
> Now very much love, dearest Mother. I am so glad that you are there. And I know that God who watches over the spirits of his children is close to you all.
>
> Your loving son,
>
> King[68]

Mary died two weeks later.

12

The UN: Human Rights and the Prisoner of War Commission

The issue of human rights had, in one form or another, been central to Gordon's interest since his student days at Oxford, forming a substratum of energy that fueled his social action. During his years of reporting for the CBC, he was constantly drawn to following the course of the human rights debates, and he was present at the Third General Assembly in Paris when the Universal Declaration of Human Rights was passed in December of 1948. In this context, it was natural that his earlier friendship with John Humphrey should be rekindled, and they met frequently for lunch, vigorously discussing relevant topics of mutual interest such as the role of the press in international crises, "I attacking and he defending," Humphrey wrote in his diary.[1] King was also fond of John's charming wife, Jeanne, and he occasionally proofread pieces she had written, or accepted the Humphreys' invitation to dinner after driving John home from the temporary headquarters of the Secretariat at Hunter College. When Humphrey invited Gordon to join the Secretariat as a member of his senior staff, one of five section chiefs – "we called it the Information Section"[2] – in December of 1949, he was delighted to accept, and he began work in mid-January 1950.

Since Gordon's most recent experience had been in communications, writing, and editing, it was logical that he would put these skills to work in the areas of public information and publications, including the writing of speeches and reports. The new position was something of a change of pace for Gordon and at first he found it rather restricting. Working for the CBC, he had been free to roam, covering the waterfront, as he put it. He had met informally with delegates in the lounge, met fellow correspondents in corridors, and concluded his day at 6 p.m. sharp, with his daily script ready to be broadcast over the circuit to Toronto or Montreal.

Now his roaming days were over and he found himself knowing less about the organization as a whole, having become an international civil servant with a specific job – "one of the hundred jobs or thousand jobs that were being done by the international staff."[3] There were other restrictions as well. He arrived in his new office on his first day with a simple request for a typewriter, only to be told by his (also new) secretary that he would now have to dictate. In alarm, he protested that he could only think on a typewriter and, although he eventually learned to dictate, he brought in his trusty portable from home.

Humphrey's first plan for Gordon was for him to give a series of lectures across Western Canada publicizing the UN, specifically the work of the Division of Human Rights. Under the auspices of the Canadian Institute of International Affairs, the tour would include lectures to women's branches (afternoons), men's branches (evenings), UN Associations, and radio addresses. His itinerary included Winnipeg, Regina, Saskatoon, Calgary, Edmonton, Vancouver, and Victoria. There must have been a reassuring sense of familiarity as once again Gordon stumped across the Prairies. He was buoyed up by what he considered to be a "useful piece of educational activity," and he reported to Humphrey that he had covered nearly 10,000 km, giving twelve addresses in seven western Canadian cities.[4] Winter weather on the Prairies is rarely auspicious for travel, and 1950 was a particularly bad year. The morning Gordon left Saskatoon for Edmonton, the thermometer stood at -46°, and because his train was delayed by four hours, his audience had all gone home by the time he arrived. Doughty as they were, however, they reassembled for a luncheon the next day in a balmy temperature of -32°. Even the West Coast did not escape the weather, and it was blanketed with snow for over a month, a shortage of fuel adding to the misery. Nevertheless, with the exception of Victoria, his meetings were well attended. Perhaps King might be forgiven for the tone of pride that crept into his report to Humphrey, as he took pleasure in the hardiness and good judgment of these western folk, and in his own ability to draw a crowd in such harsh weather. Only "Red Victoria" had remained impervious to his charms.

He was scarcely back from the western tour when Humphrey once again sent Gordon to Canada, this time to Ottawa to testify before a Senate committee on a Canadian bill of rights. The invitation had come to Humphrey from Senator Arthur Roebuck, a member of the Senate Committee on Human Rights and Fundamental Freedoms. Although it was thirteen years since Gordon had left Canada, it was clear that his reputation lived on. Humphrey wrote in his diary, "Mr. Himel [Irving Himel, Canadian lawyer and civil libertarian] wrote to me objecting to my designation of King Gordon as the man to represent me at the Canadian Senate meeting. Says that King Gordon is too closely connected with the C.C.F., that F. R. Scott will appear, etc. I rejected the objection and King will go."[5] Gordon was delighted with the honour and, perhaps feeling the sting of Mr. Himel's challenge to his political impartiality, he assured the committee of his neutrality: "It is perhaps not necessary to remind you that while, as a Canadian, I am particularly happy to be asked to give testimony before a Senate Committee, I am here not primarily as a Canadian but as an international official. My testimony, I know, will be considered in that light."[6]

There was nothing neutral, however, about Gordon's unflagging loyalty to the division or to the principles of the Universal Declaration of Human Rights, and in speech after speech, such as the one he delivered to the Wellesley Summer Institute of Social Progress that July, there was a familiar theme: that he did not expect the UN to provide the answer to history or to usher in the Kingdom (a term that, after 1939, he no longer used) any more than he had expected the Church or the CCF to accomplish this. Like them, it was a step along the way, "an emergent creation in the historical process carrying along obsolescent elements from the past, and daringly putting forth fresh shoots that may grow and harden into the reality of tomorrow."[7]

In another assignment during his first months with the division, Gordon was given the responsibility of writing a book on human rights, an educational endeavour to interpret the Universal Declaration of Human Rights and to stress its significance and likely impact. The book was published in July of 1950 by the United Nations Department of Public Information as *These Rights and Freedoms.*[8]

The drafting of the Declaration itself had been a complicated process, and part of Gordon's task was to sort through the somewhat tangled accounts of its coming into being. John Humphrey had been appointed to the United Nations Secretariat as the first director of the Human Rights Division in August 1946, and the Commission on Human Rights first met in January 1947. At this initial meeting, the commission elected Eleanor Roosevelt, the US representative to both the General Assembly and the Commission on Human Rights, as chairman, with P.C. Chang of China (Taiwan) and René Cassin of France as vice-chairmen; Charles Malik, the Lebanese representative on the commission, became the rapporteur. The first task of the commission was to draft an international bill of rights, the precursor of the Universal Declaration of Human Rights, which was passed by the General Assembly in Paris the following December. In *These Rights and Freedoms,* Gordon meticulously traced the history of the various drafts of each article of the Declaration: the Secretariat draft (written by Humphrey); the version by a drafting committee set up by Mrs Roosevelt to meet the objections of the French and Russian delegations that they were being excluded from the drafting process; the commission's version as drafted in the second and third sessions; and a summary of the General Assembly debate and the final text of each article.

A controversy developed later among scholars over just where the credit for the actual writing of the first draft of the Declaration should lie. It is argued that René Cassin (later recipient of the Nobel Peace Prize in 1968 and generally recognized as the father of the Universal Declaration of Human Rights) may have exaggerated his claim to have written the first draft, which was actually written by Humphrey. The proponents of this point of view claimed that Cassin spent merely a single weekend going over the Secretariat (Humphrey's) draft, making only minor changes that dealt with order and phraseology and not substance.[9] Gordon, understandably, did not touch on this issue, as Cassin's reputation as author was still nascent at the time of writing and so the controversy was not yet public.

In the introduction to the book, Gordon gave his readers a brief history of the concept of human rights and of the attempts, stretching as far back as Hammurabi and the ancient Hebrews, to protect the individual against oppression by the strong. These rights, which have taken their peculiarly modern shape since the Enlightenment, had suffered a "ruthless challenge" with the rise of fascism and Nazism: "During the war, a campaign of systematic extermination of the members of the Jewish race was carried on in Germany, a savage campaign for which human history could provide no parallel. Political freedom disappeared. The power of the State became absolute."[10] The Allied leaders and their governments insisted that the foundations of the peace must be built upon respect for human rights, a determination reflected in wartime statements such as the Atlantic Charter of 1941. These efforts reached fruition in 1945 at San Francisco with the adoption of the United Nations Charter, which vested the task of promoting respect for human rights in the General Assembly and in the UN Educational, Scientific and Cultural Organization (UNESCO). Gordon then raised two fundamental issues concerning the Declaration as it was subsequently passed by the

General Assembly in 1948. First, what is the status of individual human rights vis a vis the traditional right of the nation state (or ruling body) to speak for its citizens? The implication of this question is clear: How are the rights of citizens to be protected from violation by their own governments? And secondly, what legal standing does the Declaration have in international law?

Regarding the first issue, Gordon wrote: "It is perhaps significant that [in the Charter of the UN] it is not 'the High Contracting Parties' who re-affirm their faith in fundamental rights in the dignity and worth of the human person, in the equal rights of men and women and of nations large and small. It is rather 'We, the peoples of the United Nations' who assume this great responsibility."[11] In adopting the Universal Declaration of Human Rights, it is clear that the United Nations intended that, for the first time, the rights of individuals, formerly vested in nation states, now become an *international* responsibility.[12]

Concerning the matter of the implementation of this principle, Gordon described the proposed International Covenant on Civil and Political Rights, which would ensure that the signatory states would provide protection of human rights both by acting individually within their own territories, and by acting in cooperation with other member states of the United Nations. For example, national action might take the form of incorporating the provisions of the Covenant in the internal laws of the state; and international action might include mechanisms for receiving petitions and investigation and settling grievances arising out of complaints that the Covenant had been violated.[13]

Humphrey also addressed this issue in a 1945 article, "The Parent of Anarchy," in which he envisioned an international government, based on the principles of federalism, that would possess the power to enforce the protection of rights within (otherwise) sovereign nations: "States would retain their sovereignty, subject to limited powers granted to the international government," through radical amendments to the Charter of the United Nations, thus enabling individual states to co-exist within "still larger loyalities."[14] However, by 1971 Humphrey had come to the conclusion that his earlier view of such a world government had been utopian, and that such plans for international states based on the federal principle inevitably come to grief at the point of surrendering sovereignty.[15]

In his appearance before the Canadian Senate committee in April 1950, Gordon had raised the question of the moral and political authority of the Declaration, which, he stated, could not be overestimated.[16] First of all, he argued, its moral authority sprang from the nature of the document itself in its appeal to natural human rights. Furthermore, both its moral and political legitimacy lay in the fact that its passage was an act of the world's most important political organ; that it was a synthesis of opinion throughout diverse races, nationalities, and religions; that the vote for adoption was cast by forty-eight nations of the Third General Assembly of the UN, with eight abstentions and no dissensions; and that, following its adoption, it had continued to receive an unofficial consensus of support from churches, private organizations and individuals all over the world. Curling back to his initial premise of the claim of natural rights, he concluded that the character of the principles enunciated in the Declaration gave it inherent authority. This argument drew heavily on western post-Enlightenment thought, of course, and might be seen to beg the question. One must keep in mind that these were the early days of the interpretation of the Declaration, and the issue of its moral claim on nation states was widely debated in the years following the Second World War. King returned to the question repeatedly throughout his life.

The second fundamental question Gordon had raised in his book, that of the legal status of the Universal Declaration in international law, still remained to be addressed, and here he, like Humphrey, appealed to its actual application in international actions: citations of the Declaration in numerous important United Nations resolutions; its use in new national constitutions and international statutes and agreements in which it was sometimes quoted verbatim; and actions by the Trusteeship Council in writing human rights provisions into the trust agreements of former colonies.[17]

Ronald St John Macdonald argues that in contrast to the agonizing process with respect to the covenants, which were *intended* to be legally binding in international law, the relative ease with which the Universal Declaration was adopted by the General Assembly in 1948 was due to the fact that most states took the view that the Declaration would *not* be a binding part of positive law. However, this clearly was not Humphrey's view, and Macdonald quotes him as saying that while the Declaration had been adopted by the General Assembly as a "common standard of achievement for all peoples and nations … [i]t would be a great mistake to think that the Declaration is without legal significance."[18] And in a letter to Macdonald in 1986, Gordon stated that Humphrey "forbade any of his staff to describe the Universal Declaration as without legal authority."[19] Macdonald writes:

> For Humphrey, the Universal Declaration has immense political and moral authority equal to that of the Charter itself – and its impact on

> world opinion has been very great indeed ... Having been constantly invoked and referred to inside and outside of the United Nations, he has argued that the Declaration is now part of the customary law of nations and thus binding on all states. Whether or not the rules of the Declaration are *jus cogens,* he emphasizes that "the Declaration is, of course, more important than any convention or treaty could ever be, because a convention or treaty is only binding on those states which ratify it."[20]

While Gordon's own thinking on these issues at the time was largely reactive and pragmatic, Humphrey, along with Percy Corbett, had a profound influence on his thinking in the area of international theory. Gordon's subsequent years in the field – Korea, the Middle East, the Congo – would provide further strands of experience that, upon reflection, he eventually wove into his own coherent and integrated point of view.

Gordon continued to carry a heavy writing load for the division and was in particular demand as a speechwriter. John Humphrey referred in his diary to an "important speech" that Gordon had written for Henri Laugier (assistant secretary general of the United Nations, responsible for the Department of Social Affairs within the Secretariat) combining Laugier's style with Humphrey's ideas.[21] It could not have failed to please Gordon that his careful attention to research and his ability to communicate complex matters clearly but without over-simplification was recognized. He also made a sincere effort to write in the "voice" of the speaker, not always an easy task, particularly later when he was in Korea and found the style of some of the American military speakers somewhat "bombastic."

Gordon was assigned two other responsibilities during his tenure with the Human Rights Division: liaison officer with UNESCO (which, like the Human Rights Division, operated under the parent body of the Economic and Social Council, or ECOSOC); and secretary to the Ad Hoc Commission on Prisoners of War. The meetings for both these assignments necessitated two or three lengthy trips to Europe each year, initiating the long separations from Ruth and the children that continued throughout his years with the United Nations. Often, Gordon was able to combine the meetings into one trip, as UNESCO met in France (usually in Paris), and the commission met in Geneva. By this time the family had moved from Garrison to Barney Park, Irvington-on-Hudson, where they had bought a spacious colonial-style house built in 1915, for $23,000.[22] The Westchester County location, only 30 km from midtown Manhattan, made for a much shorter commute for Gordon. It also eased Ruth's sense of isolation when King was away, and she quickly became involved in community and school activities.

While most prisoners of war had been accounted for and repatriated by 1950 in accordance with the Geneva Conventions, the United Nations Ad Hoc Commission on Prisoners of War was established by the General Assembly Resolution 427 (V) of 14 December 1950, in response to protests from Germany, Italy, and Japan that, even at this late date, the USSR and China were continuing to hold prisoners of war. These actions violated the Geneva Conventions of 1929 and 1949, which required that a full accounting be made of all prisoners of war held or detained in the custody of a foreign power. The new Ad Hoc Commission defined "full accounting" to include provision of full information on all prisoners still detained as well as those prisoners who had died under detention. It was not enough to give total figures, whether of the detained or of the dead. The names and other relevant information were of decisive importance. "Human beings are not mere units in statistical totals."[23]

The commission comprised three individuals who answered directly to the secretary general and did not serve as representatives of their own nations: Judge Gustavo Guerrero of El Salvador, the chairman and a member of the International Court of Justice in the Hague; American-born Countess Estelle Bernadotte of Sweden, widow of Count Folke Bernadotte (the United Nations mediator who had been assassinated in Jerusalem in September of 1948); and Judge Aung Khine of the High Court of Burma. Gordon was asked to join the commission as its secretary and he was responsible for all reports submitted to the secretary general's office.

The commission began its work in July of 1951 with the painstaking task of fact-finding. Prior to the first meeting, the secretary general's office had sent a request for information to eighty governments (of which sixty-three eventually responded) asking for names of prisoners still held by them, the names of those who had been repatriated, and the names of those who had died under detention. If a nation had not fought in the war or had repatriated all its prisoners, this was also noted.[24] The numbers were appalling. As of March 1950, there were still some 1,300,000 German soldiers registered as missing in the Eastern and Western theatres of war.[25] The Japanese government stated that out of about 2,726,000 nationals who were in areas occupied by Soviet forces at the end of the war, approximately 370,000 had not been repatriated or otherwise accounted for. These Japanese nationals were said to be alive in the USSR, North Korea, and China.[26] The Germans and Japanese had been meticulous in their record-keeping and produced lists of names. This was in contrast to the Italian delegation, headed by a mother who had lost three sons on the Russian front, which was able to produce only about 400 names.[27]

These German, Italian, and Japanese nationals still being held included not only combatants but civilians as well. For example, in 1951 the government of the Federal Republic of Germany reported that some 750,000 German civilians had been deported to the USSR, of whom 23,515 were known to still be alive and living in "compulsory settlements." Civilians were also being held in Czechoslovakia and in Poland. Of those held in Poland, 3,240 were children, detained against the wishes of their parents.[28]

The commission relied heavily on the authenticated lists of names voluntarily submitted by the governments of the Axis powers. Although the USSR and China also submitted reports, these were not always reliable – particularly in the case of the USSR, which claimed at one point that all prisoners of war had been repatriated. The commission provided the information it received to the relevant governments, the International Committee of the Red Cross, the League of Red Cross Societies, and the Red Crescent Societies. The reports of the commission to the secretary general were publicized and undoubtedly exerted pressure on the governments concerned. Interrogations of those released helped to fill in gaps, and reports from families who had received communications (especially in letters) proved to be an invaluable source of information. A broadcast over Peking radio on 1 December 1952, prior to the mass repatriation of Japanese nationals from the Chinese mainland, indicated that in addition to some 30,000 Japanese residents, there remained an undisclosed number of Japanese "war criminals."[29]

Still, as in all wars, there were hundreds of thousands who would never be accounted for. The Federal Republic of Germany obtained the consent of some countries to open the graves of unknown soldiers in order to identify as many of the unknown dead as possible. By these methods the German government was able to present the commission with a list of the graves of Soviet nationals buried in the Federal Republic.[30]

The archival files of the reports and letters tell heartrending stories of families searching for lost members. King preserved a copy in his files of a letter to Estelle Bernadotte in March 1954 from "The Association of Families of Japanese in the Soviet Union," which tells the story of many.

The letter, signed by four Japanese women, solicited Bernadotte's help, beseeching her to intercede with the authorities of the Soviet Union in order to bring about a speedy release and repatriation of Japanese prisoners, "our dear ones," of whom a great number nothing at all was known. They wrote:

> Spring is returning for the ninth year since the war's end. But our husbands, our sons, and our brothers are still held in captivity on the cold steppes of Siberia ... Our anxieties know no bounds.
>
> Deprived of the mainstay of the family we have lived these long years, struggling for subsistence and suffering indescribable miseries and privations. Aged parents are living in the one hope of seeing some day their sons once more. Children now in school yearn for their fathers gone since their infancy.

The women appealed to the countess in her position as a member of a commission established by the United Nations; as a pre-eminent representative of a great neutral nation; and finally, "because we are women, and you, too, are one."[31]

By the time the commission wound up its work in September 1954, some 60,000 prisoners and civilians had been repatriated through its efforts. The commission did not claim sole credit for this result, but Gordon felt that the independence of its members, who operated free from political constraints, made their work far more effective than would have been the case had they represented the interests of specific governments.

As for himself, King reported to Ruth that he found it a "rather tricky business" being secretary.[32] In many ways, as representative of the Secretariat and also as a natural administrator who liked to get things done, Gordon became the de facto convener of the meetings – an arrangement implicitly acceptable to the "grand old man," as the members affectionately called Guerrero. To begin with, there was the problem of language among the commissioners, and King also became the de facto translator, as he explained: "I helped keep them talking. The Chairman of the Commission [Guerrero] understood very little English. He was Spanish speaking, lived in France, and spoke French with a Spanish accent. Countess Bernadotte spoke French with a good American private school accent. Judge Khine spoke no French at all. So I translated the Spanish-French of the Chairman into English, and the American-French into Spanish. Interesting."[33]

One wonders why a UN commission at this level would not be provided a professional translator. One explanation might be that they wished to keep their meetings informal and so did not ask for one; or they may not have wished to admit that they needed one. The group was small and intimate, and Gordon felt himself fully a member. He always arrived early to prepare for the meetings in Geneva, helped by the efficient and courteous UN staff and welcomed at the Eden Hotel, where the concierge remembered the Gordon family's visit in the winter of 1948. He then waited for the commissioners to arrive (usually over an interval of several days), filling the time with concerts, art galleries, and even skiing trips. He also called on the government delegations to the commission – the Russians never arrived until the last minute – and had "working teas" with the International Red Cross. And he even found time to visit Sir Stafford Cripps, who was recovering from a mysterious illness in a clinic in Zurich.

Once everyone had arrived, the long days began: from nine in the morning until seven in the evening, and often much longer for Gordon. Most of the days were filled with hearing all kinds of evidence from the governmental representatives, information that Gordon then had to analyze and get into some kind of shape for the commission to study. It was detailed and sometimes tedious work.

There were also political sensitivities and manoeuverings to be considered, particularly between the Russians and the Germans, who rejected the claims by the Soviets that they no longer held any German prisoners, and seized any occasion they could to publicize their plight. Gordon pointed out to Countess Bernadotte, that in fairness to the Germans, "one must assume that governments are interested in the return of their citizens from captivity and you will recall that all three governments, Germany, Japan, and Italy, urged very moderate action on the Commission in regard to its approach to the USSR and Communist China."[34] The commission acceded to the more reasonable demands of Germany, such as passing on names to western governments, but nevertheless, in the judgment of the commissioners, the Germans often went too far. Gordon gave the countess an account of an instance when he himself was subject to such pressure when the German assistant observer called on Gordon to inform him that the German minister of state would be calling on the secretary general later in the day to take up the work of the commission with him. He asked for what Gordon considered "inside information" so that his minister might have an "informed" conversation with the secretary general. Gordon replied that although Secretary General Dag

Hammarskjöld was new on the job, he was well informed on all Secretariat matters, and the German minister could be fully confident that he would be versed on all relevant matters when they met. Gordon clearly resented this request and felt it was a subtle attempt to circumvent the commission by going to the higher authority. In general, however, he was satisfied that the commission had "resisted the more extravagant requests" of the Germans and withstood their political pressure; still, he acknowledged that the panel was walking a tightrope between the legitimate right of the Germans to have their prisoners returned and the exigencies of Cold War politics.[35]

Dynamics within the commission itself could be complicated, although not bitter. For instance, King felt that the commissioners needed to be more persistent in their questioning, and the countess was sometimes engulfed by a feeling of futility that not enough was being accomplished. Indeed, in view of Soviet inflexibility, she questioned whether she would even attend the final meetings: "I personally don't entertain any hopes whatsoever as to a change of policy due to the recent death of Stalin," she wrote to Gordon.[36] In his reply, he pointed out to her that her absence would almost certainly be interpreted as suggesting a division of opinion within the commission, giving an unfortunate impression.[37] The countess yielded and she attended the meetings.

Ernest Hamburger, an international lawyer and a social affairs officer in the Division of Human Rights, who had been sent over to Geneva to help Gordon with the workload, described his view of King's role: "It's getting to be like a family group: Khine the uncle, the Countess the daughter, Guerrero the father, and you the wise family advisor that's called in when they don't know where to go!"[38] On the whole, they were a happy family who worked together harmoniously, and combined their duties with a lively social life including the countess's luncheons and the chairman's "grand smoking" [i.e., black tie] dinners. Typically, Gordon also had numerous other friends and contacts among the press and UN staff whom he saw socially.

When, at the request of the secretary general, Gordon left the commission in the summer of 1954 to begin his tour with the United Nations Korean Reconstruction Agency, its members were dismayed. Judge Guerrero, angry that the secretary general had made this decision without first consulting him, protested in a formal note, asking that the Secretariat should be "stabilized." As King noted to Ruth, it was a bit late for that. However, he was excused from his new duties in Korea to attend a last session of the commission in September 1954, finishing up the final report and staying over the weekend to give the chairman a final bit of help: "The Chairman is giving a press conference [Monday] and I'm afraid he might boggle with the figures under questioning and it is really the Secretariat's job to give him the kind of technical assistance that he requires for just such occasions."[39]

Gordon welcomed his second assignment as the Human Rights Division's liaison with UNESCO, particularly as he had established several unofficial relations with the UNESCO staff in Paris while covering the Third General Assembly for the CBC. In addition, since its headquarters were in Paris, the meetings could be coordinated with the commission's meetings in Geneva. In the larger organizational picture of the United Nations, the Human Rights Commission and UNESCO (a "specialized agency") both came under the umbrella of the Economic and Social Council (ECOSOC). Gordon's duties as the liaison officer between these two bodies largely involved attending meetings at the Paris Headquarters of UNESCO as an observer, with the dual purpose of keeping the Human Rights Division informed of UNESCO's programs and, at the same time, acting as a watchdog and publicist for human rights. His attendance at the meetings was not without controversy, however, and an entry in John Humphrey's diary for 5 October 1950, illuminates something of the tensions and turf wars among departments of the UN bureaucracy, claims not yet clearly defined or easily surrendered. Humphrey wrote that, "King Gordon is learning what it is to be a United Nations official. Every obstacle has been put in the way of his proposed trip to Paris." On the one hand, there was pressure from the Social Department of the Secretariat to send its top-ranking director, Alva Myrdal, to the UNESCO meeting; on the other hand, Tor Gjesdal, the principal director of the UN department of public information, jealously guarding his territory and fearing that Gordon might speak for his department by making public statements, strongly objected to King's going. Humphrey put his foot down: "Tor Gjsedal notwithstanding Gordon is off for Paris tomorrow."[40]

It was in his public relations role – "selling human rights,"[41] as he called it – that in August 1952 Gordon attended two UNESCO seminars that focused on human rights, the first in Woutschoten, the Netherlands, and the second two weeks later near Compiègne, France. The Woutschoten seminar occasioned King's first trans-Atlantic flight. He loved new adventures and, writing on KLM stationery over Iceland, he told Ruth, "The whole thing is pretty surreal. But it is an introduction to an aspect of the modern world that I'd known about but hadn't realized."[42] On his arrival at the conference, he discovered that Queen Juliana would be entertaining the members of the seminar, but that, alas, his name had inadvertently been left off the list of guests, whereupon Gordon suggested to the UNESCO staff that the secretary general might not be pleased if the UN representative weren't included in the party. A hasty telephone to the palace ensued and King went and enjoyed a special introduction to the queen as "the UN representative." Speaking in this capacity, he enjoyed a chatty visit with Queen Juliana and described her to Ruth: "She is a very nice, simple, charming intelligent woman. One of the aides had mentioned that Alison's birthday was the same day as Princess Margriet's. So we had a talk about our children: she wanted to know who arrived first. And – although I was not sure – said, 'I believe it was the princess, your majesty.' She said, 'Well, was it about 7 o'clock?'"[43]

He returned home with two signed pictures of Princess Margriet and her sisters for Alison. He went on to tour Amsterdam and The Hague and had his first view of *The Night Watch* and Vermeer's *Milkmaid* at the Reichsmuseum, followed by Vermeer's *View of Delft* at the Mauritshuis. He walked on the beach at Scheveningen, and in his very old age he still recalled eating mussels in one of its narrow streets. The mayor of Delft received the delegates in the old town hall, and the only blight on an otherwise perfect trip was the sight of war damage still evident in Rotterdam.

Gordon often stopped in London on his way home from his European meetings, staying with the Sprys and renewing acquaintance with old friends. "London is so satisfying to come to," he wrote to Ruth: "In Paris and Geneva I have the feeling of camping out: I've decided that that is what is wrong with most foreigners in Paris – they are just campers and a camping trip can be too long. But in London you feel you are on solid ground – politically, socially, spiritually. There is a depth to this people; and a scheme of values which is respected. I would like being here for a while – with you."[44]

He renewed CBC contacts and took the train to Oxford to see Gilbert Ryle ("balder and more lined") and Isaiah Berlin ("bustling and full of words and good stories. An excellent lunch"). In February 1952, he joined the Sprys in London just after the death of King George VI: "London is still recovering from the week of mourning. Apparently it was quite an exhausting week. Graham and Irene [Biss Spry] were at the funeral at Windsor. Graham said the spirit and mood of the people reminded him of nothing so much as Dunkirk."[45]

Meanwhile, Ruth and the children carried on at home in Irvington. Ruth and King exchanged daily letters filled with descriptive details of their activities, that common fabric of life they shared. King talked about his work, international politics, friends, and events. Ruth's letters were replete with details about the children, and a charming, often self-deprecating, wit. They discussed books, though one wonders when they found time to read so many. Alison advised her father, "Eat plenty of fruit and you'll keep healthy."[46] Charley told his Dad, "I wish you were here for my birthday," confiding, "I am beginning to miss you more and more."[47] There is a poignant note running through King's letters as well, and he missed Ruth and the children keenly. Aboard the *RMS Queen Mary* in January 1952, he wrote to Ruth: "It was depressing leaving you and Alison. I'm afraid that in spite of your picture of me as a carefree world traveller, I'm a home person and don't like going away and being away from my family. Alison at the boat looked about the way I felt. I suppose it's because I love you very much and also, in a different way, love Alison and Charley."[48]

A summer day in Paris, with clear sunshine and billowy clouds, reminded him of Birkencraig; and he felt a shaft of loneliness in Geneva as he looked at the mountains sharply etched against the sky in brilliant moonlight. He wandered down to the lakefront by himself and wrote to Ruth, "It was all very lovely – not quite so lovely though as the same moon rising over the Island just 4 weeks ago."[49]

Many more separations from his family still lay ahead.

Members of the United Nations Secretariat were not immune from the general paranoia of the McCarthy years, and King himself had a gentle brush with it. The occasion was his application to the Bureau of Personnel for a permanent contract with the Secretariat. The matter of its approval came to Egon Schwelb, the assistant director of the Human Rights Division. In response to his application, Schwelb had asked for additional information about his radical past. Gordon responded with some heat:

> It may be of some interest to you to know that as part of the preparation of my "case" before the Committee reviewing contracts ... Miss Howe of the Bureau of Personnel phoned to ask me to "fill up some gaps in my application." I was asked to say what I was doing between 1927 and 1929 and again between 1934 and 1937. It seems to me that, unless we are being subjected to something resembling an FBI check by the Bureau of Personnel, it is in the

> nature of an affront to insist upon such information from a senior employee after three years' service ... I don't think I need to add for your information that the years under investigation were not entirely dishonourable and had in fact some positive bearing on my fitness to be accepted as an officer in the Division of Human Rights.[50]

There is no reply on record, and it seems to have been the last of the matter.

The offer to join the staff of the United Nations Korean Reconstruction Agency (UNKRA), Gordon's first field assignment, came quite "out of the blue." As he recounted the story, he was working in his office on the 32nd floor of the new UN building when a friend, George Janocek (ironically, assistant director of the Department of Public Information, John Humphrey's nemesis) walked in and sat down for a chat. The conversation turned to Korea. It was June of 1954 and the armistice had been in place for nearly a year. Particularly because of his friendship with Pearson, Gordon had followed the negotiations closely and was glad to talk about the post-war reconstruction going on under the United Nations. Suddenly Janocek said, "Well look, we've been looking through your record and I see you have done quite a bit of information work in the past. Our Director of Information for UNKRA has just quit and we need to replace him pretty fast. Perhaps you'd better go out there."[51] Gordon laughed off the suggestion, but Janocek insisted he was serious and Gordon agreed to give the idea some thought. It didn't take long to decide. That evening he and Ruth had dinner guests and, as they cleared the plates between courses, King found a moment in the kitchen to ask Ruth what she thought of the idea. Within three weeks, Gordon was on his way to Seoul.

13

Gordon in Korea: The Devastation of War and the Face of Human Suffering

In requesting Humphrey's agreement to release Gordon to join the staff of the United Nations Korean Reconstruction Agency, General Alfred G. Katzin[1] presented his case tersely: "Such a loan, the Secretary-General assures us, would not exceed a two-year period. It would also be made with the assurance that Mr. Gordon would be available for the meetings of the Ad Hoc Commission on Prisoners of War in Geneva September 6–10."[2] A week later Katzin elaborated the secretary general's wishes that "the Secretariat not be deprived of Mr. King Gordon's services longer than possible, as he regards him as a most valuable senior member of the staff here."[3]

Gordon recalled that, unlike Judge Guerrero, "John Humphrey didn't protest very loudly when I informed him of the invitation."[4] He based this rather breezy recollection (written sometime in the 1980s) on his perception that, with the completion of the Declaration of Human Rights and its subsequent public presentation in *These Rights and Freedoms*, work in the Human Rights Division had slowed. Humphrey, however, saw his leaving in quite a different light. Years later, Ronald Macdonald recalled that Humphrey had, in fact, felt personally hurt by King's leaving, feeling that he had been let down during what he considered the division's greatest hour of need. In July 1958, when King and Ruth included the Humphreys as guests in a small dinner party in New York, Humphrey wrote in his diary: "It was a good party and I enjoyed myself. But my relationship with King will never be confident and frank again. Whenever I am with him I am on my guard, full of hesitations and even distrust. I remember Jeanne once saying about King – in the early McGill and L.S.R. days – that if she ever lost her confidence in him she wouldn't have much belief left in the human race. What a hero he then seemed, almost a paragon of virtue and moral courage."[5]

Still, Gordon and Humphrey met cordially many times over the years, crossing paths at conferences and meetings, and King frequently dropped in to Humphrey's office with informal reports of his work in the field. They also met at Humphrey's initiative once Gordon was back in New York.

Ruth and the children, unable to accompany King to Korea, would nevertheless be able to live in Japan. In his "Notes for an Autobiography," written in the 1980s, King recorded their reaction: "My family, Ruth, Charley 13, Alison 11, were a bit shocked but accepted the challenge bravely – and with some interest."[6] Ruth, while supportive, recalled standing in her kitchen and feeling stunned at the idea of having to arrange for renting the house, packing up, and setting off with the children by train and boat to meet King in Tokyo.[7]

After three days with the family at Birkencraig, King left for Japan and Korea in mid-July 1954, while Ruth and the children remained at the island. It was not an easy departure, and it was not helped by the fact that he was stopped for speeding as he drove up to Winnipeg to catch the plane. When he explained to the Mountie that he was leaving for Japan and Korea, he got off with just a warning – "I'm afraid I won't live it down soon," he wrote back to Ruth while in flight. He confessed that it had been a lonely day, with a quality of unreality. As he flew over the Prairies, he remembered that earlier trip thirty years before as he had ventured forth to test a vocation as a student missionary in British Columbia; and he recollected having similar feelings then of loneliness and apprehension. But he had survived and it had proven a fruitful and worthwhile experience. "I have a hunch this may be too – not only for me but for us all."[8]

The plan was that he spend August in Seoul, familiarizing himself with UNKRA and setting up his staff, and then return to New York via Geneva to help arrange family plans for the move to Japan. Of the UNKRA staff, only the agent general's wife was allowed to live in Korea; all other dependents lived in Japan, with "rest and rehabilitation" visits provided (with considerable irregularity and exceptions) about every six weeks. On his arrival in Tokyo – he kept his watch on Birkencraig time – he was taken to the UNKRA office, where he met the staff and had a long conversation with Harold E. Eastwood, the American general who was second in command to John B. Coulter, the agent general. General Eastwood also took him for lunch at the Press Club and to the Canadian Embassy, where he was welcomed warmly by Ambassador R.W. Mayhew – a delightful coincidence for Gordon, as this was that same Mayhew who had defeated him in the Victoria by-election in the spring of 1937, and to whom he felt a debt of gratitude for the happy course his life had taken as a result of that defeat. The Mayhews had King for lunch the next day, and they visited amicably around the pool in their beautiful garden, before driving him back to his hotel in the Embassy car, their previous political differences now seemingly forgotten.[9]

Gordon also met with two members of the Japanese foreign office, who presented him with their latest report concerning the Commission on Prisoners of War, and one of the officials invited him to his home for dinner – "I must say it is extraordinarily lucky to be invited into a Japanese home the second day I am in Tokyo,"[10] he told Ruth. His luck held, and his host also took him to a Japanese restaurant where they were waited on by geishas, "a pleasant form of male chauvinism to be waited on by these delightful geisha who looked after every need."[11] He also made inquiries concerning schools for Charley and Alison and housing for the family, and he was reassured that with the help of UNKRA, the embassy, and the Japanese Foreign Office, Ruth and the children would be well taken care of in Toyko. He closed his long letter to Ruth by asking her to assure his mother that he had already met some of her missionary friends.[12]

He arrived in Seoul in a heat wave and settled into his digs in the part of the US compound where UNKRA personnel were housed, which meant familiar food in the mess and plenty of company. The only drawback in his accommodation – apart from the oppressive heat – was a window that opened out onto a Buddhist temple where, just before four each morning, "the priest starts kicking up a terrible row first with a small drum which he hits with either increasing or diminishing tempo. I may get used to it, but it certainly wakened me this morning."[13] The first things to strike him about Korea, apart from this unwelcome morning alarm, were the war damage – shattered buildings, twisted bridges, military traffic everywhere, and beggars on the streets – and the energy of the people. As he watched the small (by North American standards) Korean men carrying enormous loads on A-frames, a sight that looked to him like "Alaska packboards with wooden legs," he marvelled at their strength. The women strapped their babies to their backs and carried bundles on their heads, and many of them wore white clothing that they kept spotlessly clean. "You come out from Canada," he observed, "with a kind of self-righteousness idea that you are doing a wonderful job for the poor Korean people. You aren't there long before you realize that they are doing the main job: we are just helping out with the things not available in Korea."[14]

UNKRA had been established by the UN General Assembly in December 1950, under the direction of an agent general who reported to the secretary general. Its mandate was "to assist the Korean people to relieve the suffering and to repair the devastation caused by aggression."[15] An advisory committee of five member states appointed by the General Assembly – Canada, India, the United Kingdom, the United States, and Uruguay – advised the agent general on major financial, procurement, distribution, and other economic matters. Initially, the most urgent need was for food, shelter, and medical treatment for the large population dislodged from their homes by the war. The task of providing this emergency care rested mainly with the United Nations Command, which was largely American, but UNKRA also contributed to this work by lending skilled staff for disease control, relief, and welfare. Much of this direct work – orphanages, clinics, hospitals – was done by missionaries, the YMCA, and the Red Cross, supported by grants-in-aid from UNKRA. UNKRA's fundamental mandate, however, was to support long-range reconstruction in the areas of agriculture, industry, mining, and education.

UNKRA's operations were funded by voluntary contributions from member governments of the UN, and Gordon's first duty as director of public information was to publicize the agency's need for money. In this task, he was helped by his invaluable assistant, Elma Ferguson, a Scotswoman, formerly a correspondent for the *London Sunday Times*, who had been with UNKRA from its beginning. Ferguson was held in the highest regard, and Gordon described her having "an excellent sense of values and a good sense of humour."[16] She was an immense help to King and became a lifelong friend, as she continued to work in various UN and international agencies long after the disbanding of UNKRA. Together, Gordon and Ferguson set out on a public relations blitz to disseminate information about UNKRA and make known its need for financial support. Back in New York in October, Gordon wrote to Sir Arthur Rucker, UNKRA's first agent general – that initially prospects for support did not look too favourable, with the British and Americans holding back until there was evidence that there would be commensurate support from other nations. Gordon and Ferguson set about doing their part to help UN delegations become aware of the important job UNKRA was doing and how disastrous – politically and economically – it would be for the program to fail. Using the limited means at hand, they mounted a large exhibit of photographs and big project maps in the delegates' section of the General Assembly building, then used radio, press, and television coverage to spread the contents of the agent general's report. A number of copies of the printed text of the report were flown to the UN Information Centre in London for distribution to the London press and for sale to other organizations and individuals.[17]

Encouraged by indications that both the British and the Americans were broadening their initial formula of financial contributions, and that the Canadian cabinet would be meeting shortly to consider support to UNKRA, Gordon began doing some politicking on his own. He appeared on CBC television discussing a CBC UN-Day program for schools, and he did a nine-minute speaker-of-the-week segment on CBC Radio. He spoke to the Ottawa UN Association, and addressed three hundred teachers in a UN workshop sponsored by the Trusteeship Council.[18] And, once again, he engaged in a little private lobbying to Mike Pearson, writing him an "epistle of Pauline proportions" as he called it, arguing that the stakes in Korea were high, and that "those nations who appreciate most the nature of freedom are going to have to be prepared to pay most for its survival."[19] Small wonder that he described himself to Sir Arthur Rucker as "over my head in Public Information and Public Relations work in connection with the Report and other matters relating to the items on the agenda."[20] He spoke modestly of his efforts and hoped they had proven of some use.

By the time Gordon returned to New York after that first month in Korea, images of war devastation and human suffering burned in his mind, giving credence and motivation to his crusade. During August, as part of familiarizing himself with the work of UNKRA, he and his Australian photographer, Mike O'Halloran, had visited Pusan, the port city at the southern tip of the Korean peninsula, still the home for hundreds of thousands of refugees who had been driven there during the northern assault. It was Gordon's first exposure to a kind and degree of suffering he had not experienced or imagined. They travelled from Seoul by the night train, and as they pulled in at first light, the big diesel engine blowing its horn to warn people off the tracks, they were met by appalling squalour. Small children stood by the tracks, the younger ones naked and the older ones barely clothed. Behind the children stretched their homes, rows of dilapidated shacks and packing boxes, and many more shelters made from cardboard boxes. Mothers cooked rice for breakfast over open fires, while an open ditch served as a source of water and a depository for refuse.[21]

By contrast, he wrote to Ruth, the compound where the army officers and UNKRA staff in Pusan lived was "luxurious" with a very pleasant mess hall (far better than Seoul), comfortable homes with hot and cold running water, and a PX in the compound where one could buy all the usual things, from pineapple juice to Kodachrome film. "I have a feeling that most people who live here don't see much of Pusan, but I'm probably wrong. Or too sensitive."[22]

He and O'Halloran visited a clinic run by the Maryknoll Sisters and supported by UNKRA, which gave aid for medical supplies and equipment. They found people by the hundreds, lined up since the night before, spilling into the surrounding alleys and courtyards. As nurses and doctors, both Korean and international, attended medical needs, the sisters handed out bundles of clothing and food with a cheery compassion and tenderness. King wanted to take some pictures, "but I just didn't have the nerve," he wrote to Ruth. It was like nothing he had ever seen before. "This Pusan is a place that I can't get used to. I've been in places that I just did not think existed anywhere."[23]

In spite of the almost unbearable heat and humidity and his own reaction to the appalling suffering that he saw, by the time Gordon left for New York in September he had established contact with the newspaper editors in Seoul, organized the publicity effort for New York, and begun writing press releases for both the Korean and international press. His trip home took him through Thailand and India, where he contacted UN officials and also did some informal campaigning for UNKRA. In Thailand, an official of the UN Food and Agriculture Organization told him about a highly successful experimental fishpond project, an idea that he thought might usefully be introduced to Korea. Along with Korea's hot climate, however, there was another factor that might make its transplantation unfeasible: the lack of a royal patron. It appeared that the King of Thailand himself had become so enamoured of the fish that he had had them introduced into his own pool in the palace grounds. There they had multiplied so rapidly that he had then distributed the fish to any farmers who wished to have them and, as might be expected, there was tremendous competition for "the King's fish."[24] Whether Syngman Rhee, the first president of the Republic of Korea, could function in this symbolic fashion, Gordon was not sure. Interestingly, when he was later asked if Syngman Rhee had attempted in any way to use UNKRA for personal whim, he replied that he had not, with one exception: Rhee had asked UNKRA if he might have some fish for the lake at his summer place.[25]

In Bombay, King was once again appalled by the poverty he saw. From there he proceeded to Rome, where he attended a meeting of UN Department of Information field officers and, with the group, had an audience with the pope. He arrived in Geneva for the meeting of the Commission on Prisoners of War, haunted by the face of a child beggar he had seen in Bombay.

Among the many activities during his frenzied two months home was a gala dinner given by the City of New York to honour the UN delegates, held in the grand ballroom of the Waldorf Astoria. Ruth, who found herself generally "living in a curious state of half-reality," during these days when the routines of ordinary life seemed suspended, described their evening to her mother-in-law: an evening that included a visit with Eleanor Roosevelt on their way in, being seated in the company of Ralph Bunche and Andrey Vyshinsky, the Soviet representative to the UN, and listening to speeches by Henry Cabot Lodge and Dag Hammarskjöld. The dinner was followed by entertainment and dancing until three in the morning.[26] One wonders how King reconciled these two experiences in his mind, the world of the little beggar in Bombay and the Maryknoll nuns in Pusan, and the lavish provender of the Astoria's grand ballroom in New York City, happening as they did in such proximity. Perhaps he too, for the time being, was living in that state of "half reality."

Little had been arranged as far as family matters were concerned when King once again left for Korea on 3 December. Ruth plunged into renting the house and preparing for their first lonely Christmas apart. Two days before Christmas, Charley reassured his father, "Today Alison and I brought in our Christmas tree with no trouble at all. Tomorrow night we decorate it as usual."[27] Ruth reported that Alison kept saying, "Oh – I love Christmas!" and that on her own part, "it [Christmas Day] went really better than I expected, but I hope we never have to do it again. It seemed *so* odd without you, like part of my heart were missing."[28] In the midst of these brave festivities, King's cable arrived: "FINE HOUSE TOKYO SOONEST CAR AC REFRIGERATOR GAS STOVE SPACE HEATER BLOWER SEARS ROEBUCK LOVE KING."[29] Ruth understood this rather cryptic message to mean: order a refrigerator and stove from Sears Roebuck, ship the car, and pack up for the Far East.

Describing herself with her usual modesty and understated humour as a shy housewife with very little travelling experience on her own beyond taking the children up to Kenora by train, Ruth rallied gallantly. Within the month she, with Alison, twelve, and Charley, fourteen, was en route to San Francisco where they boarded the *SS President Wilson* for Tokyo.

Ruth, having confessed her apprehension about embarking on this great adventure on her own, wrote to her mother-in-law as the train approached San Francisco, "now there is nothing but joy and gratefulness in my heart that it is all possible."[30]

King was waiting for them as the boat docked, with two UNKRA drivers, a station wagon and a car, and after a few days in a hotel (and a miserable case of flu for Ruth and Alison) they moved into a Japanese duplex in the Tokyo suburb of Denenchofu. Their landlords, the Watanabe family, along with Jimmy the houseboy and Toshiko the cook, became firm friends of all the Gordon family. Ruth's first impression of Japan was how courteous the people were: "You spend your whole time being bowed to."[31] By the time King left for Korea at the end of January, the family was settled (but with no heat) and the children were enrolled at the International School in Naka Megaro. Communication by phone from Seoul to Tokyo was rare and uncertain but, with some delays, the mail was reliable and the daily letters began once again. King hoped to return for his "rest and rehabilitation" break by the end of March.

Once back on the job, Gordon found that his work varied. A major component of his responsibility was assisting in the writing of the agent general's reports, which were submitted both to the secretary general and to the Third Committee of the General Assembly (which dealt with social, humanitarian, and cultural issues). These reports went through many drafts and, on at least one occasion, Gordon received special commendation for their clarity and content from the secretary general himself.[32] He was a press liaison with both the Korean and foreign media and a "publicist" in the days before public relations was a clearly defined category. As UNKRA was a $140,000,000 effort, a large part of his work involved field coverage of operations and escorting visiting dignitaries (of whom there were many) around the sites where UNKRA was providing support. It was within this context that two of his old friends showed up: Sam Keeney, the roving ambassador for humanitarian efforts on behalf of children; and the redoubtable Sherwood Eddy of his Union/McGill days, still championing the causes of liberalism. Gordon described him as elderly but still spry at eighty-four years of age, and much the same as ever. Eddy did most of the talking but in saying goodbye commented, "Well, King, I'm glad to see you're still a good liberal!"[33] It was a happy rekindling of an old friendship.

Another of Gordon's responsibilities was covering ceremonial occasions such as the "spontaneous demonstration" in support of UNKRA by the city of Seoul, the "big show" as he called it. In searing heat, a commandeered crowd of 8,000 or more gathered in front of City Hall: city officials; school children; "mamsans and papsans" with babies strapped to their backs, turned out by their block captains; and a good representation of UNKRA staff. A huge colourful banner of congratulations to UNKRA draped the doorway of the city hall. The agent general delivered a speech composed by Ferguson and spoken "like a senator from Texas (he's certainly improving)," and charming little girls in Korean costumes of yellow, green, and red presented flowers to the UNKRA representatives. Gordon saw to it that the event received good coverage in the Korean press, followed by a radio broadcast. This was perhaps the first, but certainly not the last, of tightly organized "spontaneous" outbursts of support that Gordon witnessed over his years in Korea. With some amusement, but without cynicism, he noted that, "the whole thing was good for UNKRA and something of a boost to staff morale."[34]

Gordon and his staff covered numerous military events and parades (replete with top brass) including the British final divisional parade in March 1956, with the British ambassador on hand, "looking an awful ass in gray top hat when he stood up to take the royal salute – they said it is what you have to wear when you represent the Queen but I can't believe it."[35] It began to snow right after the parade, and by the time they got to the Canadian mess it was a real blizzard. The Canadian soldiers were not enjoying the weather – or Korea, for that matter. As Gordon recorded interviews to be aired on both Korean radio and the CBC, he "tried to make them say how much they liked Korea and the Koreans but they were chiefly interested in saying how glad they would be to get home and I couldn't blame them."[36]

He also discovered the vagaries of life as a field reporter. In October of 1955 he travelled to Pusan for a ceremony welcoming two ships from Pakistan and Chile, one bringing rice, the other nitrates for fertilizer. "Those damn boats!" he complained to Ruth on the evening before he left Seoul. "They are constantly changing their time of arrival, particularly the Korean boat 'Yosu' that is carrying a cargo of rice from Pakistan."[37] The boat from Chile carrying the nitrates was also causing problems by threatening to unload its cargo out in the harbour. All of this uncertainty complicated the planned ceremony, but since the press release had already been written he and Mike O'Halloran left for Pusan hoping for the best. The boat from Pakistan waited for them at the dock, but the boat from Chile was nowhere in sight, despite predictions from the port authority that it was on its way and a report from the outer harbourmaster that it had arrived the day before. (The "outer harbour has a big mouth,"[38] Gordon observed.) With the Chilean representative to UNKRA on hand to make a speech and the local dignitaries waiting in the stands, they decided to go ahead with the ceremony. "Things went all right," King reported to Ruth. "I appointed myself chairman and George Hall gave a speech."[39] Presumably the ship from Chile eventually arrived.

Gordon was aided in his labours by an enthusiastic and capable staff, starting with Ferguson and her competent successor, Janet Lewis, who had a remarkable knowledge of Korea and the Korean people. Mike O'Halloran travelled with him as photographer and always addressed him as "Skipper," and Ted Conant, the brilliant and eccentric son of James Conant, president of Harvard, served as his sound man. King was especially fond of this young friend and they often talked long into the night. "He convinces me that I really am an intellectual," he confided rather shyly to Ruth.[40] In spite of having secretaries, a storywriter, a researcher, and a translator, they always felt short-handed and pinched, and from time to time temporary help was sent over from New York.

By the time Gordon arrived in Korea, the UN forces had largely been reduced to American units, and while he described the army as "just an army, some good and some bad," he had nothing but praise for the Americans at the administrative level, their relief effort and generosity. He particularly admired Ambassador Carl Strom who, along with his wife Camilla, he got to know on a friendly basis and who more than once kindly offered him a ride in their plane from Seoul to Tokyo. Gordon particularly appreciated this consideration. In spite of the fact that, as director of information, he had an "assimilated rank" of brigadier, which meant that when he hitched a ride on a military plane he could bump anybody up to and including the rank of colonel, transportation back to see his family was sometimes uncertain. Ambassador Strom, it turned out, shared an alma mater (Luther College in Decorah, Iowa) with Ruth's father, Isaac Anderson. Gordon described him as "the very best, generous, unbigoted, and sympathetic."[41]

His field coverage began in earnest in the spring of 1955 with visits to a textile mill, two irrigation projects, and the site for a cement factory. Previously, much of Korea's industry and mining had been in the North and UNKRA was investing heavily in establishing and rebuilding an industrial base. Gordon first travelled to the Anyang mill, rebuilt by the Koreans themselves, re-equipped with new spinning machinery purchased by UNKRA in England and installed under the direction of an engineer from Lancashire. (He claimed that he detected a slight Lancashire accent in the English of those Koreans he interviewed.) Irrigation was crucial for agriculture – as well as a source of power to run the mills – and he and Mike O'Halloran travelled by jeep to visit these projects also. In many places, as the roads had been washed out by heavy rains, they were forced to ford streams, eventually driving along the tops of the narrow earthen dykes that bordered the fields. The sides of the dykes were planted with coarse grass to hold the soil, and as they drove further into the countryside, they looked down from their rather precarious prospect onto a landscape patterned with green rice paddies, rows of soybeans, and ripening fields of barley. King loved being out in the countryside with ordinary, simple country people. He sent long descriptions home to his mother, letters filled with details of planting and harvesting, methods of getting water onto the fields, always extolling the energy and hard work of the Koreans.

Along with water, coal was an essential resource for the development and rehabilitation of the South, and in January 1956 Gordon undertook what was surely his most rigorous trip to visit three of the mines in eastern Korea – one near Machari, one near Changsung, and a new field at Mambak, just north of Yongwal.[42] He described the mountainous area where the coal was found as similar to the Adirondacks or the Great Smokies, only barer and starker, with narrower valleys and ridges that were closer together. O'Halloran and Gordon, with a Korean driver, started their trip north early on a mid-winter Sunday morning, both in high spirits. Even the breakdown of their first jeep did not particularly dash their hopes. By Monday, freshly re-equipped with a new jeep, they were once again winding their way over the second big pass – the Taebaek – awed by the scenery and the precariousness of the narrow hairpin roads chiselled into the sides of the steep slopes. They tried to resist looking directly down to the floor of the valley.

As the Changsung mine was the farthest in, they went there first and found themselves warmly welcomed by the only three foreigners in the town, mining consultants from Wales, Scotland, and England. Changsung also lay at the bottom of a cup in the mountains, so that they found themselves in virtual darkness at two in the afternoon. Tuesday morning they were up by first light to begin their tour, this time welcomed by bitter cold and 32-kph winds that tore through the valley. Equipped with a helmet and a feeble lamp, Gordon doubled over his tall frame of 1.9 m ("It's no sweat for the smaller Koreans."[43]) and walked through the tunnel. Eventually, with twelve others, he climbed aboard a small mine locomotive, a cramped car about 2.4 m long, and rattled through a pitch-black tunnel for about 1,000 m. Escaping into what was left of daylight, they had a look at the village and inspected the hospital and school. The next morning he found himself wakened at 6 a.m. by a loudspeaker playing selections from Handel's *Messiah*, followed by the Korean national anthem, "Jingle Bells," and Sousa marches, the mountains forming an amphitheatre for the sound. In between musical selections, he heard speeches in Korean that he discovered upon translation were exhortations to the men to get up and be on time, and to produce more coal. For the women, there were quotations of prices of eggs, vegetables, and rice.[44]

After this bright beginning, they loaded themselves into the jeep for a return trip over the two passes. There were two shallow rivers to be forded. The first, being frozen, proved to be no problem. The second river was iced only at the edges, with water about 20 cm deep. They started out cautiously but soon discovered that a rise in the middle of the riverbed had lifted their wheels off the ground and they were soon stuck. No amount of pushing and pulling by Mike and King could dislodge the vehicle and so, in the bitter cold and wind, ankle deep in water, they had to jack up the front wheels and shove stones underneath. That got them going again, and the two men tramped the rest of the way across on what ice they could find, while An, the driver, took the jeep. Not that they were home free. Then the brake bands had become iced up, which meant that they had no brakes going over the pass. However, since they had a four-wheel drive, King assured Ruth (who was happy to hear of their adventures only after the fact) that they had been quite safe.[45] At the remaining two mine sites they relied largely on the managers for descriptions of the interior workings.

Gordon rejoiced in the international character of the humanitarian and rehabilitative effort in Korea. He wrote of this internationalism, "It has produced an understanding that could not have been produced in any other way."[46] He described the cooperation of a Peruvian and a Korean engineer inspecting a British dam together; an Australian nurse and a Korean doctor caring for tubercular children; and an American designer planning a new school building with a Korean school inspector. He concluded that differences of nationality or cultural background raised no barriers for these international workers. "For them, international understanding is no mere phrase. They have found a meeting ground in a common task." Throughout his career, Gordon returned again and again to this theme of the common interest of all humanity, and of international cooperation at the grassroots level as the means to achieve common goals.

It was therefore not surprising that on these trips into the field Gordon was always alert to the human dimension, sharply observant of the lives of the ordinary people. His trip to the mines provided an occasion for such concern. When he gave his films to his Korean photographer for developing, Mr Kim confided that he was having trouble with his stomach. With typical dispatch, Gordon made an appointment for him with a doctor at the Red Cross hospital. Coincidentally, he told Ruth, he was having splendid results with his photographs – "Very sharp, sir, very good exposure"[47] – a rather suspect evaluation, King felt. But along with the humour, there was often a note of sadness that crept into his accounts, and he marvelled at the will of these people, caught in the displacement of war, to survive. He was particularly sensitive to the children in these circumstances, and he recounted an example of the same quality of resourcefulness in them that he saw in the adults. In a letter to his mother, he described encountering a small girl on the railroad platform in Seoul who, along with her brother, was shining shoes. Gordon asked if she would shine his, and they set to work. The children were well-mannered and merry, visiting and laughing with the passengers, who were nearly all American soldiers. They could not have been more than ten years old, and they spent their days riding troop trains and shining shoes. But while he was taken with their resourcefulness, King added to his mother, "I must say that it's quite a shock to see a kiddie about the size of Susan [his niece back in Canada] looking quite self-reliant and talking very maturely, and with her brother running a profitable business by herself."[48]

UNKRA also imported building materials for the expansion and repair of orphanages in six cities, and for some fifty other child-care institutions. The actual running of these facilities and the care for the hundreds of children was left in the hands of private humanitarian groups. Gordon had visited several orphanages in his travels and he had, with the help of Ted Conant, even taped a group of children singing carols and Welsh songs that were played over the CBC. One of these trips took him and Ken Marshall (who coordinated UNKRA grants-in-aid to many relief and welfare organizations, including Christian missions) down to Kwanju in Cholla Namdo province to participate in the opening of a girls' dormitory built by the YMCA working directly with the Koreans. As they entered the compound, they met women and girls carrying sand, bricks, and mortar, in an effort to complete the new building, which was already occupied. From inside a large old Korean house, they heard singing: hymns in English and then a Korean version of "Home Sweet Home."

One hundred and thirty-five girls, all orphans, were accommodated in these two crowded buildings.

The irony of the orphans singing "Home Sweet Home" was not lost on King. It was his birthday and he himself was missing his own home. They had tea and Korean candy cakes and, in honour of Gordon's special day, one of the smaller girls sang "The Sands of Duna," coincidentally a favourite of King's father. At that point Mike O'Halloran took pictures for both the Korean and the International press. "So I told them they had given me the best possible birthday party," King told Ruth. "They were really a wonderful crowd, both the grown-ups and the girls. I sent a memo to the A[gent] G[eneral] today saying that we should help them some more, at least give them the $2,000 they need to finish their dormitory."[49]

Given Gordon's sensitivity to the plight and courage of the children of Korea, it is again not surprising that he found himself uniquely involved with an orphan. It was in June 1955 when, for a whole twenty-four hours, he was responsible for an orphan of his own.[50] And so unfolded the story of Gloria. He was waiting for his car when a little girl of about eleven approached him and said she was hungry and asked Gordon for money for food. She had clearly been well cared for and was not a "tough little beggar" such as one would see around the railroad station. When his car arrived, he took her to the Canadian Mission where she was given clean clothes and food. Then Gordon and the matron, Miss Sittler, who also worked with the Christian Children's Fund, discussed orphanages. The child was not impressed. After dinner, however, she agreed to try the one they recommended, and the three of them drove there in Miss Sittler's jeep. The girl was well-received and seemed happy with their choice. It was agreed that Gordon would come to see her the following Monday. In his eagerness to be assured of her happy condition, however, he drove out Sunday evening and learned she had disappeared a few hours earlier. King searched for her for a few days, but concluded that she had probably had a bad time in earlier orphanages and had gone to find another army camp with a kind chaplain to take care of her. "She may come back," he wrote forlornly to his mother.[51]

In his anxiety, King told his good friend Helen McArthur, a Canadian Red Cross nurse, about his loss. Helen's response was somewhat less than sympathetic as she "blasted" King for being sentimental. In Gordon's telling, McArthur said, "That was a hell of a thing to do King! Let that little girl alone. It was a crazy damn fool thing to do."[52]

Ruth made the same point more gently. After telling him that she was "very upset" by his letter, she went on to reassure him that such a compassionate but impulsive action was "one of the hundreds of things I love about you, that you would do just what you are doing." But she urged King not to think that the orphan was hungry and scared somewhere: "It doesn't follow her behavior with you. She will land on her feet somewhere, and it probably won't be the kind of landing you or I would hope for, but it will doubtless be a landing much more natural for her, and therefore more suitable. Of course, I can talk this way not having seen her, or talked with her, or held her hand, and you know perfectly well if I had, I would be much more irrational on the subject than you have been."[53]

In her generous way, Ruth assured King that in his kindness he had given the child a belief and trust in human beings that should carry her along until she found a solution for her problems "which are not, and never have been, the problems we make them into."[54]

Ruth was right, and the story ended in September on King's return by train from another ribbon-cutting, silver-spike ceremony opening a new railroad. When they arrived at the Seoul station, Gordon had a surprise encounter. As he walked to the exit, he noticed two little girls playing together. Something in one of their voices sounded familiar and he asked her name. Then he asked, "Aren't you the little girl I took to the orphanage?" She acknowledged cheerfully that she was, but that all they did was act and sing and she couldn't do either, so she ran away. Gordon had to admit that she looked healthy and well-dressed, happy, and independent. She was now a shoeshine girl on the trains, making 2,000 hwan a day. "I feel very happy about the whole thing even if it isn't a very good ending for a missionary story," he told Ruth. "And it's pretty evident that the Pygmalion role is not for her."[55]

Although the UNKRA staff worked long hours, there were still many hours to be filled and, away from their families, often the need to combat loneliness. Life in Seoul provided a variety of opportunities for social life, with the many international workers, the diplomatic corps and the international press, as well as some socializing with representatives of the Korean government and the remaining military units. Gordon never lacked for company. He was frequently included in dinners and parties in honour of visitors and, as a popular guest, he often left his driver, Mr Yang, waiting at the curb long after the pick-up time he had specified. Small groups met for drinks before dinner, or a nightcap, often leading to conversations that continued long into the night.

Naturally gregarious though he was, King savoured these late hours as time to spend with Ruth, writing to her as he listened to Vagabond (the local English radio station), filling his pages with comments on her latest news and giving her the details of his own busy life. The frequent – often daily – letters strengthened the bond between them, providing reassurance that the ordinary events of their lives had significance and were treasured by the reader. They wrote with easy intimacy and enjoyment. After a long, rather tedious day, King wrote: "Now I must get to bed. I'm afraid this has been a poor little letter but I love you, darling, and I like writing to you."[56]

Gordon also enjoyed a nightly ritual of a game of Scrabble with anyone who would play, but his favourite partner was Ken Marshall. He described his brilliant plays, his victories, and his losses, in considerable detail to Ruth, who was capable of brilliant plays of her own. Their mutual love for language and for the apt word was an endless source of enjoyment, to the extent that long into their retirement the verandahs of Birkencraig rang with the cries of battle. In the fall of 1955 King wrote to Ruth: "I bumped into Ken Marshall after dinner and he was my scrabble victim."[57] But he was not satisfied with victories in the Scrabble foothills. He had higher conquests in his sights. He wrote to his father-in-law as Vagabond signed off at midnight that same evening, commenting on a visit with their mutual friends, the Stroms, and suggesting that to induce "proper humility" in the ambadassor, he planned to invite him over for a game of Scrabble, adding, "They are really out of my class, I fear."[58] This sentence clearly referred to their diplomatic status only. When the infamous match took place, Gordon trounced the ambassador by forty points.

Gordon derived particular pleasure from his contacts with Canadian troops stationed in Korea, and he spent a night up at the Demilitarized Zone as guest of the Canadian Guards Regiment, which was stationed about 3 km back from the DMZ. It was guest night and they served dinner formally with china, linen, and silver, course after course, with three wines. In the bar following dinner, they let down some of their reserve and invited Gordon to join in a new game of darts they had devised: "You stood facing your opponent three paces and threw darts at his feet to see how close you could come without hitting him. Drinks were on the loser. I did pretty well. I was put up against the Colonel and I won by about one-half inch."[59] The Colonel got his revenge the next day, however, giving Gordon his most hair-raising ride in Korea, down from the front to Seoul, washboard all the way, at a steady 80 km per hour.

In March of 1956 Gordon travelled back up to the DMZ area with Ken Marshall to say goodbye to the Canadian UNKRA workers, who were having their final party before pulling out. He and Marshall fought their way up along rain-soaked roads that dissolved from time to time into pure mud, but the party was well worth the effort. All the Canadians and their friends from miles around were present. The chef put together a fine buffet supper (on a somewhat more modest scale than the Guards) followed by spirited dancing including an eight-some reel and the hearty singing of Scotch and English folk songs. "Today I'm croaking like a frog," he told Ruth the next day. And then it was time to bid goodbye to these new friends who seemed like old friends in all the shared memories of home. He continued to Ruth, "It is the breakup of relationships like this that is one of the sad things in this Korean experience."[60]

King and Ruth kept up their lively conversation about books, and he told Ruth he was reading a Canadian novel, *Leaven of Malice*, by someone called Robertson Davies, "a light satirical thing on Toronto but quite well written."[61] He had also found a good book on ideographs and worked away at them. And he took up sketching and painting once again, a hobby that followed him into old age and which he described as a "solitary soul-searching kind of job."[62] Coming home from a long day in the field, as a way of resting, he would get out his brushes and rework a canvas, noticing his lights and colours and attempting to make it look more like Korea. He supposed it was a form of escape, but he needed something more than textile mills and dams to compensate for the loneliness and all that was frustrating about his present existence, "for the loss of our family life, for being away from you."[63]

They both reflected on these separations. Ruth wrote King about an evening she had spent alone, listening to the radio, Toshiko on her day off and the children out at parties. King responded: "Your Saturday's letter was so wonderful when you were sitting alone, with the children at their parties. I felt I wanted to be with you. Because these are the times we should be having together and we shouldn't be alone. I think that one compensation of this time apart will be that we have thought a lot about one another and about ourselves and what our life has meant and means and will mean again."[64]

Ruth felt the brevity of the years until the children would be leaving home, as she shared every detail of their daily lives by letter. She never got used to King's departures: "The minute you are gone," she wrote, "the house seems to pull in a notch or two."[65] But she determined to make the best of it, and she continued: "I think these short visits together are wonderful, but not quite of this world. It's all so abnormal in a way, isn't it? But we seem to grasp at life in a kind of frantic way. But again, I suppose we are really new at this and will learn to take it in our stride." The separations were exacerbated by the repeated postponements of King's rest-and-rehabilitation breaks. In part, these were due to factors neither could control; but Ruth argued that in part the fault also lay with King's excessive sense of duty. "He has such a conscience," she told her mother-in-law, "I'm never sure he's coming til he's here."[66] After one disappointing postponement, she wrote to King:

> I don't know if I can explain it to you … in essence, you fit your r and r's into your busy life there, while we fit our rather unbusy life around the busy r and r's. The last thing I want to sound like is someone who sits here waiting unhappily for your visits, because that isn't true, but they do loom very large for us, and they are sort of targets for us. I don't mean that you don't look forward to them too, but the life you are leading there is so much more important and frankly more interesting than ours.[67]

Ruth, clearly uneasy with her complaint, hastened to assure King that she did not mean to be shrewish. "When I say *our* and *we*, I mean UNKRA wives, not the kids and myself, because they take everything in their stride – school is pretty all-encompassing for them, and while they are disappointed if you don't come one week as opposed to the next, they are very philosophical." It was a theme they would return to during the twelve years of their extended separations.

It was true, as Ruth said, that their times together were wonderful – a whole sunny November day spent together in their small, enclosed Japanese garden, writing Christmas cards. Or their splendid holiday to Nojiri in August, at one of the most beautiful lakes in Japan in the mountainous country, five hours by train from Tokyo. There were sunny days of tennis, golf (King did his nine holes before breakfast), swimming, and sailing, and simply enjoying the pleasure of all being together. Ruth's attempt to write her mother-in-law was disrupted by King's singing "the William goat song, and the children are convulsed."[68] Nojiri was the vacation centre for most of the missionary families, which meant there was a constant social round in the evenings with friends and acquaintances of Helen Gordon. King marvelled at the older missionaries' ease and facility with the language. Overhearing a conversation between Toshiko (who had come along to cook and shop) and an elderly lady who he assumed to be Japanese until, rounding a corner, he saw that she was a Canadian friend. The children had new cameras and the company of a crowd of their school friends from Tokyo. But they all missed Kenora. Charley noticed that the kitchen of their cottage smelled like the kitchen at Birkencraig – probably due to the hibachi that Toshiko used for cooking, which produced an aroma similar to a wood stove. There was also the Blue Willow patterned china that was used at the island. One Saturday they planned a picnic by canoe, "But not to Smugglers Cove. That's what I miss," commented Alison.[69]

Ruth filled her days alone with the children in Tokyo with activities typical of expatriate wives of that time – meeting with the other UNKRA wives to sew for the Korean orphans, social events with the Canadian Embassy wives, concerts at the Tokyo Women's Club, flower arranging, and Japanese lessons – but she did so with an enthusiasm and goodwill not always typical of many women in her situation, who were tempted to retreat into their loneliness. Ted and Peggy Newton, of the Canadian embassy, became close friends and Ruth was often included in dinners for visiting dignitaries. She described to her mother-in-law one such occasion in June of 1955 when Herbert Norman, newly appointed high commissioner to New Zealand, was the guest of honour. Although King and Norman had crossed paths numerous times, this seems to have been Ruth's first introduction to him. "We had an excellent dinner, with lots of good conversation; Dr Norman is very charming – he knows King and asked about him, and also knew Walter Riddell."[70] Their paths would soon cross again, tragically, in Cairo.

Gordon was in Tokyo for the Dominion Day celebration at the Embassy on 1 July 1955, and thus able to accompany Ruth to the reception. Ruth's reaction to diplomatic life in her account to her mother-in-law is singularly revealing and perhaps helps to explain her willingness to bear the separations from King. After describing the splendour of the occasion, the great halls, the garden with its Japanese lanterns and kimono-clad girls moving gracefully among the guests with trays filled with delicacies, the military attachés in dress uniform, the Prince and Princess casting their royal luster over it all, she concluded with shrewd self-perception: "Each time I go to one of these affairs I am so thankful that King did not get into the diplomatic embassy kind of world. It seems such a waste of money and good brains! These people have to spend a large part of their time attending functions like this (not so large) where they see the same people all the time. I don't think I could stand it! We both breathed a sigh of relief when it was over, and got back to our little unpretentious house for a nice quiet supper."[71]

This was probably a shrewd piece of self-perception on Ruth's part. Her charm lay in her quiet sophistication and in the authenticity of her interest; her wit was quick, but her kindness kept her from being caustic in her observations. She found it difficult to make "cocktail talk," the superficial niceties that are often required on occasions such as the one she described.

The children, as Ruth had told King, seemed to take their lives in Tokyo in stride, busy with school and their friends. Along with Toshiko, their house boy and driver Jimmy was a happy part of the family, ferrying Ruth and Alison around the city (Charley used public transportation with a confidence that astonished his parents), even finding them a new car and negotiating the price when their own car was stolen. The dining room of their small house in Tokyo rang with shouts as Charley hosted ping-pong events for his friends, and celebrated his birthday with a jitterbug party. He was an honours student and a keen athlete. Alison, as a lively and vivacious thirteen-year-old, was a great joy to Ruth. Like Charley, she played sports at school, and she threw herself into Girl Scouts and sleepovers. She loved to garden. "You should see your daughter," Ruth wrote to King: "It's pouring rain and she is out in the garden, with a big straw hat on, and Charley's blue trench coat, looking just like Huckleberry Finn, doing something, I can't figure out what. She's completely black-footed and black-handed, and now she wants to come in, but I just told her she'll have to stay out there all day!"[72]

Alison adored her father and missed him keenly, admitting, however, that it was easier to say goodbye in Tokyo than it had been in Irvington.

In September 1955 Gordon received a letter from John Humphrey saying that his name was being considered for two jobs in the UN, one in Geneva as a liaison officer between the Department of Social Affairs and the non-governmental agencies, and the other an administrative position in New York with the Department of Social Affairs. Neither sounded quite right to King, but he admitted to Ruth that it was nice to think one had not been forgotten.[73] (One wonders if Gordon's reluctance to consider either of these positions further exacerbated Humphrey's sense of disappointment at his leaving the division in 1954.) Although he knew that UNKRA would gradually be phased out, Gordon felt that he likely had another eight or nine months doing what was needed and what he enjoyed doing in Korea. As for the future, Ferguson, back in New York for a short tour of duty, assured him that everywhere she went people enquired about him and he would have no trouble fitting in somewhere. "Anyway," he concluded philosophically, "I think we have always worked on the principle that the way is opened up when the decision has to be made."[74]

That decision arrived sooner than anticipated, when Gordon received a letter early in December 1955 from J.A.C. Robertson, director of personnel at the UN Headquarters in New York, asking him to become director of the United Nations Information Center for the Middle East in Cairo.[75] He spent a miserable Christmas break in Tokyo mulling – in a rather non-Calvinist frame of mind – over the premature job offer, and returned to Seoul at the beginning of January still in a quandary. A copy of Robertson's letter had gone to the agent general, who assured Gordon that, despite his concern for the continuation of the UNKRA work, he would not stand in his way. Nevertheless, Gordon vacillated. Ruth, in her usual sustaining way and perhaps with more Calvinist faith than her husband, urged him not to worry. "Things will work out, as they always do, somehow. We've had a good 16 years – and lots of it just *happened*!"[76] Nevertheless, she balked at a four-year appointment that would see Charley into college and Alison through her high-school years, and she wanted reassurance that the children could finish their school term in June. The next day, King had decided. "After a couple more days of wrestling with God and destiny and my own soul I've decided that we should take on Cairo."[77] It seemed to him not only a useful job, but one that could provide an interesting life for them all. Looking at it from the point of view of the family, he considered it a fine opportunity to see the cradle of civilization, with remnants of the ancient world all around them. Moreover, the new world of the Middle East was as potent a force as any in the modern world. But, how would such a move affect his career? "I have no very clear feelings," he continued to Ruth:

> Anyway, what is my career? I've done so many things. I suppose when I have time to review my life there will emerge a great consistency in all my ventures – I was going to say choices but frequently the choice did not seem to be mine. I suppose my career if anything has been a continuous effort to understand our world and help other people to understand it – perhaps make it a little better. Since the arrival of the United Nations, it has been the main focus of my interest and its work has been the thing that has been carrying me on … As you know, there has always been the nostalgic pull back to Canada. But when I label it "nostalgic" I think I am picking the right

> word. It is a pull back to a smaller comfortable world. But, let's face it, the big world has become the small world and we in our own personal experience are learning that. What is that old hymn: "In him there is no East and West ..." It's been the view of Christianity through the ages and now modern political thinking, through dire and urgent necessity, is catching up ... Perhaps, it was not so inconsistent that I started in the church, went into radical politics in the hope of doing something to make a better social order, and then went on into the one great movement that may make reality of the dreams of the great thinkers and visionaries.[78]

In this statement he achieved a clarification and a distillation of his own vision. Would he ever say it better? Though he may not have realized it, his decision at this time was a defining moment for King. But in this confiding moment with Ruth, he then pulled back in sudden embarrassment. "This is talking much too big. My part in all this has been very small ... We [ourselves] can't make the kind of world that will assure a better life for Charley and Alison, but we can do something with others and with a great organization to assure it." Ruth replied, "There are some places I don't want to go with you, but there aren't many!"[79]

Nevertheless, Ruth responded with some heat when, a few days later, King got cold feet and wondered after all if he should turn down Cairo to see UNKRA through to its end. "Cairo means we would be together ... The separation is not good for a marriage, of this I am very sure. And it is not good for the children."[80] Even aside from this, she argued, it was not good for the Agency itself. "If the Agency were not folding up, it might be a different question, but yours is not the kind of mind and spirit that enjoys a tapering off of anything." King agreed, admitting that usually the things that happen to you are the ones to be encouraged. And so, once again, the die was cast.

The date of the move to Cairo was moved from September 1956 back to June, putting in jeopardy a trip to New York and Birkencraig; but at least, it was hoped, still allowing the children to finish their school year. There was a growing sense of urgency in the letters from New York, however, and strong assurances that Gordon was considered the appropriate person for the job. Early in March, Robertson wrote from Headquarters in New York: "You point out that you want your children to complete their school years in Toyko in June, and you mention the fact that you were hoping to take home leave in 1956, the year in which it falls due. Unfortunately, events do not stand still in the Middle East and the Secretary-General has decided that it is a matter of the first importance to get you to Cairo before June, if possible."[81]

Robertson enclosed details concerning housing, schooling, transportation, domestic help, and cost of living in Cairo. On the heels of this letter came one from Alfred G. Katzin, Office of the Secretary-General:

> The fact of the matter is that you have yourself to blame. You should not be so darned efficient and thereby come under the purview of our ultimate lord and master, the S. G. However, as things are, you are regarded as the right man to head the office in a ticklish area where right men are best needed and where it is of the utmost importance at the present time for the S. G. to have an Information Centre headed by a level-headed bloke with good overall judgement and pretty ways viz-a-viz both governments and the peoples who have to be approached and served respectively in the region.[82]

Kazin went on to explain that the secretary general had already gained the confidence of the governmental parties in dispute, and that General E.L.M. "Tommy" Burns and Henry Labouisse, who were carrying the responsibility on the political and refugee fronts, were having significant success in building a basis of trust in the region. The Information Centre in Cairo would provide the final link in the chain, following up and capitalizing on Hammarskjöld's philosophy of moderation. Katzin followed shortly with another letter reassuring him that his own interests and needs had not been lightly set aside for any matter of mere expedience.[83]

In response to these letters, King wrote to Ruth: "The enclosed letter from Alf Katzin attacks me through my ego. Knowing myself much better than Alf I kept wondering who he was talking about to do this outstanding and invaluable job in Cairo! I can only think that Mr. Hammarskjöld's recent visit to India and the Middle East made him revise his plans as far as I was concerned and he wants the Center manned as soon as possible."[84]

On 12 April Gordon suddenly received word that he was to travel to Rome for a meeting of information directors, and from there proceed directly to New York for a briefing. "I had hoped for a decent and orderly departure: now that is almost impossible ... If the closing up in Tokyo is not as irksome as it would appear to be from this angle, and if you are not too exhausted when you get on the plane and don't mind too much arriving in Rome really tuckered out, then we can do it together."[85] After four days of "unholy rat-race" and parties, he was ready to leave for Tokyo.

On his departure, the agent general, John B. Coulter, congratulated Gordon on his outstanding performance of duty as director of the Public Information Division:

> You arrived at a time when UNKRA publicity was at its lowest ebb and by your intelligence, ingenuity, tact, persistence and efforts, the accomplishments of the agency are not only known and recognized by the Korean Government and people, but in many nations throughout the world.
>
> Through your work as director, you have contributed immeasurably to the prestige of the Agency and the United Nations Organization.[86]

By the end of April King and the family were on their way to Rome, London, and New York, and by 13 June they were in Cairo.

14

Gordon in Egypt: The Suez Crisis and Peacekeeping

Long after his three dramatic years in the Middle East, King concluded a Christmastide of happy family festivities with a reflection he called "Twelfth Night: 1987–1988."[1] He and Ruth had taken down the tree and put away the decorations, restoring order; the family had resumed their ordinary activities. "Another Christmas past. But not quite," he wrote. For on the mantle there remained a crèche that contained figures gathered from many countries as mementos of their long years together. And on this Eve of the Feast of the Epiphany, he found himself musing on these figures, almost, in this setting, reviewing his life – their life – with the UN. There was the tiny spiral wire tree decorated with coloured glass balls and a miniature star, bought at Wanamaker's in 1940 to celebrate their first Christmas as a family in their Greenwich Village apartment. One could spot a tiny carved medicine man from a village in Kasai, Zaire, hidden in the spiral where Alison had gently tucked him. And there was the olive wood crèche itself bought by King in Manger Square, Bethlehem on his first visit in 1957. It was a dignified little group, the baby at the centre in the cradle, Mary, Joseph, and a shepherd kneeling, three kings identified by their crowns, two donkeys, one lamb, and three camels led by a wooden looped chain. The group had expanded to include the UN General Assembly in Paris, 1948, a group of figures that suggested they had come from a circus: a clown, two dancers, and an assortment of talented performers – a horse, a dog, a rooster, and a bear. A second camel train, purchased in Cairo and lacking the fine craftsmanship of the first one, recalled to his mind trips across the desert sands (albeit, mostly by plane) from Baghdad to Tripoli and down the Nile to Sudan and Ethopia. On the other side of the Holy Family and just in front of the Cairo camels, one saw a small white lion, and above him a

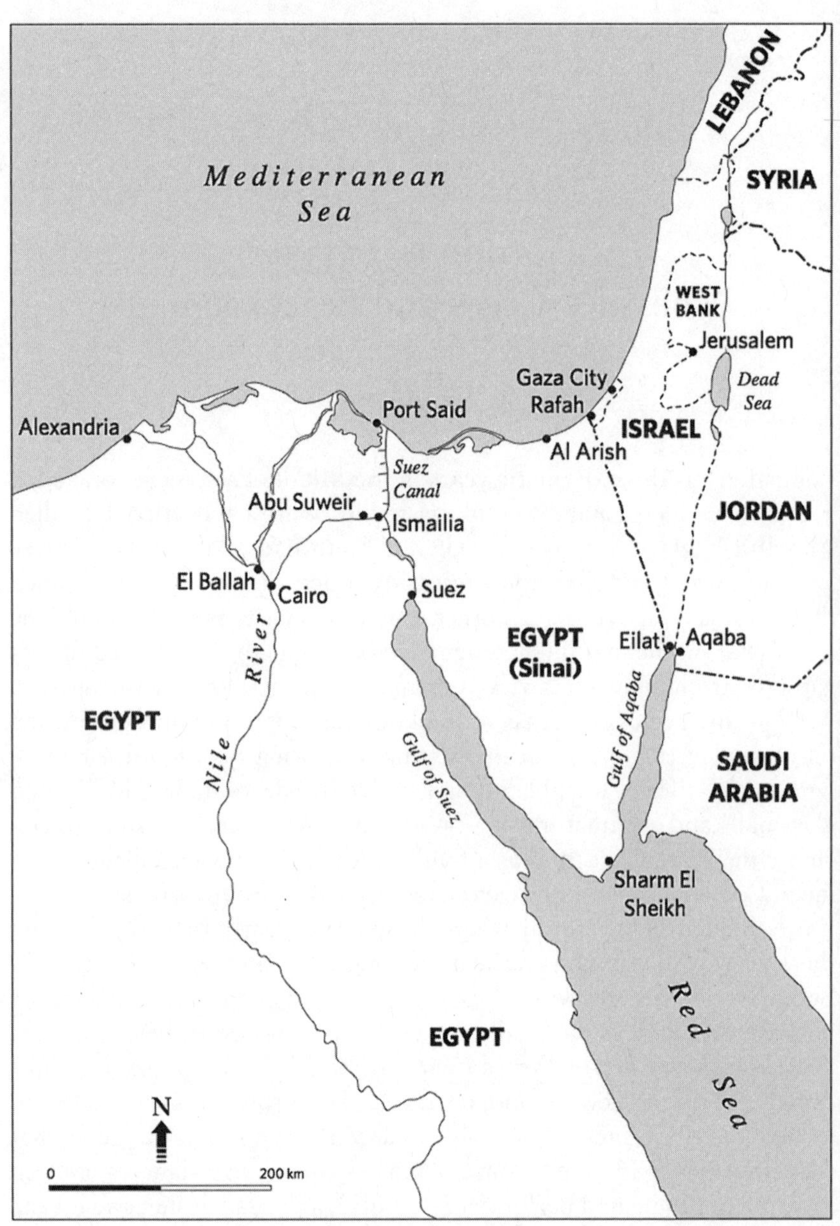

Egypt/Gaza/Israel 1956–57 (Barry Levely, cartographer)

miniature elephant, carved out of dark wood, neither of which seemed at home in the environs of the Middle East or even of Korea or Japan. These last treasures would come in later from the Congo; but if King found himself returning to dwell on that Cairo camel train, it would be to recall the tumultuous events of his years in Egypt.

In June 1956, King, Ruth, and the children arrived in Cairo and began a hot summer that presaged an explosive autumn. The brief visit to New York after leaving Korea in the late spring of 1956 had included a few days up to Winnipeg to see the family, briefings on the new posting, and shopping for household items to be shipped to Egypt. They also bought a car, duly transported on a British ship bound for Alexandria; but the ship arrived in the Mediterranean just as the British and French invasion began in late October, and the last Gordon heard of his car, it had been diverted to Bombay. "So the Cairo taxis will continue to be the gainers."[2] (UNEF – United Nations Emergency Force – later provided him with a car, complete with UN insignia and flag, which led him to hope that they might also find him a typewriter.) In New York, Gordon was given a personal briefing by Hammarskjöld, who had recently returned from a tour of the Middle East where he had conducted private discussions with government leaders, trying to work out the basis for an armistice. Gordon quoted him as saying that while in the short term he was dealing with the ceasefire issue, a break in the violence could perhaps in the long term open the door to a solution to the Palestinian refugee problem.[3]

Buoyed up by these words, Gordon left for his new assignment as director of the United Nations Information Centre for the Middle East with a feeling of optimism. Hammarskjöld had also offered words of wisdom to Gordon: the main task of anyone representing the UN in that region was to develop a relationship of mutual trust. "Never lose your temper," he added. "Personal relationships count a great deal."[4] Gordon later recalled that he had heeded Hammarsjold's advice, losing his temper only once. His lapse of civility occurred with correspondents "flocking around like vultures" while he was trying to arrange for their safe passage across the Sinai, at the same time that the Egyptian authorities, for no apparent reason, repeatedly changed the regulations, "just being bloody minded about it all."[5] He was embarrassed and chagrined by his outburst but, as he explained to Ruth, "It was bloody hot!"[6]

Their first task on their arrival in Cairo was to find an apartment and get the children registered for the fall term at the American School. They found a spacious apartment on the seventh floor of an apartment house in Zamalek, on Mahad el Swissri. From their balcony they looked out over the Nile and across the bridges to the Citadel and the Mokattem Hills. The tall sails of the *feluccas* on the river cast shadows in the living room as they passed. In the evenings they sat on the balcony, catching the cool breezes and watching egrets skim across the water. Gradually they learned their way around Cairo itself, the modern city and the old market area, where they bought brass, silver, and camel saddles. They visited museums and the Mouski or Khan Lhalil, and went to the pyramids and on to Saqqara and its step pyramid and third-dynasty tombs. Later, they travelled to Luxor and Karnak.

But they were not tourists for long. The Gordons had arrived in Egypt at a time of political tension and violence stemming from unresolved issues of the 1948 Arab–Israeli War. In May of 1948, the UN Security Council had appointed Count Folke Bernadotte as mediator to work out the terms of a ceasefire that could become the basis of a lasting settlement. With help from military officers from Sweden, the United States, Belgium, and France, Bernadotte had drafted a truce and the Security Council established a United Nations Truce Supervision Organization (UNTSO) to be headed by the count.[7] The truce had gone into effect on 11 June 1948 followed by a meeting between the mediator and both sides on the island of Rhodes, where a settlement was proposed based on a federation of Jewish and Arab states. Not surprisingly, both sides rejected the proposal and, within a month, fighting resumed. On Bernadotte's recommendation, on 15 July the Security Council ordered an immediate ceasefire under the threat of sanctions. The two sides complied, but on 17 September Count Bernadotte was assassinated in Jerusalem by Jewish extremists. Notwithstanding, by the summer of 1949 the armistice was in place, supervised by UNTSO, and eventually Major-General Burns of Canada became that organization's chief of staff. In 1950, the United States, France, and Britain reached an agreement guaranteeing the boundaries established in the armistice. The Arab states, however, continued to refuse to recognize Israel, and border incidents continued with increasing frequency.

By the middle of the 1950s, when the Gordon family arrived in Cairo, most Arab countries that had been under colonial rule had become independent. With the polarization of the Cold War, these states now faced the decision of whether their new desire for Arab unity could best be achieved within the framework of an alliance with the Western powers or independent of them.[8] Since the Western powers all recognized Israel, such an alliance was not a foregone conclusion. In fact, the formation of a neutral coalition with ties to both Western and Eastern blocs was seen by some Arab leaders as a means of increasing the political weight of the Arab states. India and Yugoslavia both encouraged this policy of non-alignment. In 1954 Egyptian president Gamal Abdel Nasser had embarked on such a course, seizing power in the aftermath of the military coup that overthrew the monarchy of King Farouk, and pursuing a distinctly nationalistic set of objectives with the goal of modernizing Egypt. Nasser clearly perceived himself as a leader of the coalition of Arab states confronting Israel. The impending sense of crisis was intensified by Egypt's agreement in 1955 to accept arms from the Soviet Union and its satellites, and by its continuing denial of Israeli access to the use of the Suez Canal. By the time of Hammarskjöld's visit in the spring of 1956, attacks by Arab guerillas (*fedayeen*) across Israel's borders with Gaza, Jordan, and particularly Egypt, had become almost daily occurrences.

In June 1956, on the expiration of Britain's 1936 treaty with Egypt that had allowed them a military base defending the Suez Canal, the last British troops left the Canal Zone. While seeming to remove a possible source of conflict, in that it made Egypt independent of foreign occupation, this withdrawal opened the door for new misunderstandings.[9] Part of Nasser's plan for modernizing Egypt involved the building of a massive dam on the Lower Nile at Aswan, providing electrification and irrigation for the entire Nile delta. Initially, the project was to be funded by an international consortium led by the United States and Britain, including loans financed through the World Bank. Nasser, however, in his flirtation with the Soviet Union and the Eastern bloc, compounded by his recognition of the People's Republic of China in May, had overplayed his cards and aroused the ire of the Republican administration in Washington. Moreover, 1956 was an election year for President Eisenhower. On 19 July the US abruptly announced its withdrawal from the whole Aswan project, insulting Egypt by casting doubts on her "good faith and on her ability to follow through with the project."[10]

The British Foreign Office followed suit the next day, stating that the project was no longer feasible; and the World Bank then announced that in consequence, its proposal for a loan of two hundred million dollars automatically expired. Nasser's response was equally abrupt. On 24 July he assaulted America verbally with his "let them choke with rage" speech, and on 26 July he nationalized the Canal. Pandora's box was now wide open, as the nationalization of the Canal "shook the foundations of peace in the Middle East."[11] Not only had Nasser seized valuable and strategic property largely owned by Britain and France, he had now threatened European access to the Middle Eastern oil on which they depended, and, as a result, Egypt was now in a position to cut off this supply without warning. Throughout the early autumn of 1956, the Western powers began a process of negotiations with Egypt to try to reach a treaty that would guarantee the free use of the Canal by those nations affected (including Israel), but to no avail. Nasser, secure in backing from the Soviet Union, proved unrelenting. This was the alarming diplomatic impasse, fraught with danger, that King and Ruth found weighing heavily on all concerned as they entered the hot Egyptian summer.

The immediate impact on Gordon was to curtail his movements. The territory for which he was responsible as director of the UN Information Centre for the Middle East included the area from Libya in the west to Baghdad in the east, and stretched south to Sudan and Ethiopia. He had spent his first weeks in Cairo getting acquainted with other UN Agencies and their staffs: Resident Representative Manuel Perez Guerrero, head of UN Technical Assistance for the Middle East, and the heads of UNESCO, UNICEF, and WHO (Alexandria) missions. He had also made the necessary contacts with the diplomatic corps and the press. These contacts were developed both by formal meetings and by a plethora of social events. He then planned to travel throughout the region to establish contacts in each country with the same groups, whose cooperation would be essential in carrying out his responsibility to provide information and publicize the work of the UN. He was also charged with overseeing the accreditation of journalists and implementing United Nations information policy and practice. With the political upheaval and the demands placed on him as a consequence, he made just one trip – to Beirut with a short stop in Damascus – before the Israeli attack on the Canal Zone at the end of October radically sidelined these professional responsibilities.

The other claim on Gordon's attention at this time was to prepare a detailed plan for the evacuation of UN staff and families should circumstances require it. On 15 August, General Burns wrote Gordon to tell him that the secretary general had informed the Egyptian delegation that, as a United Nations member, Egypt must assume responsibility for the safety of the UN personnel. Burns continued, "I would appreciate your views on the present situation and any concrete suggestions you intend to put to the secretary general concerning the safety of the United Nations Staff. In particular is there any way that UNTSO could help?"[12] As a result, a committee of four was set up consisting of Manual Perez

Guerrero; Alex Squadrilli of UNWRA; Colonel David Ely of UNTSO; and Gordon from UNIC. American Richard Niehoff, head of the UN Public Administration Program in Egypt, also worked closely with Gordon, particularly in sorting out logistical details. On 31 August a draft plan was submitted to the secretary general, and the committee continued to work on the plan throughout September and October.

The draft plan drawn up by the committee defined the circumstances, such as invasion or riots, under which evacuation might be necessary and established codes for "alerts" and "message to execute." Personnel were free to make arrangements through their own embassies; however, in such cases the UN would not accept financial or other responsibility unless the action had been approved by the agency concerned. The plan sounded a note of urgency in an addendum urging that certain arrangements should be made immediately and, where appropriate, should be kept up to date. These included items such as passports, travel funds, storage arrangements for valuables that could not be carried, and special food for children. Following the "alert" or "execute," UNTSO, under the direction of General Burns, was to be responsible for maintaining continuous communications between Geneva/Jerusalem/Cairo until all arrangements had been completed.[13] It was a huge undertaking, both to organize and, as it turned out, to implement, particularly considering the relatively primitive means of communication available at that time, even when all technical resources were in working order – something that could not be assumed to be the case.

Meanwhile, denunciations of Nasser's action in nationalizing the Canal were coming from all directions. For the governments of France, Britain, and the United States, and for the shareholders of the Suez Canal Company, Nasser's action was a flagrant violation of the 1888 Treaty of Constantinople that had guaranteed both the private jurisdiction and international operation of the Canal. From Nasser's point of view, his action in seizing the Canal was a blow struck for national pride in paying back the Western powers for their breach of faith in pulling out of the Aswan Dam project. Moreover, tolls from the Canal could now be used to help offset the cost of the dam. In late September, Britain and France, followed immediately by Egypt, took the dispute to the UN, the upshot being a resolution adopted unanimously by the Security Council that laid down principles as a basis for settlement of the Canal dispute: free and open passage through the Canal; respect for Egypt's sovereignty; fair tolls agreed upon by Egypt and users of the canal; and arbitration between Egypt and the old Canal Company.[14]

Everyone breathed more easily. Gordon wrote, "The news of this action brought great relief to us in Cairo. It had been a long, hot summer. We were never quite sure whether the Suez Crisis could be resolved without armed conflict."[15] During the last days of October, the evacuation committee even considered winding up their meetings, when suddenly, on 29 October, the Israelis moved against Egypt in a lightning attack on the Canal Zone.

The Israeli attack was followed by an ultimatum from London and Paris to both sides to withdraw their units 16 km back from each side of the Canal and to permit British and French forces to occupy Port Said, Ismailia, and Suez temporarily. Israel consented, but the demand was unacceptable to Egypt. On the 31st, the British Royal Air Force began bombing Egyptian positions in the Canal Zone and in Cairo a blackout went into effect. Gordon recalled driving along the lightless Corniche, crossing the Nile at the Fouad Bridge, and turning into Sharia Mahad el Swissri where their apartment house was located. He found their seventh floor apartment entirely dark, and the family sitting on the balcony looking out across the Nile toward the airport where flashes of light were followed by bumping sounds. They hadn't heard the news, but one of the children remarked that it was pretty funny, having fireworks in a blackout. Gordon explained that these were flares over the airport, lighting up the target for the bombers.[16] When Ruth learned a few days later that the bombs they watched blowing up the airport were British, she found it "very tough for us to take."[17] The next morning the evacuation plan so painstakingly prepared went into effect, and a convoy of the United Nations' family set out across the desert for Alexandria. From there they were taken to Naples by the American Sixth Fleet, and then by bus to Rome. Port Said came under attack from British and French naval forces, and landings were made the following day, 2 November. At this time, King began another long separation from his family, this time for seven months.

Gordon was one of seven UN personnel remaining in Cairo to keep open the offices based there, and he persevered with a feeling of grim reality, surrounded by blackouts and bombings and experiencing his own close calls. On the morning of 7 November, the day that the ceasefire passed by an emergency session of the UN General Assembly was to go into effect, Gordon was awakened at 6 a.m. by the air-raid siren. He decided to go out to the airport at Heliopolis, taking along a friend from the US Embassy and a soldier, looking for evidence that the agreement would in fact be effected. It was a calm and bright morning and they set out under the protective flag of the UN. As they made their way past the train station with the big Ramses statue, "there was a hell of a bang and gravel blew into the side of our car. A little bomb had fallen right in the main track just for our benefit as UN observers." They pressed on, talking their way through roadblocks, "but it got more and more noisy since we were the only car on the road and as the Brits had been strafing cars that looked at all military we showed more discretion than valour and turned back." He reported that the Cairenes were going on with their lives in their own calm and apparently untroubled way, with no sign of panic or of discourtesy to foreigners. They asked a villager near Heliopolis how it had been and were told, "Well, you can only die once." Gordon commented, "There is a faith in these people that is something more than fatalism."[18]

Gordon also felt a sense of profound sadness that it was at the hands of the British that they were suffering these events. On 11 November he listened to the BBC carrying the Armistice Day service from a village church in England commemorating the dead who died for a great cause. He thought back to his feelings of patriotism on previous days of remembrance. And then he thought of the paratroopers on Port Said only a few days before, their planes strafing and bombing the streets, and the pictures he later looked at with sheer horror, taken by a Swedish correspondent just after the ceasefire. He wrote to Ruth: "You will be hearing some of the British side of the case but you will not have seen Port Said, nor will [they] believe that it was British troops – not Russians – who carried out that massacre. I wince every time now that I listen to the suave tones of the BBC, so civilized, so reassuring, so damnably hypocritical. The Stewarts accused me of being anti-British. Well, I am anti those who planned and executed that brutal crime."[19]

Meanwhile, on 4 November the General Assembly in New York passed a resolution submitted by the Canadian delegation headed by Lester Pearson, proposing the creation of an interpositionary United Nations Emergency Force (UNEF). Hammarskjöld specified that "of course" the force would be put under the command of General Burns, head of UNTSO, at least initially.[20] On 5 November the General Assembly authorized the establishment of the force, and a more detailed plan was presented to the Assembly on 7 November. By the time the plan was authorized by the General Assembly three days later, the British and French forces had occupied Port Said on the Canal. The Assembly also specified that Egypt's consent to the intervention of UNEF and its continuing acquiescence to its presence would be a fundamental condition of its operation.

Gordon and his friends in Cairo followed closely as these events unfolded in New York, staying up all night on the 7th listening to the radio as it brought news from the UN. The next day, Gordon wrote, "About 7 o'clock in the morning we stepped out on the patio for a breath of air. Against a clear blue sky a big Canberra bomber was tracing a lazy figure 8 – but was dropping no bombs."[21] It was a good omen.

Of the twenty-four states offering troops to the newly formed UNEF, ten were notified that their offers were accepted – including Canada. Hammarskjöld immediately instructed General Burns to fly to Cairo to establish contact and, if possible, negotiate the terms of operation with the Egyptian government. Burns flew into Cairo on the 8th in the UN's white-painted Dakota, the first aircraft to land at the Cairo airport since the Anglo-French attacks. Gordon met him at the airport and, according to Burns, "testified to the remarkable accuracy of the air attacks, mostly by low-flying fighter aircraft with rocket and heavy machine-gun. There had been a few stray bombs, but not many."[22]

The most difficult problem that met Burns in his talks with the Egyptians concerned the composition and nature of the force that would operate in Egypt. He received a "considerable shock" when Mahmoud Fawzi, the Egyptian foreign minister, intimated that the inclusion of a Canadian contingent in UNEF might not be acceptable. Fawzi explained that while the Egyptian government appreciated Lester Pearson's helpful efforts and recognized Canada's independence in foreign policy, the fact remained that the Canadian soldiers were dressed like British soldiers, they were subjects of the same Queen, and the ordinary Egyptian would not understand the difference. There could be unfortunate incidents. Burns replied that any decision to exclude the Canadians would be regrettable and, in such a case he himself, as a Canadian, naturally would not be able to act as commander of UNEF. Fawzi was quick to assure Burns of the Egyptian government's confidence in his impartiality as a servant of the United Nations, and of his own concern that such a consequence should not follow.[23]

Back in New York, Hammarskjöld responded forcefully to Fawzi's objections to including Canadians in the peacekeeping forces, stating that there was no possibility of compromise.[24] But in view of the fact that the regiment Ottawa intended to send was the Queen's Own Rifles, wearing what was essentially a British uniform with UN badges, Pearson found the Egyptian reaction entirely predictable. With typical wryness he later wrote that what they needed was the "First Kootenay Anti-Imperialist Rifles!"[25] In fact, Pearson had been forewarned of Nasser's attitude by Herbert Norman, the Canadian ambassador in Egypt, who believed that the real reason behind the objection was the suspicion that if the Canadians settled down along the Suez Canal the effect would be the same as if the Anglo-French forces had remained, and that while the heart of the complaint lay in Canada's Commonwealth association, the Egyptians, not wanting to offend Canada, had stressed the risk of incidents.[26]

The Egyptian foreign minister, however, had raised a fundamental problem concerning areas of jurisdiction of an international force operating within a sovereign state, an entirely new concept in international law. The question confronting Hammarskjöld concerned whether, in fact, Egypt had the authority to reject a particular member of the United Nations – in this case Canada – from operating on its sovereign territory. Hammarskjöld stated that he found it constitutionally impossible to accept such an action on Egypt's part, as it would infringe upon his authority under the Assembly resolution. However, as a practical matter, he continued, the UN must give consideration to the wishes of Egypt on this point.[27] Once again, Pearson stepped into the fray and proposed a solution: substituting Canadian supply units for infantry battalions.[28]

It remained therefore, for the secretary general to work out an agreement with the Egyptians as to the terms of Canadian involvement. By 17 November, Hammarskjöld was able to get Nasser's agreement that the Royal Canadian Air Force should supply a transport squadron of C-119 aircraft to move UNEF troops from Naples to Egypt; and that the supporting military staff organized by Canada for the Queen's Own Rifles should be used to fill the very urgent need for administrative troops. It was agreed that Canada could provide air transport, administration, signals, transport, engineers, and medical units, as well as a signals unit with excellent mobile radio equipment that provided essential communication service in the Sinai and the Gaza Strip. However, these service units were accepted in place of the battalion, and Egypt would not agree to the dispatch of the Queen's Own Rifles. In retrospect, Burns felt that Nasser's refusal had been a blessing in disguise, "for the administrative and supporting troops Canada provided then and subsequently were absolutely essential, and the force could not have operated without them. It was not feasible for other contributing nations to furnish technical and administrative troops of the kinds needed."[29] Burns admitted that while he would have been "extremely glad" to have a Canadian infantry battalion in the force, given the choice between an infantry battalion and technical troops, he would have been obliged to accept the latter.

On 15 November 1956, Gordon took on his second assignment in the Middle East when he was seconded to General Burns's staff as public information officer for UNEF, and moved to the UNEF headquarters at El Ballah, a former British camp 20 km north of Ismailia on the western side of the Suez Canal. The British and French were farther north in Port Said, at the entrance to the Canal; and the Israelis occupied the Sinai across the Canal to the east, extending south to Sharm El Shaikh at the southern tip of the Sinai. Gordon spent seven months with UNEF, travelling up and down the Canal in Otter aircraft flown by RCAF pilots or driving by jeep and truck over the impossibly bad roads that connected El Ballah with El Arish, the advance headquarters of UNEF on the Mediterranean to the north; or down the shore of the Gulf of Suez to the tip of the Red Sea. He was in and out of Port Said, with forays by jeep and plane across the Sinai Desert as far as Aqaba. Finally, he moved with General Burns and UNEF into Gaza. In between, there were short trips to Cairo to attend to business at the Centre, and to check on the apartment where he was welcomed and fed hot home-cooked meals by their faithful servant, Hassan.

Gordon's first and very pressing assignment as a member of Burns's staff was the accreditation of journalists, and his first crisis came with the initial arrival of troops. He was in Cairo on 14 November, in the midst of a blackout, when word came that the first contingents would arrive the next day. Gordon, incredulous that the arrangements could have been made so quickly, was having a languid drink with a UP correspondent at the Semiramis Hotel when an AP reporter called to say that the troops were on their way. He immediately called Lieutenant-Colonel C.F. Moe of the Norwegian Army, Acting Commander of UNEF in Burn's absence, who urged him to wait for confirmation from Burns' headquarters in Jerusalem. Another urgent call from the AP reporter told Gordon that a convoy of correspondents was leaving at 6 a.m., for Abu Suweir on the Canal where the troops would be arriving, and they wanted to know where the accreditation cards for the journalists were. Gordon left post haste for his office, where the accreditation cards were safely under lock and key – unfortunately not Gordon's. This required a "jimmying job," and Gordon filled out and signed the cards until 1 a.m., just in time to receive a phone call from Burns's headquarters saying that three Swiss Air planes would be landing at 10 a.m.

In view of the busy day that lay ahead, King thought it wise to catch a few hours sleep. He was up at 6 a.m., and ready to leave, but alas, his driver was nowhere to be seen. He contacted Brigadier Salah Gohar, the press liaison between UNEF and the Egyptian government, who had heard nothing and was in "an awful sweat," with panicked visions of UN planes being shot down. Gordon and Colonel Moe, accreditation cards in hand, sped down the Canal at 140 km an hour; but they were late, and on their arrival they found the first Swiss Air plane already on the ground. Hundreds of reporters were milling around, and a "very cocky and publicity minded" Egyptian was giving an on-the-field press conference. As Gordon set about trying to sort things out, the second and third planes arrived.[30]

Within three days, he had accredited 126 correspondents, and both the Egyptians and the press seemed appreciative of his efforts.[31] Two days later they were up to over 160 correspondents, and by 29 November Gordon was complaining that the correspondents, by now far less appreciative, just kept pouring in: "We have a hell of a problem and just haven't the staff to deal with it. Over 200 correspondents have now been accredited and are located in five places – Cairo, Abu Suweir, El Ballah, El Cap, and Port Said.[32]

The correspondents, however, had good reason to be grateful to Gordon's organizational skills. This was clearly demonstrated the day that the British and French evacuated Port Said and the UNEF forces entered. It was a day they had all been waiting for, and although the British still controlled the entrance to Port Said, they had agreed that all correspondents could be allowed in. Gordon, however, insisted that all the journalists must have UNEF ID cards before he cleared them for entry. He blithely turned back the press attaché of the Soviet Union and a few legitimate correspondents who had not been accredited previously; and he arranged for an Indian major to check in all who came along against a list that he provided. "There was some squawking but not much. I have learned a little toughness in this experience." Gordon meanwhile waited inside the barrier, and after the cars that had been checked by the major had come through, he led a contingent of about seventy correspondents down the Canal to the final checkpoint at the entrance to Port Said. At this point, the British officials objected to the entry of two particular reporters. Gordon responded by pointing out that all correspondents checked by him should be allowed in, and he put in a call to the British Corps headquarters. A brisk reply came back saying that they went in on Gordon's responsibility. "I took it, and across the bridge we went."[33]

At the same time, Gordon was giving interviews to international journalists (the Canadian journalist, Blair Fraser, had just been through), meeting film crews for the Canadian Film Board and American correspondents who were filming for television, and trying to get the communications network set up by which the reporters could get their news out. The link out of Abu Suweir depended on the overloaded and inadequate Egyptian telephone system; messages sent by mobile radios, while invaluable, were often victims of delay or error owing to differences in radio procedure. UNEF itself had major difficulty with intercommunications before the arrival of the Canadian signal unit, being entirely dependent on the UN international radio service, which linked Cairo to New York through Jerusalem and Geneva. This slow and uncertain technology caused many difficulties, often keeping UNEF headquarters uninformed about when flights would arrive and what they were carrying.[34]

Gordon had also launched into the larger part of his new job, which was organizing the information office for UNEF. He wrote to Alfred Katzin in New York asking for more help, and he explained to Ruth that in many ways he considered this the biggest information challenge that they had met in the UN so far, and that they could not afford to fail: "It is something to be part of it. Daily things happen that change the pattern of our world. I am one of the little factors in the changing shape of things: the big forces and the big personalities give things their bend."[35] He travelled constantly with General Burns, and the general came to rely on King, appreciating the vital role he played in communicating UNEF to the world with accuracy and fairness – and tact. After Gordon left his staff to return to the Centre in Cairo, Burns expressed concern that UNEF no longer had a functioning information office, and he wrote to Gordon after a visit by the latter: "We are always very glad to see you in Gaza and only wish that you could be with us here permanently. I don't suppose you wish that however!"[36] The relationship between these two Canadians, both of them modest, extremely capable, and reserved at heart, developed into one of deep mutual respect.

In spite of his late arrival in welcoming them at Abu Suweir, Gordon was thrilled to be present when the first UNEF contingents arrived. "I was there," he told the CBC listeners when he sent out his first report on 19 November. "Their coming has been welcomed. The United Nations stands for something in this land. As we drive through the villages on the Ismailia road our [UN] flag is cheered by the people along the way."[37]

This welcome by the common Egyptians continued. Later, Gordon described driving through the streets of Cairo, stopped by a traffic light right beside a bus marked *Nasr School formerly English School*, when a couple of young boys leaned out the window and started shouting, smiling at King and pointing to the UN flag. They asked King's name and then, as the bus pulled away, one boy called out: "All our girls *love* the United Nations! Keep it up!"[38]

On 22 November, Gordon travelled with General Burns to Port Said to discuss the timetable of the British and French evacuation with General Sir Charles Keightley, commander-in-chief of the British–French Expeditionary Force. They flew down the Rosetta Nile, the river below them twisting like a big silver and green snake through the Delta.[39] It would have been shorter to follow the Damietta branch, but it seemed wise to avoid the nervous Egyptian gunners who might not recognize the white Dakota with UN markings. General Keightley and Lieutenant-General Hugh Stockwell, commander of the British contingent in the Allied Force, along with a French general and a French admiral, met them at the control tower.

The general staff of the Expeditionary Force – with considerable aplomb – had established its headquarters in the luxurious offices of the Suez Canal Company, and General Burns and Gordon were taken to the boardroom, which was filled with British and French officers. A British officer whom Gordon had known in Korea greeted him a little self-consciously. The conference was largely a formality as the format of the withdrawal had already been discussed at UN headquarters in New York and covered by correspondence. General Burns went through his list, and General Keightley and his staff confirmed the arrangements. As the meeting was about to end, General Burns raised the question of what vehicles and stores the "enemy" could furnish to the United Nations Emergency Force; perhaps the British might like to save themselves the trouble of taking home their trucks? (UNEF's expeditious arrival had meant that they still lacked ground transportation, and at that time the HMCS *Magnificent* had not yet arrived with its supplies.) Burns observed the distinctly "Gilbertarian" aspect of this transaction in which UNEF, while it was not supposed to drive the invaders out, was at the very least expected to usher them out politely. However, his inquiry had logic in view of the British decision that when a United Nations force was established, they would gracefully withdraw.[40]

The UNEF group was then invited to lunch with the British and French officers in the Suez Canal Company's dining room across the courtyard. The officers deposited their hats on a table on their way in to a splendid lunch, with cordial conversation about everything except the issue at hand. Gordon recalled that as they left the dining room, stopping to pick up their hats, General Keightley remarked to General Burns, "We wear the same hat," referring to the characteristic red band of the British staff officer. Gordon recollected that the next time Burns came to Port Said, he wore a different uniform, designed by himself in grey blue and bearing some resemblance to that worn by the UN Field Service, but with no offending red band around the hat. When pressed by correspondents to identify who was responsible for this creation Burns replied, "Dior!" and walked on.[41]

The first Canadians came by air on 24 November, followed on 10 January by the arrival of the HMCS *Magnificent* bringing the rest of the Royal Canadian Engineers detachment: 56th Reconnaissance Squadron; 56th Signal Squadron; 56th Transport Squadron (including 230 vehicles); 56th Infantry Workshop; and 115th Air Transport Unit (Dakotas, Caribous and Otters), with accompanying personnel of 400 officers and men.[42] The CBC asked Gordon for thirteen minutes on UNEF with special reference to Canadians, a request he readily obliged. "I must say the Canadians are into it everywhere so it shouldn't be too hard to write about them," he wrote to Ruth.[43] In typical fashion, he set the scene for his listeners back in Canada, describing the flight over the Sinai Desert, a desolate landscape of low hills and dry wadis, where the earlier torrential rains had left patterns like the veins on a withered leaf. A Canadian major, sitting across from Gordon on the light plane, commented, "It's like the face of the moon."[44] Looking down from 150 m, Gordon reflected on the young peacekeeper from Denmark, Yugoslavia, or Indonesia standing guard in the bleak coldness of a desert night, wondering what he was doing there: "And in the cold, and loneliness, and the wind drifting the sand so that it gets into your eyes and your hair and your mouth and your rations, it's hard to realize that *you* are the *United Nations*. And when a world statesman in New York speaks of UNEF he means *you*."[45]

He would leave it to historians, he told his listeners in Canada, to one day tell what these boys in the blue helmets had done. For those involved, it had been a matter of more practical problems of supply, transport, and communications. It was the Canadians who were performing these special services for the whole force. Since Gordon was speaking to Canadians, he was free to combine his heartfelt pride in his homeland with his immense admiration for the peacekeeping forces. He concluded his CBC broadcast with a typically homey touch, an account of a

Canadian corporal doing a "grease job" on his vehicle, looking up with the comment, "Well, if it brings peace, it will be worthwhile – nobody wants war."[46]

On 1 December, the Israelis agreed to pull back 50 km from the east side of the Canal, and Burns received instructions from Hammarskjöld to move UNEF troops across to occupy the area vacated by Israel's withdrawal. Gordon accompanied General Burns and witnessed another occasion that bolstered his growing admiration for the general. They arrived to find a newly arrived Yugoslav unit making camp at El Ballah. Their commander, Colonel Radosevic, expected the customary time allotted for settling in before being given a major task. But while Burns and Radosevic, with Gordon, shared a glass of slivovitz, Burns explained the situation. When Radosevic suggested that he should be able to get some troops across to the evacuated area in a few days, Burns replied that there was a camel ferry just up the Canal at El Qantara and that Radosevic should not have too much difficulty getting some troops over quickly. Radosevic suggested "possibly tomorrow." Burns replied, "What about today?" Suddenly it dawned on Radosevic that this was an order. Gordon later recalled that this was how Burns worked: "He said it with a bit of a twinkle in his eye – but not much. At the same time this was a man with an extraordinary sense of humor, rather sardonic and Lincolnesque. He was never effusive, and did not talk a great deal; but the more you got to know him, the easier it was to talk and this humor was just under the surface."[47]

Despite his appreciation of subtlety and humour, and his sheer enjoyment of the human interactions that he witnessed, Gordon was never far from the ironic. Early in January, he accompanied correspondents to the site of an alleged atrocity in the Sinai as the Israelis withdrew. They found no evidence of an atrocity, only the detritus of war, bones and shoes and articles of abandoned clothing. He sent Ruth a page from his notebook, written out in the desert, telling her that the site had been named by the Romans and was purported to be the meeting place of Caesar and Cleopatra. "But the desert has conquered and will conquer, the symbol of remorseless time, of man's emphemerality, futility."[48]

The Israeli withdrawal continued in stages throughout the rest of December and into January 1957. As the Israelis withdrew across the desert, they systematically destroyed surfaced roads, the railway, the telephone lines, and any buildings along their path, hoping to prevent the Egyptians from re-establishing their army on the border of Israel. "God had scorched the Sinai earth," Burns commented, "and His chosen people removed whatever stood above it."[49] In a letter to Ruth, King described what he had seen on a trip down to El Tor on the Gulf of Suez, plowing along a sand road by jeep, and finding more detritus of war hastily cast aside by the retreating army: suitcases, boxes, shoes, probably thrown off trucks and then looted. They came to Ras el Sudr, stretching along the Canal and surrounded by oil wells. It had been a model village of Shell Egypt with charming villas for the international staff and sturdy homes for the Egyptian workers. Now they found it totally deserted, homes ransacked, broken windows, filthy. They bedded down with a unit of Indian peacekeepers and ate curry around the campfire. At daybreak they continued their journey southward, moving into spectacular scenery with magnificent canyons painted pink and gold in the sunrise.[50] In a touching note to his mother, King identified the route of the Exodus from Egypt, "picking it up on a map at the back of my bible last night and following the story in Exodus."[51]

Finally, they came through a rocky pass out onto the seacoast, finding more deserted oil towns, one with an Italian flag flying over it. Sixteen Italian soldiers camped nearby; they had come in on 6 December as the Israelis retreated and claimed that the Israelis had taken away with them over a million dollars of equipment. Gordon described the Israeli armies as "tough, ruthless fighters, from all accounts vastly better soldiers than the Egyptians, giving no quarter and asking none." In another of those ironies of war, on their return trip Gordon and his escort overtook the last vehicle of the retreating Israelis, finding themselves somewhat embarrassed and a little surprised by the encounter. They had a friendly chat, opened a couple of tins of C rations, and had lunch together. In their entire drive down to El Tor, they did not see a single person apart from soldiers: "[E]ight camels and one bird the only living things we saw that belonged to the country. We heard there were about 5,000 Bedouin in the region close to El Tor, but we did not see them."[52]

On another "desert safari" a week later, they approached El Arish to the north of El Ballah, again following the retreating Israelis. They camped 6 km from the town, and the Swedes showed their "boy scout efficiency" by getting the tents up and a fire going in about four minutes. After C rations augmented by some extras from the Scandinavian countries – special bread, good biscuits, and paté that you squeezed from a tube – they found themselves in a tent pleasantly warmed by a heater, air mattresses, and sleeping bags. And over all, "the great dome of the sky filled with stars and the bright moon shining. And not a sound except our voices, and far away over the hill the sound of the surf."[53]

The last of the British and French forces departed from Port Said on 22 December; El Tor to the far south was evacuated by the Israelis on 16 January; and El Arish on the Mediterranean was evacuated the following week. The first phase of the UNEF operation appeared to be nearly finished. The only invaded territory still in the possession of Israel's armed forces was Gaza on the Mediterranean, and Sharm El Sheikh at the southern tip of Sinai. The long hiatus between UNEF's arrival at the International Frontier on 22 January and their entry into the Gaza Strip on 6 March, was occupied by high-level negotiations in the United Nations General Assembly and in Washington. For those in the field, it was a time in the doldrums. King wrote to Ruth, "We have reached a marking time stage and it is bad for the morale of all of us."[54] They had their first sandstorm, rattling the tents, filling in the roads, sifting into their eyes and their food. "The sun was there all right but somehow it didn't mean very much and the wind howled like a banshee."[55]

As they waited for some break on the Gaza question, the information staff was getting "mopey and broody." Gordon reflected that the stalemate was affecting people in different ways – some bored, some exasperated, some simply relaxing, some drinking more. And so, in an effort to raise morale, the *Sand Dune* was born. Gordon called a meeting of all the PR men of each UNEF contingent, with General Burns in attendance, and they agreed to put out a paper. They encouraged everyone to send in news. Originally, names high on the list for the new paper included "The Ballah Bugle" and the "Sinai Sentinel," which the general liked. By the time of its first edition, however, Burns had chosen *Sand Dune*. There were local interest stories and references to what was happening at the UN in New York. The *Sand Dune* came out weekly, a four-page mimeographed publication. Gordon complained, "I have been doing what I decided not to do again ... editing a weekly newspaper ... Today I was contributor, editor, compositor and typist. I even helped design the Camel on the masthead. I hope the boys like it. When it is mimeographed it looks so easy."[56]

At the top of the front page one finds the drawing of a UNEF soldier mounted on Gordon's camel, holding a UN flag. He looks across the sand dunes into a smiling sun. Ruth suggested that as a collector of first editions, Frank Scott might be happy to receive a copy. The paper flourished, built morale, and became the prototype for the *Tom Tom,* which later raised the spirits of the peacekeepers in the Congo.

King's thoughts were never far from his family during these days of unanticipated separation as both he and Ruth struggled to make the best of it. Letters, as always, flew back and forth, King's filled with details of his busy life in Egypt and the Sinai, and Ruth's containing descriptions of the children's activities and her own efforts to make a somewhat normal life for them in Rome. After their evacuation from Egypt the previous November, Ruth had written a long letter to her father describing what the experience had been like for her and the children.[57] While uncomplaining, it provides a glimpse into the cost, however willingly borne, by the families of those in international service. According to her account, amid much confusion as they gathered at the American embassy early in the morning of 1 November, a convoy of about one hundred cars pulled away for Alexandria across open desert (the road was closed because of bomb damage). They travelled with an Egyptian escort, and each car carried a UN flag; the lead car also carried an American flag. Hours later, they arrived in Alexandria during a blackout, and they spent the night in the stifling heat of a small darkened hotel room, listening to the noise of falling bombs that shook the building. Morning brought relief along with a feeling of unreality. They peeked through the shutters and saw the beautiful harbour, the blue sea calm and ethereal, while in the distance they could see flames, with planes circling overhead. In more confusion, they were ferried out to the USS *Chilton*, part of the Sixth Fleet. There were hundreds of small children, infants in arms, and pregnant women, with everyone carrying coats and bundles and small bags, with nowhere to sit. Finally, they climbed up a steep gangplank to the ship's deck where they were greeted with a sign: "If we'd known you were coming, we'd have baked a cake!" That was the keynote for their two days on the ship, as 1,500 marines gave up their sleeping quarters to the weary, dazed travellers, carried and fed babies, played with children and, without grumbling, did everything they could do to help. They set sail in late afternoon during an air raid, with full escort, everyone wearing a life preserver until they were clear of the area mined by the British.

After two nights, they transferred to the USS *General Patch*, when everything changed, including the weather. Ruth recounted that they were ordered around like cattle with loudspeakers blaring at them every moment, and they slept in troop quarters, about 200 to a room, with seasickness adding to their misery. Throughout, the Gordon children seemed to be taking it all in their stride. Charley assured his father that, "Our evacuation was really a lot of fun, although with the international situation the way it was, it seemed almost wrong for it to be."[58] After enjoying the run of the ship on the USS *Chilton*, Charley too found that things had changed as he and his friends found themselves "volunteered" for mess duty, waiting on tables and washing trays for 2,500 people, a 2-½ hour operation during which he caught a cold. Still, he told his father, "It was good to do some work for a change."[59]

They disembarked at Naples on Tuesday, 6 November (King and Ruth's wedding anniversary), and after several hours of red tape they were put on buses for Rome. There they were greeted warmly at FAO headquarters of the UN and given coffee and hotel assignments. Happily for the Gordon family, their good friends Dick and Helen Niehoff and their son David settled in with them at the Casa Pallotti on the Via Pellinari where, to Charley's satisfaction, he and David shared a room on the floor below the others. Alison shared a room with Ruth. They were crowded and short on hot water and heat, but safe. The children started classes at the Overseas School of Rome. Back in Cairo, their father was heartened to hear that they were safe, and no doubt he was amused to hear from Charley that they had seen his picture in the *Rome Daily American*, "with your *Marty* face on ... Alison said it looked like you were dead and they propped you up."[60]

Ruth hoped to return to Cairo soon, but was not too sanguine about the prospects of doing so. She confessed to her father that she had mixed emotions about going back, fearing it would never be the same again. She worried that there would be no school for the children. Even if the British school reopened, she could not imagine sending the children there: "I don't even want to eat British candy, and smoke British cigarettes! There is tremendous bitterness among many of us." She admitted being overcome by fatigue and uncertainty. Nevertheless, she concluded to her father, that while she would never want to do it again, now that the danger was over for the moment, she was grateful to have had the experience. "It gives an understanding of what people have faced all over the world."

Especially in the early weeks of their exile, communication was uncertain, and when King did write (which was often), his letters were frequently preoccupied with details of his busy day and not particularly responsive to Ruth's family news or her questions. Ruth wrote, "I have never felt so incomplete on any correspondence we have had." She felt sure that not all her letters were getting through to King, or if they were, that he was not mentioning them – "which is very unlike you." Ruth found herself unsettled by this uncertainty of communication. "I almost feel," she wrote, "I am writing into a void ... as though you are a stranger ... living in a very interesting period, in a very interesting and dangerous section of the world."[61] But soon mail delivery (mostly by diplomatic pouch) became more reliable, and life gradually settled into a daily pattern: school and related activities for the children, skiing trips, movies, fellowship meetings at the church (mostly dancing, Ruth gathered), all with many friends. "It is all shades of Cairo, but the kids are so happy to see old friends."[62] The Niehoffs became family for Ruth and the children, and Helen Niehoff and Ruth became constant companions, exploring the cultural riches of Rome together. Dick Niehoff's base of operations was the FAO office, and each day he brought home news and letters (if there were any). After drinks, usually Dick, Helen, and Ruth went out for dinner, with or without children and often joined by other UN friends. Helen and Ruth cooked Thanksgiving dinner in the apartment of friends, and Dick brought "the boys" from FAO, which added to the festivities. "Except for one thing, it was a lovely day." Ruth told King. "I guess you can guess what that one thing was!"[63] For Christmas, Ruth and the children trimmed a tree in the hallway, there being no room for it elsewhere. The sun came out, showing Rome's nicer side, as Ruth put it, and she and the children, along with the Niehoffs, went to see an exhibit of Eskimo sculpture. On Christmas morning, they opened their gifts from King – an ebony carving from the Sudan for Charley, and Nefertiti jewelry for Alison and Ruth. King also sent along Charley's baseball glove, which he had spied on the shelf of Charley's bedroom.[64] Gordon meanwhile spent Christmas with the troops at El Ballah being serenaded by an Indian pipe band.[65]

One thing they both worried about was the children's schooling. Charley pointed out that he had now attended four different high schools, a situation of some concern as he was approaching matriculation for university in another year. In the meantime, he excelled at his studies, particularly English and history. They consoled themselves that any deficits in schooling that the children might experience were compensated for and enriched by their international experience, and that certainly was the case. (They might also have considered the cultural bounty of their home environment and the careful tutelage of Ruth.) Much later, King reflected on the effect of these years abroad on the children. He valued the cultural richness and the breadth of perspective, as well as the self-reliance that the experience had given them; and he also treasured what he felt was the deep loyalty and family solidarity that developed during these difficult years when the close family bonds were sustained over long periods of separation.[66] At the time, he reassured Ruth that the children were all right "in terms of the essentials," and that she shouldn't worry over details like Alison's algebra.

While he missed hearing about the moments when she bubbled over, he told Ruth that he had to admit "in terms of physical sacrifice we haven't suffered during these last three years. But we have sacrificed in terms of the spiritual values that come from shared life in our family. And the children have too."[67]

In his birthday letter to Alison, he tried to explain the necessity of his absence from the family:

> I had been hoping that I might be able to get away to be with you on your birthday. But I'm afraid that it won't be possible. It isn't that it is more important for me to be here: I like to think it is more important for me to be with you and Charley and Mummy. But it is just that I have a responsibility here and I cannot walk out on it. You see, I am working now with soldiers and in an army, a peace army, not a war army. But a soldier can't say: "I think I'd like to go away now and see my family." He may feel it and all of us do. But we can't say it, and we can't do it.[68]

Ruth wrote wistfully, "Remember the days when you used to catch a train to NY and home at night?"[69]

King came to Rome for two weeks at Easter, and they enjoyed the city together in the April sunshine, taking a car trip to Florence with stops at Sienna and St Gingnano. There were crosswords and word games and moments of fun. King admired Charley's impressive collection of ash-trays, twenty-five or thirty from different hotels and pensiones, including one from the school bus. They discussed the possibility of school in Beirut for Charley the following year, and they made plans for their summer leave to New York and Birkencraig. When King left for Cairo they all felt it would be for a short separation this time, which it was. Ruth and the children were back in Cairo by 2 June, and King was at the airport to meet them with the Gordon Dodge, complete with the blue UN flag.

After the delays and uncertainties regarding Israel's withdrawal from Gaza, King wrote to Ruth on 5 March 1957, "I have a just-before-the-battle-mother kind of feeling tonight. Tomorrow at this time we should be moving into Gaza."[70] At this point, Gordon was frantically trying to set up a functioning infrastructure for covering the news of the move into Gaza and for getting it out quickly. UNEF's ready access to the telegraph facilities meant that they could connect to all wire services and newspapers, but these messages would have to be short because of priority signals crowding the lines. Longer stories would have to be sent out by plane, and the technician doing recordings and radio work would need to fly out to get on the shortwave to New York.

An unexpected twist developed with the Israeli journalists, who were also eager to get stories out. On at least three occasions after the Israeli withdrawal from Gaza, the correspondents at the Israeli border a kilometer or two away from the Gaza headquarters asked Gordon and his assistant to meet them at the demarcation line and tell them what was going on, amicably discussing events and managing to "bat down some of the bad propaganda on both sides." Gordon felt the device they had worked out was "quite dramatic and quite effective – one of the many cockeyed developments in this whole affair."[71]

Altogether, Gordon's "devices" at getting out the news appear to have been remarkably efficient, and he received a letter from J.V. Stavridi, director of External Services, at UN headquarters in New York complaining that his dispatches were in fact coming through *too* quickly. In one or two cases, Gordon's press statements, "with highly commendable speed," had come on the wires before General Burns' official reports were received on the 38th floor. "It puts us in a bad position here if the release has to be held up, or if no comment can be added at headquarters on the ground that no report has been received by the Commander."[72] Never one to drag his feet, however, Gordon proceeded to set up a "photographic spree" for General Burns and Ralph Bunche (acting mediator for Palestine, who had recently arrived from New York) with *Life*, CBS, and NBC all clicking briskly. He then suggested that both photographers and film could be carried out on the general's plane, so that no time would be lost in getting the pictures to the waiting world. "We can't do very much for our correspondents here, cut off as they are from communication, but we do our best."[73]

Gordon's modesty belies the effectiveness of his efforts. In fact, George Ivan Smith, director of the UN Information Office in London, and a close friend and confidant of Dag Hammarskjöld, wrote a letter of appreciation to him for the "first class job" he was doing in difficult circumstances. "Believe me," he wrote, "people at Headquarters are aware of these conditions, and have been made so largely through the activities of you and your colleagues." Smith went on to assure Gordon that during the long night sessions "on the 38th floor," his cables were read personally by the secretary general and his inner circle, often becoming topics of conversation at different times day after day. Even when the cables were not of high news value, "every word that is sent brings the atmosphere of the area closer to Headquarters at all levels, whether or not the material finds its way into a press release."[74]

General Moshe Dayan, chief of staff of the Israeli Defense Force, and General Burns arranged that the takeover of the Gaza Strip by UNEF should take place on 6 March during the hours of darkness. Gordon flew with General Burns into El Arish where the units – Danors (Danes and Norwegians), Indians, Colombians, and Swedes – formed up in trucks at the last checkpoint before Gaza. It was a bit eerie, according to Gordon, the long line of trucks, troops moving around talking, smoking, waiting; and overhead, a sliver of moon. There were a few Bedouin and refugees alongside the road, wondering what it was all about. The convoy got underway at 8:15 p.m. Gordon and his assistant were in one jeep, followed by two other assistants in two more jeeps, all carrying correspondents, and all sandwiched in between the six-wheel trucks They followed the stream of red tail lights past the Israelis at the checkpoint of Rafah and then wended their way at about 29 km per hour through the dark countryside between rows of cactus hedges for over an hour.

The convoy, with the Danor battalion in charge, reached Gaza City at 9:30 p.m., and found themselves surrounded by the popping of flashbulbs and a mass of correspondents from Israel, with armed Israeli soldiers backed by tanks. A huge dust storm in the afternoon had now been replaced by a cold, driving rain. Gordon and his crew didn't know where to go, and neither did most of the trucks. They were prowling around the Israeli headquarters when an Israeli officer offered to take them to a vacant house close by, which included not a stick of furniture, simply a phone. The joke of the evening was when one of the correspondents picked up the phone and said, "Give me Tel Aviv!" He was connected immediately and he and the other correspondents with them sent out their copy via Tel Aviv, beating the Israeli journalists who had gone back to Jerusalem by bus.

Gordon returned to the police station and saw the handover by the Israeli forces to UNEF, General Dayan himself being present. King described the scene to Ruth: "a darkened city, Israeli soldiers, men and women, Israeli tanks, correspondents, UNEF troops in blue helmets, trucks and jeeps racing through streets in general confusion, and rain pouring down in a cold deluge."[75] Nevertheless, General Burns was able to report to the secretary general by 3:35 a.m., that UNEF troops were in position in all camps and centres of population in the Gaza Strip; and that the last Israelis were out by 6 a.m.

In the days leading up to the Israeli withdrawal, the degree to which the UN would undertake control of the civil administration in Gaza had not been clarified. At the last minute, however, the government of Israel had agreed to withdraw its forces from the Gaza Strip on the understanding that UNEF would be deployed throughout Gaza and that the transfer of military and civil control would be exclusively to UNEF and not immediately to Egypt; and that the United Nations would be in charge of civil administration for an indeterminate period until an arrangement for Egyptian administration could be agreed upon.[76] General Burns left Gaza for El Arish on 10 March confident that the issue had been settled for the time being, and noting that the streets were filled with crowds celebrating the Israeli withdrawal. A day later he received the unsettling news that Egyptian agitators were active in Gaza. He flew back immediately, and when Gordon met him at the Gaza airport, they were surrounded by quite a different kind of crowd, now protesting the delay in turning the civil government over to the Egyptians. Gordon had to push through the throngs with his jeep on the way to the police station, now the UNEF headquarters. Of particular concern to Gordon was the fact that the three principle agitators had come into Gaza from Egypt as journalists, their credentials in order. The principle upon which the United Nations Information Service (UNIS) worked was that any journalist in Cairo who represented a responsible newspaper or other medium of information was allowed to enter with UNEF, and Gordon would have had no means of ferreting out their true intent.

The crowd eventually had to be broken up with tear gas, and shots were fired into the air when the protestors surged against the gates of the police station. Unfortunately, one young Arab was struck by a ricocheting bullet and died two days later. It was not a happy situation for UNEF, but by the next morning all was quiet again, with open markets and people moving about the streets naturally. Gordon hitched a ride with Ralph Bunche back to Cairo for the night to check up on the office and to write to Ruth. After nearly a week of bedding down in his sleeping bag wherever and with whomever he could find a dry spot, his own bed felt good.[77] General Burns remained at the UNEF headquarters in Gaza where he received news that, in the wake of threatened violence following the death of the young Arab, the Egyptian government had abruptly appointed an administrative governor, who would take up his functions at once. This coincided with an attack on the Canadian forces in the

Cairo press, claiming that the Arab in question, while innocently climbing a flagpole to get a better view during the demonstration at the police station, had been fired on by a Canadian.

While Gordon was back in Cairo for his brief overnight respite, he had an hour's talk with Canada's ambassador to Egypt, Herbert Norman, who was "quite upset about the present anti-Canadian trend of Egyptian opinion."[78] Gordon himself was indignant but not too upset. "I'm sure if the Canadians had been in the position of the Danes and Norwegians [in holding back the demonstrators] they would have been firing off guns in the air. But it so happened that they were only driving trucks, running signals, and pounding typewriters." Nevertheless, in the protestors' minds the Canadians were at fault.

As it turned out, at the urging of Ralph Bunche, Nasser agreed to persuade his cabinet to allow UNEF's Canadian reconnaissance squadron into Gaza and the immediate crisis appeared to have passed. Still, when he flew back to Gaza the next day, Gordon looked down on two demonstrations and streets spanned with banners carrying slogans, "Egypt is our Mother," and "We will never be separated from Egypt."[79] They landed just as the general was taking off back to Cairo to see Bunche. Gordon commented to Burns in passing that he had heard there had been a demonstration but he supposed it was a quiet one. Burns barked, "Quiet! It was noisy as hell!"[80]

The crisis had, in fact, passed, and the demonstrations were followed by an abrupt change in the public attitude of the Egyptians, Nasser perhaps fearing that if hostility to UNEF went too far there was a danger that the force might be withdrawn, leaving the Egyptians to face the Israelis on their own. Therefore, when Major-General Mohammed Abd el Latif, the new administrative governor, made his entry into Gaza on 14 March, he quickly put a damper on local hostility, pointing out to the chanting crowds that UNEF was there with the consent of the Egyptian government and should, therefore, be treated with traditional Arab hospitality.

On 21 March, George Ivan Smith arrived in Cairo with Hammarskjöld, and it fell to Gordon to give Smith an introduction to the Gaza Strip and the work of UNEF. Gordon was not enthusiastic. From his perspective, "[George Ivan Smith] has been dealing so long in the airy realms of Assembly resolutions that he is always falling back when the newsmen ask him an awkward question. I have a feeling [exposure to the field] will be a wholesome experience for George."[81] The truth behind this uncharacteristically dyspeptic comment lay in the fact that after four and a half months of unrelenting crisis, Gordon was exhausted. Moreover, with the winding down of the Gaza assignment, he faced returning to Cairo and what seemed to him the mundane task of getting the Centre in shape after his long absence. "The field was quite different," he wrote to Ruth as he turned to this task: "There I was with my 'old comrades' who were all in the same boat with jobs to do all related to the same effort. There was activity and practical problems to deal with. Here, however, I am by myself in a big city from which the very life seems to have gone out. This is a subjective judgment, I know: because what I miss now acutely is you and the children and the life we had."[82]

However, social life gradually resumed in Cairo, with many of the old UN friends returning; and George Ivan Smith turned out to be amenable, telling Gordon, "You must remember [King], that your job is vital until we round this curve in history." The hyperbole was not entirely lost on King who observed to Ruth that the sharp elbow of this curve lay somewhere on the Cairo–Gaza–Tel Aviv axis.[83] With a return to more work in Gaza ("rather pleased to be with my chums again for a day or two") and a shot of penicillin for his sore throat, King recovered completely from both his cold and his low spirits. Within a few days of Smith's visit, Gordon and an Indian major travelled along the demarcation line between Israel and Gaza, visiting UNEF outposts as they went. The first outpost, situated high above a valley, gave them a view of Israel below. King commented to Ruth, "It was all so peaceful, with sheep and goats and shepherds and shepherdesses that it seemed incredible that this should be one of the most bitter pieces of land in the whole world."[84] They reached the Indian outpost just at sunset and this time they looked down on the Palestinian territory, watching the Bedouin taking their flocks home for the night, and listening to larks singing high up in the sky.

Meanwhile, the Canal was being cleared. The final ship to be raised at the beginning of April was the *Edgar Bonnet*, sunk near Ismailia. Gordon and his information team had received instructions from headquarters in New York as to how to cover the dramatic moment: crowds on the bank awaiting the raising; cheers when the secretary general and General Burns appeared; and the tremendous cheer when the *Edgar Bonnet* was finally lifted from the Canal bottom. On the big day, when Gordon's crew arrived, it appeared that the cheering crowd consisted only of two nuns with picturesque headdresses standing on the bank quietly observing the preparations. Undeterred, Gordon and company boarded a tugboat along with the dignitaries to get good coverage of the event. The

Edgar Bonnet emerged steadily (and apparently without fanfare) and as the bow appeared, so did something written just above the water line. With some squinting, the VPs deciphered: KILROY WAS HERE. Feeling pleased with their copy, Gordon observed: "It seemed to us that the Suez Crisis was over."[85]

It was in that same month, April 1957, that the diplomatic community in Cairo and in the larger world was shattered by the death of Herbert Norman. During their first months in Cairo, King and Ruth had renewed their friendship with the Normans, who had arrived in August 1956, with Herbert's appointment as Canadian ambassador to Egypt and minister to Lebanon. With their fellow compatriots in Egypt and throughout the world, they shared the horror and confusion that surrounded Norman's suicide the following April, a victim of his own despair and of the long arm of McCarthyism.

Herbert Norman had been born in Japan of Canadian Methodist missionaries, and spent his formative years there.[86] After he graduated from the University of Toronto he completed a second degree at Trinity College, Cambridge, and it was in the heady atmosphere of political ideas of the 1930s, that he, like several contemporaries, "found Marx" and joined the Communist party. After the Second World War he joined the Foreign Service and served as head of the Canadian Liaison to Japan. It was at this time that the first challenge to Norman's loyalty came, growing out of suspicion within American intelligence branches that he had remained a communist after he had left Cambridge in 1935 or, perhaps even worse, had ties with the Soviet Union and operated as a spy. After his appointment as ambassador to Egypt, McCarthyism struck a second blow when the US Senate Internal Security subcommittee released to the press a text of their hearings that included previous information about Norman. Lester Pearson, as secretary of state for External Affairs, sent a strongly worded note of protest to his American counterpart, John Foster Dulles, pointing out that the Canadian government had examined similar allegations as long ago as 1951, and confirming the Canadian government's full confidence in Mr Norman.[87]

The support of his government notwithstanding, Norman fell into a deep depression at the prospect of further inquisition. On the morning of 4 April he left his Cairo residence, climbed to the roof of an eight-storey building, and jumped to his death. Gordon flew back to Cairo from Gaza that afternoon and wrote to Ruth in Rome: "I got the news of Herbert's death just about one o'clock today … All the way across the desert – I was sitting up in the cockpit with the pilot – I kept asking why, why, why, it should happen to one who seemed so rational, so considerate, so experienced in the ways of the world, even the ways of evil men."[88]

Three days later, Gordon wrote a long letter to Pearson: "As you probably know I saw a great deal of Herbert during his first months in Cairo … During these months … I got to know him much better and my appreciation of him and affection for him deepened enormously … We had a great many talks … In [them] there was no 'other side' of Herbert that came out. The man was transparently sincere and of complete integrity."[89]

In response to the story of the Senate subcommittee's report breaking in the western press, King had called in to see Herbert on the Monday of 1 April, three days before his death. In his letter to Pearson, Gordon tried to reconstruct their conversation, describing Norman's dread at once again falling prey to the distortions of the FBI and the US Senate subcommittee. Furthermore, Norman was acutely aware of his position in the Department of External Affairs and as a representative of Canada, and he feared bringing embarrassment to those who were standing so loyally behind him. At that point in their conversation, Herbert had said: "King, I wakened up the other night suddenly with the phrase going through my head, 'Innocence is not enough.' I have, I believe, served the Department with complete integrity. I have been completely scrupulous and discreet in everything that I have done and said in carrying out my job. But that is not enough. If this thing comes up again I don't think I can go on."[90]

They talked for over an hour, and Norman seemed to grow relaxed. But King, like other friends, was deceived by Norman's high degree of rationality and, like them, was convinced he would snap out of his despondency. "With the terrible wisdom of hindsight," Gordon told Pearson, "I now feel that if we had realized how horror-stricken was his world, by our concerted efforts we might have saved him." Then, reflecting on the ambiguities and compromises of public service that, in a way, recalled the issues Reinhold Niebuhr had wrestled with in *Moral Man and Immoral Society*, Gordon went on: "Of course, Herbert's very integrity may have been his undoing. Most of us, with less integrity, make our mental compromises with evil … It is an accepted fact in the world. We cultivate thick skins to protect ourselves and with some resignation or optimism shrug off its corroding impact, never admitting its malignant power. Herbert refused this easy way out which would have given him protection."

Gordon quoted Norman's wife as saying, "Perhaps if [Herbert's death] results in bringing an end to this kind of thing it will have been worthwhile." He closed his letter to Pearson: "My God, let us hope so, or at least make us all aware of the devastating results of the disregard for human sensitivities and human decencies. Of course, this line of thinking must go beyond hatred of the methods and the men who destroyed Hebert, through to something positive, more creative. But all this is beyond my present horizon."[91]

Gordon left General Burns's staff in May, reluctantly but with the recognition that his job with UNEF had been completed. In June, shortly after Ruth and the children returned from Rome, the family left for home leave and a summer of restoration at Birkencraig, with meetings and briefings in New York for Gordon. With Charley's impending enrollment at the American Community School of Beirut scheduled for September, this time together as a family was both happy and poignant.

Ruth Gordon with Charley and Alison, Birkencraig, 1945. (Courtesy of the Gordon family)

At the office of *The Nation*, circa 1946. Left to right: Keith Hutchinson, J. King Gordon, Joseph Wood Crutch, Freda Kirchwey, Maxwell Stewart, I.F. Stone. (Permission granted by Schlesinger Library, Radcliffe Institute, Harvard University)

King Gordon and Frank Scott, North Hatley, 1955. (Courtesy of the Gordon family)

Ruth Gordon in Japan, 1955. (Courtesy of the Gordon family)

Carte No. 296 ٢٩٦ تذكرة رقم

ممنوحة الى مستر جون كنج جوردون

مدير مركز الامم المتحدة للانباء

بالشرق الاوسط

délivrée à Mr. John King Gordon

Directeur, Centre d'Information des Nations Unies pour le Moyen Orient.

القاهرة في ١٥ اكتوبر سنة ١٩٥٦

إمضاء حامل التذكرة

Signature du Titulaire

Le Chef du Protocole — مدير المراسم

Assimilé à un chef de mission diplomatique.

يعتبر مثل رئيس بعثة دبلوماسية أجنبية

King Gordon's 1957 Carte d'identité, issued by Egyptian government (Courtesy of Alison Gordon)

UNEF peacekeepers in the Sinai, taken by King Gordon, 1957. (Courtesy of the Gordon family)

King Gordon with UNEF peacekeepers and assistant, 1956. (Courtesy of the Gordon family)

Clearing the Suez Canal, Egypt 1957. "KILROY WAS HERE!" (Courtesy of the Gordon family)

King Gordon with his mother Helen at Birkencraig, 1958. (Courtesy of the Gordon family)

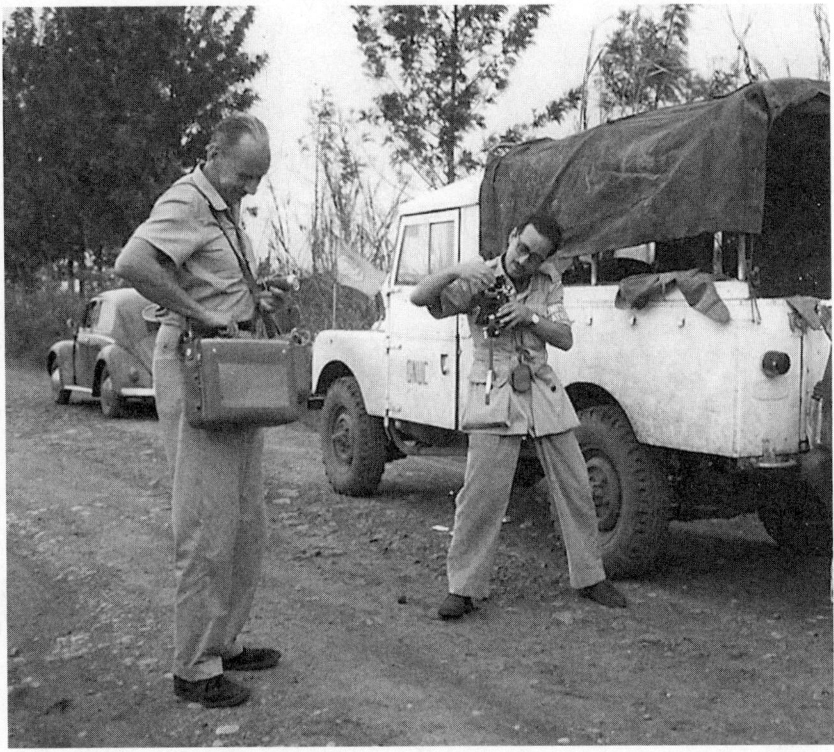

King Gordon with his photographer Freddy Bayat, on the road to Goma, Congo, 1960. (Courtesy of the Gordon family)

King Gordon, 1957. (Courtesy of the Gordon family)

Dr J. King Gordon receives Pearson Peace Medal from Governor General Edward Schreyer at Rideau Hall, 1980. (Tim O'Lett/*Ottawa Citizen*. Reprinted by permission)

15

Field Work in the Middle East

Gordon's summer leave included a brief visit with Frank Scott in August 1957 when their paths crossed in Montreal. As always, King found it "extraordinarily good" to see Frank once again, and after their conversation, easily resumed from when they were last together, he and Alison boarded their plane for the short flight down to Boston to rejoin Ruth's family in Hingham. About half an hour from Boston, Alison (now a world traveller and scornful of the small plane) nudged King and pointed to the engine on the port wing. It was stopped. "I told you so," she said in disgust. They "sailed through the murk" on to the Boston airport where waiting fire trucks greeted them, and they deplaned rapidly and without ceremony: "Get 'em out and never mind their coats!" the captain shouted. They watched from the tarmac as the smoldering wing was doused with carbon monoxide, and shortly they were on their way. The event, following as it did the heart-to-heart talk of the two old friends, provoked King to reflection. He wrote to Scott the following day:

> The H-bomb and the intercontinental missile should, I suppose, have a greater apocalyptic impact on me than they do. Perhaps my years in the Far and Middle East have induced a kind of fatalism that doesn't disturb my dreams. But the port engine on fire on a two-motor Northeastern aircraft for a perennially airborne family has a more personal apocalyptic significance and I admit I slept badly last night. You think of the things left undone that you should have done – not just the untidy mess that somebody, and perhaps a lot of people, would have to tidy up but the surface character of so much of the life we lead. Perhaps an international civil servant is more appalled by this reflection than one who has cultivated his own

> vineyard. (You have that ancient maple to look out on; it is there when you leave in the morning and when you return at night. I watch the *faluccas* [sic] drift down and sail up on the Nile but when each has passed my window I am never sure that I shall see it again.)[1]

He concluded his letter voicing the recurrent hope that he would return to Canada one day soon, and he asked Frank to pass on any leads concerning suitable jobs that he might hear about. "If and when we return I shall plant a young maple at our door!"

The family returned to Cairo in September, Ruth once again settling in to her life in the international community, Alison happily returning to school and her friends. King travelled to Lebanon with Charley, getting him settled in the American Community School – which was, Charley noted, now his fifth high school. Gordon wrote Scott again, this time to discuss the possibility of Charley's entering a Canadian university the following year and to ask him to garner information about academic prerequisites. He confided to Frank that he favoured Carleton, but as it had no boarding facilities, he asked for information from Queen's. He also expressed his concern for Charley's safety in the politically unstable situation in Lebanon.[2] As a result of the Suez crisis and the forced withdrawal of the British and French forces, Nasser had gained political stature in the surrounding Arab countries, and Western fears of a Soviet-sponsored takeover by Nasser in the Middle East increased.[3] Throughout the region, the split between pro-Western and pro-Nasser opinion was deepening, dangerously inflaming local rivalries, a division exacerbated in Lebanon by the growing imbalance between Christians and Muslims with the influx of Palestinian refugees, and the pro-Western policies of President Camille Charmoun rested on a steadily weakening base. Gordon was justified in feeling apprehensive about his son's safety. In April, with the area careening into rebellion and civil war, the American Community School closed, fearing that it could no longer assure the safety of its students, and Charley returned to Cairo.

Gordon returned to Cairo, finding it somewhat drabber than usual; nevertheless, he was eager to take up his duties at the UN Information Centre for the Middle East. The tense circumstances preceding the Suez crisis the previous year, combined with his lengthy assignment on General Burns's staff as chief information officer for UNEF, had meant that his movements had been curtailed and that so far he had had little opportunity to fulfill his original assignment in the vast territory of his mandate.

There were two aspects to his work at the Centre: first, to supply the region with information about the United Nations; and second, to report back to UN headquarters in New York, from his first-hand observations in the field on what the UN was doing through its technical and educational projects.

The first set of responsibilities could be carried out from the headquarters in Cairo: press releases, pamphlets, publications and documents, radio recordings, pictures and films. The Centre's library provided an effective medium for the transmission of information, and was heavily patronized by professors, students, government officials, and the press. The staff published a weekly newsletter in Arabic, combining useful information about the United Nations programs and activities throughout the world, paying special attention to local projects. They also issued news stories and photos to be carried in the local press, and radio scripts for the news services, and they hoped to produce films but the lack of working projectors throughout the region made that unattainable for the time being. The Centre worked through the resident representative of the UN Mission in each of the capitals, and the residents in turn relied heavily on the Information Centre in Cairo to assist in them in publicizing the work being carried on in their particular countries. There was also a necessary public relations aspect to the program, an art not yet formalized into a recognized function, and Gordon felt that it was vitally important to go beyond the "cordial welcome, shoulder-patting, coffee-drinking practices of this region"[4] to present a clear and detailed explanation of the goals of the UN programs.

Gordon found the bureaucratic and secretarial aspects of his job less to his liking than being out in the field, where he felt the real work of the UN was being accomplished. Nevertheless, he recognized the necessity and value of the more mundane work and, underneath his grousing, he enjoyed it. Still, it was in travelling around the region, observing in concrete terms the working out of the UN's program of technical assistance that gave him the greatest pleasure. As he began to cover his territory, he focused as always on the human face of need. "What do we mean by human need?" he asked a New York audience shortly after his final return from Egypt in 1959. He thought in pictures, he told his listeners: the sickly child at his mother's breast in a mud-walled village in the Nile Delta, his eyes covered with flies, destined for blindness; the father, standing in an irrigation canal scooping up pails of polluted water, the soles of his feet offering host to parasites that would lodge in his bloodstream and eventually destroy his kidneys. "Human need is the cloak of ignorance that cuts a man off from the knowledge that may save him and leaves him victim of fears and superstitions, his life haunted, as was the life of his ancestors for thousands of years by spirits and witchcraft and black magic,"[5] he told his audience.

As he began to familiarize himself with his territory, his first port of call was right at home: Cairo and the Public Administration Institute, training Egyptian civil servants and helping to organize government bureaucracy. He marvelled at the matter-of-fact attitude of the international experts sent out at the requests of governments requiring aid; and at the students, themselves government officials, who added their training to an already busy schedule. Gradually, as the Institute in Cairo expanded, he anticipated that Egyptians would replace the foreign experts, and that year by year the benefits would be passed on to new generations of government workers, many of whom would qualify for periods of study abroad. Nothing spectacular, he noted, just the steady building of a stable, enlightened, and efficient bureaucracy, to be repeated over and over in other developing nations as the program succeeded.[6]

The other countries of the Middle East then claimed his attention, and these trips followed a pattern. The UN resident representative in each country organized the itinerary, which invariably included interviews with government officials, and the local press. Gordon was often billeted in lavish hotels, but he had his share of shabby local accommodation; once in the field, his nights on dirt or wooden floors reminded him of his days with UNEF. There was always a tour of the cultural riches of the cities and lavish dinners with local UN dignitaries and diplomatic personnel. But most of his time was spent with the representatives, observing the work of the UN agencies in the region, visiting experimental farms and factories, vocational schools, mother and child care centres, clinics and hospitals.

In the late fall of 1957 Gordon travelled to Amman and Jordanian Jerusalem where he visited refugee camps and attended a United Nations Relief and Works Agency for Palestine Refugees (UNRWA) meeting in Bethlehem. He also caught up with his old UNEF buddies as he talked with friends at the Jerusalem headquarters of UNTSO. Amman's geographical setting pleased King, and he pointed out to Ruth that an ancient Hellenic city, Philadelphia, had flourished on this site about 2,000 years before William Penn was born. Once again he was enchanted by the land and by its history. "This is the spot where Uriah died about 3,000 years ago. He was the lad that King David decided was expendable after he had seen his wife [Bathsheba] having a bath in Jerusalem and asked his chief of staff to arrange that he be left in the forefront of the battle when his forces were besieging Rabbah Ammon."[7] From Amman he pressed on to Iraq. "What is Baghdad like?" he posed to Ruth. He contrasted the old Baghdad with its *souks* and second class hotels with the new spacious and modern city of wide streets and modern villas (where, happily, he was staying), predicting that within five years Baghdad would climb out of its old skin and establish itself in the region.[8] (In fact, Iraq was moving into a period of political instability. In July 1958, within a year of Gordon's prediction, a military coup overthrew the ruling Hashemite kingdom and established a republic.[9]) At the time of his visit, he described Iraq as "an astonishing piece of development," and the UN groups – he counted fifty-four – were "riding the tide."[10]

He also travelled to Syria where he repeated his customary pattern of interviews and inspections. His route took him through Jerash, where he stopped to explore the remains of an old Graeco-Roman city built around the first century. "It must have been a splendid place in its day, with great temples and public buildings and forums. There are still a great many columns standing and as you may imagine my camera was active."[11] He reported that the road to Damascus was "quite clear" and despite the fact that he travelled by taxi and without incident, he admitted that he felt a certain kinship with that earlier traveller to Damascus, Saul of Tarsus.

After a restless night in his rather derelict hotel in Damascus where he was less than charmed by the indifferent waiter who ruined his breakfast eggs, an administrative officer from UNWRA rescued him and guided him through his interviews. To his surprise, he found himself warmly embraced by one newspaper editor who kissed him on both cheeks while quoting volubly from the Prophet. As far as Gordon could gather through the translator, his enthusiastic assailant recalled meeting him on an earlier visit. He visited his favourite mosque built by the Ummaya caliphs on the site of a Christian basilica, itself on the site of a Roman temple. Finally, he made a quick trip to St Paul's Gate where the Apostle Paul was let down in a basket to escape the wrath of the Jews (a red arrow pointed to the window). "But who knows?" he asked generously. "Paul came to Damascus; it is the site of an old gate, and in the Holy Land you can't be too choosy about the authenticity of the location."[12] Gordon crisscrossed his Middle Eastern territory several times, revelling in the richness of its history, genuinely (and perhaps somewhat relentlessly) optimistic about the future he saw rising from the steady effort of the UN programs.

By the time Gordon was able to return to Beirut the following June, unrest in Lebanon had reached alarming levels. This political crisis, precipitated the previous February by the union of Egypt and Syria into the United Arab Republic, had strengthened the pro-Nasser forces in the region. The two Hashemite kingdoms of Jordan and Iraq, both harbouring significant dissenting populations, had responded by forming the opposing pro-Western Arab Union. In May, President Charmoun of Lebanon appealed for help to President Eisenhower, whose evasive answer reflected Western fears of a hostile response by the Soviet Union. The Beirut government then appealed to the UN Security Council. As a result, the Council voted to send UN Observers to Lebanon (UNOGIL – UN Observer Group in Lebanon) in an effort to isolate its internal struggle from the outside influences of the Cold War.[13]

The first Observers began arriving in Beirut at the beginning of June 1958, coinciding with Gordon's visit, and he found himself penned up in a hotel because of the curfew. He described the situation as being quite different from the UNEF operation, telling Ruth, "the task of this new UN force is going to be quite a bit more complicated. The situation is absolutely fantastic. It's not civil war so much as a confounded anarchy."[14] Nevertheless, Beirut was superficially calm, going about its business in a restricted way, King told Ruth, who was back in Cairo preparing for their summer leave home. There was no need for worry, he assured her. While in the long view of things, the situation might not look good, in the short term they were learning that just as events blew up fast, they also had a habit of calming down quickly. "I feel that this rather spectacular UN action may speed up the process of settlement."[15]

Others shared this optimism, including Dag Hammarskjöld, who made a trip to Lebanon and the other Middle East capitals in what he hoped was "a classical case of preventive diplomacy."[16] Because of the urgent need that had suddenly developed for press releases, the resident representative asked Gordon to stay in Lebanon for the time being and coordinate the gathering of UN information. Gordon gladly complied and cancelled a scheduled trip to North Africa. He returned to Cairo at the end of June, collected Ruth and the children and left for New York and then the cool, sweet summer mornings of Birkencraig. Meanwhile, in Lebanon, with the continuing support of the insurgents by Egypt and Syria, and the threat of Soviet involvement, Eisenhower ordered the landing of US marines in Lebanon in mid-July.

In September of 1958 Gordon returned alone to Cairo, leaving Ruth and Alison back in Irvington, New York, and Charley at Queen's University in Kingston. It was time for him to explore another corner of his vineyard and to make the North African trip that he had cancelled during the Lebanese crisis in June. Therefore, in mid-autumn, Hassan packed King's bags, fed him three eggs for breakfast, and put him on the plane for Libya. "Here is another time I pinch myself and say, 'Benghazi? What the dickens are you doing in Benghazi?' Yet here I am, courtesy of Swissair and" – as he had come to refer, in moments of frustration, to the often cumbersome UN bureaucracy – "Grandmother UN."[17]

His itinerary the first day followed the usual frenzied pattern, ending with a cocktail party with diplomats and UN bureaucrats, and dinner with a director of the National Bank. In his weary bedtime note to Ruth he wrote, "[I]t's the sort of day I used to spend campaigning for the LSR and CCF. Now it's the UN. Perhaps I haven't changed. But I must say I feel like bed."[18] He described Libya as a "prize piece," the UN having been largely responsible for its existence and rebuilding following the ravages of the marching armies during the Second World War, when it changed hands four times. In spite of the fact that there seemed to be very little in the way of a Libyan professional class, and a dearth of local technicians or public services, the people as a whole seemed comparatively well-off, and he attributed this largely to the delicate but sustainable balance between population and resources. There was no doubt that the large contingent of UN workers contributed significantly to the well-being of the population, and that the Libyans themselves worked "as if toward a glorious future."[19] Gordon also found this imbedded optimism among UN personnel wherever he went, and used as an example a UNICEF–WHO program training Bedouin girls from the desert as midwives and assistant midwives so that under the developing public health system they could go back and provide maternity services in their villages. This was a remarkable achievement, given the traditional and strongly held Arab view that nursing of any kind was inappropriate for young women. He had seen these Bedouin children many times in the Sinai and in Gaza, "bright eyed children with a sense of humor, with the metal ornaments jangling before their faces, chasing their herds of goats with shouts and laughter." Now he watched in wonder as their sisters, dressed as nurses, studied modern medicine and childcare.[20]

From Benghazi he travelled on to Tripoli where he was struck by the sight of women completely draped in burkas so that as he passed even their eyes were hidden. He spent most of his time in Tripoli with representatives from FAO and UNESCO, happily inspecting a date farm and a vocational school. And then, it was off to the ruins: *Leptis Magna*. Gordon identified himself as somewhat of an authority on ruins by this time, but he was stunned by the immense glory of this ancient Phoenician/Roman treasure, judging it next only to Luxor and the Roman Forum in grandeur, despite centuries of habitation and war. He felt himself being pulled back 2,000 years. Far from being the travel-weary international civil servant, at nearly fifty-eight years of age King still viewed the world with the fresh eyes of a boy, eagerly sharing his newfound wonders with Ruth as he wrote to her each evening.[21]

Although Gordon had visited Khartoum, he considered his trip to Ethiopia, where there were about sixty UN experts of various kinds, his first real contact with Africa and with the Bantu region south of the Sahara. In meeting with the press, Gordon had another of those serendipitous encounters that cheered his heart and seemed to satisfy his sense of being at home in the world: Percy Richards, a Canadian journalist and editor of the English/Amharic *Voice of Ethiopia*, had covered Gordon's three political campaigns in Victoria in the 1930s when he ran as the CCF candidate. Their reminiscences together reminded King of what he called the "happy accidents" of his life: had he won the seat for the CCF, he would not be in Ethiopia now, and he would not have met Ruth.

After his official duties, Gordon was treated to his most memorable Ethiopian experience, a visit to a UNESCO-sponsored educational centre located far into the wilderness about 300 km west of Addis Ababa. They travelled in a Land Rover, bumping along the dirt road that crossed the rolling plains of the 2,440-meter plateau on which Addis Ababa stood. The trip took seven hours, and the calluses and bruises that the ride produced reminded Gordon of rowing at Oxford. The countryside, with the large roving herds of cattle, reminded him of Alberta. A sudden gap in the mountain barrier revealed a green and rolling world with tiny farms along the river basins 1,220 m below. They drove through a tunnel built by Mussolini and descended to the valley floor where they were greeted by a herd of baboons, monkeys, hundreds of donkeys, cattle and horses, and flocks of brilliantly coloured birds. They passed by villages of round houses with thatched roofs, called *turkels*. He described the people as primitive, poor, and ignorant, living as they always had; nominally Christian, many with crosses tattooed on their foreheads or arms.

About 16 km from the main road they came across the centre, modern buildings built of mud blocks. Their hosts, a French couple with two young children – the only Europeans for miles around – all spoke Arabic, though they welcomed their guests in English, delighted to have companionship in this lonely outpost. As they ate a dinner of roast pig and local vegetables, the couple described their work with students recruited from nearby villages, teaching courses in literacy, sanitation, farming methods, techniques for better house construction, and treatment for simple diseases. Gordon listened with focused intensity, taking in information while at another level dwelling in a state of reflection, once again touched in that deep part of himself that waited for the (metaphorical) Kingdom: the old social gospel of the LSR and the CCF now experienced in the heart of Africa. Abruptly, a wild laughing yell from the darkened forest shattered the mood. They rushed to the balcony and with a flashlight picked out the two gleaming eyes of a hyena on the other side of the brush fence.[22] The next day Gordon watched a UNESCO specialist who had worked out a simplified system that enabled students to learn to read in Amharic, the official language of Ethiopia. As Gordon's party left for their long trip back to Addis Ababa, he experienced a sense of fulfillment: "For the first time in a thousand years a ray of light is being let in."[23]

Gordon's last major assignment during his final year of travelling in the Middle East and North Africa was serving as chief of information for the inaugural meeting of the UN Economic Commission for Africa (ECA) in Addis Ababa, which opened on 29 December 1958. The conference took place within the "avalanche of independence"[24] occurring in Africa during this period (at the time the ECA conference met there were ten UN member states from Africa; by 1960 there were twenty-seven), and Hammarskjöld had become increasingly preoccupied with the economic, social, and political challenges of the new Africa. Hammarskjöld's biographer, Brian Urquhart, describes him as "brooding" over the necessity of training the right kind of staff to carry out a global economic development program with the resources of the UN, which he considered "pathetically small" in relation to the vast and complex problems of world poverty.[25] As the colonial structures were being dismantled, there was an increasing involvement in the new African states by UNESCO and the UN Specialized Agencies such as WHO (World Health Organization), FAO (Food and Agriculture Organization), ILO (International Labour Organization), and UNICEF, which operated under the authority of the General Assembly. Hammarskjöld, realizing the direction the UN must take in aiding the developing nations, made a point of travelling around Africa after the Addis conference, meeting leaders, and estimating needs and potentialities. Once back at headquarters in New York, he began to speak about the crucial time when the maximum assistance must be at hand from the United Nations.[26] In a 1988 letter to Erskine Childers, senior advisor to the administrator of

UNDP (United Nations Development Programme), Gordon described Hammarskjöld at the Addis Ababa conference as being "a different man" than the one he had met on previous occasions: "he had just discovered the Third World."[27] Africa was to hold Hammarskjöld's interest – and as a consequence, Gordon's also – until his tragic death in the Congo in 1961.

Gordon began lining up his staff and support systems for the UN Economic Commission early in December and, after the technical travails of UNEF and Gaza, he found reporting the Addis conference demanding but straightforward. Happily for him, the Niehoffs were now in Addis Ababa where Dick was in charge of a UN project setting up a public administration institute, very much the same as the one he had established in Cairo. Gordon stayed with the Niehoffs, and they all celebrated Christmas together, gathering at the home of a Quaker family to sing carols.

On Christmas Day the Niehoffs organized an excursion for about fifty people so that delegates and personnel far from home need not spend a lonely holiday. The picnic lunch included a special rum punch, and the crowd, increasingly jolly, enjoyed the warmth and clear air of the high plateau. In spite of the celebrations and the busy week ahead, Gordon could not quite shut out a wistful moment as he thought of Ruth, Alison, and Charley back in New York, joined by Dick Niehoff's son David who had come from a boarding school in nearby Poughkeepsie to spend his vacation at the Gordon home. He imagined their day, sitting down to dinner, visiting as they walked in the park, trying out new records on the record player, watching TV in the evening.[28] Ruth described the day to King as a time of "much gaiety, much spirit, much loneliness, much work."[29] The holidays ended on a sad note for Ruth and Alison, with the death of Alison's new puppy Abdul shortly after everyone had left. The poignancy of King's absence pierced Ruth. "It struck me last night that is the first thing, of this particular kind, that we haven't shared. He is, or was, a real member of the family, but you never even knew him, or never will."[30]

The UN conference opened on 28 December with a grand reception at the Jubilee Palace given by His Imperial Majesty Haile Salassie. After a dinner for the entire conference, the emperor, whom Gordon found to be a "wonderful combination of old world formality and democracy," shook the hand of each guest. And then it was on to the flurry of press releases and radio reports, arranging for translators, receptions for the foreign press and interviews with foreign leaders. "In general," he reported to Ruth, "our shop is running pretty well."[31]

At the end of the conference, Gordon had one adventure left: a crocodile hunt. He and a UN cohort from Sweden, Arne Rubin, launched an inflatable rubber boat down the Awash River, their goal being not only to hunt crocodiles, but also to visit a falls that Arne was keen on seeing, further down river. King sat in the stern, with Arne, holding the gun, in the bow. The only crocodile that approached them came right up to their raft, but since one could see only its eyes and its snout it did not make a suitable target for these big game hunters, who appeared to be completely oblivious to the irony of their situation. A bit farther down the river they saw two nostrils and the pricks of two miniature ears. Hippos. At this point the Awash was a "deep quiet little river, about twenty-five yards across; big trees with branches like banyans growing down to the water; all kinds of birds – hawks, and herons, kingfishers and others, mostly brightly colored."[32] In the warmth of the afternoon they floated along sleepily. Suddenly, at the sound of rushing water ahead, they snapped to full alert, and leapt out of their boat, hauling it, paddles, and gun around the falls. Back on board, King inadvertently took the boat, swirling in the current, backwards down a 4-foot (1.2 m) falls. Giddy with success, he told Arne he thought he would just "take the next one" as well.

This questionable helmsmanship became the new pattern of navigation until they found themselves in the gorge heading for the big falls. At this moment it became obvious that Arne had never, in fact, been this far down the Awash River, and certainly not in a rubber boat. So they scrambled ashore, let the air out of the raft and rolled it up, took off their wet clothes, and climbed up the 40-foot (12-meter) bank, King carrying the paddles and gun. They hiked happily through the forest along game trails made by wart hogs, antelopes, and hippos, back to the designated meeting spot where Arne's wife and children waited for them with a car.

By this time the sun had gone down and as they made their way to the car they met a tall Galla with a hide over his shoulder and two long spears, followed by two boys with spears and a smaller boy and three young girls, all making their way along the path toward them. The Rubin children talked to the Africans in Galla and King offered them candy which they chewed, paper and all. Arne negotiated for the skin and bought it for a dollar, and they started back to Addis Ababa over the worst possible road – perhaps in all of Africa, according to Gordon. At one point they hit a stone, causing the car door to fly open, and Arne's wife Carmen was thrown out, hitting her head on a rock. "However, these Swedes are very tough and although it raised a large bump she swore it didn't hurt." The rest of the trip was mercifully uneventful except for seeing two hyenas, a jackal, and several baboons, and they arrived home, Arne and King looking like two boiled lobsters, to find two very worried Niehoffs waiting for them. Helen fixed a cold supper, and King ended the day reporting their adventure to Ruth: "What a wonderful day it was. I feel tired and exercised and full of fresh air and sunshine and satisfied with our little adventure. And I don't worry that we didn't get any crocs."[33] Perhaps, like Teddy Roosevelt as he neared retirement, King felt it was his last chance to be a boy.

The circumstances that found Ruth and Alison back in Irvington while King soldiered on in Cairo had resulted from a decision made by "Grandmother UN" that, following their home leave in the summer of 1958, Gordon should return alone to Cairo to wind up his work there, and then return to New York for the last months before his mandatory retirement when he turned sixty in December. Headquarters estimated that he would be back in New York by mid-autumn, certainly by Christmas. There was logic to this decision that applied also to their family situation: Alison was starting her third year in high school, and Charley would enter Queen's University in September. At the same time, however, it meant more separation for Ruth and King and, as they only heard the news in Geneva on their way home to the United States in June, it also brought an abrupt end to Ruth's life in Cairo. This meant that she could play no part in the sorting and packing up of their family belongings, leaving the task to King, for whom it was a considerable burden; nor would she have an opportunity to take leave of their many friends in Cairo.

Early in September, therefore, Gordon left for Cairo via Geneva, and Ruth remained in Irvington, lonely and often feeling overwhelmed. She faced a delay of over a month in getting back into their house and, when she did, she was confronted by four years of repairs, painting, and cleaning. "My what a big house," she told King. "Please send Hassan by airmail!"[34] Gradually, their furniture began arriving from Egypt, often broken, or with parts missing. She had bouts of loneliness, discovering that in her absence others had filled her old place among her friends. She hung onto news of the Middle East, particularly Beirut, giving thanks that she had Alison safely with her in Irvington; but the lack of interest in other parts of the world that she encountered among her friends also added to her sense of isolation, "although I suppose I should have realized it would be so."[35] In her letters to King, she struggled with the issue of whether she should come out and join him, particularly if his stay were going to extend beyond six months; perhaps, she suggested, they should have been more thorough in their thinking before he left. Never mind, she told him. Everything would straighten out once she was busy again. And then, in a rare crumbling of resolve, Ruth wrote, "It seems so idiotic for us to be living in separate parts of the world at our age. Sometimes I would like to throw the whole thing in, as I am sure you would, and say, 'to hell with the UN!'" But unable to leave it on that note, she continued: "but there is a great deal of pride involved with the UN, and I take full share of it. In fact, it is the only hope today."[36] Ruth's claims of frailty belie her steady courage, and she closed her letter with a postscript, assuring King that by the time he read it she would be over her discouragement.

With typical aplomb, Ruth donned the stylishly-cut blue suit she had bought in Rome and took the train into New York with a friend to enjoy an afternoon at the Museum of Modern Art, shopping in the new Takashimaya store, and concluding the "lovely afternoon" at a Japanese restaurant where she introduced her friend to tempura, sukiyaki, and sake. Gradually other friends returned. She resumed her volunteer duties at Graham School. More furniture arrived, and in the bureau drawers she discovered all sorts of Cairo treasures where King had carefully packed them.[37]

Charley wrote regularly to both Ruth and King, telling them that he had adjusted to college life and was wearing a sports coat and smoking a pipe. He had joined the Queen's jazz society and tried out for the varsity basketball team. As he began courses in political science and comparative government, he found that many of the ingrained bits of American School propaganda were being displaced by knowledge of a more "useful – and possibly more truthful – nature."[38]

On Gordon's arrival in Cairo in September 1958 he stepped off the plane to a dubious welcome. In contrast to the pure Canadian air of Birkencraig, he was greeted by a blast of dust and heat and then a customs line, often stationary, where he stood for an hour and a half. He was perplexed to find that while he was moving forward at a snail's pace, the line was thinning out *behind* him. Casual observation revealed enterprising officials, including airport police, collecting passports (for a consideration) and getting them cleared. In spite of his best efforts to be tolerant, Gordon was depressed by the corruption and perhaps most of all by the implicit acceptance of this means of doing government business. Finding no sign of his driver, he took a taxi to the apartment where he looked down on the "muddiest Nile yet" rolling by the windows, "a nasty brown swirling mess."[39] The local radio blared out Victorian French ballads and the green and red bistro lights across the river reminded him of New York traffic lights. Hassan produced two meals remarkably alike for lunch and dinner, and moped around the apartment, depressed about running the house without Ruth, Alison, and "Mr. Jolly." In contrast to this dreary homecoming, Gordon was greeted at the office by an embarrassing display of affection, and when he made a wry face and said that he was not at all happy about the prospect of being away from Ruth and the children, one of the secretaries assured him, "But Mr. Gordon, we will do anything to look after you in your evenings – anything!"[40] All in all, he had not anticipated how lonely he would be without Ruth.

Gordon did not stay down for long, and he threw himself into his travels to Jordan, Lebanon, Syria, across North Africa and down to Ethiopia, keenly enjoying his work after all, and his preparation for the Economic Commission on Africa. Getting out into the field always worked as an elixir for his gloom. His work at the Centre, largely bureaucratic and organizational as he prepared for his successor, he enjoyed less. And then, there was the "Black Hole of Calcutta," his metaphor for the sorting and packing that had to be done and which he attacked with dread: what to sell, what to keep, and what to buy that they might want as mementos of their days in Egypt. He kept the pictures on the walls as the apartment gradually emptied out, and he and Hassan made do with borrowed domestic articles. He found that he vacillated between moods of loneliness for New York and nostalgia at leaving Egypt. At other times he plunged into introspection about his life and work, asking himself what he had accomplished. A large part of his angst arose from his apprehension at the nature of his next assignment at headquarters in New York and, most particularly, his keen feelings of loss at leaving the field.

This love of being at "ground level" of any project, part of a team, suited Gordon's temperament for, like his father and many of the Gordons, King preferred action to introspection. Even in his retirement, he would not brood unduly about the meaning of his life or "what it all added up to." To the contrary, he would attend meetings all over the world, recount stories, write letters, and participate in citizen groups,bringing pressure to bear on the government for policies consistent with human rights. It was the independence and the practical nature of work on the ground that he liked; history with a human face. He felt that he was living amid the richness of history, reporting a social revolution. He relished the contingencies and ironies of working with people, and the discrepancies that being an eyewitness allowed him to see. He harkened back to the raising of the last barge at the Suez Canal in the spring of 1957, remembering that news reporters had been asked to focus on cheering crowds while in reality the audience consisted largely of two nuns in elaborate habits, watching silently from the bank.[41] Most of all, perhaps, he experienced fulfillment in spreading the news of what could be accomplished by the harnessing of goodwill and technology.

Among his happiest days in the field were those spent on General Burns's staff with UNEF. He loved the camaraderie and common effort, the sharing of rations, sleeping in the open air and lumbering over bumpy roads in white trucks bearing the UN insignia. His own depression on returning to the Centre in March of 1957, when his UNEF assignment ended, lifted when he spent a few days "back with my chums" in Gaza. He gloried in driving an open jeep with the troops once again, a confirmation that he was not an intellectual but "a jeep driver and a newspaper man!"[42] In the fall of 1958, at the request of General Burns, who was distressed that they no longer had an information officer covering UNEF activities, he returned to Gaza "for too few days" to help with "the information end of things," flying in on an UNRWA plane.[43]

Undoubtedly, one of his most intense and treasured experiences in the field occurred over Christmas in 1957 when he accompanied Dag Hammarskjöld as he visited the UNEF troops in Gaza. Gordon shared Hammarskjöld's flight in a light Otter aircraft as they flew to visit a Yugoslav platoon camped out on a desert oasis, which they used as a base for the armor patrols along the sand trails. They flew with a Yugoslav colonel, bumped down on the desert sand and walked over to the tents sheltered by palm trees. There, in preparation for their visit, they found a table laden with choice Yugoslav dishes prepared by the cook in his outdoor kitchen, and graced by champagne and Yugoslav slivovitz (plum brandy). Hammarskjöld was delighted and visited with the men, relaxed and informal. But the heart of the visit was the Christmas Eve service at the Swedish headquarters on the sand dunes near the beach at Gaza, in the new Swedish chapel. Lacking spruce boughs, the soldiers had decorated it with palm branches. Some of the soldiers had trained as a choir and sang the responses in the Lutheran liturgy. The chaplain talked of the significance of the day and of their duty on a mission so far from home; and then he reminded them that this same evening, across all of Sweden, this same service was being held. Led by the choir, they closed with Martin Luther's hymn, "A Mighty Fortress is Our God." Gordon walked out with Hammarskjöld who said to him, "You know they say the Swedes are a very formal people. They are right. We have great respect for form." Hammarskjöld's eyes were filled with tears.[44]

In what may have been an attempt to respect Gordon's dedication to fieldwork and to provide for its continuation by extending his stay in the Middle East, George Ivan Smith, by this time his superior in New York, stumbled clumsily into a tangle of misunderstanding and hurt feelings. In early December 1958, Gordon contacted Smith with a somewhat impatient inquiry concerning his replacement at the Centre, the timing of his own moving to headquarters in New York, and the nature of his new assignment there. Smith responded on 29 December 1958, telling him that while they wanted to use his experience to the fullest extent, and that he and everyone at headquarters had the highest regard for Gordon, it would not be realistic at this point to indicate what his next assignment might be. Gordon could be confident, Smith assured him, that they would spare no effort to place him where he could be of optimum service. Smith hoped to have details by the end of January.[45]

For King and Ruth, this indecision and apparent indifference to their domestic plight was another example of the slow and frustrating, stumbling progress of the UN bureaucracy that they came to refer to as "Grandmother UN." Smith concluded his letter by congratulating Gordon on the breaking news of his excellent covering of the Economic Commission on Africa, a grand climax to his work in Cairo. But at the end of January, as Gordon waited for the promised details, he received instead a cable suggesting that he might be interested in replacing the information officer in Gaza, entailing an additional nine months in the Middle East.[46] Gordon was astonished, insulted, and then furious: "the implications behind the suggestion have left me rather shaken and I must admit resentful at UN personnel policy that would come up with this one after my record during the past four and a half years." He replied to Smith: "Let me be clear that I have been consistent in believing that a member of the Secretariat should accept assignments in the field even if it means inconvenience to him and a disruption of family life. But I believe equally firmly that one's own self respect requires that an assignment to be acceptable must be one that takes into account past experience and achievement and is consistent with past personnel decisions. This suggestion seems to me to be irresponsible on both counts."

Then his frustration boiled over. Pointing out that he had put up with repeated delays concerning his next assignment "in view of the uncertainty in the organizational pattern of the Department," and that the Gaza assignment would entail nine more months separation from his family and bore no relation whatsoever to any reasonable appraisal of his experience, he concluded: "I have looked forward to finishing my career in a post that reflects to some extent my experience in and service to the Organization. If that is not in the books I had better know now."[47] When Ruth heard, she commented: "What colossal nerve!"[48]

Smith was completely taken aback. "I need only say that you have misjudged the motives and intentions of my cable," which was intended only to suggest the faint possibility that it might suit Gordon to spend a little more time in the area. No one was asking King to go to Gaza, much less pressing it. He merely meant to be helpful. Surely if he looked at this whole thing again, he would see that he had had the telescope the wrong way round. In spite of Smith's assurances however, Gordon may perhaps be forgiven a certain cynicism, as Smith still offered no clearly defined position for King, merely assuring him that "we shall be relying on you to keep us covered and advised on an important sector here."[49]

King confided to Ruth that he had been closer to sending in a letter of resignation than ever before and, with uncharacteristic bitterness, told her, "They surely could not suppose that I could seriously consider this and keep my self-respect. There is something awfully rotten in that whole set-up and I am of the opinion that the sooner I get out the better."[50] Two days later, as he "reflected upon the callous vagaries of UN policy," he told her that he had hammered out a letter to Frank Scott asking his opinion about the possibilities of starting a new magazine in Canada along the lines of the *Reporter* or the *New Statesman*. It would be an exciting way to make his exit from the UN, and as he had told Frank, "I have had so much of the emasculating propriety of thought that the UN insists upon that I'd like to know whether I have any creative tissue left."[51]

One grasps the depth of Gordon's discouragement, and the demoralizing effect of the long period of indecision and indifference on the part of his superiors in the UN bureaucracy can be grasped by observing how his mood had deteriorated since the previous October when he nostalgically described Cairo as lovely, with a full moon rising over the receding flood waters of the Nile, yellowing leaves, and orange juice right from the trees. At that time he told Ruth he found himself looking at ordinary sights with fresh eyes: the donkeys and the coloured carts, the flower sellers going to the market with the roses and dahlias strapped on the back of their bicycles, the little beggars running up smiling when the car stopped at the corner of Hassan Sabri and Fouad, the coffee sellers with their big glass jugs hawking their brew, the host of flunkies at the club greeting him like an ambassador even when they knew there was no business for them.

As he was writing on the eve of their nineteenth wedding anniversary in November, he continued, "You know, we really have had quite a life, haven't we – lots of fun, some sorrow, perhaps some useful work done, perhaps some people happy because we have been we. And still a lot to do together, *inshallah*."[52]

In contrast to this mood of contentment, by the following February he was writing to Ruth, "I mean I don't think, even speaking professionally, my life has been entirely wasted. But it has not been the best, and there have been inherent factors which have prevented it from being the best."[53] He did not elaborate, but one wonders what part (if any) a heated conversation with his sister Marjorie during her visit to him in Cairo in December might have contributed to his despondency. She had stopped on her way back to Australia from a family visit in Canada and they spent several happy days together filled with sightseeing, shopping, and talking long into the night. Then, as he was driving her to the airport, there erupted "one of those emotional storms which from time to time swirl into our family without any warning," and which appeared to have grown out of "some pretty emotional talks" earlier in the week on the subject of religion, with King being accused of "going back on my earlier love (Mother quotes me)."[54] Whether or not this had any connection with King's vocation and the giving up of his ordination to the ministry of the United Church, can only be surmised. To a large extent, he had more or less "drifted" out of the ministry, at no point specifically renouncing his orders but simply moving into secular work. It does not appear then that the change in the mode of his service to the "Kingdom of God" from sacred to secular gave Gordon himself qualms of conscience, but perhaps it left vestiges of unease among other members of his family. One cannot know all the factors that brought about this struggle with self-doubt in Gordon's thinking at this time. One can be sure, however, that it was a period of anxiety for him as he approached retirement.

After her first indignant outburst in response to Smith's suggestion that King take up an assignment in Gaza, Ruth reacted with her usual calm wisdom and support. She liked the idea of starting a new magazine in Canada, particularly as it would mean she could share in the enterprise by contributing her editing skills. Of course, it might not work out. She herself would be perfectly happy if he were to teach at a university, something she thought he would enjoy. "What I am trying to say, King, is that I am not in the position of wanting you to stay with the UN in a job which you would find not to your liking, just to round out the two years left ... You should work at what is important to you. So much happiness comes out of a person doing a job he likes!" Then she cautioned him: "One other thing I must say. Your last letter was rather bitter about the UN – and with good reason I feel – but since Charley has set his idealistic sights on the UN as his future, we must be awfully careful what we say. I do think he himself will probably change his ideas and ideals in the next few years – but I would hate to have any sourness come from us. Don't you agree?"[55]

Gordon did not stay out of sorts for long. In early February, he made a farewell swing through Lebanon, Syria, and Jordan, and spent an enchanting few hours by himself touring the Old City of Jerusalem: the Dome of the Rock and Al Aqsa, St Anne's, built on the site of the Pool of Bethesda, and the Via Dolorosa. He thanked Ruth for her wise counsel and told her that he had received George Ivan Smith's pained letter, much hurt that he had misinterpreted the Gaza suggestion – "which I'm sure I didn't."[56] The job they were holding for him at headquarters would fall somewhere between regular Public Information and Information for Technical Assistance, and he felt it might have possibilities if they gave him enough elbow room and some budget.

He returned to Cairo to a bevy of farewell dinners and parties and the hectic process of extrication, as he called it. Once again, he became nostalgic on a sunny, spring-like day, as he watched the polo players at the club and Monsur, the golf instructor, trying to teach a lady in a pink sweater and khaki slacks how to hit a golf ball. The Cairo letters home ended abruptly in mid-February as Gordon at last began his journey home – not directly, of course, as he had friends, colleagues, and UN agencies to visit in Athens, Rome, Geneva, Paris, and London. On 14 March, he arrived in New York where he was greeted by his happy wife and daughter.

Gordon's title for his new job at UN headquarters in New York was Chief Public Information Officer for Technical Assistance and the Special Fund. It was a newly created position for which Gordon's experience in the field uniquely prepared him. (This may, in part, have accounted for the delay in assigning Gordon's new responsibilities – Grandmother getting her ducks in a row, so to speak, in these early days of the UN.) In 1965, these two UN programs were merged into the United Nations Development Program, but at the time Gordon returned to New York, neither had an independent informational organization, although they were somewhat served by the Department of Public Information as part of the general UN coverage. The considerable overlapping and confusion in the area of communications and public relations was understandable and made more complicated by the inevitable competition among agencies for limited resources. It was this niche that Gordon filled by applying his particular experience and skills. It was actually a prestigious and necessary role, and he was quite mistaken in thinking that he was being sidelined on his way out to pasture – something he came to appreciate as he worked into the new job.

When he first reported for work, he discovered that some pioneering efforts had been begun by Norma Globerman, later chief of the Asia desk in UNDP, who put together a newsletter that appeared about once every two months; it was a beginning, however modest. Gordon began to develop an information base from interviews with returning or outgoing experts. His extensive experience in Korea and the Middle East; his remarkable organizational and technical skills in communications; his familiarity with the UN specialized agencies and their work; and, perhaps most of all, his wide range of contacts, built a foundation for the later emergence of the elaborate information network of the UNDP. Among his other duties, he attended weekly meetings of the Technical Assistance Board, which was chaired by Bruce Stedman and attended by David Owen, director of the Expanded Program of Technical Assistance; and Paul Hoffmann, who directed the Special Fund. These meetings provided Gordon with a front-row seat as the administrative details of the new United Nations Development Program were hammered out.

Gordon worked in this position from his arrival home in March 1959 to August 1960, the date of his official retirement. In spite of his occasional claustrophobic grumbling that he was back to the in-basket and the out-basket, and despite his unabashed longing for meals in army messes and travelling by jeep along Suez watching the raising of sunken ships, he was not unhappy. He felt he was doing useful work. Nevertheless, it was with a sigh of relief and an expectant eye on the future that he left with his family in August for a retirement celebration at Birkencraig. One can imagine his anticipation of summer at the lake, with evenings on the verandah, the children tucked into their cots, the grownups at the big table with their crosswords and books, hissing gas lamps casting their shadows. Or the bright summer mornings when everyone fell so easily into the domestic routine: his sister Ruthie up before everyone, cooking oatmeal over the wood stove, his sister Alison sweeping the verandah with unhurried rhythm, the calling back and forth of grocery items that the men would fetch from town by boat. And then, he and Ruth would move together into a long and fulfilling retirement. But not yet, not quite yet.

16

The Congo: Hammarskjöld and Beyond

It was an August morning at Birkencraig in the summer of 1960 and Gordon was enjoying the first days of his retirement. Ruth and Charley were with him, while Alison remained behind in New York at her summer job. King and his mother sat visiting on the verandah, looking down through the spruce and pine onto the lake as cool breezes rippled its surface into sparkling patterns. The humming of a motorboat broke their reverie as an RCMP launch pulled in close to shore. King immediately thought guiltily of the family's dereliction in not purchasing fishing licenses, a rather modern intrusion of state regulation considering their long tenure of fishing off their island. He raised the alarm and, as Alison pictured it in a letter back to her mother, "I can see the whole camp in a state of terror, madly tearing around hiding fishing rods and tackle, Ronnie hiding the boat, and [five-year-old] Sheila ready to protect the house!"[1]

The law-abiding Gordons need not have feared this unwarranted intrusion. When the Mounties had tied up at the dock, it turned out that they were delivering a message: would Mr Gordon please get in touch with the United Nations Department of Information without delay. King rowed over to the neighbouring island to place the phone call and through the static deciphered the request that he report to New York for assignment to the Congo as quickly as possible. Within two days he was on a plane for New York and, after a short briefing at UN Headquarters, boarded a Paris-bound jet ("you see we really are important,"[2] he noted to Ruth, having expected the usual eleven-hour prop-driven flight), and from there he flew to Brazzaville. On 10 August, he found himself crossing the wide, muddy Congo River from Brazzaville to Leopoldville (modern-day Kinshasa), the ferry pushing its way through floating islands of water lilies and clumps of hyacinth.[3]

The Congo 1960 (Barry Levely, cartographer)

In many ways, the Congo proved to be the most challenging of Gordon's assignments with the UN, and all his gifts came together to make it a success. He found himself thrown abruptly into a situation of political instability and increasing violence as the Congo disintegrated into civil war. The Byzantine complexities of political relationships – the fluidity and the confusion – strained credulity. Gordon depended on primitive, even nonexistent, technical means in accomplishing his task of collecting and disseminating information even as he coped with the often chaotic French dialects, not to mention his own struggle with the language. The suffering of the Congolese people in their refugee camps called for a combination of compassion, which came naturally to Gordon, and detachment, which did not. Through it all, he experienced a suffocating loneliness for Ruth and the children. The climate and the rough terrain as he travelled through jungle and mountains tested his rugged constitution, and his mandate as chief public information officer tested his organization skills. It was a challenge that might have caused even younger men to quail, but with his remarkably buoyant and willing spirit, his sturdy physical stamina, and his enduring appetite for new challenges, he thrived.

The crisis in the Congo had erupted almost immediately after Belgium granted independence on 1 July 1960. The roots of the tragic events that followed lay in its colonial history described by Joseph Conrad as "the vilest scramble for loot that ever disfigured the history of human consciousness."[4] Belgium's interest in the Congo had developed in the context of Europe's reviving drive for colonies in the 1870s when King Leopold of the Belgians sent Henry M. Stanley to establish trading stations along the Congo River. Leopold's claim to the vast mineral wealth of the Congo was formalized in 1885 at the Congress of Berlin when thirteen European states, under the ostensibly benign "honest brokerage" of German Chancellor Otto von Bismarck, met to define their territorial claims in Africa. At that time the European powers recognized Leopold's private dominion over the ironically named "Congo Free State." By ruthlessly exploiting African labour, Leopold turned the Congo into a personally profitable investment; but his barbarous methods fueled a widespread humanitarian protest throughout Europe. As a result, in 1908 the Belgian government assumed full colonial responsibility for the Congo.[5]

Gradually, a policy of state paternalism replaced the brutalities of the Leopold period. Workers on the plantations and in the mines experienced better working conditions and wages than those in other African territories. Primary education expanded, largely through government-subsidized Catholic schools. Health services treated the sick and brought many epidemic diseases under control. Even in agriculture, in a country where most inhabitants lived at a subsistence level cultivating small plots of land, the Belgians established thousands of *paysannats*, which provided larger plots of land for communal farming and allowed for some degree of mechanization. By the 1950s, the industrial and commercial development of the Congo had attracted a larger proportion of Africans to the cities than in any other African country. These remarkable and technological achievements, however, took place within the fold of colonial exploitation and paternalism, and Belgium's complete disregard of the need to train the Congolese for self-rule and the independence that would inevitably come.

In his 1962 study for the Carnegie Endowment for International Peace, Gordon noted that, perhaps not surprisingly, until 1958 the Congo was singularly free from the political unrest that characterized many of the other African colonies.[6] However, the first municipal elections, held in 1957 in the three largest cities, Leopoldville, Elisabethville, and Jadotville, marked the formation of the first Congolese political parties and the emergence of Joseph Kasavubu and Patrice Lumumba as national leaders. In late 1958 and early 1959, when the Belgians attempted to ban meetings by the two major parties headed by Kasavubu and Lumumba, rioting broke out and was brutally put down by the police. As a result of the violence, the Belgian government was forced to abandon its still nascent plan of gradual independence for the Congo, and set the date of independence for 30 June, 1960. In the hastily written *Loi fondamentale* outlining the structure of the new constitution, the Belgium parliament failed to clearly define the relationship between the executive and the legislative branches; nor did they adequately delineate the division of powers between the central and provincial governments, equally important in this new nation of strong tribal loyalties. After the May 1960 elections, the resident minister of the Belgian government in the Congo asked Kasavubu to become president and Lumuba, his bitter rival, prime minister.

The mainstay of law and order within the new republic was to be the *Force Publique*, an army of more than 25,000 men whose officers were exclusively Belgian. Within five days of independence, however, the Congolese in the *Force* mutinied against their Belgian officers, resulting in the spread of atrocities against white civilians. Panic erupted within the European population, and from all parts of the Congo they fled to the nearest point of exit, leaving behind schools, hospitals, plantations, and suburbs of elegant homes that in many cases had been occupied by families for three generations. Because the Europeans had been responsible for the maintenance of the administration, technical facilities, and health services, the Congo faced a complete social and economic breakdown.[7] In an effort to protect its nationals, Belgian warships and planes attacked the port city of Matafi on 11 July. On the same day, the province of Kantanga declared its independence, an additional blow to the new republic as Katanga was the richest (and most heavily European) province, with its huge deposits of copper, cobalt, and uranium.

The secessionist leader, Moise Tshombe, was backed by the powerful Belgian-owned mining company, the Union Minière du Haut-Katanga, and fueled by European mercenaries, who were flooding into Tshombe's army, the Katanga gendarmerie.

At this point, the central government in Leopoldville appealed to the United States for 2,000 troops to intervene under the UN flag. The US took the position that any aid should come through the United Nations. Consequently, the Security Council met on the hot, humid evening of 13 July, and early the next morning passed *Resolution 143 (1960)*, creating ONUC: Operation des Nations Unies au Congo.[8] By its original mandate, ONUC was to ensure the withdrawal of Belgian forces from the Republic of the Congo, to assist the government in maintaining law and order, and to provide technical assistance. Initially, ONUC was not authorized to act except in self-defence or to take any action that would make it a party to internal conflicts.[9] Later, however, its mandate was strengthened to include maintaining the territorial integrity and political independence of the Congo against Belgian encroachments and to prevent the occurrence of civil war. In such circumstances it was authorized to use force, if necessary, as a last resort.[10] Hammarskjöld clearly had in mind some analogue to UNEF's action in Gaza, but the situation in the Congo and its implications for ONUC proved far more complicated than that in the Suez crisis.

With the arrival of the ONUC Force, the prime minister, Patrice Lumumba, increasingly interpreted its task as supporting the central government in subduing Katanga. Hammarskjöld, however, held firm in his view that the Security Council had authorized him to send ONUC troops into Katanga to preserve order as the Belgian troops withdrew, and that there was no question of sharing this mandate with the Congo government or of embarking on any action that would make ONUC party to internal conflicts. In thus holding firm, Gordon wrote, "the Secretary-General was embarking on a highly delicate venture which, given the explosive elements in the Congo, risked disaster."[11]

By August of 1960, Lumumba and his central government were implacably at war with Hammarskjöld. To further complicate matters, the Congo dispute was rapidly becoming a flash point in the Cold War, with the USSR placing itself squarely behind Lumumba's complaint and his demand for military assistance to crush the Katanga secession. In light of Lumumba's threats to turn to the Soviet Union if he did not get concessions from the West, and because of his bitter attacks on Western financial interests in Katanga, the Western powers openly supported Kasavubu, who remained accessible to their representatives and appeared to be a man of moderation and reason.

With convolutions of the plot already straining credulity, in September 1960 President Kasavubu fired Prime Minister Lumumba. At this point, another (and ultimately dangerous) player became active on the stage, Lumumba's chief of staff and deputy-commander of the Congolese army, Colonel Joseph Mobutu, who announced that the army was taking command of the government by a "peaceful revolution" – that is, a military coup. Mobutu expelled the Soviet embassy and arrested Lumumba, who was later taken prisoner and mysteriously killed. Such was the swirling caldron of politics, intrigue, and human tragedy that Gordon entered when, ferried upon lily pads through clumps of water hyacinth, he arrived in Leopoldville on 10 August 1960.

Gordon had three assignments in the Congo. The first extended from August to the end of December 1960, at which time his mother's serious illness required an emergency return to Winnipeg. During this first stretch he served as senior information officer under the information director, Grenville Fletcher. He returned to Leopoldville in mid-March 1961, assuming the role of chief information officer, and remained until 15 July. He made his third trip to the Congo in June 1962 to direct a UN documentary focusing on UN civilian operations and refugees, an assignment that lasted into August and at the end of which he finally said goodbye to the Congo.

Gordon described Leopoldville as one of the most modern African cities he had seen, with skyscrapers, fine hotels and restaurants, air-conditioned offices, and well-lighted streets. He found the Congolese pleasant and friendly, and "much less highly strung than the Egyptians."[12] As he met UN personnel he had known in Cairo and Gaza, and even in Korea, he told Ruth that he had begun to feel at home. Initially he stayed in the Memling Hotel, but soon he moved to cheaper quarters that were more than adequate as they provided both a spectacular view across the Congo River and air conditioning. The UN offices and ONUC headquarters were similarly modern and cool. He and his assistant explored the residential section of the city, "great broad streets with private homes looking like the best in Winnipeg, Toronto or Westchester," now empty, abandoned by the fleeing Belgians.[13] They rescued a dog, a beautiful boxer, which had been left behind, and found a home for him with one of the UN personnel. The first Saturday night, there was a party that struck Gordon with its similarity to UN parties in Korea, El Ballah, and Gaza. After the party, someone suggested that they go to a Congolese nightclub – just a record player and a loudspeaker out on an open plaza, but they were welcomed warmly and invited to dance. (King preferred conversation.) The music was Americanized African rock-and-roll, with lively rhythm. It was an entirely new experience for Gordon and he contrasted it with a dinner given the next evening at the Memling Hotel for a few UN people and some of the remaining Belgians. The elegant meal, served formally, was marred by the anger of the Belgians when a UNESCO worker brought a Congolese guest with him. The unpleasant episode jarred Gordon, and he found himself suffering a sense of displacement, enhanced by jetlag and fatigue. Had he been at Birkencraig only a week ago? Would there be some fishing going on, he wondered? He would love to be there, he told Ruth, but "as you know, I don't exactly pine away under conditions like this."[14]

There was little time for nostalgia or homesickness, however, as they worked long hours, not always with air conditioning. Gordon's first duty was to set up radio broadcasts directed mainly at the UN troops who were stationed in isolated outposts, almost entirely cut off from the outside world and in some cases not even receiving mail. The UN Forces broadcast aired three times a day and was built around UN news: normal military information (which Gordon collected from headquarters in the Royal Hotel) including troop movements; news from the field; interviews with visiting dignitaries and upper-level UN personnel; and music. King's assistant, identified only as Sam, scoured the record library for musical numbers, coming up with "Me and My Shadow," and "Rum and Coca Cola." (King preferred classical music.) The broadcasts went out in French and English, Gordon voicing the latter. From time to time, the programs would be cut off without explanation. "But nothing out here proceeds by logic," he told Charley, as censorship of the UN Forces program was frequent and erratic, making it difficult to carry out their operation.[15] The broadcasts did go out, however, if somewhat irregularly at the beginning, and Gordon was gratified in mid-October when he received letters from as far away as Nigeria and Cameroon responding to the Forces program that they had picked up on their radios.

This erratic censorship was part and parcel of government policy, along with "Belgian hunts," which took the form of checking identity cards by banging on hotel doors in the middle of the night. In his letter to Charley, King wrote, "The situation is utterly fantastic. An enormous country with no political experience of any kind suddenly facing the problems of independence." Lumumba, described by his French doctor as paranoid, had taken on a personal vendetta with the secretary general and when the Security Council backed Hammarskjöld, the situation only grew more ominous. King concluded his letter to Charley: "We all had an accelerated education during our first weeks in Egypt but that was nothing compared with the Congo. This is the biggest task so far."[16]

Gordon was also responsible for issuing press releases, conducting and recording interviews, covering press conferences held by the "top brass," and putting out a daily bulletin based on the monitoring of troop movements. His greatest challenge, however, or perhaps his greatest headache, proved to be the setting up and publishing of an ONUC newspaper, the *Tom Tom/Tam Tam,* chiefly directed to the troops scattered throughout the Congo. The newspaper was modelled on *Sand Dune*, but the problems in producing the *Tom Tom* were at once easier and more difficult. The UN Force in the Congo was much larger than that of UNEF, 20,000 compared with 6,000; the geographical area to be covered was huge; and at least half the troops spoke French, requiring the paper to be bilingual. The original name was an obvious and appropriate choice in English, the drum being the customary African instrument of communication and entertainment. But after the first issue there were complaints from the French readers that *Tom Tom* meant nothing in French and that *Tam Tam* was the appropriate word. The printer suggested a way out of the linguistic problem by making it two papers: under the English heading *Tom Tom*, pages one and two would be entirely in English. The reader would turn the paper over and upside down and find *Tam Tam* heading pages three and four written entirely in French.[17] For the masthead, Gordon had the idea of having one miniature ONUC soldier beating out a message on the drum, and the message being picked up by another soldier with earphones clamped to his head. A sketch artist who was an interpreter at the N'Djili (Leopoldville) airport created a professional drawing that included the name as well.

The *Tom Tom/Tam Tam* was produced on a good modern press with facilities not only for printing but also for photo reproduction – something Gordon regarded not only as effective journalism, but a blessing in that pictures filled space. But having professional printing rather than a mimeograph also meant that copy had to be written or cut to length, and the staff of two, one English-speaking and one French-speaking, had to do the work of an entire editorial and production team, under a deadline. In fact, Gordon complained, while he had myriad brilliant suggestions for its production, when it came down to it, "there was just the French typewriter and me," and he not uncommonly pecked out 7,000 words a week. "I might as well be running *The Nation* again," he complained to

Ruth.[18] Norma Globerman, who had worked with Gordon in Technical Assistance in New York, arrived early in September, assigned to Civilian Operations, and she was able to give him some help, particularly in sending over snippets of news from their office. Gordon frequently found himself correcting the French copy with what he acknowledged were his rudimentary language skills, a burden eased when he acquired a more reliable translator.

The content of the *Tom Tom* had much in common with the *Sand Dune*, "some generously and regularly supplied by conscientious local correspondents, some the result of desperate appeals from the editors."[19] There were stories about the contingents and their countries of origin, background information about the Congo supplied by scholars and missionaries, and news features that concerned the Force as a whole. And then, there were photographs, largely the work of Gordon's talented and trusty photographer, Freddy Bayat. A complete set of editions of the *Tom Tom/Tam Tam* survive in Gordon's papers, and one is struck by their sophistication, both in production and content.[20]

And so the *Tom Tom* was born on 24 September, with Gordon concluding that it seemed like a "pretty feeble effort."[21] By the third edition at the beginning of October, however, they had far too much news and had to drop articles. They were also having more success at getting stories from the field, particularly from the Irish at Goma, who reported a lioness having been sighted in the bush just outside the perimeter of their camp, a discovery the Irish claimed had been made by a Private Foxe and a Private Wolfe. The crowning touch was their first sports column, written by a Frenchman who had had twenty years experience as a sports writer in France. King did the translation into English and afterwards the writer complimented him, not for his facility in French, but for his impressive knowledge of sports. King thought Charley would like that.[22]

In the haste of Gordon's departure for the Congo, the issue of his proposed length of term there was left uncertain. In mid-September he received a letter from the chief administrative officer in the Office of Public Information in New York about extending his contract for another year, until December 1961 – which was, eventually, what was done. In the meantime, King and Ruth were left once again with the unresolved issues of his length of stay and whether or not Ruth would join him.

After King's departure in August, Ruth maintained her morale as long as she was at Birkencraig surrounded by family, most particularly King's mother. She returned to Barney Park at the end of August to pack up the children and send them to Queen's University, where Alison was joining Charley. "I wish you were here to share the going-to-college process with Alison. She is wonderful – but I feel you have missed so much of this phase."[23] Once the children had left for Kingston, however, Ruth found herself unable to bear the big empty house, and she went up to Hingham, Massachusetts, where her father lived with her brother Alan and his wife Sally. There she did crosswords and played Scrabble with her father, waiting anxiously for news from the Congo. While Sally and Alan had their kitchen renovated, Ruth and her father went up to North Pembroke to stay with her sister Marie. While they were there her father, unsettled by the move, suddenly became completely disoriented to the extent of not being able to carry out the tasks of everyday life. Ruth was devastated. With remarkable restraint, she told King, "I seem to feel awfully in need of moral support right now."[24] She tried to account for her feelings: the children's leaving ("it seems such a final step, really the beginning of the end of our family as a foursome in the same way"); her fiftieth birthday in August; the suddenness of King's departure; and the way she had bottled up her loneliness while she was at the lake. And then, there was her reluctance to leave her father to join King in the Congo. She confessed to him that she simply could not imagine coming to Leopoldville at this time, her memories of closing up the house and going off to Japan on her own still fresh in her mind. "If you really want to stay, and can get home for Christmas, I of course would go back with you," she wrote. "But just please don't ask me to do any more completely on my own, because I don't think I can. I'm sorry dearest, because I'm afraid I am a disappointment to you."[25] King replied immediately, "I can understand your feelings very well and I am sorry if my suggestions about Leo have proved just too much to consider. Don't worry about them and let's just see what develops in the next month or so." "After all," he assured her, "I can resign at any time."[26]

Ruth finally returned to Barney Park, Irvington, at the beginning of November, leaving her father (somewhat improved) in the care of a private nurse at Alan and Sally's. King's cousin "Mar" (daughter of Gilbert Gordon, his father's older brother), a close friend of both King and Ruth, came up from New York to spend part of each week with Ruth. As she had done after King had returned to Egypt on his own, she once again threw herself into activities – volunteering at Graham School, the League of Women Voters, many social engagements, calls and letters to the children. Her letters were once again filled with local news and commentary on the children's lives and on the coming election. But the cold reality of

King's absence remained: "I have never felt before that we are in such *entirely* different worlds, you and I," she wrote.[27] King did not come for Christmas after all, and for the first time Ruth prepared for the holiday entirely on her own, even buying and decorating the tree. There was a joyful reunion when Alison and Charley arrived home from college, but on 22 December Ruth told King, "When you read this, we will have missed you terribly."[28]

Gordon's first trip into the field was a three-day swing at the end of August through the eastern provinces of Katanga and Kivu. It was an opportunity to gain some idea of the deployment of the troops and to visit them in their camps. He flew with the force commander, Lieutenant-General Carl C. von Horn (of Sweden) to Elizabethville. The general was called back to Leopoldville almost immediately, and Gordon and Freddy Bayat spent the night at the "swish" Sabena resthouse. An argument with the manager erupted when he tried to eject Freddy from the bar for unsuitable attire: no tie and a short-sleeved bush jacket. Gordon got his Scots temper up, but Freddy, being reasonable and diplomatic, charmed the manager into an apology and they had an excellent meal.[29] Mollified and well-fed, they flew by Cessna with Lieutenant-General Sean MacEoin to Kabalo in North Katanga, ONUC's Ethiopian base on the Lualaba River. Gordon was thrilled to fly in a light plane once again, but when they arrived at Kabalo they found a miserable town, bleak and deserted, with tall elephant grass and poor Baluba huts encroaching on its perimeters. Bare-breasted mothers walked around with babies on their backs and huge loads on their heads, while the young men with feathers in their hats and sticks in their hands (the mark of Balubakat warriors) danced and chanted. "They looked rather pathetic, not very fierce."[30]

The Ethiopians, who had been at this post for eight months, greeted the visitors hospitably with what they had to offer – shared C rations – and they settled in for a miserable night battling mosquitoes. "It was the best Kabalo has to offer and we were here for one night and not for eight months."[31] While there, General MacEoin presented Congo medals to members of the ONUC unit. Under the blistering hot sky, about twenty soldiers and officers lined up to receive their medals. After a formal salute and a speech by General MacEoin, the Ethiopian colonel raised three cheers for the Emperor Haile Selassie whereupon two Congolese came forward and read a formal statement in French thanking ONUC for sending these disciplined troops for their protection against a massacre.

One Congolese then moved forward and invoking the blessing of divine providence, offered the general a leopard skin, the highest honour they could offer. And then the party started with drums, dancing, songs storytelling and finally champagne and toasts to the UN, the general, the Ethiopian brigade, and the emperor.[32]

Gordon and the general travelled on to visit the Irish platoon at Kilubi in Kantanga province where ONUC troops guarded the powerhouse that supplied electricity for the Kamina base about 100 km away. They flew over flat, treeless land with rivers marked by the thick growth of jungle along their banks.[33] They found the Irish guardpost at the bottom of the narrow gorge near the power house where the blue-helmeted and fair-skinned Irish soldiers sheltered themselves from the blazing sun in a small tent that was equally hot but shaded. The soldiers' tour of duty in Kilubi would last for just one week, but they claimed they liked it, this quiet spot with friendly villagers. It was trips like these that refreshed Gordon's spirit and offered him hope. As his party flew back to the Kamina base, they suddenly spotted a herd of eleven elephants, the babies pressing into the sides of their mothers as the old daddy of the herd flapped his ears and waved his trunk in the air. In spite of the noise of the heliocopter, Gordon thought he could hear his trumpeting rage at having been disturbed.

It was on this trip that Gordon developed a genuine affection for the Irish troops. Of all the European contingents, he found them the most at ease with the Congolese, with little sense of a colour barrier. He remembered being in a discussion with Irish officers who said they could identify with the Congolese better than any other troops because they understood colonial oppression. The British officers present protested vigorously, and the Irish responded by shouting, "Yes! Oppression!"[34] He recalled an occasion when the Irish were replacing a contingent of Mali troops, and the Irish pipe band serenaded the black Mali soldiers as they lined up to get on the train. The sun was setting, and when the pipes stopped the Cathedral bells of Albertville rang out the Angelus – a dramatic moment. On the morning of 1 September, as Gordon and his companions prepared to return to Leopoldville, they were treated to their own pipe-band parade into the town, with Congolese children following them through the streets, stretching their little legs and throwing sticks into the air to imitate the drum major. It was an early example of the friendliness between the Congolese and the UN troops in the early days of ONUC, one that, sadly, did not prevail in the succeeding months.[35] "These Irish are wonderful!" King told Ruth.[36]

In October, at the invitation by Sture Linner, UN Chief of Civilian Operations, Gordon added Information Officer for Civilian Operations to his already heavy load. Under the Technical Assistance Program with which Gordon had worked in New York, the UN had been ready to meet the technical demands in the Congo well before the crisis precipitated by independence. Once the Belgians had fled, however, the technical aid program quickly became unworkable, and it was immediately apparent that unless the UN could implement an emergency program to train Congolese to assume responsibilities previously carried out by foreigners, the Congo faced a collapse of technical and public services. Until this base of competent Congolese could be built, international technicians had to be recruited and brought in to restore, operate, and maintain the services.

Understandably, the mutinies, violence, and political instability overshadowed the United Nations' efforts in the area of civilian operations. In an effort to regain necessary publicity, at the end of October Gordon travelled to Coquilhatville, a city of 40,000 on the Congo River in the province of Équateur, to report on the progress being made in restoring the infrastructure.[37] He was most interested in investigating the health services, which under the Belgians had not only provided care for the sick but had also kept epidemic and endemic diseases under control. The flight of the foreign doctors and professional staff having left the hospitals in dire straits, WHO was overwhelmed in trying to cope with the problem. In response to an appeal by the secretary general, national Red Cross societies in twenty nations had responded with medical teams to keep the hospitals running. The Canadian Red Cross had sent two doctors and two nurses to the hospital at Coquilhatville, where the doctors gave Gordon a tour of the facilities including the leprosarium.[38] He found some of the cases horrifying, but, encouraged by the doctors, he tried to identify that element of hope among the patients that one day they might return to society. In his report, he addressed the "shockingly distorted idea" that with the high death rate, particularly among children, in undeveloped countries, "life is cheap."[39] He described a mother bringing her baby into the clinic, her grief and despair no different from that of a North American mother in the same situation, and he pointed out that it was not a reverence for life that the Western world was called upon to teach the African, but a belief in medical science, knowledge of the rules of health, and confidence that they could learn to care for their own sick.

One afternoon while Gordon was in Coquilhatville, a friend from the Royal Canadian Corps of Signals took him for a speedboat trip along the Congo River. As they travelled close to shore along the thick and tangled foliage of the jungle, waving at the Congolese fishermen who called back to them, he felt he was on the edge of Africa. They stopped at one of the villages, where the young headman wanted to know why they were in Africa. How to explain, Gordon wondered, how to cross the barriers of culture, geography, and language? On his return to Leopoldville, King wrote to Ruth that he felt he had come closer to knowing the Congo than ever before and, after weeks in Leopoldville, he felt more hopeful about its prospects, having been out in the field. His only complaint about Coquilhatville was that there were just two restaurants, miserable and terribly noisy, with bad food and blaring radios. Still, the people were friendly and "terrific talkers."[40]

During the autumn, ONUC faced a particularly tragic situation in the province of Kasai, whose southern border was contiguous with the rebel province of Kantanga. The Luala tribe of southern Kasai, traditional enemies of the Kantaga Baluba, had taken advantage of the breakdown of central authority to revive their age-old feud. The Baluba, less aggressive than the Luala and inclined toward education and training, had been moving northward into Luala land where they established themselves as farmers, merchants, and clerks. In August 1960, the tribal conflict took on greater significance as the Luala, backed by the central government of Lumumba, attacked the Baluba, burning their villages and massacring their people.[41] Within the limits of its original mandate, ONUC was powerless to intervene; but in early September, Hammarskjöld authorized the interposing of UN troops, using force if necessary to stop the massacre.[42]

In late November, Gordon was placed on a committee to determine what ONUC could do about the crisis situation of the Baluba refugees, estimated to be about 100,000 living in famine conditions. As information officer, he felt he should go in to see the situation for himself and on 6 December (his sixtieth birthday), he flew in to Bakwanga with two UN relief coordinators. They arrived at Bakwanga in the afternoon and immediately made contact with the head of the Congolese Red Cross, a doctor for the Forminière (the Belgian company in charge of the big diamond mines at Bakwanga), and the Ghanian ONUC troops with whom they were billeted. They were then taken to the refugee shelter. Gordon was stunned. "Death by starvation is a quiet death," he reported in his first CBC report. "A dead child in its father's arms, a baby too feeble to get a drop of milk from its mother's breast. The hospital unnaturally quiet because there is no longer life to cry out."[43]

The next morning they travelled 100 km west of Bakwanga to Lake Mukamba where the main group of new refugees was concentrated. About 50 km out they came upon a village market where the majority of the people were refugees, most of them women and children, all with the characteristic marks of starvation. The refugees had put up a shelter of sticks and mud that housed sixty or seventy of them. Farther along they turned off the main road to visit a dispensary and saw a woman lying at the edge of the road, shrivelled and sunken and covered by flies. "She looked like an ancient hag. But she might have been thirty." As he stood numbly looking down at her, her eyes moved. "She's alive!" he shouted. They flagged down a Red Cross van that took her to the dispensary, only 274 m away. There they laid her on the ground under a tree and began to feed her liquid out of a spoon, and gradually she began to swallow. To King, it had a curious Gothic flavour, like an early German print of the raising of Lazarus.[44]

They continued on their way and came upon a government feeding station. Each refugee was entitled to one bowl of manioc flour per week for each member of the family, three fish, and a couple of cups of palm oil. A refugee centre of 30,000 had once been a village of 300. It had a decent, well-equipped hospital, with 150 beds and more than 1,000 patients, no doctors or nurses, and just one Congolese medical assistant and his helper. They learned that this was one of five regional hospitals, the other four having a total of 600 beds, and not a single doctor for any one of them. On Thursday, they talked with government leaders in Bakwanga, the prime minister of Kasai, the ministers of economy and health, the head of the Kasai Red Cross, the bishop of Bakwanga, and the chief of the Protestant Relief. They talked of practical details – questions of warehouse space, distribution centres, distribution personnel, transport. After three hours of discussion, they reached an agreement on the organization and plan of distribution of a massive food airlift backed by the UN. By the time the meeting ended, a C-119 was in with five more tons of food. Once unloaded, it was ready to take Gordon's party back to Leopoldville.[45]

The trip home had its own moment of drama for Gordon. The plane, not designed for passenger travel, swerved suddenly, and getting up to see what was happening, he "came croppers." The next thing King remembered, after half an hour of unconsciousness, was being taken to the ONUC hospital in Leopoldville to have the "hole in the top of my head" stitched up. He was really quite all right, he assured Ruth, and he spent his few days in the hospital rereading *Brideshead Revisited*, which he liked better this time: it didn't make him as angry as when he had first read it (this not being Oxford as he remembered it), and it kept his mind occupied.[46]

It was hardly a surprise that he would not be home for Christmas (he promised Ruth that this would be the last time), and in fact he spent perhaps the most momentous Christmas of his life, with the refugees in Kasai. By Christmas week, five or six planes a day were airlifting in food, trucks had been ordered, three WHO doctors were on the job, and nutrition and childcare experts had arrived. There was not enough help to supervise the handling and distribution of the airlifted food over the holidays, and Gordon was asked to go to Bakwanga. Once again, he was billeted with the Ghanian regiment and their British officers, and as he sat with the major sipping drinks before dinner on the 23rd, they heard music drifting in and saw lights through the palm trees, a land rover with four lanterns on top, bright red flowers decorating the hood, and Father Christmas with his snowy beard in the driver's seat. A dozen soldiers wearing surplices of mosquito netting to look like angels sang English carols and then Ghanian carols "marvelously reconstructed from some of the old missionary hymns to resemble Gregorian chants."[47]

The next morning, Christmas Eve, the big planes began arriving with loads of beans and rice that were stored in the ONUC warehouse in the Forminière compound, and by noon the convoy of three five-ton trucks was loaded and ready to leave. First came the Red Cross truck carrying milk and both tinned and dried fish. Its crew comprised twenty youngsters from the Junior Red Cross, eager, energetic, and "with a propensity for song." This was followed by the Ghanian five-ton truck, loaded with rice, beans, and maize flour, with its crew of Ghana soldiers stripped to the waist, their blue helmets glistening in the hot sun. Finally, the third truck, in which Gordon rode, driven by the Mennonite missionary, Archie Graber, carried ten drums of palm oil and fish. The staff car brought up the rear, carrying the deputy commissaire of refugees, the UN refugee coordinator and his assistant, an International Red Cross representative, and two WHO doctors. The convoy drove west and north, back to Lake Makumba, the heart of the famine area where Gordon had visited earlier. As they distributed their life-giving cargo they once again came face to face with kwashiorkor, the malnutrition of starvation, something no one could never get used to or forget. He wrote, "Starvation is such an individual experience and, somehow, as the flesh recedes and the body is reduced to a skeleton, the individuality of each child asserts itself, making a private appeal."[48]

Back in Bakwanga that night they got a signal from Leopoldville that on Christmas morning the representatives of the secretary general, accompanied by twenty newsmen, would pay a visit. The team had advised against it when it was first proposed, but had been overruled. So at the crack of dawn on Christmas morning, Gordon, Graber, and a young Scottish doctor from WHO, made their way to the hospital nearest Bakwanga (one that they had not had time to reach with supplies the day before) to alert the staff of the impending arrival of their distinguished visitors. To their horror, in a hospital built to accommodate 300, they found 1,200 starving refugees with no one in charge. The entire staff of medical assistants (there were no doctors) had gone home for Christmas Day. The patients had had no food at all that day. Gordon and the two others scrounged around and found some powdered milk that they stirred up in a big tub and took around the wards. "It was quite a sight: three or four to a bed, some lying on the floor. Many of them had hardly enough strength to be interested in a drink of milk." At about that time the journalists and dignitaries arrived, and Gordon, Archie, and the young Scottish doctor gave the members of the Western press "a clinical tour on what famine really meant in human terms."[49] During the tour, the black sky split open and the rain began in a deluge. A photographer said, "It's tragic. All that material and no light."[50]

They had Christmas dinner back at the Ghana camp. No one was in a mood to celebrate. Their pilot stalked in muttering and angry: he had come from the infirmary with the other pilots, having taken sweets they had brought with them especially for the children. Two babies had died just before they arrived and the sisters didn't think the Father Christmas act was appropriate. Gordon and the assembled company all knew how the pilot felt, having spent the last two days looking at children with big eyes and starved bodies. They wished each other Merry Christmas with little enthusiasm as they parted.

Helen Gordon had suffered a stroke in the summer of 1959 that had slowed her down somewhat but had not disabled her. Shortly before he left for Kasai, King received a cable from his sister Ruthie in Winnipeg, saying that she had taken a turn for the worse, followed by a phone call saying she was somewhat better. On Christmas Day, while he was in Kasai, King received a telegram saying that she was extremely ill, and as he had already made contingency plans to return to Canada in such an event, he left Leopoldville immediately on returning there. He spent two and a half months in Winnipeg, visiting his mother daily, attending to family business, and, unable to settle, reading with desultory concentration the novels stacked by Ruthie on the guestroom bedside table. He also used his spare time in what he described to Ruth as "discreet agitation" on behalf of the Kasai refugees, turning down invitations to lecture publicly as he thought it would not be fitting with "the boss" (Hammarskjöld) in the middle of a delicate situation in the Congo. This discreet agitation included contacting his wide network of friends and acquaintances in the university, church, and political communities, and he received responses from each contact assuring him of support. He also accepted an invitation from the CBC to report on the South Kasai famine on its national radio program, "Trans-Canada Matinee."[51]

As his mother's condition appeared to have stabilized, King returned to the Congo on March 10. In his letter telling his mother that he had arrived safely, a letter she probably never read, he visited cheerily much in the manner he always had with her. He told her about attending church that morning. He talked about the churches' contributions to the famine effort, and assured her about the safety of the missionaries, always her keen concern. He told of taping a concert of Africans singing spirituals, and of how an unfortunate baby crying through one number sadly strained his Christian forbearance. He concluded, "Very much love, dearest Mother. I shall be looking forward to Ruthie's first letter giving news of you. You are very much in my thoughts and in my heart."[52]

On 17 March, Gordon was paying a visit to his friends, the Irish ONUC contingent at Kamina, when he received word that his mother had died. The Irish were, of course, celebrating St Patrick's Day. The soldiers had become interested in the missionaries' work with children in the surrounding villages, and they had been volunteering with educational work, also teaching Irish songs and dances. On this special day, they put on a party for about two hundred of their young charges. Although the news Gordon received in the midst of the merriment was not unexpected, he felt it a "crushing blow." He described his reaction:

> My immediate reaction was to withdraw to be alone by myself. And that's what I did. But then I thought: it's hardly fair to absent myself or to impose my grief on my hosts in their day of celebration. So I went to the bonfire. The Chaplain sang "Oh Danny Boy," and some of the boys performed. And then the little Congolese children took over the show. They sang, alternating the songs they had learned from the missionaries with their own music ... It was a marvelous, joyous celebration. Mother would have loved it.[53]

King continued to Ruth the next day en route to Leopoldville:

> All day I have been living in two worlds. I have told nobody because I didn't want to speak of it. And while I have been alone, I have been thinking back and recalling. But most of the time I have been with people … I attended mass this morning and for the first time got some comfort out of it, the church packed with khaki and the Gregorian chanting in deep male voices. They are a fine lot and St Patrick's Day with them was quite an experience. It's ironical that I was celebrating St Patrick's Day with all the guns and activities and a big bonfire and concert at night. But in the spirit of joy and friendliness and play and faith there was no contrast in what Mother was in her life. With her health she would have enjoyed the day at Kamina. The Irish would have loved her.[54]

Ruth wrote:

> You must know how I long to be with you now. If I find it so very hard to bear, how must you be feeling! And yet, loving her so much, I am happy to think that her struggling is over and that she is peaceful at last … She couldn't have helped but know how greatly she was loved and how much happiness she gave to many *many* people.
>
> … And it is good to know that there is a part of her in you and in our children. They are so lucky to have had her for a grandmother, as I have been to be a part of her family, which she truly made me feel.[55]

By the time Gordon returned to Leopoldville in March of 1961, Patrice Lumumba had been assassinated and there were four rival governments in the Congo: Leopoldville under President Kasavubu ("neutralized" but not removed during Mobuto's coup the preceding September),[56] recognized by the UN as the legitimate government; Stanleyville in the north-eastern province of Orientale, under Antoine Gizenga, former supporter of Lumumba; Katanga under the secessionist leader Moise Tshombe; and Bakwanga under the Baluba king, Albert Kalonji. The military forces were likewise fragmented. The Congolese army (ANC) had split into two factions, half of it under the command of General Mobutu in Leopoldville, and the other half under General Lundula in Stanleyville. In Katanga, Tshombe's *gendarmerie* of 10,000 supported Leopoldville, while in neighbouring South Kasai, an army of 5,000, supported the Baluba king. Both armies were trained by white officers, many of whom were mercenaries.[57] Intertribal rivalries flared into open warfare, and the withdrawal of a number of national contingents had reduced the ONUC Force to less than 15,000. ONUC detachments on the Atlantic ports had been savagely attacked, creating severe logistical problems for the UN. With the strengthening of the UNOC mandate authorizing the use of force to maintain order and prevent civil war (Security Council Resolution 161 [1961]) however, reinforcements began to arrive, resulting in a turning of the tide. By mid-summer the force was once again up to 20,000 troops, with twenty bases spread throughout all six provinces.

Gordon gradually settled back in to his Congo routines. With the loss of his mother still fresh in his heart, he found himself preferring an evening of reading to socializing, enjoying Harold Nicholson's *Some People* and the novels of C.P. Snow. And, as he noted sardonically, "of course, there is always the *Courier d'Afrique* to improve one's French in a kind of basic way and keep up one's blood pressure."[58] Over Easter, remembering his mother with particularly poignancy, he had what he described as "quite an experience." Against his inclination, he agreed to join Freddy Bayat and a group of Irish friends at a restaurant. While there, he met an American ex-army pilot whom he had known in Korea, along with his French wife and two young daughters. It was a hot night, and someone suggested that they all go for a swim, but by the time they got to the Club they found it completely dark. They asked the Congolese caretaker if they could swim, and he said "Why not?" "It was a beautiful experience," he told Ruth:

> There were no lights but the moon, just about full, was directly overhead. And the water was just lukewarm. It is a big pool with palm trees around it. I swam around keeping my eye like a retriever on the two youngsters, one of whom could swim fairly well and the other had a rubber ring … John Farrar I know would have some Freudian explanation to the whole thing but it was just so satisfying and so right for my mood … I came home and slept as I haven't slept in weeks.[59]

He began to feel like himself again.

In mid-April, Gordon returned to Bakwanga in South Kasai where he had helped feed refugees at Christmas. It was a story with a happy ending, a successful UN project. He flew in with Xavier Cabellero, head of the relief operation, six Austrian medics, and five tons of very smelly dried fish. When Gordon told Caballero that he wanted to see Miabi, the large refugee centre in the Lake Mukamba region that he had visited the previous December, the affable Bolivian shrugged and said, "There's nothing to see."[60] Nevertheless, they started out along the dusty trail through elephant grass growing high on both sides, a different landscape from the sea of mud their five-ton truck had struggled through on Christmas Day. They began to spot patches of corn growing by thatched roofed huts, and women in colourful costumes with babies on their backs and loads of maniok, wood, or washing on their heads. Soon they came to a group of buildings, a hospital, and a sign that read "Commune Miabi." The surgeon and the director of the commune came out to meet them, and when the formalities of the welcome were over, Gordon asked to be taken through the wards where he and Archie Graber had ladled reconstituted milk from tubs to feed the neglected patients, four or five to a bed, on Christmas Day. The wards were clean. There were perhaps fifteen patients. The children playing on the hospital grounds appeared to be healthy and well fed. When Gordon asked about kwashiorkor, the starvation disease, the doctor said that they saw very little of it now and the three babies in their care who suffered from it had been brought in from an outlying area.

Gordon visited other hospitals in the area, and the story he heard from the WHO doctors and FAO nutritionists was the same: the famine was over. It had disappeared in the aftermath of a stunning undertaking of international cooperation that combined compassion, organization, and imagination. To Gordon, it was another example of the resilience of the African people and he marvelled at their ability to recover, both physically and psychologically, in view of the loss of thousands of their Baluba tribesmen and families who had died by starvation and violence.

Gordon made one more trip in April, again travelling with the Force commander, Lieutenant-General Sean MacEoin, to Bukavu and Goma in Kivu province, on the border of Rwanda and Uganda. Once again they visited Kabalo, the heart of the Baluba resistance under the control of the Ethiopian ONUC soldiers. Gordon found the outpost as miserable as on his earlier visit the previous fall when General MacEoin had passed out medals and received a leopard skin and declarations of love for the UN. "What a godforsaken place!" he complained. "Nothing but elephant grass growing all around."[61] The people were poor and simple, but tough and spirited, sometimes going into battle against Tshombe's gendarmerie armed only with sticks and the belief that the special medicine of the witch doctors would protect them against bullets. La jeunesse Balubakat, little boys with "Davy Crockett bands of fur around their heads," were led into battle by twelve- to fourteen-year-old warriors.[62]

He returned to Leopoldville to what was his most difficult period in the Congo. A cable arrived telling him of the sudden death of his sister Marjorie's husband in Australia. Following so closely on the death of his mother, King was devastated, feeling his sister's grief, and cut off and isolated from the family, with nothing he could do to help. "This is a characteristic of 'the field,'" he wrote Ruth. "There is nothing one can do: you are isolated. And so you just go on without brooding too much."[63] By this time, word had also come of the massacre of the more than forty ONUC Ghanian and Swedish soldiers at Port-Francqui in April. Following on the heels of this bad news, he learned that in view of the danger, ONUC had pulled its relief workers out of South Kasai. "This is a little short of tragic but with the security situation what it is there was no alternative."[64] Food would continue to be shipped to the borders of the state, and the relief coordinator who had stayed behind was attempting to get the government authorities there to set up their own distribution system. Then, at the end of June, he learned that eight Irish soldiers had been killed by Balubas.[65]

Meanwhile, the date of Gordon's departure for New York and the appointment of his successor remained uncertain – more of "Grandmother UN." Morale in the office suffered because of the delays and the general unhappiness on the part of his staff about his leaving. Moving to the more trivial but not less frustrating, when one of his editors of the *Tom Tom/Tam Tam* mutinied and refused to work because of criticism directed at his work (not by Gordon but by a member of the Department of Public Information in New York), Gordon himself put out two issues on his own before the problem was resolved. Even his digestion suffered. And so, he wandered out to the zoo for a solitary meal, feeling that nobody loved him (as he said to Ruth in mocking self-deprecation), comforted by a sense of the animals out in the darkness beyond the lights of the restaurant. He had nearly finished eating, rather enjoying his melancholy, when a friend came along – also by himself, which surprised Gordon "since he is such a gay and sociable dog."[66] They passed an hour of fraternal misery that, after a few drinks, gave way to a certain degree of good cheer, and he pronounced the evening a success. Nevertheless, King was ready to go home.

There were moments of wistfulness, though not regret, as he entered the last two weeks of farewell dinners. As he left his many friends, he wrote to Ruth, "It will be so good to see you again. And this time there will be no sense of guilt for an uncompleted job. It's good bye to the Congo."[67] The family was waiting for him when he arrived at Birkencraig. This time, Gordon finished his vacation at the lake, and then returned to New York in September to complete the four months remaining on his contract with the UN. He was there when the tragic news of Hammarskjöld's death in Africa arrived on 17 September.

By June of 1961, the central government in Leopoldville had been restored and was recognized by the United Nations as having authority over the entire country, including the rebel province Katanga. It appeared that a chapter in the Congo had been closed.[68] However, Belgian army officers and mercenaries continued to pour into the renegade province and were serving in the Kantanganese gendarmerie. To make matters worse, the Belgians in many cases distributed arms to the population and the Luala, under the direction of Belgian officers, once again began terrorizing the Baluba around Elizabethville. In an attempt to resolve the crisis, Tshombe had requested a meeting with Hammarskjöld at Ndola in Northern Rhodesia. When Hammarskjöld did not hear further from Tshombe concerning the conditions that must be met before the meeting could take place, and was informed that Tshombe had already chartered a plane to fly to the agreed-upon meeting place, he decided to fly to Ndola on the assumption that Tshombe would show up.[69]

Hammarskjöld left Leopoldville with his staff at five o'clock in the afternoon of 17 September. Normally UN planes did not fly at night, but the threat to small aircraft from the Kantanganese Fouga Magister jets made daytime flights dangerous, and Hammarskjöld flew across the entire expanse of the Congo in darkness. His plane crashed in the jungle about 16 km short of its destination.

Gordon was devastated by the death of Hammarskjöld. He wrote: "He had come to personify and symbolize the world organization, which, in a time of mounting crisis, still held the best hopes for peace."[70] That October, during United Nations Week, he told an audience, "the personal impact of his death has been like nothing that I have experienced in my lifetime." Gordon had been brought both to Cairo and to Leopoldville at Hammarskjöld's request; and although the secretary general's role in the Congo later became a subject of debate, Gordon remained loyal both to Hammarskjöld's policies and to his person,[71] feeling that he had directed a highly complex and difficult course of operation in a manner consistent with the principles of the Charter and the decisions of the United Nations organs.[72] Until his own death many years later, Gordon spoke of Hammarskjöld with admiration. It was as though, along with the copy of the UN Charter that he always carried in his pocket, he continued to carry Hammarskjöld in his heart.[73]

Gordon retired from the UN at the end of 1961, having just turned sixty-one. At the request of Ann Winslow, editor-in-chief of the Carnegie Endowment for International Peace, he spent the first months of 1962 writing a book, *The United Nations in the Congo: A Quest for Peace*. He worked in New York with access to United Nations documents; his interviews with UN officials who were participants in the Congo Operation, and his own experience there gave the account warmth and clarity. The book was widely praised by reviewers, the major exception appearing in *The American Academy of Political and Social Science*.[74] The reviewer, a retired foreign service officer, accused Gordon – and those like him who supported the central government in Leopoldville – of being unwise and short-sighted in supporting the idea that the "vast, sprawling, illiterate, socially disparate and politically unprepared Congo" could realistically come to be viewed as a nation state.

This argument regarding the post-colonial creation of nation states in Africa and other developing nations continued, and in his later writings Gordon addressed the issue. At the time he wrote the book, however, he stood firmly behind the UN position. He titled his second last chapter, "The Issue is Secession," and in it he described Secretary-General U Thant's appeal on 31 July 1962 to Belgium, the United Kingdom, and the United States to bring pressure on Tshombe to accept reunification. He concluded the chapter with a degree of optimism that with peace restored, the Congo would no longer be a "problem child," but would assume its place among the new nations of the world.[75] This hope, however fragile, was shared by all concerned when in June 1964, with Kantanga once again reintegrated into the national territory of the Congo, the last of the ONUC Force was completely withdrawn.

By the time he wrote his book for the Carnegie Foundation, Gordon had experienced two major United Nations peacekeeping operations, UNEF in Egypt and Gaza, and ONUC in the Congo. (UNKRA, the United Nations Korean Reconstruction Agency was not, of course, a peacekeeping operation.) He reflected on these two experiences as he returned home from Leopoldville, acknowledging that the story of ONUC was still incomplete. In both cases, the UN force was charged with supervising the withdrawal of foreign troops; neither force had military objectives; both came into being with the agreement of the parties in dispute; and each was forbidden to interfere in the internal affairs of the country. UNEF was a tidy, efficient operation noted for the smooth functioning of its military units under a strong, centralized command and for the effectiveness of its administration. By contrast, ONUC appeared to be diffused, cumbersome, and at times confused, and the magnitude and complexities of its tasks became increasingly apparent as the Congo operation developed.[76] While UNEF functioned clear of all involvement in the politics of the host country, ONUC was thrust into the midst of a turbulent political whirlpool in which political authority was disintegrating or actively hostile. At times, ONUC had no legal government at all to deal with as it tried to preserve order in a vast area plagued by political conflicts, tribal fighting, civil war, and undisciplined and frequently leaderless armies. Moreover, UNEF operated in sparsely populated open desert, while ONUC covered a huge densely populated territory of jungle, savannah, and highlands. In view of these challenges, Gordon found it amazing that ONUC had been able to discharge its central task of separating armies and maintaining order (with its mandate later expanded to include expelling Belgians and mercenaries) as well as it had.[77]

Reflecting more generally on the experience of UNEF, in an article he wrote in 1970 for *The International Journal* of the Canadian Institute of International Affairs,[78] Gordon identified the necessary elements at the core of successful peacekeeping: political consensus, particularly unanimity among the great powers in the Security Council, as well as among the states immediately involved; the availability of military resources; and the efficient and disciplined conduct of the Force itself under experienced command. As long as the political consensus held, the authority of UNEF's mandate remained intact; but once the great-power consensus in the Security Council dissolved, and attention was diverted to the perceived communist threat in Asia, and once Egypt determined that the arrangement agreed upon no longer served its interests, war ensued between Israel and Egypt in 1967. While the formation of UNEF constituted a significant stage in the evolution of dealing with international conflict, it could not be applied as a multi-purpose model for all peacekeeping operations. For example, in the case of ONUC, neither consensus held. Gordon rightly pointed out that in spite of the genuine contribution of the UN operation in the Congo, the problems of internal conflict and lack of political coherence, and the interference of outside national interests, had serious consequences for the future of peacekeeping.[79]

What then was the prospect for UN peacekeeping? Gordon argued that there was value in returning to the Security Council, as Hammarskjöld did again and again; but ultimately, only great-power consensus, and agreement by the host government that such action serves its interest, could provide legitimacy and the practical support necessary for success. He concluded that the work of *peacekeeping* would ultimately be judged by the *peacemaking* that ensued. Had Gordon lived to see the collapse of the Soviet Union in 1989, and the complexities that dogged UN peacekeeping in the 1990s, one wonders what he would have written.

In June of 1962, Gordon returned to the Congo to direct the filming of a documentary for the UN International Zone series. The film covered two aspects of the mission, the refugee situation among the Baluba and the Watutsi populations, and the progress being made in the Civilian Operations area. It was a happy trip for Gordon, without the uncertainty and apprehension of his earlier tours, and as he sat on the Brazzaville side of the Congo River enjoying a cool breeze and waiting once again for the ferry across to Leopoldville, he confided his only complaint to Ruth, that his bags and equipment remained behind at the Orly airport in Paris.[80]

On his return to Leopoldville, his welcome by his friends left him exhausted and he slept all the way to Elisabethville lying on the floor of a military C54 plane filled with cargo.[81] He arrived just in time for another party, this one held for a group of Cuban entertainers. He told Charley, "It might have been Korea, El Ballah, Gaza."[82] And then he and his crew set to work, lining up the first part of the refugee section of the film.

They found the situation around Elisabethville depressingly grim, with about 50,000 Balubas living in a camp on the edge of town that had formerly been the botanical garden. Now, it was just a bleak area of red dust with a few big trees like umbrellas rising above it. The refugees were crowded together in a jumble of messy huts made of cloth, cartons, corrugated iron, and mud. The UN provided rations and water. Gordon found it particularly sad that these refugees had formerly been part of the work force in the Belgian mines and they had lived in communes, receiving fairly good wages and services such as schools and hospitals. By the time Gordon and his crew arrived, the UN had decided that the only solution to the problem of the swelling refugee camp was to relocate the refugees back to the tribal areas from which the Belgians had brought them as labourers in the first place, and they were now being "repatriated" by train and by plane at the rate of 8,000 to 9,000 a week. But the tragedy did not end there. Those Baluba being shipped out of Elisabethville had been used to a comparatively advanced standard of living, and they were now going back to primitive tribal lands. Gordon watched as they arrived with their bundles to have them weighed, leaving behind possessions that they had considered indispensable. "There is a stack of thousands of bicycles that have been left behind and a healthy market in iron beds which obviously they cannot take. I've been a lot in the camp during these days and saw a trainload go off to Kamina today and it is really heartrending."[83]

The plan for the film was to find a refugee family from the camp at Elisabethville and follow them through the whole evacuation process. It seemed a fairly straightforward assignment, and Gordon was overjoyed have the help of his old friend, the Mennonite missionary Archie Graber, in finding the perfect family. As it turned out, the likelihood of finding an ideal family in a Congolese refugee camp was no greater than in the population at large. Graber thought he had located a fine family, but the elder daughter turned out to be the second wife and this was too much for Archie's "good Christian conscience." Gordon found a mother of two babies who looked like a Madonna, but she turned out to be divorced and this did not meet the UN mandate, which required a family with a father. Finally, in desperation, Gordon appealed to a UN social worker, who found the perfect family: a mother, two babies, and two handsome boys. The father, it turned out, had already gone to Bakwanga, so they changed their story line to having a happy reunion at the other end. Gordon's Barbadian friend, Oliver Jackman, himself a man of colour, ventured the observation that the nursing baby had a light complexion and fairish hair and might possibly have a Swede for a father; but Gordon discounted this canard, only suggesting that, if true, the family reunion might have an interesting UN denouement.

As the filming proceeded, Gordon and the crew became enchanted with their choice. They filmed for ten days in Elisabethville and then flew to Bakwanga with a planeload of refugees, including their own film star, the mother, Mbuyi, with her children. Gordon rhapsodized, "The film boys have done excellent work and unless I miss my guess the UN has some footage like they have never had before."[84] Indeed they had. The crew found the husband in the new refugee village and prepared to film the joyful reunion. "But, of course, things are never quite as planned in Hollywood,"[85] King explained to Ruth. With the husband was his second wife, and not only that, but both husband and second wife had their heads shaved and were in mourning for a baby who had died. At this point, Mbuyi retired with the second wife into the hut for about half an hour of traditional wailing. Fortunately, the husband's brother was at hand, so he volunteered to play the part of the husband: "It was all very homey and a little earthy; they killed a chicken for the feast in a very direct and brutal way by banging it on the ground – this we didn't film – and then had a simple meal under a small tree in front of the mud house. I recorded some noises – a homemade xylophone called a madimba, and kids singing and got a wonderful interview between Archie and a former refugee."[86] Not as planned, perhaps, but a successful conclusion in any case.[87]

The crew now had to find a suitable civilian operation to film and, after considerable initial frustration looking for something with more popular appeal than the Leopoldville farm machinery school, Gordon found a project that he felt demonstrated that given some equipment and training the Congolese could capably cope with things. This happy day of filming took place at a mechanized farm in the Thysville area, about 160 km from Leopoldville, one of the few successful mechanized agricultural projects in the Congo. The Groupe d'Economie Rurale, as it was called, provided and maintained equipment for farmers to rent for producing their crops that they then sold for profit. There were about 2,500 farmers in the Groupe, working 9,000 acres and renting mechanized equipment from eight machinery and tractor centres. They made good livings, having broken away from the subsistence pattern, and it was a model that Gordon felt the UN should be supporting.

The "star" of their film was Kanza Albert, a young graduate of the Mechanical Agriculture Center. The plot of the film traced the clearing of the land by a big D7 caterpillar bulldozer that would, on cue, break down and be repaired by none other than Kanza Albert, with his young brother looking on admiringly. This would be followed by an inspection of various fields – peanuts, corn, tobacco, bananas – and a filming of the village of well-built houses where the workers lived, each covered with brightly coloured plaster. The filming was entirely successful, with no surprise visits from second wives or missing husbands. After a lunch of bananas and beer, they drove back to Leopoldville, delivering Kanza Albert and his brother to their commune just as the early, sudden equatorial darkness fell. A completely satisfactory day, Gordon reported, spent entirely with Congolese.[88]

Gordon's third tour in the Congo proved to be a seven-day-a-week assignment as, in addition to making the film, he prepared broadcasts for the UN Radio and the CBC. He had anticipated that the work he planned to do while there on the last chapter of his book would be routine, just a wrapping up of details. The book was scheduled for publication in October, and his editor, Ann Winslow, had expressed pleasure with the manuscript, asking only for minor revisions and, of course, the conclusion. But on his return to the Congo, Gordon encountered the complexities and ambiguities faced by any author who writes about contemporary political events. "Altogether, the Congo situation is not very happy," he wrote to Ruth on his arrival. "On the total situation, my feelings are now very mixed. The story is not nearly as simple as I wrote it down after the study of UN documents ... And I would like to bet that nobody, but nobody, knows just where we are going to come out."[89] Part of the trouble, he explained to Ruth, was that once back in the field, the words on the page seemed irrelevant. "That has always been the trouble: the Congo is in a different world. It doesn't make much sense and the more orderly you are in your attempt to describe it the farther you probably are from the truth."[90] Finally, King concluded, the Congo confounded one. Too soon for reflection and the benefit of perspective that it would bring, he found it hard to say what this mission had accomplished.

On returning home, he wrote his last chapter, called "An Interim Appraisal," suggesting that with political and constitutional unity achieved and the army integrated, the phase-out of the United Nations Force should be possible, leaving a civilian operation with an expanded program of economic aid. But in spite of his optimism, he was uneasy, adding a caveat: "[T]he story is still incomplete; all the facts are not yet available. We are still too close to it to see the international operation in its historical context."[91]

Ottawa 1988, Twelfth Night: Standing in front of the Cairo camels on the mantel are the small white lion and the miniature elephant carved out of dark wood. Once there had also been five elephants, an ivory drummer, and a sad, badly carved antelope. It was the same antelope that had first caught Gordon's eye as he browsed through the Leopoldville market in May 1961, feeling rather sad and badly carved himself. The asking price was 600 francs, about $12.00, but King eventually got it for sixty francs, protesting to the boy, "Mais, regardez, elle est malade." The boy shouted with laughter. "Mais non, patron, elle n'est pas malade."

Gordon then tried, "Mais, elle est faim." The boy answered, "Oui, elle est femme." Gordon tried again, "Oui, mais la femme est faim." Again, roars of laughter. Gordon's friend strolled over and offered the boy ten francs, and at that point to save "elle" from humiliation, Gordon stepped in quickly and got her for sixty. "She really is quite sweet although a somewhat curious shape. And I didn't have to pay for the baby she is apt to have at any moment," he recounted to Ruth.[92] Eventually, four of the elephants and the dubious antelope went missing, probably as mementos to friends; but the lion and the drummer, together with the remaining elephant, watched over by the medicine man from Kasai hiding in the Wanamaker's tree, seemed to bring King full circle. Once again, on leaving the Congo, it would seem that it was time to retire. But who are these four colourful peasants made out of corn husks? And the moose, dominating the scene with his dignified height as he stands guard over the Madonna and child? Where do they come from? Or, rather, from what further peregrinations are they added to the collection? Gordon's story appears not to be over.

17

Retirement in an Expanding World

In 1977, King Gordon received the honorary degree of Doctor of Laws from Carleton University in Ottawa. In his citation, university president Michael Oliver briefly summarized Gordon's career and accomplishments, concluding:

> The unifying element in this remarkably diverse career has been King Gordon's commitment to serve mankind as a fighter for social justice, as a promoter of peace, and as a champion of a more equitable distribution of the material elements of civilized existence. Trained as a theologian, he has manifested his religion largely through humanitarian action. King Gordon's career both at home and abroad demonstrates that there is no inconsistency between being a good Canadian and a dedicated internationalist. Indeed, Mr. Chancellor, King Gordon would agree with your predecessor (Lester Pearson) who suggested that one cannot be a good Canadian *unless* one is also a good internationalist, and a supporter of universal peace and equity.[1]

Three years later, in October 1980, Gordon became the second recipient of the Pearson Peace Medal, being presented to the governor general, Edward Schreyer, by his old friend George Ignatieff. The Pearson Peace Medal had been established by the United Nations Association of Canada to honour individuals who "by voluntary effort, personally most contributed to those causes for which Lester Pearson stood: aid to the developing world, mediation between those confronting one another with arms, succor to refugees and others in need, and peaceful change through world law and world organization."[2]

In his acceptance speech, Gordon identified two basic elements in Pearson's world view: a deep abhorrence of war and a commitment to building peace; and a realistic recognition that in the modern world any nation's security and well-being were to be found only within a peaceful and just world community.[3]

These remarks articulate the defining elements of Gordon's own understanding of his mission in the world. Until his retirement in 1962, and despite his varied interests and commitments, his vocation had been more or less tethered to one or another particular place and time by his professional responsibilities. Upon his retirement, one might have anticipated Gordon settling into a quieter life, perhaps filled with reflection and writing and the casting of a weather eye toward UN affairs. Quite to the contrary: his sphere of activity appeared to become global. Gordon was now beginning perhaps the most productive period of his long life, now tethered only by personal choice and by unswerving commitment to those goals of which Oliver and Ignatieff had spoken.

In the immediate future however, he and Ruth faced the decisions typical of retirees: where to live and what to do. It was in this context there occurred one of those happy accidents of life that Gordon enjoyed; and, as always, there was a story recounting the ironies of providence. Gordon had a strong preference for returning to Canada (fully supported by Ruth), and this had been a priority in his mind since his move to New York in 1937. Charley, now graduating from Queen's University, had chosen Canadian citizenship; and Alison, with two years left in university, was leaning in that direction. (After visiting Alison in her first term at Queen's, her Aunt Lois reported to King that it had taken her "only about a week to become a Canadian!"[4] Alison herself told her father, "I am becoming Canadianized – I practically say *oot* and *aboot*!"[5]) Ever since J.S. Woodsworth had written to him in 1940 urging him to return to Canada "to help give guidance in the serious days which undoubtedly lie before us,"[6] Gordon had received invitations from the CCF to run for election. In 1952, M.J. Coldwell, leader of the party, had written to Gordon that Manitoba was ripe for a CCF victory providing a leader could be found who would command the respect of the people. "Naturally," he wrote, "our thoughts turn to you."[7] Now, as word of Gordon's retirement spread, he received requests from two of the New Democratic Party (NDP) Riding Associations in Toronto: Rosedale and High Park. His replies indicated that his interests had shifted beyond local politics to supporting Canada's role in international development. He began to contact his network of friends about the possibility of returning to university teaching. "I have long had the feeling," he wrote in a letter to President W.H. Johns of the University of Alberta after their first meeting, "that those of us who have had the good fortune to serve abroad with the United Nations may have something to contribute to the group of Canadians who are coming up through our universities and perhaps to a wider constituency of Canadians who have a vital interest in the large–small world in which we are all involved."[8]

It was in the late winter of 1962 that the opportunity came about – almost by coincidence. Under the auspices of the Canadian Institute of International Affairs, Gordon undertook a brief speaking tour across Canada, attempting the Herculean task of explaining the UN's role in the Congo. The lectures began in Toronto where, over dinner, he discussed his future prospects with John Holmes, who encouraged him to look into university possibilities. With this advice in mind, he continued to Winnipeg where he "spoke to the ladies" in a nostalgic return to the "lovely big living room" in the stately old house at 54 Westgate (now West Gate), now the University Women's Club. His sense of the past was heightened by the presence of his sisters, Ruthie, Greta, and Alison.[9] However, his arrival in Edmonton on 16 February jolted him back into the present. He had scarcely unpacked when he received a call from the British information officer, John Chaplin, telling him that he would be entertaining him for dinner – a rather large one, as it turned out. King wrote to Ruth the next day:

> Here's another crocodile hunt letter![10] I'm going up to the University in about half an hour to look into the matter of a teaching job. It happened that after last night's meeting – which was the biggest yet and one of the best – that a man who I had talked to through dinner and was impressed [by the lecture] came up to me and after congratulating me on the clear presentation etc. etc. said: "And if you are ever thinking of a university job get in touch with me." I thanked him and said that as a matter of fact I was thinking of one right now. It seemed to shake him a bit to be called so quick but he said: "Well, I'll be in my office all morning and if you would like to come up and talk about it give me a ring." He left then and I said to somebody, by the way who was that I was talking to? He looked a bit surprised and said: "Oh, that was President Johns of the University."[11]

He confessed to Ruth that he knew little more about the University of Alberta than he did about the Awash River when he began his crocodile hunting adventure with Arne Rubin; but as he thought about the possibility it occurred to him that it might be a good thing. "I've always been a westerner in thinking and this would be a new start in the West."[12]

Later in the day, King reported on his visit to President Johns and that "as far as the President has anything to say about it, they would be very happy to have me come on the staff." He explained to Ruth, who had never been west of Winnipeg, that while Edmonton had none of the attraction of Montreal or Ottawa, it was a beautiful city with a big river (the North Saskatchewan) running through it and within about 160 km from the Rockies – "a kind of Texas, but with plains, foothills and mountains" – and, he added, just far enough off the main beat to have some appeal. The one thing against it was that it would pull him away physically from the main centres of international activity, Ottawa and New York. He concluded: "It is odd that when I saw that they had given me a weekend in Edmonton of all places I mentally cursed them for not arranging that I should have the extra time in Vancouver. There's always something interesting cropping up, isn't there?"[13]

The decision was almost made. However, as usually happened when providence/fate offered opportunities, Gordon mulled over the decision. In Vancouver, he explored possibilities at the University of British Columbia and had second thoughts about Edmonton. He wrote to Ruth in flight to Toronto: "I'm in quite a quandary – if that's the word – about a job."[14] He was still attracted by the Alberta offer, he assured her, but asked whether he was taking it to avoid having to look further. Saying no to the position would, of course, also cut off alternatives that they had been considering; but the factors in its favour were not likely to be clarified by any talks with easterners, who would be all too ready to advise caution.

And then King raised a surprising question: "Of course, there is the big question that I haven't really gone into: Do we really want to go to Canada?" There was realism in his question and in the admission that he had not really plumbed its depths. The fact was that Gordon had been away from Canada for twenty-five years. The bulk of his professional career, and the entire period of his international experience, had taken place in the United States and abroad, and in spite of his many friends and contacts he was not widely known in Canada at this time. Canada was only now emerging onto the international stage as a "middle power"; and while it had its international "stars," the internationalism that later became its hallmark had not yet been fully articulated. Prescience could have told Gordon that he was coming back to Canada at exactly the most propitious moment in his country's growth and in his own part in it; but providence had not included this gift of foresight among its happy accidents.

By the time Gordon returned from his last assignment in the Congo in August of 1962, the commitment had been made, and as of 1 September he became Visiting Professor of International Affairs at the University of Alberta in Edmonton. With Ruth once again doing the heavy lifting, they were able to put their New York house on the market in time for three weeks at the lake in August. Ruth had mixed feelings about leaving the big house in Barney Park, which they sold at a price considerably higher than the $23,000.00 they had paid ten years before. For Ruth, the house held many emotions: memories of family life and the happy network of friends and community activities mingled with loneliness and times of feeling overwhelmed in King's absences. But over the years of her marriage, she had become rooted and loved in the Gordon family, and at home in Canada during summers at the island. Through her wide reading and attention to political and cultural affairs, she was also well-informed about life north of the border. Furthermore, she anticipated that her children's futures would be lived out in Canada. So it was with a sense of relief that the retirement plans were settled and in anticipation of this new phase of their lives together that she left for Birkencraig.

As Gordon had predicted, the move to Edmonton would mean cutting off other possibilities. They were scarcely settled in Edmonton when, on 20 September, he received a letter from the United Kingdom's high commissioner to Canada, asking whether he, with the agreement of the Department of External Affairs, would agree to become a member of a British government commission to report on a dispute in the Northern Frontier District of Kenya.[15] (With the granting of independence to Kenya, the district, whose 70,000 inhabitants were nearly all Somali Muslims, had requested that it be allowed to join the Somali Republic.) Much later, Gordon admitted that had this invitation, with its opportunity to return to Africa, come sooner, he would have accepted it over the invitation to Edmonton.[16] However, he had no regrets at this and other missed opportunities.

Once settled near the University of Alberta campus, the Gordons received a warm western welcome. By December, Gordon was writing to Reinhold Niebuhr that academic life seemed to be agreeing with him, his only complaint being the quality of the typewriters provided. The mood in Edmonton was buoyant, the region was booming on oil, and the climate was vigorous and refreshing. After many years of exile in the East, Gordon was rediscovering the clear, western sunshine.[17]

For Ruth, the days were quickly filled with activities at the university, and by correspondence with friends back in New York and their many UN friends abroad. As always, she read avidly, and she resumed the editing that she had sporadically continued since her days at Farrar and Rinehart. (Requests for her skilled blue pencil continued long into retirement.) Gordon meanwhile was enjoying an enthusiastic response to his book on the Congo, hearing from UN friends, and he was particularly gratified to receive compliments from John Humphrey and his wife Jeanne, who had dinner with the Gordons on a trip through Edmonton. Perhaps the letter that Gordon most appreciated was from Brian Urquhart, whom he had known in the Congo and in New York and who was soon to write the definitive account of Dag Hammarskjöld's tenure as secretary general. "Dear King," he wrote, "I don't think I ever congratulated you on your book. I gave a copy to Walter Lippmann who was here the other day; he was very pleased with it and has since said how useful it has been to him in understanding the problem."[18] Edmonton, it seemed, was not so distant from the world after all, and in spite of the intense cold and long dark winter nights, it was proving to be a good move for them both.

Gordon described his return to university teaching as an education for himself as well as for his students, noting that during his years in the field he had not had time to keep up his reading on Canadian policy and international political theory. He also admitted that, as a practitioner, he had developed reservations about self-confident model-builders who predicted the future, as opposed to traditional theorists who based their understanding of relations between nations on historical knowledge and interpretation of national interest.[19] His courses in international relations and international organization offered him wide scope and opportunity for fresh thinking. Each lecture was delivered from a full, carefully prepared manuscript and supported by a voluminous list of required reading. He peppered his talks with lively illustrations from his own experience and contemporary politics. His content was informed by his classical education in Modern Greats at Oxford and illuminated by a lifetime of reading (despite his disclaimer), experience, and reflection. He did not draw back from presenting a point of view, but neither did he attempt to impose an ideological interpretation, working rather from the historical data, raising questions, and inviting student participation.

Irene Biss Spry, who later taught with Gordon at the University of Ottawa, described him as a lively, accessible teacher: "The students loved King and found him intensely interesting."[20] Throughout, he remained grounded in the humanities and in the tradition of humane letters, with a liberal sprinkling of examples from the ancient world and frequent excursions into Greek and Latin etymologies. For Gordon, his new role as professor was a return to an earlier love: teaching. Now, however, the lectern replaced the CBC microphone, his audience not isolated farm families around a kitchen table but a classroom of young Canadians whom he hoped to imbue with international vision.

Gordon's first task in his international relations class was to define and articulate theories that described and explained the principles that formed the basis of relations between states. Clearly, for as long as societies had traded and fought wars statesmen and philosophers had concerned themselves with conventions of engagement. However, it was only in modern times that international relations came to be regarded as an academic discipline that could identify and formulate guidelines for foreign policy. Theorizing about international affairs after the League of Nations was established was characterized by emphasis on reason, morality, and orderly patterns of international behaviour – Woodrow Wilson's "moral diplomacy" being a case in point. The reaction to the breakdown of the League of Nations system and the utopian assumptions of its supporters led to a focusing on power over against reason and morality in relations between states. This "realism" approach reached its apotheosis in the writings of Hans Morgenthau and his *Politics Among Nations*,[21] which dominated the theory of international relations at the time Gordon took up his teaching assignment in the 1960s.[22]

Writing after the Second World War, Morgenthau expressed disillusionment with the utopianism of the idealist school, and on the basis of an empirical approach he described the foreign policy of states as pursuit of national interest defined in terms of power. He argued that objective laws stemming from human nature govern politics; and national interest, thus defined, encompassed all levels of social interaction – individual, domestic, and international. The realist was not indifferent to morality, but moral principles could at best only be approximated in practice. Morgenthau was, in short, a true follower of Machiavelli and Hobbes, postulating an evil world, with the root of conflict found in man's desire for power. Power was the immediate end of all politics, and only secondarily could it be a means to achieving other (moral) goals. On the international scene, it was therefore only natural that each state should follow its national interest, stated in terms of power.[23] Did this single-factor approach to relations between states therefore preclude all possibility for "moral dignity"? Since there was no existing integrated international society that could preserve order and realize moral values, Morgenthau argued that self-preservation on the part of a state itself constituted moral duty. International government did not provide the answer to the problem of peace: the United Nations could not be expected to achieve what its predecessors had not. In his view, peace could be maintained only by a balance of power among individual states.[24]

Earlier in his career, of course, Gordon himself had been exposed to and deeply influenced by another "realist" pioneer, Reinhold Niebuhr. However, Niebuhr did not go as far as Morgenthau in insisting on the irrelevance of ethics in international relations. Politics for Niebuhr was not Morganthau's realm of amorality but a sphere of moral ambiguity because moral man remained caught in a constant state of tension, required to act in an immoral society. In December 1962, Niebuhr wrote to Gordon, "You are right, there is considerable difference between Morgenthau's and my 'realism' because he makes the 'national interest' into the ultimate form."[25]

By the mid-1930s, Gordon himself had moved beyond Niebuhr's early influence, rejecting his absolute dichotomy between the Christian ethic and the requirements of political action.[26] Niebuhr's 1934 collection of essays, *Reflections on the End of an Era*, expressed his deepening pessimism, portraying humanity as a desperate but futile contender in a warring world. Gordon parted company with Niebuhr at this point, rejecting Niebuhr's fatalism on two grounds. First, he objected to Niebuhr's distrust of human nature, arguing that the individual and the environment interact, neither being determinant; and that good as well as evil can be the outcome of human action. The Christian is obliged, Gordon argued, to throw his strength and resources wholeheartedly into the fight for moral action. Secondly, he rejected Niebuhr's despair of gaining social-ethical advance in the field of politics.[27] To the end of his life Gordon held to his conviction of the possibility of moral action between individuals *and* among nations.[28]

Gordon continued to refine his ideas concerning moral action in the international sphere. Writing in 1979,[29] he stated that in order to discover any meaning in the phrase, "morality and foreign policy," one had to go back to that normative period before the rise of the nation state when rulers were generally considered to be subject to a universal *natural* law that dictated certain rules of conduct. With the rise of secularism and the nation state, this idea was eventually superseded by the positivist doctrine that rulers and governments of states were completely free to pursue their own interests, governed only by considerations of expediency. The decline of natural law theory did not lead to anarchy, however, as concern for one's citizens, and a preference for peace, led to the rise of professional diplomats who followed the lines of generally accepted practice. Moreover, in the course of the twentieth century conditions emerged between nation states that were closely analogous to those internal to these states, and along with those new conditions emerged stable international institutions and infrastructures. "In other words," Gordon concluded, "we are beginning to see the emergence of something resembling an international community within which moral norms tend to govern actions of individuals and eventually find expression in accepted forms of behavior and are consolidated in acceptable and enforceable international law."[30] With the spread of democracy and participation in government, citizens could hold their elected officials to certain moral principles in external relations within this framework of a global community.

In this debate over the possibility of moral action in the international sphere and the shape of the institutions that might support such action, Gordon was finally indebted to the internationalism of Percy Corbett, who was part of what has been described as the McGill Faculty of Law's "remarkable tradition in international law."[31] In their brief years together in Montreal in the 1930s Gordon and Corbett came to share many friends in the leftist group gathered around Scott at that time and, while Corbett shared many of the goals of the LSR, he was primarily interested in international law and participated only peripherally in the group. Later, like Gordon, he broke with the intellectual left on the isolationist policy of the new CCF party, remaining faithful to his conviction that the best road to peace could be found through international collaboration.

In 1943, Corbett moved to Yale University as Professor of Government and Jurisprudence. By this time Gordon was non-fiction editor at Farrar and Rinehart, which published Corbett's book, *The Postwar World*, and the two men became further acquainted as they participated in a number of organizations concerned with the shape of the post-war world. When Gordon moved to *The Nation*, Corbett became one of its writers, doing what Gordon considered some of the "finest writing in the whole field."[32]

One evening while he was managing editor at *The Nation*, Gordon invited Corbett and Niebuhr (who was also writing for the journal) for dinner at the Gordon home; whereupon the two invited guests launched into a vigorous argument.[33] Corbett defended the principles of political institutions based on constitutions, while Niebuhr held that in the international arena one had to rely on power interests and could not count on the development of democracy or the rule of law. In 1971 (just before Niebuhr's death), Gordon visited Corbett at his summer home in Magog, and in their conversation it became evident that Corbett was still using Niebuhr as an example of the ideas he was attacking. Perhaps one can hear echoes of the earlier dinner party contretemps between Corbett and Niebuhr, and the tone of the 1971 conversation between Gordon and Corbettt on the shores of Lake Memphremagog, in Corbett's comments in *The Growth of World Law*,[34] published that same year:

> Where I do not follow [Niebuhr] is in his belittlement of the liberal's faith in progress, and in his extreme skepticism about man's ultimate ability to establish institutions capable of rendering him service on the universal plane commensurate with that now rendered by the state in national community. Not being obsessed with original sin, and full of wonder at the civilization that the human animal has been able to contrive, I find in history no more basis for the conclusion that he cannot learn to control international violence and to live under supranational law than for the belief that he can do so in a decade or generation.[35]

Accordingly, Corbett concluded that Niebuhr's insistence that the United Nations was not, and could not be, a constitutional world order, or that the chaos in international relations could not be overcome by a system of collective security, was in effect saying that man is "finally unmanageable."[36]

Much later, Gordon concluded that the argument between Corbett and Niebuhr had been a debate between a humanist lawyer with a rigorous intellectual mind and one of the greatest and most courageous moral thinkers of our time.[37] As for Gordon himself, in spite of rare moods of genuine pessimism he found his deeper beliefs in the possibility of human endeavour and his own natural optimism breaking through the Niebuhrian gloom, and he could not abandon mankind to a tragic fate. He confessed that he came down on the side of Corbett. "You aren't faced with the crassness of applied power and the utopianism of international idealism," he told Ernest Dick in a July 1976 interview. "You are somewhere in between. You have the application of power and the expression of idealism, and out of this blend you'll have the emergence of a more stable international order. I tended to go along with Corbett and I still do."[38]

The question remains: Was Gordon a world federalist, a popular concept of the period, and did he support a supranational form of world government? The short answer is no. He was not a world federalist; and he did not (as Corbett did) believe that the sense of community emerging among nations was strong enough to tolerate and support the mechanisms that would be necessary for the enforcement of such a federation's laws. Gordon did, however, anticipate a "new world order," which he often wrote and spoke about, based on Hammarskjöld's enunciation of the founding principles of the United Nations: political equality among nations; equal opportunity and access to the world's resources; the rule of law; the outlawing of war; and the peaceful settlement of international disputes.[39] In 1976, Gordon wrote an article entitled "The New International Economic Order" for the CIIA series, *Behind the Headlines,* in which he asked, "What is this New International Economic Order? How much is rhetoric, how much reality?" By the end of his argument Gordon concluded that a longer view of history suggested that there were times of global crisis when assertion of political will must determine whether nations choose to follow positive factors in the political environment or to fall back into anarchy.[40] But while he believed that the principles spelled out in the UN Charter provided this normative framework for moral action, and that their realization was possible and not utopian, Gordon was by no means blind to the failures of the United Nations. In spite of this acknowledgment, however, it was as Ruth had put it during the frustrating days in Cairo with "Grandmother UN," "it is the only hope today."[41]

Gordon could never sit still for long and in spite of a busy university schedule, his years in Alberta were marked by a good deal of off-campus activity. Upon arriving in Edmonton he immediately became involved in the local branch of the United Nations Association, and this brought about his involvement in the Annual Banff Conference on World Affairs. In the fall of 1962, the executive of the Edmonton branch of the UNA proposed starting an annual seminar on world affairs, and with the enthusiastic backing of both the local and national branches of the Canadian Institute of International Affairs (Gordon belonged to both), the idea became a reality. In August 1963, the first conference (with Gordon as its director) was held on the theme, *The Challenge of World Development.*[42] As a result of the conference, the participants submitted a number of proposals to the prime minister and the minister for External Affairs. Gordon received a prompt reply from Prime Minister Pearson, thanking the conference participants for their valuable contributions and wishing them success in future similar conferences in the future.[43] The prime minister's encouragement was sincere and, at Gordon's invitation and urging, Pearson gave the opening speech at the 1964 Conference on *Latin America: Challenge and Response*.

The Banff Conference reached its apex in 1965 when 120 participants gathered to discuss the theme "Canada's Role as a Middle Power." The topic was particularly timely, coming as it did on the eve of Canada's centenary, a period of changes and tensions in Canada's political and cultural life. It was followed by four more conferences, drawing from a growing list of internationally prominent speakers. After the 1969 conference, Gordon (by then living in Ottawa) was elected honorary director and continued as a member of the Banff Planning Committee. Early in 1970 a dispute arose between the Alberta branches of the CIIA and the central office in Toronto concerning financial support for the conference. The disagreement resulted in the cancellation of the 1970 conference, showing the extent to which the first six conferences had been due to Gordon's steady leadership.

The factors leading to the demise of the Banff Conference following Gordon's departure for Ottawa are significant in the story of Gordon's life for the way in which they reveal the deep core of his intense loyalty to the Canadian West. At the heart of the issue was a misunderstanding between the director of branch relations and development at the CIIA headquarters in Toronto and Gordon's replacement as director of the conference, who felt he had been slighted in correspondence with the central office. Gordon, fearing that the conference was in danger of being cancelled over pique on one side and rudeness on the other, tended to be sympathetic to the new director while John Holmes pleaded that his employee in Toronto had meant no offence.

If Gordon seemed to be over-reacting to what Holmes argued was an unintended semantic slight, the explanation appears to lie in a deeper sensitivity to a slight of longer duration. Gordon wrote to Holmes: "I am most unhappy to think that the Banff conference should end on this sour note. As a misplaced Westerner, I feel strongly that there is a great need to be served by an annual conference devoted to a discussion of world affairs in Western Canada ... I have grave doubts about the influence of the CIAA in the West."[44] Holmes, in an attempt to mitigate the damage, replied by describing the longstanding frustration of the central office in dealing with the Calgary branch on financial matters,[45] and at this point in his letter, the normally long-suffering Holmes lapsed into "a little steam-blowing-off exercise:"

> Dealing with the West, however, as a long line of CIIA staff members can tell you, means being prepared to listen in patience to a constant stream of grievances, complaints and some pretty unreasonable demands. The Winnipeg branch alone has taken years off the lives of all of us ... Of course we are concerned and should be concerned about a threat to the influence of the CIIA in the West but quite frankly our work here would be made a great deal easier and the mission of the Institute would be furthered if we could just skip the prairies. It was different when Gordon was in the West.[46]

Despite this assuasive compliment and his closing comment that "I wish I could emulate you and grow more rather than less tolerant as I age," Holmes had stirred the pot. Gordon gave vent to his fundamental grievance:

> Finally, I must return to my original leitmotif of the CIIA in the West. There your exasperation came out full blast: "the mission of the Institute would be furthered if we could just skip the prairies." I say "exasperation" because I do not believe that this is a considered opinion ... If, as I understand, the new [1970] White Paper is going to restate Canadian foreign policy as a true reflection of the interests and aspirations of the totality of the Canadian people then it is time that the prairies be drawn into the dialogue. Have you ever thought of having a CIIA office or presence in the West as you now have in Quebec City?[47]

Gordon's letter caught Holmes as he prepared to leave for London, but he took time to get off a "Personal and Confidential" reply: "As for the West, I am now running out of time and will have to put that off. Of course what I said was written in exasperation and not to be taken seriously ... It was only because you were a real bosom friend that I indulged in that little outburst. My devotion to Regina [the CCF and its principles] remains boundless."[48]

Sadly for both Gordon and Holmes, the new director – who, as an American, was oblivious to the East–West debate he had stumbled into – called off the 1970 Banff Conference as "unwise and even impractical" given his lack of confidence that there could be effective cooperation between the CIIA central office and others of the Banff Committee.[49] Several proposals were put forth as possibilities for reconstituting the conference, but the Banff Conference, as originally conceived by the Edmonton branch of the CIIA and directed by Gordon, was over. It had not, after all, ended on a "sour note," as Gordon feared; at least certainly not as far as the friendship between Gordon and Holmes was concerned. Almost twenty years later in his eulogy on Holmes's death, Gordon compared him with Mike Pearson and Dag Hammarskjöld in his understanding and vision of a new community of nations.[50]

In the spring of 1962, as he negotiated with the University of Alberta, Gordon had written to President Johns that he hoped to impart to young Canadians an awareness of the larger world and the contributions they might make to it.[51] Through his work with the Canadian University Service Overseas (CUSO), this goal was realized, and in a letter to Pearson in 1966 he described his personal involvement in the recruiting of university graduates for the program as "one of the most rewarding experiences I have ever had."[52] Gordon had been contacted by the executive committee of CUSO as early as 1961 asking if he would be willing to consider the position of executive secretary for the newly formed organization. Gordon could not make a commitment at that point, still being under contract to the UN, but he did write to John Holmes asking for more information about CUSO, its objectives and its practical backing.[53] It sounded like a promising vehicle for Gordon's own interest and many contacts in technical assistance work in the developing world. While the organization mirrored its counterpart in the Peace Corps, CUSO remained a non-governmental organization, eventually heavily funded by the Canadian International Development Agency (CIDA), with the Canadian National Committee for UNESCO initially acting as its executive agency.[54] In its early years, university graduates spent two years in developing countries, usually as teachers in rural areas. Within a short time, however, it became clear that more technically trained volunteers were needed and recruiting shifted to those with professional skills.

On his arrival at the University of Alberta, Gordon became the senior faculty advisor for CUSO, and in 1964 he succeeded Francis Leddy as chairman of the national executive, a position he held until 1969. With typical efficiency and enthusiasm, he threw himself into the task of recruiting. The student newspaper, *Gateway*, wrote an article on CUSO in December 1964, requesting that applications be directed to Professor

J. King Gordon.[55] The article featured an early recruit, one of the university's own graduates in agriculture, who had written back to friends from the leper colony where he was serving in India. There is a degree of wry (though not facetious) humour in his account of the life of a volunteer. There was, first of all, the problem of weather and marauding animals: the monsoon rains got most of the maize, and two female elephants and a baby took the rest one night. Then, there was the problem of the labour force that knew nothing of agriculture and had an efficiency rate between 10 and 15 percent of that of a normal Indian worker. "But then," he concluded, "I couldn't work very hard either if I had no fingers to work with."

In spite of this testimonial, applications poured in, and President Johns wrote to Gordon: "regarding the CUSO program, I knew it had being going well and indeed I have heard some firsthand reports of students who have been serving under the program in remote parts of the world. I had not been aware, however, that we ranked so well among Canadian universities and Canadian cities."[56]

Gordon took a personal interest in the recruits. He inquired into the living conditions of the volunteers and, in cases when there was money to send families, what arrangements would be made for the children's education. Two students died in an accident, and he drove down to Lethbridge for the funerals.[57] He was delighted with a romance and marriage between two volunteers. Gordon's pride broke through his Scottish reserve after a visit to the orientation course in Quebec for forty French-speaking Canadians in preparation for their overseas assignment with CUSO. He reported to Pearson: "They were dedicated all right but in a down-to-earth unsentimental sort of way. They are going to do a great job for Canadians overseas and inject something new into their communities when they return."[58] He urged Pearson to pay them a visit, assuring him that he would get a thrill if he did.

There was no doubt that during these early years CUSO achieved considerable success. By 1969, when Gordon retired from his position as chairman of the national executive, it had nearly 1,200 workers in 45 countries, and in several countries from Zambia to Colombia it was the main Canadian presence. Moreover, unlike the Peace Corps, it had never been asked to leave a country.[59] Gordon wrote, "In a way, it was to keep myself part of that world that I had come to call my world that I became interested in CUSO in Alberta."[60] Gordon was enormously proud of these young volunteers; forty years earlier he might well have been one of them.

In the spring of 1966, Gordon travelled to Europe with a group from the University of Alberta with the apparent intention of making international connections that would be helpful in establishing a Centre of International Studies at the University of Alberta. While the proposed centre did not come to fruition, the failure of the project and the trip to Europe renewing his contacts in the international field seem to have awakened a restlessness in Gordon, and a desire to become active once again in a more immediate manner than his teaching responsibilities allowed. He had written Ruth from Geneva, "It's work, this trip ... but I feel like an old pro."[61]

Once again, the changes in Gordon's circumstances seemed to come about serendipitously, as a result of meeting a young political science professor from the University of Ottawa, Louis Sabourin, at one of the Banff Conferences. Sabourin told Gordon about a new program of training in administration at the University of Ottawa, designed especially for intermediate- and senior-level civil servants coming from French-speaking developing countries. The university planned to expand the program to establish a Centre for International Cooperation at the University of Ottawa that would be devoted to development assistance, and would extend the training program to Canadians who were about to take overseas assignments or work with national and international agencies dealing with development. Gordon responded with interest, and the result was an invitation to come to Ottawa as assistant director of the new Centre in the fall of 1967. He would also teach courses in international relations and Canadian foreign policy part-time at the university. Gordon would not, however, be involved in the actual teaching in the Centre as this was all to be done in French. The Centre for International Cooperation was officially inaugurated on 11 October 1968.[62]

On leaving Edmonton, Gordon left behind a bevy of new friends and contacts, and expressions of regret were forthcoming on both sides. There would be many trips back over the years for speaking engagements, seminars, and conferences, frequently under the auspices of the CIIA, the United Nations Association, or CUSO. There was family in Winnipeg and there would be summers at the lake. Charley had married Nancy Thain of Fort William in 1965 and they had settled in Brandon, where Charley had been hired by the *Brandon Sun* as its editorial page editor, becoming the paper's managing editor five years later. Their two children, John and Mary, became the joy of King and Ruth's lives much as their own children had been. Alison had left Queen's in 1965 and was working in London, England. Although his geographical location had changed once again, King remained tied to his western roots.

The move to Ottawa for King and Ruth in late August 1967, after a summer at the lake, promised a return to past interests. Happily, it also issued in another beginning. "When I left the United Nations, I felt that my traveling days had ended," he wrote in his 1987–88 reflection, "Twelfth Night." "Looking back ... I realize that they had just begun."[63] In 1967, the crèche on the mantle was still by no means complete.

If the move needed further evidence of its felicity, it was surely received when they moved into the Ignatieffs' vacant house at 55 Julianna Road, in Rockcliffe Park. The house, inspired by the Bauhaus movement in Germany, was designed and built for the Ignatieffs by Alison Ignatieff's cousin Hart Massey and reflected the Bauhaus values of simplified forms and unadorned functionalism. "Set in a wood, it looked like two finely detailed white cubes pushed together. It had a flat roof and broad expanses of windows."[64] Inside, the nine-foot high ceilings gave a sense of space, with beautifully proportioned rooms flowing from one to the other. King and Ruth loved their new home, and they lived there until 1979.

Julianna Road had developed in an avant-garde fashion, but some in the neighbourhood were more traditional. The eighty-year-old former Conservative prime minister, John Diefenbaker, walked his Cairn terrier McAndy each morning through the exclusive suburb of Rockcliffe Park. In the fall of 1978 the *Ottawa Citizen* reported that on one such morning a large black Lab (none other than the Gordons' elderly Simba) appeared and attempted to take on the terrier. Diefenbaker intervened. The lab jumped up, laid his paws on the former prime minister's chest, licked his face, and in the process of this unwelcome display of affection knocked the old gentleman off his feet. Gordon quickly caught up with his runaway dog, helped Diefenbaker up, apologized, and received assurances the ex-prime minister was fine. In the circumstances, no political views were exchanged. Dr P.B. Reynard (member of Parliament for Simcoe North) diagnosed a bad sprain, but Diefenbaker insisted on hobbling to his place in the House of Commons the next day.[65]

As part of his duties at the new institute, Gordon served on the Commission on Canadian Universities and International Development, and undertook a consultancy for CIDA, preparing a lengthy report on "The Briefing of Experts" for service abroad. In spite of an aching arthritic hip that caused him to limp, his last major trip on behalf of the Institute in the summer of 1972 found him in full travelling fettle. This time accompanied by Ruth and at the invitation of French economist Paul-Marc Henri, he attended meetings at the Organization for Economic Co-operation and Development (OECD) in Paris. Henri had been Gordon's colleague and friend at the UN where he had been chief of operations – overlapping with Gordon's tenure as chief information officer for technical assistance – of the United Nations Development Program and Special Fund. This invitation from Henri is an example of Gordon's numerous contacts already established that would now launch him into perhaps his happiest years of international activity. Travelling on to Malta, the Gordons also attended the third annual conference – Gordon's first – of the International Ocean Institute called *Pacem in Maribus*; and their itinerary included visits to international development centres as they made contacts for the Centre for International Co-operation. Typically, they worked in visits to friends, foremost a stopover with the Ignatieffs in Geneva, where George was now ambassador to the Permanent Mission of Canada to the European Office of the UN. Finally, in London and Oxford, they met with Malcolm MacDonald and Gilbert Ryle. Gordon was in his element once again.

Except for one short and chilly overnight visit in 1975 ("Oh, those cold English houses!"[66] he lamented to Ruth), this was the last time that Gordon saw his old friend Gilbert Ryle. On a trip to England in September 1976, he called Ryle at his home in Islip to say that he was coming to see him. Ryle's sister Mary answered the phone and explained regretfully that Gilbert had just left for a hiking trip in Yorkshire. King had missed him by ten minutes. Ryle died of a stroke while on the walking tour.

When King heard of his friend's death on his return to Ottawa, he spent the evening reading through a folder of old Oxford letters, reliving memories of their days at Queen's – long talks before the smoky fireplace in Gilbert's room; hiking through the German countryside and climbing the intellectual mountains of Kant and Hegel as they struggled to learn the German language. There is poignancy in these early letters from Ryle to his friend as King sets out for the mountains and forests of British Columbia and, presumably, the life of ordinary people. Referring to King and his Canadian friends, Ryle added later that same year, "You all brought something to the life of Oxford (and certainly of me) which makes it richer."[67]

In his reply to the invitation from Gilbert's nephew John Ryle to attend the memorial service, Gordon wrote: "I won't attempt to say how deeply

I feel Gilbert's loss. It brings to a close a friendship that extends over more than half a century – an active and ongoing friendship, rooted of course in the nostalgic past but constantly renewing itself in the living present."[68] A mutual friend sent Gordon a copy of the service, commenting, "The Cathedral was full. As you may imagine, had a bomb been dropped, Oxford, and indeed England, would have lost all its philosophers."[69]

During the years at the University of Ottawa, King and Ruth were saddened by the deaths of three other old friends: Frank Underhill, Reinhold Niebuhr, and Lester Pearson. Frank Underhill died in September 1971.[70] Joe Parkinson, a friend from LSR days, gave the eulogy, and Gordon conducted the service. In his remarks (surely as lengthy as the eulogy), King quoted the comment from an editorial of the previous day: "Let there be no wry charity in what is said of Frank Underhill. This was a man who never tried to wrap up his meaning, who despised insincerity, a dissenter by temperament, his conformity only to intellectual honesty."[71] He added that Underhill was a scholar who built a reputation for an antipathy to "the sacred cows who cluttered our green pastures, crowded our city streets and even strayed into our university corridors." Yet, Underhill was, like Gordon, a man of deep enduring convictions and beliefs, hopeful in spite of his sharp criticism. Although Underhill had moved back to the Liberal Party from those days of heady socialism that he shared with the LSR and CCF, he had not moved out of King's affection and deep regard.

After a lengthy illness, Reinhold Niebuhr died in Stockbridge, Massachusetts on 1 June 1972. For forty-three years, Gordon had been in intellectual conversation and bound in friendship with Niebuhr. After all the years, since that first dramatic meeting with Niebuhr in the Union Seminary common room in 1929, King still regarded his old teacher with profound respect and affection, and admired him as a profoundly courageous philosopher and prophet. Until the end of his own life, Gordon continued to quote Niebuhr: "Faith builds its citadels on the edge of the abyss of despair."[72]

King and Ruth heard of Pearson's death on 27 December 1972, while on their Christmas visit with Charley and Nancy in Brandon. The news did not come as a surprise, but it was received with "a very great personal sorrow."[73] King and Ruth had seen the Pearsons regularly during their mutual years of retirement in Ottawa, enjoying times together with other old friends – Graham Spry's seventieth birthday party, for instance. Pearson had given a humorous speech at Gordon's own seventieth party and the Pearsons had been invited to dinner, along with the Ignatieffs, at the Gordons' home earlier in December. As it turned out, Mike had been too tired to join the party, and his wife Maryon had come by herself.

The first volume of Pearson's memoirs, *Mike*, had come out in the fall of 1972, and in November Gordon wrote to him enthusiastically, "That's a great book you've written. I've been using every spare minute since I saw you on Sunday to read it and I've just finished." Gordon praised it as being an "inspiring testament" to him personally, and added, "in being honest, you have not forgotten how to be generous."[74] In his letter, Gordon ranged back in memory to the 1930s and recalled the gossip around LSR and CCF circles that "Mike Pearson if not one of us was very sympathetic"; and he recalled Mike's hockey career at Oxford (where he had first met Mike) and their shared passion for baseball. He recounted an occasion in the late autumn of 1947, when he was covering the UN for the CBC and Mike, as head of the Canadian delegation to the UN, was heavily involved in its debates. The World Series had just begun and Gordon listened in the pressroom as the radio reported the game inning by inning. He began to suspect that the Canadian representative might be experiencing a certain frustrated anxiety, locked in debate in the General Assembly. "A particularly dramatic play changed the fortunes of the game we were listening to so avidly and I thought it was important enough to type out a little note, find a messenger, and send it in to the head of the Canadian delegation." Gordon ended his letter with a tender formality typical of their generation: "If there is anything I can do to help in any way, I would count it a great privilege if you would call on me."

Gordon was asked to be an honorary pallbearer at the funeral and he walked with the cortège in the driving rain from the Parliament Buildings to Christ Church Cathedral, a forty-five-minute trek. His sister Mary's son, Peter Carver, who was standing in the silent crowd, later wrote a note to his uncle expressing his admiration for him, knowing the degree of pain that his hip was causing and to which he gave no quarter.[75] The procession was led by a twenty-five-man mounted RCMP escort, the Mounties in their fur hats and dark blue winter coats over their scarlet tunics, while a military band played the "Dead March" from *Saul*. Mike Pearson was buried in a country graveyard sheltered by spruce and birch, on a hillside looking out over the Gatineau River.

While Gordon himself moved ahead into a period of energetic activity, as is often the case for one who lives into a healthy old age, he celebrated anniversaries and mourned deaths with increasing frequency. In March 1973 it was a celebration, a conference on "The Social Gospel in

Canada," held at the University of Regina. Richard Allen, at that time associate professor of history at McMaster University, later edited the conference papers, which were published by The National Museum of Man Mercury Series as *The Social Gospel in Canada* (1975). Gordon's contribution, organized for him by Ruth, was entitled "A Christian Socialist in the 1930's," and it traced his own road to socialism as it had begun in his youth in his father's house in Winnipeg, through Oxford, Union, United College and his years as the travelling executive secretary of the Fellowship for a Christian Social Order. It was – typically – filled with charming anecdotes and humour, and it represents one of Gordon's first attempts to bring his own experience and intellectual growth together into a coherent narrative.

Again in 1983, Gordon found himself celebrating an event from those early years of socialist activity, this time the fiftieth anniversary of the Regina convention of the CCF in 1933. The celebratory dinner was held in the Regina fairgrounds on the Saturday evening of the New Democratic Party convention. As he and Ruth entered the hall, King discovered to his dismay that he knew no one. "I don't know what friends I expected to see. For days I had been immersed in memories of those meetings [fifty years ago] in the Regina city hall, the debates, the personalities, the excitement. It was all very real."[76] Then he spotted a frail, bright woman in a wheel chair: the daughter of J.S. Woodsworth and former MP, Grace MacInnis. She had been at the Regina meeting in 1933. Happily, they found themselves seated at the head table with two other old friends from 1933, Tommy Douglas and Stanley Knowles.

Only two years later, it was Tommy Douglas whom they mourned. Gordon's eulogy captured the essence of that first shared vision in Regina.[77] He recalled his own complete surprise in hearing about the CCF victory in Saskatchewan in the 1944 election, and admitted that as managing editor of *The Nation* in New York he had lost close touch with the party at that time. However, he had hopped on a plane for Regina, with the result that two August 1946 issues *The Nation* carried lengthy articles entitled, "Prairie Socialism." In his eulogy for Douglas, Gordon recalled Douglas asking his 1983 audience in Regina to remember their roots and the challenging vision shared in that hot prairie city in 1933. King closed his eulogy by quoting from William Blake's poem, "Jerusalem," that in its musical setting was a favourite hymn of Tommy Douglas: "I will not cease from mental flight / nor shall my sword sleep in my hand / 'Til we have built Jerusalem / in this our green and pleasant land."

Gordon had not strayed so very far from those roots.

The move to Ottawa marked the beginning of a period of remarkable activity for Gordon in the sphere of international development. Once in Ottawa, he was in daily contact with friends and contacts from earlier days and, through his teaching at the Center for International Cooperation at the University of Ottawa and his consultancies with CIDA, he quickly made new ones. It was natural therefore that, when he was offered a position in 1973 with the recently formed International Development Research Centre (IDRC), he accepted it.

With the rise to independent nationhood of former European colonies during the 1950s and 1960s, the landscape of international relations had changed dramatically. As a result, countries like Canada had developed large – and largely uncoordinated – aid programs. Prior to 1968, Canada's foreign aid had been managed and administered by a division of the Department of External Affairs, the External Aid Office (EAO).[78] In September 1968, the Trudeau government brought together the various budgets and aid programs of the EAO and created a new Crown corporation, CIDA. By 1984, CIDA had become a major bureaucratic organization, and Gordon described its creation as one of the most important decisions taken by the Canadian government in the field of international relations.[79]

In 1970, an Act of Parliament created CIDA's "research twin," the IDRC. IDRC's mandate was to support applied scientific research in developing countries on issues identified by local scientists and carried out in their own institutions – universities, government departments, and research centres. Initially, projects in agriculture, food production, and nutrition got the most money, with health services, economics, and education following closely behind. Ivan Head, IDRC's second president, described the Centre as "a superb example of what could be done when all political parties agreed," and judged its efforts as reflecting "the decency and purpose of the greatest proportion of Canadians, as well as by the majority of human kind."[80]

Gordon was surprised and pleased when David Hopper approached him with an invitation to join the Centre's staff in 1973. He accepted quickly and without the soul-searching that had bedevilled so many of his earlier decisions. He was given the title of Senior Advisor on University Relations and he reported to the vice-president, Dr Louis Berlinguet, Office of Canada and Donor Agency Relations, with whom he enjoyed a relationship of mutual respect and cordiality. Gordon was to advise the vice-president on IDRC relations with universities and other academic institutions in Canada and to develop a policy and program implementing cooperation between the Centre and the universities in research on development problems.

Carrying out this mandate involved establishing and strengthening personal contacts with the administration and faculty of Canadian universities committed to development research or other forms of cooperation with developing countries, such as the Economic Council of Canada and the North–South Institute. This goal would be accomplished through visits, correspondence, appointments by the universities of IDRC liaison personnel, and attendance at meetings of learned societies and the Association of Universities and Colleges in Canada (AUCC).

Gordon also had to become familiar with the broader scheme of cooperation and development research in other countries, most notably those in the United Kingdom and Western Europe. To achieve this end, he served as the IDRC representative at numerous international seminars that brought together the directors of development research institutes from both industrialized and developing countries. Gordon felt that a great value of these conferences was not only in the development of practical policies, but also in confirming the impression of a global academic community working for social justice, of which Canada was a part. This was a hefty – and at times rather undefined – assignment, to be invented as it went along. It demanded stamina, diplomacy, attention to detail, tolerance for meetings and committees, and a remarkable schedule of travel. Indefatigable as always, Gordon thrived. At the same time, he accepted consultancies with CIDA, often combining assignments on a single trip as the interests of the "research twins" overlapped.

Gordon had scarcely signed his contract with IDRC when he was launched into his new life of travel, finding himself on Air Canada en route to London, this time flying first class, which he described to Ruth as "comfortable, but in a kind of vulgar way."[81] He was less impressed when Air Canada lost his bag, leaving him to rinse out his drip-dry shirt in his hotel bathroom in preparation for his first meeting. It all ended well, however, when Air Canada assured him that his bag had been found – once again, in a metaphorical Moscow. With the same fresh curiosity and enjoyment of his Oxford days, Gordon used every spare minute as he travelled to revisit and explore his surroundings. In every city he walked, sending descriptions home to Ruth of how Geneva had changed since his student days, popping into art museums and cathedrals and finding unexpected pleasure in an organ recital. On one occasion he got a last-minute ticket to *Aida*. He toured historical sites, particularly pleased with the restoration of Europe from the war. He delighted in small restaurants like the "Mussel Man" on the beach at Scheveningen. Then too, there was the natural beauty of a full moon in Geneva or a country walk in England. In Africa he took time to visit the Serengeti, listing each animal he had seen, like Noah taking roll. "You must come soon," he wrote Ruth. "It would be fun if you were here."[82]

This first trip for IDRC included a conference in Castellabate, Italy, organized under the auspices of the International Ocean Institute, which discussed ocean management – a topic of increasing interest to Gordon and one that would continue to the end of his life. It was during this conference that he met Aurelio Peccei, the founder and president of the Club of Rome, a small society of professionals from the fields of diplomacy, industry, academia, and civil society who came together because of their common concern that population growth would overwhelm diminishing resources. These meetings illustrate how, as Gordon's interests in development became focused, he made contacts with their institutional expression, those organizations, overlapping and many-layered, that worked tirelessly to preserve the environment and distribute its resources fairly. He also attended several meetings of the North–South Round Table, a forum that met once a year to discuss problems concerning "problems and possibilities in the North-South equation."[83]

But it was in Belgrade, while attending still another conference, once again invited by his friend Paul-Marc Henri, that Gordon had a unique experience of the magic of travel; and where he found the four engaging corn-peasant dolls that joined his Twelfth Night crèche. On the ground floor of the hotel where the conference was being held, Gordon came across an exhibit of what was called "naïve art," consisting for the most part of crafts and paintings of peasants cultivating their fields with wooden plows drawn by white oxen. As the conference ended, a bus took the participants on a tour of the rural countryside where, only 30 km from the city, Gordon saw for himself the landscape of the naïve artists: "peasants working in their field, no machinery, white oxen everywhere, dragging loads along the roads, and helping out in the fields."[84]

Once again, his trip home took him through Geneva, Paris, London, and Sussex as he contacted friends and colleagues at research centres. By early January of 1974 he was on his way, as IDRC representative, to a conference of university vice-chancellors in Ibadan, Nigeria, this time stopping in London for a consultation with a Harley Street surgeon about his aching hip. (Later in the year, he had surgery in Canada and before long he was walking without a limp, preferring the odd tumble to the use of a cane.) His relentless pace continued: another trip to Malta to attend *Pacem in Maribus*; meetings in London with Sir Hugh Springer, president of the Association of Commonwealth Universities, and Arnold Smith, secretary-general of the Commonwealth Secretariat; a lunch with Isaiah Berlin, now president of the new Wolfson College at Oxford, a graduate school whose fifty-five Fellows were all scientists, making it an institution Gordon felt it particularly important for the IDRC to establish contact with.[85] He wound up his trip by joining over two hundred representatives from western European countries at the European Association for Third World Development meetings in Ghent. (Apart from the usefulness of making contacts, he found the discussion at these meetings a waste of time: rather superficial and "heavy on the subjunctive.") In this manner, networks formed on behalf of IDRC – "moving around on a highly stratospheric plane" as Gordon described it to Ruth. For Gordon, with his easy charm, confidence, and genuine interest in people and in the causes he represented, "networking" was still his meat and drink.

Gordon was always happy for the opportunity to revisit Africa. In 1975 he had been appointed chairman of a small committee known as the Evaluation Group of UN Educational and Training Programs for Southern Africa. UNETPSA had grown out of the UN involvement in decolonization during the 1960s. Under this program, nearly 12,000 young people, mostly refugees, from Southern Rhodesia, Mozambique, Angola, Guina-Bissau, Namibia, and South Africa, had received education and technical training at universities throughout the world. In addition to its concern to recognize human rights, a major goal of the program was to help provide trained personnel for the newly independent states once the European bureaucracies had left.

King wrote to Ruth from Nairobi: "The trip is proving fascinating and it's exciting being in Africa again."[86] The group flew from Addis Ababa over the Sahara on a daytime flight, and he was awed by the vastness of the desert and the shifting patterns of light across its surface. In Addis, he revelled in the strong sun and the clear, cool nights, listening to the hyenas, the wild dogs, and the lions from the comfort of his bed. Once again he met old friends, delighted particularly in meeting Swedes who knew Arne Rubin of the crocodile-hunting trip on the Awash River. The UN High Commissioner for Refugees drove him out to the lake where he had picnicked years earlier with Dick and Helen Niehoff. But even as he breathed deeply of the clear African air, he was once again stunned by the poverty of village life. He mused sadly in a letter to Ruth on whether, if one were to come back again in fifty years, one would find it still unchanged.

In his last letter to Ruth from Africa, written from Dar El Salaam on the Indian Ocean, Gordon had the feeling that Somerset Maughan was looking over his shoulder as he struggled with the claustrophobic humid heat. "After Nairobi and Luksaka, Dar is really Africa – like when you move from Beirut to Damascus ... this whole trip has been fascinating and I certainly know much more about East Africa than I did before."[87]

While at the IDRC, it was Gordon's habit to file a monthly report chronicling his activities. His report for April 1980, a month he did not travel abroad, gives one a fair idea of his day-to-day life at the Centre. As representative of IDRC he was involved in the following activities: UNESCO National Commission, Annual Meeting; University of Guelph Symposium; Canadian Association of University Research Administrators annual meeting; Institute for Environmental Studies, University of Toronto Seminar; UN Institute for Training and Research (UNITAR), Seminar on Development Strategies for the 1980s, Carleton University. His report on work as liaison with Canadian Universities and other institutions shows a similarly full calendar. His report was followed later in the year by his attendance at *Pacem X* in Slovenia, and a UNESCO seminar in Paris. His agenda is all the more impressive when one takes into account that Gordon was now in his eightieth year.

In 1979 the Ignatieffs finally claimed their house in Rockcliffe, and King and Ruth moved to their last home together on Fairlawn Avenue on the west side of Ottawa. It was more modest than most of their previous houses, but it suited them perfectly, made charming by all the mementos of their travels, their paintings, books, and King's piles of papers. Very shortly, Gordon was on a first-name basis with waiters, clerks, and bank tellers (or, at least, he addressed them all by their first names), and he and Ruth enjoyed the ethnic foods available at neighbourhood restaurants. They were closer to Charley and Nancy, who now lived in Ottawa, and they revelled in the company and accomplishments of their grandchildren, John and Mary. There was room in the small garden for King to dig and plant, his specialty being tulips.

The move to Fairlawn coincided with the winding down of Gordon's consultancy with IDRC. In 1977, David Hopper resigned his position as president of IDRC to join the World Bank as a vice-president. He was replaced in March 1978, by Ivan Head, the brilliant international law professor who had been Pierre Trudeau's foreign policy advisor. Gordon and Ivan Head had first worked together back in the days of the Banff

Conferences, at that time both on the faculty of the University of Alberta in Edmonton. They had met socially over the years and shared many interests. Head later described Gordon as "a close friend for many years, a person whom I greatly admired."[88] In February, once it had been announced that Head would be the new president of IDRC, he penned a P.S. on a letter to Gordon from the prime minister's office, "and many thanks for the pleasant lunch. I am delighted that the old partnership has been revived, and count heavily – as I always have – on your wise counsel. I."[89] Head's wife Anne, his executive secretary for many years, recalled Gordon's courtly formality in the IDRC office, despite the informality of their friendship.[90]

Nevertheless, Gordon was deeply disappointed when, in November of 1979, Head made the decision to disband the Office of Canada and Donor Agency Relations headed by Louis Berlinguet. In a report to Berlinguet, Gordon protested: "I would suggest that some serious rethinking might be directed to the decision at this strategically and politically critical moment to disband the Office which has been largely responsible for [the above mentioned] positive developments and which has a special competence to ensure that the present momentum continue with the greater involvement of Canadian science and technology in international cooperation and development."[91]

Head's decision stood, however. At Christmas, King wrote to Marjorie in Australia: "I approach the New Year with some uncertainty. I am not too happy with the developments at the IDRC, but will probably stay on for a few months. But with the abolition of the section with which I have been associated, it will be more difficult."[92] His contract continued through June, after which he acted as a consultant for both IDRC and CIDA on an ad hoc basis. In July he tidied up his office and left a note for Ivan Head, who was on vacation, assuring him that he would be "glad to be of any service to whoever is in charge of the new Canadian universities program."[93] Then King left for the summer at Birkencraig.

Gordon turned eighty that December, but if there was any slowing down as he grew into old age, it was barely perceptible. Two commitments – one could almost say callings – continued to occupy him until the end of his life nearly ten years later: the Law of the Sea (*Pacem in Maribus)*, and the Group of 78.

18

The Last Decade

Gordon's interest in a UN Law of the Sea flowed naturally out of his concern for the preservation of the oceans and his commitment to an equitable distribution of seabed resources. These issues first came to prominence at the UN in November 1967 when Arvid Pardo, Malta's representative to the United Nations, delivered an impassioned speech to the General Assembly. Dr Pardo focused on the vast riches hidden on the deep floor of the world's oceans, beyond the sovereignty of any nation, which the technological revolution was rapidly making accessible to exploration, comparing the impending race to carve up this no man's land of resources to the sectioning of the African continent by the colonial powers in 1885 at the Congress of Berlin. Describing how the old law of the sea based on sovereignty of coastal waters and on freedom of the seas had become outmoded, Pardo argued that the resources of the seabed beyond the limits of national jurisdiction should be regarded as the common heritage of mankind.

Gordon's involvement in this new venture began early in 1971 with a phone call from his friend, the socialist peer Lord Peter Ritchie-Calder of Balmashanner, an author, journalist, and academic. They had first met in the Congo in 1960 and Ritchie-Calder was active in many of the same humanist causes. By the time of the phone call, Gordon was already familiar with the international conference called in Malta in 1970 to discuss, at a nongovernmental level, the issues raised by Dr Pardo. This conference was called *Pacem in Maribus* (an adaptation, perhaps, of Pope John XXIII's 1963 encyclical, *Pacem in Terris*) and it turned out to be the first of a long series of annual meetings called convocations. It soon became apparent that something more basic than an annual conference was needed, and in 1972 the International Ocean Institute (IOI) was founded with the cooperation of the University of Malta and the United Nations Development Program.[1] The IOI was structured around two major responsibilities: organizing the annual *Pacem in Maribus* convocations and running research programs and providing technical training seminars focusing on particular projects. The results of these research programs formed the basis for discussion at the annual conferences. Over the years, many of the resolutions and proposals first discussed at *Pacem in Maribus* subsequently found their way into the *United Nations Convention on the Law of the Sea* (1982), which became one of the most comprehensive instruments of international law.[2] At its founding meeting, Gordon was named to the planning council of the IOI, a broadly representative group of twenty-four members that included marine scientists and oceanographers, economists, and international lawyers, who later played leading roles in the United Nations Conference on the Law of the Sea (convened in 1973). Gordon described his participation in the IOI as "a very exciting association that lasted for nearly eighteen years."[3]

Ritchie-Calder's aim was to have Canada and Canadians involved in these yearly convocations, and he asked Gordon if he could arrange a meeting with Lester Pearson, who had recently completed his study on international development for the World Bank, *Partners in Development*. Pearson was also at that time chairman of the board of the newly established IDRC. It was an interesting lunch that Gordon arranged as Ritchie-Calder, ever the propagandist, tried to persuade Pearson to promise IDRC support for *Pacem*. Pearson was interested, but doubtful that ocean management could be included on the agenda of the new Centre. However, he told Ritchie-Calder that he would be happy to talk with Elizabeth Mann Borgese, the chairwoman of *Pacem in Maribus*, should she come to Ottawa.

Borgese did, in fact, come to Ottawa within a month of Gordon's lunch with Pearson and Ritchie-Calder. Pearson invited her to lunch along with the minister of external affairs, Paul Martin, and Gordon. It was a good meeting with considerable interest shared in lively conversation; but with the IDRC's established priorities, Pearson was still doubtful of direct support. However, he suggested, why not send Gordon to a *Pacem* convocation as a consultant for the Centre? The following April, Gordon received an invitation to attend the Third Convocation of *Pacem in Maribus* to be held in Malta in late June. Between 1972 and 1987, Gordon attended twelve *Pacem* convocations at various sites around the world: Malta, Japan, Algeria, Mexico, Cameroon, Slovenia, and Canada. He remained a member of the IOI Planning Committee until his death, and from 1984 he was also a member of its board of governors. As the IOI planning committee met in the months preceding each annual *Pacem* meeting, this meant a considerable amount of travel for Gordon, particularly when combined with his other international responsibilities. It was also an opportunity to meet new acquaintances and to see old friends, keeping the network alive.

Accompanied by Ruth, Gordon left in mid-June 1972 for the first IOI meeting in Castellabate, an old seaside fishing village on the southwestern coast of Italy. Before proceeding to Malta for *Pacem in Maribus III*, he attended a meeting of the Club of Rome. Gordon attended several meetings of the Club of Rome, usually in collaboration with the IOI, and over the years he developed deep admiration and respect for its founder, Aurelio Peccei.[4]

But undoubtedly, the high point of this trip – both professionally and aesthetically – was the *Pacem* convocation and the enchanting beauty of Malta. Gordon wrote: "*Pacem in Maribus* never became academic or purely theoretical. There was the ocean all around. In the little harbors the painted fishing boats lay at anchor. Clear blue water rolled over the beaches."[5] Sitting with Arvid Pardo over a cup of bitter black caffé on the terrace of the Corinthian Hotel, he felt lucky to be invited.

Particular convocations of *Pacem in Maribus* stood out in Gordon's mind, some because of his interest in the topics discussed, and others perhaps because of their exotic locations. *Pacem VI*, which met in Okinawa in October 1975, stood out for both reasons. Once again, Gordon met with his colleagues Avrid Pardo, Elisabeth Mann Borgese, Ritchie-Calder, and Aurelio Peccei; but what struck him as remarkable about this non-governmental conference was the number of governmental delegates in attendance. Some of these statesmen had served as their countries' representatives on committees of the UN Law of the Sea Conference, including those from Cameroon, El Salvador, Bulgaria, Canada, Jamaica, Tanzania, Indonesia, and Turkey. Lord Hugh Caradon, the former British ambassador to the UN, was there, as were several Japanese policy makers.

The Okinawa meeting was the first *Pacem* convocation held away from its home base in the International Ocean Institute at the University of Malta. The site was chosen because of its proximity to Expo 75, an extraordinary international exhibition in Okinawa dealing with all aspects of ocean science, conservation, and management with more than thirty nations, including Canada, participating. Gordon described Expo 75 as perhaps less exciting than a big world's fair, but dramatic nevertheless in its depiction of human dependency on the sea, and the threat that modern civilization posed to this source of human survival.[6] At the invitation of their Japanese hosts, the participants took a glass-bottomed boat from a pier close to an aluminum pyramid housing a 30-meter chunk of Arctic ice, to the Aquapolis, a huge floating city that rode high on its sixteen cylindrical columns. They crossed a small footbridge onto the Aquapolis itself for a reception and a tour of what was intended as a vision of the future: a self-contained habitat, generating its own power, distilling its own water supply, processing its own waste, and providing comfortable quarters for its staff of forty. Gordon wrote, "One day we shall be moving out to sea from our overcrowded land-based world. And the Aquapolis will be the prototype."[7]

The *Pacem* discussions on this occasion concentrated on early drafts of the Law of the Sea, which to the participants seemed to veer away from the concept of the sea as the common heritage of humankind toward a carving up of the seabed among a small number of wealthy coastal states. This would give these large states effective jurisdiction over "ocean space" up to 200 miles (320 km) offshore, allowing them to claim exclusive economic rights over the resources of the sea and the seabed.[8] In addition, for states with a continental shelf, similar rights might extend for several hundred kilometers beyond the 200-mile limit, depending on continental submarine topography and interpretations of continental margins.[9] With some concern, Gordon wrote that Canada, which had been one of the earliest campaigners for the common heritage principle, would now – with its huge continental shelves – find itself numbered as one of the greediest of the shelf countries; and he saw this to be at variance with Prime Minister Pierre Trudeau's recent speech at Mansion House in London in which he talked of dividing up Canada's rich resources with the developing world.[10] Within a decade, however, after a plethora of meetings and negotiations among both governmental and non-governmental bodies, these issues were resolved by the United Nations Convention on the Law of the Sea (1982);[11] and within a few years of Gordon's death, the Convention's rules had gained near-universal acceptance, governing all activities in the oceans and the use of their resources.[12]

Gordon found reason for hope, as well as alarm, in the discussions at the convocation. For him, this optimism was captured in the stance of his new friend, Aurelio Peccei. On the return trip from the Aquapolis to the mainland in the glass-bottomed boat, Gordon saw Peccei standing by the rail, looking thoughtfully toward the Aquapolis shining brilliant in the setting sun. Gordon snapped his camera and revisited the photograph many times over the years. In it, there is a half-smile on his friend's face. A hopeful omen.[13]

The 101 Planning Committee meeting in Malta in December 1978 provided a nostalgic moment for Gordon. In his letter to Ruth, he wrote, "We ate at the restaurant where we ate in 1973." It had been a good meeting, he told her, and he reminded her of the beauty of Malta: "You forget about the shape and color of the houses and the twisting narrow streets and the marvelous light."[14] He had scarcely returned home when he left once again for Yaounde, Cameroon, where the *Pacem in Maribus IX* Convocation met in January 1979. He always welcomed a trip to Africa. "It's Africa, all right," he wrote. "Not just the temperature – 25 degrees [Celsius] after the minus 25 degrees in Ottawa last Friday – but everything about it."[15] It was the slow pace, the friendliness, the confusion and the inefficiency, the "wonderful mixture of strong arm assertion of rights and the utter nonchalance," that captivated him. One had to remember that this was Africa and things would fall in place eventually if one had enough patience, he explained. Africa's charm diminished and his patience was sorely tried, however, by missing vouchers, taxi drivers who did not turn up, altered plane schedules, and missing luggage or, perhaps even more frustrating, luggage being searched as the passengers stood on the tarmac in the hot sun.

Gordon attended more 101 Planning Committee meetings and *Pacem in Maribus* convocations around the world, and his commitment to fair use of the resources of the sea and its protection from exploitation never flagged. In 1979, he wrote that in looking back over the past three decades of close contact with a number of international, as well as national, non-governmental organizations concerned with international cooperation and development, none surpassed the International Ocean Institute in effectiveness, realistic understanding, and commitment.[16] Now nearly eighty, however, Gordon increasingly focused his energy on Canadian foreign policy, concentrating his efforts in The Group of 78.

The spirit in which Gordon pursued his interest in Canada's foreign policy is nicely captured in a comment by Michael Oliver, president of Carleton University, during a lunchtime conversation with Ronald Macdonald in 1976. As Macdonald recounted in a letter to the author, Oliver remarked:

> When King Gordon returned to Canada from the United States he drew up a list of 8–10 people of influence, mostly leaders in the

> political parties and in the bureaucracy, people he knew and who knew him and who, in his opinion, had influence in Ottawa. Whenever anything started to go wrong within the country or at the international level, which of course happened frequently, King would sit down and telephone each of the people on his list. Since he was so well known he was always put through right away. His opening remark was, "Now just listen, this is the situation." He would then give a little speech and his closing remark would be, "Now what are you going to do about it?"

Macdonald added: "Michael Oliver and I both feel this brief account encapsulates a very great deal about King Gordon."[17] Indeed it does.

Gordon had arrived back in Canada during a period of transition in government policy and a rethinking of Canada's status and identity in the postwar world. The prevailing paradigm of Canadian foreign policy that greeted him on his arrival was that of Canada as a "middle power" – the topic of the 1965 Banff Conference. This powerful metaphor for Canadian foreign policy had come into use during what John Holmes has called "the remarkably swift transition from the status of a wartime junior partner in 1945 to that of a sure-footed middle power with an acknowledged and applauded role in world affairs ten years later."[18] Canada had emerged from the war as the third strongest of the western countries, and was faced with the problem – along with other countries of middle stature such as Australia, Sweden, and Brazil – of finding a place at the international table as "something less than major and something more than minor powers."[19] Lester Pearson, as Prime Minister St Laurent's secretary of state for external affairs, had strengthened Canada's middle-power status with his strong support of the UN and NATO and other international bodies such as the Commonwealth; and Canada's new role was also encouraged by a growing sense of national pride as the country entered the period of unparalleled national expansion that followed the war. Pearson's reputation within the international community also positioned Canada as an actor on the world stage, as did the sophistication of Canadian diplomats. Historian Robert Bothwell points out that although these diplomats might not, understandably, prevail in international discussions in which the great powers were particularly invested, nevertheless, because of their prodigious preparation and competence, they in fact exercised an influence commensurate with their contribution rather than their size.[20] In this context, Canada began to develop a reputation as a mediator, and by the time of Pearson's famous intervention in the Suez Crisis in 1956 Canada had already played major mediatory roles in Palestine, Indonesia, and Indochina, leading some Canadian commentators to note that the country was becoming something of a "busybody."[21]

The metaphor was also enthusiastically embraced by Canadians, following Canada's participation in the discussions leading up to the founding of the United Nations at the San Francisco Conference in 1945; and part of this ready acceptance lay in its portrayal of the country as a good international citizen, associated with an active foreign policy, a moderate tone, a preference for multilateral solutions, and mediatory roles. Historian Adam Chapnick refers to the strong role of Canadian politicians, academics, and journalists in popularizing the image as they "spoke and wrote wistfully of their country's new position as a middle power leader," evidence of Canada's new, elevated position in the world.[22] In this, they had a ready ally in Lester Pearson himself who, in a 1944 External Affairs memo,[23] became the first Canadian official to formally refer to Canada as a "middle power." His skill as a communicator and his growing reputation as a diplomat also added ballast to the new image: he (along with others of the Canadian delegation) gave regular explanations of proceedings to the press, and leading journalists of the time "all shared an affection and respect bordering on hero worship for Lester Pearson."[24] Finally, there was the moral force of Pearson's idealism and vision of Canada. As his biographer, John English, writes of him at this time, "Mike's concerns had become Canada's";[25] and by the time King Gordon returned to Canada in 1962, the image of itself as a middle power was well-established in the Canadian psyche.

But the story was not over. History was not only being made, it was being interpreted into a narrative of middle power.[26] John Holmes raised an early voice of caution concerning the eager acceptance of the middle-power metaphor at the 1965 Banff Conference when he said, "I think we must look at the future of our foreign policy with hard realism, but without cynicism. We cannot live by old slogans."[27] Ten years later, he wrote that the idea of such a vocation reinforced Canadian confidence in diplomacy and served a purpose, "until it became over-stuffed."[28] He explained that while for some the mediation implied by the metaphor failed to defend the national interest with sufficient vigour, for others it suggested an over-eagerness to solicit mediatory business for Canada through peacekeeping, that "quintessence of the middle role."

Gordon, however, continued to defend Pearson's internationalism and, in an interview in 1976, he rejected what he called the simplistic and increasingly popular interpretation of Canada's middle-power status as an inflated understanding of its own role in the world as a "helper–fixer" (a step up, perhaps, from "busybody"), when in fact its prominence was merely a function of the power vacuum following the Second World War.[29] It was logical, even natural, that Gordon would find the middle-role interpretation appealing. To begin with, he was not a scholar of Canadian foreign policy, as John Holmes was, and he had not been privy to the debates among the Canadian delegation at the Dumbarton Oaks and San Francisco conferences. Moreover, having recently returned from twelve years in the field, with experience of peacekeeping in both the Middle East and the Congo, he was fully committed to Pearson's internationalism and what could be accomplished by the participation of the smaller nations. The skill and commitment that he saw among Canada's diplomats and peacekeepers fit his opinion of the decency and generous spirit of Canadians – an understanding of the Canadian character forged by his own experience during his years of ministry and travel in Canada during the 1920s and 1930s. Finally, of course, there was his deep admiration for Lester Pearson and his enduring vision.

As the Trudeau administration replaced that of Lester Pearson in 1968, the dominant metaphor of Canada as a "middle power" was replaced with the image of Canada as an "actor" on the world stage with strategic national interests in its relationship with other nations. On becoming prime minister, Pierre Trudeau fulsomely praised what he called the "extraordinary" contributions made by Canada in the shaping of the peace since the Second World War, and the "Canadian vision of a decent, fair, and stable international community expressed by brilliant, competent public servants of an earlier generation."[30] But he argued that circumstances in international relations had changed drastically and that it was time to take a fresh look at Canada's foreign policy. In June 1968, in his new capacity as prime minister (but before his first election), Trudeau used his convocation address on receiving an honorary degree from the University of Alberta to signal a shift in policy. The speech, devoted to North–South issues, carried the subtext that assistance to developing countries was not charity, but in Canada's own long-term interests, and that Canadians must never forget that they were beneficiaries as well as benefactors. "If at the same time our consciences – our humanitarian instincts – are served, as they are and should be, then so much the better."[31] Trudeau argued that this was a double mandate: a moral obligation to cooperate with the developing nations in their pursuit for equity, and at the same time an obligation to reach this goal through programs that would also realize Canada's national interests. For too long, Canada's role as a "helper-fixer" had ignored urgent issues at home, such as its own economic challenges and the French-English question, and he concluded that Canada's involvement in international affairs and its own national interests must be congruent as, under Pearson, they had not been.[32]

The "new look" at foreign policy also took form in the government's White Paper of 1970, "International Development: Foreign Policy for Canadians," which outlined the policies that the government intended to adopt in the field of development assistance; and it raised the question of how assistance to the less-developed nations could be expected to serve Canada's interest – apart from developing the moral character of its citizens. The White Paper answered the question by proposing that the government provide an initial source of financing for exporting goods and services and help support expansion of Canadian commercial interest overseas. At the same time, successful economic development in the less-advantaged countries would benefit world trade as a whole: Trudeau applied the metaphor "a rising tide floats all boats."[33] Critics, however, quickly identified a shift from Pearson's policies and by implication a rejection of the helper-fixer model as suggesting that national interest took precedence over social justice, "the past being abandoned for a strange new god of national interest," as historians J.L. Granatstein and Robert Bothwell put it.[34]

Although Gordon had been favourably impressed by Trudeau's 1968 speech at the University of Alberta, he was skeptical about the new direction presaged by the White Paper, and he leapt to Pearson's defence. He summarized his misgivings in his concluding lecture in international relations at the University of Ottawa in April 1973. His criticism was not aimed primarily at the new reorganization of the aid programs, with Trudeau's creation of CIDA and the IDRC – in fact, he was in the process of moving to the IDRC and he had already represented the IDRC at CIDA conferences – but at the "new look's" decreased emphasis on multilateral bodies such as NATO, the UN, and the Commonwealth.[35] Out of his own experience, as well as his loyalty to Pearson, Gordon told his students that formerly, when Canada played a role not only in providing peacekeeping forces but also in formulating the new concept of peacekeeping, Canada had been involved in significant international diplomacy. This was not the "helper-fixer" role that its critics decried, but a realistic recognition that Canada's own security depended on the prevention of world war. Canada might have little to offer in the way of troops for

NATO, but as a voice in international decision-making, Canada had substantial influence.[36]

With the new policy outlined in the White Paper, Gordon argued, Canada had deliberately decided to base its policy on a narrowly defined national interest with a concern for world peace on the periphery of its priorities. The *Foreign Policy Review* had asserted that future conflicts would more likely have their roots in subversion and insurgency not easily resolved through the use of international peacekeeping forces. Addressing his students, Gordon referred to those days "when it was more than a pious gesture to state that support of the United Nations was the central concern of Canadian foreign policy." The White Paper suggested to him that in the future, foreign policy would be more closely related to domestic issues – economic growth, national sovereignty, quality of life, natural environment – and less committed to working for peace and security and social justice abroad. Gordon feared that Trudeau was now abandoning the idealism of his 1968 speech in Alberta in which he had nailed his colours to the mast in saying that aid, though necessary, was only an intermediate step, and that trade and self-reliance must be the essential goal so that developing countries could become independent of powerful industrialized states.

In Gordon's view, Trudeau further muddied the waters in a speech he delivered in March 1975, when the Lord Mayor of London conferred upon him the Freedom of the City of London. In addressing the dignitaries assembled in the Mansion House, it seemed to him, Trudeau was circling back to the idealism of the Alberta speech when he said, "Now, possibly as never before, moral principle has become the defining element in effective policy."[37] It was time, Trudeau continued, to embrace a global ethic that would repair the imbalance in basic human conditions: access to health care, a nutritious diet, shelter, and education.

As Gordon threaded his way through Trudeau's foreign policy speeches and statements, he found himself beguiled, perplexed, and finally, in many ways, disenchanted. In this, he was apparently not alone.[38] But was Gordon's own optimism *cum* utopianism out of step with the political and economic realities of Canada's position at this time? Had Canada, in fact, passed the point of being able to play a middle power, "helper-fixer" role when, as Trudeau frequently declared (his Mansion House speech notwithstanding), it was now time for Canada to attend to its own interests? Bothwell presents the view that Trudeau and his foreign policy advisor, Ivan Head, understood that there would be a cost to Canada of an effective program of development assistance: politically, the country faced a crisis over Quebec and the Constitution; and economically, with prosperity waning, Canada found itself coping with rising oil prices and stagnation. Canadians were becoming increasingly convinced that "charity began at home." In both cases it was, as Trudeau put it, time for Canada to heal itself.[39]

But Gordon was not oblivious to political and economic realities and their implications for foreign policy; and by the following year it was clear that his initial optimism following the Mansion House speech had been tempered. In a September 1976 article,[40] he criticized the Canadian government's positions and actions at the United Nations as being out of step with the growing consensus within the General Assembly and UN conferences calling for the establishment of a new international economic order; and he asserted that these policies reflected strong domestic political and economic pressures, ignoring wider international implications and lacking the principles that had characterized the Pearsonian tradition. Perhaps, he concluded rather sadly, the expression of a grand design just takes time; but his enthusiasm had clearly been curbed by the trajectory of Trudeau's policies, and by the emerging political realities and changing nature of politics within Canada.

And so, the currents of hope and caution alternated and at times conflated in Gordon's thinking as he attempted to sort out what appeared to him to be the conflicting messages of Trudeau's foreign policy. In speeches like that delivered at the Mansion House, Gordon felt there was nothing that Pearson had ever said in terms of Canada's global frame of reference that wasn't touched upon and amplified by Trudeau. And yet, Gordon told Ernest Dick in 1976, when it came to the specifics of policy, "it's almost as if a different crowd takes over. It's almost as if the Department of Industry and Commerce moves in and says no, you can't modify your trade policy because that's going to affect the textile industry in Drummondville."[41] Shortly after this interview, Gordon told an audience at the Dalhousie Conference on Canadian Foreign Policy that, "It would almost appear as if the global issues, given high priority by the prime minister and other cabinet spokesmen, are somehow beyond the parameters of the practical policy-makers who act in terms of traditional patterns and more immediate political pressures."[42] And he concluded the 1976 interview by saying, "In case after case our immediate policy runs counter to our declaratory policy. I don't think there was the same inconsistency in the Pearson period."

Gordon was left, finally, unresolved, but not alienated. Throughout the duration of Trudeau's four governments, Gordon and Trudeau remained on terms of mutual respect, admiration, and cordiality, as an exchange of letters begun in late 1974 and early 1975 demonstrates. Their initial form of address, "Dear Mr Trudeau" and "Dear Mr Gordon," quickly changed to "Dear Pierre," and "Dear King," and many of the letters to Gordon had PERSONAL AND CONFIDENTIAL above the salutation.

One of the first subjects of their correspondence concerned the government's decision to push the sale of CANDU reactors to both Asian and Latin American countries. These pressurized heavy water reactors, developed by Atomic Energy of Canada Ltd in the late 1950s and early 1960s, were used in nuclear power plants to produce nuclear power from nuclear fuel. As he launched this new engagement with Trudeau, Gordon opened his letter by confessing that he was frightened about the expansion of nuclear power before it was absolutely necessary and before all research efforts to develop alternative sources of energy, including fusion, had been exhausted. It seemed to Gordon that the danger of the spread of nuclear weapons and, in consequence, of nuclear war, came specifically from those states that, in refusing to sign and ratify the UN Non-Proliferation Treaty, were keeping their options open to develop a nuclear bomb. He then put the question directly: why had the Canadian government not been faithful to the spirit of the Treaty and refused to sell CANDU reactors – with their technological potential for producing nuclear weapons – to states that had not signed and ratified it?

Trudeau's reply, remarkably prompt when one considers the agenda of a prime minister, opened by assuring Gordon: "We enter this discussion on common ground." He continued with "an argument of equal force," that it was countries like Canada that possessed advanced technology that must share this technology with the developing world if those nations were to raise the living standards of their own people. Ideally, those countries, particularly India (which had conducted its first nuclear explosion earlier that year using CANDU reactor technology supplied by Canada), would adhere to and eventually ratify the Non-Proliferation Treaty; but in its present form, Trudeau thought this was unlikely. In the meantime, the International Atomic Energy Agency and the involvement in its work by a number of countries, including India, was sometimes overlooked in the efforts to promote the Non-Proliferation Treaty.[43]

But it was not only the CANDU reactors that were bothering Gordon. Budget cutbacks the government felt it must make at the expense of international programs, Canada's commercial whaling operations that supported a watered-down moratorium on a depleted stock, and unresolved tension between Canada and Europe in areas of trade and defence, also weighed heavily on his mind.[44] As a result, in the early spring of 1980 Murray Thomson received one of Gordon's something-must-be-done-about-it phone calls. Thomson described the conversation: "King was angry, perturbed, agitated – all words to describe King at his best – concerning the drift of Canadian foreign policy at a time when super power relations were deteriorating. The Soviets had just gone into Afghanistan, and NATO embarked on its two-track policy, placing Pershing IIs and Cruise missiles in Europe. Canada went along meekly with the US, as it has done so often in recent years."[45]

Gordon was alarmed and wanted to get a few people together immediately. In Thomson's recollection, a small group including himself, Gordon, and MP Andrew Brewin, and his wife Peggy, met in downtown Ottawa, their only decision being to meet again and to draft a statement on foreign policy to be sent to the prime minister. Robert McClure, former moderator of the United Church, joined them at the second meeting, which was held at the Brewins' home. In November 1981, the statement drafted by this little committee, *Canadian Foreign Policy in the 80s*, was sent to Prime Minister Trudeau, signed by seventy-eight Canadians, hence the name Group of 78. The founding members who signed the original statement comprised, as Thomson described them, "the illustrious and wise," as well as those with sympathetic views – hopefully also not lacking in wisdom – all of whom had access to mass constituencies. They included church leaders, both Protestant and Catholic; members of academia; political leaders; artists and writers; and many of King's old friends who had international connections. The list exemplified a wide range of intellectual gifts, skills, and accomplishments, and a dedication to social justice. It also illustrated the reach of Gordon's network of connections among the "illustrious and wise."

Canadian Foreign Policy in the 80s set out three inter-related objectives: removing the threat of nuclear war; mobilizing world resources to achieve a more equitable internal order and bring an end to the crushing poverty the Third World; and strengthening and reforming the United Nations and other global institutions to bring about a peaceful settlement of disputes, foster international cooperation, promote the growth of world law and the protection of basic human rights.[46] Thus began the long conversation between the Group of 78 and the Canadian government.

Murray Thomson complained that the Group waited for weeks for a reply to their initial statement to Trudeau in November 1981. But considering the demands on the prime minister's time, the delay does not strike one as unseemly, as Trudeau wrote to Andrew Brewin addressing its critique and proposals on 27 December. The following April, Trudeau wrote to Gordon on two of the issues that had particularly concerned Gordon, the inward-looking direction of the government's foreign policy, and the prime minister's position on disarmament and arms control. Trudeau wrote: "First, you suggest that, by insisting that Canadian foreign policy address the needs of Canada and Canadians, I am arguing for a narrow, selfish policy directed to the pursuit of 'isolated and insulated interests which can best be served even if the rest of the world goes to pot.'"[47] Trudeau attempted to refute this accusation by using the long and difficult negotiations on the Law of the Sea, where the issue of national claims to the continental shelves particularly concerned Canada's economic interests, even as they conflicted with Canada's principles of fair international access to the wealth of the seabed; and he appealed to the obvious fact that there was a direct link between the establishment of a stable and just international order and the peace and prosperity of Canada. It is unlikely that this rather vague defence and appeal to truism would have satisfied Gordon, as in cases like this, "the devil was in the details." Still, it was a courteous response that assured Gordon that Trudeau was aware of the narrow line he was walking and that in this instance, as in so many others, they entered the discussion "on common ground."

As to Gordon's second concern alleging a conflict between Canada's commitment to a strong NATO alliance and its dedication to arms control and disarmament, Trudeau once again claimed to see no contradiction in the two, arguing that a strong Western deterrent was justified on the grounds of the threat from the Warsaw Pact and as a precondition for bringing the Soviet Union to the negotiating table on arms control. It was this security through membership in NATO and Canada's proximity to the United States, he continued, that in fact enabled Canada to speak credibly and forcefully on the issues of disarmament and arms control. Perhaps in an allusion to middle-power aspirations, he pointed out that while Canada must be steadfast in its pursuit of its ideals, it must also be realistic in acknowledging its limitations in influencing the super powers.

Given the unity and coherence of Gordon's approach to the three objectives defined by the Group of 78, it is difficult – and unnecessary – to sort the strands of Gordon's thinking into rigid categories. The fact remained that the conflict, as perceived by the Group of 78, between Canada's commitment to NATO and the issues of nuclear power and disarmament, continued to be of paramount concern, and the Group as a whole was not assuaged by Trudeau's reassurances. Canada had a long history in the area of nuclear technological development: in 1945 the first nuclear reactor outside the US began to function in Chalk River, Ontario. Canada's interest remained the peaceful application of nuclear technology – power generation and medical therapy, for example – with no consideration of developing or acquiring atomic weapons. However, Canada's charter membership in NATO in 1948 raised the question of what part its military forces should be committed to play in its alliance with the western nuclear powers, and Canada's stand in this regard varied during the next twenty years as different governments changed policies.

Soon after Trudeau's first election as prime minister in 1968, his government made the decision to relinquish nuclear weapons in any form. However, NATO policy under US leadership was to strengthen the nuclear capability in western Europe and to threaten nuclear retaliation to break up armoured formations of the Warsaw Pact should they be deemed a threat to western Europe. Convinced that nuclear-weapons use in Europe could not be kept separate from the use of strategic [first strike] weapons, Trudeau became determined that Canada should withdraw from all nuclear roles in Europe.[48] By January 1972, Canada's NATO forces in Europe had been restructured: the Canadian forces would consist of 5,000 personnel; the mechanized battle group would be non-nuclear, and the air element would forego its nuclear-strike role. This withdrawal from nuclear weaponry begun in 1969 was completed in Canada in the early 1980s.

In 1978, Trudeau further clarified his position in a speech to the UN on a strategy of "nuclear suffocation," in which he proposed that new developments should be stopped in the laboratory while nuclear nations worked to reduce existing stockpiles. To "cut off the oxygen" on which the arms race fed, he proposed a comprehensive test ban to stop the flight testing of all new strategic missiles, to prohibit all production of nuclear material for weapons purposes, and to limit and then reduce military spending on new strategic nuclear weapons systems.[49] While his speech was well-received in the UN, allies at the NATO summit that followed a few days later were less enthusiastic. At that point NATO was launching a two-track strategy of pursuing peace overtures with the Soviets on the one hand and meeting any new Soviet weapons threat "arm for arm, gun for gun" on the other. As a result, the Europeans were prepared to allow the introduction of a new American missile, and Canada was asked to allow testing of the cruise missile in the Canadian North, an area that replicated as much as possible the terrain of Siberia.

Because the missile was accurate and difficult to detect, it was argued that it would increase the uncertainty of Soviet military planners; but critics, including Gordon and the Group of 78, argued that heightened Soviet anxiety in a nuclear-armed world was dangerous and that the deployment of what they saw as a "first strike" weapon such as the cruise missile would contribute to the further escalation of the nuclear arms race.[50]

In February 1983, the issue of testing the cruise missile in Canadian territory exploded into a crisis of public opinion. In an exchange of notes, Canada and the US established the Canada–US Test and Evaluation Program to allow the US to request the testing of unarmed air-launched cruise missiles and certain other military systems in Canada. The response among Canadian peace groups was rapid and intense, including that of the Group of 78. Gordon himself had, of course, long opposed the development and deployment of nuclear weapons, dating back to his days at *The Nation* in the aftermath of Hiroshima and Nagasaki. Ever since his first dust-up with Trudeau over the sale of CANDU reactors in 1974, Gordon had supported Trudeau on as many occasions as he felt he could, and offered criticism as he had felt necessary – exercising, as he wrote, "the freedom of the academic which you will understand."[51] Now, Gordon, along with his cohorts, responded with fury and a flurry of activity. In Gordon's words, "it was not exactly five days that shook the world but they demonstrated what can be done by a concerted effort of a few determined people."[52]

At the end of January, Gordon was invited by Murray Thomson to attend a luncheon meeting of the Ottawa executive of Ploughshares. First on the agenda was the strategy for organizing a vigil on Parliament Hill for the coming Tuesday or Wednesday, since it was believed that a cabinet decision on the cruise missile would be taken on Thursday. Group of 78 members would be called to ask that they write, telegraph, or phone the prime minister urging him not to ratify cruise testing in Canada and to give stronger leadership in disarmament dialogue. Gordon's campaign began that evening at a benefit showing of the film *Gandhi*, where he was able to contact three Group of 78 members, including the mayor of Ottawa, Marion Dewar. During the next three days he phoned or contacted twenty-two members of the Group including his old friends Tommy Douglas, the Scotts, George Ignatieff, and Elisabeth Borgese. Meanwhile, Murray Thomson contacted Toronto members and another member of the Group did the Montreal detail.

As Gordon talked with his son on Monday evening, the latter, with his journalist's eye, raised the question of press contacts and notifications and mentioned that the French press was particularly interested. Murray Thomson provided press releases in both English and French in the press gallery in the House of Commons and in the Press Club on Wellington Street. Gordon also contacted his friends at IDRC, a number of whom became actively involved.

All in all, Gordon concluded, the protest was quite successful with about sixty coming and going at the steps in front of the Peace Tower – Ploughshares standbys as well as MPs and, of course, members of the Group. There was a big banner pointing out that fifty-two per cent of Canadians opposed the testing, with some coverage by the CBC, CTV, and the *Globe and Mail.* Murray Thomson was "fairly satisfied," but urged a further step in a signed statement by the Group. Gordon also sent a telegram to the prime minister, urging indefinite postponement of the decision to allow US testing of the cruise missile on Canadian soil: "to go ahead with testing would commit Canada to a new phase of arms escalation completely at variance with your policy of suffocation and mounting world pressure for nuclear disarmament."[53]

Gordon received a response from the Prime Minister's Office at the end of April (with a later apology from Trudeau for not having been able to respond personally)[54] summarizing the views that appeared in Trudeau's "Open Letter to All Canadians" in early May.[55] In this Open Letter, Trudeau responded to the inter-related issues of permitting the testing of American cruise missiles over western Canadian territory, and of joining NATO in the deploying of American Pershing II cruise missiles carrying nuclear warheads to protect western European nations against the Soviet nuclear threat. To Gordon's charge that he was going back on his "policy of nuclear suffocation," Trudeau defended himself by saying that obviously his proposal had to apply to both sides or to neither. Since the Soviet Union had rejected such a strategy, there could be no question of urging its acceptance by NATO. Moreover, at present it was hardly fair to rely on the Americans to protect the West, but refuse to lend them a hand; some Canadians seemed eager to take refuge under the American umbrella, he asserted, without wanting to help hold it. In his view, it behooved Canada to bear its fair share of the burden falling upon NATO.

In his response to Trudeau, Gordon pointed out that the American administration's approach to global security, based on the escalation of more and more sophisticated weaponry to match a real or imagined

Soviet arms buildup was "of course" widely familiar. However, he asked: "Is this what you refer to as the American defense umbrella under which 'some Canadians' are eager to take refuge? If you are identifying these Canadians as belonging to the peace movement, I should think that for them the 'umbrella' has the curious shape of a mushroom cloud. Moreover, to describe their attitude as 'anti-American' is wide of the mark – witness the strong movement for a nuclear freeze and the difficulty Ronald Reagan is encountering in Congress in getting approval for his military buildup."[56]

Trudeau, however, was not content to leave his argument at the level of simple logic – that the success of nuclear suffocation strategy was dependent on reciprocity with the Soviet Union – and he continued his letter by reaching for moral justification:

> I do not deny that there is an element of truth, and validity in an unconditionally pacifist position. I simply say that it is simplistic to ignore the real, complex and often immoral world to which our choices must apply …
>
> I believe that the Soviet peoples desire peace just as much as the peoples of the free world. But I also know that the Soviets are very heavily armed. In these circumstances, it would be almost suicidal for the West to adopt a policy of unilateral disarmament, or a policy of suffocating the development of new means of defending ourselves against the Soviet SS-20s. *That is the kind of heroic moral choice which an individual could make in his personal life, but does anyone have the right to impose that choice upon a whole nation, or upon the community of free countries?* [Italics added.]

Gordon would have recognized the Niebuhrian turn in Trudeau's logic at this point, although he surely would have had difficulty in reconciling it with both earlier and later statements by Trudeau. Gordon had settled his argument with Niebuhr long ago, and in the current context he once again offered a caveat to the moral man/immoral society debate: to the traditional view that states that make foreign policy are impersonal entities and therefore cannot be considered capable of moral action, he countered that citizens in democracies can hold their *elected* governments to certain moral principles in external relations.[57] An aspect of the argument not acknowledged by Trudeau's question, *but does anyone have the right to impose that choice upon a whole nation?* is that when Gordon refers to the rights of citizens to hold their governments to certain moral principles in external relations he is speaking of individual citizens *as members of a democratic community* in which action is taken by majority consensus. While the individual has a right to be heard, the idea that Gordon would support his own – or any individual's – right to impose his choice upon a whole nation is absurd. Speaking with a *citizen's right to be heard* then, Gordon replied to Trudeau, "Canadian security does not depend on accreditations to American military might and there is no moral obligation to cooperate in the testing of additional weapons."[58]

Despite the Niebuhrian turn reflected in Trudeau's Open Letter in May, Trudeau seems more generally to have shared, in his own way, Gordon's assumption concerning the bearing of a democratic populace's values on policies of state. In 1995, writing in their last chapter of *The Canadian Way: Shaping Canada's Foreign Policy 1968–1984*, Head and Trudeau reflected on the goals of the foreign policy White Paper of 1970,[59] arguing that these goals illustrated that principle and interest – idealism and realism – need not be inconsistent, and that ethical considerations were not simply tolerable, they were necessary: "We were not willing to accept Niebuhr's reluctant conclusion that irony was the prevailing characteristic of history,"[60] and they posited that Canadians should not be asked to tolerate a moral distinction between their own moral behaviour and that of their government. Moreover, "Consistency of moral standards and actual practice would hopefully also enhance the influence that Canada could bring to bear within the international community for the pursuit by other actors with similar goals."[61] Gordon and others like him were justified in their perplexity as they looked for consistency in Trudeau's statements. At the same time, one cannot fail to appreciate Trudeau's seeming willingness to be caught in the ambiguity between his own idealism and political realities, or, perhaps one could say, his philosophical ideals and his kingly responsibilities.

In any case, in this instance Gordon's arguments did not prevail. In July 1983, the Canadian government announced that in response to the US request it had agreed to allow the testing of the AGM-86B air-launched cruise missile in Canada, a five-year agreement that was automatically extended for a further five years in 1988. Nevertheless, Gordon pressed on in his dialogue on disarmament with the prime minister, offering criticism, advice, and support. Trudeau responded to all three with varying degrees of appreciation but always with a listening ear. On his way to the Special Conference on Disarmament at the UN in 1982, for example, he wrote to Gordon thanking him for his encouragement: "Your most eloquent analysis of what might be achieved with the right approach and the right motivation was a refreshing change from the sombre and pessimistic forecasts which are put forward so often today. Like you, I have an abiding faith in the intelligence of the human race and I believe we will some day find an alternative to the balance of terror as our guarantee of security."[62]

Gordon's respect and admiration for Trudeau were reciprocated. The following responses were not untypical: "Thank you for your extremely thoughtful letter. It is encouraging to see that such civilized and perceptive attitudes are still alive and well in Canada."[63] And again, on having missed a letter early in his "peace initiative": "The thoughts which you wanted to share with me would have been helpful indeed during my Asian journey. However, their pertinence and wisdom transcend the limits of time and I do want to thank you warmly for allowing me to meditate on them."[64]

Trudeau announced his intention to resign on 1 March 1984. King wrote to Marian Scott, "Well, I feel today that we've stepped into a new era. And I feel a bit depressed by it. I think we all felt that one of these days Pierre would do what he has done and that in the current partisan political situation it was probably inevitable. But that does not cheer me. And in my opinion, despite all there is to criticize, we've lost a political leader of pretty large dimensions."[65] Of course, King told Marian, he wasn't always an effective political leader, and frequently his enlightened declarations found no expression in actual Canadian policy. "But in time I think it would have."[66] To Trudeau, Gordon wrote sincerely, "You have played a significant role in this global process out of which will come a more equitable and secure world community."[67]

In their last exchange of letters during Trudeau's tenure as prime minister, and in his response to Gordon's invitation to be the opening speaker at the annual conference of the Group of 78 at Stony Lake, Ontario, Trudeau wrote, "Since the Group of 78 took out its first advertisement on 6 June 1982, I believe that we have come a long way together."[68] He admitted that while the views of the government and the Group of 78 members may have differed on specific issues such as cruise missile testing in Canada and a declaration of Canada as a nuclear-weapon-free zone, they shared a belief in the need to press for productive and verifiable arms control and disarmament agreements. He concluded, "I am very appreciative of the support and encouragement provided by members of the Group of 78."

It is interesting to note that in their years of conversation Gordon did not engage in perhaps the central issue of Trudeau's tenure as prime minister – and, indeed, of his whole professional life: the role of Quebec within the Canadian Constitution. In response to the author's query concerning this omission, King's son replied: "I would say that generally, [Dad] didn't have strong views on Quebec. He liked Levesque personally but I think his admiration for Trudeau would overpower that. When Dad returned to Canada, his focus continued to be international. He was not deeply involved in domestic issues and I don't recall ever having a discussion of Quebec. Trudeau respected him and they used to correspond, but mostly that was about international affairs."[69]

The founding of the Group of 78 had brought great satisfaction to Gordon, bringing together as it did a community sharing those concerns that occupied him most deeply. For the first three years Gordon co-chaired the Group with Murray Thomson, and later with Ann Gertler. Membership rapidly expanded to over 250, and the Group gradually developed an infrastructure of conferences and workshops, an expanding program of publications, and ad hoc and working committees to research and draw up reports on specific issues. The Group also made presentations to parliamentary committees and published a newsletter. In September 1984, with a new Conservative government in office, an expanded Group met for a three-day conference at Stony Lake, and produced a consensus statement entitled *A Foreign Policy for the 80s* that updated and expanded on the statement of 1981. This publication consisted of a substantial collection of articles and under the editorial committee of Ruth Gordon, Clyde Sanger, and Tim Brodhead, the Group began an ambitious practice of producing similar collections each year, publicizing the topic and outcome of the annual conferences. Gordon played a significant part in the recruitment of speakers and authors, frequently contributing an article of his own or writing the introduction to the collection. In fact, his introduction to its 1989 book, *Alternative Defence Policy*, would be among the last pieces that he wrote before his death. After his death, the Group of 78 established the *Lester B. Pearson College of the Pacific Endowment Fund*, which provided scholarships in his memory.

Did Gordon's letters and urgings, along with those of the Group of 78, have any significant influence on Pierre Trudeau and the shaping of Canadian foreign policy? The nature of the circumstances and the imponderables of political power make it difficult to know. How much does an individual citizen count in the political community? Gordon was no ordinary "common man" in this respect, but a sophisticated thinker, informed, experienced, and well-known. It is clear from his correspondence with the prime minister that he was heard and respected – and answered. While Trudeau often disagreed, he was happy to acknowledge that he and Gordon shared common values. When it came right down to it – Trudeau's love of process and his commitment to the rationalization of policy notwithstanding – he and Gordon shared many elements of the romantic tradition in politics that grew out of the Enlightenment: a challenge of conventional orthodoxy and power structures; a belief in the essential goodness and dignity of human beings; a deep commitment to freedom and the ability of people to shape their own lives; and a utopian vision that life in the political community could improve – an apotheosis of the cry at the heart of the French Revolution for liberty, equality, and fraternity.

Then too, in his discussions of morality in international relations Gordon insisted on a modern recognition that in a democratic society citizens are expected – and indeed required – to hold their elected government to certain moral principles. This is a mandate to both individuals *and* groups. This conviction on Gordon's part surely must have counted heavily in his sense of urgency – that something-must-be-done energy – that led to the formation of the Group of 78. For, of course, Gordon was not a voice crying in the wilderness and he did not speak alone: he had behind him the voices of seventy-eight (and many more) informed and articulate citizens with deep faith in the democratic process and the courage to speak out.

Invariably, citizens tend to depersonalize their leaders, forgetting that even the most confident benefit from encouragement, and even the most politically cynical rely on favourable public opinion. Gordon always approached Trudeau in personal terms, as a fellow human being committed to the welfare of the people, and his respect and admiration for him were genuine, as was his generous encouragement. How much does such personal support and encouragement by individual citizens affect a leader as he "bears the burdens of office?" Another imponderable. By upbringing, training, and experience, Gordon was eager to participate in the political process by providing such support, motivated by his duty as a citizen and firm in his conviction that short of perfection, a great deal can be achieved.

Gordon received many honours during his retirement years, and accepted each honour with deep appreciation and modesty. In 1977 he was appointed a Member of the Order of Canada, an order created by the

Canadian government in 1967 to recognize "outstanding achievement and honouring those who have given service to Canada, to their fellow citizens or to humanity at large."[70] The Investiture of Honours took place at Government House on 26 October 1977, and for King and Ruth the occasion was immortalized in a picture of them, beaming happily in their formal dress, that sat on the piano of their Fairlawn home. Gordon received a plethora of congratulations from his friends of many years, taking their kind comments in his stride but by no means as his due. He responded to an exultant letter from the former rector of the Université de Montréal, Roger Gaudy: "I must confess it is a somewhat unnerving experience after my chequered career to find myself honoured by the Establishment. If I were more arrogant I would be led to believe that the truths which I espoused and expounded in earlier years of radical revolt were at length being accounted as relevant!"[71]

He received honorary degrees from five Canadian universities: Carleton, Brandon, Winnipeg, Manitoba, and St Francis Xavier. But the honour that he treasured most deeply was undoubtedly the Pearson Peace Medal he was awarded in 1980. He began his acceptance speech with charming reminiscences about Pearson and baseball, his abhorrence of war and commitment to peace, and his own years in the field. He then moved quickly to celebrate the peacekeepers and aid workers, the technicians working on water, electricity, transportation, banking, civil aviation, and all those mundane and sometimes dreary tasks that build the infrastructure of a civil community. These were the ones he said, who deserved a Pearson Peace Medal. He himself was only a witness.[72]

In January of 1985, Frank Scott died. He had been Gordon's friend for over fifty years, and King described him as "the Canadian who has had the most impact on my life and thinking."[73] They had both returned from Oxford with a new vision of the world, and of their homeland, and by the time they met in Montreal, each had become involved in radical politics. Half a century later, Gordon recalled being struck by Scott's self-confidence and his natural bearing of authority With youthful enthusiasm and endless discussions they had "planned programs" (King's words), meeting to draft letters, newspaper ads, manifestos, and whatever might be required in achieving their determined goal, whether over lunch at the Ritz Hotel in Montreal or at a diner in Regina where they hammered out the details of the Regina Manifesto on humble "oil cloth." In all of it, they shared a profound commitment to the principles of social and economic justice, and confidence in the efficacy of their actions.

When Gordon married, Ruth was welcomed into the Scott friendship and, with letters flying back and forth and visits whenever possible, they kept in touch through the years of separation. In reminiscing after Scott's death, Gordon recalled a somewhat atypical, though not unfitting, evening together in 1982. It was the day on which the Queen came to Ottawa to sign the the Canada Act 1982 giving Canada its own Constitution and Charter of Rights and Freedoms. Frank and Marian had come from Montreal for the festivities and, with the Gordons in their Fairlawn home, they watched the proceedings on television, lifting their glasses in a toast. They had to speak up to hear one another over the pounding rain against the windows. They also contended with the noise made by the television crew in their midst who were making a film on Frank Scott for the National Film Board of Canada. The glaring camera lights lit up the living room, adding to the air of festivity – and perhaps also to the jolly confusion.

In their early years together, during which "the old orthodoxies were unraveling [and] the sacred cows were out of their pasture and cluttering the highways,"[74] Gordon and Scott, along with their peers, focused on the human tragedy of everyday working people caught in economic forces beyond their understanding or control. The universal nature of this problem became explicit for them only in the period of political change following the Second World War, with the rebuilding of Europe and the emergence of the newly independent nations.

The poetry of Scott's mature years reflects this expanding consciousness, as he increasingly focused on the integration of the human community with the natural environment. Gordon's thinking had moved steadily in this direction as well. In his *Twelfth Night* reflection written the year before he died, King identifies a final figure that has strayed into the family crèche:

> At first he seemed a bit strange, as if he didn't belong. But over the years he seems to feel – in fact appears to be – more and more at home. He's a moose ... In a sense you could say he represents nature – the world of nature. But that's a rather strange concept, as if it is a reality quite separate from humans – from 'human nature.' And there is something in that idea, that separation. I am reminded of Frank Scott's poem, 'Surfaces.'
>
> This rock-bound river, ever flowing
> Obedient to the ineluctable laws,

Brings a reminder from the barren north
Of the eternal lifeless processes.
There is an argument that will prevail
In this calm stretch of the current, slowly drawn
Toward its final equilibrium.

Come, flaunt the brief prerogative of life,
Dip your small civilized foot in this cold water
And ripple, for a moment, the smooth surface of time.[75]

> This conception of the close relationship between man and nature ... has come to be recognized as one of the great questions we face today. Its full implications are only now being recognized.[76]

In an article written the summer after Frank's death, Gordon pointed out that Scott had always been drawn to nature, even in his earlier poetry.[77] But it was his assignment to Burma as a UN technical-aid representative in 1952 that brought Frank in touch with a world he had never seen – "crowded lands, deep poverty, ancient cultures, lush environment" – all tumbled together. King felt that this experience in Southeast Asia deepened Scott's sense, expressed perhaps most tellingly in his poem "A Grain of Rice," that the evolution of the good society was linked to the eternal processes of nature.

In a draft version of a review that Gordon had written in 1983 of a collection of essays honouring Scott's contributions to law, literature, and politics, he explored the role of the poet in realizing this just society.[78] Tracing the original Greek meaning of the word *poet* [*poietes*, "maker"], Gordon wrote that the poet is "both interpreter and creator, the one who discovers and reveals meaning" as he observes nature's majesty and "ineluctable" laws. But humans are also part of this universe – *dip your small civilized foot in this cold water* – and Scott, he observed, increasingly recognized human beings as participating in this cosmic order, sharing with one another – "with the grain of the universe"[79] – in the creation of order and justice in human society. Gordon continued, "[t]he poet's concern in injustice, powers, the suppression of human rights is a natural concern since they represent the exclusion of large sections of humanity from order and fulfillment. Law naturally represents order and justice. But Scott goes further, in seeing law as the servant of emerging order. Law has a creative function,"[80] as providing the basis of freedom for the creative life of human beings.

In his address at the memorial service held for Scott at McGill shortly after his death, Gordon noted that the poet is more than an observer: he is a participant – "dipping his foot into the cold water and rippling for a moment, the smooth surface of time" – part of the political process, "a co-partner in a creative universe."[81] King quoted the poem that, for him, crystallized Frank's vision:

... Yet always we find
Such ordered purpose in cell and in galaxy,
So great a glory in life-thrust and mind-range,
Such widening frontiers to draw our longings,
We grow to one world
Through enlargement of wonder.[82]

In a sense, Gordon postulated, Frank Scott was already living in the good society he had worked to build: "He was able to see things as a whole. His emancipated spirit found expression in his poetry, in his sense of humor, in his enthusiasm ... for he was the living expression of that human spirit that would build the new society."[83] Scott's poetry encapsulated the vision of social justice that King had spent his own life living out. "There will be other Frank Scotts in many lands," he wrote, "and with them, millions of people in a world that is becoming one to combine their efforts to build that good society."[84] He was not, of course, referring to Scott's poetic brilliance, but to the vision and intention and goodwill of those who, though in other endeavours, joined the ranks of poets as *poietai*, "makers." In fact, there had already been many in Canada's own tradition who could be included in this company: King's own father and those visionaries of the social gospel; J.S. Woodsworth; the young scholars returning from Oxford, imbued with the ideas of the Fabians; the founders of the CCF, the League for Social Reconstruction, and the Fellowship for a Christian Social Order; the liberal tradition of Lester Pearson, and of Pierre Trudeau who urged a global ethic and drew on the philosophy of the French Jesuit, Pierre Teilhard de Chardin: "Love one another, or you will perish ... We have reached a critical point in human evolution in which the only path open to us is to move towards a common passion, a 'conspiracy' of love."[85] It was a vision that would be passed on to future generations of Canadians.

Throughout his life, Gordon's logic habitually worked from the particular – a boy with a donkey, a nativity scene of figures gathered from around the world – to the abstract principle, then curved back again to the incarnation of that principle in human society. He concluded his *Twelfth Night* reflection:

> We seem to have got far away from the moose as representative of the world of nature in which humanity lives and moves and has its being. But perhaps not. The original Bethlehem crèche represents a human family – mother, father, baby – in a friendly setting with farm animals and visitors, bringing with them good will from homes far away. And those who have joined the crèche – including the moose – emphasize the essential nature of a secure and supportive community in a friendly world.

19

Home to Birkencraig

King Gordon's thinking and his actions describe an elegant arc, stretching from his early exposure to the social gospel at his father's table in Winnipeg to the poetry reading with friends just days before his death, when he listened to Frank Scott's, "We Grow to One World." Gordon defined moral action as "response to the imperative to put into practice the principles and purposes to which one is committed."[1] In his own actions, one finds a seamless connection between handing out cocoa and other food to hungry refugees in Vienna in 1922, serving in the UN Secretariat on the Prisoner of War Commission in 1952, and mixing powdered milk on Christmas Day in 1960 for abandoned patients in a field hospital in the Congo.

Gordon's search for vocation began early. On a visit to Lord Aberdeen's estate in Scotland shortly before leaving Oxford and returning to Canada in July 1924, he struggled "with my conscience and with a great darkness as to where lies my course in life."[2] At first he thought that his immediate plan must be to follow his father into the Presbyterian ministry. But as he continued to wrestle in this darkness, it dawned on him that

> all my deepest interests have become centered in the League [of Nations], in the possibility of averting war. I believe that the time of international statesmanship is not past but is just beginning. I believe that surely I shall find an opportunity of realizing my best self in that sphere of service.
>
> May I never allow the beacon which for many years has been smoldering and to-night has burst into flame to die out. May God help me.

He signed his name as if to a covenant.

After his early career in the church, politics, and publishing, he found that vocation with the formation of the United Nations in 1945, first as a correspondent for *The Nation* and the CBC, and then in 1952 as a member of the UN Secretariat, Division of Human Rights. Both familial background and temperament had predisposed him to this vocation as an international civil servant. In his eulogy for King in 1989, his brother-in-law Humphrey Carver spoke of the "glowing and powerful bonds of affection" within the Gordon family. Carver suggested that it was this kind of love that laid the foundation for all the friendships Gordon made in many parts of the world, and formed the basis of his genuine respect for those of all social classes and circumstances, equally at ease with the Queen of Holland and the fishermen and miners of Nova Scotia. For King, "the distinguished internationalist, the expression 'The Family of Man' was not just a cliché."[3]

By temperament Gordon simply enjoyed people – although he had little patience with pomposity or guile. Carver felt that this genius for making friends wherever he went lay in Gordon's sense of the uniqueness of ordinary people, sharing family news with taxi drivers and teenage waitresses. At Gordon's memorial service, Carver told a story to his listeners: "The last time Anne and I saw King, about a week ago, we went out to dinner at a small restaurant in Ottawa kept by a man and wife who came from the other end of the earth. She is the chef and they had just had twins. King and our host embraced with the enthusiasm of old friends. And when the time came to leave, King and Ruth disappeared into the kitchen to see the twins and wouldn't go home until they found out how much weight the twins had gained since birth."

Gordon's own view of his role in this world of international figures and events, and his way of taking himself in this role, bespoke a blend of modesty and self-assurance. By nature sunny and hopeful, he was only rarely given to introspection or second-guessing himself, and with remarkable self-confidence he was always eager to get on with the job. He liked to refer to himself with humorous self-deprecation, and would make a point of his status as an amateur. In his reply to the affectionate congratulations of his friends at his seventieth birthday party on 6 December 1970, he claimed that he had never actually had a career at all: "I have done many things," he said. "I have worked along side professionals; but my status has always been an amateur status – and I use the word *amateur* in the French [from *amare, to love*] as well as in the English sense."[4] He demonstrated this by recounting a story from the winter of 1923–24 when he and his Oxford friends, on a skiing vacation to Chamonix, attempted to qualify for a third-class certificate in downhill skiing – not a prairie boy's forte. There were three heats and King was in the third. As he waited for his signal to start, he found himself feeling increasingly lonely as he watched the skiers disappearing down the slope to the finish line over 600 m below. As each skier was free to pick his course, King felt that gravity was on his side, and he pointed his skis straight downhill. In spite of a few spectacular falls, he made terrific speed, overtaking both the second and first contingents, finally skidding over the finish line in a great cloud of powder. The judge looked at him in amazement. "But you are with the third heat." King replied, "Yes, sir." "But this is the first heat." King responded, "Is it, sir? I qualify then?" "Yes, of course you qualify!"

This unexpected triumph had a deleterious effect on him in giving him the impression that he could ski well – although, with some credit to gravity, he certainly could ski fast. At a deeper level, however, it confirmed in him an amateur approach to life, and to the unintended blessings that could come through a succession of amateur roles.

> Had I settled at any time on a permanent professional career, I would not have met my wife. We would not have had our children. These, looking back over seventy years, must be counted as the greatest blessings that have come to me, undeserved … The disquieting thing is that while I should be ashamed of this disgraceful masquerade, so often repeated in different roles, and at this very moment I should be recalling with remorse my wasted years, I am not. And perhaps, as an amateur, there may be one more role for me to play.[5]

When he was asked by Ernest Dick in 1976 if he had any personal regrets about what he was able to do, he replied, "No. We all regretted that we didn't do a better job, but I would have had those regrets anywhere."[6]

Gordon's taciturn responses to Dick belie his struggles and, at times, self-doubt about whether he was, in fact, doing all that he could with his life and whether, for that matter, the UN itself was being as effective as it might be. In the midst of wrestling with Hammarskjöld's request in 1956 that he leave Korea and move to Cairo where the Suez crisis was building, he had wondered to Ruth how such a move would affect his career, adding, "Anyway, what is my career? I have done so many things. I suppose when I have time to review my life there will emerge great consistency in all my ventures – I was going to say choices but frequently the choice did not seem to be mine ... Perhaps, it was not so inconsistent that I started in the church, went into radical politics in the hope of doing something to make a better social order, and then went on into the one great movement that may make reality of the dreams of the great thinkers and visionaries."[7]

In the spring of 1957, waiting for Egyptian officers (who never showed up) in the Sinai, he had another of his rare bouts of soul-searching as he contemplated the detritus of warfare lying on the desert floor: "A heap of stone – a smell of decay – a few bones – two left shoes – two soldiers' caps – a legging – the inevitable toll of war; all these the symbol of remorseless time, of man's ephermerality, futility." He admitted to Ruth, "I think we still believe what we are here for, but we don't confess it."[8] Still later, in the spring of 1959 as he waited for "Grandmother UN" to make a decision about his next assignment, he complained to Ruth about the "policy of drift" concerning his future and spoke of "that sudden moment of clarity when some realities of one's situation are revealed." Not that his life had been wasted by any means, but perhaps some creative possibilities had not been realized. Still, he concluded, "the fault, dear Brutus, lies not within our stars but in ourselves. Well, it's not too late and perhaps the next ten years will be the best."[9] Gordon lived for another thirty years, a period of increasing commitment to the goals of the United Nations. He carried a copy of the United Nations Charter in the pocket of his jacket until the time of his death.[10]

King was not unaware of the cost to Ruth and the children of the long separations and the frequent moves from school to school for Charley and Alison. "I certainly haven't given you an easy life," he wrote to Ruth while he was struggling with the decision to move to Cairo, and he often admitted the demands that his work made on her and the children.[11] Ruth for her part supported King; and as for Charley and Alison, it was their parents' hope that international experience had both broadened and enriched their knowledge of the world and strengthened the bonds of family.

To identify those elements that determined the course Gordon's life would take, one must return again to his reveries at the Aberdeen estate in the summers of 1923 and 1924 when he searched in the "great darkness" for his vocation. At that time he identified volition and consent in response to "the highest purpose for which one is in this world" as central to moral action. Gordon often spoke of *duty*, of what *ought* to be done. He also spoke of *destiny*, of bringing one's life in line with Providence.

But there was another essential ingredient that, in Gordon's view, determined the course of his life: *happy accident*. As he put the matter to Ruth, "Usually, but not always, the things that *happen* to you are the things that should be encouraged."[12] And in another context he wrote, "It is the accidents on the road rather than careful planning and accurate map-reading that frequently determine the course of one's life."[13] Gordon revelled in serendipity, the happy coincidence, the chance meeting, such as sitting beside President W.H. Johns at dinner and landing himself a teaching position at the University of Alberta. At times it was almost as though he suspected a wizard behind the curtain, something less than determinism and far more playful, a joyful interplay between human freedom and circumstance. For above all, it was the dynamic nature of human existence that delighted King. Writing to Ruth in 1955, he summed it up:

> I'm coming to the mature conclusion that a great many situations if patiently waited out will solve themselves. In fact, no situation which represents a head-on clash of principles or personalities is capable of logical solution ... But somehow, amoeba-like, we can absorb them and move on. And we often find that our very logical description of the situation hides intangibles that eventually assert themselves.
> I suppose that is simply saying that life and persons are very complex and there is a gratifying process of accommodation that is going on all the time ... I also thought how many of the poignant novels of young intellectuals are based on the false assumption that facts are facts, logic is logic, and the insoluble is insoluble. I suppose the main fallacy is to state things in terms of solutions. There is no solution. But there somehow is growth and development. The irresistible force and the immovable object are mechanistic terms and life is organic and creative.[14]

The arc of King's life. A superficial survey suggests his life to be a "succession of many things;" but each one is a particular embodiment and pursuit of "that one thing I do," informing not only *what* he did at a given period in his life, but the *spirit* and intention in which he did it. There is an Aristotelian logic in its shape, reflected in his Aberdeen reverie: self-realization.

Gordon's death on 24 February 1989 was sudden, and in its manner fitting. He died of a massive stroke on Wellington Street in Ottawa, while driving past the Parliament buildings, as he and Ruth returned home from an afternoon visit with friends. He was at the wheel of his car which eased itself into a parked vehicle near the National Library and Archives. Strangers rushed to help a stricken Ruth. Charley later remarked to the Reverend David MacDonald, as they planned the funeral service, that the only improvement on the event from King's point of view would have been if it had happened in a canoe on Lake of the Woods.[15] His memorial service took place on 27 February in Dominion-Chalmers United Church in Ottawa, attended by friends, including many notables, with tributes by Murray Thomson and Humphrey Carver, and hymns and scripture reflecting Gordon's sturdy Christian heritage. The ceremony closed with "And did those feet in ancient time," set to the tune "Jerusalem," the hymn shared by King Gordon and Frank Scott in the glory days of the Regina Manifesto in 1933, and it concludes:

Bring me my bow of burning gold!
Bring me my arrows of desire!
Bring me my spear! O clouds unfold!
Bring me my chariot of fire!
I will not cease from mortal fight,
Nor shall my sword sleep in my hand,
Till we have built Jerusalem
In this our green and pleasant land.

The weekend before his death, King and Ruth had met with a dozen friends to read favourite poems. While some read love poems (the gathering followed Valentine's Day), King read only from Frank Scott. Shortly after King's death, Clyde Sanger wrote:

The best moment came when our host played a record of Scott reading his poem, *Surfaces*, and King's eyes glistened at those final lines:

Come, flaunt the brief prerogative of life,
Dip your small foot in this cold water
And ripple, for a moment, the smooth surface of time.

The ripples King Gordon made will last with many of us for all our days.[16]

Ruth was devastated by King's death. She soldiered on through illness and despair, eventually regaining, in her son Charley's words, "her most memorable quality," her sense of humour. She exhibited this quality not by telling jokes, but "in a way of looking at life, seeing the absurdities of it, finding something to chuckle about in the darkest of moments."[17] Eventually, Ruth moved from Fairlawn Avenue to Central Park Lodge in Ottawa. The large windows of her apartment looked northward toward the Ottawa River, with the Gatineau Hills beyond. When I last visited her there in 1995, I found her seated in her armchair by the window, a pile of books on the floor reaching to the arm of her chair, and on the other side, a table holding clippings of Charley's daily columns. Alison recalled her mother's love of reading and remarked that nothing pleased Ruth more than watching her children discover the wonders between the covers of books. Throughout their childhood, Alison and Charley found that their mother's editing skills did not depend on a blue pencil. Alison remembered: "At the dinner table, where we shared our news each evening, I might tell with great excitement, about my best friend Patsy and me catching a frog by Glenn's pond. 'That's nice, dear,' she'd say, dishing out the lima beans. Then after a small pause, she would add: 'Patsy and I.'"[18]

Nancy and the grandchildren, John and Mary, came to visit frequently, as did Alison from Toronto. Charley stopped in on his way home from work. And friends once again enjoyed her warm intelligence, always clothed in a genuine humility. Ruth died on 21 June 1996.

In the summer following Gordon's death, the family gathered at their island in Lake of the Woods to bury King's ashes. Years before, he and his cousin Chile had cleared paths across the island and, more recently, he had cleared a shorter path from the highest point on the island over to the flagpole, about 7 m away. This path ended on the bare rock face covered with ground balsam and sumac.[19] It was the spot where he used to work or paint watercolours, and it offered him a magnificent view looking down the lake.[20]

On this warm summer day, the family climbed up the paths cleared by King and Chile and gathered on the high point near the flagpole where, Charley recalled, "there was a little family ceremony on the hillside with my cousin-in-law Bill Millar presiding."[21] King Gordon's ashes now rest in the ground of Birkencraig.

Notes

PREFACE

1 J.S. Woodsworth to JKG, December 3, 1938, MG30C241. v. 73 (LAC)
2 Eugene Forsey, *A Life on the Fringe: The Memoirs of Eugene Forsey* (Toronto: Oxford University Press, 1990), 133.
3 JKG, "A Visit: E.M.B. in Ottawa, Dec. 12–14, 1982," JKGP.
4 Eileen Janzen, diary entry, December 6, 1979.

CHAPTER ONE

1 Charles W. Gordon, *Postscript to Adventure: The Autobiography of Ralph Connor* (Toronto: McClelland and Stewart Limited, 1975), 22.
2 J. King Gordon, review of *The Kirk in Glengarry*, by Donald MacMillan, *The Citizen*, 3 November 1984.
3 Charles W. Gordon, *Postscript*, 24–5.
4 Donald MacMillan, *The Kirk in Glengarry* (Ste-Anne de Bellevue, Quebec: Imprimerie Cooperative Harpell, 1984), 180–1.
5 Charles W. Gordon, *Postscript*, 17.
6 Ibid., 5.
7 Ibid., 6.
8 Ibid., 8.
9 Ibid., 10.
10 P.W. Wilson, review of *Postscript to Adventure: The Autobiography of Ralph Connor*, by Charles W. Gordon, *The New York Times Book Review*, 22 May 1938.
11 J. King Gordon, *The Citizen*, 3 November 1984.
12 Charles W. Gordon, *Postscript*, 53.

13 Ibid., 48.
14 Quoted by J. Lee Thompson and John H. Thompson, in "Ralph Connor and the Canadian Identity," *Queen's Quarterly* 2 (1962): 160.
15 Ibid., 161ff.
16 J. King Gordon to Charles Gordon, 4 May 1958. JKGP.
17 Charles Gordon, "Ralph Connor and the New Generation," *Mosaic* 3 (1970): 12.
18 The following account is based on J. King Gordon, "The World of Helen Gordon," *Manitoba Pageant*, 71 (Autumn 1978): 1–15.
19 Charles W. Gordon, *Postscript*, 416.
20 Ibid.
21 Ibid., 417.
22 J. King Gordon, "The World of Helen Gordon," 4.
23 Charles W. Gordon, *Postscript*, 422.
24 The phrase is, of course, from Wordsworth's "Immortality Ode," as identifying the deeper-than-human "ancestry" attending anyone's birth.

CHAPTER TWO

1 Charles W. Gordon, *Postscript to Adventure: The Autobiography of Ralph Connor* (Toronto: McClelland and Stewart Limited, 1975), 138.
2 Ibid., 301.
3 Ernest Dick Interview, November 22, 1974. Sound Archives, J. King Gordon Collection, Acc. 1974-121 (LAC).
4 Ibid.
5 C. W. Gordon to JKG, April 19, 1907, MG30C241, v. 89 (LAC).
6 Helen Gordon to JKG, June 1913, MG30C241, v. 88 (LAC).
7 JKG, "Birkencraig," unpublished manuscript, JKGP.
8 Malcolm M. MacDonald, "The Lake of the Woods," n.d., MG30C241, v. 10 (LAC).
9 JKG to CWG, June 29, 1915, MG30C241, v. 87 (LAC).
10 JKG, "The Bonfire," unpublished manuscript, JKGP.
11 Dick Interview, November 28, 1974. Sound Archives, J. King Gordon Collection, Acc. 1974–121 (LAC).
12 J. King Gordon, "St Stephen's," unpublished manuscript, 1984, JKGP, 4.
13 Dick Interview, November 28, 1974.
14 Following C.W. Gordon's death in October 1937, Helen Gordon and her daughters Ruth and Alison moved to a smaller house on Grosvenor Avenue. In 1938, the University Women's Club of Winnipeg rented

54 Westgate for their clubhouse, renaming it the Ralph Connor House; and in 1945 they bought the house as a permanent home for the UWCW. Under their custodial care, the house flourished in its new role and in 1983 it was designated an historic site by the City of Winnipeg. In 2004, it was named a Provincial Historical Site; and in 2009, it received national heritage designation status as a National Historical Site of Canada. I am indebted to Celine Kear, president of the Manitoba chapter of the Canadian Federation of University Women (2009–11), for her interest in King Gordon's story and for sending me an excellent source in 2011 about the House and the family history: *54 West Gate: Stories of Ralph Connor House* (Winnipeg: Friends of Ralph Connor House Inc., 2005).

15 Ibid., 161ff.

16 *Canadian Annual Review,* 1914, 188. Quoted in Richard Allen, *The Social Passion: Religion and Social Reform in Canada 1914–1928* (Toronto: University of Toronto Press, 1973) 34.

17 Ibid.

18 Charles W. Gordon, *Postscript*, 256.

19 "Silver Jubilee of St Stephen's," 18.

20 Dick Interview, November 22, 1974. Sound Archives, J. King Gordon Collection, Acc. 1974-121 (LAC). See also, George H. Doran, *Chronicles of Barabbas, 1884–1934* (New York: Harcourt, Brace and Company, 1935), 205.

21 JKG, "The World of Helen Gordon," *Manitoba Pageant* 71 (Autumn 1978): 6.

22 C.W. Gordon to JKG, July 28, [1916], MG30C241, v. 89 (LAC). This letter is almost certainly misdated 1917, as C.W. Gordon had returned to Canada in late 1916, after the Battle of the Somme.

23 JKG to Ruth Gordon, March 14, 1956, JKGP.

24 JKG to CWG, December 2, 1917, MG30C241, v. 87 (LAC).

25 Dick Interview, November 28, 1974. Sound Archives, J. King Gordon Collection, Acc. 1974–121 (LAC).

26 Desmond Morton, *A Short History of Canada*, 3rd ed. (Toronto: McClelland and Stewart Inc., 1997), 179.

27 Richard Allen, *The Social Passion Religion:Religion and Reform in Canada, 1914–1928* (Toronto and Buffalo: Toronto University Press, 1973), 87.

28 Desmond Morton, *A Short History of Canada*, 179.

29 Kenneth McNaught, *A Prophet in Politics: A Biography of J. S. Woodsworth* (Toronto: University of Toronto Press, 1959), 105.

30 Richard Allen, *The Social Passion*, 88; see also Kenneth McNaught, *A Prophet in Politics*, 100–5, for an analysis of major historical interpretations of the Winnipeg Strike.
31 Dick Interview, November 28, 1974.

CHAPTER THREE

1 Charles Ritchie, *An Appetite for Life: the Education of a Young Diarist 1924–1927* (Toronto: MacMillan of Canada, 1977), Entry for October 15, 1926, 111.
2 "At a time when the undergraduate population [of Oxford] never exceeded 3,000, nearly 2,700 members of the University were killed in that war." Jan Morris, *Oxford* (Oxford: at the University Press, 1988), 252.
3 Quoted in Christopher Hollis, *Oxford in the Twenties: Recollections of Five Friends* (London: Heinemann, 1976), 45.
4 Ibid., 17.
5 Lester B. Pearson, *Mike: The Memoirs of the Right Honorable Lester B. Pearson, Volume 1: 1897–1948* (Toronto: University of Toronto Press, 1972), 44.
6 Frank R. Scott, Diary, October 5, 1920, MG30D211, v. 90 (LAC).
7 Charles Ritchie, *An Appetite for Life*, Entry for October 26, 1926, 109.
8 J. King Gordon, "Oxford: recap," n.d., MG30C241, v. 86 (LAC).
9 JKG, "Going to Oxford: Being a personal account of what happened in the daily life of one John King Gordon – from that night on which he left his home-city and circle of friends in quest of further learning in a far off country during that time when he did sojourn away from his family and home," n.d., MG30C241, v. 86 (LAC).
10 Ibid.
11 Ibid.
12 CWG to JKG, October 5, 1921, MG30C241, v. 89 (LAC).
13 JKG letter to "Kay," October 11, 1921, MG30C241, v. 1 (LAC).
14 Ibid.
15 Ibid.
16 JKG to CWG, November 18, 1921, MG30C241, v. 87 (LAC).
17 Ibid.
18 *Handbook to the University of Oxford* (Oxford at the Clarendon Press, 1932), 249–51.
19 Stephen Leacock, *My Discovery of England* (London: John Lane The Bodley Head Ltd., 1922), 80.
20 Charles Ritchie, *An Appetite for Life*, 129.

21 *Handbook to the University of Oxford*, 251.
22 Dick Interview, November 28, 1974 (LAC).
23 JKG to CWG, February 3, 1922, MG30C241, v. 87 (LAC).
24 Ibid.
25 Ernest Dick Interview, November 28, 1974. Sound Archives, J. King Gordon Collection, Acc. 1974-121 (LAC).
26 JKG to CWG, May 16, 1923, MG30C241, v. 87 (LAC).
27 JKG to CWG, December 17, 1921, MG30C241, v. 87 (LAC).
28 Ramsay MacDonald became the first Labour prime minister in January 1924, a term in office that lasted only 9 months. He returned as Labour prime minister in 1929; in 1931 he was expelled from the Labour Party for forming a National Government with the Conservatives. He continued as prime minister until 1935. C.W. Gordon first met him in 1913, when MacDonald was the leader of the parliamentary Labour Party and, in *Postscript to Adventure*, Gordon described him as "belonging to the Fabian school, and a pronounced pacifist," (191). In later years, the Gordons enjoyed many visits to the Prime Minister's residence in London and to his county estate, Chequers. During his father's tenure as prime minister, Malcolm MacDonald often spent vacations at Birkencraig.
29 JKG to CWG, November 18, 1921, MG30C241, v. 87 (LAC).
30 Aberdeen and Temair to C.W. Gordon, November 23, 1921, MG30C241, v. 2 (LAC).
31 JKG, review of Sandra Djwa, *The Politics of the Imagination: A Life of F. R. Scott*, in *Dalhousie Law Journal*, November 1989, 570–1.
32 JKG to CWG, December 17, 1921, MG30C241, v. 87 (LAC).
33 JKG, "A New Internationalism in Action," *The Canadian Student*, n.d., MG30C241, v. 2 (LAC).
34 Ibid.
35 JKG to CWG, February 3, 1922, MG30C241, v. 87 (LAC).
36 JKG, "A New Internationalist in Action."
37 JKG, "Oxford: 1921–22: First Vacation, Discovery of Post-war Europe," MG30C241, v. 87 (LAC)
38 JKG, "A New Internationalism in Action."
39 R.H. Tawney, *The Acquisitive Society* (New York: A Harvest Book: Harcourt, Brace and World, 1948. Original publication, 1920).
40 JKG, "A Christian Socialist in the 1930's." Richard Allen, ed., *The Social Gospel in Canada; Papers of the Interdisciplinary Conference on the Social Gospel in Canada, March 21–4, 1973, at the University of Regina* (Ottawa: National Museums of Canada, 1975), 122–53.
41 Ibid., 123–4.

42 JKG to CWG, June 21, 1922, MG30C241, v. 87 (LAC)
43 Ibid.
44 JKG, "Chamonix," December 30–31, 1922; January 1–2, 1923, MG30C241, v. 4 (LAC).
45 John English, *Shadow of Heaven: The Life of Lester Pearson, Volume One: 1897–1948* (London: Vintage UK, 1990), 149.
46 Dick Interview, November 28, 1974. Sound Archives, J. King Gordon Collection, Acc. 1974-121 (LAC).
47 JKG, "Universities League of Nations Federation," *The Oxford Chronicle*, September 11, 1923, MG30C241, v. 3 (LAC).
48 JKG, "In the Beginning, Ryle," 1976, MG30C241, v. 72 (LAC).
49 JKG, review of Sandra Djwa, *The Politics of the Imagination: A Life of F.R. Scott*, 571.
50 JKG, "Graham Spry – Renaissance Man," 1983, MG30C241, v. 70 (LAC).
51 Dick Interview, November 28, 1974. Sound Archives, J. King Gordon Collection, Acc. 1974-121 (LAC).
52 JKG, "Graham Spry – Renaissance Man," 1983.
53 JKG to CWG, January 29, 1924, MG30C241, v. 86 (LAC)
54 JKG, July 10, 1923, MG30C241, v. 2 (LAC). While King liked both the Aberdeens, he became especially devoted to Ishbel, Lady Aberdeen, who is described as "affable and generous, with a critical mind, whose religious background led her to see the true worship of God in the service of man." She was a "democratic aristocrat," identified as a Liberal in politics. (John T. Saywell, ed., *The Canadian journal of Lady Aberdeen 1893–1898*, xvi.) She and King maintained a sporadic correspondence until her death in 1939.
55 JKG, "July 10," JKGP.
56 JKG, July 31, 1924, MG30C241, v. 2 (LAC)

CHAPTER FOUR

1 Scott Diary, November 10, 1923, MG30D211, v. 90 (LAC).
2 Ernest Dick Interview, December 12, 1974. Sound Archives, J. King Gordon Collection, Acc. 1974-121 (LAC).
3 Gilbert Ryle to JKG, October 25, 1924, MG30C241, v. 72 (LAC).
4 JKG, "Giscome, B. C. 1924–25: A Year in the Bush," MG30C241, v. 4 (LAC).
5 JKG, "Fraser River Missionary," MG30C241, v. 4 (LAC).
6 JKG to Helen Gordon, November 8, 1924, MG30C241, v. 87 (LAC).

7 JKG to HG, November 30, 1924, MG30C241, v. 87 (LAC).
8 Ibid.
9 Dick Interview, December 12, 1974. Sound Archives, J. King Gordon Collection, Acc. 1974-121 (LAC).
10 JKG to CWG, February 22, 1925, MG30C241, v. 87 (LAC).
11 JKG to HG, August 4, 1925, MG30C241, v. 87 (LAC).
12 JKG to HG, January 14, 1925, MG30C241, v. 87 (LAC).
13 JKG, "The Death of Giscome," n.d., MG30C241, v. 87 (LAC).
14 Dick Interview, December 12, 1974.
15 JKG to HG, May 10, 1925, MG30C241, v. 87 (LAC).
16 JKG to CWG, March 9, 1925, MG30C241, v. 87 (LAC).
17 Malcolm MacDonald to JKG, January 7, 1925, MG30C241, v. 3 (LAC). See also, Clyde Sanger. *Malcolm MacDonald: Bringing an End to Empire* (Montreal and Kingston: McGill-Queen's University Press), 1995.
18 Gilbert Ryle to JKG, December 15, 1924, MG30C241, v. 3 (LAC).
19 JKG, "Gilbert Ryle: The Beginning of Wisdom," n.d., MG30C241. v. 3 (LAC).
20 JKG to HG, August 9, 1925, MG30C241, v. 87 (LAC).
21 JKG, "Giscome, B. C. 1924-1925: A Year in the Bush," MG30C241, v. 4 (LAC).
22 Dick Interview, December 12, 1974. Sound Archives, J. King Gordon Collection, Acc. 1974-121 (LAC).
23 Ibid.
24 JKG, "An Athletic Diversion: 1926–28," MG30C241, v. 4 (LAC).
25 Gilbert Ryle to JKG, December 22, 1925, MG30C241, v. 4 (LAC).
26 JKG to HG, November 15, 1926, MG30C241, v. 87 (LAC).
27 JKG, "A Discussion of the Industrial and Social Conditions of Pine Falls, a Company Town Owned and Operated by the Manitoba Paper Company," 1930, MG30C241, v. 6 (LAC).
28 JKG to HG, January 10, 1928, MG30C241, v. 87 (LAC).
29 JKG to HG, November 26, 1926, MG30C241, v. 87 (LAC).
30 JKG to CWG, September 11, 1928, MG30C241, v. 87 (LAC).
31 JKG to CWG, September 11, 1928, MG30C241, v. 87 (LAC).
32 JKG to HG, November 1927, MG30C241, v. 87 (LAC).
33 CWG to JKG, March 3, 1929, MG30C241. v. 87 (LAC). See also, "JKG letters to Betty," 1929, MG30C241, v. 5 (LAC).
34 JKG to CWG, May 6, 1929, MG30C241, v. 87 (LAC).
35 JKG, "Autobiographical Notes on Pine Falls," MG30C241, v. 4 (LAC).
36 JKG, "Notes for an Autobiography," MG30C241, v. 5 (LAC).

CHAPTER FIVE

1 JKG, "Notes for an Autobiography," MG30C241, v. 5 (LAC).
2 Richard Wightman Fox, *Reinhold Niebuhr: A Biography* (New York: Pantheon Books, 1985), 105.
3 Ibid., 11.
4 JKG to CWG, February 17, 1930, MG30C241, v. 87 (LAC).
5 JKG, "Notes for an Autobiography," MG30C241, v. 5 (LAC).
6 Ibid.
7 JKG, "Reinhold Niebuhr, Portrait of a Christian Realist," *The Ottawa Journal*, June 1971.
8 JKG to CWG, November 25, 1930, MG30C241, v. 87 (LAC).
9 JKG, "A Christian Socialist in the 1930s." Richard Allen, ed., *The Social Gospel in Canada: Papers of the Interdisciplinary Conference on the Social Gospel in Canada, March 21–24, at the University of Regina* (Ottawa; National Museums of Canada, 1975), 125.
10 Beverly W. Harrison, review of Eugene P. Link, *Labour-Religion Prophet: The Times and Life of Harry F. Ward*, in *Union Seminary Quarterly Review* 39, no. 4 (1984), 319.
11 Ernest Dick Interview, January 17, 1975. J. King Gordon Collection, Sound Archives Acc. 1975-12 (LAC).
12 Robert H. Craig, "An Introduction to the Life and Thought of Harry F. Ward," in Martin E. Marty, ed., *Modern American Protestantism and Its World: Historical Articles on Protestantism in American Religious Life* (New York: K.G. Saur, 1992), 258.
13 Craig, 258ff.
14 Craig, 271.
15 JKG to CWG, November 25, 1930, MG30C241, v. 87 (LAC).
16 Richard Fox, *Reinhold Niebuhr: A Biography*, 125.
17 Ibid.
18 Eberhard Bethage, *Dietrich Bonhoeffer: A Biography*, Revised and Edited by Victoria J. Barnett (Minneapolis: Fortress Press, 2000), 157.
19 *Dietrich Bonhoeffer Works*, Volume 10: Barcelona, Berlin, New York 1928–1931, English Edition Edited by Clifford J. Green (Minneapolis: Fortress Press, 2008), 34. See also, Clifford Green, "Bonhoeffer at Union. Critical Turning Points: 1931 and 1939," in *Union Seminary Quarterly Review* 62, nos. 3–4 (2010): 1–16.
20 Erdman Harris, "Hungry Men in an Empty Gymnasium," *Christian Century*, December 3, 1930.

21 JKG to CWG, November 25, 1930, MG30C241, v. 87 (LAC).
22 JKG, "All Quiet on the Waterfront: A Seminary Faces Unemployment," *The Christian Advocate,* January 22, 1931; and, "Union Waterfront Project," n.d., MG30C241, v. 6 (LAC).
23 Ibid.
24 Dick Interview, January 24, 1975. J. King Gordon Collection, Sound Archives, Acc. 1975-12 (LAC).
25 JKG to HG, January 22, 1931, MG30C241, v. 87 (LAC).
26 JKG, "Vagabonds of Time," sermon May 25, 1930, MG30C241, v. 6 (LAC).
27 JKG, "Children's Sermons," February 9, 1930, MG30C241, v. 6 (LAC).
28 JKG to HG, July 13, 1930, MG30C241, v. 87 (LAC).
29 Dick Interview, January 24, 1975. J. King Gordon Collection, Sound Archives, Acc. 1975-12 (LAC).
30 30 JKG to HG, July 13, 1930, MG30C241, v. 87 (LAC).
31 JKG to CWG, December 16, 1930, MG30C241, v. 87 (LAC).
32 Richard Allen, *The Social Passion: Religion and Reform in Canada 1914–1928* (Toronto: University of Toronto Press, 1973), 10.
33 Dick Interview, January 24, 1975. J. King Gordon Collection, Sound Archives, Acc. 1975-12 (LAC).
34 Salem Bland to JKG, April 4, 1931, MG30C241, v. 6 (LAC).
35 Graham Spry to JKG, April 2, 1931, MG30C241, copy in v. 6 (LAC).
36 John Farthing to JKG, April 1931, read into Dick Interview, January 24, 1975. King Gordon Collection, Sound Archives, Acc. 1975-12 (LAC).
37 JKG to HG, June 21, 1931, MG30C241, v. 87 (LAC).
38 JKG to HG, June 21, 1931, MG30C241, v. 87 (LAC).
39 JKG, "Notes for an Autobiography," MG30C241, v. 5 (LAC).

CHAPTER SIX

1 JKG to CWG, October 6, 1931, MG30C241, v. 86 (LAC).
2 JKG to The Reverend Principle James Smyth, March 1931, MG30C241, v. 5 (LAC).
3 W.A. Gifford to Harry F. Ward, March 12, 1931, MG30C241, v. 7 (LAC).
4 JKG to HG, October 7, 1931, MG30C241, v. 87 (LAC).
5 The following information about Montreal is based on Wendell MacLeod, Libbie Park and Stanley Ryerson, *Bethune: The Montreal Years: An Informal Portrait* (Toronto: James Lorimer and company, Publishers, 1978), 86–7.

6 Laura Brandon, *Pegi by Herself: The Life of Pegi Nicol MacLeod, Canadian Artist* (Kingston and Montreal: McGill-Queen's University Press, 2005), 58; Pegi Nicol to JKG, early in 1932, MG30C241, v. 8 (LAC).
7 JKG, "The Politics of Poetry," in eds., Sandra Djwa and R. St J. Macdonald, *On F.R. Scott* (Kingston and Montreal: McGill-Queen's University Press, 1983), 19.
8 JKG, "F.R. Scott Remembered," *Saturday Night*, July 1985, 22–3.
9 JKG, "The Politics of Poetry," 21.
10 F.H. Underhill, *In Search of Canadian Liberalism* (Toronto: The Macmillan Company of Canada Limited, 1961), x.
11 Ibid.
12 Ibid., 150.
13 Michiel Horn, *The League for Social Reconstruction: Intellectual Origins of the Democratic Left in Canada 1930–1942* (Toronto: University of Toronto Press, 1980), 21ff.
14 Frank R. Scott, "F.H.U. and the Manifestos," *The Canadian Forum*, November, 1971.
15 I am working with the text of the LSR manifesto found in F.R. Scott *et al.*, *Social Planning for Canada* (Toronto: Thomas Nelson and Sons Limited, 1935), ix–xi.
16 *Social Planning for Canada* (Toronto and Buffalo: University of Toronto Press, 1976), ix.
17 This statement is based on a scholarly consensus put forth, for example, in the following works: Paul Fox, "Early Socialism in Canada," in J.H. Aitchison, ed., in *The Political Process in Canada; Essays in Honour of R. Macgregor Dawson* (Toronto: University of Toronto Press, 1963), 79–98; Evelyn Eager, *Saskatchewan Government: Politics and Pragmatism* (Saskatoon: Western Producer Prairie, 1980); Michiel Horn, *The League for Social Reconstruction: Intellectual Origins of the Democratic Left in Canada 1930–1942* (Toronto: University of Toronto Press, 1980); Gad Horowitz, *Canadian Labor in Politics* (Toronto: University Press, 1968); Seymour M. Lipset, *Agrarian Socialism: The Cooperative Commonwealth Federation in Saskatchewan* (New York: Doubleday and Company, Inc., 1968); R.T. Naylor, "Appendix" to "The Ideological Foundations of Social Democracy and Social Credit," in Gary Teeple, ed., *Capitalism and the National Question in Canada* (Toronto: University of Toronto Press, 1972), 252–6; Martin Robin, *Radical Politics and Canadian Labour 1880–1930* (Kingston: Industrial Relations Centre, Queen's University, 1968); Walter Young, *The Anatomy of a Party: The National* CCF *1932–1961* (Toronto: University of Toronto Press, 1969). Note that Norman Penner,

The Canadian Left (Scarborough: Prentice Hall of Canada, 1977), argues for and documents a Marxist influence on Canadian socialism in the years preceding the First World War.

18 *Social Planning for Canada*, 16.

19 Quoted in Sandra Djwa, *The Politics of the Imagination: A Life of F.R. Scott* (Toronto: McClelland and Stewart, 1987), 139.

20 JKG Diary, 1932–33, MG30C241, v. 7 (LAC).

21 JKG to HG, October 26, 1932, MG30C241, v. 87 (LAC).

22 JKG, "The Growing Threats to Religious Liberty," Lecture, 1932, MG30C241, v. 7 (LAC).

23 JKG, "Dare the Church Be Christian?" *New Outlook*, March 22, 1933.

24 JKG, Sermon delivered at UTC 1931–32, MG30C241, v. 7 (LAC).

25 JKG, "The Relevance of the LSR," n.d., MG30C241, v. 70 (LAC).

26 JKG, "F.R. Scott Remembered," 2.

27 JKG, "The LSR – Thirty Years After."

28 Sandra Djwa, *The Politics of the Imagination: A Life of F.R. Scott*, 135.

29 JKG, "F.R. Scott Remembered," 25.

30 H. Blair Neatby, *The Politics of Chaos: Canada in the Thirties* (Toronto: Macmillan of Canada, 1972), 56ff.

31 Ibid., 63.

32 J.R. McLean, "Bennett of Tarsus," *Forum: Canadian Life and Letters 1920–1970, Selections from the Canadian Forum*, eds., J.L. Granatstein and Peter Stevens (Toronto: University of Toronto Press, 1972), 132–3.

33 Quoted in H. Blair Neatby, *The Politics of Chaos*, 65.

34 H. Blair Neatby, *The Politics of Chaos,* 64–5.

35 F.R. Scott, "The Privy Council and Mr Bennett's 'New Deal' Legislation," *Essays of the Constitution: Aspects of Canadian Law and Politics* (Toronto and Buffalo: University of Toronto Press, 1977, 90–101.

36 *Information Bulletin* published by the Committee on Social and Economic Research of the Montreal Presbytery, United Church of Canada. Committee: J. King Gordon–Eugene Forsey–J. M. Coote. MG30C241, v. 7 (LAC).

37 J. S. Woodsworth to JKG, February 12, 1932, MG30C241, v. 11 (LAC).

38 For a comprehensive discussion of the controversy concerning the *Information Bulletin* see Frank Milligan, *Eugene A. Forsey: An Intellectual Biography* (Calgary: University of Calgary Press, 2004), 77ff.

39 William Munroe, Secretary of the Montreal Presbytery, to JKG, May 5, 1933, MG30C241, v. 7 (LAC).

40 J.A. Ewing to JKG, June 29, 1933, MG30C241, v. 7 (LAC).

41 Alexander McA. Murphy, Esq., to JKG, June 29, 1933, MG30C241, v. 7 (LAC).

42 JKG to Alexander McA., Murphy, Esq., to JKG, July 13, 1933, MG30C241, v. 7 (LAC).

43 Dick Interview, April 30, 1975, Sound Archives, J. King Gordon Collection, Acc. 1975–73 (LAC); also, William Munroe, Secretary of the Montreal Presbytery, to JKG, May 5, 1933, MG30C241, v. 7 (LAC).

44 JKG, "A Christian Socialist in the 1930's," 136.

45 Frank R. Scott, Travel Diary, January 1961, MG30D211, v. 91 (LAC).

46 Michiel Horn, *The League for Social Reconstruction*, 43.

47 CWG to JKG, June 4, 1933, MG30C231. v. 89 (LAC)

48 Dick Interview, May 28, 1975, Sound Archives, J. King Gordon Collection, Acc. 1975–73.

49 During the Dick Interview of May 28, 1975, JKG had with him – and read from it into the tape – his own copy of Underhill's draft Manifesto with the pencil editing on it. A xeroxed copy of this document and an excerpt from Underhill's draft on Agriculture and Social Justice with King Gordon's handwritten revisions on the back of the page, can both be found in MG30C241, v. 9 (LAC).

50 Ronald St John Macdonald, in reading the draft of this chapter, wrote to the author regarding King Gordon's participation in going over Frank Underhill's draft and in the final wording of the Regina Manifesto (see footnote 66): "This in my opinion is an extremely important paragraph and part of the history of the Manifesto… . For one thing, as M.J. Coldwell said, the content [of the final wording of the Manifesto] worked greatly to the detriment of the CCF party. For another, you have here the best evidence we will ever have of an extremely important specific contribution of King Gordon to the final wording of the Manifesto." Ronald St J. Macdonald to Eileen Janzen, July 21, 1998.

51 Michiel Horn, *The League for Social Reconstruction*, 43.

52 Walter Young, *The Anatomy of a Party: The National* CCF *1932–1961* (Toronto; University of Toronto Press, 1969), 44.

53 Eugene Forsey, *A Life on the Fringe: The Memoirs of Eugene Forsey* (Toronto: Oxford University Press, 1990), 54.

54 Walter Young, *The Anatomy of a Party*, 44.

55 Ibid., n.d., 16.

56 F.H. Underhill, "Political Radicalism in the 'Thirties," Seminar 3. Text deposited with the Institute of Canadian Studies, Carleton University, Ottawa, 1959; manuscript also called, "The Angry 'Thirties," MG30D204, v. 18 (LAC).

57 JKG to FRS, Easter Sunday 1979, photocopy in FRSP, MG30D211, v. 73 (LAC). I also have a copy of this letter, sent to me by King Gordon.

58 Quoted by FRS in a conversation with this author in December 1979, in which he agreed with JKG that they probably had written that last offending paragraph.
59 Walter Young, *The Anatomy of a Party*, 44.
60 G.V. Ferguson, "C.C.F. 'Brain Trust,'" *Winnipeg Free Press*, July 25, 1933.
61 Michiel Horn, *The League for Social Reconstruction*, 44.
62 Ibid., 47.
63 Walter Young, *The Anatomy of a Party*, 72.
64 Original clipping, n.d., JKGP.
65 Norman F. Priestly to JKG, October 10, 1933, MG30C241, v. 9 (LAC).
66 F.H. Underhill, Notes for a speech, his eightieth birthday dinner, November 26, 1969, MG30D204, v. 26 (LAC).
67 JKG, "The Relevance of the LSR," MG30C241, v. 70 (LAC).
68 Article 10, "External Relations," Regina Manifesto.
69 C.W. Gordon, *Postscript to Adventure*, 379.
70 Ibid., 381.
71 JKG, "Biographical Fragment," MG30C241, v. 86 (LAC).
72 JKG, "The Imperatives of Social Democracy: Then and Now," MG30C241, v. 67 (LAC). In correspondence between R. St J. Macdonald and this author, Professor Macdonald contributed two examples from his own experience that support my interpretation of JKG's reluctance to go along wholeheartedly with the 1933 position of the CCF on foreign policy. In July of 1998, he wrote:

> The first example concerns John Humphrey. He was a student at McGill in the early '20s and joined the Law Faculty in the 1930s. He was a close friend of Frank Scott, Percy Corbett, Eugene Forsey, and he almost ran as a Labour candidate in one of the east end constituencies. As you know, he knew King Gordon and later worked with him. Yet he was never active in the LSR, which he fully supported. Why? Because, as he told me at least half a dozen times, the people in the LSR were really not interested in international affairs, which was where his own interests lay. So, while sympathetic and generally supportive, Humphrey did not participate in the work of the LSR.
>
> The second example is even more persuasive coming as it does from the horse's mouth, so to speak. I once asked Frank Scott why he and his pals did not take more interest in international affairs and even before he completed his answer I could tell by the look in his eye and the tone of his voice that he was irritated by the question. "I am not against internationalism," he replied, "I am in favour of Canada joining the OAS." Well, if ever one needed reaffirmation of the statements in your text I think this is it.

Ronald St J. Macdonald to Eileen Janzen, July, 21, 1998. Letter in author's possession.

CHAPTER SEVEN

1 JKG, "Dare the Church Be Christian?" Sermon preached at the Metropolitan Church, Toronto, Sunday, March 12, 1933; published in *New Outlook*, March 22, 1933.
2 CWG to JKG, April 4, 1931, MG30C241, v. 89 (LAC).
3 JKG, "A Christian Socialist in the 1930's," Richard Allen, ed., *The Social Gospel in Canada: Papers of the Indisciplinary Conference on the Social Gospel in Canada, March 21–4, 1973, at the University of Regina* (Ottawa: National Museums of Canada, 1975), 128.
4 JKG, "Russian Travel Diary," June 1, 1932, MG30C241, v. 11 (LAC).
5 Ibid.
6 Eugene Forsey, *A Life on the Fringe: The Memoirs of Eugene Forsey* (Toronto: Oxford University Press, 1990), 52.
7 Ibid., 51.
8 JKG, "Russian Diary: Kharkof, the Ukraine, July 30th," MG30C241, v. 7 (LAC).
9 Ibid.
10 Dick Interview, April 30, 1975, Sound Archives, J. King Gordon Collection, Acc. 1975–73 (LAC).
11 Dick Interview, April 30, 1975.
12 Ibid.
13 Ibid. Regarding Forsey's response to what he saw in the Soviet Union, see also, Frank Milligan, *Eugene A. Forsey: An Intellectual Biography* (Calgary: University of Calgary Press, 2004), 111–17.
14 Rose Potvin, ed., *Passion and Conviction: The Letters of Graham Spry* (Regina: Canadian Plains Research Centre, 1992), 102.
15 Ibid.
16 Kenneth McNaught, *A Prophet in Politics; A Biography of J.S. Woodsworth* (Toronto: University of Toronto Press, 1959), 233.
17 Sandra Djwa, *The Politics of the Imagination: A Life of F.R. Scott* (Toronto: McClelland and Stewart, 1987), 154.
18 Frank R. Scott, "Impressions of a Tour in the U.S.S.R." *The Canadian Forum*, December 1935.
19 Norman and Jeanne MacKenzie, *The Fabians* (New York: Simon and Schuster, 1977), 406.

20 Ross Terrill, *R.H. Tawney and His Times: Socialism as Fellowship* (Cambridge: Harvard University Press, 1975), 75.
21 Dick Interview, April 30, 1975.
22 "Real Religion in Russia Discovered: No More Puritanical Group Than Communist, Says Prof. King Gordon," *Montreal Gazette*, October 3, 1932; clipping, MG30C241, v. 11 (LAC).
23 "Religion in Russia and in Canada," *The Witness and Canadian Homestead*, October 5, 1932, MG30C241, v. 11 (LAC).
24 JKG to HG, October 26, 1932, MG30C241, v. 89 (LAC).
25 Ibid.
26 Sir Arthur Currie to JKG, March 21, 1933, MG30C241, v. 11 (LAC).
27 JKG to Sir Arthur Currie, March 23, 1933, MG30C241, v. 7 (LAC).
28 For this reference I am indebted to Michiel Horn, *Academic Freedom in Canada: A History* (Toronto: University of Toronto Press, 1999), 129.
29 William Bovey to Major General J.H. MacBrien, December 17, 1932. Copy, MG30C241, v. 81 (LAC). Regarding UTC's affiliation with McGill University, four Montreal theological colleges had become affiliated to McGill: the Congregational in 1865, the Presbyterian in 1867, the Methodist in 1879, and the Anglican in 1880. In 1925, with the creation of the United Church of Canada, the Congregational, Methodist and Presbyterian Colleges joined to form United Theological College. UTC's affiliation to McGill continued until 1948 when UTC and the Anglican Diocesan College, the Joint Board of the Theological Colleges, and McGill University came to an agreement establishing the Faculty of Divinity (now Religious Studies). "R.G. 90: Affiliated Educational Institutions," http://www.archives.mcgill.ca/resources/guide/vol1/rg90.htm.
30 J.H. MacBrien to Arthur Currie, February, February 13, 1933. Copy, MG30C241, v. 81 (LAC).
31 The letters referred to include those used in writing this chapter, copies sent to me by JKG and also in MG30C241, v. 81 (LAC).
32 As an example of the growing polarization within the United Church: in 1932, responding to the growing tensions between conservatives and radicals in the Church, the General Council of the United Church established a Commission on Christianizing the Social Order, chaired by Sir Robert Falconer—hence its name, the Falconer Commission. The Commission divided itself into sixteen small geographic groups to study the various issues of concern. The Montreal Study Group, led by Professor R.B.Y. Scott and the Reverend J.L. Smith, included Gordon and Forsey, and was mandated to report to the Commission on the "merits of capitalism within the

scope of Christian society." The submission by Forsey and Gordon on their findings was considered on the radical fringe when compared to the submission of the moderates who urged a "cooperative reconciliation with capitalism." Cf. Frank Milligan, *Eugene A. Forsey: An Intellectual Biography* (Calgary: University of Calgary Press, 2004), 85–7.

33 Chapter 6, note 9.

34 "Policy in Church Bulletins Scored – Articles in United Church Periodicals Criticized at Presbytery," *Montreal Star*, March 2, 1933.

35 Michiel Horn, *Academic Freedom in Canada*, 114–15.

36 JKG to Chairman of the Board, February 22, 1933, MG30C241, v. 11 (LAC).

37 *The Montreal Gazette*, March 31, 1933.

38 JKG to HG, April 9, 1933, MG30C241, v. 89 (LAC).

39 Ernest Deane, "Trying to Teach Christians Ethics," *The Canadian Forum*, June 1933.

40 "The Front Page," *Saturday Night*, April 8, 1933.

41 Deane, "Trying to Teach Christians Ethics," *The Canadian Forum*, June 1933.

42 J.C. Ewing K.C., *The Clubman*, Montreal, January 22, 1934. Quoted in Roger C. Hutchinson, "The Fellowship for a Christian Social Order: A Social Ethical Analysis of a Christian Socialist Movement," unpublished dissertation, Victoria University, Toronto, 1975, 34.

43 R.H. Barron, Secretary, Board of Governors, to JKG, March 24, 1934, MG30C241, v. 11 (LAC).

44 "The Matter of the Montreal College," *New Outlook*, May 9, 1934.

45 JKG to HG, May 30, 1934, MG30C241, v. 89 (LAC).

46 "The Case of the Montreal College," *New Outlook*, April 11, 1934.

47 "King Gordon Loses Chair," *The Christian Century*, April 11, 1934.

48 Gregory Vlastos to *The Christian Century*, October 7, 1934. Copy to JKG, MG30C241, v. 7 (LAC).

49 JKG to Michiel Horn, October 2, 1972, Quoted by Horn in *Academic Freedom in Canada*, 116.

50 Dick Interview, April 30, 1975.

51 JKG, "A Christian Socialist in the 1930's" 143.

52 JKG, "July 24," *New Outlook*, September 5, 1934, 750–1.

53 JKG, "Black Sea Holiday," MG30C241, v. 7 (LAC).

54 Ibid.

55 Ibid.

56 Ibid.

57 JKG, "July 31: Yalta: The Last Day of July," unpublished poem, MG30C241, v. 22 (LAC).

CHAPTER EIGHT

1 Richard Allen, *The Social Passion: Religion and Social Reform in Canada 1914–1928* (Toronto: University of Toronto Press, 1973), 143; 146–7. See also Roger G. Hutchinson, "The Fellowship for a Christian Social Order: A Social Ethical Analysis of a Christian Socialist Movement," Ph.D. dissertation, Victoria University, 1975.
2 Roger Hutchinson, "The Fellowship for a Christian Social Order," 27ff.
3 JKG to Reinhold Niebuhr, April 26, 1934, MG30C241, v. 10 (LAC).
4 Hutchinson, "The Fellowship for a Christian Social Order," 96.
5 Reinhold Niebuhr, review of *Towards the Christian Revolution*, in *Radical Religion* (Spring 1937), 42–4.
6 R.B.Y. Scott and Gregory Vlastos, eds., *Towards the Christian Revolution* (Chicago: Willett, Clark and Company, 1936).
7 JKG, "A Christian Socialist in the 1930's," in Richard Allen, ed., *The Social Gospel in Canada: Papers of the Interdisciplinary Conference on the Social Gospel in Canada, March 21–24, 1973, at the University of Regina* (Ottawa: National Museums of Canada, 1975), 125.
8 JKG to Professor R.B.Y. Scott, June, 1937. The following series of letters from JKG to RBY Scott, describing his tour of the Maritimes, are found in MG30C241, v. 10 (LAC).
9 See James D. Cameron, *For the People: A History of St Francis Xavier University* (Montreal and Kingston: McGill-Queen's University Press, 1996). See also Gregory Baum, "Social Catholicism in Nova Scotia: The Thirties," in *Religion and Culture in Canada,* ed. Peter Slater (Waterloo: Wilfred Laurier Press, 1977), and ibid., "Catholics in Eastern Nova Scotia," in Gregory Baum, *Catholics and Canadian Socialism: Political Thought in the Thirties and Forties* (Toronto: James Lorimer and Company, Publishers, 1980), 189–211.
10 JKG to R.B.Y. Scott, June 17, 1937.
11 JKG to R.B.Y. Scott, June 22, 1937.
12 Ibid.
13 JKG to R.B.Y. Scott, June 22, 1937.
14 Walter Young, *The Anatomy of a Party: The National* CCF *1932–1961* (Toronto: University of Toronto Press, 1969), 256.
15 JKG to R.B.Y. Scott, June 17, 1937.

16 JKG, "Notes on the FCSO in the Thirties," MG30C241, v. 10 (LAC).
17 JKG, The LSR—Thirty Years After," MG30C241, v. 7 (LAC).
18 JKG, "St Francis of Antigonish," *The Canadian Forum*, May 1936.
19 James Cameron, *For the People: A History of St Francis Xavier University*, 169–71.
20 Ibid.
21 Ibid.
22 Rose Potvin, ed., *Passion and Conviction: The Letters of Graham Spry* (Canadian Plains Research Center: University of Regina, 1992), 104.
23 Dr Norman Bethune was frequently part of the group that gathered at the home of Frank and Marian Scott on Oxenden Avenue, although he was considerably further left in his political views than the CCF and LSR. He joined the Communist Party in 1936.
24 Poitvin, *Passion and Conviction*, 105.
25 JKG, "Fascist Week-end in Montreal," *The Christian Century*, November 25, 1936.
26 Ibid.
27 Michiel Horn, *The League for Social Reconstruction: Intellectual Origins of the Democratic Left in Canada 1930–1942* (Toronto: University of Toronto Press, 1980), 136.
28 JKG, "Church or State: To Stand or Run," n.d., King's own recollection of his "Battle of Victoria," MG30C241, v. 9 (LAC); see also, JKG, "Battle of Victoria," *The Canadian Forum*, January 1938.
29 JKG, "Church or State: to Stand or Run," 3.
30 Quoted in JKG, "Church or State: to Stand or Run," 3.
31 Ibid., 4.
32 Ibid.
33 Ibid., 5.
34 Ibid.
35 Ibid.
36 Ibid., 6.
37 JKG, "Church or State: To Stand or Run," 6.
38 W.A. Gifford to JKG, May 11, 1935, MG30C241, v. 7 (LAC).
39 JKG, "Church or State: To Stand or Run," 6.
40 Ibid., 8.
41 J.S. Woodsworth to JKG, May 13, 1935, MG30C241, v. 7 (LAC)
42 Quoted in JKG, "Church or State: To Stand or Run," 14.
43 Ibid., 16.
44 T. Albert Moore to JKG, May 28, 1935, MG30C241, v. 7 (LAC).
45 T. Albert Moore to JKG, June 8, 1935, MG30C241, v. 7 (LAC).

46 T. Albert Moore to JKG, July 8, 1935, MG30C241, v. 7 (LAC).
47 T. Albert Moore to JKG, August 1, 1935, MG30C241, v.7 (LAC).
48 JKG, "A Christian Socialist in the 1930's," 147.
49 JKG, "Church or State: To Stand or Run," 13.
50 JKG to HG, July 7, 1935, MG30C241, v. 87 (LAC).
51 *The New Era*, Victoria, October 12, 1935; published by the Victoria Federation CCF Campaign Committee. MG30C241, v. 9 (LAC).
52 JKG to HG, September 22, 1935, MG30C241, v. 87 (LAC).
53 JKG to C. W. Gordon, October 3, 1935, JKGP.
54 Kenneth McNaught, *A Prophet in Politics: A Biography of J. S. Woodsworth* (Toronto: University of Toronto Press, 1959), 275–6.
55 JKG to HG, November 13, 1935, MG30C241, v. 87 (LAC).
56 JKG, "A Christian Socialist in the 1930's" 148.
57 Ibid., 149.
58 JKG, Introduction to C.W. Gordon, *Postscript to Adventure*, xiii.
59 Ibid., xv.
60 Ibid., xvi.
61 Ibid., xvii.
62 J.S. Woodsworth to JKG, December 30, 1938, MG30C241, v. 10 (LAC).
63 J.S. Woodsworth to JKG, December 3, 1938, MG30C241, v. 10 (LAC).
64 F.R. Scott to JKG, March 27, 1938, MG30C241, v. 73 (LAC).

CHAPTER NINE

1 This chapter is based in part on Eileen Janzen, "King Gordon's Christian Socialism and the Kingdom of God," *Studies in Religion/Sciences Religieuses*, 16, no. 3 (1987): 347–61.
2 J. King Gordon, "A Christian Socialist in the 1930's," Richard Allen, ed., *The Social Gospel in Canada: Papers on the Interdisciplinary Conference on the Social Gospel in Canada, March 21–24, 1973, at the University of Regina* (Ottawa: National Museums of Canada, 1975), 122.
3 The following discussion is based on Richard Allen, *The Social Passion: Religion and Social Reform in Canada 1914–1928* (Toronto: University of Toronto Press, 1973); and Richard Allen, "The Background of the Social Gospel in Canada," in *The Social Gospel in Canada*, 2–25.
4 Benjamin G. Smillie, "The Social Gospel in Canada: A Theological Critique," in *The Social Gospel in Canada*, 318–20.
5 JKG, "A Christian Socialist in the 1930's," 122.
6 Richard Allen, *The Social Passion*, 33.
7 Ibid., 5.

8 Ernest Dick Interview, December 4, 1975. Sound Archives, J. King Gordon Collection, Acc. 1975-195 (LAC).
9 JKG, "The Twilight of This Age," review of Reinhold Niebuhr, *Reflections on the End of an Era* (New York: Charles Scribners' Sons, 1934), in *The World Tomorrow*, March 1, 1934.
10 JKG's published articles from this period include: *The Nation*, "Prairie Socialism," August 17 and August 24, 1946; *The Canadian Forum*, "St Francis of Antigonish" (May 1936); "A Marxist Explains the World" (October 1936); "The CCF Convention" (September 1937); "Battle for Victoria" (January 1938); in *The Christian Century*, "Nova Scotia See a Great Light" (May 27, 1936); *The New Outlook*, "Dare the Church Be Christian?" (March 22, 1933); "Moscow, July 24, 1934" (September 5, 1934); "Christianity and Social Revolution" (June 12, 1935 and June 19, 1935); "The World of Books: A Christian Socialist Reflects Upon His Ancestors" (February 26, 1937); *Saskatchewan CCF Research*, "Christianity and Socialism" (May 1934); *The World Tomorrow*, "The Twilight of This Age," a review of Reinhold Niebuhr, *Reflections on the End of an Era* (March 1, 1934). He signed his name to the preface of *Social Planning for Canada* (Toronto: The League for Social Reconstruction, 1935), thus assuming responsibility with other members of the research committee for the book as a whole, and he wrote "The Political Task," chapter seven in *Towards the Christian Revolution* (Toronto: The Fellowship for a Christian Social Order, 1936).
11 JKG, "Easter Sermon," n.d., MG30C241, v. 6 (LAC).
12 JKG, "Sermon," n.d., MG30C241, v. 6 (LAC).
13 JKG, "The Religion of the Kingdom," Lecture Series, 1934, MG30C241, v. 11 (LAC).
14 JKG, "The Religion of the Kingdom," MG30C241, v. 11 (LAC).
15 JKG, "The Preacher at the End of an Era," sermon, n.d., MG30C241, v. 11 (LAC).
16 Dick Interview, December 4, 1975. Sound Archives, J. King Gordon Collection, Acc. 1975-195 (LAC).
17 JKG, "The Twilight of This Age," review of Reinhold Niebuhr, *Reflections on the End of an Era* (New York: Charles Scribners' Sons, 1934), in *The World Tomorrow*, March 1, 1934.
18 JKG to RN, February 23, 1934, MG30C241, v. 10 (LAC).
19 JKG, "The Twilight of This Age."
20 Quoted in JKG, "The Twilight of This Age."
21 JKG, "The Twilight of This Age."

22 Dick Interview, January 24, 1975. Sound Archives, J. King Gordon Collection, Acc. 1975-12 (LAC).
23 JKG, "Beyond Tragedy," review of Reinhold Niebuhr, *Beyond Tragedy: Essays on the Christian Interpretation of History* (New York: Charles Scribners' Sons, 1937). Manuscript, 1938, MG30C241, v. 11 (LAC).
24 Northrope Frye, "The Critical Path: An Essay on the Social Context of Literary Criticism," *Daedalus* 99, no. 2 (Spring 1970): 332–3.
25 JKG, "Christianity and Socialism," *Saskatchewan CCF Research Bureau*, May 1934, 4–9.
26 Ibid., 9.
27 See JKG, "St Francis of Antigonish," 21; "Nova Scotia Sees a Great Light," 764–7; "How Relevant is Coady?" address delivered at St Francis Xavier University, October 1978, MG30C241, v. 87 (LAC). For a discussion of the place of the Antigonish Movement in Canadian religious and social life, see Gregory Baum, "Social Catholicism in Nova Scotia: The Thirties," in Peter Slater, ed., *Religion and Culture in Canada* (Waterloo: Wilfred Laurier Press, 1977); and Gregory Baum, "Catholics in Eastern Nova Scotia, in *Catholics and Canadian Socialism* (New York; Paulist Press, 1980). Baum points out that the Antigonish Movement was a cooperative, not a socialist, movement and that Moses Coady, its founder, was himself a Liberal. See also, James Cameron, *For the People: A History of St Francis Xavier University* (Montreal and Kingston: McGill-Queen's University Press, 1996).
28 JKG, "The Political Task," 146.
29 JKG, "Prairie Socialism," *The Nation*, August 17, 1946.
30 Author's conversation with JKG on cooperatives, October 1978.
31 JKG, "The CCF Convention," *The Canadian Forum*, September 1937.
32 JKG, "Prairie Socialism," 183.
33 Report of the First National Convention, 1933, CCF Papers, MG28IV1, v. 1 (LAC).
34 Frank R. Scott, "A Note on Canadian War Poetry," *Preview I*, November 1942, 3.
35 JKG, "Easter Sermon," n.d., and sermon, "The Christian Shape of Things to Come," n.d., MG30C241, v. 6 (LAC).

CHAPTER TEN

1 JKG to HG, September 24, 1938, MG30C241, v. 87 (LAC).
2 JKG, "Reflections on Oxford," September 1937, MG30C241, v. 11 (LAC).

3 Along with acquaintances and friends in the larger context of Oxford, JGK mentions in particular Gilbert Ryle, P.I. Bell, Malcolm MacDonald, W. Hurst Brown, Graham Spry, and Gilbert Murray Webb.
4 JKG, "Reflections on Oxford."
5 Ibid.
6 Ibid.
7 Alison Gordon, reminiscing at the time of her mother's death, June 1996.
8 HG to JKG, July 19, 1939, MG30C241, v. 87 (LAC).
9 JKG, "Reflections on Oxford," September 1937, MG30C241, v. 11 (LAC).
10 JKG to HG, July 24, 1939, MG30C241, v. 87 (LAC).
11 HG to JKG, July 1939, MG30C241, v. 89 (LAC).
12 JKG, "Eulogy for Charles William Gordon," MG30C241, v. 93 (LAC).
13 RAG to HG, November 7, 1939, MG30C241, v. 86 (LAC).
14 HG to Ruth and King Gordon, December 2, 1939, JKGP.
15 JKG to F.H. Barlow, K.C., December 1942, MG30C241, v. 16 (LAC).
16 Minority Report, *Royal Commission on Steel*, Dissenting Opinion of J. King Gordon, Commissioner, MG30C241, v. 17 (LAC).
17 FRS to JKG, December 23, 1942, FRSP, MG30D211, v. 82 (LAC).
18 JKG to HG, February 7, 1943, MG30C241, v. 88 (LAC).
19 John English, *Shadow of Heaven; the Life of Lester Pearson, Volume One: 1897–1948* (London: Vintage U. K., 1989), 248.
20 David Jay Bercuson, *True Patriot: The Life of Brooke Claxton, 1898–1960* (Toronto: University of Toronto Press, 1993), 83.
21 JKG to Brooke Claxton, April 10, 1941, MG30C241, v. 13 (LAC).
22 Brooke Claxton to JGJ, April 1941, MG30C241, v. 88 (LAC).
23 FRS to JKG, April 20, 1942, F.R. Scott Papers, MG30D211, v. 73 (LAC).
24 Ernest Dick Interview, January 28, 1976. Sound Archives, J. King Gordon Collection, Acc. 1976-115 (LAC).
25 Quoted in Michiel Horn, *The League for Social Reconstruction: Intellectual Origins of the Democratic Left in Canada 1930–1942* (Toronto: University of Toronto Press, 1980), 146.
26 *Social Planning for Canada*, 517–8.
27 David Jay Bercuson, *True Patriot: The Life of Brooke Claxton 1898–1960*, 89–90.
28 See *Social Planning for Canada*, 518ff.
29 Kenneth McNaught, *A Prophet in Politics*, 302.
30 JKG to HG, September 4, 1939, MG30C241, v. 87 (LAC).
31 Richard Wightman Fox, *Reinhold Niebuhr: A Biography* (New York: Pantheon Books, 1985), 194.

32 Provisional Committee of the Union for Democratic Action to JKG, March 29, 1941, MG30C241, v. 13 (LAC).
33 Richard Wightman Fox, *Reinhold Niebuhr*, 193.
34 JKG to Reinhold Niebuhr, April 4, 1941, MG30C241, v. 13 (LAC).
35 Richard Wightman Fox, *Reinhold Niebuhr*, 230–1.
36 Frank R. Scott to JKG, December 23, 1942, FRSP, M30D211, v. 82 (LAC).
37 JKG to Frank R. Scott, February 4, 1944, FRSP, MG30D211, v. 73 (LAC).
38 Frank R. Scott to JKG, February 8, 1944, FRSP, MG30D211, v. 73 (LAC).
39 JKG, "CCF: Awakening in the North," *Assembly*, published by the U. S. Student Assembly, November 1943, MG30C241, v. 14 (LAC).
40 Walter Young, *The Anatomy of a Party*, 109.
41 JKG, "Prairie Socialism," *The Nation*, August 17 and August 24, 1946.
42 S.M. Lipset, *Agrarian Socialism: The Cooperative Commonwealth Federation in Saskatchewan* (Berkeley: University of California Press, 1971), 362.
43 JKG to Ruth Gordon, July 26, 1945, RAGP.
44 Ross Terrill, *R.H. Tawney and His Times: Socialism as Fellowship* (Cambridge: Harvard University Press, 1973), 92.
45 JKG to F.R. Scott, December 7, 1945, FRSP, MG30D211, v. 73 (LAC).
46 For a fuller discussion of the Frank H. Underhill affair, see Michiel Horn, *The League for Social Reconstruction*, 187ff, and *Academic Freedom in Canada: A History* (Toronto: University of Toronto Press, 1999), Chapter 6; Carl Berger, *The Writing of Canadian History: Aspects of English-Canadian Historical Writing 1900–1970* (Toronto: Oxford University Press, 1976); R. Douglas Francis, *Frank H. Underhill: Intellectual Provocateur* (Toronto: University of Toronto Press, 1986).

CHAPTER ELEVEN

1 Sara Alpern, *Freda Kirchwey: A Woman of the Nation* (Cambridge: Harvard University Press, 1987), vii–viii.
2 JKG to HG, September 27. 1943, MG30C241, v. 88 (LAC).
3 Frank R. Scott to JKG, February 8, 1944, FRSP, MG30D211, v. 73 (LAC).
4 *The Nation*, March 11, 1944.
5 JKG's two articles on the Saskatchewan CCF in 1946 fell into this category, articles which in retrospect he called "much too optimistic." Ernest Dick Interview, December 16, 1975.
6 Ernest Dick Interview, December 16, 1975. Sound Archives, J. King Gordon Collection, Acc. 1975-195 (LAC).

7 The American Forum of the Air, September 27, 1944.
8 Sara Alpern, *Freda Kirchwey*, 117–18.
9 JKG, "The Political Task," in R.B.Y. Scott and Gregory Vlastos, eds., *Towards the Christian Revolution* (Chicago: Willett, Clark and Company, 1936). Chapter VII.
10 Sara Alpern, *Freda Kirchwey*, 123.
11 Ibid., 183.
12 Dick Interview, February 4, 1976. Sound Archives, J. King Collection, Acc. 1976-115 (LAC).
13 cf. JKG, "Big States, Little Men," *The Nation*, April 6, 1946; and JKG, "Two World Debate," *The Nation*, October 18, 1947.
14 Dick Interview, February 4, 1976.
15 JKG to HG, August 16, 1945, MG30C241, v. 88 (LAC).
16 Freda Kirchwey, "One World or None," *The Nation*, August 18, 1945.
17 JKG, "The Bomb is a World Affair," *The Nation*, November 24, 1945.
18 JKG to Frank R. Scott, April 3, 1947, FRSP, MG30D211, v. 73 (LAC).
19 Freda Kirchwey to JKG, February 16, 1947, MG30C241, v. 18 (LAC).
20 Freda Kirchwey to JKG, July 6, 1947, MG30C241, v. 18 (LAC).
21 RG to Mary Gordon Carver, July 17, 1947, MG30C241, v. 88 (LAC).
22 JKG to Helen Gordon, August 10, 1947, MG30C241, v. 88 (LAC).
23 Stanley Knowles to David Lewis, September 25, 1947, MG30C241, v. 19 (LAC).
24 JKG to HG, September 22, 1947, MG30C241, v. 88 (LAC).
25 Notes for Reporters, MG30C241, v. 20 (LAC).
26 Stuart W. Griffiths to JKG, September 4, 1947, MG30C241, v. 20 (LAC).
27 JKG to Ernie Bushnell, December 19, 1949, MG30C241, v. 20 (LAC).
28 Autobiographical Notes, MG30C241, v. 20 (LAC).
29 Ibid.
30 CBC Talks and Public Affairs Department, "Tips to Talkers," MG30C241, v. 21 (LAC).
31 JKG, CBC Scripts, February 12, 1947, MG30C241, v. 21 (LAC).
32 JKG, CBC Scripts, March 20, 1948, MG30C241, v. 21 (LAC).
33 JKG, CBC Scripts, April 13, 1950, MG30C241, v. 22 (LAC).
34 JKG, CBC Scripts, September 21, 1948, MG30C241, v. 22 (LAC).
35 JKG, CBC Scripts, December 24, 1947, MG30C241, v. 21 (LAC).
36 JKG to HG, February 27, 1949, MG30C241, v. 88 (LAC).
37 JKG, "Wind-up at Flushing," *The Nation*, December 6, 1947.
38 L.B. Pearson, *Mike: The Memoirs of the Right Honourable Lester B. Pearson: Volume 2 1948–1957*, eds., John A Munro and Alex I. Inglis (Toronto: University of Toronto Press, 1973) 122–3.

39 JKG to HG, October 22, 1947, MG30C241, v. 88 (LAC).
40 JKG to HG, July 9, 1947, MG30C241, v. 88 (LAC).
41 JKG, "The Making of a Peacemaker," n.d., *The Ottawa Journal*, MG30C241, v. 67 (LAC).
42 JKG to HG, June 6 and June 20, 1948, MG30C241, v. 88 (LAC).
43 "King Gordon Leaves CBC to work for 'Human Rights'." *The Ottawa Journal*, February 23, 1950.
44 Count Folke Bernadotte (1895–1948), a Swedish diplomat, was appointed UN mediator in Palestine in May 1948. He was assassinated in Jerusalem on September 17, 1948, by extreme Zionists, members of the Stern Gang. Count Bernadotte, a member of the Swedish royal family, was married to an American heiress, Estelle Manville, who became Countess Bernadotte upon her marriage. She and King worked together on the Prisoner of War Commission, in the UN Division of Human Rights. She became close friends with Ruth and King.
45 JKG to HG, September 25, 1948, MG30C241, v. 88 (LAC).
46 Ruth Gordon to HG, November 15, 1948, MG30C241, v. 88 (LAC).
47 JKG to HG, November 11, 1948, MG30C241, v. 88 (LAC).
48 Ibid.
49 Ruth Gordon to HG, November 15, 1948, MG30C241, v. 88 (LAC).
50 JKG to HG, November 30, 1948, MG30C241 v. 88 (LAC).
51 JKG to Ruthie Gordon, November 10, 1986, JKGP; and, "Confessions of a Europhile: Charles Gordon makes a grudging trip back to his childhood Europe only to find ... he likes it." *The Citizen's Weekly*, May 2, 2004.
52 Ruth Gordon to HG, November 15, 1948, MG30C241, v. 88 (LAC).
53 JKG to HG, November 30, 1948, MG30C241, v. 88 (LAC).
54 JKG, Capital Report, Geneva, December 14, 1948, MG30C241, v. 21 (LAC).
55 JKG, CBC United Nations Commentary, Rome, December 20, 1948, MG 30C241, v. 22 (LAC).
56 Ibid.
57 JKG to HG, January 9, 1949, MG30C241, v. 88 (LAC).
58 JKG, International Commentary, Edinburgh, January 19, 1949, MG30C241, v. 22 (LAC).
59 See R. St J. Macdonald, "Leadership in Law: John P. Humphrey and the Development of the International Law of Human Rights." *The Canadian Yearbook of International Law* 29 (1991): 3–92.
60 JKG to Ira Dilworth, December 26, 1949, MG 30C241, v. 20 (LAC).
61 I. Dilworth to JKG, December 27, 1949, MG30C241, v. 20 (LAC).
62 JKG to HG, December 1, 1940, MG30C241, v. 88 (LAC).

63 JKG to HG, February 26, 1945, MG30C241, v. 88 (LAC).
64 JKG to HG, October 8, 1945, MG30C241, v. 88 (LAC).
65 JKG to HG, July 32, 1947, MG30C241, v. 88 (LAC).
66 Ruth Gordon to HG, July 26, 1944, MG30C241, v. 88 (LAC).
67 JKG to HG, September 13, 1945, MG30C241, v. 88 (LAC).
68 JKG to HG, December 30, 1947, MG30C241, v. 88 (LAC).

CHAPTER TWELVE

1 A.J. Hobbins, ed., *On the Edge of Greatness: The Diaries of John Humphrey, Volume* 2 (Montreal: McGill University Libraries, 1996), 28.
2 Ernest Dick Interview, February 16, 1976. Sound Archives, J. King Gordon Collection, Acc. 1976-115 (LAC).
3 Elspeth Chisholm, CBC Interview, 1962, MG30C241, v. 34 (LAC).
4 JKG to John Humphrey, February 1950, MG30C241, v. 23 (LAC).
5 A.J. Hobbins, ed., *On the Edge of Greatness, Volume* 2, 44.
6 JKG, "Brief on Human Rights," presented to the Canadian Senate, April 25, 1950, MG30C241, v. 23 (LAC).
7 JKG, "The United Nations and the World Crisis," Wellesley Summer Institute of Social Progress, 3 July 1950, MG30C241, v. 23 (LAC).
8 JKG, *These Rights and Freedoms* (New York: United Nations Department of Public Information, 1950).
9 Ronald St John Macdonald, "Leadership in Law: John P. Humphrey and the Development of the International Law of Human Rights," *The Canadian Yearbook of International Law* 29 (1991): 3–92.
10 JKG, *These Rights and Freedoms*, 2.
11 Ibid., 3. A parallel might be drawn from American constitutional theory in which the issue of whether the Union was established by "We the people of the United States," [U.S. Constitution, Preamble, 1787] or, as the Confederacy of southern states argued in 1861, by a compact of the states which spoke for their citizens. This difference in interpretation led, of course, to the prolonged and bloody Civil War of 1861–1865.
12 Ibid.
13 Ibid., 90.
14 John P. Humphrey, "The Parent of Anarchy," *International Journal* 1946. Quoted in Ronald St J. Macdonald, "Leadership in Law: John P. Humphrey and the Developemnt of the International Law of Human Rights," 23.
15 John P. Humphrey, "The United Nations in the Year 2000 A.D." Quoted in Ronald St J. Macdonald, "Leadership in Law: John P. Humphrey and the Development of the International Law of Human Rights," 23.

16 JKG, "Brief on Human Rights," presentation to the Canadian Senate, April 25, 1950, MG30C241, v. 23 (LAC).
17 Ibid.
18 Macdonald, "Leadership in Law: John P. Humphrey and the Development of the International Law of Human Rights," 59.
19 JKG to R. St J. Macdonald, September 21, 1986, quoted in, "Leadership in Law: John P. Humphrey and the Development of the International Law of Human Rights," n. 184, 59.
20 Macdonald, "Leadership in Law: John P. Humphrey and the Development of the International Law of Human Rights," 60–1; On this topic see also Michael Ignatieff, *Human Rights as Politics and Idolatry* (Princeton: Princeton University Press, 2001), 8; John P. Humphrey, *Human Rights and the United Nations: A Great Adventure* (Dobbs Ferry, N.Y.: Transnational, 1984); and Mary Ann Glendon, *A World Made New: Eleanor Roosevelt and the Universal Declaration of Human Rights* (New York: Random House, 2001).
21 A.J. Hobbins, ed., *On the Edge of Greatness, Volume* 2, 41.
22 Notes, MG30C241, v. 23 (LAC).
23 *United Nations General Assembly:"Declaration" Fifth Session, AD HOC Commission on Prisoners of War*, A/AC.46/15, 2 April 1954.
24 *United Nations General Assembly, "Report on the AD HOC Commission of Prisoners of War on the Work of Its Seventh Session,"* A/AC.41/21, 19 September 1957.
25 Ibid.
26 Ibid.
27 Ibid.
28 United Nations General Assembly *"Report of the AD HOC Commission on Prisoners of War,"* A/AC.46/17, 30 September 1954.
29 Ibid.
30 Ibid.
31 The Association of Families of Japanese Nationals in the Soviet Union to Countess Estelle Bernadotte, March 11, 1954, MG30C241, v. 24 (LAC).
32 JKG to Ruth Gordon, January 29, 1952, RAGP.
33 Dick Interview, February 16, 1976. Sound Archives, J. King Gordon Collection, Acc. 1976-115 (LAC).
34 JKG to Estelle Bernadotte, April 16, MG30C241, v. 24 (LAC).
35 JKG to Estelle Bernadotte, April 16, MG30C241, v. 24 (LAC).
36 Estelle Bernadotte to JKG, March 18, 1953, MG30C241, v. 24 (LAC).
37 JKG to Estelle Bernadotte, March 24, 1953, MG30C241, v. 24 (LAC).
38 JKG to Ruth Gordon, January 30, 1952, RAGP.

39 JKG to Ruth Gordon, September 17, 1954, RAGP.
40 J.H. Hobbins, ed., *On the Edge of Greatness, Volume* 2, October 5, 1950.
41 JKG to Ruth Gordon, August 18, 1952, RAGP.
42 JKG to Ruth Gordon, August 1–2, 1952, RAGP.
43 JKG to Ruth Gordon, August 6, 1952, RAGP.
44 JKG to Ruth Gordon, February 17, 1952, RAGP.
45 JKG to RG, February 17, 1952, RAGP.
46 Alison Gordon to JKG, January 15, 1952, RAGP.
47 Charles Gordon to JKG, November 17, 1952, RAGP.
48 JKG to Ruth Gordon, January 7, 1952, RAGP.
49 JKG to Ruth Gordon, August 23, 1953, RAGP
50 JKG to Egon Schwelb, 1953, MG30C241, v. 23 (LAC).
51 Dick Interview, March 3, 1976. Sound Archives, J. King Gordon Collection, Acc. 1976-115 (LAC).

CHAPTER THIRTEEN

1 Colonel Alfred G. Katzin, South African, Director of the UN Bureau of Personnel, and former Representative of UN Secretary-General Trygve Lie in Korea, 1950–1953.
2 Alfred Katzin to JKG, July 9, 1954, MG30C241, v. 25 (LAC).
3 Alfred Katzin to JKG, July 13, 1954, MG30C241, v. 25 (LAC).
4 JKG, "Notes for an Autobiography," MG30C241, v. 32 (LAC).
5 Humphrey Diaries, July 6, 1958, quoted note 54, page 18, A.J. Hobbins, "Mentor and Protégé: Percy Ellwood Corbett's Relationship with John Peters Humphrey," *The Canadian Yearbook of International Law* (1991): 3–56.
6 JKG, "Notes for an Autobiography," MG30C241, v. 32 (LAC).
7 Eileen Janzen conversation with Ruth Gordon, October 1985.
8 JKG to Ruth Gordon, July 28, 1954, RAGP.
9 JKG to Ruth Gordon, July 31, 1954, RAGP.
10 Ibid.
11 Ernest Dick Interview, March 3, 1976. Sound Archives, J. King Gordon Collection, Acc. 1976-115 (LAC).
12 JKG to Ruth Gordon, July 31, 1954, RAGP.
13 JKG to Ruth Gordon, August 3, 1954, RAGP.
14 JKG, "Korea 1954–1956," MG30C241, v. 87 (LAC).
15 United Nations, Department of Public Information, 19 September 1955: "UN Fact Series UNKRA." A brochure prepared by King and his staff. MG30C241, v. 25 (LAC).

16 JKG, "Korea 1954–1956."
17 JKG to Sir Arthur Rucker, UN Liaison and Procurement Office, London, October 14, 1954, MG30C241, v. 25 (LAC).
18 JKG to Elma Ferguson, October 13, 1954, MG30C241, v. 25. (LAC).
19 JKG to Lester Pearson, December 31, 1955, MG30C241, v. 25 (LAC).
20 JKG to Sir Arthur Rucker, October 14, 1954, MG30C241, v. 25 (LAC).
21 JKG, "Korea 1954–1956."
22 JKG to Ruth Gordon, August 17, 1954, JKGP.
23 JKG, "Korea 1954–1956."
24 JKG to John B. Coulter, September 4, 1954, MG30C241, v. 25 (LAC).
25 Dick Interview, March 3, 1976. Sound Archives, J. King Gordon Collection, Acc. 1976-115 (LAC).
26 Ruth Gordon to Helen Gordon, October 11, 1954, RAGP.
27 Charley Gordon to JKG, December 23, 1954, RAGP
28 Ruth Gordon to JKG, December 26, 1954, RAGP.
29 JKG to Ruth Gordon, December 17, 1954, RAGP.
30 Ruth Gordon to Helen Gordon, January 10, 1955, RAGP.
31 Ruth Gordon to Helen Gordon, January 29, 1955, RAGP.
32 JKG to Ruth Gordon, September 21, 1955, RAGP.
33 JKG to Ruth Gordon, October 10, 1955, RAGP.
34 JKG to Ruth Gordon, July 22, 1955, RAGP.
35 JKG to Ruth Gordon, March 11, 1956, RAGP.
36 Ibid.
37 JKG to Ruth Gordon, October 13, 1955, RAGP.
38 Ibid.
39 JKG to Ruth Gordon, October 16, 1955, RAGP.
40 JKG to Ruth Gordon, December 13, 1955, RAGP.
41 Dick Interview, March 3, 1976. Sound Archives, J. King Gordon Collection, Acc. 1976-115 (LAC)
42 JKG, "Korea 1954–1956."
43 JKG to Ruth Gordon, January 26, 1956, RAGP.
44 Ibid.
45 Ibid.
46 JKG, "Korea 1954–1956."
47 JKG to Ruth Gordon, January 30, 1956, RAGP.
48 JKG to Helen Gordon, January 1956, MG30C241, v. 88 (LAC).
49 JKG to Ruth Gordon, December 8, 1955, RAGP.
50 Dick Interview, March 3, 1976. Sound Archives, J. King Gordon Collection, Acc. 1976-115 (LAC).
51 JKG to Helen Gordon, June 10, 1955, MG30C241, v. 88 (LAC).

52 Dick Interview, March 3, 1976. Sound Archives, J. King Collection, Acc. 1976-115 (LAC).
53 Ruth Gordon to JKG, June 12, 1955, RAGP.
54 Ibid.
55 JKG to Ruth Gordon, September 15, 1955, RAGP.
56 JKG to Ruth Gordon, November 7, 1955, RAGP.
57 JKG to Ruth Gordon, September 27, 1955, RAGP.
58 JKG to Isaac Anderson, September 27, 1955, RAGP.
59 Dick Interview, March 3, 1976.
60 JKG to Ruth Gordon, March 25, 1956, RAGP.
61 JKG to Ruth Gordon, February 3, 1956, RAGP.
62 JKG to Ruth Gordon, August 15, 1955, RAGP.
63 JKG to Ruth Gordon, August 7, 1955, RAGP.
64 JKG to Ruth Gordon, February 9, 1956, RAGP.
65 Ruth Gordon to JKG, May 17, 1955, RAGP.
66 Ruth Gordon to JKG, May 18, 1955, RAGP.
67 Ruth Gordon to JKG, October 12, 1955, RAGP.
68 Ruth Gordon to Helen Gordon, August 30, 1955, JKGP.
69 JKG to Helen Gordon, August 24, 1955, MG30C241, v. 88 (LAC)
70 Ruth Gordon to Helen Gordon, June 13, 1955, RAGP.
71 Ibid.
72 Ruth Gordon to JKG, May 29, 1955, RAGP.
73 JKG to Ruth Gordon, September 28, 1955, RAGP.
74 JKG to Ruth Gordon, "Wednesday," November 1955, RAGP.
75 J.A.C. Robertson to JKG, December 9, 1955, MG30C241, v. 26 (LAC).
76 Ruth Gordon to JKG, January 4, 1956, RAGP.
77 JKG to Ruth Gordon, January 5, 1956, RAGP.
78 Ibid.
79 Ruth Gordon to JKG, January 11, 1956, RAGP.
80 Ruth Gordon to JKG, January 20, 1956, RAGP.
81 J.A.C. Robertson to JKG, March 8, 1956, MG30C241, v. 26 (LAC).
82 Alfred G. Katzin to JKG, March 9, 1956, MG30C241, v. 26 (LAC).
83 Alfred G. Katzin to JKG, March 23, 1956, MG30C241, v. 26 (LAC).
84 JKG to Ruth Gordon, March 14, 1956, RAGP.
85 JKG to Ruth Gordon, April 12, 1956, JKGP.
86 Alfred G. Katzin to JKG, April 18, 1956, MG30C241, v. 26 (LAC).

CHAPTER FOURTEEN

1 JKG, "Twelfth Night 1987–1988," MG30C241, v. 87 (LAC).
2 JKG to Alfred G. Katzin, August 23, 1956, MG30C241, v. 27 (LAC).

3 Quoted in Ernest Dick Interview, May 6, 1976. Sound Archives, J. King Gordon Collection, Acc. 1976-115 (LAC).
4 Ibid.
5 Ibid.
6 JKG to Ruth Gordon, March 12, 1957, RAGP.
7 Cf. Norrie MacQueen, *The United Nations Since 1945: Peacekeeping and the Cold War* (London and New York: Longman, 1999), 26.
8 Albert Hourani, *A History of the Arab Peoples* (Cambridge: The Belknap Press of Harvard University Press, 1991), 365ff.
9 Lester B. Pearson, *Mike: The Memoirs of the Right Honourable Lester B. Pearson, Volume 2, 1948–1957*, edited by John A. Munro and Alex I. Inglis (Toronto and Buffalo: University of Toronto Press, 1973), 219.
10 Ibid., 226.
11 Brian Urquhart, *Hammarskjöld* (New York: Harper Colophon Books, Harper and Row, 1972), 163.
12 E.L.M. Burns to JKG, August 15, 1956, MG30C241, v. 26 (LAC).
13 "Draft United Nations: Plan for the Evacuation of United Nations Personnel Stationed in Egypt," MG30C241, v. 27 (LAC).
14 L.B. Pearson, *Mike, v.* 2, 236.
15 JKG, "The United Nations and Suez," MG30C241, v. 35 (LAC).
16 JKG, "Biographical Fragment," MG30C241, v. 87 (LAC).
17 Ruth Gordon to Isaac Anderson, November 8, 1956, RAGP.
18 JKG to Ruth Gordon, November 8, 1956, RAGP.
19 JKG to Ruth Gordon, November 11, 1956, RAGP.
20 E.L.M. Burns, *Between Arab and Israeli* (Toronto: Clarke, Irwin & Company Limited, 1962), 187.
21 JKG, "The UN and Suez."
22 E.L.M. Burns, *Between Arab and Israeli*, 196.
23 Ibid., 198.
24 Brian Urquhart, *Hammarskjöld*, 186.
25 Lester B. Pearson, *Mike*, v. 2, 262.
26 Ibid.
27 Brian Urquhart, *Hammarskjöld*, 186–7.
28 Lester B. Pearson, *Mike*, v. 2, 269–71.
29 E.L.M. Burns, *Between Arab and Israeli*, 215.
30 JKG to Ruth Gordon, November 18, 1956, RAGP.
31 Ibid.
32 JKG to Ruth Gordon, November 29, 1956, RAGP.
33 JKG to Ruth Gordon, December 19, 1956, RAGP.
34 E.L.M. Burns, *Between Arab and Israeli*, 219.
35 JKG to Ruth Gordon, November 18, 1956, RAGP.

36 E.L.M. Burns to JKG, December 30, 1957, MG30C241, v. 27 (LAC).
37 JKG, CBC Script, November 19, 1956, MG30C241, v. 29 (LAC).
38 JKG to Ruth Gordon, October 30, 1958, RAGP.
39 J. King Gordon, "Prospects for Peacekeeping," *International Journal* (CIIA), no, 2 (1970): 370–87.
40 E.L.M. Burns, *Between Arab and Israeli*, 212.
41 J. King Gordon, "Prospects for Peacekeeping," 372.
42 "United Nations Emergency Force (Egypt) – UNEF," Department of Veterans Affairs, Government of Canada.
43 JKG to Ruth Gordon, January 29, 1957, RAGP.
44 JKG, CBC Script, n.d., G30C241, v. 26 (LAC).
45 Ibid.
46 Ibid.
47 J. King Gordon, "Not So Far East of Suez," ed., Clyde Sanger, *Canadians and the United Nations* (Ottawa: Department of External Affairs, 1988), 58–9.
48 JKG to Ruth Gordon, January 5, 1957, RAGP.
49 E.L.M. Burns, *Between Arab and Israeli*, 243.
50 JKG to Ruth Gordon, January 10, 1957, RAGP.
51 JKG to Helen Gordon, March 3, 1957, RAGP.
52 JKG to Ruth Gordon, January 10, 1957, RAGP.
53 Ibid.
54 JKG to Ruth Gordon, January 29, 1957, RAGP.
55 JKG to Ruth Gordon, February 1, 1957, RAGP.
56 JKG to Ruth Gordon, February 25, 1957, RAGP.
57 Ruth Gordon to Isaac Anderson, November 10, 1956, RAGP.
58 Charley Gordon to JKG, November 21, 1956, JKGP.
59 Ibid.
60 Ibid.
61 Ruth Gordon to JKG, December 20, 1956, RAGP.
62 Ruth Gordon to JKG, November 23, 1956, RAGP.
63 Ibid.
64 JKG to Charley Gordon, "Thursday," December 1956, RAGP.
65 JKG to Ruth Gordon, December 20, 1956, RAGP.
66 JKG, conversation with Eileen Janzen, December 1979.
67 JKG to Ruth Gordon, March 24, 1957, RAGP.
68 JKG to Alison Gordon, January 17, 1957, RAGP.
69 Ruth Gordon to JKG, February 19, 1957, RAGP.
70 JKG to Ruth Gordon, March 5, 1957, RAGP.
71 JKG to Ruth Gordon, March 13, 1957, RAGP.

72 J.G. Stavridi to JKG, February 8, 1957, MG30C241, v. 26 (LAC).
73 JKG to Ruth Gordon, March 17, 1957, RAGP.
74 George Ivan Smith to JKG, February 26, 1957, MG30C241, v. 27 (LAC).
75 JKG to Ruth Gordon, March 12, 1957, RAGP.
76 E.L.M. Burns, *Between Arab and Israeli*, 253.
77 JKG to Ruth Gordon, March 12, 1957, RAGP.
78 JKG to Ruth Gordon, March 13, 1957, RAGP.
79 E.L.M. Burns, *Between Arab and Israeli*, 264.
80 JKG to Ruth Gordon, March 13, 1957, RAGP.
81 JKG to Ruth Gordon, March 24, 1957, RAGP.
82 JKG to Ruth Gordon, March 31, 1957, RAGP.
83 JKG to Ruth Gordon, March 24, 1957, RAGP.
84 JKG to Ruth Gordon, March 17, 1957, RAGP.
85 JKG, "The United Nations and Suez," MG30C241, v. 35 (LAC).
86 Cf. Roger Bowen, ed., *E.H. Norman: His Life and Scholarship* (Toronto: University of Toronto Press, 1984), ix ff. Further discussion of Norman's suicide is found in Roger Bowen, *Innocence Is Not Enough: The Life and Death of Herbert Norman* (Vancouver/Toronto: Douglas & McIntyre, 1986).
87 Ibid., 169–70.
88 JKG to Ruth Gordon, April 4, 1957, RAGP.
89 JKG to Lester B. Pearson, April 7, 1957, Xeroxed copy, MG30C241, v. 71 (LAC).
90 Ibid.
91 Ibid.

CHAPTER FIFTEEN

1 JKG to Frank R. Scott, August 31, 1957, FRSP, MG30D211, v. 73 (LAC).
2 JKG to Frank R. Scott, September 29, 1957, FRSP, MG30D211, v. 73 (LAC).
3 Brian Urquhart, *Hammarskjöld* (New York: Harper Colophon books, 1972), 262ff.
4 JKG, "Some Notes on UN Information Program in the Middle East," 30 January 1959, MG30C241, v. 27 (LAC).
5 JKG, "The United Nations and Human Need," Tarrytown, April 1959, MG30C241, v. 28 (LAC).
6 JKG, CBC Interview with Elspeth Chisholm, 1962, MG30C241, v. 34 (LAC).
7 JKG to Ruth Gordon, December 11, 1957, RAGP.
8 JKG to Ruth Gordon, December 14, 1957, RAGP.

9 Albert Hourani, *A History of the Arab Peoples* (Cambridge, MA: The Belnap Press of Harvard University Press, 1991), 368.
10 Ibid.
11 JKG to Ruth Gordon, November 16, 1958, RAGP.
12 Ibid.
13 Brian Urquhart, *Hammarskjöld*, 263.
14 JKG to Ruth Gordon, June 12, 1958, RAGP.
15 Ibid.
16 Brian Urquhart, *Hammarskjöld*, 265.
17 JKG to Ruth Gordon, November 17, 1958, RAGP.
18 Ibid.
19 Ibid.
20 JKG, CBC Interview with Elspeth Chisholm, 1962, MG30C241, v. 34 (LAC).
21 JKG to Ruth Gordon, November 21, 1958, RAGP.
22 JKG to Ruth Gordon, March 8, 1958, RAGP.
23 JKG, "The United Nations and Human Need," MG30C241, v. 28 (LAC).
24 Brian Urquhart, *Hammarskjöld*, 377.
25 Ibid.
26 JKG to Erskine Childers, October 15, 1988, MG30C241, v. 86 (LAC).
27 JKG to Erskine Childers, July 30, 1988, MG30C241, v. 86 (LAC).
28 JKG to Ruth Gordon, December 25, 1958, RAGP.
29 Ruth Gordon to JKG, December 30, 1958, RAGP.
30 Ruth Gordon to JKG, January 11, 1959, RAGP.
31 JKG to Ruth Gordon, December 31, 1958, RAGP.
32 JKG to Ruth Gordon, January 4, 1959, RAGP.
33 Ibid.
34 Ruth Gordon to JKG, October 14, 1958, RAGP.
35 Ruth Gordon to JKG, September 22, 1958, RAGP.
36 Ibid.
37 Ruth Gordon to JKG, October 19, 1958, RAGP.
38 Charley Gordon to JKG, December 8, 1958, RAGP.
39 JKG to Ruth Gordon, September 16, 1958, RAGP.
40 Ibid.
41 Ibid.
42 JKG to Ruth Gordon, May 7, 1957, RAGP.
43 JKG to Ruth Gordon, October 8, 1958, RAGP.
44 JKG, address to St Barnabas Church, October 22, 1961, MG30C241, v. 30 (LAC).
45 George Ivan Smith to JKG, December 29, 1958, MG30C241, v. 27 (LAC).
46 JKG to Ruth Gordon, February 3, 1959, RAGP.

47 JKG to George Ivan Smith, January 30, 1959, MG30C241, v. 27 (LAC).
48 Ruth Gordon to JKG, February 9, 1959, RAGP.
49 George Ivan Smith to JKG, February 3, 1958, MG30C241, v. 27 (LAC).
50 JKG to Ruth Gordon, February 1, 1959, RAGP.
51 JKG to Ruth Gordon, February 3, 1959, RAGP.
52 JKG to Ruth Gordon, October 28, 1958, RAGP.
53 JKG to Ruth Gordon, February 3, 1959, RAGP.
54 JKG to Ruth Gordon, December 13, 1958, RAGP.
55 Ruth Gordon to JKG, February 9, 1959, RAGP.
56 JKG to Ruth Gordon, February 16, 1959, RAGP.

CHAPTER SIXTEEN

1 Alison Gordon to Ruth Gordon, August 10, 1960, RAGP.
2 JKG to Ruth Gordon, August 10, 1960, RAGP.
3 JKG, CBC Interview, 1962, MG30C241, v. 34 (LAC).
4 Joseph Conrad, "Geography and Some Explorers," in *Last Essays* (London: J.M. Dent, 1926), 25.
5 Adam Hochschild, *King Leopold's Ghost: A Story of Greed, Terror, and Heroism in Colonial Africa* (Boston: A Mariner Book, Houghton Mifflin Company, 1999).
6 JKG, *The UN in the Congo: A Quest for Peace* (Carnegie Endowment for International Peace, 1962), 9–10.
7 Ibid., 15.
8 Brian Urquhart, *Hammarskjöld* (New York: Harper Colophon Books, 1972), 397.
9 JKG, *The UN in the Congo*, 24.
10 Resolution 161 (1961), February 21, 1961; Resolution 169 (1961), November 24, 1961.
11 JKG, *The UN in the Congo*, 41.
12 JKG to Charley Gordon, August 19, 1960, RAGP.
13 JKG to Ruth Gordon, August 12, 1960, RAGP.
14 JKG to Ruth Gordon, August 13, 1960. RAGP.
15 JKG to Charley Gordon, August 19, 1960, RAGP.
16 Ibid.
17 JKG to Ruth Gordon, September 29, 1960, RAGP.
18 JKG to Ruth Gordon, September 18, 1960, RAGP.
19 JKG to "Jerry," n.d., MG30C241, v. 29 (LAC).
20 Copies of the *Tom Tom/Tam Tam* can be found in MG30C241, v. 94 (LAC).

21 JKG to Ruth Gordon, September 23, 1960, RAGP.
22 JKG to Ruth Gordon, October 6, 1960, RAGP.
23 Ruth Gordon to JKG, September 1960, RAGP.
24 Ruth Gordon to JKG, October 12, 1960, RAGP.
25 Ibid.
26 JKG to Ruth Gordon, October 17, 1960, RAGP.
27 Ruth Gordon to JKG, November 22, 1960, RAGP.
28 Ruth Gordon to JKG, December 22, 1960, RAGP.
29 JKG to Ruth Gordon, August 29, 1960, RAGP.
30 JKG, CBC Script, September 1960, MG30C241, v. 30 (LAC).
31 Ibid.
32 Ibid.
33 Ibid.
34 Ernest Dick Interview, May 14, 1976. Sound Archives, J. King Gordon Collection, Acc. 1976-115 (LAC).
35 JKG, CBC Interview with Elspeth Chisholm, 1962.
36 JKG to Ruth Gordon, September 1, 1960, RAGP.
37 JKG, "Congo Diary: October 28, Coquilhatville," MG30C241, v. 29 (LAC).
38 JKG to Ruth Gordon, October 26, 1960, RAGP.
39 JKG, "Congo Diary: October 28, Coquilhatville," MG30C241, v. 29 (LAC).
40 JKG to Ruth Gordon, November 4, 1960, RAGP.
41 Brian Urquhart, *Hammarskjöld*, 435.
42 Ibid., 438.
43 JKG, CBC Report, "South Kasai Refugee Problem – Script I," MG30C241, v. 29 (LAC).
44 JKG, CBC Report, "South Kasai Refugee Problem – Script II," MG30C241, v. 29 (LAC).
45 JKG, CBC Report, "South Kasai Refugee Problem – Script III," MG30c241, v. 29 (LAC).
46 JKG to Ruth Gordon, December 11, 1960, RAGP.
47 JKG, "Christmas in Kasai," December 26, 1960, MG30C241, v. 87 (LAC).
48 Ibid.
49 Ibid.
50 Ibid.
51 JKG to Ruth Gordon, January 5, 1961, RAGP.
52 JKG to Helen Gordon, March 12, 1961, RAGP.
53 JKG, "The World of Helen Gordon," *Manitoba Pageant*, Autumn 1978, 14.
54 JKG to Ruth Gordon, March 19, 1961, RAGP.
55 Ruth Gordon to JKG, March 17, 1961, RAGP.
56 Brian Urquhart, *Hammarskjöld*, 451.

57 JKG, *UN in the Congo*, 103.
58 JKG to Ruth Gordon, March 31, 1961, RAGP.
59 Ibid.
60 JKG, CBC Script, April 1961, MG30C241, v. 30 (LAC).
61 JKG to Ruth Gordon, April 30, 1961, RAGP.
62 Ibid.
63 JKG to Ruth Gordon, May 9, 1961, RAGP.
64 JKG to Ruth Gordon, May 14, 1961, RAGP.
65 JKG to Ruth Gordon, June 24, 1961, RAGP.
66 JKG to Ruth Gordon, June 20, 1961, RAGP.
67 JKG to Ruth Gordon, July 1961, RAGP.
68 JKG, *UN in the Congo*, 121.
69 Ibid., 127–8.
70 JKG, *UN in the Congo*, 129.
71 Ernest Dick Interview, May 14, 1976. Sound Archives, J. King Gordon Collection, Acc. 1976-115 (LAC).
72 JKG, *UN in the Congo*, 129.
73 D.R.F. Taylor, "Tribute to King Gordon," June 1, 1990, JKGP.
74 Smith Simpson review, *The American Academy of Political and Social Science*, "The Annals," v. 351, January 1964, copy in MG30C241, v. 30 (LAC).
75 JKG, *UN in the Congo*, 184.
76 Ibid., 182.
77 JKG, "An International Police Force," Special Studies prepared for the Special Committee of the House of Commons on Matters Relating to Defence: Supplement 1964-65 (Ottawa: Queen's Printer, 1965).
78 JKG, "Prospects for Peacekeeping," *International Journal* (CIIA), XXV, no. 2 (1970): 370–87.
79 Ibid., 377–9.
80 JKG to Ruth Gordon, June 14, 1962, RAGP.
81 JKG to Ruth Gordon, June 19, 1962, RAGP.
82 JKG to Charley Gordon, June 22, 1962, RAGP.
83 Ibid.
84 JKG to Ruth Gordon, June 27, 1962, RAGP.
85 JKG to Ruth Gordon, July 1, 1962, RAGP.
86 Ibid.
87 JKG to Ruth Gordon, July 31, 1962, RAGP.
88 JKG to Ruth Gordon, July 11, 1962, RAGP.
89 JKG to Ruth Gordon, July 1, 1962, RAGP.
90 JKG to Ruth Gordon, July 7, 1962, RAGP.

91 JKG, *UN in the Congo*, 182.
92 JKG to Ruth Gordon, May 27, 1961, RAGP.

CHAPTER SEVENTEEN

1 Michael Oliver, "Citation for Professor John King Gordon," November 17, 1977, MG30C241, v. 86 (LAC).
2 George Ignatieff, Presentation of J. King Gordon for the Pearson Peace Medal 1980, October 23, 1980, MG30C241, v. 86 (LAC).
3 JKG, October 23, 1980, MG30C241, v. 86 (LAC).
4 Lois Gordon to JKG, October 22, 1960, RAGP.
5 Alison Gordon to JKG, November 22, 1960, RAGP.
6 J.S. Woodsworth to JKG, March 27, 1940, MG30C241, v. 19 (LAC).
7 M.J. Coldwell to JKG, December 23, 1952, MG30C241, v. 24 (LAC).
8 JKG to W.H. Johns, March 5, 1962, MG30C241, v. 30 (LAC)
9 JKG to Ruth Gordon, February 14, 1962, RAGP.
10 King's story of hunting crocodiles with Arne Rubin on the Awash River in Ethiopia is recounted in chapter 15.
11 JKG to Ruth Gordon, February 17, 1962, RAGP.
12 Ibid.
13 Ibid.
14 JKG to Ruth Gordon, February 23, 1962, RAGP.
15 R.W.D. Fowler to JKG, September 20, 1962, MG30C241, v. 75 (LAC).
16 Ernest Dick Interview, July 14, 1976. Sound Archives, J. King Gordon Collection, Acc. 1976-115 (LAC).
17 JKG to Reinhold Niebuhr, December 3, 1962, MG30C241, v. 75 (LAC).
18 Brian Urquhart to JKG, January 15, 1963, MG30C241, v. 75 (LAC).
19 Ernest Dick Interview, July 14, 1976. Sound Archives, J. King Collection, Acc. 1976-115 (LAC).
20 This author's conversation with Irene Biss Spry, Ottawa, March 28, 1995.
21 Hans J. Morgenthau, *Politics Among Nations: The Struggle for Power and Peace* (New York: Alfred A. Knofp, Inc., 1948).
22 Lecture Notes for International Relations 360, University of Alberta; and International Relations 3062, University of Ottawa. MG30C241, v. 39 (LAC).
23 Ghazi A.R. Algosaibi, "The Theory of International Relations: Hans J. Morgenthau and His Critics," in *Background: Journal of the International Studies Association*, v. 8, no. 4 (1965), 231.
24 Hans Morgenthau, *In the Defense of the National Interest* (New York: Alfred A. Knopf, 1951), 38.

25 Reinhold Niebuhr to JKG, December 8, 1962, MG30C241, v. 75 (LAC).
26 Dick Interview, December 4, 1975. Sound Archives, J. King Gordon Collection, Acc. 1975-195 (LAC).
27 JKG, "The Twilight of This Age," review of Reinhold Niebuhr, *Reflections on the End of an Era*, in *The World of Tomorrow*, March 1, 1934, 115–17.
28 Dick Interview, January 24, 1975. Sound Archives, J. King Gordon Collection, Acc. 1975-12 (LAC).
29 JKG, "Morality and Foreign Policy," 1979, MG30C241, v. 81 (LAC).
30 Ibid.
31 A.J. Hobbins, "Mentor and Protégé: Percy Ellwood Corbett's Relationship with John Peters Humphrey," in *The Canadian Yearbook of International Law 1999*, 4. I am also indebted to Kathleen E. Fisher for allowing me to consult her unpublished research and essays on Percy Corbett.
32 Dick Interview, December 16, 1975. Sound Archives, J. King Gordon Collection, Acc. 1975-195 (LAC).
33 Dick Interview, January 28, 1976. Sound Archives, J. King Gordon Collection, Acc. 1976-115 (LAC).
34 Percy E. Corbett, *The Growth of World Law* (Princeton, N.J.: Princeton University Press, 1971).
35 Ibid., 3-4.
36 Ibid., 12.
37 Dick Interview, January 28, 1976. Sound Archives, J. King Gordon Collection, Acc. 1976-115 (LAC).
38 Ibid.
39 JKG, "The Myth of World Government," MG30C241, v. 67 (LAC).
40 JKG, "The New International Order," *behind the headlines*, CIIA XXXIV (1976): 28.
41 Ruth Gordon to JKG, September 22, 1958, RAGP.
42 Foreword to J. King Gordon ed., *Canada's Role as a Middle Power: Papers given at the Third Annual Banff Conference on World Development, August 1965* (Toronto: Canadian Institute of International Affairs, 1966).
43 L.B. Pearson to JKG, September 6, 1963, MG30C241, v. 59 (LAC).
44 JKG to John W. Holmes, April 4, 1970, MG30C241, v. 60 (LAC).
45 John W. Holmes to JKG, April 3, 1970, MG30C241, v. 60 (LAC).
46 Ibid.
47 JKG to John W. Holmes, April 25, 1970, MG30C241, v. 60 (LAC).
48 John W. Holmes to JKG, April 29, 1970, MG30C241, v. 60 (LAC).
49 James Barrington to John Sokol, April 16, 1970, MG30C2441, v. 60 (LAC).
50 JKG, "John W. Holmes: Canadian Peace-Shaper" 1988, MG30C241, v. 64 (LAC).

51 JKG to W. H. Johns, March 5, 1962, MG30C241, v. 30 (LAC).
52 JKG to L. B. Pearson, February 10, 1966, MG30C241, v. 41 (LAC).
53 JKG to John W. Holmes, October 26, 1961, MG30C241, v. 32 (LAC).
54 For a history of CUSO, see Ian Smillie, *The Land of Lost Content: A History of CUSO* (Toronto: Deneau Publishers, 1985).
55 A copy of the *Gateway* article can be found in MG30C241, v. 39 (LAC).
56 W.H. Johns to JKG, August 15, 1967, MG30C241, v. 41 (LAC).
57 Ibid.
58 JKG to L.B. Pearson, July 12, 1966, MG30C241, v. 41 (LAC).
59 Clyde Sanger, "Turbulence in CUSO Over Its Goals," *The Globe and Mail*, November 6, 1969.
60 JKG, Notes for a Speech, MG30C241, v. 43 (LAC).
61 JKG to Ruth Gordon, March 13, 1966, RAGP.
62 Brochure, "Centre for International Cooperation, First Annual Conference, October 1968." MG30C241, v. 37 (LAC).
63 JKG, "Twelfth Night 1987–1988," MG30C241, v. 87 (LAC).
64 "Mister Modern: Architect Hart Massey introduced the city to the Bauhaus movement," *The Ottawa Citizen*, April 3, 2004.
65 JKG's personal reminiscence to Eileen Janzen.
66 JKG to Ruth Gordon, February 17, 1975, RAGP.
67 Gilbert Ryle to JKG, October 25, 1924, MG30C241, v. 72 (LAC).
68 JKG to Dr John Ryle, November 15, 1976, Mg30C241, v. 72 (LAC).
69 Peter Ady to JKG, November 29, 1976, MG30C241, v. 72 (LAC).
70 R. Doug Francis, *Frank H. Underhill; Intellectual Provocateur* (Toronto: University of Toronto Press, 1986), 175.
71 JKG, "FHU 1889–1971, September 18, 1971" MG30C241, v. 74 (LAC).
72 As quoted by JKG in "The Global Imperative," a speech to the Society for International Development, Toronto Branch, September 23, 1982, MG30C241, v. 67 (LAC). Original found in Reinhold Niebuhr, *Moral Man and Immoral Society* (New York: Charles Scribner's Sons, 1932), 62: "Religion is always a citadel of hope, which is built on the edge of despair."
73 JKG to Marjorie Gordon, January 8, 1973, MG30C241, v. 78 (LAC).
74 JKG to L.B. Pearson, November 17, 1972, MG30C241, v. 72 (LAC).
75 Peter Carver to JKG, January 1973, MG30C241, v. 72 (LAC). Peter wrote: "Dear King, I wanted to drop a note to you, in a kind of formal way, to say how much I admired your walking in the cortège Sunday and, secondly, how I enjoyed your article on the editorial page of tonight's Citizen … I have certainly never felt as devastated as I have in the past week, with the sudden understanding of what he represented and was to us Gordons, and, I imagine to all kinds of other people in the country and in the world …

I hope that you felt you represented on the formal occasion Sunday, not only your own associations with Mike Pearson, but the affection and respect which all of us in the Gordon clan have felt over the years."

76 JKG, "Tommy Douglas: a Great Canadian," Eulogy, March 3, 1986, JKGP.
77 Ibid.
78 J.L. Granatstein and Robert Bothwell, *Pirouette: Pierre Trudeau and Canadian Foreign Policy* (Toronto: University of Toronto Press, 1991), 286.
79 JKG, "Citizens of a World Community: Tommy Douglas and John Bene," Address to the Group of 78, MG30C241, v. 67 (LAC).
80 Ivan Head and Pierre Trudeau, *The Canadian Way: Shaping Canada's Foreign Policy, 1968–1984*, 162–3.
81 JKG to Ruth Gordon, September 19, 1973, RAGP.
82 Ibid.
83 Brochure, North South Round Table, First Session, Rome, 1978, MG30C241, v. 62 (LAC).
84 JKG, "Twelfth Night 1987–1988," MG30C241, v. 87 (LAC).
85 JKG to David Hopper, "Special Report of European Trip, September 8–29, 1974," MG30C241, v. 54 (LAC).
86 JKG to Ruth Gordon, March 3, 1975, RAGP.
87 JKG to Ruth Gordon, March 7, 1975, RAGP.
88 Ivan Head to Eileen Janzen, June 14, 2000.
89 Ivan Head to JKG, February 24, 1978, MG30C241, v. 80 (LAC).
90 Author's conversation with R. St J. Macdonald, March 2006.
91 JKG to Louis Berlinguet. November 13, 1979, MG30C241, v. 50 (LAC).
92 JKG to Marjorie Gordon Smart, December 30, 1979, MG30C241, v. 80 (LAC).
93 JKG to Ivan Head, June 30, 1980, MG30C241, v. 52 (LAC).

CHAPTER EIGHTEEN

1 Elizabeth Mann Borgese, "International Ocean Institute," reprinted from OCEANS, January/February 1977.
2 *Basic Facts About the United Nations* (New York: The United Nations Department of Public Information, 2004), 274.
3 JKG, "Twelfth Night: 1987–1988," MG20C241, v. 87 (LAC).
4 JKG, "Aurelio Peccei and the World Tomorrow," n.d., MG30C241, v. 62 (LAC).
5 JKG, "Seeking Peace on the Seas," *The Ottawa Journal*, July 14, 1972.
6 JKG, "Towards a New Order for the Oceans: Notes on a Recent Conference in Okinawa, 1975," MG30C241, v. 56 (LAC).

7 Ibid.
8 Ibid.
9 Ibid.
10 Pierre Elliott Trudeau, Remarks, Mansion House, London, March 13, 1975.
11 See *United Nations Convention on Law of the Sea* (1982), "Exclusive Economic Zones," and "Continental Shelf."
12 *Basic Facts About the United Nations*, 275.
13 JKG, "Aurelio Peccei and the World Tomorrow."
14 JKG to Ruth Gordon, December 7, 1978, RAGP.
15 JKG, "African Diary, January 16, 1979," MG30C241, v. 81 (LAC).
16 JKG, *The International Ocean Institute*, 26 February 1979, MG30C241, v. 52 (LAC).
17 Ronald St J. Macdonald to Eileen Janzen, March 18, 2003.
18 John W. Holmes, "A Diplomatic Assessment," in J.L. Granatstein, ed., *Canadian Foreign Policy Since 1945: Middle Power or Satellite?* (Toronto: Copp Clark, 1970), 35.
19 Ibid., 36.
20 Robert Bothwell, *Alliance and Illusion: Canada and the World, 1945–1984* (Vancouver: UBC Press, 2007), 17–18.
21 Jonathan Bays, "Fire-Proof House to Middle Power: Metaphor, Identity, and Canadian Foreign Policy, 1939–1950," D. Phil thesis, Balliol College, University of Oxford, 1999, 69. See also, Blair Fraser, "Canada: Mediator or Busybody?" in J. King Gordon, ed., *Canada's Role as a Middle Power* (Toronto: The Canadian Institute of International Affairs, 1966), 4–12.
22 Adam Chapnick, *The Middle Power Project: Canada and the Founding of the United Nations* (Vancouver, Toronto: UBC Press, 2005), 6.
23 Ibid., 69.
24 Patrick H. Brennan, *Reporting the Nations Business: Press-Government Relations during the Liberal Years, 1935–1957* (Toronto: University of Toronto Press, 1994), xi. Quoted in Adam Chapnik, *The Middle Power Project*, 144.
25 John English, *Shadow of Heaven: The Life of Lester Pearson, Volume One: 1897–1948* (London: Vintage UK, 1990), 268.
26 Adam Chapnik, *The Middle Power Project*, 6.
27 John Holmes, "Is There a Future for Middlepowership," ed., J. King Gordon, *Canada's Role as a Middle Power: papers given at the Banff Conference on World Development, August 1965* (Toronto: the Canadian Institute of International Affairs, 1966), 28.
28 John W. Holmes, *Canada: A Middle-Aged Power* (Toronto: McClelland and Stewart, 1976, The Carleton Library No. 98), vi.

29 Ernest Dick Interview, July 14, 1976. Sound Archives, J. King Gordon Collection, Acc. 1976-115 (LAC).

30 Ivan L. Head, Pierre Elliottt Trudeau, *The Canadian Way: Shaping Canada's Foreign Policy, 1968–1984* (Toronto: McClelland & Stewart, 1995), 7.

31 Quoted in Ivan L. Head, Pierre Trudeau, *The Canadian Way: Shaping Canada's Foreign Policy 1968–1984*, 139–40.

32 John English, *Just Watch Me: The Life of Pierre Elliott Trudeau 1968–2000* (Toronto: Knopf Canada, 2009), 62.

33 *International Development: Foreign Policy for Canadians* (Published by authority of the Honourable Mitchell Sharp, Secretary of State for External Affairs, Ottawa, Canada, 1970), 10.

34 J.L. Granatstein and Robert Bothwell, *Pirouette: Pierre Trudeau and Canadian Foreign Policy* (Toronto: University of Toronto Press, 1990), 33.

35 It is interesting to note George Ignatieff's comment regarding Trudeau's attitude to the UN while he was serving as Canada's representative on the UN Security Council: "Though he visited me from time to time in New York, I think it is fair to say that the Trudeau government was not UN-oriented; the emphasis was on developing relations with the People's Republic of China and building a 'just society' at home rather than cultivating traditional channels of international relations." George Ignatieff, *The Making of a Peacemonger: The Memoirs of George Ignatieff* (Penguin Books, 1987), 240.

36 JKG, Typescript of Lecture, University of Ottawa, April 2, 1973, MG30C241, v. 39 (LAC).

37 Pierre Elliott Trudeau, Remarks, Mansion House, London, March 13, 1975.

38 J.L. Granatstein and Robert Bothwell explore at length perplexing aspects of Trudeau's foreign policy in *Pirouette: Pierre Trudeau and Canadian Foreign Policy*.

39 Robert Bothwell, *Alliance and Illusion*, 352–3.

40 JKG, "Canada at the United Nations: Specific policies must reflect a return of global perspective," *International Perspectives: A Journal of Opinion on World Affairs* (Ottawa: The Department of External Affairs, September/October 1976), 3–6.

41 Ernest Dick Interview, July 14, 1976.

42 JKG, "Past is Prologue," Address at Dalhousie Conference on Canadian Foreign Policy, May 1979, RAGP.

43 Pierre Trudeau to JKG, 31 January 1975, MG30C241, v. 74 (LAC).

44 JKG to Pierre Trudeau, June 21, 1978 and October 22, 1978. MG30C241, v. 80 (LAC).

45 Murray Thomson to Bernard Wood, May 28, 1991, copy in my possession given to me by Murray Thomson, March 1995.
46 "Group of 78: Statement on Canadian Foreign Policy in the 1980's," *BULLETIN*, United Nations Association, February 1982 Copy in MG30C241, v. 56 (LAC).
47 Pierre Trudeau to JKG, 5 April 1982, MG30C241, v. 82 (LAC).
48 Ivan L. Head and Pierre Trudeau, *The Canadian Way: Shaping of Canada's Foreign Policy 1968–1984*, 92.
49 Pierre Elliott Trudeau, *Memoirs* (Toronto: McClelland & Stewart Inc, 1993), 333.
50 Government of Canada, Parliamentary Research Branch, "Cruise Missile Test in Canada: the Post-Cold War Debate," 1994, http://publications.gc.ca/Collection-R/LoPBdP/MR/mr114-e.htm.
51 JKG to Pierre Trudeau, November 29, 1979, MG30C241, v. 80 (LAC).
52 JKG, "January 28–February 1, 1983," MG30C241, v. 56 (LAC).
53 Ibid.
54 Office of the Prime Minster to JKG, April 29, 1983, MG30C241, v. 74 (LAC).
55 Pierre Trudeau, "An Open Letter to All Canadians," reprinted in *Bulletin of the Atomic Scientists*, 39, 8 (October 1983), 2–3, http://tinyurl.com/cljqf99.
56 JKG to Pierre Trudeau, May 16, 1983, MG30C241, v. 74 (LAC).
57 JKG, "Morality and Foreign Policy," 1979, MG30C241, v. 81 (LAC).
58 JKG to Pierre Trudeau, May 16, 1983, MG30C241, v. 74 (LAC).
59 *Foreign Policy for Canadians 1970*.
60 Ivan L. Head and Pierre Trudeau, *The Canadian Way: Shaping Canada's Foreign Policy, 1968–1984*, 313–5.
61 Ibid., 316.
62 Pierre Trudeau to JKG, 7 September 1982, MG30C241, v. 88 (LAC).
63 Pierre Trudeau to JKG, June 19, 1984, MG30C241, v. 74 (LAC).
64 Pierre Trudeau to JKG, March 21, 1983, MG30C241, v. 74 (LAC).
65 JKG to Marian Scott, March 1, 1984, MG30C241, v. 83 (LAC).
66 Ibid.
67 JKG to Pierre Trudeau, June 15, 1984, MG30C241, v. 84 (LAC).
68 Pierre Trudeau, June 19, 1984, MG30C241, v. 84 (LAC).
69 Charles W. Gordon to Eileen Janzen, October 17, 2010.
70 Roger de C. Nantel, Director of Honours, to JKG, 11 May 1977, informing JKG of his recommendation for appointment, MG30C241, v. 80 (LAC)
71 JKG to The Reverend Roger Gaudy, C.C., O.M.I., August 12, 1977, MG30C241, v. 80 (LAC).

72 Brandt Commission, *North-South: A Programme for Survival, the Report of the Independent Commission on International Development Issues under the Chairmanship of Willy Brandt,* 1980, copy in MG30C241, v. 64 (LAC).
73 Dick Interview, July 14, 1976. Sound Archives, J. King Gordon Collection, Acc. 1976-115 (LAC).
74 JKG, "Eulogy," FHU 1889–1971, September 18, 1973, JKGP.
75 F.R. Scott, "Surfaces," *The Collected Poems of F.R. Scott* (Toronto: McClelland and Stewart, 1981), 39.
76 JKG, "Twelfth Night: 1987–1988," MG30C241, v. 87 (LAC).
77 *Saturday Night*, 25.
78 JKG, "In Praise of Frank Scott," draft review, *On F.R. Scott: Essays on His Contributions to Law, Literature, and Politics*, eds. Sandra Djwa and R. St J. Macdonald (Kingston and Montreal: McGill-Queen's University Press, 1983), JKGP.
79 I borrow the phrase from John Howard Yoder, "The Political Meaning of Hope," in *The War of the Lamb: The Ethics of Nonviolence and Peacemaking*, eds. Glen Stassen and Mark Thiessen (Grand Rapids, MI: Brazos Press, 2009), 62.
80 JKG, "In Praise of Frank Scott."
81 JKG, "We Grow Old to One World," MG30C241, v. 72 (LAC).
82 F.R. Scott, "A Grain of Rice," *The Collected Poems of F.R. Scott*, 126.
83 JKG, "Politics and the Good Society."
84 Ibid.
85 Quoted in Ivan L. Head and Pierre Trudeau, *The Canadian Way: Shaping Canada's Foreign Policy, 1968–1984*, 318.

CHAPTER NINETEEN

1 JKG, "The Religion of the Kingdom," Lecture Series, 1934, MG30C241, v. 11 (LAC).
2 JKG, "July 31, 1924," MG30C241, v. 2 (LAC).
3 Humphrey Carver, "King Gordon and His Family," February 27, 1989, JKGP.
4 JKG, "On Being Seventy," MG30C241, v. 77 (LAC).
5 Ibid.
6 Ernest Dick Interview, July 14, 1976. Sound Archives, J. King Gordon Collection, Acc. 1976-115 (LAC).
7 JKG to Ruth Gordon, January 5, 1956, RAGP.

8 Ibid.
9 JKG to Ruth Gordon, February 3, 1959, RAGP.
10 D.R.F. Taylor, "Tribute to King Gordon," June 1, 1990, JKGP.
11 JKG to Ruth Gordon, January 5, 1956, RAGP.
12 JKG to Ruth Gordon, January 20, 1956, RAGP.
13 JKG Review, R. Douglas Francis, *Frank H. Underhill: Intellectual Provocateur, in The Ottawa Citizen,* September 27, 1986.
14 JKG to Ruth Gordon, Wednesday, November 1955, RAGP.
15 The Reverend David MacDonald, "Meditation," February 27, 1989, JKGP.
16 Clyde Sanger, "Gordon's Legacy," *The Ottawa Citizen*, February 28, 1989.
17 Charles Gordon, "Remarks by Charley," June 24, 1996, JKGP.
18 Alison Gordon, "Remarks by Alison," June 24, 1996, JKGP.
19 JKG, "Birkencraig 1907–1983," JKGP.
20 Charles Gordon to Eileen Janzen, January 20, 2010.
21 Ibid., The Reverend Bill Millar of Winnipeg is a minister of the United Church of Canada.

Bibliography

UNPUBLISHED SOURCES

Archival Materials

CCF Papers, MG28IV1 (LAC).
J. King Gordon Papers, MG30C241 (LAC).
F.R. Scott Papers (FRSP), MG30D211 (LAC).
F.H. Underhill Papers, MG30D204 (LAC).
Ernest Dick, J. King Gordon Interviews, 1974–1976, Sound Archives (LAC).
J. King Gordon Papers (JKGP), privately held by the Gordon family.
Ruth Anderson Papers (RAGP), privately held by the Gordon family.

Theses and Dissertations

Bays, Jonathan. "Fire-Proof to Middle Power: Metaphor, Identity, and Canadian Foreign Policy, 1939–1950." D.Phil thesis, Balliol College, University of Oxford, 1999.

Buttars, D.M.J. "A Comparison of the Principles and Program of the Fellowship for a Christian Social Order in Canada, with those of the Christian Socialist Movement in England Under Kingsley and Maurice," S.T.M. thesis, Union Theological Seminary, 1941.

Hutchinson, Roger G. "The Fellowship for a Christian Social Order: A Social Ethical Analysis of a Christian Socialist Movement," Ph.D., dissertation, Victoria University, 1975.

Wood, Edward H. "Ralph Connor and the Canadian West." M.A. thesis, University of Saskatchewan, 1975.

Interviews, Correspondence, and Conversations

In the writing of this biography I have drawn on material provided by the following:

Irene Biss, March 1995, Ottawa.
Andrew and Peggy Brewin, November–December 1978, Ottawa.
Humphrey and Anne Carver, October 1985; March 1995, Ottawa.
T.C. Douglas, November 1978, Ottawa.
Kathleen Fisher, August 1996; July 1998, Edmonton.
Eugene Forsey, May 1978, Ottawa.
Charles W. and Nancy Gordon, July 1984–June 2013, Ottawa.
J. King Gordon, April 1978–February 1989, Ottawa and Kenora.
Gordon family members, July 1984; August 1985; July 1989; Kenora.
Ruth Anderson Gordon, October 1978–March 1996, Ottawa and Kenora.
Ivan Head, June 2000, Vancouver.
Michiel Horn, August–September 1996, Toronto.
David Lewis, December 1978, Ottawa.
Ronald St J. Macdonald, March 1994–August 2005, Ottawa and Halifax.
Michael Oliver, December 1978, Ottawa.
Clyde Sanger, August 2000, Ottawa.
F.R. Scott, September 1977–April 1980, Montreal.
Marian Scott, September 1977–January 1986, Montreal.
Graham Spry, June, 1978, Ottawa.
Murray Thomson, March 1995, Ottawa.
Sydney Wise, December 1978, Ottawa.

Other Interviews

With J. King Gordon:
Elspeth Chisholm, 1963, J. King Gordon Papers, MG30C241, LAC.
Ernest Dick, 1974–1976, Sound Archives, LAC.
With F.R. Scott:
Elspeth Chisholm, 1963, F.R. Scott Papers, MG30D211, LAC.
Anne Scotton, 1978, Douglas-Coldwell Foundation.
With F.H. Underhill:
Paul Fox, June, 1960, F.H. Underhill Papers, MG30D204, LAC.
With former members of the LSR:
Ontario Woodsworth Memorial Foundation, 1977. Taped interviews with Andrew Brewin, Graham Spry, Leonard Marsh, J.F. Parkinson, Humphrey Carver, J. King Gordon, E.A. Forsey, and others, LAC.

SECONDARY SOURCES

Algosaibi, Ghazi A.R. "The Theory of International Relations: Hans J. Morgenthau and His Critics." *Background: Journal of the International Studies Association* 8, 4. (1965): 221–56.

Allen, Richard. *The Social Passion: Religion and Reform in Canada, 1914–1928*. Toronto and Buffalo: Toronto University Press, 1973.

– ed. *The Social Gospel in Canada; Papers of the Interdisciplinary Conference on the Social Gospel in Canada, March 21–24, 1973, at the University of Regina*. Ottawa: National Museums of Canada, 1975.

– "The Background of the Social Gospel in Canada." *The Social Gospel in Canada: Papers on the Interdisciplinary Conference on the Social Gospel in Canada, March 21–24, 1973, at the University of Regina*, ed., Richard Allen. Ottawa: National Museums of Canada, 1975: 2–35.

Alpern, Sara. *Freda Kirchwey: A Woman of the Nation*. Cambridge: Harvard University Press, 1987.

Basic Facts About the United Nations. New York: The United Nations Department of Public Information, 2004.

Baum, Gregory. "Social Catholicism in Nova Scotia: The Thirties." *Religion and Culture in Canada*, ed., Peter Slater. Waterloo: Wilfred Laurier Press, 1977: 117–28.

– "Catholics in Eastern Nova Scotia." *Catholics and Canadian Socialism Political Thought in the Thirties and Forties*. Toronto: James Lorimer and Company, Publishers, 1980: 189–211.

Bercuson, David Jay. *True Patriot: The Life of Brooke Claxton, 1898–1960*. Toronto: University of Toronto Press, 1993.

Berger, Carl. *The Writing of Canadian History: Aspects of English-Canadian Historical Writing 1900–1970*. Toronto: Oxford University Press, 1976.

Bethge, Eberhard. *Dietrich Bonhoeffer: A Biography*, revised and edited by Victoria J. Barnett. Minneapolis: Fortress Press, 2000.

Borgese, Elizabeth Mann. "International Ocean Institute." *OCEANS* (January/February 1977): 2–7.

Bothwell, Robert. *Alliance and Illusion: Canada and the World, 1945–1984*. Vancouver-Toronto: UBC Press, 2007.

Bowen, Roger. *Innocence is Not Enough: The Life and Death of Herbert Norman*. Vancouver/Toronto: Douglas & McIntyre, 1986.

Burns, E.L.M. *Between Arab and Israeli*. Toronto: Clarke, Irwin & Company Limited, 1962.

Cameron, James D. *For the People: A History of St Francis Xavier University*. Montreal and Kingston: McGill-Queen's University Press, 1996.

Caplan, Gerald L. *The Dilemma of Canadian Socialism: The CCF in Ontario.* Toronto: McClelland and Stewart Limited, 1973.

Chapnik, Adam. *The Middle Power Project: Canada and the Founding of the United Nations.* Vancouver, Toronto: UBC Press, 2005.

Coady, Moses M. *Masters of Their Own Destiny: The Story of the Antigonish Movement of Adult Education Through Economic Cooperation.* New York: Harper & Brothers, 1939.

Corbett, Percy E. *The Growth of World Law.* Princeton: Princeton University Press, 1971.

Craig, Robert H. "An Introduction to the Life and Thought of Harry F. Ward." *Modern American Protestantism and Its World: Historical Articles on Protestantism in American Religious Life*, ed., E. Marty. New York: K.G. Saur, 1992: 258–83.

Deane, Ernest. "Trying to Teach Christians Ethics." *The Canadian Forum*, June (1933): 331.

Dietrich Bonhoeffer Works, Volume 10: Barcelona, Berlin, New York 1928–1931, English edition edited by Clifford J. Green. Minneapolis: Fortress Press, 2008.

Sandra Djwa and R. St J. Macdonald, eds. *On F.R. Scott: Essays on His Contributions to Law, Literature, and Politics.* Kingston and Montreal: McGill-Queen's University Press, 1983.

Djwa, Sandra. *The Politics of the Imagination: A Life of F.R. Scott.* Toronto: McClelland and Stewart, 1987.

Eager, Evelyn. *Saskatchewan Government: Politics and Pragmatism.* Saskatoon: Western Producer Prairie, 1980.

English, John. *Shadow of Heaven: The Life of Lester Pearson, Volume One: 1897–1948.* London: Vintage UK, 1990.

– *The Worldly Years: The Life of Lester Pearson, Volume Two: 1949–1972.*

– *Citizen of the World: The Life of Pierre Elliott Trudeau, Volume One: 1919–1968.* Toronto: Knopf Canada, 2006.

– *Just Watch Me: The Life of Pierre Elliott Trudeau, Volume Two: 1968–2000.* Toronto: Knopf Canada, 2009.

Forsey, Eugene. *A Life on the Fringe: The Memoirs of Eugene Forsey.* Toronto: Oxford University Press, 1990.

Fox, Paul. "Early Socialism in Canada." *The Political Process in Canada: Essays in Honour of R. Macgregor Dawson,* ed. J.H. Aitchison. Toronto: University of Toronto Press, 1963.

Fox, Richard Wightman. *Reinhold Niebuhr: A Biography.* New York: Pantheon Books, 1985.

Fraser, Blair. "Canada: Mediator or Busybody?" In *Canada's Role as a Middle Power: papers given at the Third Annual Banff Conference on World*

Development, August 1965, ed., J. King Gordon. Toronto: Canadian Institute of International Affairs, 1966: 4–12.

Friesen, Gerald. *The Canadian Prairies: A History*. Toronto: University of Toronto Press, 1984.

Frost, Robert. "The Constant Symbol," in *Selected Prose of Robert Frost,* eds. Hyde Cox and Edward Connery Lathem. New York, Chicago, San Francisco: Holt, Rinehart and Winston, 1966.

Frye, Northrop. "The Critical Path: An Essay on the Social Context of Literary Criticism." *Daedalus* 99 (1970): 268–342.

Gelber, Lionel. "Canada's New Stature." *Foreign Affairs* 24, 2 (January 1946): 277–89.

Glendon, Mary Ann. *A World Made New: Eleanor Roosevelt and the Universal Declaration of Human Rights*. New York: Random House, 2001.

Gordon, Charles W. "Ralph Connor and the New Generation." *Mosaic* 3, 1970.

Gordon Charles W. *Postscript to Adventure: The Autobiography of Ralph Connor*. Toronto: McClelland and Stewart Limited, 1975.

Gordon, J. King. "All Quiet on the Waterfront: A Seminary Unemployment." *The Christian Advocate*, Pacific Edition, January 22, 1931.

– "Dare the Church Be Christian?" *The New Outlook*, March 22, 1933.

– "The Twilight of This Age." Review of *Reflections on the End of an Era* by Reinhold Niebuhr. New York: Charles Scribners' Sons, 1934. *The World of Tomorrow*, March 1, 1934: 115–17.

– "Christianity and Socialism." *Saskatchewan* CCF *Research Bureau*, May 1934.

– "Moscow, July 24, 1934." *New Outlook* September 5, 1934.

– "Christianity and Social Revolution." *The New Outlook*, June 12 and 19, 1935.

– "St Francis of Antigonish." *The Canadian Forum*, May 1936.

– "Nova Scotia Sees a Great Light." *Christian Century*, May 1936.

– "A Marxist Explains the World." *The Canadian Forum*, October 1936.

– "Fascist Week-end in Montreal." *The Christian Century*, November 1936.

– "Preface" and "The Political Task." In *Towards the Christian Revolution*, edited by R.B.Y. Scott and Gregory Vlastos, ix and 146–74. Chicago: Willett, Clark and Company, 1936.

– "The World of Books: A Christian Socialist Reflects Upon His Ancestors." *The New Outlook*, February 26, 1937.

– "The CCF Convention." *The Canadian Forum*, September 1937.

– "Battle for Victoria." *The Canadian Forum*, January 1938.

– "The Bomb is a World Affair." *The Nation*, November 24, 1945.

– "Big States, Little Men." *The Nation*, April 6, 1946.

– "Prairie Socialism." *The Nation*, August 17 and August 24, 1946.
– "Two-World Debate." *The Nation*, October 18, 1947.
– "Wind-up at Flushing." *The Nation*, December 6, 1947.
– *These Rights and Freedoms*. New York: United Nations Department of Public Information, 1950.
– *The UN in the Congo: A Quest for Peace*. Carnegie Endowment for International Peace, 1962.
– "An International Police Force," *Special Studies Prepared for the Special Committee of the House of Commons on Matters Relating to Defence: Supplement 1964–65*. Ottawa: Queen's Printer, 1965.
– "Forward." *Canada's Role as a Middle Power: Papers given at the Third Annual Banff Conference on World Development, August 1965*, ed., J. King Gordon. Toronto: Canadian Institute of International Affairs, 1966: i–v.
– "Prospects for Peacekeeping." *International Journal* (CIIA), no. 2 (1970): 370–87.
– "Reinhold Niebuhr, Portrait of a Christian Realist." *The Ottawa Journal*, June 21, 1971.
– "A Christian Socialist in the 1930's." *The Social Gospel in Canada; Papers of the Interdisciplinary Conference on the Social Gospel in Canada, March 21–24, 1973, at the University of Regina*, ed., Richard Allen. Ottawa: National Museums of Canada, 1975: 122–53.
– "The New International Economic Order." *Behind the Headlines*, CIIA XXXIV (1976): 1–28.
– "Canada at the UN: Return to a Global Perspective." *International Perspectives*. Ottawa: Department of External Affairs, September/October 1976: 6.
– "The World of Helen Gordon." *Manitoba Pageant* 71 (Autumn 1978). The Manitoba Historical Society: 1–14.
– "The Politics of Poetry." *On F.R. Scott: Essays on His Contributions to Law, Literature, and Politics*, eds., Sandra Djwa and R. St J. Macdonald. Kingston and Montreal: McGill-Queen's University Press, 1983: 17–28.
– "We Grow Old to One World," review of *On F.R. Scott: Essays on His Contributions to Law, Literature, and Politics*, eds., Sandra Djwa and R. St J. Macdonald. Kingston and Montreal: McGill-Queen's University Press, 1983. *The Citizen*, Ottawa, Saturday September 24, 1988.
– Review of Donald MacMillan, *The Kirk in Glengarry*. Ste-Anne de Bellevue, Quebec: Imprimie Cooperative Harpell, 1984. *The Citizen*, Ottawa, 3 November 1984.
– "F.R. Scott Remembered." *Saturday Night*, July 1985: 22.
– "Not So Far East of Suez." In *Canadians and the United Nations*, ed., Clyde Sanger. Ottawa: Department of External Affairs, 1988: 58–9.

– Review of Sandra Djwa, *The Politics of the Imagination: A Life of F. R. Scott*. Toronto: McClelland and Stewart, 1987. *Dalhousie Law Journal* 12, no. 2 (1989): 570–1.

Government of Canada, Parliamentary Research Branch, "Cruise Missile Test in Canada: the Post-Cold War Debate," 1994, http://publications.gc.ca/Collection-R/LoPBdP/MR/mr114-e.htm.

Granatstein, J.L. *Canadian Foreign Policy Since 1945: Middle Power or Satellite*. Toronto: Copp Clark, 1970.

Granatstein, J.L., and Robert Bothwell. *Pirouette: Pierre Trudeau and Canadian Foreign Policy*. Toronto: University of Toronto Press, 1991.

Green, Clifford. "Bonhoeffer at Union. Critical Turning Points: 1931 and 1939." *Union Seminary Quarterly Review* 62, 2010: 1–16.

Green, Martin. *Children of the Sun: A Narrative of 'Decadence' in England After 1918*. New York: Basic Books, 1976.

Handbook to the University of Oxford. Oxford at the Clarendon Press, 1932.

Harris, Erdman. "Hungry Men in an Empty Gymnasium." *Christian Century*, December 3, 1930.

Harrison, Beverly W. Review of Eugene P. Link, *Labor–Religion Prophet: The Times and Life of Harry F. Ward* (Boulder, Colorado: Westview Press, 1984). *Union Seminary Quarterly Review* 39, 1984: 319.

Head, Ivan, and Trudeau, Pierre. *The Canadian Way: Shaping Canada's Foreign Policy, 1968–1984*. Toronto: McClelland & Stewart Inc., 1995.

Hillmer, Norman and J.L. Granatstein. *Empire to Umpire: Canada and the World to the 1990's*. Toronto: Copp, Clark, Longman, 1994.

Hobbins, A. J. "Mentor and Protégé: Percy Ellwood Corbett's Relationship with John Peters Humphrey," *The Canadian Yearbook of International Law*, 1991: 3–56.

– ed. *On the Edge of Greatness: The Diaries of John Humphrey, Volume 2*. Montreal: McGill University Libraries, 1996.

Hochschild, Adam. *King Leopold's Ghost: A Story of Greed, Terror, and Heroism in Colonial Africa*. Boston: A Mariner Book, Houghton Mifflin Company, 1999.

Hollis, Christopher. *Oxford in the Twenties: Recollections of Five Friends*. London: Heinemann, 1976.

Holmes, John W. "Is There a Future for Middlepowership?" *Canada's Role as a Middle Power: papers given at the Third Annual Banff Conference on World Development, August 1965*, ed., J. King Gordon. Toronto: Canadian Institute of International Affairs, 1966: 13–28.

– *Canada: A Middle Aged Power*. Toronto: McClelland and Stewart Limited, 1976 (Carleton Library, no. 98).

– "A Diplomatic Assessment." *Canadian Foreign Policy Since 1945: Middle Power or Satellite?* ed., J.L. Granatstein. Toronto: Copp Clark, 1970: 35–42.

Horn, Michiel. *The League for Social Reconstruction: Intellectual Origins of the Democratic Left in Canada 1930–1942*. Toronto: University of Toronto Press, 1980.

– *Academic Freedom in Canada: A History*. Toronto: University of Toronto Press, 1999.

Horowitz, Gad. *Canadian Labour in Politics*. Toronto: University of Toronto Press, 1968.

Hourani, Albert. *A History of the Arab Peoples*. Cambridge: The Belnap Press of Harvard University Press, 1991.

Humphrey, John P. *Human Rights and the United Nations: A Great Adventure*. Dobbs Ferry, NY: Transnational, 1984.

Ignatieff, George. *The Making of a Peacemonger: the Memoirs of George Ignatieff*. London: Penguin Books, 1987.

Ignatieff, Michael. *Human Rights as Politics and Idolatry*. Princeton: Princeton University Press, 2001.

International Development: Foreign Policy for Canadians. Published by authority of the Honourable Mitchell Sharp, Secretary of State for External Affairs, Ottawa, Canada, 1970.

Janzen, Eileen R. "J. King Gordon's Christian Socialism and the Kingdom of God." *Studies in Religion* 16, (1987): 347–61.

"King Gordon Loses Chair." *The Christian Century*, April 11, 1934.

Leacock, Stephen. *My Discovery of England*. London: John Lane The Bodley Head Ltd., 1922.

Lewis, David and Scott, Frank. *Make This Your Canada: A Review of C.C.F. History and Policy.* Toronto: Central Publishing, 1943.

Lipset, Seymour M. *Agrarian Socialism: The Cooperative Commonwealth Federation in Saskatchewan*. New York: Doubleday and Company, Inc., 1968.

Lotz, Jim, and Welton, Michael R. *Father Jimmy: Life and Times of Jimmy Tomkins*. Wreck Cove: Nova Scotia: Breton books, 1997.

Macdonald, R. St J. "Leadership in Law: John P. Humphrey and the Development of the International Law of Human Rights." *The Canadian Yearbook of International Law* 29, (1991): 3–92.

Mackenzie, Norman and Jeanne. *The Fabians*. New York: Simon and Schuster, 1977.

MacLeod, Wendell, Libbie Park, and Stanley Ryerson. *Bethune, the Montreal Years: An Informal Portrait*. Toronto: James Lorimer and company, Publishers, 1978.

MacMillan, Donald. *The Kirk in Glengarry*. Ste-Anne de Bellevue, Quebec: Imprimerie Cooperative Harpell, 1984.

MacQueen, Norrie. *The United Nations Since 1945: Peacekeeping and the Cold War*. London and New York: Longman, 1999.

McNaught, Kenneth. *A Prophet in Politics: A Biography of J.S. Woodsworth*. Toronto: University of Toronto Press, 1959.

Milligan, Frank. *Eugene A. Forsey: An Intellectual Biography*. Calgary: University of Calgary Press, 2004.

Morgenthau, Hans J. *Politics Among Nations: The Struggle for Power and Peace*. New York: Alfred A. Knofp, Inc., 1948.

– *In the Defense of the National Interest*. New York: Alfred A. Knopf, 1951.

Morris, Jan. *Oxford*. Oxford: at the University Press, 1988.

Morton, Desmond. *A Short History of Canada*, 3rd ed. Toronto: McClelland and Stewart Inc., 1997.

Morton, W.L. *Manitoba: A History*. Toronto: University of Toronto Press, 1957.

Naylor, R.T. "Appendix: The Ideological Foundations of Social Democracy and Social Credit." *Capitalism and the National Question in Canada*, ed., Gary Teeple. Toronto: University of Toronto Press, 1972: 251–6.

Neatby, H. Blair. *The Politics of Chaos: Canada in the Thirties*. Toronto: Macmillan of Canada, 1972.

Niebuhr, Reinhold. Review of *Towards the Christian Revolution*, ed. R.B.Y. Scott and Gregory Vlastos. Chicago: Willett, Clark and Company, 1936. *Radical Religion*, Spring 1937.

– "Intellectual Autobiography." *Reinhold Niebuhr: His Religious, Social and Political Thought*, eds., Charles Kegley and Robert W. Bretall. New York: Macmillan, 1956: 1–23.

– *Moral Man and Immoral Society*. New York: Charles Scribner's Sons, 1960.

Pearson, Lester B. *Mike: The Memoirs of the Right Honorable Lester B. Pearson, Volume 1: 1897–1948*. Toronto: University of Toronto Press, 1972.

– Mike: *The Memoirs of the Right Honourable Lester B. Pearson: Volume* 2 *1948–1957*. Toronto: University of Toronto Press, 1973.

– *Mike: The Memoirs of the Right Honourable Lester B. Pearson, Volume 3, 1957–1968*. Toronto: University of Toronto Press, 1975.

Potvin, Rose, ed. *Passion and Conviction: The Letters of Graham Spry*. Regina: Canadian Plains Research Center, 1992.

Regina Manifesto: Programme of the Co-operative Commonwealth Federation adopted at First National Convention. Regina, Saskatchewan, July 1933.

"Religion in Russia and in Canada." *The Witness and Canadian Homestead*, October 5, 1932.

Ritchie, Charles. *An Appetite for Life: the Education of a Young Diarist 1924–1927*. Toronto: MacMillan of Canada, 1977.

Ross, Douglas A. *In the Interests of Peace: Canada and Vietnam 1954–1973*. Toronto, Buffalo, London: University of Toronto Press, 1984.

Safarian, A.Z. *The Canadian Economy in the Great Depression*, Third Edition. Montreal and Kingston: McGill-Queen's University Press, 2009 (Carleton Library, no. 217).

Sanger, Clyde. *Malcolm MacDonald: Bringing an End to Empire*. Montreal and Kingston: McGill-Queen's University Press, 1995.

Saywell, John T., ed. *The Canadian Journal of Lady Aberdeen 1893–1898*. Toronto: The Champlain Society, 1960.

Scott, Frank R. "A Note on Canadian War Poetry." *Preview I*, November 1942: 3.

– *Essays on the Constitution*. Toronto: University of Toronto Press, 1977.

– "F.H.U. and the Manifestos." *The Canadian Forum*, November 1971.

– and others. *Social Planning for Canada*. Toronto: Thomas Nelson and Sons Limited, 1935.

– "Impressions of a Tour in the U.S.S.R." *The Canadian Forum*, December 1935:

– "Surfaces," *The Collected Poems of F.R. Scott*. Toronto: McClelland and Stewart, 1981: 39.

– "A Grain of Rice," *The Collected Poems of F.R. Scott*. Toronto: McClelland and Stewart, 1981: 126.

Scott, R.B.Y., and Gregory Vlastos, eds. *Towards the Christian Revolution*. Chicago: Willett, Clark and Company, 1936.

Scotton, Anne, ed. *Bibliography of All Sources Relating to the Cooperative Commonwealth Federation, and the New Democratic Party in Canada*. Published by the Woodsworth Archives Project with the Assistance of the Boag Foundation, 1977. Copyright Anne Scotton.

"Silver Jubilee 1895–1920 of St Stephen's. Winnipeg," booklet privately printed, n.d., JKGP.

Smillie, Benjamin G. "The Social Gospel in Canada: A Theological Critique." *The Social Gospel in Canada: Papers on the Interdisciplinary Conference on the Social Gospel in Canada, March 21–24, 1973, at the University of Regina*, ed., Richard Allen. Ottawa: National Museums of Canada, 1975: 317–40.

Smillie, Ian. *The Land of Lost Content: A History of CUSO*. Toronto: Deneau Publishers, 1985.

Smith, Simpson. Review of *The UN in the Congo: A Quest for Peace*, by J. King Gordon. Carnegie Endowment for International Peace, 1962.

The American Academy of Political and Social Science: THE ANNALS, v. 351 (January 1964): 225.

Stairs, Dennis. "The Political Culture of Canadian Foreign Policy." *The Canadian Journal of Political Science* 15, 4 (December 1982): 667–90.

– "Trends in Canadian Foreign Policy: Past, Present, and Future." *Behind the Headlines* 59, 3 (Spring 2002): 1–7.

Tawney, R.H. *The Acquisitive Society*. New York: A Harvest Book: Harcourt, Brace and World, 1948. Original publication, 1920.

– *Religion and the Rise of Capitalism*. New York: Harcourt, Brace and Company, 1926.

Terrill, Ross. *R.H. Tawney and His Times: Socialism as Fellowship*. Cambridge: Harvard University Press, 1975.

"The Case of the Montreal College." *New Outlook*, April 11, 1934.

"The Matter of the Montreal College." *New Outlook*, May 9, 1934.

Thompson, J. Lee, and John H. Thompson. "Ralph Connor and the Canadian Identity." *Queen's Quarterly* 2, 160 (1962): 159–70.

Trudeau, Pierre Elliott. *Memoirs*. Toronto: McClelland & Stewart Inc, 1993.

– "Trudeau's Statement on Cruise Missile Testing," http://tinyurl.com/cljqf99.

Underhill, F. H. *In Search of Canadian Liberalism*. Toronto: The Macmillan Company of Canada Limited, 1961.

United Nations General Assembly: "*First Interim Report of the AD HOC Commission on Prisoners of War*," A/AC.46/5, 27 August 1951.

United Nations General Assembly: "*Declaration*" *Fifth Session, AD HOC Commission on Prisoners of War*, A/AC.46/15, 2 April 1954.

United Nations General Assembly: "*Report of the AD HOC Commission on Prisoners of War*," A/AC.46/17, 30 September 1954.

United Nations, Department of Public Information, 19 September 1955: "UN Fact Series UNKRA."

United Nations General Assembly: "*Report on the AD HOC Commission of Prisoners of War on the Work of Its Seventh Session*," A/AC.41/21, 19 September 1957.

United Nations Security Council *Resolution 161 (1961)*, February 21, 1961; *Resolution 169 (1961)*, November 24, 1961.

United Nations General Assembly: *Convention on the Law of the Sea* (1982), "Exclusive Economic Zones," and "Continental Shelf."

"United Nations Emergency Force (Egypt) – UNEF," Department of Veterans Affairs, Government of Canada.

Urquhart, Brian. *Hammarskjöld*. New York: Harper Colophon Books, Harper and Row, 1972.

Vlastos, Gregory. Letter to *The Christian Century*, October 7, 1934.

Watt, F.W. "Western Myth: The World of Ralph Connor." *Writers of the Prairies*, ed., Donald Stephens. Victoria: University of British Columbia Press, 1973: 7–16.

Wilson, P.W. Review of Charles W. Gordon, *Postscript to Adventure: The Autobiography of Ralph Connor* (Toronto: McClelland and Stewart Limited, 1975). *The New York Times Book Review*, 22 May 1938.

Yoder, John Howard. "The Political Meaning of Hope." *The War of the Lamb: The Ethics of Nonviolence and Peacemaking*, ed., Glen Stassen and Mark Thiessen. Grand Rapids, MI: Brazos Press, 2009: 53–65.

Young, Walter. *The Anatomy of a Party; the National* CCF *1932–1961*. Toronto: University of Toronto Press, 1969.

Index

Note: The initials KG refer to King Gordon in this index. Page numbers followed by an italic *f* indicate a figure.